GETAWAYS
— FOR —
GOURMETS
In the Northeast

By Nancy Webster & Richard Woodworth

A guide to the best dining and
lodging in 22 areas appealing
to the gourmet in all of us.

Wood Pond Press
West Hartford, Conn. 06107

Prices, menus, hours, and days closed in restaurants and inns change season-ally and with business conditions. Places in this book are assumed to be open year-round, unless otherwise noted. Readers are advised to call or write ahead to avoid disappointment. Prices quoted are for peak periods and were correct as this edition went to press. They are offered as a relative guide to what to expect and are, of course, subject to change.

Lodging rates are for double occupancy and include breakfast, unless speci-fied to the contrary. EP (European Plan) means no meals. MAP (Modified American Plan) means breakfast and dinner.

The authors have personally visited the places recommended in this book. There is no charge for inclusion.

Readers' comments and suggestions are welcomed.

Please Note: The telephone area code for the Southeastern Connecticut chapter changed in 1995 from 203 to 860.

Sci.
Ref.
TX
907
W4
1994

Twelfth Printing, June 1996.

Cover Photo: Breakfast at Geneva on the Lake, resort in Geneva, N.Y.

Cover Design by Bob Smith the Artsmith.

Contents

New Year's calling treats are on display for Yuletide at Winterthur.

Brandywine Valley

A Feast for All the Senses

Mention the Brandywine Valley and most people think of gardens, house museums and art, probably in that order. And with good reason, for the region is unsurpassed on the East Coast in its extraordinary combination of the three.

This is an area of exceptional visual appeal, especially during spring when the gardens burst into bloom, and in summer, when the renowned mansions and art museums are at their crowded height.

But the area straddling the Delaware-Pennsylvania border from Wilmington to West Chester is more than a treat for the eyes and more than a seasonal tourist destination. It's a feast for all the senses — especially so during the holiday season, which arrives early and leaves late.

Experiencing a Brandywine Christmas is like coming upon an oasis of color and sensation in the midst of a stark Andrew Wyeth landscape. Simply incredible are the museum treasures within half a dozen miles of each other in this valley that the du Ponts and the Wyeths have made famous. All the museums put on their best holiday spread, and Yuletide at Winterthur is the year's highlight for food lovers, who get to see and smell the feasts recreated from yesteryear.

Strangely for such a touristy area, this region long lagged in providing country inns and exceptional restaurants in which travelers could rest their weary bones and sate their appetites between expeditions to the valley's attractions. The situation has improved lately, however.

Most visitors are aware of the valley's museums and gardens. But they may not know the treats they offer those with special interests in food, wine (the area has

1

two wineries), decorating and gardening (locally grown mushrooms are a specialty). And they probably are not aware of the newer inns and fine dining opportunities away from the tourist attractions.

Dining

The Best of the Best

Vickers, Gordon Drive, Lionville, Pa. (610) 363-6336.
The rural building that houses this sophisticated country restaurant reached through an industrial park has quite a history. When John Vickers, a famous potter, owned it in the mid-19th century, it was one of the main stops on the Underground Railroad. A nice touch was that until lately a potter was usually in residence in the room that houses the bar — her work still graces the tables and also is for sale.

Proprietor Arturo Burigatto, a suave Venetian, opened the restaurant in 1972 shortly after his arrival from Italy when he "saw what they did to Italian food here — it was a travesty." Taking over an 1800 farmhouse, he fashioned five historic dining rooms, a classic continental menu and a superb wine list. His chef is from Ethiopia and the food is on the expensive side, with most dinner entrées over $20 and lunch, $7.75 to $11.50.

For lunch, we were seated in a room with a brick floor, a wall of barn siding with coaching lanterns, a beamed ceiling and a huge fireplace with a roaring fire. Small bouquets of fresh flowers adorned the tables covered in beige and blue.

The lengthy list of possibilities included stuffed fillet of sole, veal piccante and beef diana as well as eggs benedict, assorted omelets and fettuccine.

From the huge, heavy wine book as thick as a telephone directory and displaying an incredible array of labels, we chose a Liberty School chardonnay. Prices start in the teens and rise to $180 for a Chateau Latour.

Our only disappointment was a shared hors d'oeuvre, mushrooms stuffed with crab meat; $6.25 seemed rather pricey for four diminutive mushrooms you could barely see, especially when they are grown right in Chester County.

The spinach salad ($2.25) was nicely arranged with tomatoes, black olives and green beans, and the entrées were lovely: a soufflé of fresh rainbow trout topped with a seafood mousse and scampi provençal, four large shrimp with a buttery and garlicky rice. With the trout came crisp cubed potatoes and green beans and julienned strips of leeks and carrots. We barely had room for dessert — cherry cheesecake, a choice of five fruit tarts or crème caramel — but shared a grand-marnier layer cake.

Arturo Burigatto says he serves lunch as "a convenience" to businessmen and tourists. It's at night when he feels Vickers is at its best with candlelight, formal service by waiters and much flambéeing at tableside.

The continental menu (written in French) seldom changes, but is supplemented by specials. Among main courses are dover sole with three-citrus sauce, frog's legs provençal, navarin of rabbit, sautéed quail with rosemary and sherry vinegar sauce, sweetbreads with madeira and truffle sauce, beef wellington and a medallion of buffalo sautéed with medoc — the priciest single entrée at $25.95 except for rack of lamb, $53 for two. Desserts start with French pastries ($4.50) and include cherries jubilee, bananas foster and crêpes suzette for two.

Lunch, Monday-Friday 11:30 to 2; dinner, Monday-Saturday 5:30 to 11.

Vickers Tavern is visible through window in old stone wall.

Dilworthtown Inn, Old Wilmington Pike at Brinton Bridge Road, Dilworthtown, Pa. (610) 399-1390.

In the quaint hamlet of Dilworthtown, this large old wood, stone and brick inn has a classic French menu and what is considered to be the area's best wine list. Winner of the Wine Spectator award, its vast selections start at $18 for Georges Duboeuf beaujolais and rise rapidly to $1,100 for a 1945 Chateau Lafite-Rothschild. There are 110 cabernets from the Napa Valley alone.

The original 1758 inn and its late 18th-century wing were restored in 1972 into a warren of fifteen dining rooms, a bar and a lobby, complete with plate-glass windows and plantings in a mini-atrium. Eleven fireplaces, stenciling, oriental rugs, artworks by Andrew Wyeth, rich wood tables with woven mats, antique furnishings and candlelight combine for a romantic, historic atmosphere. The place shows no effects from a kitchen fire that required its closing for eight months in 1993.

The leather-like, eight-page dinner menu starts with fourteen appetizers ($5.50 for the house pâté of duck liver, port wine and truffles to $8.25 for shrimp cocktail or hickory-smoked salmon).

Among the entrées ($14.25 to $22.95) are three kinds of steaks, South African lobster tail, Maryland crab casserole, and specialties like lobster thermidor, Long Island duck with apricot-nectar sauce, rack of lamb and medallions of veal with local mushrooms. Many consider the kitchen at its best on its nightly specials: perhaps homemade crab cakes with a spicy green sauce, pâté of pheasant and goose, and angel-hair pasta with wild mushrooms for appetizers; salmon poached with ginger, quail sautéed with fresh pears and venison with green-peppercorn sauce for entrées. The special of smoked chicken and lobster with basil and asparagus tips over fettuccine proved so popular that it was a fixture on the menu at our last visit. Desserts range from chocolate mousse to crème caramel and include wonderful homemade sorbets and ice creams of exotic flavors (the white-chocolate/macadamia-nut is a favorite).

Except for the specials, the inn embraces the traditional. That's fine with its regular clientele, who rate it their favorite all-around spot for consistency, charm and service.

Dinner nightly, 5:30 to 10:30, Sunday 3 to 9.

Chadds Ford Inn, Routes 1 and 100, Chadds Ford, Pa. (610) 388-7361.

Andrew Wyeth and his wife sometimes dine at this restaurant, which was founded in 1736 and looks it, and several of his works grace the dining rooms. It's also particularly popular with tourists. People started beating down the doors for lunch at 11:30 on the Saturday we were there, and the two long dining rooms on either side of the center entry hall soon were filled. So were three upstairs dining rooms. Only the tavern was empty and that filled up later, no doubt. Service by a young staff is geared to handling the crowds, however.

One yellow rose in a slender vase adorned our table, nicely set in beige and brown. The candles were lit at noon, though they were scarcely needed with sunlight streaming through the alcove windows. The low beamed ceiling and wainscoting enhanced the Wyeths on the walls.

It was here we first learned that the area's popular snapper soup ($3.50) is not made with red snapper but with snapper turtle. Thick and spicy, it tastes like the turtle soup we've had in New Orleans. We also enjoyed chicken crêpes garnished with carrots, coleslaw and a piece of melon. Cantaloupe stuffed with chicken and fruit salad was another good choice.

The dessert tray held old favorites like pecan and pumpkin pies, chocolate éclairs, blueberry shortcake and a sour-cream peach pie. The changing selection included chocolate-mousse cake and a strawberry-kiwi tart at our latest visit.

The lengthy wine list is priced mainly in the twenties. And the bill came on a doily, with a dollop of M&Ms.

At night, the historic atmosphere is grand, the presentation stylish and the service leisurely, at least the midweek evening we dined. Almost everything on the short dinner menu ($14.25 to $22.95) appealed, from the pistachio catfish with ginger-honey glaze to the grilled duck breast with andouille sausage and spiced peach sauce. We especially liked the mustard-sauced Australian loin of lamb and the tender grilled venison steaks topped with port wine and plum sauce. These were accompanied by broccoli and roasted potatoes. A hot popover came first; a key lime puff finished.

Lunch, Monday-Saturday 11:30 to 2; dinner, 5:30 to 10 or 10:30; Sunday, brunch 11:30 to 2, dinner 4 to 8.

Chadds Ford Cafe, Route 1 at Heyburn Road, Chadds Ford, Pa. (610) 558-3960.

Some of the Brandywine area's most exciting cuisine has been served up lately by an ex-Philadelphia Main Line chef amidst simple, plain-Jane surroundings. Don't let the nondescript facade or the neon cafe light in the window deceive you. From chef Jeff Schaeffer's sparkling kitchen come innovative treats at bargain-for-the-area prices.

Gone is the deli that was originally the focus of the Chadds Ford Deli Cafe opened by sisters Barbara Cohen and Joan Winchester in 1991. Gone also is the earlier menu emphasis on breakfast and family dining. The straightforward dining

Table for two at Chadds Ford Inn.   Hearthside dining at Dilworthtown Inn.

room remains, with its Wyeth prints on the walls, Amish-made table tops and a bench and a corner cupboard also made by Amish farmers. Now the partners proclaim "a rustic spot for the informal gourmand."

Chef Schaeffer's ambitious menu gets more innovative with every writing. Consider some of his November dinner offerings: roasted monkfish served over lyonnaise potatoes, grilled tuna with a mango-ginger-lime vinaigrette garnished with baby greens, grilled lobster tail served with a pumpkin-lobster sage cream, chicken wellington, rabbit fricassee with a mushroom-leek tart, grilled buffalo steak with a sweet-corn/pepper relish and roasted New Zealand venison on a bed of green-lentil and mushroom ragout with red-currant glaze and chestnut mousse. The pastas could include chicken penne and pheasant ravioli. We gladly would have ordered any of the 25 choices, pleasantly priced from $12.95 to $18.95.

Appetizers ($5.75 to $8.95) are equally complex and alluring: cured salmon tartare with cucumber dill yogurt sauce and ginger soy sauce, duck and potato napoleon, mousseline of veal sweetbreads wrapped in black truffle shavings, and pan-seared foie gras over French lentils and wild mushroom ragout. The royal imperial here is royal indeed: shrimp and crab served with Japanese mushrooms and snow peas with a sundried tomato sauce and horseradish cream. The soup of the day is a "split bowl" -- perhaps black bean and cream of jalapeño cheese with smoked pepper cream.

Getting the meal off to a redolent start is a head of roasted garlic served with the dinner rolls. "It's our signature," says Jeff. "We go through 50 pounds of garlic a week. I like the smell throughout the dining room."

Sweet endings include grand-marnier napoleon, a seven-layer hazelnut napoleon, a white chocolate sundried cherry timbaline and a "chocolate tower" of mousse wrapped in a lattice of chocolate.

Innovation continues at weekend breakfasts (shrimp benedict, wild mushroom and leek frittata) and daily lunch (a gourmet burger with spinach and brie, a steak sandwich with smoked mozzarella and wild mushrooms), when nothing costs more than $6.

As Jeff rattles off some of his game specialties -- caribou, bear, antelope, rattlesnake and rabbit -- you wonder how he can do all this at such reasonable prices and how a cafe clientele will support it. Yet this was named the year's best new restaurant by a Wilmington newspaper and diners have proved receptive. Breakfast, weekends from 8; lunch, Monday-Friday 11 to 2:30; dinner, Wednesday-Saturday 5 to 9. BYOB.

Buckley's Tavern, 5812 Kennett Pike (Route 52), Centreville, Del. (302) 656-9776.

Immensely popular locally is this tavern built in the late 1700s, all spiffed up with a pretty, white-linened interior dining room and an airy garden-room addition. The singles head for the tavern, where snacks and light entrées are available all day, or the appealing open-air bar on two upper outside levels.

Lately, the former tavern and dinner menus have been combined into one short, interesting menu appealing to a variety of tastes. We ate light at our most recent visit. One enjoyed spring rolls and a half serving of an addictive pasta of farfalle with smoked salmon and roquefort. The other liked the caesar salad and porchetta (sliced pork roasted with garlic and rosemary, served on an onion roll with roasted peppers). With a $12.75 Round Hill chardonnay and a slice of key lime pie, the bill came to a modest $38 before tip.

You also could try, as we did on an earlier occasion, one of the handful of entrées, priced from $12.95 for lemon chicken or pork medallions with grapefruit and pinenuts to $18.95 for delmonico steak with shiitake mushrooms. We liked the crab cakes, their flavor heightened by a dill mayonnaise laced with orange, and the linguini with smoked chicken and red peppers. Votive candles cast shadows on bare, rich wood tables flanked by comfortable, cushioned chairs as we lingered over a Hogue Cellars chardonnay from Washington State for $13.50.

With a wine store located in the front of the building and operated by Collier's of Wilmington, you would expect the tavern's selection to be excellent. It's also very reasonably priced, and many wines are available by the glass.

The special cappuccino-pecan-praline ice cream was a hit among desserts ($3 to $5). They included a light lemon-ginger cake and chocolate cups filled with raspberry mousse and served on a pool of crème anglaise. The cheesecake studded with black raspberries and strawberries is to groan over. Lunch, Monday-Saturday 11:30 to 2:30; dinner nightly, 5:30 to 9; Sunday brunch.

The Back Burner, Old Lancaster Pike, Hockessin Corner, Del. (302) 239-2314.

Started as a cooking school, this quickly became a local favorite for interesting American cuisine in a country setting. The casual, barn-style establishment is part of the wonderful Everything But the Kitchen Sink culinary complex. "This area was farmland fifteen years ago when we opened," said owner Missy Lickle. "So we began a cooking school and started serving lunch to get people out here." A full-fledged restaurant was the next step, followed by a thriving deli operation called The Back Burner to Go.

The dining-room menu changes every two weeks. For dinner ($14.95 to $19.95), you might find Acadian shrimp and scallop sauté, grilled yellowfin tuna served over red-chile linguini, baked red snapper en papillote, sautéed halibut with crystallized ginger and lobster in a sherried cream sauce, grilled calves liver with sherried onions and bacon, roasted rack of lamb with five-berry sauce and filet mignon forestière. Start with baked brie or crab-stuffed mushrooms. Finish with chocolate-amaretto cake or tirami su. The wine and beer lists are as good as everything else about this fascinating place. The only jarring note: glass tops over some of the blue tablecloths.

Lunch, Monday-Saturday 11:30 to 2:15; dinner, Monday-Thursday 5 to 8:45, Friday and Saturday, 5:30 to 9:45. No smoking.

Other Dining Choices

La Cocotte, 124 West Gay St., West Chester, Pa. (610) 436-6722.

Chef Henri Noebes has sold the charming French restaurant he started in 1974 in downtown West Chester to Jeff Lonsdale, who worked with him for nine years. Very little has changed, according to satisfied patrons. Beamed walls, lace curtains and white linens convey an authentic country French atmosphere. The biggest pepper grinder we ever saw is utilitarian as well as a conversation piece.

The dinner menu starts with ten soups and appetizers, ranging from onion soup and mushroom consommé to country-style pâté and crayfish mousse nantua. Entrées run from $18 for free-range chicken with roasted garlic to $23 for lobster thermidor. Salmon en papillote, sweetbreads grenobloise, breast of pheasant baked in pastry with wild mushroom duxelles, grilled barbary duck with chestnut glaze and grilled veal tenderloin with sundried tomato sauce are other favorites.

For dessert, how about hazelnut cheesecake, napoleons, chocolate mousse, baked alaska or pear pernod? The wine list is priced mainly from $20 to $40.

The lunch menu here is fairly classic French, that is to say substantial and pricey ($6 to $12). Light eaters can settle for an omelet or an oriental shrimp salad.

Lunch, Monday-Friday 11:30 to 2; dinner, Monday-Saturday 6 to 9:30 or 10.

Vincent's, 10 East Gay St., West Chester, Pa. (610) 696-4262-4246.

There's a jazz club upstairs, and a well-known jazz pianist plays downstairs on weekends at this musical place named for a former owner long gone. Fans like its New Yorkish atmosphere and its straightforward international fare.

The dinner menu is up-to-date yet of the old school, before the "with" syndrome took hold. Here the food names are not embellished: crab cakes, mussels marinara, Louisiana catfish, Santa Fe chicken diablo, Brazilian pork medallions, grilled lamb chops and filet of beef langoustine, although the servers will elaborate on the day's presentations. Prices for entrées are $14 to $17.95. Appetizers go from $4.75 for marinated artichoke hearts to $6.50 for three shrimp dishes. Desserts could be New York cheesecake, frozen raspberry soufflé, almond tart and crème caramel.

The blackboard menu at lunch time lists such main courses as roasted pork marsala and cheese ravioli with homemade meatballs in a madeira-peppercorn sauce. Light fare is served upstairs in the jazz club.

Photos of jazz figures adorn the walls of the main-floor dining room, attractive with brick, pine wainscoting and hunter green walls.

Open Monday-Saturday, lunch, 11:30 to 2; dinner, 5:30 to 9:30.

The Farm House Restaurant, McCue Road, Avondale, Pa. (610) 268-2235.

A former chef from Wilmington's Hotel du Pont was putting this rather ordinary-looking restaurant on the lower floor of the clubhouse at Loch Nairn Golf Course on the local culinary map. We particularly liked the canopied outdoor

Ted Pace pours wine at Pace One.

patio, glamorously set for dinner with white linens on the large, well-spaced tables flanked by heavy wooden chairs.

The blackboard menu lists dinner entrées from $15 for roast pheasant to $22 for surf and turf. Salmon florentine, shrimp provençal, veal madeira, chargrilled venison, baby rack of lamb and steak au poivre were other possibilities. Among appetizers were escargots in garlic butter, clams casino, chilled smoked breast of duck with cumberland sauce and a "duet" of caviar and crab meat. The chef also will prepare any dish to order, we were informed.

Homemade desserts include chocolate-pecan tart, poppyseed butter-lemon cream cake and strawberries romanoff with slivered almonds. Finish with the specialty Loch Nairn Irish coffee.

The lunch menu is fairly standard, except perhaps for sautéed Norwegian salmon on a kaiser roll. But you can't beat the outdoor patio for location.

Lunch daily, 11 to 3; dinner, Thursday-Monday 5 to 9.

Pizza by Elizabeths, 4019A Kennett Pike, Greenville, Del. (302) 654-4478.

Two Elizabeths -- Greenville residents Betsy Stoltz and Betty Snyder -- opened this high-style, gourmet pizza parlor in the heart of du Pont country in the summer of 1993. No ordinary pizza parlor, this. The place is a beauty in beige and green, with a Mediterranean terrà-cotta tile floor, oversize dried-flower wreaths on the walls and half a dozen booths and tables. The pizza toppings are displayed in containers at the pizza bar. The crisp, chewy crusts are baked in a wood-fired oven. And the beverage list includes not only Evian and cappuccino but Samuel Adams beer and a connoisseur's selection of wines, priced up to $39.

You can try some of the owners' favorite pizza creations named after famous Elizabeths, from $7.50 for the Barrett Browning to $11 for the Taylor (with goat cheese, rosemary onion sauté, sundried tomatoes and black olives). Or you can create your own pizza from a selection of three sauces and about three dozen toppings. Breadstick appetizers, green salads and cookies make up the rest of the menu.

Open Monday-Saturday, 11 to 8:30 or 9. No smoking.

Bed and Board

The Inn at Montchanin Village, Route 100 at Kirk Road, Box 134, Montchanin, Del. 19710. (302) 888-2133.

A deluxe inn and restaurant were scheduled to open in the fall of 1994 on the site of a charming 19th-century workers' village. Local preservationists Missy and Daniel Lickle planned 26 bedrooms and suites plus a 55-seat restaurant in eleven buildings on a twenty-acre site formerly occupied by mill laborers who worked at the nearby du Pont powder mills and factories along the Brandywine River.

Guest rooms were emerging in a row of turn-of-the-century duplexes facing Rockland Road and the railroad station that helped make this a thriving workers' village in the midst of du Pont country. One house has four bedrooms, a living room and a dining room and will operate as a true B&B, said Missy, with guests taking breakfast there. Most of the other units in various duplexes and dependencies are one- or two-bedroom suites with sitting areas. These have kitchenettes with microwaves and refrigerators; guests are served a continental breakfast at the restaurant. Missy planned to furnish the rooms in formal Victorian style, each with private bath and fancy toiletries, TV-VCR, handpainted wardrobes, Frette bed linens from Italy, terrycloth robes and the like. Guests will register in an 1890 stone schoolhouse, home of a resident innkeeper.

Dining for inn guests -- and the public on a space-available basis -- is offered in **Crazy Cat's Cafe.** It occupies an old blacksmith shop and is named for an old maid who once lived there "and was crazy as a cat," as Missy's grandmother described her. Serving dinner nightly, the restaurant offers regional American fare in the $13.95 to $24.95 range. It is more formal than her other restaurant, The Back Burner, part of her huge gourmet emporium known as Everything But the Kitchen Sink in nearby Hockessin.

The inn site, a rural area sloping toward the Brandywine, is architecturally notable for 19th-century stone, frame and stucco construction and paths, gardens, carriage ways and such. It represents the core of the old village named in honor of Ann Alexandrine de Montchanin, mother of Pierre Samuel du Pont de Nemours.

Talk about location! Almost next door are Winterthur and the Hagley Museum, and not far away are the Brandywine River Museum and Longwood Gardens. "We're surrounded by treasures and have everything right here," says Dan Lickle. "How could we miss?"

Dinner nightly, 5:30 to 9:30. Doubles, approximately $100 to $250.

Pace One, Thornton and Glen Mill Roads, Thornton, Pa. 19373. (610) 459-3702.

For sixteen years, creative chef Ted Pace has been serving fine meals in the basement of a 250-year-old fieldstone barn in the hamlet of Thornton. Since 1985, in the newly restored upper levels, he has offered six guest rooms and a suite as well.

Rooms are distinguished for the Lancaster oak beds made by the carpenter who built the inn, the original watercolors of Brandywine Valley scenes by a local artist, and the variety of striking wreaths created by the decorator. Though different in each room, all the sheets, pillowcases, comforters and shower curtains in the private baths match. All rooms have handsome tables and chairs, and you'll likely be struck by the beautiful carpentry throughout.

A continental breakfast of fresh fruit, juice and breakfast cake is set out in an upstairs sitting room for overnight guests.

Ted Pace, who hails from a Pittsburgh restaurant family, is the guiding light behind the downstairs restaurant, which is known for consistency and creativity.

Diners sit in a dimly lit interior room with stucco walls, bare pine floors and low ceilings or in a bright outer room enclosed like a porch. Inside, good artworks and vases of fresh flowers provide color; pierced lanterns cast neat shadows.

A recent luncheon began with a cup of the locally ubiquitous snapper soup ($3.25, served with a small pitcher of sherry) and a terrific vegetable pâté that looked like a colorful mosaic. The generous seafood salad niçoise ($7.95) and the puff pastry filled with crab meat, spinach and red peppers ($9.50) were excellent. We also remember fondly a Sunday brunch that included a lobster, crab and shrimp casserole. The pumpkin-brandy cheesecake was as delicious as the menu said it was.

Dinner entrées run from $16.50 for baked flounder with a saffron-cream sauce and Beluga caviar to $26.95 for rack of lamb with a mushroom demi-glace. Other choices are roast stuffed pork tenderloin, roast duckling with an orange-coconut sauce, grilled veal chop with a red-pepper vinaigrette and mixed grill, a combination of lamb, venison, sausage and quail served with apple-pepper chutney. Lighter (and less pricey) entrées are available, as are half a dozen appetizers. Most folks opt for the soup cart, which offers all you care to eat of, perhaps, squash-apple bisque, shrimp and corn chowder, and clear mushroom soup. Acclaimed are such desserts as hazelnut cheesecake, key lime pie and kiwi crêpes. The wine list contains good values, particularly among California whites, and there are numerous half bottles.

Lunch, Monday-Friday 11:30 to 2; dinner, Monday-Saturday 5:30 to 10; Sunday, brunch 10:30 to 2:30, dinner 5 to 9. Doubles, $65 to $85.

Duling-Kurtz House and Country Inn, 146 South Whitford Road, Exton, Pa. 19341. (610) 524-1830.

When this opened in 1983 as the area's first real country inn, it was out in the country. It since has been surrounded by encroaching commercial development, but remains a serene retreat No expense was spared by the original owners, local developers whose venture combined the maiden names of each of their late mothers. The place was rescued from financial difficulty in 1992 by Michael and Gertie Person, who also own the huge Lenape Inn restaurant nearby.

The eighteen guest rooms·on three floors of the restored 1830s barn are named for American historic figures and decorated for the period, with a slightly ersatz feel. Some of the rooms are exceedingly small. One of us, who thinks her day is lost if it doesn't begin with a hot bath, was appalled to find only one guest room with a tub. Luckily, the staff was accommodating and we were able to switch to that room (the George Washington, $120), but it didn't have a shower, which made the other half of our party rather cross. But we had a kingsize canopy bed,

Outer dining room at Duling-Kurtz House.

two red wing chairs (the room was done in red, white and blue, with a portrait of George), telephone and TV, and an enormous sunken bathroom with a couple of oriental rugs atop the hardwood floors. The only common areas are a small lobby and an intimate upstairs sun porch outfitted with garden furniture. Fresh fruit and cookies were set out in the lobby in the afternoon. A continental breakfast of fresh orange juice and homemade banana and cranberry breads was served on a tray in our room the next morning.

Dinner in the adjacent restaurant, made up of several small, beautifully decorated dining rooms and a long enclosed porch, plus a second-floor veranda, is an elaborate affair.

Delicious, piping-hot popovers were served from a basket by a waitress in a tuxedo shirt and black pants. One of the best salads we've had in a long time — small spinach leaves with avocado, pinenuts and mustard vinaigrette ($3.95) — came with a chilled salad fork.

Main courses are priced from $14.50 to $24.95 and were served, at our visit, with an interesting selection of vegetables like cauliflower in half a tomato, cubed potatoes and butternut squash. We very much liked a special of grilled pork medallions served with an apple fritter and fall chutney and the medallions of veal with lots of local mushrooms. Other possibilities include brook trout (caught in the inn's stream), shrimp with cilantro-poppyseed sauce over angel-hair pasta, chicken roulade, roasted pheasant and rack of lamb dijon. Among appetizers in the $7.95 range are escargots; salmon in phyllo and a smoked fish sampler.

The beehive oven near the front entrance, restored to working order, is used for baking the bread, rolls and muffins served at Duling-Kurtz.

Lunch, Monday-Friday 11:30 to 2; dinner, Monday-Saturday 5 to 10. Doubles, $80 to $120.

Lodging

Fairville Inn, Route 52 (Kennett Pike), Box 219, Mendenhall, Pa. 19357. (610) 388-5900.

The most convenient and most luxurious of the Brandywine Valley's small inns was opened in 1986 by Swedish-born Ole Retlev and his wife Patti, transplanted Vermonters who ran the acclaimed Deerhill Inn in West Dover. Their latest pride and joy is fortuitously situated between Winterthur and Longwood Gardens. If the Fairville bears more than a faint resemblance to Deerhill, that's because it was designed by Patti's uncle, architect Rodney Williams, owner of Vermont's Inn at Sawmill Farm. And Patti, who did the decorating, seems to have inherited her aunt Ione Williams's design flair.

No expense has been spared in the conversion of the former private home. Ask Ole to tell you about the "Retlev Memorial Highway," which is what he calls Route 52 since he had to shell out $38,000 to lower the roadway for better sight lines in the long haul toward zoning approval.

The original 1826 house contains five guest rooms, a spacious living room with a stunning copper table, and a cozy breakfast room with pink and white linens and copper utensils hanging about.

Most choice rooms are the ten out back in the Carriage House, built by an Amish family, and in the nearby Barn. Each is the epitome of elegant comfort. Accented with barnwood, beams and occasional cathedral ceilings, seven rooms have fireplaces, and some boast decks looking across three acres of fields toward a pond. Lamps with pierced shades made by Patti and her mother cast pleasant shadows. All possess spacious full baths (our suite had two vanities and a separate dressing area; the towels were thick and matched the decor), oversize closets, unobtrusive TVs, phones, elegant country furnishings, crisp and colorful chintzes, and flowers from Patti's prolific garden. Both spacious suites have a balcony with wrought-iron furniture, a sitting room with a love seat, and a bedroom with a kingsize canopy bed and two wing chairs by the fire. Their pale yellow and moss green decor are altogether cheerful, enhanced by pink bud roses in clear vases.

On fine linens and china in the main house, the inn serves a continental-plus breakfast which included, when we were there, a generous fresh fruit cup of kiwi, melon, grapes and strawberries, as well as fresh orange juice, cinnamon-raisin muffins, sticky buns and Swedish coffee bread. Afternoon tea with at least ten kinds of homemade Swedish butter cookies is a culinary treat as well.

Doubles, $100 to $165; suites, $175.

Brandywine River Hotel, Route 1 at Route 100, Box 1058, Chadds Ford, Pa. 19317. (610) 388-1200.

Set back on a hill adjacent to the rustic Chadds Ford Barn Shops and the historic Chadds Ford Inn is this brick and shingle hotel, which opened in 1987 with 40 deluxe guest rooms, among them ten suites with fireplaces and jacuzzi baths.

Room appointments were designed to resemble a wealthy Colonial home: Queen Anne reproduction furnishings in cherry and classic English chintz, wing chairs, oriental rugs, brass sconces and paintings in the Brandywine tradition. Telephones, bathrooms and remote-control TVs hidden in armoires are thoroughly up to date.

A complimentary buffet continental breakfast of granola, corn or blueberry muffins, croissants and danish is served in the fireplaced hospitality room, decorated in the style of a Colonial meeting hall. It also is used for meetings and

Main 1826 house at Fairville Inn.

functions. Afternoon tea (iced tea on a warm day), tea sandwiches, pastries and cookies are set out by the fireplace in the lobby.

Doubles, $105; suites, $130.

Scarlett House Bed & Breakfast, 503 West State St., Kennett Square, Pa. 19348. (610) 444-9592.

Victoriana reigns in this stone house with rust-colored shutters astride a hill at the edge of Kennett Square. Susan Lalli Ascoci left a career in marketing at the University of Pennsylania Hospital to open a B&B in 1990 with her husband, an engineer. They and their lively young son are only the second family to occupy the house purchased from the Scarlett family, to which the lady of the house came as a bride in 1923.

The wide entry foyer is notable for chestnut woodwork, doors and stairs. Each of two window nooks on either side of the door contains facing benches that are replicas of originals in the old Quaker Meeting House in Kennett Square. Off the foyer are two fireplaced parlors. One is Susan's "fantasy room," an explosion of red, from the floral maxi-print wallpaper to the velvet chairs and sofas. The other -- less Victorian with a country feeling, comfortable seating and a TV/VCR -- is where she chats with guests.

Upstairs is another sitting area, this one beside sunny windows full of plants on the landing, and a suite and three guest rooms (two of the rooms share a bath). A dish of candies, a basket of fruit, a guest diary, bathrobes and Gilbert & Soames toiletries are in each room, and a fresh flower is put on the pillow at turndown. The suite offers a queensize bed with the head of Shakespeare carved in the top of its solid walnut headboard and a sofa in the rear sitting area. A Victorian lady's face is carved into the furniture in the Victorian Rose room. Miniatures collected on the couple's travels are displayed in a hallway cabinet.

A continental-plus breakfast is served by candlelight in the dining room or, in summer, on the broad wraparound porch with its white Adirondack chairs and rockers. Susan uses low-fat recipes for all the fare, even the chocolate-chip scones and cookies. One day's repast might be clafouti, which she describes as a French

13

breakfast pie with pears, apples and a touch of brandy, pumpkin-raisin muffins, sweet-potato/walnut cake and a fruit cup with yogurt sauce and a splash of amaretto. Two bread puddings (one cinnamon-raisin and the other chocolate-amaretto) are frequent special requests. The interesting coffee turns out to be a special blend with vanilla, walnut and Irish cream. "I did it once by accident and everybody liked it," says its originator. She serves tea and cookies in the afternoon.

Doubles, $65 to $85; suite, $95. No smoking

Sweetwater Farm, Sweetwater Road, Box 86, Glen Mills, Pa. 19342. (610) 459-4711.

Fifty acres of woodlands and meadows surround the farm and 1734 stone mansion in which this B&B is ensconced. Part of a William Penn land grant to the Hemphill family, the inviting house has ten working fireplaces, a sweeping center-hall staircase, a formal parlor, a comfy library with TV and stereo, and six guest rooms, four with private baths.

Rooms vary considerably in size and decor, but all are handsomely furnished in styles from Williamsburg to Laura Ashley and accented with Wyeth prints, dried or fresh flowers, quilts and eyelet-ruffled pillows. Lafayette's portrait is over the fireplace in the room in which he once stayed. The master bedroom with a queensize canopy bed and fireplace has three windows onto the sunrise. We enjoyed the fan-window suite, private and peaceful, where you can watch the sun set and the queen bed feels as if it's in the treetops.

Off to the side of the house are four "cottages" fashioned from farm buildings and farmhand quarters. The Hideaway has a living room with a corner fireplace, a kitchen and an upstairs bedroom with a canopied four-poster. Like most cottage rooms, it has a telephone and TV. The grounds include a lovely swimming pool.

Breakfast is served family style by a resident innkeeper in the dining room. It might involve shirred eggs or puff pancakes, fresh fruit and homemade muffins.

Doubles, $145 to $165.

Faunbrook, 699 West Rosedale Ave., West Chester, Pa. 19382. (610) 436-5788.

Victoriana and fine art are in their element in this Italian Federal-style villa built about 1860, long the family home of Smedley Darlington, banker and Congress-man, who was known as the "autocrat of Chester County." Today, the awe-inspiring structure houses a seven-bedroom B&B operated by energetic Judi and John Cummings, who have furnished it with sweat equity and T.L.C.

The place was a wreck when the couple bought it in 1982. They undertook a gradual restoration and stocked it with items acquired from here and there. When guests leave for the day they sometimes return to find that Judi has redecorated their room in the interim. There's a lot of dramatic art, much of it the work of a lifelong friend, Harry Dunn, whose works are for sale here.

Monticello windows (patterned after Thomas Jefferson's invention) slide up to open the main floor onto the wraparound porches, full of decorative wrought iron and looking onto grounds dotted with fountains and statuary. Guests find plenty of room in which to spread out: the formal parlor with two facing love seats and an antique grand piano, the comfortable library and a front sun room. The last, all paneled in fine wood (even the ceiling), contains a maroon velvet love seat and two matching chairs.

The library opens onto a fancy dining room in which Judy serves an elaborate breakfast around 9 a.m. Typical fare would be juice, fruits, homemade breads

Sweetwater Farm occupies a 1754 stone mansion.

and sticky buns, and perhaps orange-croissant french toast with bacon or frittata with sausage and peppers.

The second floor harbors a master bedroom with a full bath, working fireplace, feather bed, a chaise lounge, a mirrored dressing table and an armoire. Two smaller bedrooms, dark and intimate and each with fancy stenciling, share a second-floor bath. Four bedrooms on the third floor share one bath. Each is decorated imaginatively.

Doubles, $65 to $75; master bedroom, $95. No smoking.

Meadow Spring Farm, 201 East Street Road (Route 926), Kennett Square, Pa. 19348. (610) 444-3903.

There's a Noah's ark on the fireplace mantel of this farmhouse-turned-B&B, along with animals in all guises everywhere, inside and out, not to mention 150 Santas at Christmas and a fine collection of dolls in the attic. We were partial to the hundreds of cows of all varieties, many sent by guests.

Innkeeper Anne Hicks has lived on the farm for 45 years; it was here that daughter Sissy Hicks, chef and co-owner of the Dorset Inn in Vermont, grew up. With her brood gone, Anne opened the farmhouse to guests in six air-conditioned rooms, four with private baths and all with TVs. The Chippendale has a crocheted canopy bed and a huge bathroom that was converted from a bedroom. Two rooms over the garage are newer and furnished in country contemporary style.

Guests here enjoy the living room full of inanimate animals, a dining room with a long table centered by a carved cow and her calf, a lovely porch with garden furniture looking onto gardens and a swimming pool, and another enclosed porch with a hot tub. Mushroom omelet with scrapple or sausage is Anne's specialty at breakfast, taken in the dining room or on the porch, where she offers tea or wine in the afternoons. She also puts up 200 jars of jam a year with local fruit.

Guests may fish in the farm pond or play ping-pong or pool in the downstairs game room. Families particularly like the feel of a 200-acre working farm.

Doubles, $65 to $75.

Museums and Gardens

Yuletide at Winterthur, Winterthur Museum and Gardens, Route 52, Winterthur, Del. (302) 654-1548.

In late fall, you can't see much in Henry Francis du Pont's prized gardens besides a bunch of Canada geese by the pond, but what could be more festive than to visit when the vast Winterthur mansion-museum is decorated with Christmas trees, flowers and the appropriate foods of each era represented in the rooms?

The special Yuletide tour takes about an hour and must be booked in advance. Groups of ten get escorted away every four minutes and the popular tour season is usually more than half booked before it starts about Nov. 10.

The tour theme is holiday dining and entertaining of the 18th and 19th centuries, as well as the ways the du Ponts entertained in the home they occupied until 1951. Interestingly, most of the food is so well preserved (some of it freeze-dried by the Smithsonian Institution) that it not only looks real but smells so, too.

Yuletide celebrations are recreated in more than 20 period rooms, from a parlor prepared for an evening musicale to a nursery prepared for an infant's holiday christening. When we visited, the du Pont dining room was set up for Christmas meals as the family would have had them in the 1930s and 1940s. You got to see the lunch of persimmon melon, broiled lobster, asparagus in aspic, and mince and pumpkin pies. The dinner was terrapin stew, pheasant with grape stuffing, cauliflower with hollandaise, a celery, apple and walnut salad, and plum pudding with ice cream.

Other rooms are set for everything from a Maryland hunt breakfast — with Brunswick stew made of rabbit or squirrel, trout and a large half ball of butter — to a tea party in the Baltimore drawing room, with eggnog, Queens cakes and meringues decorated with angelica. A bedroom is set up for breakfast, with poached eggs on rusks, tongue and pickles, and toast cooked in front of the fire.

Several rooms are ready for the New Year's Day calling — an occasion when the ladies stayed home to entertain the gentlemen who made the rounds to call (the 300 or so du Ponts in the area continue the family custom to this day, our guide said). The Winterthur du Ponts always served white and chocolate cakes, according to the precise records Mr. du Pont kept, and one year 39 cakes were consumed.

You can smell the confections in some of these rooms as you ogle displays of pound cake decorated with marzipan roses, cherry cake, sugared fruits and a great steamed plum pudding. Especially interesting are the oysters on the half shell made by the du Pont Co. husband of one of the tour guides, as well as the darling green marzipan peas in pods.

If all this makes you hungry, stop after the tour in the Pavilion Cafeteria in the Visitor Pavilion, where breakfast and lunch are available in a large and handsome room, with floor-to-ceiling windows looking onto the gardens. A salad bar ($2.95 small, $3.95 large) has just about everything you could imagine, and we enjoyed the Thursday Mexican fiesta bar where we made our own tacos and salads. Prepared sandwiches and salads and a few items like a hamburger and smoked salmon plate are in the $3 to $5 range. The restaurant devotes one section to a fancy garden setting where afternoon tea and Sunday brunch are served. The tea, featuring American holiday desserts displayed on the Yuletide Tour, is served Tuesday-Sunday from 2:30 to 4:30 for $8.50. The Sunday champagne brunch, $16.95 for quite a spread, is served from 10 to 1:45. The cafeteria is open Tuesday-Saturday 8 to 4 and Sunday noon to 4.

The gift shop is full of wonderful books, cards and wrapping papers. A "Sugarplum" room in back has a good selection of children's books as well as Christmas decorations of impeccable taste.

Yuletide at Winterthur: Nov. 10 through Jan. 2, Tuesday-Friday 10 to 5, Saturday 10 to 7 and Sunday noon to 7; adults, $12. Other tours and hours vary; open Tuesday-Saturday 9 to 5, Sunday noon to 5.

Longwood Gardens, Route 1, Kennett Square, Pa. (610) 388-6741.

For years the 350-acre private preserve of Pierre S. du Pont, the horticultural legacy he left is the area's single most popular showplace.

The year-round focal points are the Crystal Palace-type conservatories in which spring begins in January and the spectacle changes monthly through Christmas. How appealing they were on the blustery December day we first visited, brightened by 3,000 perfect poinsettias in red, pink and cream, unusually large and grown singly and in clusters. Outdoors after dark, 200,000 lights glitter in Longwood's trees and colorful fountain displays are set to music.

The indoor plants alone — from bonsai to cacti to impatiens to orchids — are so lush and spectacular as to boggle the mind as to what's outside the rest of the year, which, we discovered on later visits, is plenty.

Longwood's large shop is filled with items for the gardener — small pots of herbs, orchids (around $20), tiles, garden chimes, books, placemats and cookbooks, many with an herbal theme. Packets of Brandywine bayberries smell heavenly; tins of various sizes are decorated with flowers and horticultural notes.

Restaurant Associates runs the appealing Terrace Restaurant. A formal, sit-down restaurant plus a cafeteria that can accommodate 300 at a time, it is done in fine taste in shades of pink and brown, with walls of windows looking onto the gardens and black wrought-iron furniture on delightful dining terraces.

The cafeteria does all its own baking and boasts mushroom specialties, chili, deli sandwiches ($3.75 to $4.95), and local wines and beers. A separate line leads to the desserts, among them a luscious hazelnut torte and, at one visit, a celestial cheesecake topped with almonds, whipped cream and all kinds of fruit, including kiwi, in a decorative pattern. Lunch and brunch (and dinner on the nights the gardens are open) are served in the plant-filled dining room. You could start with double mushroom soup with pernod and tarragon, go on to wild mushroom salad, and for your main course have sliced tenderloin of beef with zinfandel sauce ($12.95). Finish with a pastry or one of the Terrace sundaes.

Open daily, conservatories 10 to 5, outdoor gardens 9 to 6, to 5 in winter. Holiday hours in December, 10 to 9 (gardens), 11 to 8 (restaurant). Adults, $10.

Hagley Museum, off Route 52, Wilmington, Del. (302) 658-2400.

The aroma of fresh cookies emanates all year from the woodburning stove in a typical worker's house, part of this fascinating restoration of the early mill community where E.I. du Pont started the du Pont Company as a gunpowder manufacturer in 1802.

Eleutherian Mills, the first du Pont family home in Delaware, offers special candlelight tours and decorations during the holidays. The Georgian-style residence of 1802 is furnished to reflect the tastes of five generations of du Ponts. We particularly liked the basement keeping room, left as it was furnished by Louise du Pont Crowninshield when she died in 1958. The formal dining room is remarkable for its scenic American wallpaper, a curious hand-blocked print with Spanish moss adorning trees around Boston Harbor. At Yuletide, it's set for

Basement keeping room at Hagley Museum's Eleutherian Mills.

a Twelfth Night celebration. A children's tea set with silver spoons is a highlight of the master bedroom in this house, which impresses because it feels like a home rather than a museum. (The French garden outside has been restored with espaliered fruit trees and organic fruits and vegetables — in season, it's not only beautiful, but functional.)

In keeping with the period, the simple Belin House Coffee Shop on Blacksmith Hill offers sandwiches, beverages and homemade desserts daily from 11 to 4. You can get a hot dog or a hoagie, lemonade and a piece of pie, and quite imagine yourself back nearly 200 years in time.

Open daily, 9:30 to 4:30, March 15 through December; same hours weekends and one tour at 1:30 on weekdays, January to March 14. Adults, $9.75.

Brandywine River Museum, Route 1, Chadds Ford, Pa. (610) 388-7601.

This special place made famous by the Wyeth family is extra-special during the holiday season when you not only can gaze at paintings but watch an elaborate model-train layout, enjoy a fabulous collection of dolls, see a ram made of grapevines, magnolia leaves, cattails and goldenrod, and eat roasted chestnuts.

Inside a century-old gristmill with white plastered walls and curved glass windows are three floors of beamed galleries that make up a permanent repository of the works of artists inspired by the Brandywine Valley.

The paintings of three generations of Wyeths — Andrew, who lives nearby, his father N.C. and his son Jamie — fill the second floor. The first floor houses the permanent collection, including works of Howard Pyle, Maxfield Parrish and a hundred other artists of the region. Much of the third floor is devoted to changing theme exhibits. The third-floor gallery in the new wing has a dramatic, state-of-the-art skylighting system aiming controlled natural light at the works of art.

At Christmas, the entire museum is decorated with swags of pine cones, mobiles made from grapevines, and pots of scarlet and white poinsettias contrasting with the stark view of the Brandywine River through floor-to-ceiling glass windows.

An attractive cafeteria-style restaurant, also part of the new wing that greatly expands the museum facility, has bentwood chairs and little round tables on a floor of old paving bricks in a glass tower that affords a great view of the Brandywine River. It's open from 11 to 3, serving main dishes, salads and wine or beer. Try the Brandywine melt: an open-face sandwich of roast beef, turkey, coleslaw and swiss cheese. The ploughman's lunch brings sausage pâté, cheese and breads. Chicken and dumplings, London broil and lasagna are hearty lunches, and you can finish with one of Rachel's brownies.

Open daily, 9:30 to 4:30. Admission, $4.

Gourmet Treats

Chaddsford Winery, Route 1, Chadds Ford, Pa. (610) 388-6221.

Eric Miller explains why he started his winery in this location and why he expends much effort making elegant chardonnays that are finished in French oak barrels and retail for $24 to $26 a bottle: "Well, this isn't Disneyland, you know. We've got a lot of traveling connoisseurs who know their wines."

Eric, who comes from a winemaking family (his father owns Benmarl Vineyards in New York's Hudson Valley), and his wife Lee, author of a book about wine, live next door in a house whose image is imprinted on some of the labels that mark their bottles. They have a private tasting room where they cater dinner parties. A cabernet sauvignon is offered for $21, and the winery bottles spiced apple wine ("good with ham," they say) and a sparkling blanc de blanc for $27.

After hearing the Millers talk about the chardonnay ("it's a good dinner companion and keeps your mouth fresh for the food") and tasting it ("showing honey and vanilla in the nose"), we splurged and laid down a bottle for a special occasion.

Open Tuesday-Saturday 10 to 5:30, Sunday noon to 5. Guided tours offered on weekends.

Phillips Place, Route 1, Kennett Square, Pa. (610) 388-6082.

This area is a center for the cultivation of mushrooms (you find mushroom specialties at most local restaurants) and the best place to find out about them is at Phillips Place, which has a deli (The Market Place) and a mushroom museum (the Mushroom Place), where you can see them growing at all stages. The museum has a new film, which it says justifies the $1.25 admission charge, but unless you're really into mushrooms, you'll likely find it a letdown. The adjacent Cap and Stem Gift Shop offers gift items with a mushroom motif, from bumper stickers to neckties.

At **The Market Place** behind the museum, you can buy specialty items like mustards, vinegars and crackers as well as foods to go. The sit-down deli offers breaded mushrooms, mushroom soup, mushroom burgers, mushroom steak, mushroom melt and marinated mushroom salad, as well as quiches, sandwiches and desserts. Also for sale are mushroom chips, mushroom ketchup and mushrooms chow mein. You can have all this inside on ice-cream parlor chairs or outside on a pleasant brick patio. Breakfast, including (of course) mushroom omelets, is served until 11; the deli stays open until 6 or 7.

You also can pick up recipes for mushrooms and pamphlets about them. Did you know that mushrooms are high in potassium? Did you know they are 99 percent fat-free? Maybe you don't want to know all these things, but the complex is fun, anyway.

Other interesting places:

Brie & Thee, Route 1 at Hickory Hill Road, Chadds Ford, offers all kinds of imported cheeses and specialty foods, plus baked goods, sandwiches, pastas and desserts to go. Pick up a croissant sandwich with ham, turkey or cheese and a slice of raspberry-chocolate cheesecake for a picnic by the river.

The main street (Route 52) of Centreville, Del., has several nice shops. **The Troll of Scandinavia,** 5808 Kennett Pike, makes up good sandwiches for $3 (small) or $4.50 (large) — one of the most popular is London broil. On our visit, chef-owner Hebba Lund's soup of the day was pumpkin-mushroom and the chocolate-hazelnut torte with raspberry filling looked delectable. We sampled the famous confetti cheese spread with carrots and celery and found it worth the raves. Next door, **Communiques** is a great card and stationery store with a difference -- an interesting selection of books and gifts, a coffee stand where you can sip a sample or something larger, and special events from art classes to poetry readings. Owners Becky and Tony Falkowski are making theirs a community focal point. Nearby, a suave gift shop, **The Horse,** is run by one of the du Ponts.

You also can pick up a sandwich or salad at the deli at **Janssen's,** a fine, family-owned market catering to the carriage trade at 4021 Kennett Pike in Greenville, Del. We liked the Brandywine chicken salad sandwich on a hard roll and another chicken version with almonds and grapes in pita.

Just a shopping complex away in 2 Greenville Crossing at 400l Kennett Pike is **The Country Mouse,** with a selection of more than 100 cheeses and pâtés. New owner Peter Sheridan expanded the original emphasis on cheese to embrace breakfast and lunch items, salads to go, smoked Virginia meats and more in a pleasant little cafe with seating inside and out.

Well worth a side trip is the hamlet of Dilworthtown, northeast of Chadds Ford, and Audrey Julian's **Dilworthtown Country Store,** chock full of American country crafts and folk art. It's been a country store since 1758 but took on its sophisticated form a decade or so ago. The owner shops craft shows to find unusual things — we fell for a tin wreath of sassy spotted cows with "Welcome" in the center and treated ourselves to an anniversary present. The store is adjacent to the Dilworthtown Inn and across the street from **A.E. Shea & Co.,** purveyor of lovely accessories.

Another worthy side trip is to the hamlet of Glen Mills, where across the tracks from the train station lies a good-looking Victorian building known as **Pratt and Company.** Inside, Joy Juliano and Margaret DeMarco display their collectibles, gifts and period home furnishings in several rooms. The store closes for the better part of a week in early November to prepare for its special Christmas extravaganza, featuring handmade gifts reflecting the spirit of Christmases past. Gorgeous Christmas items (especially the stockings), pretty linens and dried flower arrangements abound.

For those with an interest in things culinary, the best side trip of all is to Hockessin Corner, Del., and the incredible **Everything But the Kitchen Sink** complex. It's located in a warren of old warehouse buildings beside the railroad track, just off Route 41 on Old Lancaster Pike. Here, Missy Lickle oversees The Back Burner Restaurant, a cooking school and room after room of kitchenware, a fabulous array of china, MacKenzie-Childs and Lynn Chase dinnerware, cookbooks, gadgets, gourmet foods, paper goods, linens and more. We've never before seen such an interesting selection in one place.

Daffodils are signs of spring outside Black Bass Hotel in Lumberville.

Bucks County

Romance along the River

There's something very special about the Delaware River section of Bucks County, Pa., and neighboring New Jersey.

In both look and feel, from the sturdy stone houses to the profusion of daffodils proliferating down to the river in springtime, it's the closest thing this side of Great Britain to the Cotswolds we love so well. There's a welcome sense of isolation and romance along the River Road, a narrow and winding route that thwarts vehicular traffic and invites visitors to take to their feet. There are real country inns, both chic and quaint, and more good dining places than one has a right to expect. And there's the great river with its historic canal and towpath, which shapes the area's character and raises the rationale to laze along, whether by foot, bicycle or canoe.

We're not alone in our love affair with Bucks County, a meandering mosaic of suburbia and seclusion stretching north from the Philadelphia suburbs almost to

Easton and the edge of the Poconos. Places like New Hope, the artist colony, are wall-to-wall people on summer weekends. More to our liking is the scenic rivershed area stretching above New Hope to Upper Black Eddy, especially in spring or fall.

Consider Lumberville, Pa., for instance. It's so small that you can drive through in less than a minute and canoe past in a few minutes, yet so choice that a walk through with stops can take a couple of hours or all day. From our base at Lumberville's 1740 House, we walked the towpath down to Stockton and Phillips Mill, checking out inns and restaurants along the way as we rekindled memories of the British countryside (after all, the area was settled by the English Quakers and names like Solebury, Chalfont and Wycombe persist).

This chapter generally focuses on the strips of Bucks County and New Jersey along the river north of New Hope — and places within walking distance of the river. Thus we stress several river towns in New Jersey's Hunterdon County like Lambertville, which is being revitalized to the point where "there's a restaurant for almost every family," according to one local foodie.

Because liquor licenses are limited, inns and restaurants without them — most of them in Hunterdon County — invite guests to bring their own wines. The restaurants can't survive on liquor, so they have to be extra good with their food, explained one restaurateur.

And good they are. New restaurants are emerging to compete with the old, and several inns have outstanding dining rooms. At peak periods, dinner reservations often are hard to come by. Most inns require at least two-night minimum stays on weekends.

So book well ahead and prepare to relax. Here's a perfect place for a gourmet getaway, especially for anyone with an iota of British blood in his body and a bit of romance in his heart.

Dining

The Best of the Best

The Frenchtown Inn, 7 Bridge St., Frenchtown, N.J. (201) 996-3300.

Young restaurateurs Robert and Holly Long from Chatham, N.J., were looking for their own place in Hunterdon County, the emerging hot spot, and found it in the 19th-century, red-brick Frenchtown Inn. "It had the charm and location we wanted," said Robert, who apprenticed at Le Français in Wheeling, Ill., and in France before becoming a chef at the Tarragon Tree in Chatham. "And we thought we could make some heads turn in the area."

Heads indeed have turned since the Longs opened their French restaurant on New Year's Day, 1986. Critics have lavished ratings of three and four stars, fellow restaurateurs accord the highest accolades and the growing clientele books far in advance for weekend tables. Best of all, the establishment — though elegant and refined — is not pretentious, the menu is adventurous and the far-ranging wine list offers good values.

Arriving without reservations for a Friday lunch, we were greeted by a maître-d' who holds forth in a reception hall in front of a couple of stuffed foxes, outfitted in hunting clothes and perched on the stairway banister. The cozy front dining room with its beamed ceiling, brick walls and carpeted floors was full, so we were seated in a more austere columned dining room in the rear. Austrian curtains drape the tall windows, walls are brick or covered with green and pink wallpaper,

Chef-owner Robert Long has won acclaim for Frenchtown Inn.

and crisp white linens, Villeroy & Boch china in the Florida pattern, two sets of wine glasses and fresh flowers are on the luxuriously spaced tables.

Everything on the menu looked great. We enjoyed an unusual black-bean soup with an almost fluffy texture, the selection of pâtés and terrines ($7.50 — small but very smooth and good, presented nouvelle style on a large plate with three croutons, mustard and cumberland sauce), the corned-beef sandwich on brown bread, and a sensational salad of duck and smoked pheasant with a warm cider vinaigrette ($9.25), loaded with meat and mixed greens like radicchio and arugula. A layered pear-raspberry tart with whipped cream was a perfect dessert ($5.25).

At dinner, the menu arrives with complimentary hors d'oeuvre, perhaps hot puff-pastry morsels and belgian-endive spears dabbed with lemon-scented cream cheese and decorated with button-size potato roses. Appetizers ($7.50 to $10.75) include a signature house-smoked salmon, served two ways (layered between blinis and chervil-cured, resting on lotus chips), raviolis of prawns on a nest of roasted savoy cabbage, and a baked strudel filled with wild mushrooms, duck confit, roquefort, duck sausage and green-peppercorn sauce.

Augmented by nightly specials, the seven entrées go from $19.50 for roast pork loin with cranberry, pumpkin flan and a wild-rice-apple-pecan compote to $25.75 for rack of lamb with a curried vegetable-lentil ratatouille, braised swiss chard and garlic whipped potatoes. Other possibilities are herb-crusted Atlantic salmon with a smoked-shrimp cornet and black-bean coulis, roasted halibut atop a nest of spaghetti squash tossed with Dungeness crab meat and bay scallops, and filet of beef with a spinach, roasted-pepper and three-cheese soufflé and organic carrots. Dinner on Saturday night is prix-fixe only, $45 for four courses with five or six choices.

The pastry chef is known for dessert treats ($6.50) like crème brûlée napoleon, chocolate cylinder (layers of cheesecake and butternut-chocolate dacquoise, wrapped in a chocolate leaf) and apple-cranberry-pear compote with homemade honey-vanilla ice cream. Summer brings more homemade ice creams, including fresh mint and chocolate with white-chocolate chips.

Although friends who have eaten there lately demur, others say that the combination of inspired cuisine, friendly service and appealing decor propels this restaurant from the ranks of merely excellent to exceptional.

Lunch, Tuesday-Saturday noon to 2; dinner, Tuesday-Friday 6 to 9, Saturday 5:30 to 9:30; Sunday, brunch noon to 3, dinner 5:30 to 8:30.

The Ferry House, 21 Ferry St., Lambertville, N.J. (609) 397-9222.

The newest culinary gem in Lambertville -- which has more than its share -- occupies a restored 18th-century house built at the site where the original Coryell ferry crossed the Delaware River to New Hope. The dining experience here is historic, all right, but not in the way you might expect. The interior is sleekly contemporary, as is the menu, and chef-owner Bobby Trigg is creating pinnacles on the area's culinary landscape.

The dining room, neatly divided into two by a half-wall divider, is a beauty in white and black. White walls with dramatic local art (including, at our visit, a couple of distracting nudes), black enameled upholstered chairs and tables crisply dressed in double white cloths and topped with salmon-colored Villeroy & Boch faux-marble service plates and napkins, and unique black fabric drapery panels create a stunning backdrop.

It proved a stylish, refined setting for a lunch of distinction. Only salads and sandwiches are offered, but what treats they are. One of us enjoyed a sandwich of roasted red pepper, prosciutto, marinated goat cheese and arugula on toasted focaccia ($6). The other was amazed by a salmon BLT with ginger and cilantro ($7), an explosion of tastes lurking between slices of a man-size English muffin. Each was artistically presented on parsley-flecked plates with crispy sweet-potato fries and garnishes of fresh strawberries and raspberries. We would have liked one of the homemade ice creams (perhaps ginger or passion fruit) or the tequila-lime sorbet, but, alas, they weren't to be ready that day until dinner time.

Our lunch testified, however, to what delights this talented young chef might whip up in the evening. The press reviews have raved over the likes of sautéed halibut on a cilantro-butter sauce topped with a fresh fruit salsa, grilled shrimp and sautéed cucumbers and snow-pea shoots on a tomato and coriander coulis, grilled chicken set on sautéed spinach and curried couscous with a garlic-rosemary sauce, and roast rack of lamb on a glazed shallot and pepper sauté with mint au jus. Prices of the ten entrées range from $15.50 for the vegetable preparation of the day accompanied by a grilled portobello mushroom to $24.50 for the Ferry House's rendition of surf and turf, sautéed crab cake with citrus butter and grilled filet topped with foie gras.

Starters ($7 to $11) are equally arresting, perhaps oriental duck salad on sautéed bok choy and snow-pea shoots, pan-roasted quail set on sautéed arugula and couscous with a black-currant and coriander sauce, grilled shrimp and wilted greens bruschetta, and chilled farm-raised oysters topped with wasabi flying-fish roe mignonette. The dessert tray includes an acclaimed crème brûlée, lemon-mousse cake, caramel nut torte and a signature miniature bittersweet-chocolate canoe (patterned after the restaurant's logo) filled with small scoops of chocolate ice cream and laden with strawberries and raspberries.

The chef, an area native, left his job as an investment banker with Salomon Brothers in 1987. He was flush with an early-retirement package that put him through a year's crash course at the Philadelphia Restaurant School and a two-year apprenticeship with award-winning chef Jean-Pierre Tardy in nearby Newtown, Pa. "I was 26 and the clock was ticking," he recalls. Four years later he had his own restaurant and a young staff of admirers.

Chef Bobby Trigg with an array of desserts at The Ferry House.

Although it opened in 1992, the Ferry House remains a work in progress. At our visit in November 1993, construction was underway to enclose the front foyer in glass for a dining alcove and to create a side patio for outdoor dining. The owner was about to appear before the zoning board to seek approval for an upstairs bistro serving a lighter menu. He also stages frequent special events, ranging from a chile-pepper fiesta (the dessert was soft banana taco with papaya and strawberry salsa and black-pepper ice cream) to a shellfish and truffles dinner.

Open Friday-Tuesday, lunch noon to 2, dinner 5:30 to 9:30 or 10; Sunday, brunch noon to 2:30, dinner 4:30 to 8:30. BYOB. No smoking.

Hamilton's Grill Room, 8 Coryell St., Lambertville, N.J. (609) 397-4343.

Hidden at the end of an alley in the Porkyard complex, this is run by former Broadway set designer Jim Hamilton and his daughter Melissa. "I designed the place," said Jim, an architect who designs other restaurants, "and Melissa established the food service." He installed an open grill beside the entrance and built the wood-fired pizza oven himself. Melissa produced a menu featuring Mediterranean grill fare from the south of France, northern Italy and northern Africa, with a touch of Greek and Spanish.

Patrons dine at tables rather close together in the grill room, the Bishop's Room beneath angels and clouds surrounding a huge gilt-framed mirror on the ceiling, a gallery (taking space from an art gallery next door) and, in season, outdoors around the fountain on the courtyard. Seafood is the specialty, the shellfish delivered twice weekly from Boston and the other fish coming from Philadelphia.

Seated at tables covered with stiff white paper over white linen in the convivial, candlelit Bishop's Room, we began a winter dinner with grilled shrimp with anchovy sauce and a crab cake with wilted greens and sweet red-pepper sauce, chosen among appetizers priced from $6.75 to $9.25 (except $23.75 for Jim's iced seafood extravaganza for two). Other possibilities might be duck and barley soup, grilled black tiger shrimp with anchovy sauce, grilled brie stuffed with black olives wrapped in grape leaves, and warm salad of grilled quail, fennel and prosciutto with a sundried-tomato vinaigrette.

Entrées are priced from $16.75 for roasted chicken with black olives to $24.75 for grilled rack of lamb with mint oil. Most run about $18.75. We sampled an exceptional grilled duck on bitter greens with pancetta and honey-mustard glaze, one of the best duck dishes we've had, but thought the marinated lamb brochette could have been more tender. The oversize plates were filled with fanned razor-thin sliced potatoes, grilled zucchini, and green and red peppers.

Melissa and a Swiss baker are responsible for the delectable mini-baguettes and the desserts, which might include grappa torta with fresh fruit, white-chocolate mousse cake and zabaglione with fresh berries. The dense chocolate-almond meringue torte was almost too rich (and we couldn't detect any meringue). Two biscotti came with the bill.

Hamilton's is BYOB with a twist. It serves its regular menu weekends at the **Wine Bar** annex, a small house across the courtyard for folks who want full liquor service from the adjacent Boat House wine bar. In the main grill, the white wine we toted was set in a pail full of ice, and red wines and even water are poured in large hand-blown globes made locally.

Dinner, nightly 6 to 10 or 11, Sunday 5 to 10. BYOB.

Anton's at the Swan, 43 South Main St., Lambertville, N.J. (609) 397-1960.

Anton Dodel, a very young-looking 35, doesn't appear old enough to have his own restaurant. But he has a vision, and he certainly seems to know what he is doing in the establishment he opened in 1990 in the Swan Hotel. Shortly afterward, the New York Times picked Anton's as one of the year's ten best in New Jersey.

Trained at La Bonne Auberge in New Hope and with the renowned Bruce Frankel at the former Panache in Cambridge, Mass., Anton is, in his words, spontaneous and eclectic. His short menu changes monthly. The one we salivated over mentioned entrées ($21 to $25) like steamed salmon on a tamarind-peanut sauce, sautéed lobster with ginger, grilled partridge with wild mushrooms, grilled veal loin and truffle cream, and grilled rack of lamb with garlic risotto. Starters ($7.50 to $12) included crabmeat flan with a lobster and cider cream, fried green tomatoes and goat-cheese gnocchi, sautéed foie gras with apples, and a potato, olive and sundried-tomato tart. Polenta sticks fried in goose fat and sugar-snap peas might accompany the skillet-roasted beef tenderloin. "This restaurant is not for those who worry about butter and fat," says Anton. He makes his own butter and says it's much fresher than the norm.

Dessert ($5) always includes something chocolate and always a flan, but you might find a poached pear in caramel sauce or a cornbread pudding.

All this takes place in a subdued room with paneled wainscoting, a wall of mirrors, hurricane lamps atop white-linened tables and step-down windsor chairs.

Melissa Hamilton readies food in front of open grill at Hamilton's Grill Room.

Anton rebuilt the hotel's kitchen in order to produce a sophisticated menu and style, "one like a well-established restaurant in France." He cooks more casual fare for the hotel's bar, where the short menu might offer pizza with Ely Farms sausage and grilled scallops with pumpkin sauce and pasta, $7 to $14.

The good, pricey wine list ranges from $18 to $95.

Dinner, Wednesday-Saturday 6 to 10, Sunday 4:30 to 8. Bar, Tuesday-Sunday 5 to 11.

La Bonne Auberge, Village 2, New Hope, Pa. (215) 862-2462.

"Four-star everything," report people who have eaten here and consider it comparable to the best in New York or Philadelphia. Those doing the reporting happen to be from New York or Philadelphia, where they expect four-star dining and are willing to pay for it. Many of the people around New Hope aren't, nor were we, after we saw the menu prices.

There's no denying the food. The restaurant "seems a strong contender for 'best in Bucks,'" wrote Bon Appétit magazine. "Chef Gerard Caronello, originally from Lyons, makes the kitchen sing. His gracious, soft-spoken wife, Rozanne, sees to things up front. It all translates into some very good French."

There's no denying the setting, either. The pretty stone house is surrounded by beautifully landscaped grounds and formal gardens atop a hill at the edge of the Village 2 condominium complex (through which you must pass — and can easily get lost, coming or going). The contemporary, airy, wood-paneled dining room at the rear is gracious and gorgeous, its large and well-spaced tables flanked by comfortably upholstered rattan chairs. Wines are stacked in a corner cabinet, windows look out onto the gardens, fresh flowers grace the tables and salmon-colored napkins stand tall in twin peaks in the wine glasses.

Downstairs is a cozy hideaway bar that even some regular diners don't know about. Nestled in wing chairs in a candlelit corner, couples sipping after-dinner cognacs (at $12 and up a snifter) think they've died and gone to heaven.

Count on spending $150 to $200 on dinner for two with a bottle of wine. Except for melon glacé or avocado vinaigrette (both $9), appetizers start at $13 for escargots provençal. Soups are $9 and the house salad, $10. Big-spenders can go for Beluga caviar ($52).

Entrées are $30 to $33, except grilled chicken dijonnaise, which is $27. The French classics (grilled salmon armoricaine, dover sole with capers, escalopes of veal with morels, rack of lamb provençal and entrecôte of beef) are prepared to perfection, we understand.

Desserts are in keeping, and the wine prices hurt, starting in the $30 range.

In addition to the regular menu, on Wednesday and Thursday evenings the chef offers a four-course, table-d'hôte dinner with a limited choice for $40.

For twenty years, La Bonne Auberge has been doing very nicely with a loyal clientele that appreciates the best.

Dinner, Wednesday-Saturday 6 to 10, Sunday 5:30 to 9. Jackets required.

Manon, 19 North Union St., Lambertville, N.J. (609) 397-2596.

Dining here is reminiscent of the south of France, which comes as no surprise when you learn that young chef-owner Jean-Michel Dumas grew up in Provence. He and his American wife Susan gave a provençal name to the 32-seat charmer they opened in 1990 in the tiny space vacated by The Cafe, whose owner moved her cafe to Rosemont, near Stockton.

The downtown storefront has tables rather close together, outfitted with white butcher paper over white cloths. Each has a basket of crayons and a candle in a tall hurricane lamp, which leaves little room for the gutsy food served in robust portions. In back is a refrigerated case displaying desserts and, through an open door, one can see into the kitchen.

Jean-Michel, who was a chef at the Inn at Phillips Mill in New Hope, relies on fresh ingredients cooked simply. At dinner, you might start with his trademark anchovy relish with an assortment of raw vegetables ($6.50), the house pâté or one of the three salads (caesar, goat cheese or watercress, endive, apples and walnuts with roquefort). Soup of the day could be garlicky mussel or pistou ($4). That's it for starters, unless a special is offered (there are a few each night, and they tend to be more interesting than the menu items).

Among the eleven entrées ($15 to $20) are red bouillabaisse, roasted monkfish with pernod and tomato fondue, grilled salmon with red-pepper oil, grilled chicken with cilantro and lime butter, duck with green-peppercorn sauce and sautéed lamb chop with roasted garlic. Desserts include a classic crème caramel, tarte tatin, chocolate mousse, marjolaine and nougat ice cream with raspberry sauce.

Similar fare is offered at wallet-pleasing prices for Sunday brunch. The $15.50 tab is all the more pleasant because you can bring your own wine.

Dinner, Wednesday-Sunday 5:30 to 9 or 10; Sunday brunch, 11 to 2:30. No credit cards. BYOB.

28

Forager House, 1600 River Road, New Hope, Pa. (215) 862-9477.

Contemporary decor with track lighting, white scalloped china on floral cloths, well-spaced tables and good art along the walls distinguish this restaurant south of town. So does the food, which tends to be in the vanguard, if not quite so exotic as that of some of its peers. Forager House was the first to offer Spanish tapas to Bucks County. The different ethnic and regional dinners served Thursday nights have become a winter tradition.

Given their out-of-the-way location, chef-owner Dick Barrows and his wife Sue, the hostess, have to be innovative to attract patrons to the pleasant restaurant they have owned since 1983. Innkeepers often recommend the Forager House for consistently good food in chic surroundings; the three dining rooms here are not steeped in history, as are most in the area.

The changing, hand-written menu offers such entrées ($18 to $19.50) as mesquite-grilled salmon with roasted potatoes and asparagus, seared sea scallops with saffron risotto and sweet-pepper vinaigrette, Thai chicken curry with basmati rice and pineapple chutney, Southwestern pork loin with ancho-chile sauce and black-bean salad, breast of muscovy duck with peppered pineapple, and grilled beef tenderloin with fried potatoes and spinach. Appetizers ($6.25 to $7.25) could be a corn and cilantro crêpe filled with spiced duck, deep-fried calamari with sweet and sour cabbage, baked goat-cheese salad and penne with sweet sausage and peppers. Desserts ($4.50) include fresh fruit sorbet, crème caramel, meringue glacé, pumpkin cheesecake and apple galette.

The house wine is Trefethen. Some other excellent Californias (Groth sauvignon blanc and Mill Creek merlot) are in the $20 range.

Dinner, Wednesday-Saturday from 6, Sunday from 5.

The Landing, 22 North Main St., New Hope, Pa. (215) 862-5711.

The only restaurant right in New Hope with a river view is tucked back off the main street in a small house with windows onto the water and a brick courtyard at the side, offering patio dining in season. Christopher and Leslie Bollenbacher, owners for seventeen years, are known for the most consistent food in town.

"This is a no-smoking building," says the sign at the door, a declaration we applaud. Inside on either side of a quite luxurious small bar are two dining areas. The front room, welcoming in barnwood, contains booths and two tables for two with wing chairs at each and hanging stained-glass lamps. The rear room has picture windows overlooking the river.

The changing menu (which comes in a picture frame) is creative. Entrées ($18.95 to $22.95) range from seared grouper with pineapple sour cream and grilled yellowfin tuna with capers and sundried tomatoes to roast Peking duckling with calvados and apples, loin lamb chops with mint and lingonberry sauce, wild Swedish boar roasted with red and black currants, and venison medallions wrapped with bacon and rosemary in a red wine sauce.

Among appetizers ($7.95 to $9.95) you might try beef carpaccio, smoked duck on a green-peppercorn vinaigrette, or Pine Island oysters broiled with smoked goose and champagne sauce. Desserts are luscious: cranberry-walnut tartlet, chocolate-macadamia cake, truffle torte with grand marnier and a frozen mousse with tia maria. A good wine list is priced from $15 to $65.

The luncheon menu might yield a white-bean with bacon soup, a brussels-sprouts quiche with sundried tomatoes, warm lentil and duck-sausage salad, beer-batter chicken and grilled flank steak with jerked spices, black beans and tropical fruit salsa.

29

Lunch daily, 11 to 4; dinner, 5 to 10 or 11. Closed Monday and Tuesday in winter. No smoking.

Chef Tell's Harrow Inne, 8340 Easton Road (Route 611), Ottsville, Pa. (215) 847-2464.

Master chef and TV personality Tell Erhardt took over Bucks County's oldest inn in 1993 as a new showcase for his contemporary continental cuisine. The 1744 stone landmark, once a stagecoach stop, provides a charming rural setting for food that is nicely presented and represents good value (dinner appetizers, $4.75 to $6.75; entrées, $11.95 to $19.95).

Chef Tell is well known locally through his earlier Philadelphia restaurants and appearances on the syndicated Evening/PM Magazine television show. Until lately he had been spending much time traveling to promote his own line of stainless-steel cookware and running his other restaurant, Chef Tell's Grand Old House on Grand Cayman Island.

His opening menu in Bucks County reflected some Caribbean influences, as in an appetizer of grouper beignets with yogurt-curry mint sauce or main courses of grilled mahi-mahi Cayman style with tomatoes, peppers and onions and almond-crusted red snapper with a mango-peach melange. International influences surface in such items as Cuban black-bean soup with andouille sausage, Greek salad, Thai meat dumpling with teriyaki-ginger glaze, and chicken and lobster in a curry sauce with raita and pappadums.

Chef Tell is nothing if not versatile. He still offers such traditional specialties as venison pâté with cumberland sauce, roast duck "my way" with red cabbage and spaëtzle, and schweinepfeffer, the specialty that won him a gold medal in the 1970 cooking Olympics. It combines pork, red peppers, mushrooms, onions and cracked peppercorns and is served with spaëtzle and sautéed sugar-snap peas. These share the spotlight with changing specials like grilled swordfish with shiitake-balsamic vinaigrette and potato-crusted pheasant with a caramelized pearl-onion relish.

Desserts might be espresso-mousse pie, banana-toffee torte, German apple cake, cappuccino terrine and white-chocolate cheesecake.

The main dining room is attractive with white linens and soft track lighting illuminating the fine paintings from Chef Tell's private collection.

Lunch, 11:30 to 2:30; dinner, 6 to 10; Sunday, brunch 10:30 to 2:30, dinner 5 to 10. Closed Wednesday.

Other Dining Choices

Lambertville Station, 11 Bridge St., Lambertville, N.J. (609) 397-8300.

An abandoned train station has been transformed into a stylish Victorian restaurant and lounge that fairly oozes atmosphere. Diners on several levels of the glass-enclosed Platform Room can watch geese glide by on the Delaware Raritan Canal and see tiny lights reflecting off the water.

The casual ambiance gives little hint of the gourmet treats to come, whether they be a fine carpaccio of buffalo appetizer or the braised sweetbreads served with brandy cream, as good as any we've had and bearing a gentle $12.95 price tag. Also good at our latest visit were a robust venison special with smoked walnuts, brie and apple and the house spinach and tropical salads.

On another occasion, our party of four sampled what was then an unusual appetizer of alligator strips ($6.95), which you dip into a mustard and green

Old railroad platform has been enclosed for dining at Lambertville Station.

peppercorn sauce — interesting, if not the kind of thing we'd want every day. But it proved so popular that alligator is now offered as a main course as well, sautéed with lemon butter for $15.75. Among entrées ($11.95 to $16.50), the jambalaya was spicy, the boneless roast duck was properly crispy and had a raspberry sauce, the seafood fettuccine was more than ample, and the veal medallions with jumbo shrimp in garlic butter were excellent. The honey-mustard dressing on the spinach salad was super and the coconut bread tasty. For dessert, we liked the lime-almond cheesecake even better than an old favorite, key lime mousse pie.

The latest appetizer for the adventuresome is rattlesnake Arizona ($7.75), a combination of rattlesnake and seasonings served over kidney beans and corn with a flour tortilla. Also available are grilled buffalo sirloin and sautéed medallions of wild boar in a wild mushroom sauce. The chef pulls out all the stops for the annual winter game festival: perhaps a warm bear salad with pears, boneless moose sirloin, elk strip steak and filet of yak.

The early-bird special, called Sunset on the Delaware and served weekdays from 4 to 6:30, is considered one of the best bargains around: soup or salad, entrée and dessert for $9.95. A Victorian lounge is on the mezzanine, and a dance club on the lower level is open every night.

Lunch, Monday-Saturday 11:30 to 3; dinner, Monday-Thursday and Sunday 4 to 10, Friday and Saturday 5 to 11; Sunday brunch, 11 to 3.

Mothers, 34 North Main St., New Hope, Pa. (215) 862-9354.

Desserts here are highly recommended, followed by breakfast, lunch and dinner in that order, according to many who have dined at Mothers over the years. Get there early, they advise, for the best dessert choice.

The printed dessert menu, listing chocolate delicacies plus fruit and nut creations, is augmented by daily specials. Indulge in a black and white chocolate pavé, mocha-hazelnut cake, an apricot-almond roulade, trifle, a white-chocolate raspberry gâteau or a banana-hazelnut torte, all great and all in the $3.50 to $5 range. Mothers specializes in coffee drinks -- like Cafe Monk (a nutty concoction of frangelico, kahlua and brandy, $4.75) -- to go with.

Omelets, spuds and eggs, griddle cakes, frittatas, smoked fish and bagels are the fare at breakfast, along with drinks by the glass and pitcher (bloody mary, $14.50; mimosa, $16). Seafood benedict with salmon is the most expensive dish at $10.95, although we thought all the prices to be on the high side. Our cheddar omelet special and an order of two poached eggs on an English muffin came to a cool $13 with coffee and tip.

Everything from pizzas and sandwiches to pastas and entrées is available on the international menu at lunch and dinner. For appetizers, as an example, how about mushrooms à la campagnarde, beef satay or fried chestnut balls with a cranberry dipping sauce? Entrées ($13.95 to $16.95) include Java duck, pepper-crusted salmon and leg of lamb. The inventive menu changes frequently.

There's full bar service, and the menu warns that "Momma don't allow no cigar or pipe smoking here." The several small dining rooms, all tile and brick with beamed ceilings, are lively and intimate, and there's courtyard dining in back.

Breakfast daily, 8 to 2; lunch, 11 to 5; dinner, 5 to 10 or midnight; summer, late-night menu 10 to 2.

David's Yellow Brick Toad, Route 179, Lambertville, N.J. (609) 397-3100.

We'd always been intrigued by the name and the ads touting creative cooking and a special "menu for wellness." When we drove up the hill for Sunday brunch, we were quite unprepared for so large an establishment in what resembled the clubhouse of a country club, surrounded by verdant vistas.

It was built as the restaurant for the old Lambertville Music Circus, the first in the country, owner David Duthie Jr. advised. We've never seen such a jungle of plants hanging from the skylit cathedral ceilings, and the holiday season generated an array of twinkling lights at midday. Posts and beams, dark wood and white stucco walls, track lighting and mats in a pumpkin shade over white linens create a casual, pretty setting.

Smokey and the Benedict (eggs benedict in puff pastry with smoked salmon), a ham and cheese puff with the house salad, and the Toad's Treasure Chest (a garlicky crouton box filled with spinach, broccoli and mushrooms topped with poached eggs and cheese sauce) made a fine brunch for three.

The dinner menu is American-continental. Main courses are priced from $12.50 for vegetable pasta to $25.95 for seafood mixed grill. Specials of the week might include Irish lamb stew and venison with poached pears and juniper. Entrées come with salad and homemade blue cheese, peach vinaigrette, double-mustard or dill-yogurt dressings. Light suppers are offered nightly except Saturday, seven choices from $6.95 for pasta alfredo to $10.25 for scallop scampi on linguini.

Wine tastings, holiday feasts, gourmet dinners and wonderful-sounding picnic baskets -- even brunch with Santa -- are detailed in the Toad's eight-page quarterly newsletter — there's always something going on to lure customers to "go the extra mile" beyond Lambertville. Owner Duthie is proud of his vast wine selection, many available by the glass and many for under $20 a bottle.

Lunch, Tuesday-Saturday 11:30 to 2:30; dinner, Tuesday-Saturday 5 to 10; Sunday, brunch 11 to 3, dinner 11 to 8.

Siam, 61 North Main St., Lambertville, N.J. (609) 397-8128.

This small and highly rated storefront Thai eatery is run by an American and her Thai husband, who cooks with his two brothers and a sister-in-law. Musical instruments from the hill tribes in northern Thailand and swaths of Thai fabrics on the high walls comprise the decor.

Specials of stir-fried beef with oriental eggplant, bamboo shoots, curry paste and basil and a grilled whole baby red snapper with sweet-chile sauce were offered the night we visited. The food is true Thai, much of it flavored with garlic, onion, lime juice, lemon grass, ginger and hot pepper, and garnished with peanut and cucumber sauces. Appetizers are in the $3.75 to $6 range; entrées, $8.50 to $13. The stir-fried pork with spicy peanut sauce on a bed of stir-fried watercress sounds especially appealing. Thai coconut custard, sticky rice, kiwi and mango are among desserts.

Lunch, Wednesday-Sunday 11 to 2; dinner, Tuesday-Saturday 6 to 9 or 10, Sunday 4 to 9. BYOB.

Bucks Bounty, 989 River Road, Erwinna, Pa. (215) 294-8106.

The Adirondacks meet the Southwest in this casual American restaurant put together by a Dutch chef. Johan Van der Linden, who used to be at the old Wilson Inn in Lambertville, N.J., opened his own restaurant here in 1991. It's notable for the unique vaulted ceiling, extravagantly colorful in yellow, red, turquoise and black — the design taken from an Alaskan Indian blanket. Long, narrow mirrors atop the wood wainscoting that doubles as the back for banquettes are bordered by Adirondack scenes. Sturdy Adirondack chairs are at green-clothed tables covered by glass tops.

It's a trendy, unexpected setting for food that Johan calls American-continental with German influences and Italian specialties. He's at his best at dinner, when a lengthy list of specials augments the basic menu. For starters, you might find garlic shrimp or mussels marinara. Entrées ($12.95 to $16.95) could be flounder stuffed with scallops and crab meat, sweetbreads sautéed with cognac and wild mushrooms, chicken saltimbocca, roast pork with oven-roasted potatoes or steak pizzaola. There are pizzas and pastas as well. Favorite desserts are crème brûlée, peach cobbler and shoofly pie.

The lunch menu ($4.75 to $8.95) is not as interesting, although the food is good. One of us had an excellent tuna-salad sandwich, while the other got the soup and half-sandwich special. The onion soup was tasty and the half liverwurst sandwich with a big slice of raw onion more than substantial.

Breakfast, Tuesday-Friday 7:30 to 11:30; lunch daily, 11:30 to 3; dinner nightly, 6 to 10 (fewer nights in off-season), Sunday 5 to 8.

Olde Mill Ford Oyster House, 17 Bridge St., Milford, N.J. (201) 995-9411.

You know the seafood is fresh as can be in this informal restaurant with two small dining rooms downstairs and one upstairs, because the two couples who own it also own the attached fish market and supply many restaurants in the area. Their Nature's Cornucopia outdoor produce market also provides fresh vegetables and herbs. The decor is rather plain but country fresh, with a few oriental rugs on wide-planked floors and blue and white cloths on the tables.

Poached mussels, sautéed mushrooms, pierogies and vegetarian cossack pie might be the night's appetizers. Prices are a pleasant surprise, entrées ranging from $14.95 to $17.95 (for shellfish stew). The menu lists dishes like shrimp in beer batter, New England baked scallops and stuffed flounder with shrimp sauce, but the nightly specials could be crab Norfolk, grilled salmon with watercress-shallot butter, grilled swordfish with rouille, beer-braised rabbit and, at our spring visit, fresh shad roe broiled with bacon on toast points. Entrées come with homey things like little red potatoes and pickled beets.

A local woman makes the pies, maybe pineapple or raspberry, and there's an ice-cream crêpe with chocolate-rum sauce.

Lunch, Thursday-Sunday 11:30 to 3, dinner, Thursday-Saturday 5 to 9 or 9:30, Sunday 5 to 8. No credit cards; BYOB.

Meil's Restaurant, Bridge and Main Streets, Stockton, N.J. (609) 397-8033.

Behind the facade of an old gasoline station housing a bakery and restaurant is one of the area's more versatile eateries. Meil's moved here in 1990 from Lambertville, where it started in the dining room behind Mitchell's bar. The prices are right, the menu extensive and the decor jaunty: colorful balloon curtains over the windows, quilts on the walls (one wall contains a montage of black muffin pans) and tables covered with mint-colored oilcloths.

We sampled a classic salade niçoise ($6.95) and a not-so-classic huevos rancheros ($7.95), the salsa lacking coriander and the eggs resting on a heap of chili (we prefer our eggs resting on the tortilla). Interesting salads (warm sesame-duck and poached-salmon platter), sandwiches and egg dishes are featured at lunch, along with comfort food like chicken pot pie, beef stew and chili with cornbread in the $9 range. Something called "Day after Thanksgiving" (you know what that means) for $9.95 was on the menu at our December visit.

Night brings some of the daytime fare (more salads and suppers) as well as hefty pastas and main courses from $12.95 for meatloaf with mashed potatoes and gravy to $19.95 for peanut shrimp or grilled duck breast. Mustard chicken, pork chops and sautéed crab cakes are mainstays.

Breakfast daily, 9 to 3; lunch, 11 to 3; dinner, 4:30 to 9 or 10. No credit cards.

The Cafe, Route 510 at Route 604, Rosemont, N.J. (609) 397-4097.

Lola Tindell and Peg Peterson moved their little cafe from Lambertville to Rosemont in 1990. In the 1885 old general store, they have a lot more room to offer "fresh food at its simple best," as their business card attests.

It's a casual, drop-in kind of place with bare floors, wooden tables, a mix of chair styles and, we found, rather laid-back service. Shelves are filled with the cookbooks they use, plus items for sale like gourmet foods, Botanicus soaps and striking ceramics, some done by one of the waitresses. A case along one side displays cheeses, desserts and baked goods. Things get more formal for dinner on weekends with candles, cloth napkins and 1940s tablecloths on the tables.

Stop in for a breakfast burrito or the Adirondack breakfast, muesli and a bran muffin, which "gives you the strength to climb mountains," says the menu. Omelets include Russian peasant and rhubarb-ginger chutney with cream cheese. Potatoes from heaven are grilled with olive oil, rosemary, garlic, onion and cayenne.

For lunch we enjoyed an excellent turkey quesadilla ($6) and a hefty turkey sandwich on whole wheat ($4.75) from a menu that included eggplant and mozzarella boboli, pasta with wild-mushroom sauce and red-pepper ravioli with olive oil and garlic, most in the $6 to $7 range.

At dinnertime, when entrées range from $13 to $16.50, you can still find sandwiches and omelets for much less. Try broiled flounder with herbs, chicken brailia or pasta Wilhemina, named for the resident ghost, with chicken, broccoli, mushrooms and garlic. There's a large selection of natural soft drinks, mineral waters, teas, coffees and juices, and you may BYOB. Mocha pot de crème and cranberry flan are popular desserts, and Peg's cheesecakes (maybe rum-raisin or espresso) are also in demand.

Open weekdays at 8, weekends from 9; dinner, Thursday-Sunday to 9. Closed Monday. BYOB.

Victoriana prevails at Evermay on the Delaware.

The Bridge Cafe, 8 Bridge St., Frenchtown, N.J. (908) 996-6040.

If you're not up to the prices and the complexity of the Frenchtown Inn across the street, this small cafe with a large screened porch facing the river is a good bet for breakfast, lunch and occasional dinners. Sip a mochaccino while you try an omelet (the Greek has roast eggplant, feta and tomato) or "better than french toast bread pudding," which is served with orange butter.

At lunch, a turkey burger comes on a toasted homemade roll with gourmet sprouts and curried mayonnaise. Other sandwiches and salads (in the $5.50 to $7.50 range) include a vegetarian stuffed pita and a Mediterranean hero. Soup of the day might be red bean and sausage, and a special of grilled fish cakes on nippy greens sounded interesting. A chocolate-buttermilk bundt cake and frozen non-fat yogurt with fresh berries are a couple of the good desserts.

"Mainstay" dinners, including cafe bread, fresh vegetables and salad with balsamic vinaigrette, are around $15 for the likes of sautéed soft-shell crabs or herbed-crusted salmon fillet.

Open daily, 7 to 4 for breakfast and lunch, to 9 in summer for dinner; rest of year, no dinner except Friday and Saturday. BYOB.

Bed and Board

Evermay on the Delaware, River Road, Erwinna, Pa. 18920. (215) 294-9100.

Dinner at this charming country inn is served only on Friday, Saturday and Sunday nights at one 7:30 seating, and is in such demand that usually you must book far in advance. The six-course meal costs $48, with little choice except between two entrées and two desserts.

Owners Ron Strouse and Fred Cresson gained a reputation for fine cuisine at the Sign of the Sorrel Horse in Quakertown, which they sold to concentrate on Evermay.

The main dining room has been enhanced by new draperies and matching upholstered chairs. Out back is a porch-conservatory pretty in pink, with tables

35

for two set up in the narrow room (a bit too narrow, we thought, since you could overhear others' conversations and the waiter's recitation of every course to every table). Also, a chilly evening was made chillier by the stone floors and wide expanse of windows.

But not to quibble. The meal was one of the best we've had, nicely presented and paced. Hors d'oeuvre of smoked-trout salad, sundried-tomato crostini and country pâté with green peppercorns were served first. After these came in order a suave chicken and leek soup, sautéed chanterelles on a saffron crouton, and a salad of boston and mache lettuces, garnished with violets and toasted walnuts and dressed with a fine balsamic vinaigrette.

Thank goodness all these courses were small, for we needed room for chef Ron's main courses: tender lamb noisettes wrapped in bacon and topped with a green-peppercorn butter, and Norwegian salmon poached in white wine, served with hollandaise sauce and garnished with shrimp. These came with thin, crisp asparagus from Chile, a mixture of white and wild rice, and sprigs of watercress.

A cheese course of perhaps St. André, montrachet and gorgonzola precedes dessert. Ours was a perfect poached pear, set atop vanilla ice cream, butterscotch sauce, golden raisins and pecans. These days a choice is offered, perhaps chocolate cones filled with white-chocolate mousse and raspberries, a linzer torte with fresh raspberries and thirteen ingredients in the crust, a pecan tart made without flour but with kahlua, or coffee-kahlua-honey-almond ice cream. Fred does all the baking, makes his own sorbets and ice creams, and is responsible for the knockout flower arrangements all around.

Twenty chardonnays are on the well-chosen, primarily California wine list, which contains some not-often-seen vintages.

Evermay is more than a memorable dinner. It's an inn with sixteen rooms (one named for Pearl S. Buck, longtime resident of the area) on the second and third floors, a newer loft suite on the fourth floor, and in a carriage house and a cottage. They are furnished in Victoriana, as befits the era when this structure became a hotel (the original house dates from the early 1700s). All have private baths and telephones, and many have queensize beds. Fresh flowers and a large bowl of fruit decorate each room, and at bedtime you may find fruit and candy and a liqueur in a little glass with a doily on top.

A fire burns in the fireplace in the double parlor, and decanters of sherry are placed on tables in front of the Victorian sofas. Afternoon tea with watercress or cucumber sandwiches and cookies is served at 4 p.m.

Although continental, breakfast is quite special, with orange juice, incredibly flaky croissants and pastries, one with cream cheese in the center, and the pièce de résistance at our visit: a compote of fresh strawberries, red seedless grapes, bananas and honeydew melon, garnished with a sprig of mint and dusted with confectioners' sugar — colorful and pretty.

Evermay also has one of the strangest bathtubs in which we've bathed. It's in the carriage house and is, we assume, a Victorian number, with oak trim around the rim. It's narrow, so long that a six-footer can stretch out and so deep that you can barely see out. We would not recommend it for anyone with a touch of arthritis — it could take a crane to get you in or out.

We would recommend Fred's and Ron's cooking to anyone, however. It's so good that it could practically cure what ails you.

Dinner, Friday-Sunday at 7:30. Jackets required. Doubles, $80 to $155; two-bedroom suite, $185.

Golden Pheasant Inn, River Road, Erwinna, Pa. 18920. (215) 294-9595.

A more stunningly romantic spot than the solarium of the Golden Pheasant is hard to imagine. Beneath the stars is a rainbow of orange chairs, green cloths, hanging lamps, a large vat of colorful mums and tiny twinkling lights all around. The place is so dim that we had to ask for an extra candle to read the menu. The canal bank beyond is illuminated at night, and it's all rather magical.

Well-known local chef Michel Faure from Grenoble and his wife Barbara, who took over in 1986, have refurbished the two inner dining rooms from dark Victorian to the inn's original 1850s period, brightened with accents of copper pots, oriental rugs and their extensive Quimper collection from Brittany. The bar is in the front of the wallpapered main dining room, which contains a working fireplace. The inner Blaise Room claims hardwood floors, a beamed ceiling, recessed windows and exposed stone walls. The family live upstairs, and they have renovated six guest rooms to offer "a taste of France on the banks of the Delaware," according to Barbara.

She has decorated the rooms with country touches, antiques and four-poster beds, one so high that you need a stool to climb up. We were particularly impressed with the main-floor suite with its private deck and a stereo set. Overnight guests enjoy a rear patio beside the canal.

The geese along the canal don't end up on the menu, though pheasant occasionally does, roasted and flambéed with calvados, shallots and apples. French-born Michel, who was formerly at the Carversville Inn and worked in a number of French restaurants, including Philadelphia's esteemed Le Bec Fin and New Hope's Odette's, presents a classic French menu rich with sauces.

Start with the pheasant pâté ($9.95), snails sautéed with hazelnut-garlic butter or Michel's acclaimed lobster bisque. Entrées range from $19.95 for sautéed chicken with tarragon sauce or medallions of pork dijonnaise to $27.95 for veal cutlets with morels and crème fraîche. Steak au poivre is flamed with brandy and crème fraîche, lump crab cake is served with a light mustard hollandaise, and rack of lamb comes with a rosemary, garlic and mint demi-glaze. Cassoulet of seafood bears a lobster sauce. Roast boneless duck might be sauced with raspberry, ginger and rum.

Desserts include cappuccino cheesecake, pecan pie, crème caramel, home-made sorbets and a specialty, Belgian white-chocolate mousse with a raspberry coulis.

Dinner, Tuesday-Sunday 5:30 to 9 or 10. Doubles, $110 to $145.

The Inn at Phillips Mill, North River Road, New Hope, Pa. 18938. (215) 862-9919 (dining) and 862-2984 (lodging).

Depending on the season, hanging pots overflowing with fuchsias or wooden casks filled with all colors of mums mark the entrance to this small and adorable yet sophisticated inn. When you see its facade of local gray stone, smack up against an S-turn bend in River Road, with its copper pig hanging over the entrance, you would almost swear you were in Britain's Cotswolds.

Inside, that impression is heightened, as you take in the low-ceilinged rooms with dark beams, pewter service plates and water goblets, and a gigantic leather couch in front of a massive fireplace, on which you can recline while waiting for your table. Candles augment the light from the fireplace, and arrangements of fresh and dried flowers are all around.

The French menu is short and to the point, and the prices reasonable. The house terrine, foie gras with truffles in phyllo and a salad of warm goat cheese and roasted peppers on watercress are among appetizers ($5.50 to $9.50). We started with a springtime special, Maryland crab meat in half an avocado; it was indeed special, garnished with shredded carrots and black olives.

Main courses range from $14.50 for chicken breast with lentils and herbs to $22 for rack of lamb dijonnaise. We have never tasted such a tender filet mignon with such a delectable béarnaise sauce (and artichoke heart) nor such perfect sweetbreads in a light brown sauce as on our first visit. The sautéed calves liver in a cider-vinegar sauce and the filet of veal with roasted garlic and scallions were excellent the second time around.

A basket of crusty French bread (with which you are tempted to sop up the wonderful sauces) and sweet butter comes before dinner. Try to save room for one of the super desserts ($4) — once a lemon ice-cream meringue pie, about six inches high and wonderfully refreshing, and later a vanilla mousse with big chips of chocolate and a fudge sauce.

Sometimes it is hazardous to bring your own wine. The host at a table of four next to ours was wondering where his expensive bottle of Clos du Val had gone when we noticed the waitress on the verge of pouring it into our glasses. We caught her in time and reconciled ourselves to our modest bottle of California zinfandel.

Upstairs are four cozy guest rooms and a suite, cheerily decorated by innkeeper Joyce Kaufman (her husband Brooks is an architect who did the restoration of the 1750 structure). The rooms are usually booked far in advance. One has its own sitting room. Honeymooners ask for the third-floor hideaway suite, where fabric covers the ceiling. Most beds are four-posters or brass and iron and are covered with quilts. They don't advertise it, but sometimes the Kaufmans rent a cottage in back of the inn, and share their small swimming pool with house guests.

A continental breakfast (juice, croissants and coffee) is delivered to your room in a basket for $3.50 a person.

Dinner nightly, 5:30 to 9:30 or 10. BYOB. No credit cards. Doubles, $75; suite, $85; cottage, $125.

Hotel du Village, River Road at Phillips Mill Road, New Hope, Pa. 18938. (215) 862-9911.

The French name is a bit misleading, since the chef-owner is Algerian and his hostelry is English Tudor in an early boarding-school setting. The dining room is in the former Lower Campus building of Solebury School and looks exactly like one in an English manor house, with a glowing fire at each end, a beamed ceiling, small-paned windows and a fine Persian carpet on the floor. Candles, fresh flowers and crisp linens add to the luxurious feeling.

Country French cuisine is the forte of 44-year-old Omar Arbani, who arrived in Bucks County from Algeria by way of culinary endeavors in France, Denmark, London and Washington, D.C. His menu seldom changes. Partial to fine sauces, he shuns nouvelle to provide "the kind of home-style country cuisine you'd find in the restaurants of Bordeaux or Burgundy on a Sunday afternoon," in the words of his wife Barbara, a former New Jersey teacher, who manages the dining room and inn.

Prices remain among the more reasonable in the area, although some find the portions small. Appetizers, including escargots, shrimp sautéed in garlic butter, clams casino and mushrooms rémoulade, are $5.50 to $5.95, except $6.50 for lamb sausage, one of the few additions to the menu since we dined here ten

1740 House backs up to canal towpath and Delaware River.

years earlier. Main courses run from $13.95 for chicken tarragon to $18.95 for tournedos or steak au poivre. The house salad is $3.50 extra.

Our tournedos Henry IV, with artichoke heart and béarnaise sauce, was heavenly. So were the sweetbreads financière, with green olives, mushrooms and madeira sauce. Potatoes sautéed with lots of rosemary, crisp beans and grilled tomato with a crumb topping were worthy accompaniments.

Bread was piping hot and crusty — grand when spread with the house pâté ($5.50 for a small crock as an appetizer). Moist black-forest cake, crammed with cherries, and café royale were sweet endings to a rich, romantic meal.

The pre-dinner drinks were huge and one of us, who shall be nameless, ordered a bottle of Mill Creek merlot, which was ever-so-smooth. The trouble was he had forgotten his glasses and thought the price to be $10 (this was years ago); when the bill came it was twice what he had expected. Moral: bring along your glasses.

Hotel du Village serves dinner in the main dining room, paneled in rare American chestnut pieced together from other sections of the building, and in an adjacent room that was originally a sun porch, with windows on three sides. Beyond the bar is a small room with more dining tables on two levels, candles in hurricane lamps and a wood stove in the corner.

Accommodations in twenty rather spare rooms in a converted stable in the rear reflect their boarding-school heritage, although all have private baths and air-conditioning. Guests get continental breakfast and have access to a pool, two tennis courts and gorgeous grounds.

Dinner, 5:30 to 9, Friday and Saturday to 10:30, Sunday 3 to 9. Restaurant closed Monday and Tuesday, and mid-January to mid-February. Doubles, $85 to $100.

1740 House, River Road, Lumberville, Pa. 18933. (215) 297-5661.

The first time we tried to book at this delightful inn we were turned away, trying for Easter weekend a month in advance. So the following spring we were pleasantly surprised to get a choice of rooms only a week ahead.

Twenty-four spacious, individually decorated rooms on two floors overlook the canal and, beyond the towpath, the river. Glass doors open onto your own brick patio or balcony. There are kingsize or twin beds, and real wooden coat hangers that detach from the rod. The chambermaid knocks on the door to turn down the bed and give you fresh towels. A complimentary breakfast is served in the garden room. You can laze in a tiny swimming pool or paddle the canal beneath your room in the inn's canoe.

All this for less than the Holiday Inn in New Hope usually charges for you know exactly what.

Lately, Robert John Vris has assumed some of the management duties long held by his grandfather, 92-year-old Harry Nessler, the ubiquitous innkeeper. The latter is a well-traveled ex-New Yorker who retired from real estate and with his late wife opened a new, built-to-look-old motel-type inn that was among the first of its genre in 1967. His patrician demeanor masks a personal interest in guests' well-being, including making reservations for dinner at other restaurants upon request — "you'll get a better table and service," he explains. Upon your return, he also asks how your dinner was and is apt to chide that his was better.

Indeed, the 1740 House serves a very good dinner (for house guests only) in the airy garden dining room, nightly except Sunday, 6:30 to 8.

Table-d'hôte prices from $25 to $29.95 include appetizer or soup and dessert. Order one of the four entrées in the morning, and bring your own wine. Avocado soup, fettuccine alfredo or seafood crêpes could start you off. Crab imperial, butterfly shrimp in cream sauce, lamb chops, filet mignon and, in spring, shad roe might be chalked up on the blackboard. We particularly liked the château-briand with béarnaise and the veal marsala on one of our not infrequent visits. Crème caramel and a lemon-orange chiffon pie were worthy endings.

Breakfast is served buffet-style from 8:30 to 10 in the cheery, flagstone-floored garden dining room, where if it's busy you'll share tables. Guests help themselves to juice, cereal, croissants and a hot dish like scrambled eggs or creamed chipped beef, and toast their own English muffins or homemade bread.

This is a place to savor the peace and quiet of the river from your balcony or porch, to read in your room (there's no television) or in a couple of small parlors, to meander up River Road to the center of Lumberville and walk the canal towpath or cross the footbridge to an island park in New Jersey.

Doubles, $70 (weekdays) to $100 (weekends). No credit cards.

The Stockton Inn, 1 Main St., Stockton, N.J. 08559. (609) 397-1250.

"There's a small hotel with a wishing well," Richard Rodgers and Lorenz Hart wrote for the 1936 Broadway show, "On Your Toes." This is that small hotel, and guests still make wishes at *the* wishing well.

Dating from 1710, the place oozes history. It was a mecca for artists and celebrities, band leader Paul Whiteman used to sign off his radio shows with the announcement that he was going there for dinner, and in 1935 it gained national fame as the press headquarters during the Lindbergh kidnapping trial. The Colligan family ran it for 55 years until 1983.

Major renovations to the guest accommodations followed, and since it was taken over in 1989 by former New York restaurant manager Andrew McDermott, the food has been upgraded as well. "I'm now proud of the cuisine," says Andy.

He and chef Stuart Pellegrino present a contemporary American menu that's trendy but, they stress, "not too trendy" — prime rib and Maine lobsters from the inn's own tank are featured along with the likes of grilled salmon with chive watercress and hearts of palm and grilled mahi-mahi with plum-tomato coulis.

For starters ($6.50 to $8.95), we found the trio of salmon -- home-cured gravlax with rillettes and smoked salmon from the inn's smoker -- a sensational presentation, thanks to an assortment of sauces, condiments and delicious homemade baguette toasts. We also enjoyed the special salad, an arrangement of arugula, goat cheese, roasted red peppers and sundried tomatoes with a complex, smoky taste.

Among entrées ($15.95 to $24.95), the boned and rolled chicken stuffed with mushroom duxelles and flanked by an array of green beans, carrots, braised red cabbage and layered potatoes was excellent. So was the veal sauté with sundried tomatoes and roasted garlic. Desserts include chocolate-truffle torte, crème caramel and deep-dish apple pie.

All this is offered in six historic dining rooms seating 175. Five have fireplaces and three are notable for murals of local scenes painted by artists during the Depression in exchange for room and board (one pictures Paul Whiteman fallen from his horse on his way home to nearby Rosemont after over-imbibing at dinner). In season, there's dining on five outside terraces amidst two waterfalls and a pond stocked with golden trout. The **Old World Garden Bar** on the upper terrace has a dance floor, and there's piano music here and in two inside bars on weekends.

The inn offers three guest rooms and eight suites, three of them upstairs and the rest in three restored buildings nearby. All come with private baths and color TV and most with queensize canopy beds. Seven have fireplaces and four have porches or balconies. We were impressed with all the amenities -- from the selection of timely magazines and a mini-refrigerator to toiletries and a mending kit -- in the comfortable upstairs suite in the Federal House. The next morning, there was quite a spread of fresh fruit (kiwi, strawberries, pineapple and cantaloupe), carafes of juices and an array of pastries from croissants to muffins to nut bread to savor for continental breakfast in one of the inn's dining rooms.

Lunch, Monday-Saturday 11:30 to 3:30; dinner, Monday-Thursday 4:30 to 9:30, weekends 5 to 10; Sunday, brunch 11 to 2:30, dinner 3:30 to 9. Doubles, $80 to $105; suites, $125 to $145.

The Black Bass Hotel, Route 32, Lumberville, Pa. 18933. (215) 297-5770 (dining) and 297-5815 (lodging).

The food is said to have improved lately at the venerable Black Bass, an inn dating from the 1740s and every traveler's idea of what a French countryside inn should look like. Harry Nessler, innkeeper of the 1740 House just down the road, likes to recall how one of his guests, Pierre Matisse, told him that the Black Bass "looks just like the inns my father painted."

Lunch may be a better bet than dinner because (1) you should take advantage of the fact the dining room with its long porch overlooks the river, (2) the food can be inconsistent, although we've had both a good dinner and a good lunch here over the years, and (3) prices at dinner are steep — entrées like the Charleston Meeting Street crab meat, a fixture on the menu, going for $24.95 at our latest visit.

Wander around the charming old inn and look at all the British memorabilia collected by innkeeper Herbert Ward as well as the pewter bar that came from Maxim's in Paris. We enjoyed our lunch of New Orleans onion soup and the house salad. The soup, thick with onions and cheese, came in a proper crock; the crisp greens in the salad were laden with homemade croutons and a nifty house dressing of homemade mayonnaise, horseradish, dijon mustard and spices. Famished after a lengthy hike along the towpath, one of us devoured seven of the nut and date mini-muffins that came in a basket. Lunch entrées range from

$6.95 for omelet of the day to $12.95 for the crabmeat or grilled salmon with potato-horseradish galette.

Dinner prices start at $19.95 for sautéed rainbow trout with curry sauce or roast duck over walnut-flavored spaëtzle. If you don't try the crabmeat, which many do, consider roast pork tenderloin with molasses-bourbon-pecan sauce and a fried grit cake or lobster française with swiss chard and tomato-saffron sauce. Finish with homemade ice creams or sorbets, walnut or rum cream pies, or chocolate mousse with raspberry coulis.

Lighted stamped-tin lanterns hang from thick beams in the various dining rooms, which are filled with antiques, collections of old china in high cabinets, and fancy wrought iron around the windows. The wood chairs look as if they've been around since 1740; it's a wonder they don't fall apart.

Upstairs are seven rooms sharing two baths and three suites with antique furnishings. Some have ornate iron balconies, upon which continental breakfast is served overlooking the river.

Lunch, Monday-Saturday noon to 1:30; dinner, 5:30 to 10; Sunday, brunch noon to 3, dinner 3:30 to 8. Doubles, $55 to 90; suites, $150 and $175.

Lodging

Whitehall Inn, 1370 Pineville Road, RD 2, Box 250, New Hope, Pa. 18938. (215) 598-7945.

In the rolling countryside about five miles from the hustle and bustle of New Hope, this 1794 manor house on twelve acres has been open as an inn since 1985. The hospitality of its owners, Oklahomans Mike and Suella Wass, who keep an electric candle always lit in one room as a symbol for peace, is such that some guests return as often as five times a year.

We can understand why, because Whitehall is a true retreat from the cares of the world. Seldom are you as coddled as here.

Four of the six antiques-filled bedrooms have working fireplaces (and the innkeepers lay a fire for you on chilly nights), four have private baths and some have canopy beds. While you are out for dinner, your bed is turned down and wonderful handmade chocolate truffles inscribed with a W for Whitehall are left beside it. Sip wine or Poland Spring mineral water (a bottle is in your room) from crystal wine glasses as you contemplate the fire. Soak in a tub made fragrant by the innkeepers' homemade bath salts before you snuggle into your flannel-sheeted bed. From large containers of shampoos and fancy soaps to extra-thick colored towels and velour robes, the Wasses have overlooked no detail.

A swimming pool and arrangements for horseback riding are other draws. We still haven't mentioned the best part — the leisurely, four- or five-course candlelight breakfasts and elegant afternoon teas. Served promptly at 9, breakfast is cooked by Suella, who arises at 6 to prepare it, and served with aplomb by Mike, surely the cheeriest morning person we have met. It usually starts with fresh juice (honey-tangerine at our last visit) and the inn's secret blend of coffee that we think has a touch of chocolate and cinnamon in it, or English and herbal teas. Next come two of Suella's breads or muffins. Once we sampled tiny carrot muffins and cinnamon ribbon bread. At a subsequent visit, the "prize-winning" butter coffee cake was a big hit. The warm apple and sweet paprika soup was unusual and tasty. A fruit course follows, perhaps a baked pear stuffed with raisins, walnuts and lemon rind on a caramel sauce, or sliced oranges with orange flower water and a dusting of powdered sugar. Then there might be an appetizer

Suella and Mike Wass pamper guests at Whitehall Inn.

of cheddar cheese and corn spoonbread, after which (can you stand it?) comes holiday french toast souffléed with eggnog and rum or a delicate spinach tart with toasted pinenuts and parmesan cheese. Just in case you're still hungry, Bucks County sausage patties might also be on the plate. And just in case you are *still* hungry, a little dish of jarlsberg cheese and chocolate-toffee crunch could finish the repast with your last sip of coffee.

All this takes about an hour and a half, and there is good camaraderie at the two formally set tables. Candles on the tables and in the wall sconces, sterling silver so pretty that it is turned over to show the gracefully scrolled backs, and Villeroy & Boch china in the Petites Fleurs pattern create a gracious atmosphere. After they have finished cooking and serving, Mike and Suella join guests for coffee to chat and advise about the day's excursions.

Three or four kinds of cookies, tea breads and cakes are served at tea time, along with perhaps open-face cucumber and blue cheese sandwiches or three-onion tarts. We especially enjoyed the currant-orange scones with devonshire cream and strawberry preserves. Daughter Sarah (who has won prizes in several baking contests) might have baked the chocolate cookies. Tea is properly brewed and poured, of course, from a silver pot.

The spacious double parlor, a fireplace blazing at one end, contains comfortable chairs and sofas, a piano and a pump organ, a stereo and lots of books, magazines and games. Guests have filled many diaries with remarks about their dining experiences, most relating that the best food and hospitality were at the Whitehall. A jigsaw puzzle is always in progress on a sun porch. A decanter of sherry is set out near the fire for returning guests in the evening. Homemade potpourri from Mike's roses is everywhere.

Is there anything these innkeepers have not thought of? They even write notes after you leave to thank you for choosing them, and send repeat guests off with gifts of coffee, bath salts or potpourri. If you are a returnee, their computer tells what you had to eat at breakfast, so you will be served something different from Suella's vast repertoire.

Could there be more? Yes. They offer spring tea concerts (one with a chocolate theme and another featuring strawberries). On summer holiday weekends, they put together gourmet picnics -- on the grounds or to go. And because they are music buffs, they host events like a baroque tea concert in May and a candlelight champagne New Year's Eve concert.

This special inn appeals to the romantic, as well as to the gourmet, in all who visit.

Doubles, $130 to $170. No smoking.

The Inn at Lambertville Station, 11 Bridge St., Lambertville, N.J. 08530. (609) 397-4400 or (800) 524-1091.

More than $3 million went into this architecturally impressive luxury inn beside the Delaware River with a three-story-high lobby and the most elegant of suites.

You check in at a counter resembling the ticket office of an old train station, perhaps tarry for tea or a drink from the honor bar in the towering lobby or on the adjacent creekside deck, and get your bags up the elevator to your room. Prized antiques are in the 45 impressive guest rooms, each named for a major city and decorated accordingly by an antiques dealer who spared no expense.

Ours was the corner New York Suite, high in the trees above a rushing waterfall that lulled us to sleep. There were chocolates at bedside, the bathroom had a whirlpool tub and a basket of good toiletries, and around the L-shaped room were heavy mahogany furniture, leather chairs facing the fireplace and TV, handsome draperies, ornate mirrors and fine art. A small continental breakfast with carrot-nut muffins arrived at our door with a newspaper the next morning.

The large Riverside Room, facing the river with windows on three sides, is used for Sunday brunch ($18.95 for quite a spread).

Doubles, $80 to $110; suites with fireplaces and whirlpool baths, $150.

Isaac Stover House, Route 32, Erwinna, Pa. 18920. (215) 294-8044.

Theatrical. That's the best way to describe this 1837 Victorian Federal mansion owned by radio-TV personality Sally Jessy Raphael, who has furnished it with flair and whimsy.

The collections acquired from her globe-trotting travels are showcased in typical Victorian clutter through the seven guest rooms, five with private baths. The owner's favorite, the third-floor Cupid's Bower, is a confection of pink ruffles and lace. Wizard of Oz paraphernalia marks the Emerald City Room, a beauty in deep greens with a fireplace. A poofed valance borders the ceiling of the Amore Room, which has a river view and the inn's only queensize bed. A big potted plant with fake flowers adorns the Secret Garden room. The Bridal Suite, all lace, has its own sitting room with a small TV. Swags, tassels, stuffed animals, oriental tapestries, crystal chandeliers — you name it, it's bound to be here somewhere.

All the red velvet chairs and settees, moiré draperies, lace antimacassars and silk pillows from Burma are a sight to behold in the formal parlor, where Balinese shadow puppets and a tapestry from Malta are showcased above the marble fireplace. There's an upstairs television nook with books and games, and a front porch is outfitted in white wicker and black wrought iron. Cookies, fruit, beverages, wine and cheese are put out in the afternoon, and truffles are at bedside. In the morning, innkeeper Susan Tettemer serves a hearty repast (perhaps potato-cheese frittata, crêpes or an asparagus omelet) amid crocheted tops, lacy cloths and crystal chandeliers in a pretty breakfast room.

Although you won't likely see the owner — she gets here only a couple of

Hunterdon House is a recently restored Italian villa in Frenchtown.

times a month, says Susan, and had the place up for sale — you can see her pictures in the bathroom of the fireplaced Loyalty Royalty room and scattered throughout the house.

Doubles, $150 to $175; suite, $250.

Hunterdon House, 12 Bridge St., Frenchtown, N.J. 08825. (908) 996-3632 or (800) 382-0375.

A $200,000 rehab and redecoration preceded the reopening in 1992 of this grand Italian villa. Previously known as the Old Hunterdon House, it was originally launched as a B&B by the owners of Evermay-on-the-Delaware across the river. An archivist did the paint scheme, coordinating yet varying the colors throughout the house, which had deteriorated under subsequent owners. The latest investment shows, inside and out, and new owners Clark Johnson and his wife, Karen Amritt, are justly proud and in an expansionist mood.

The couple offer seven guest rooms, all with private baths and furnished in Victoriana. Antiques, oriental rugs, the inn's own toiletries and queensize beds and ornate carved headboards are among the attractions. A main-floor room offers a working fireplace, while a third-floor suite comes with a wicker-appointed sitting room.

Guests gather in a formal living room, at window seats in the rooftop belvedere (with views in all directions) or on the front porch facing a manicured lawn and gardens. "Everything you can see from the porch dates from the 1800s except for the cars," Clark says of the tranquil scene along Frenchtown's main street.

A full breakfast is served at lace-covered tables for two in the dining room. The handwritten menu the day we were there gave a choice of eggs benedict with herbed red potatoes, blueberry pancakes with link sausages, asparagus and cheese omelet with bacon and a toasted bagel, and scrambled eggs with corned-beef hash. Tea and refreshments are offered in the afternoons.

With the installation of a full professional kitchen, the owners planned to offer breakfast and tea to the public. They also show off the interior on guided tours. Doubles, $100 to $145. No smoking.

Bridgeton House, River Road, Box 167, Upper Black Eddy, Pa. 18972. (215) 982-5856.

The Delaware River literally is the back yard of this comfortable B&B, just beyond a landscaped terrace and on view through french doors and the third-floor balconies. Although smack up against the road, the onetime wreck of an apartment house built in 1836 has been transformed by Bea and Charles Briggs and reoriented to the rear to take advantage of the waterside location.

A parlor with a velvet sofa looks onto the canal. Fresh or dried flowers, a decanter of sherry and potpourri grace the dining room, where breakfast is served. Following a fruit course (perhaps baked pears in cream or a fresh fruit plate) comes a main dish: waffles with strawberry butter, eggs roxanne or mushroom and cheese omelets. Fresh lemon breads, muffins and apple cake likely accompany.

Upstairs are ten guest rooms and suites overlooking the river, each exceptionally fashioned by Charles, a master carpenter and renovator, and interestingly decorated by Bea. Some have four-posters and chaise lounges; all have private baths, country antiques, colorful sheets and fresh flowers. Our main-floor room included a private porch with rockers and lovely stenciling, a feature throughout the house, done by a cousin who also did the nude paintings scattered about.

What Bea calls Bucks County's ultimate room is a huge penthouse suite with a kingsize bed beneath a twelve-foot cathedral ceiling, a black and white marble fireplace, a marble bathtub, black leather chairs, a stereo-TV center, a backgammon table and a full-length deck looking down onto the river.

Doubles, $79 to $139; suites, $149 and $199. No smoking.

York Street House, 42 York St., Lambertville, N.J. 08530. (609) 397-3007.

James Bulger of the Swan Hotel opened this large Georgian brick home as Lambertville's first B&B after it had been glamorized as a designers' showhouse.

A pillared front veranda with wrought-iron furniture welcomes guests, and the main-floor common rooms are impressively outfitted with fine art and Mercer tiles around the fireplaces. An original Waterford chandelier glitters over chintz chairs and cushions in the large living room. Tables are set for breakfast with peach napkins and white cloths in the formal dining room, and the dark, cherry-paneled library has a TV set.

Crystal knobs open the doors to the six large guest rooms, three on the second floor with private baths and three on the third sharing two baths. Some have queensize canopy beds.

Resident innkeepers Claire and Jeff Shoemaker oversee the place for his uncle. They serve a full breakfast—sometimes scrambled eggs and sometimes pancakes or french toast — with homemade muffins.

Doubles, $80 to $100.

Gourmet Treats

River Road Farms, just up River Road from EverMay in Erwinna, Pa., is a complex of buildings centered by a picturesque red wood and fieldstone barn built in 1749. **Chachka,** an interesting gift shop in the barn, is chock full of crystal

Richard deGroot features Gentleman Farmer's preserves and relishes at Chachka.

and porcelain, much of it from Portugal. The real draws here, though, are all the "food accents" and the wild and wonderful preserves and relishes made by Richard deGroot, the "Gentleman Farmer" who lives next door. From hot or sweet-pepper relish to sweet carrot relish to Colonial cranberry catsup to pickled cocktail radishes (yes, radishes), the relishes cost $3.69 and up. Most of his preserves, plum-rhubarb with amaretto, pumpkin marmalade with rum, spicy blueberry with cointreau, banana strawberry with framboise — have you ever heard of such neat combinations? — are in the $4.89 range for ten ounces. All are topped with calico bonnets so they make great hostess gifts. Pastas, sauces and condiments like a *very* hot Thai garlic sauce (opened for tasting -- we nearly choked) are dotted around. Chachka also hosts outdoor festivals with seasonal food and entertainment on certain weekends.

In an old train station, **The Little Shop,** 2 Bridge St., Milford, N.J., offers food items and gifts, and provides tables for dining or just having a cappuccino in a front room and along an outdoor deck with hot pink awnings in season. We enjoyed an excellent seafood quiche with a side salad and a homemade rhubarb pie. Proprietor Jo French, a native of England, sells wonderful paper things, preserves and sauces from Crabtree & Evelyn (and has some nice gift baskets for these products), many cheeses and a wide selection of fresh ground coffees. Try her truffle mousse or just pick up a Belgian praline if you fancy something sweet. Giant chocolate and shortbread sculpted cookies bear all kinds of messages.

At **Lambertville Trading Co.,** 43 Bridge St., Lambertville, N.J., "when we grind coffee, the whole street smells," says Dean Stephens, who ran the Black Bass Hotel for a time and started selling herbs and spices to the public and to many restaurants, whose chefs rave about them. Since then, he's added a cappuccino bar where you can sip mochaccino ($3.50) and sample a dessert (cranberry-orange cream pie, brandied apricot mousse, $3 to $4) amid an expanded selection of food baskets, chocolates, preserves, cans of almonds and such.

In New Hope, the exceptional **New Hope Cheese Shop** at 18 North Main St. purveys all kinds of usual and unusual cheeses, Tuscany toast with sundried tomatoes and wild onions, and cornichons to go with the pâtés. The smoked-salmon mousse is layered with spinach and topped with grape leaves and a fresh mozzarella roll has pepperoni or pesto sauce. Wheels of candies that look like mosaics and cost a cool $25 each brightened the windows at our latest visit, and we fell for a hefty Bucks County cookie. **Gerenser's Exotic Ice Cream** at 22 South Main offers such flavors as English mincemeat, African violet, Hungarian tokay, Swedish ollaliberry, Polish plum brandy, Greek watermelon, Indian mango, Jewish malaga and ancient Roman ambrosia ($1.75 for a cone, or $2.50 for a waffle cone). Satisfy your coffee urge at **Two Sisters Gourmet Coffee** at 11B West Bridge St. Fresh roasted and flavored Arabica coffees are offered along with hot cider, Italian cream soda, an Italian Cow (steamed or chilled milk flavored with Torani syrup), breads and sweets.

Two very well-stocked wine shops on the New Jersey side of the river help you handle the BYOB situation at restaurants. **Welsh's** at 8 South Union St. in Lambertville and **Phillips'** on Bridge Street in Stockton offer shelf after shelf of rare French vintages plus wines from most California wineries (about 75 percent of Richard Philips's 20,000 bottles are from California, including those from every boutique winery we have ever visited or heard of and many we haven't). A good selection of whites is kept refrigerated in both establishments. Prices are reasonable and the staffs are well versed to help you choose. Welsh's also has an incredible selection of cognacs, armagnacs and single-malt whiskeys.

Now open for tastings of its 100-percent vinifera wines is **Sand Castle Winery,** run by two brothers from Czechoslovakia off River Road in Erwinna, Pa. Paul and Joe Maxian started with riesling and chardonnay before adding cabernet sauvignon and pinot noir. They lead tours through their underground wine cellar in a new building patterned after a 10th-century Czech castle. The 72-acre vineyard, largest in Pennsylvania, yields about 42,000 gallons of wine annually.

Lumberville General Store, River Road, Lumberville, Pa., is a true country store run by genial proprietor Gerald Gordon. On jumbled shelves you can find anything from ketchup to chicken soup, with more upscale things like Perrier, Pennsylvania Dutch preserves, antiques and Crabtree & Evelyn goods. A post office is at the rear and upstairs is an art gallery. At the deli counter you can get good sandwiches, soups, chili, vegetarian lasagna and pasta salads.

Those in the know like to visit the **George Nakashima Studio,** 293 Aquetong Road, New Hope, where his colleagues carry on the tradition launched by the late Japanese master woodworker. If you have a thousand dollars and up to spare, you might order a custom-made table. Even if you don't, it's fun to see what the locals call "The Compound," an extension of Nakashima's Zen philosophy. It's open Saturday from 1 to 4 (or by appointment) and is closed occasionally even then. Call 862-2272 to confirm.

It's a pity (for most visitors, anyway) that the famed **Rice's Sale and Country Market** is open only on Tuesdays from dawn until 1 p.m. It's like no other open-air flea market we've seen, and provided a high point on one of our Bucks County expeditions. Amish specialties, fresh produce, seafood, meats, honeys, spices and kitchenware are available, but foods aren't the best part — the incredible bargains on quality merchandise are. We did all the Christmas shopping (Jantzen and Ralph Lauren sweaters, a set of knives, perfume, a watch and a pretty homemade wreath) that two hours and our checkbook would allow. Everything from fine luggage to Evan Picone apparel is offered. Many of the same purveyors and bargain-seekers come weekly to this great flea market, which has been going strong for more than a century. It's located along Green Hill Road off Route 263 northeast of Lahaska (watch for signs).

Lineup of verandas, a Cape May trademark, is on view from Mainstay Inn.

Cape May, N.J.
Two for B&B, Tea and Dinner

Victoriana, bed and breakfast inns, and dining par excellence. That's the rare combination that makes Cape May a model of its genre and draws visitors in increasing numbers each year from March through Christmas.

Cape May has shed its mantle as a long-slumbering seaside city that time and Atlantic City had passed by. In 1976 its potential was recognized when it was designated a National Historic Landmark city, one of five in the nation — an honor it had shunned only a few years earlier. Now its Victorian heritage is so revered that Cape May celebrates a ten-day Victorian Week in mid-October, plus a week-long Tulip Festival, a Dickens Christmas Extravaganza, a Cape May Music Festival, Victorian dinners, a Victorian fair, and various inn and house tours.

The bed-and-breakfast phenomenon started here in the late 1970s as preservationists Tom and Sue Carroll and Jay and Marianne Schatz restored their neighboring Victorian landmarks into museum-quality guest houses, setting a national standard and launching a trend that has inspired the opening of more than 100 B&B inns locally.

Besides enhancing the Victorian structures in which they are housed, some of Cape May's B&Bs elevate the level of breakfast and afternoon tea to new heights — in formal dining rooms and parlors, or on the ubiquitous front verandas that are occupied everywhere in Cape May from early morning to dusk and later. The sumptuous morning ritual draws many couples year after year, and has resulted in publication of a number of Cape May cookbooks.

Where upscale B&Bs open, restaurants are sure to follow. "Our businesses attracted a clientele that demanded good food," says Nan Hawkins of the Barnard-Good House, whose breakfast feasts are the most lavish in Cape May.

Adds Dane Wells of the Queen Victoria B&B: "When my guests arrive, I tell them I know why they're here — for the food. Seven or eight of the best restaurants in New Jersey are within a few blocks of our inn."

Since the late 1970s, more than two dozen restaurants have emerged and, remarkably for a resort town, most have survived. Besides stability, many offer creative food and convivial ambiance. Some are small (make that tiny) and, lacking liquor licenses, allow patrons to bring their own wine. Prices, in many cases, are pleasantly lower than in other resort areas.

The result is that thousands of visitors come to experience the ultimate in bed and breakfast, tea and dinner in this, the culinary capital of South Jersey.

Dining

At peak periods, many restaurants are booked far in advance (those that take reservations are so indicated). Some of the most popular do not take reservations, which may mean a long wait for a table. Some also require a minimum of one entrée per person. Be advised that parking at many Cape May restaurants is difficult to impossible. Parking meters on the street gobble up quarters every half hour until 10 p.m.; a few restaurants offer valet parking.

The Best of the Best

410 Bank Street, 410 Bank St., Cape May. (609) 884-2127.

A gumbo of New Orleans, Caribbean and French dishes, many grilled over mesquite wood, is the forte of this restaurant that opened in 1984 and is considered by many to be the best in town. (It added a companion Italian restaurant, **Frescos,** next door in 1986, and some reviewers think it's even better.)

Dining is magical on the outdoor courtyard, surrounded by plants, tiny white lights and Victorian lamps. If you can't eat outside, settle for one of the narrow screened porches or the small, intimate dining rooms done in Caribbean pastel colors inside the restored 1840 house. Owners Steve and Janet Miller are theater-set designers, so both inside and outside are quite dramatic.

For appetizers ($6.50 to $7.95), we passed up the menu's champagne crab meat crêpe, shrimp brochette and Bahamian yellowfin tuna beignets for excellent specials of ceviche and mesquite-grilled quail, now a menu staple. After those, both our entrées of blackened red snapper with pecan sauce and yellowfin tuna in Barbadian black-bean sauce with a hint of sesame and ginger, served with crisp vegetables and rice pilaf, were almost too much to eat. We had to save room for the key lime pie, which was the real thing.

Other choice entrées ($19.95 to $24.95) include coconut-battered catfish fillet in a lime-jalapeño sauce with bananas and tomatoes, sautéed soft-shell crabs grenobloise, mesquite-grilled lobster, grilled Jamaican strip steak with changing sauces, and blackened prime rib. A French-style roast is now offered nightly.

Patrons dine New Orleans-style on courtyard at 410 Bank Street.

For desserts there are chocolate-pecan pie with amaretto puree, triple- chocolate ganache with grand-marnier sauce, hazelnut cheesecake with raspberry puree and a bread pudding with hot bourbon sauce that's the best around.

Service is by knowledgeable waiters attired in black and white Batik-style shirts. With the Key West-ish atmosphere and a menu like this, who'd guess that the chef, Henry Sing Cheng, is Chinese? Experts consider him the top chef in town.

Dinner nightly, 5:30 to 10, May-October. Reservations. BYOB.

Frescos, 412 Bank St., Cape May. (609) 884-0366.

New Jersey Monthly magazine once sent two writers to cover what they said "may well be New Jersey's leading center of gourmet restaurants." What did they rate best? Frescos, with three and one-half stars of a possible four. That was one-half star more than their second-best rating, 410 Bank Street.

Crayons are on the tables for doodling on the paper overlays that cover the white tablecloths in this restored Victorian summer cottage run by Steve and Janet Miller of 410 Bank Street next door. Faux-marble columns and unusual art involving three-dimensional fish accent the spare white dining rooms, where brown leather chairs flank tables that are rather close together. We prefer the narrow wraparound porch, its tables for two far enough apart for private conversations.

Chef Tommy Thompson's pasta dishes ($12.95 to $21.95) are Cape May's most extensive, ranging from ricotta-cheese ravioli with marinara sauce to jumbo shrimp and scallops in champagne-lobster cream sauce over fettuccine. Friends who dined there rated at 9.5 on a scale of 10 both the linguini with white clam sauce and fresh littlenecks, and the fusilli with a sauce of tomatoes, anchovies, black olives, capers and garlic. Other entrée choices ($18.95 to $21.85) include grilled tuna with tomatoes and black olives, pan-grilled T-bone of veal with orzo and portobello mushrooms, and osso buco.

We hear the key-lime-cream-filled cannoli is even better than the signature dessert: a layered, rum-soaked sponge cake with imported mascarpone cream and grated chocolate.

Dinner nightly, 5 to 10; Thursday-Sunday, Oct. 15 to New Year's. Closed January-April. Reservations. BYOB.

Restaurant Maureen, 429 Beach Drive, Cape May. (609) 884-3774.

"This started as a tavern and just grew," says Maureen Horn, who with her chef-husband Steve relocated to Cape May in 1982 after operating a restaurant under the same name in Philadelphia for five years. Maureen's quickly became the best fancy restaurant in town, its status only slightly eclipsed lately by some more recent arrivals. A warm welcome, consistently good food and flawless service are its hallmarks.

This sophisticated establishment is on the second floor of a beachfront Victorian structure that was once a bathhouse and saloon. The enclosed front porch, with a great view of the ocean and boardwalk goings-on, is pristinely white with pink napkins as accents.

Inside is a long, chandeliered dining room with fringed swagged draperies, fancy wall sconces, gilt mirrors and wallpaper in an intricate English Victorian pattern called "Ribbon." The plain, white-linened tables are topped only by crystal salt and pepper shakers and a flickering candle in a small crystal vase (no flowers). We liked the lively noise level and the unobtrusive waist-high divider that nicely separates parallel lineups of tables for two, providing privacy in a setting that we ordinarily would find too close.

A zesty sauce of ginger, garlic, soy and scallions accompanied an appetizer of shrimp oriental ($7.75). The ample house salads came with gorgonzola or creamy Italian and tarragon dressings.

Chef Horn showed his deft hand with seafood and sauces in crab Abigail, fresh jumbo lump crab meat seasoned with a sauce of cream, mustard and shellfish stock and baked in a casserole, and the house specialty, poisson jardinière — at our visit, a succulent salmon baked in parchment with an array of tomatoes, leeks, carrots, basil, olives and lemons. Crisp asparagus and red potatoes sautéed with onions accompanied. Other entrées ($17.50 to $25) include scallops mango, roasted duck with pecan stuffing, veal steak with three peppers and rack of lamb sorrento.

From a pastry-laden dessert cart (we were sorry, as we are so often, that there were no refreshing frozen mousses or sorbets) we shared a strawberry tart. The limited but fairly priced wine list produced a fine Groth sauvignon blanc from California for $17. Although people were waiting for our table, we did not feel rushed as we lingered over coffee and cordials.

Dinner nightly in summer, 5 to 10; fewer days in off-season. Reservations. Open mid-April through October.

Water's Edge, Beach Drive and Pittsburgh Avenue, Cape May. (609) 884-1717.

A family restaurant and lounge in front of La Mer Motor Inn has been transformed into a sleek, hotel-style dining room run by a husband-and-wife team with a background in nouvelle cuisine and a menu that prompted us, upon discovering it, to cancel our dinner reservations elsewhere that night. Since our first visit, chef Neil Elsohn and his hostess-wife, Karen Fullerton-Elsohn, have put their somewhat out-of-the-way restaurant on South Jersey's culinary map, despite an aborted effort to open a less seasonal offshoot in suburban Atlantic City.

Enclosed porch of Restaurant Maureen overlooks beach.

Their restaurant here has winning ingredients — a well-tailored aspect of banquettes and booths dressed in white cloths with rose-colored runners, flickering votive candles, a select and reasonably priced wine list, an inspired menu and an outdoor deck with the ocean beyond. We were impressed with our initial dinner: an appetizer of strudel with escargots, mushrooms, pinenuts and an ethereal garlic-cream sauce ($7.25); the abundant house salads with romaine and red-leaf lettuce, yellow cherry tomatoes, julienned leeks and a zesty vinaigrette; the poached fillet of salmon with smoked-salmon butter, lime and salmon caviar, and sautéed sea scallops with tomatillos, cilantro and grilled jicama (unfortunately lacking any taste of cilantro), followed by key lime ice cream.

On our next visit, we grazed happily through appetizers and salads, the staff graciously foregoing the one-main-course-per-person minimum with the awareness that our sampling would cost more than a single entrée each. The scallop chowder ($3.75) was wonderfully creamy, dotted with thyme and flecked with prosciutto, and full of scallops and potato. The spicy pork and scallion empanada with pineapple-ginger chutney ($6.75), encased in a radicchio leaf, was a standout, as was the house green salad with three medallions of Coach Farm goat cheese ($5.25) and a suave balsamic dressing. We also relished the fusilli with grilled tuna, oriental vegetables and Szechuan vinaigrette ($8) and grilled chicken salad with toasted pecans, grilled red onions, mixed greens and citrus vinaigrette ($6.50). A Silverado sauvignon blanc ($17) poured in oversize wine globes helped make a delectable feast, not to mention icy grapefruit and champagne sorbet as a finale.

Main courses range in price from $16 for grilled tenderloin of pork with spicy black-bean sauce and crispy sweet plantains to $23 for grilled tournedos with classic béarnaise and madeira demi-glace -- about the only classic dish we've encountered here. You're more apt to find exotica like seared shrimp with lime, cilantro and tequila, avocado relish and crispy tortillas, or grilled loin of lamb with vegetable ragout and risotto cakes.

Desserts could be fruit shortcakes, banana-bread pudding with hot chocolate sauce, lemon-coconut cheesecake with strawberry-rum sauce, and bittersweet-chocolate-walnut pâté with espresso and vanilla sauces.

In summer, a lounge menu is served in the spacious bar. Salads and appetizers are available there anytime.

Lunch in summer, 11:30 to 3; dinner nightly, 5 to 9:30 or 10. Dinner only, Thursday-Monday, mid-October to May. Sunday brunch, 11 to 2:30. Reservations.

The Ebbitt Room, 25 Jackson St., Cape May. (609) 884-5700.

The small, candlelit dining room in the restored Virginia Hotel is elegant in peach and gray. Swagged draperies, crisply linened tables, delicate wine glasses, art-deco wall sconces and birds of paradise standing tall in vases enhance the setting. Chef Chris Hubert's menu changes seasonally, with entrées ($16.50 to $23) ranging from oven-roasted soft-shell crabs with orange couscous and curry sauce to sautéed medallions of veal with roasted tomatoes, basil and crab meat at our latest visit.

Excellent hot rolls with a crisp crust preceded appetizers, one an eggplant and gorgonzola crostini served with red-onion pesto ($4.75) and the other a very zesty caesar salad ($5.50), served on black octagonal plates. Among main dishes, we've enjoyed roast cornish game hen served on a bed of caramelized vegetables, grilled salmon with spring greens and miso dressing, and filet mignon with three-onion salad and spicy steak fries.

For dessert, we wished for something frozen, but settled for an upside-down fig cake and pecan-praline cheesecake. The Danfield Creek chardonnay ($17) had the oakey taste we like..And the live piano music emanating from the lobby lent a glamorous air to a welcome addition to the Cape May dining scene.

Dinner nightly, 6 to 10; Sunday brunch, 9 to 2:30.

Peaches at Sunset, 1 Sunset Blvd., West Cape May. (609) 898-0100.

Arguably Cape May's prettiest restaurant is this new establishment with an offbeat name, derived from chef-owner George Pechin's nickname and its location at the head of Sunset Boulevard. A decade ago, "Peach" Pechin and partner Craig Needles opened a small sidewalk cafe in downtown Cape May. Their debut as a gourmet-to-go cafe quickly evolved into a serious small restaurant, one that finally gained the space it deserved with the new location in 1992. **Peaches Cafe** remained behind, true to its beginnings with a short dinner menu priced from $12.95 for vegetarian lasagna to $18.95 for Norwegian salmon with oriental black beans, served nightly in season from 5.

A nicely restored Victorian house, striking in peach with green trim, holds Peaches at Sunset. Two small dining rooms are divided by a walnut-trimmed aquarium full of tropical fish beneath a stained-glass panel and a tropical design on the ceiling. Peach-colored napkins stand tall in wine glasses at each candlelit table. Dining is al fresco on a raised rear deck leading to a gazebo with a few pint-size tables.

The contemporary dinner menu offers eight entrées ($15.95 to $20.95), among them Caribbean grilled tuna with plantains and black beans, Bangkok seafood jambalaya, broiled scallops with gingered coconut cream sauce, breast of duck Portuguese with fig puree, and twin tournedos with gin and juniper berries. Start with the creamy clam chowder that we once savored during lunch at Peaches Cafe; an exotic Thai salad on belgian endive; corn, polenta and jalapeño fritters with sour cream and chives, or roasted garlic served with mascarpone cheese and grilled sourdough bread. Finish with bourbon-pecan pie or crème caramel.

Dinner nightly except Tuesday from 5:30. Reservations. BYOB. Closed January and February.

New Virginia Hotel offers dining in elegant Ebbitt Room.

Globe Restaurant, 110 North Broadway, West Cape May. (609) 884-2429.

Assorted flags fly out front, two globes hang in the entryway and maps of the world adorn the walls of this unassuming-looking restaurant proclaiming "global cuisine." It was opened in 1988 by two top New York chefs, Michael Colameco, who had been at the Ritz-Carlton and the Tavern on the Green, and his South Korean wife, Heijung Park, pastry chef at the Hotel Pierre.

The menu is eclectic, even odd. Representative of their ethnic roots are Italian and oriental specialties like fried squid, penne in fresh tomato sauce with ricotta and baked manicotti, and sauté of beef "hot and spicy," dumplings of shrimp and ginger, and an extraordinary lobster with a sauce of black beans and fresh water chestnuts that one local foodie says is the best entrée he's had anywhere. But the chefs draw their culinary inspiration from around the world, producing items like chilled peach soup, finnan-haddie chowder, salade niçoise, blackfish in potato crust, crab cakes with coriander and lemon mayonnaise, and grilled swordfish with tomato salsa. Specialties are lamb tagine, a Moroccan dish; chicken pot pie with corn and cheddar, and a six-ounce shrimp burger served with maui-onion rings.

The food is widely acclaimed, the decor in several dining rooms casual to the point of underwhelming, and the value received (appetizers, $5 to $7, and entrées, $12 to $18, except $23 for the lobster dish). Three different breads, including a cajun corn bread, get dinner off to an auspicious start. The dessert list is fairly modest: rice pudding, apple strudel and lemon mousse with raspberry sauce. We'd opt for the ice creams with butterscotch, chocolate, or sweet red-bean sauce. Now that last sounds interesting.

With the entrées, a vegetable and starch are served family style. The owners also added a children's menu following the birth of their son, declaring that they want to be "a family restaurant for the 1990s."

Dinner nightly in summer, 5 to 10, Wednesday-Sunday in off-season. Open mid-May to mid-October. BYOB.

55

The Washington Inn, 801 Washington St., Cape May. (609) 884-5697.

Long considered the best of the large restaurants in town, this has become even better with the new dynamic lent by David and Michael Craig, sons of the owners.

The attractive white 1840 plantation house is surrounded by banks of impatiens, and inside all is pretty as a picture. The Craig brothers redecorated, picking up the colors from their striking, custom-designed floral china. They seat 130 in several areas, including a wicker-filled front veranda done up in pink and candlelight, a Victorian conservatory filled with greenery, dark interior rooms, and a romantic, enclosed brick terrace centered by a fountain trickling over an array of plants. Off a Victorian cocktail lounge is another enclosed, L-shaped veranda with more wicker.

The menu blends the traditional with the more creative, starting with clams casino, mushroom strudel and shrimp with a trio of peppers in puff pastry ($4.95 to $6.75). Cream of crab soup and lobster and corn chowder also are worthy starters. Entrées ($15.95 to $21.95) include soft-shell crabs, seafood fettuccine, bouillabaisse, flounder imperial, three veal and three chicken dishes, Kansas steak and rack of lamb.

The menu ends with nine "romantic international coffees." The night's desserts could be frozen key lime pie, crème brûlée, pumpkin-pecan cheesecake and fresh strawberry napoleons.

David Craig likes to show the new basement wine cellar, which holds an inventory of 500 titles and won the Wine Spectator Grand Award. The wine list has a table of contents, includes a page of chardonnays, and offers a Virginia red and a Lebanese wine, with a number of offerings priced in the teens.

Dinner nightly, 5 to 10, fewer nights in off-season. Reservations.

Louisa's, 104 Jackson St., Cape May. (609) 884-5882.

Tops on everyone's list for value is this tiny storefront restaurant that packs in the cognoscenti, who covet its twenty seats despite the fact that no reservations are taken and long waits are the norm. It does have the timing down to a science, however. People who put their names on the list are told when their table will be ready and can kill time by browsing through the shops on the nearby Washington Street Mall.

From a postage-stamp-size kitchen, Louisa and Doug Dietsch -- she does the managing and the desserts, he does the cooking -- offer some of the most innovative and affordable dinners in town. Formerly with the National Geographic Society, he has a natural touch for cooking and a rare way with herbs.

Feeling as if they're sharing their meal and their conversation with everyone in the place, patrons crowd together on molded plastic chairs of vibrant colors at tables covered with a mishmash of bright calico cloths. The changing menu, posted nightly at the door, might offer curried carrot soup, smoked shad mousse or hot and spicy ginger sesame noodles to start ($3.75 to $4.50).

Entrées ($9.50 to $12) could be scallops with tamari and scallions, grilled chicken with rosemary, grilled polenta with savory greens and grilled dolphin with rouille.

For dessert ($2.75), how about kahlua-mousse pie, lime-orange chiffon pie, mango upside-down cake or pecan-walnut-caramel tart?

We understand that some people come for a week to Cape May and contentedly eat almost every night at Louisa's.

Dinner, Tuesday-Saturday 5 to 9. No smoking. No credit cards. BYOB. Open March-October.

Other Choices

Cucina Rosa, 301 Washington St. Mall, Cape May. 898-9800.

David Clemans, who has a reputation as one of the best cooks in town, opened this authentic and popular Italian restaurant in 1993 after selling the John F. Craig House, his B&B of many years. His former lodging guests may have lamented his move, but locals applauded since they now get to share the fruits of his culinary prowess. "This is my last permitted insanity, according to my wife," says David, who named it for her late grandmother. Here he teams with his stepson, Guy Portewig, who's the chef.

"We take relatively standard southern Italian dishes and make them very carefully," says David. Everything is done from scratch, from the marinara and meat sauces to semolina bread.

Prices are gentle. Appetizers run from $3.95 for eggplant parmesan to $5.95 for clams oreganata, a house favorite. Also popular is the sautéed calamari with a marinara sauce that's almost as spicy as fra diavolo. Main dishes are priced from $6.95 for basic pastas to $19.95. Widely acclaimed is the chicken portofino, stuffed with mozzarella cheese and Italian sausage specially made for the restaurant, rolled and baked with tomato sauce and served with pasta ($14.95). Other treats include grilled swordfish and lamb chops, each marinated in olive oil and Italian spices and served with fried potatoes sautéed with peppers and onions or pasta with a choice of sauce.

Desserts are David's forte. He makes fruit pies that change daily, lemon cheesecake and a rich chocolate cake. He also offers ice creams and sherbets.

The 64-seat restaurant is at a corner location along the mall, with sixteen tables spilling out onto a sidewalk patio in season. The interior decor is soft and romantic in rose and green tones, with candles flickering on white-clothed tables.

Dinner nightly, 5 to 10, Sunday from 4:30 to 9:30. Closed January to mid-February. BYOB. No smoking.

The Mad Batter, 19 Jackson St., Cape May. (609) 884-5970.

Traditionally known for some of the most innovative (others say far-out) meals in town, this eighteen-year-old mainstay has had its ups and downs.

At our first visit on an early May night, the canopied sidewalk cafe was warm enough for candlelight dining — a special treat, what with the view of the passing scene, the roar of the surf muted by classical music, and food so assertive that we returned the next morning for breakfast. We were surprised during a September lunch a year later to find food so bland as to be almost beyond redemption and service so slow that the waitress had to apologize, "we're training a new chef."

At our latest visit, here-today, gone-tomorrow executive chef Mindy Silver was gone again, but local innkeepers were still steering visitors here for brunch. We enjoyed a gorgeous fruit bowl ($5.50) and whole-wheat peach pancakes ($4.75) from a breakfast-brunch menu that included cinnamon-raisin french toast, belgian waffles, eggs benedict and morgen roësti, Swiss pan-fried potatoes and herbs enveloped by eggs and gruyère cheese ($6.50).

The dinner menu was in transition under a new chef. Prices ranged from $17 for grilled pork tenderloin with red curry sauce to $23.50 for veal oscar. From previous visits, we'll never forget the Santa Fe seafood fritter served with herbed crème fraîche and tomato-corn relish, a terrine of five seafoods, the crusty whole-wheat French bread, dancing devil shrimp stir-fried with pecans, kumquats and black-bean sauce, and a fettuccine tossed with snails, asparagus and baked garlic, all sensational.

The pastry chef's creations, as well as other light Mad Batter offerings, are available for takeout from a small shop by the door. Besides the sidewalk cafe, there's seating in a large skylit dining room divided into two parts, and in a rear garden area amid white furniture, statues and greenery.

Breakfast/brunch/lunch, daily 9 to 2:30; dinner from 5:30. Open late March-November, weekends only in spring and fall. Reservations. BYOB.

The Rose Garden Restaurant, Perry Street and Congress Place, Cape May. (609) 884-8336.

There's a new rose garden outside this gem of a restaurant, nicely ensconced since 1992 at the side of Congress Hall in quarters formerly occupied by the late, lamented Bayberry. Culinary Institute-trained chef Chris Holl and partner Jerry Emery have softened the soaring space with an abundance of hanging plants and potted greenery and -- a striking touch -- swags of roses and ivy hand-painted on the pink walls. The pair were adding latticework to the front veranda to give al-fresco diners more privacy.

The seasonal menu offers a dozen entrées, priced from $16 to $24 (for bouillabaisse alfredo). Standouts include baked Norwegian salmon with asiago pesto, veal steak au poivre and Bourbon Street filet with mustard-bourbon sauce.

Among starters at our visit were seafood boudin, clams aioli, pheasant ravioli and grilled quail with sundried tomatoes and gorgonzola polenta. The house desserts are to die for: perhaps sixteen-layer chocolate cake over champagne sabayon, mascarpone-chocolate mousse with passion fruit and raspberry sauce and, in summer, fresh fruit ices and sorbets.

Dinner nightly in summer from 5:30, Thursday-Monday rest of year. Reservations. BYOB.

Freda's Cafe, 210 Ocean St., Cape May. (609) 884-7887.

Chef Steve Howard and his baker-wife Carol moved their gourmet shop and deli in West Cape May to a downtown location behind the former La Toque restaurant. The kitchen also serves their new cafe in the old La Toque quarters.

The short dinner menu ($11.95 to $17.95) pairs a fancy item like filet mignon au poivre with valfraise cheese against earthy barbecued spare ribs, black-eyed peas and rice. Nightly specials could be pork tropical, mixed grill with whipped sweet potatoes and a medley of chicken, scallops, shrimp and lobster topped with black-bean sauce and served on a bed of grilled polenta.

Among starters are focaccia, crab meat remicks, and warm goat cheese rolled in pecans with poached pears and watercress. For dessert, Carol makes a dynamite key lime pie, chocolate-bourbon cake and tirami su.

Lunch, 11:30 to 2:30; dinner from 5. Closed Thursday except in summer. BYOB.

Lodging

Since bed and breakfast is so integral to the Cape May experience, we concentrate on a few of the more than 100 in town, particularly those with bountiful breakfasts. Most require minimum stays of two to four nights, do not allow smoking inside, and access is only via push-button combination locks installed in the doors. Breakfasts tend to be lighter in summer, more formal and filling the rest of the year. The Cape May ritual is for the innkeepers to serve —

Typical Victorian structures lead to Gothic tower of the Abbey in background.

and often sit with — guests at breakfast, and later to help with dinner plans as they review the menus during afternoon tea or beverages. So integral is the food element that many inns keep a log in which guests write comments on local restaurants; some of the reports are scathingly at odds with previous entries.

The Mainstay Inn, 635 Columbia Ave., Cape May 08204. (609) 884-8690.

The Mainstay and the Abbey are the two that led the way, and are the most likely to be filled weeks, if not months, in advance. Tom and Sue Carroll began the B&B movement in Cape May at the Windward House, now under different ownership, and purchased the Mainstay in 1975.

The Italianate villa was built in 1872 for two gentlemen gamblers and, says Tom, is one of the few Victorians in town that has gone through 100 years with no transitions. It later became a guest house run by a Baptist minister who never got rid of anything, and the collection is there for all to view. Tours of the museum-quality inn are given Tuesday, Thursday, Saturday and Sunday at 4, and upwards of 50 people gladly pay $5 to visit and join inn guests for tea. Except in summer, when it's iced tea on the veranda, tea time is inside and formal, the tea served from a copper container and accompanied by cucumber sandwiches, cheese straw daisies, toffee squares, spiced shortbread, chocolate-chip meringues and the like.

The twelve guest rooms, all with private baths and some with copper tubs, in the main inn and the 1870 Cottage next door are handsomely and formally appointed with lace curtains, stenciling, brass and iron bedsteads, armoires and rockers. In 1994, the Carrolls were adding four luxury, two-bedroom suites with double jacuzzis, fireplaced living rooms, TVs with VCRs and private porches in what they call the Officers' Quarters, an old World War I officers' house they acquired across the street on Stockton Place. Outfitted in more contemporary style, the suites are designed for families and for those who seek privacy. Modest antiques, stenciling, bright colors and plants "give a whole different atmosphere here than in the inn," says Tom. Guests in the Officers' Quarters have continental breakfast delivered to their rooms, since the Carrolls already had their hands full serving breakfasts in the main inn.

So sought-after are Sue Carroll's recipes for her breakfast and tea goodies that she has published six editions of a small cookbook called "Breakfast at Nine, Tea at Four," which has sold more than 18,000 copies. In summer, breakfast is continental-plus, served buffet-style on the veranda; other seasons it is formal and sit-down at two seatings around the table for twelve in the dining room. Strawberry french toast, chicken-pecan quiche, ham and apple pie, California egg puff and macaroni mousse are some of the offerings. Lately Sue has been doing less with meats and more with fruits like banana-pineapple crisp, cranberry-apple compote, orange crunch and banana-cream coffee cake.

Doubles, $130 to $155; suites, $195 ($295 for four); three-night minimum in season and most weekends. Open mid-March through mid-December.

Barnard-Good House, 238 Perry St., Cape May 08204. (609) 884-5381.

Breakfasts are *the* claim to fame of Nan and Tom Hawkins, whose morning feast was judged the best in the state by New Jersey Monthly magazine.

Nan never serves plain juice. "It's blended with maybe strawberry or lime juice, sometimes five different kinds." That's followed by a soup course: perhaps fresh peach, blueberry or, in fall, a hot cider soup topped with croutons and whipped cream. In lieu of soup she might serve fresh pears poached in kahlua with sour cream and chocolate curls, or hot apple crunch with applejack brandy. Breads could be brioche, Italian pepper bread, biscuits or "dogbone scones," shaped by a dogbone cutter that she uses to make dog biscuits for all the dogs in her family at Christmas.

The main course might be swiss enchilada crêpes filled with chili, chicken and tomato, with a side dish of corn pudding. Or you might have a chicken and apple strudel with pistachios, plum-chutney waffles, wild rice and walnut pancakes, or a Norwegian ham pie with sweet-potato pancakes.

For dessert -- "why *not* for breakfast?" laughs Nan -- there might be a blueberry-orange cake, sour-cream brownies or brandy crêpes with homemade ice cream.

"I create as I go," says Nan, for whom cooking is a passion and who spends hours preparing for the next breakfast after serving the last. Guests dine family-style at a lace-covered table in the formal dining room. "My ego trip is seeing the joy of my guests in the morning," she says.

In the late afternoon, she puts out more goodies like chocolate-banana cake and lemon mousse in a meringue shell to accompany tea or beverages in the parlor or outside on the veranda.

The Barnard-Good offers three guest rooms and two suites, all air-conditioned and with private baths.

Doubles, $86 to $118. Open April-October.

The Abbey, Columbia Avenue and Gurney Street, Cape May 08204. (609) 884-4506.

A steady stream of passersby gawks at this elegant Gothic villa with its 60-foot tower and incredible gingerbread trim, all painstakingly painted a soft green with deep red and ivory accents. Inside, guests and tour visitors alike admire the parlor, library (with the largest free-standing bookcase you'll ever see) and dining room on the main floor, plus seven guest rooms upstairs. They're filled with priceless items, and ceilings are ornately decorated with paint, gilt and wallpaper pieces.

We stayed in the Savannah, a summery room with white enamel bedstead, oriental carpets, a white wicker sofa with purple cushions and a small refrigerator in the bathroom. Owners Jay and Marianne Schatz have converted the cottage next door into seven more guest rooms, all with private baths, and a couple of parlors and verandas, where continental breakfast is served in the summer.

In spring and fall, guests gather in the dining room of the main villa, where fourteen people can sit around the banquet table beside a Teutonic sideboard. "We have the noisiest breakfasts in town," Marianne said, and we agree. Jay, a non-stop comic, keeps guests regaled both with his stories and his selection of hats from a closet that holds a choice of 250 -- he might pull out an Australian bush hat or a "Hagar the Horrible" beauty. His act, and Marianne's repartee, nearly upstage their fairly elaborate breakfasts: perhaps pink grapefruit juice, a dish of fresh peaches and whipped cream, an egg and ham casserole with garlic grits on the side, and English muffins. Marianne also makes a great quiche with a bisquick crust. Guests share opinions of restaurants they visited the night before.

Doubles, $80 to $175; three- to four-night minimum stay in season and most weekends. Open April through mid-December.

The Manor House, 612 Hughes St., Cape May 08204. (609) 884-4710.

This impressive, gambrel-roofed house with warm oak and chestnut foyer and striking furnishings seems almost contemporary in contrast to all the high-Victorian B&Bs in Cape May. Guests spread out for punch, cider or tea in a front room with a striking stained-glass-front player piano or a library with two plush loveseats in front of a fireplace.

Upstairs are nine guest rooms, seven with private bath, furnished in antiques, brass and wood king or queensize beds, handmade quilts and light Victorian print wallpapers. The newest is a third-floor suite with a sitting area and a whirlpool tub by the window in the bathroom. There are handmade "napping" signs for each door knob and the cookie fairy brings goodies during nightly turndown service.

Innkeeper Mary Snyder offers a choice of two seatings and two entrées (from a repertoire of about 85) for breakfast. Among favorites are "asparageggs" (poached eggs and asparagus on homemade English muffins with mornay sauce), a french-toast sandwich with raisin bread stuffed with cream cheese, breakfast pizza (shredded potatoes, zucchini and egg custard on top, dubbed "quizza"), apple crêpes, corn quiche and "perfectly thymed scrambled eggs." Juice, fresh fruit and Mary's signature sticky buns round out the meal. Noisy breakfasts also are the rule here, as Tom Snyder jokes about Mary's crumb buns in a non-stop monologue that rivals that of his colleague, Jay Schatz. In 1993, the Snyders produced a cookbook, "Mary's Buns & Tom's Puns," with an emphasis more on recipes than on humor.

Doubles, $98 to $158.

The Virginia Hotel, 25 Jackson St., Box 557, Cape May 08204. (609) 884-5700 or (800) 732-4236.

Its gingerbread restored and its interior pristine, the Virginia, built in 1879 as Cape May's first hotel, was reopened in 1989 as what general manager Curtis Bashaw, young son of the owner, calls a deluxe "boutique" hotel. Newspapers hang from a rack outside the dining room, and a pianist plays in the pleasant lounge during the dinner hour in the highly regarded Ebbitt Room.

Upstairs on the second and third floor are 24 guest rooms that vary widely in size and shape. Like the public rooms, they are furnished in a simple yet sophisticated manner, which we find refreshing after all the Victorian clutter one sees elsewhere in Cape May. On your way upstairs check the stained-glass window in the landing; a local craftsman spent a year looking for old glass with which to restore it.

Bedrooms are equipped with private baths with new fixtures, telephones, and remote-control TVs and VCRs hidden in built-in cabinets. The restful decor is mostly soft peaches and grays. Room service is available, and terry robes are provided. There are eleven standard-size rooms, eleven premium and two extra-premium at the front of the second floor with private balconies. Five have a sofa and two upholstered chairs each, though one premium room with a kingsize bed has room enough only for one chair. The wraparound balcony on the second floor gave our expansive room extra space and was particularly pleasant the next morning for a continental breakfast of fresh juice, fruit, danish pastries and croissants, delivered to the room at the time specified.

Doubles, $170 to $235; two- or three-night minimum on weekends.

The Queen Victoria, 102 Ocean St., Cape May 08204. (609) 884-8702.

Dane and Joan Wells are among Cape May's original innkeepers and are among the few who still live on their property. Over the years, they have had much experience learning what their guests wanted in their lovely 1881 corner property that has twelve rooms with private baths. In 1989, they used that experience to open a Victorian house and a carriage house next door with eleven luxury suites offering the niceties that many today seek: queensize brass or iron canopy beds, sitting rooms or areas, mini-refrigerators, whirlpool baths, air-conditioning, fireplaces and television. They also are decorated in a simpler, more comfortable style than the Cape May norm, outfitted with arts and crafts furniture but still authentic, since Joan once was executive director of the Victorian Society of Americ. They're named after neighborhoods in London; Dane is partial to the Greenwich, which, "if all the good eating at the restaurants here gets you, has a gout stool."

Each house has a living room, one in the original building with a piano and a fireplace and the new one with TV, games and jigsaw puzzles. Pantry areas are outfitted with the makings for tea, popcorn, sherry, wine glasses and such.

Breakfast is an event in two dining rooms, with either Dane or Joan presiding at each. Lately they've added a fresh fruit compote daily to great acclaim -- "I don't know what people ate before," says Joan, "because it goes like mad." There are plenty of other options, however: perhaps stuffed baked french toast with sausage patties or baked eggs and cheese with curried fruit. Always available are homemade granola, mini shredded wheat, homemade muffins and a basket of toasting breads featuring Wolferman's English muffins. Afternoon tea brings crackers and a dip, maybe blue cheese or salmon, plus cookies and brownies.

Eighty of the house favorites were compiled in 1992 in "The Queen Victoria Cookbook," exceptionally good-looking and outstanding in its genre. The recipes, scaled to serve twelve, are geared to entertaining.

Doubles, $120 to $170; suites, $180 to $210.

The John F. Craig House, 609 Columbia Ave., Cape May 08204. (609) 884-0100.

This attractive carpenter gothic cottage has long been known for some of the best breakfasts in town, and new owners Frank Felicetti, formerly a lawyer in

Family kibitzes with Joan Wells as she tends front garden at Queen Victoria.

Wilmington, Del., and his wife Connie are continuing the tradition. They live in the house, so are more involved than was former owner David Clemans, who was on hand to prepare breakfast but transferred day-to-day operations to a caring staff. David left most of the furnishings for the new owners.

Blended coffees and teas are put out for early-risers at 7. Breakfast is served at 8:30 or 9:45 in the lovely dining room with its lace tablecloth and scallop-shell wallpaper. There are always seasonal fruits on the table as well as homemade muffins and buttermilk coffee cake. The entrée, which comes out on a piping-hot plate garnished with fruit, could be anything from blueberry-stuffed french toast with ricotta cheese and almond flavoring to a bacon and gruyère cheese casserole to eggs with scallions in a ramekin. Homemade sourdough or dark molasses herb breads accompany. Frank does the cooking, while Connie serves. She also bakes the pastries and the goodies that accompany afternoon tea, perhaps baked brie with almonds and brown sugar, oatmeal-preserve bars, almond-cake squares or molasses-spice cookies. The couple gathered the recipes from their families.

The Felicettis also have launched their own traditions. In lieu of afternoon tea, they serve picnic suppers on the major summer holidays -- perhaps roasted chicken, potato or tomato-orange salad and cornbread. "It was the holiday thing we did at home," Connie explained, "and so we continue it here. One guest wrote in our guest book that it was like celebrating a holiday with a bunch of old friends." They also serve Thanksgiving dinner and Easter brunch for guests.

The house, which comes in two sections, contains nine air-conditioned guest rooms (seven with private bath) including a suite. They are done in typical Cape May style, with lots of wicker and oriental rugs, lace curtains and elaborate wallpaper. Guests have use of the parlor and the requisite Cape May porches.

Doubles, $105 to $165. Open March-December.

Gourmet Treats

Cape May is somewhat lacking in specialty-food shops, and our informant at the Visitor Center said someone would make a killing by opening one. B&B owners tell us regular guests sometimes bring certain hard-to-find items from home as favors. For wines to carry to the BYOB restaurants, most visitors head for **Collier's Liquor Store** on Jackson Street just north of the Washington Street Mall.

Lobster House Seafood Market, Fishermen's Wharf. Among the largest enterprises around, this includes an enormous restaurant that does one of the highest volumes in the nation, an outdoor raw bar, a moored schooner for lunches and cocktails in season, a take-out counter and one of the best seafood markets we have ever seen. We drool over the exotic varieties of fresh fish, which can be packed in ice to travel, and like to take home items like snapper-turtle soup ($3.50 a quart), oysters rockefeller (75 cents each), or clam pies ($1.95) to remember Cape May by. Out back, the **Dockside Take-out** offers such goodies from the seafood market as snapper soup and a soft-shell crab sandwich. You also can get snacks from the **Rigging Loft** raw bar. Open daily year-round.

La Patisserie, 524 Washington Mall, is the place for lovely fruit tarts, many breads and all kinds of sweets from chocolate croissants to raspberry puffs and cranberry squares. Located in front of Dillon's restaurant, it's open from 7:30 to 1.

Cape May Bakers offers elegant pastries, desserts and whole-grain and savory stuffed breads at 482 W. Perry St.

Our Daily Bread at 322 Washington Mall has super desserts like Kentucky derby pie, apple-crumb cheesecake and Southern pecan tarts. A piece of raspberry cheesecake and a cappuccino might hit the spot in mid-afternoon. Sandwiches are available from 11 to 5 and include Cape May shrimp, a garden or hummus pocket, and grilled chicken breast.

The Bake Shop at Carpenter's Square Mall specializes in scones, muffins, sticky buns, pies and cakes like sacher or hazelnut torte, chocolate-mousse cake and key lime cheesecake ($2.50 a slice). Try these with the house coffee (a different flavor every day), espresso or cappuccino.

We stopped for breakfast at **Bodacious Bagels,** Beach and Howard Streets, and liked the toasted pumpernickel bagel with a cream-cheese, walnut, raisin and honey spread. You can also have a Swiss fondue bagel or a pizza bagel for lunch or, for $7.95, the ultimate bagel with nova lox, tomato, vidalia onions, pickles and cream cheese.

For the ultimate omelet, head for **McGlade's,** a small restaurant with a large deck practically over the ocean. If you can face lunch after a mammoth plate full of the Uncle Tuse's omelet (with about a pound of bacon, tomatoes and sharp cheddar) plus a load of delicious homefries ($6.75) or the shrimp and garlic omelet ($7.50), you're heavier eaters than we are. We know some Cape May innkeepers who love McGlade's for dinner (entrées $9 to $18 -- BYOB). It's on the pier beside Convention Hall, just behind Morrow's Nut House.

For shopping, we head to the **Whale's Tale,** a gift shop extraordinaire, purveying everything from gourmet cookware and nifty coffee mugs to shell magnets and an outstanding collection of cards and children's items.

Culinary students nearing end of training serve breads to diners at American Bounty.

Hudson Valley
New Mecca for Gourmets

Barely an hour's drive north of New York City lies an area that represents a different world, one often overlooked by travelers destined for Manhattan's urban attractions.

The central Hudson Valley, including the Hudson Highlands, remains surprisingly rural, at times rustic. It is a mixed-bag area of steep mountains and rushing streams, noted mansions and historic houses, hip boutiques and hippie pursuits, winding country roads and a mighty river with seemingly unending, interesting traffic.

It also is an area of fine restaurants, one of which we would go so far as to say could give any restaurant in the country a run for its money. That is The American Bounty, one of four esteemed restaurants at the storied Culinary Institute of America in Hyde Park.

The area's diversions for the daytripper or weekender are known far and wide. Not so widely known are the restaurants, some of them quite new and many with connections — as you might expect — to the Culinary Institute. Chef-owner John Novi of the highly rated DePuy Canal House, a CIA graduate, attributes the array of restaurants to the arrival of the institute in 1972. The CIA created a demand for better food supplies in the area as well as a pool of teaching chefs and a ready entourage of culinary students who needed places to serve their required eighteen-week externships.

Between meals, you will find plenty to do. The Hudson Valley is the nation's oldest wine-growing region, and more than twenty wineries offer tastings and/or tours. The valley is known for its great estates and house museums, from Boscobel to Hyde Park to the new Montgomery Place, the latest of the Sleepy Hollow Restorations. Rhinebeck, Red Hook and Millbrook are upscale villages particularly attractive to tourists.

Following your own pursuits will spur an appetite for things culinary.

Dining

The Culinary Institute of America

A former Jesuit seminary high above the Hudson River at Hyde Park became the home of the nation's oldest and foremost school for professional culinary training when The Culinary Institute of America moved in 1972 from New Haven, Conn. It has been a mecca for gourmets ever since, not only for chefs but also for visiting professionals and knowledgeable diners who sample the fare cooked by students in four leading-edge restaurants.

This is not a traditional college campus, you find upon arrival as you watch budding chefs in tall white hats scurry across the green, most clutching their knife kits. It couldn't be when you learn the rallying cry for the hockey team is "mirepoix, mirepoix, roux roux, roux; slice 'em up, dice 'em up, drop 'em in the stew!"

The main red brick classroom building has an institutional tinge, but the aromas wafting from The American Bounty or The Escoffier restaurants at either end of the long main hall are tantalizing, hinting at glories to come.

The restaurants are the final courses in 21 months of study for the institute's 1,900 candidates for associate degrees, who arrive and graduate in cycles every three weeks. They work in the kitchens and then serve in the dining rooms.

Visitors don't get to see much behind-the-scenes action, except through windows into the kitchens off both restaurants. Tours for bus groups afford a glimpse into the mysteries of a variety of specialty and experimental kitchens, the pantry and the former chapel, which is now the student dining room and used for large private banquets and graduation ceremonies. Visitors may catch glimpses of the General Foods Nutrition Center (first of its kind in the country), the Sunsuke Takaki School of Baking and Pastry, and the new Conrad N. Hilton Library and Learning Resources Center. At our latest visit, a display in the main hall outlined the CIA's new Center for Advanced Studies in California's Napa Valley, where a 100-seat restaurant was scheduled to open in 1994 at Greystone Cellars in the former Christian Brothers Winery in St. Helena.

Open regularly to visitors here is an expanded gift shop and bookstore named after Craig Claiborne, stocking specialty-food items and 1,300 cookbooks on every culinary subject imaginable. They may inspire you to try at home some of the dishes cooked up in the CIA restaurants.

The American Bounty Restaurant, The Culinary Institute of America. (914) 471-6608.

We've had lunch at Lutèce, the five-star restaurant in New York, and we've had lunch at the CIA's American Bounty, and we liked The American Bounty better. Not only did we find the food more interesting and more attractively presented, but the staff is pleasant and helpful, and the cost less than half.

Opened in 1982 for the presentation of American foods (before they became

Arched opening frames view of cloister-style dining room at The American Bounty.

trendy) and wines, The American Bounty complements the noted, more formal Escoffier Restaurant at the other end of the building.

Fashioned from former offices and corridors, the high-ceilinged restaurant is the institute's largest. It is stunning, from its etched-glass doors to its cream and green draperies with a floral motif, gathered back from high arched windows. The seminary heritage is evident in the two cloister-style dining rooms, seating 110 people at tables spaced well apart.

A changing array of America's bounty is in front of the window onto the Julia Child Rotisserie Kitchen, through which you can see ducklings turning on the rotisserie as white-clad students work in the final course of their 21-month program.

The only item that appears not to be American is some of the liquor from the bar. The wines and beers are domestic and the small markup yields some bargains, though not so many as when we first dined shortly after it opened.

The menu changes slightly with every meal. Seldom have we had such a dilemma making choices as we did for a springtime lunch. Doesn't your mouth water when you contemplate appetizers like Southwestern-style stuffed chicken breast with ancho-coriander flavored coleslaw or New York State foie gras sautéed with concord-grape sauce and fried grapes?

We settled for tomato and celery mousse on cold tomato hash, a heavenly dish decorated with a floret of mayonnaise and a sprig of fresh dill, and a sampling of the day's three soups served in tiny cups: chilled strawberry, the clam chowder and New Orleans gumbo "Ya-Ya" (whatever that means).

With these appetizers was passed a basket with at least nine kinds of bread and rolls (bran muffins, corn sticks, cloverleaf rolls and biscuits were some), served with a crock of sweet butter.

For main courses, because of the season we ordered fresh asparagus on sourdough toast with creamed salmon and sweetbreads, and "baked fresh seafood variety, new garden style." The former had perfectly crisp asparagus arranged like a fan on crisp sourdough; the sauce was suave and rich. The seafood was served in an iron skillet and was pretty as a picture, rimmed by tomato wedges. Crab meat, clams, mussels, salmon and more were topped with butter and crumbs and baked. Vegetables, served family style, were stuffed cherry tomatoes, yellow squash and tiny red potatoes.

Desserts include chocolate-cheese timbales, Shaker lemon pie and, at one visit, sautéed Hudson Valley apples with praline ice cream in a walnut lace cup and pear-blueberry cobbler with Wild Turkey ice cream. We tried the popular Mississippi river boat, a shell of pastry filled with an intense chocolate mousse with kiwi fruit on top and, weird sounding but very good, fried strawberries — huge fat ones in a sort of beignet, served with a sour-cream and orange sauce.

Prices for all this are fairly reasonable. Two people having appetizers, entrées ($11 to $14) and desserts plus a bottle of wine can have a memorable lunch of dinner-size proportions for $50 to $60.

At night, when dining is by candlelight, entrées might range from $17 for sautéed pork medallions with blue-cheese polenta, zucchini and spaghetti squash to $21 for broiled lamb chops with caramelized root vegetables and white-bean/rosemary sauce.

Service, of course, is correct and cordial — after all, these kids are *graded* for this. But, as you might expect, it can be a bit slow. Not to worry. The food is worth the wait. Where else can you find New England seafood chowder, Eastern Shore backfin crab terrine with a spicy mayonnaise and New Orleans-style shrimp etouffée, all on the same menu?

Open Tuesday-Saturday, lunch noon to 1, dinner 6:30 to 8:30. No smoking.

The Escoffier Restaurant, Culinary Institute of America. (914) 471-6608.

The great French chef Auguste Escoffier would be pleased that some of his traditions are being carried on in the fine restaurant bearing his name.

The dining room is pretty in pale pinks and raspberry tones, with comfortable upholstered chairs and elaborate chandeliers and wall sconces. On spacious tables the gigantic wine glasses — globe-shaped for red, hurricane-shaped for white, and a flute for champagne — take an inordinate amount of room. With classical background music, it reminds one of a small, select and comfortable hotel dining room and seats about 90.

Menus change seasonally and are primarily à la carte, with one prix-fixe offering. The $23 prix-fixe lunch is a particular bargain, especially when compared with dinner ($40), which offers only two more courses (a second appetizer and a sorbet between courses). À la carte prices are $14.50 to $17.50 at lunch, $17.50 to $26 at dinner. Expect to spend upwards of three hours for lunch and not have any appetite for dinner that night.

The classic French menu has acquired nouvelle touches since we first dined here in 1978. Gone are the escargots bourguignonne and onion soup. In their place are things like snails with wild mushrooms and goat cheese in a potato crust, oak-leaf and frisée salad with quail breast and grapes in armagnac, and garlic soup with chives and croutons. Main courses could be sautéed dover sole meunière, sautéed chicken with shrimp and truffles, ragout of wild mushrooms flambéed with brandy, and roasted loin of venison with apples, pears and glazed chestnuts. We remember fondly an entrée of sweetbreads topped with two large

New dining room of St. Andrew's Cafe is light and airy.

slices of truffle and a subtle sauce, and chicken in a spicy curry sauce, accompanied by a large tray of outstanding chutneys, the tray decorated with white napkins folded to point up at each corner, giving it the appearance of a temple roof.

Overfull diners have been known to moan as the dessert cart laden with noble tortes, rich cakes and more rolls up. But how can one resist a taste of a silky coffee-kahlua mousse and an incredible many-layered pastry square, filled with whipped cream and raspberries?

After partaking of the prix-fixe meal, could anyone possibly have room for a full dessert? Our waiter, a former teacher whose wife was putting him through school, replied: "That's nothing. Some people have two or three."

Open Tuesday-Saturday, lunch noon to 12:45, dinner 6:30 to 8:30.

St. Andrew's Cafe, The Culinary Institute of America. (914) 471-6608.

The institute's best-kept secret had been this cafe, transformed in 1985 from the old Wechsler Coffeehouse and stressing healthy, nutritious food. Dropping in for what we expected might be a quick snack, we were astonished to partake of a memorable three-course lunch, all specially designed to be less than 1,000 calories.

It was a secret, that is, until it moved front and center into the CIA's new General Foods Nutrition Center, behind and to the side of the main building. All here is state of the art as the CIA seeks to change Americans' eating habits through greater awareness of nutrition and the availability of healthful and delicious meals. That's public-relations jargon for what this cafe really produces, "good food that's good for you."

The cafe has gone upscale in decor since its move from the former coffeehouse. Ceramic vegetables on a breakfront in the foyer greet diners, who may catch a glimpse of the tiled kitchen through windows behind the bar. Beyond is an expansive, 65-seat room with generally well-spaced tables set with white linens, heavy silver and, surprise, salt shakers that were notably missing in the old digs. A coffered ceiling, arched windows and upholstered rattan chairs add to a light, comfortable setting.

The remarkable appetizers and desserts in the $3 to $4 range are what we most remember from two lunches here. We started the first with a Mediterranean seafood terrine with the seafood in chunks, on a wonderful sauce, and a smoked-duck salad with raspberry vinaigrette, a gorgeous presentation including about six exotic lettuces topped with raspberries, ringed by sliced pears. A later visit produced a crab-meat quesadilla with a jícama and citrus salad and an extravagant presentation of carpaccio of fresh tuna and oriental mushroom salad.

Healthful breads like rye, sunflower seed and whole wheat along with butter curls were offered no less than four times — surely the fourth would have blown the calorie limit.

Among entrées ($8.50 to $11.50), barbecue-grilled chicken breast with black-bean sauce and roast medallions of lamb with wild mushrooms and a potato pancake kind of affair, came with crisp young asparagus (in November!) garnished with sesame seeds. These were preceded by salads of fancy greens, including endive, and tender peeled tomatoes. Garnishing the chicken dish was a peeled-back tomatillo filled with fresh salsa.

Desserts were, once, a pumpkin torte with cinnamon sauce and glazed pineapple madagascar, a concoction with rum, honey and peppercorns. The second visit yielded a remarkable warm apple sauté with graham-cracker crisps and apple pie glace, so ample and eye-catching when we saw it at the next table that we thought it must have been prepared for a visiting dignitary (not so), and a Hudson Valley pear strudel with amaretto glacé.

All this, with a glass of wine and a beer, came with tip to about $40 for lunch for two. And, according to the computer printout that you can request for a technical but interesting diet analysis, only the cappuccino took our meal over the 1,000-calorie limit.

The dinner menu, which also changes every three days, offers similar prices except that appetizers and wood-fired pizzas are $4.25 to $6.75 and entrées, $10.50 to $14.25. We figured you couldn't spend more than about $20 for a dinner of pheasant consommé with wild-mushroom ravioli, pan-seared salmon with citrus-chardonnay sauce and raspberry bavarian with a minted fruit salsa. Wines by the glass, beers and natural juices are available.

As well as eating delicious food cooked with a minimum of salt, sugar and fat, you are given solicitous service such as is rarely found nowadays. If we lived nearby, we'd surely be tempted to eat here several times a week.

Open Monday-Friday, lunch 11:30 to 1 and dinner 6 to 8.

The Caterina de Medici Dining Room, The Culinary Institute of America. (914) 471-6608.

Serving a varied menu of regional Italian cuisine, this is the newest and smallest of the institute's public restaurants and was closed to visitors when we last were there (as often is the case for lunch, we were told).

The room honors the Renaissance patron whose greatest contributions to European culture and culinary history were her gifts of Florentine cuisine and refinements — among them the use of the fork, the cultivation of the green bean, the creation of ice cream and the introduction of sauce-making to the French.

Today, CIA students serve up prix-fixe meals (lunch, $17; dinner, $24) that reflect a trend toward Italian cucina fresca. The antipasti might be mushroom salad with celery and parmesan, risotto with prosciutto and sautéed scallops with lemon and endive. Soup could be egg drop, Roman style, or pea with Italian bacon. For main dishes, how about oven-roasted tuna with olives and potatoes, roast pork tenderloin with sausage and pesto or grilled lamb chops with herb crust and parmesan? Dessert could be pear crêpes with mascarpone cheese and zabaglione, hazelnut torte with ricotta and chocolate, or a selection of homemade gelatos and sorbets.

Italian wines are featured, of course, in this venture's stated attempt to prove to Americans that there's more to Italian cuisine than Pizza Huts. One recent grad advised that some of his peers consider it the CIA's best restaurant.

Open Monday-Friday. Single seatings, lunch at 11:30, dinner at 6.

More Fine Dining

Xaviar's, Route 9D, Garrison. (914) 424-4228.

This restaurant, launched in 1983 by Peter X. (for Xavier) Kelly when he was 23, is so good that he opened a second restaurant across the Hudson, **Xaviar's at Piermont** (506 Piermont Ave., 359-7007), plus an adjacent and more casual Freelance Cafe and Wine Bar. Both earned the highest ratings in the Zagat Restaurant Survey, near-perfect 29s, the first ever awarded, Peter says proudly.

The Garrison restaurant is in the clubhouse overlooking the grounds at the Highlands Country Club. The long room with 25-foot-high ceilings holds a dozen or so well-spaced tables. It's a sight to behold, decked out in white china and linens, white fanned napkins, gleaming wine glasses, crystal candle-holders and white candles, with a glass stallion here and a silver pheasant there. Arrangements of exotic flowers in crystal vases on each table, on the fireplace mantels, on sideboards and even in the rest rooms add touches of bright color — the bill from the florist must be staggering. Light is provided by candles everywhere and the blazing fireplaces at each end.

In a space like this, Peter says, "you couldn't do anything else but grand dining." So in 1993 he canceled the weeknight dinners of long standing to concentrate on special-occasion dining on weekends. Dinner is prix-fixe, $65 for six courses and a pairing of six wines, with a choice between two menus. The staff suggests that a party of two order both menus to best sample Peter's culinary prowess.

Part of the special-occasion dining at Garrison is the Sunday brunch buffet, $24.50 including champagne. The buffet, lavish as you'd expect, is supplemented by any number of foods passed from the kitchen.

Dinner in Piermont also is prix-fixe, $42 for appetizer, salad, sorbet, main course, dessert and coffee, and petits fours. Peter improvises with the best of the night there when patrons order his dégustation menu for $60.

Wine Spectator gave its Best of Award of Excellence to the Xaviar's wine cellars, which contain more than 700 selections priced from about $12 to $1,000.

Peter, very much a hands-on chef, spends part of every day in both restaurants. In 1993, he tended to cook weekends in Garrison as he changed to the weekend format and during the week in Piermont.

We consider ourselves fortunate to have sampled a number of his dishes, each a triumph of taste, texture and presentation. Consider his lobster ravioli in saffron sauce, garnished with the ends of lobster tails (they look like butterflies so that's what Peter calls them) and bearing a mound of caviar in the middle and two long chives on top. Or the seared sea scallops, served with potato pancakes and raspberry vinaigrette with a few fresh raspberries for good measure. Or the New

Dramatic dining room at Xaviar's.   **Owner Harrald Boerger at Harrald's.**

York State foie gras, surrounded by sliced kiwi, strawberries and sliced pears and served with a glass of sauternes. Best of all — in fact, one of the best dishes we've had anywhere — is the seared Pacific tuna tartare with wasabi and soy sauce, resting on an oversize plate, the rim garnished all the way around with dollops of red, gold and black caviar.

Finger bowls were presented before our main courses: mignon of venison with grand veneur sauce and the best spaëtzle we've tasted, and saddle of veal with wild mushrooms and pommes parisienne, garnished with a tomato carved to look like a rose. Both came with tiny, barely cooked haricots verts.

Desserts here are hardly after-thoughts. One of us had an ethereal hot raspberry soufflé, light as air. The other tried the grand assortment, nine little samples including hazelnut dacquoise, chocolate-chestnut terrine, frozen caramel mousse, raspberry sorbet and praline ice cream. A plate of petits fours, chocolate strawberries and chocolate truffles finished a meal to remember.

The silverware that came and went with each course was as noticeable as all the extra touches that went into food and presentation. "We try to give people a little more than anyone else does," explains Peter. Indeed they do.

Xaviar's at Garrison: dinner, Friday and Saturday 5 to 9:30; Sunday brunch, noon to 3. Xaviar's at Piermont: lunch, Wednesday-Sunday noon to 2; dinner, Tuesday-Sunday 6 to 9. Freelance Cafe & Wine Bar: lunch and dinner Tuesday-Sunday.

Harrald's, Route 52, Stormville. (914) 878-6595.

Reservations are essential at this unlikely-looking establishment, one of twelve five-star Mobil Guide restaurants in the country and widely revered since its opening in 1971. We tried unsuccessfully two weeks ahead to reserve for a Friday — "we only have thirteen tables," the host reminded. There are two seatings on Saturdays, and the meal takes three hours.

Yellow lanterns and meticulous landscaping give something of a Japanese look to the Swiss-Tudor house that reflects the tastes and work of proprietor Harrald Boerger. He proudly introduced his wife, Eva Durrschmidt, "the only woman chef-owner in the United States of a five-star restaurant," who said her philosophy is that "simplicity is elegance." Until recently, hers was a kitchen in which men were not allowed to cook.

Three-foot-high blackboard menus are wheeled to the table, outlining the night's variations on six courses. Dinner is prix-fixe ($60 for six courses) and served in three small, intimate rooms by waiters who may intimidate more than the outgoing and down-to-earth Harrald, who usually visits each table during the course of the evening. The experience is designed to make guests think they are dining in a home rather than a restaurant, he says.

The meal might start with a choice of home-smoked rainbow trout, crab cakes, a galantine of veal and diced tongue with cashew nuts and green peppers, and a poached egg en cocotte with diced chicken, ham, mushrooms and truffles. The soup course involves a traditional French onion with emmenthaler and a choice of one hot and one cold each evening, perhaps pureed vegetable and a cold Russian-Polish specialty called okroshka.

A mixed green salad with the house vinaigrette or country herb dressing precedes the main course. This typically could be poached or sautéed trout au bleu with dill sauce, veal roast with pan gravy and dumplings, steak au poivre, stuffed free-range poussin, canard au cassis and zuricher rahm schnitzel served with four kinds of mushrooms.

Prior to dessert and coffee, a cart brings a selection of fresh fruits, cheeses, nuts and a glass of good port. Dessert could be chocolate-sabayon cake, chocolate mousse made with Swiss Lindt, linzer torte or fresh fruit topped with whipped or heavy cream.

Before dinner, you might have drinks on the terrace or stroll the park-like grounds. The trout come from an outdoor tank that looks like a wishing well and has water so fresh it's drinkable, says Harrald. Another special touch is a small 200-year-old farmhouse used as a wine cellar with an extensive selection that is "cheaper than any place I know, because wines should be affordable." Outside the wine house is an old-fashioned swing. Harrald explains: "My wife said she'd like a swing for her birthday. So I built her one for $12."

Harrald does not advertise because it embarrasses him and he doesn't need to. "I put the money I save back into serving our guests," he says. "We're giving them the very best of the best."

Local reviewers variously praise individual items as the best they've had, but it is the entire experience — from soup to nuts, as it were — that earns Harrald's its five stars year after year.

Dinner, Wednesday-Saturday 6 to 9 (two seatings Saturday at 6 and 9). Closed January to mid-February. Reservations and jackets required. No credit cards.

The Fine Foods Cafe, 10 Charles Colman Blvd., Pawling. (914) 855-3785.

The highest accolades go to this new cafe, a fortuitous outgrowth of the well-known **Corner Bakery.** "Excellent," declared the New York Times critic. "An all-time favorite," swooned the Poughkeepsie Journal reviewer. Young partners Shannon McKinney and Brian Doyle moved in 1992 to expanded quarters in the center of Pawling from a smaller bakery that had attracted national notice (see Gourmet Treats). Shannon continues to man the bakery, while Brian has turned his attention to the restaurant.

And what a restaurant it is! Sophisticated, stunningly executed fare is served in a comfortable, homespun atmosphere. The old-fashioned, high-ceilinged store-front cafe is a mix of booths and tables that came from an old Pawling pub, bare floors and exposed brick walls holding local memorabilia and art displays. Many and changing are the touches of whimsey: words of dining wisdom here and there; a shelf bearing bricks, shutters, a clothesline with pins and an old flag; a beehive in a ficus tree, and a window display with an amusing picture of chefs exercising amid an array of spring-form pans. Brian lends his decorating skills and laconic wit to a space that exudes personality.

His kitchen talents are equally diverse. For dinner, you might start with grilled shrimp with Thai peanut sauce over angel-hair pasta or Yukon potato-leek pie and warmed Coach Farm goat cheese on a roasted-pepper coulis. The night's entrées ($16 to $19, served with an exceptional green salad) could include fresh farmed catfish ("pan sautéed with Northern integrity"), grilled swordfish with scallop-caper butter, breast of duck with peppercorns and applejack-soaked figs, roast quail with root-vegetable cakes, and tournedos of beef with forest mushrooms and a peppercorn-brandy glace. Save room for one of the bakery's fabulous desserts, perhaps sour-cream apple pie, pumpkin cheesecake, sour cherry tart, raspberry linzer torte or Belgian-chocolate pound cake with caramel sauce.

Interesting fare also is offered at lunch ($5 to $9), perhaps a soup of shrimp and scallops in a creamy sauternes-leek broth, a sampler of several salads, Shannon's "hogbreath vegetarian chili" with grilled jalapeño cornbread or a sandwich of roasted chicken and apricot salad served on a fresh baguette. Brunch brings a panoply of egg dishes, banana pancakes, almond french toast, smoked salmon on bagels, and corned-beef hash served in its own cast-iron skillet with a shirred egg and bakery toast.

The wine list is good and affordable, with many available by the glass. Also offered are interesting ales and lagers. The adjacent bakery dispenses all kinds of baked goods as well as quite a variety of foods to take out under the logo of McKinney & Doyle.

Oktoberfest beer-tasting dinners, wine tastings, a Christmas madrigal dinner, art exhibitions, mail-order -- it takes their Word of Mouth newsletter just to follow all that these engaging guys are up to.

Lunch, Tuesday-Friday 11:30 to 3; dinner, Tuesday-Sunday 6 to 9:30; weekend brunch, 9 to 2.

DePuy Canal House, Route 213, High Falls. (914) 687-7700.

This National Historic Landmark, built of stone in 1797 by Simeon DePuy to serve travelers along the Delaware and Hudson Canal, is everyone's dream of what a cozy tavern should be.

Snowshoes, baskets, lanterns and the like hang from dark beamed ceilings, the floors are wide planked and sloping, fires are lit in season in one or all of the four big fireplaces, and antiques, dried berries, fresh flowers and chintz abound. The china is Staffordshire, the cutlery pewter, and placemats are an unusual blue slate. Dining is in two small downstairs rooms (the main dining room, reminiscent of a Colonial keeping room, seats only eighteen) and three more upstairs. Although High Falls native John Novi opened his restaurant in 1969, he's always improving, adding a new arbor-covered bluestone patio for more casual outdoor dining, opening a cabaret in the basement with a bar fashioned from a century-old bank teller's cage, and preparing a line of food products to be sold in the New York Store under construction behind the restaurant at our latest visit.

Best of all, chef-owner Novi is an imaginative cook, whom Time magazine

Shannon McKinney and Brian Doyle run Fine Foods Cafe and Corner Bakery.

called "the father of New American cooking" in a 1985 article. He likes guests to come into his elegant black and white tiled kitchen, where a table for four or six can be booked at no extra charge. You also can watch the kitchen goings-on from an upstairs balcony.

Dinner is served from a prix-fixe menu of three courses (soup or salad, entrée and dinner, $19.94), four courses ($32), seven courses ($45), or à la carte (soup and appetizers, $4 to $8.50; entrées, $15 to $19; desserts, $6, and variations thereof). The variations make for some confusion, as do some of the contents -- "smoked salmon iceberg (ready to be rolled by you)," "dandelion and meat balls" and "smelts aioli -- aioli is made with cilantro."

Meals begin with a freebie: a pissaladière (small pizza) with baby peas and fresh mozzarella cheese and a clam strip with lemon and parsley on belgian endive at a recent visit. Soups could be caramelized onion with fontina de asti on a flour tortilla, Chinese corn chowder with langoustino or "hot and spicy chicken tenderloin and fried rice ball on yellow tomato and pickled lime broth."

Instead of soup, how about a Russian pâté zakuska — smoked-ham-hock pâté served with mustard byrd sauce, Paris toast and a shot glass of Russian pepper vodka. Whew! Other appetizers might be "reel of pasta, a Canal House original" pairing carrot pasta and ricotta cheese on a diced-tomato sauce; aforementioned smelts aioli or smoked-salmon iceberg with mascarpone cheese in a seaweed crêpe with hot chile-garlic sauce, or shiitake mushroom and pumpkin flan with leeks on a ginger-wine sauce. Expect garnishes of dried day lilies, raw rhubarb or scallops soaked in beet juice and rolled in parsley and sesame seeds to look like strawberries, as we encountered at a springtime dinner (our pre-dinner manhattan came with a slice of apple instead of a maraschino cherry).

A complimentary sorbet, perhaps fennel, precedes the entrée in the four- and seven-course dinners, and at this time the waiter may suggest a stroll through the house or a look at the kitchen. Your main course might be halibut poached spa-style with two conserve sauces, seafood or all-meat jambalaya, peppercorn-crusted beef tenderloin served on roasted garlic sauce with potato galette and radicchio, or two deboned quails stuffed with pork-cornmeal sausage, served with potato, poached fennel and beet-rhubarb relish. The salad, composed of four types of greens and a mild Italian dressing, may be garnished with popcorn.

If you order the whole meal, you get a fruit bowl and a platter of three cheeses (usually including soft ripened goat cheese from Coach Farm in nearby Pine Plains) before dessert, which could be Mama Novi's chocolate cake, charlotte russe or a special chocolate soufflé with brandy cream sauce.

The extensive wine list, including a number of Hudson Valley offerings, is affordably priced, starting at $14. To celebrate the wine harvest in 1993, the Canal House staged a week-long Fête du Cochon, a French-inspired celebration, featuring Hudson Valley wines and grapevine-grilled meats.

Ever the entrepreneur, John has opened a B&B called the **Locktender Cottage** across the street. It offers two bedrooms with private baths ($85) and a second-floor suite with kitchenette and jacuzzi ($110).

Dinner, Thursday-Saturday 5:30 to 10; Sunday, brunch 11:30 to 2, dinner 4 to 9.

The Thymes, 11 Main St., Kingston. (914) 338-0434.
Chef Daniel Smith and his year-old restaurant walked off with seven awards, including the Grand Award, in the 1990 and 1991 Taste of the Hudson Valley culinary competitions. It came as no surprise to those who knew him, for he also had swept the competition two years earlier when he was chef at the Beekman Arms across the river in Rhinebeck. Indeed, this graduate of La Varenne Cooking School in Paris had won a medal in the 1980 Culinary Olympics in Frankfurt.

Awards alone weren't responsible for making this uptown Kingston establishment one of the hottest restaurants in the Hudson Valley. A comfortable, convivial atmosphere pervades the front bar and dining room beyond. Sixty patrons can be seated in both rooms at tables covered with white linens at night. The turn-of-the-century decor involves a beautiful mahogany bar, dark wood wainscoting, mauve mini-print wallpaper, a brick wall, brass sconces, high ceilings and other vestiges of the building's heritage as the City Hotel, circa 1905.

All that rich wood gives off a rosy glow after dark, as we found during a leisurely November dinner. The menu is in two parts: à la carte, $5.95 to $7.50 for appetizers, $13.95 to $17.95 for entrées, and prix-fixe $19.95 for three courses, each with several choices from the à la carte menu. Our meal began with good, crusty rolls and scoops of three different butters -- basil, tomato-garlic and lightly salted -- inspiring spirited debate over which was best. Delivering good value, the prix-fixe side yielded a huge "cup" of seafood minestrone that was unfortunately light on seafood and four skewers of spicy chicken satay, spiked like stalks into a lemon resting in a pool of peanut sauce crossed with a ribbon of onions. Main courses were an excellent pan-seared arctic char bearing a superior mushroom sauce and robust pork medallions with caramelized apples and roquefort cream. The plates were artfully presented with slivered beets, beans and carrots plus a timbale of rice. An $18 bottle of Markham sauvignon blanc accompanied from a short, expensive wine list priced up to $200. Desserts were pumpkin bread pudding and a plate of intense homemade sorbets -- pineapple-orange, green tea and mixed fruit.

Chef-owner John Novi outside DePuy Canal House.

"I can make French, German, Chinese, Italian or Mexican food and I'm free to call it modern American," says Dan. His legion of fans call it wonderful.

Lunch, Tuesday-Friday 11:30 to 3; dinner, Tuesday-Saturday 5 to 10; Sunday brunch/dinner, 11:30 to 8.

The Would Bar & Grill, 120 North Road, Highland. (914) 691-2516.

A former gin mill -- her words -- with a curious name winning the grand prize among restaurants in the Northeast in a 1993 national ranking by Restaurants & Institutions magazine? "I was just overwhelmed," said Claire Winslow, the chef who turned her parents' neighborhood bar around and firmly implanted it on the local culinary map.

Claire, a 1985 Culinary Institute grad, had planned to return to California to work for noted chef Brad Ogden, with whom she had done her externship. She decided instead to stay in her home area and apply her cooking talents to changing the image of the Applewood Bar, located in a complex of two old and undistinguished apartment buildings at the edge of nowhere. (Indeed, a rooster was chasing chickens around the exterior as we arrived and tried to find the entrance, and we thought we were on a wild goose chase.) "We started small and now it's grown around us," Claire said of her restaurant's locally high-profile mystique and its inordinate number of Taste of the Hudson Valley culinary awards.

The derivation of the restaurant's shortened name from Applewood is obscure, but there's no mistaking the quality and creativity of the food served in the main barroom, where a TV set and a pool table provide distraction, or the newer and more appealing outer dining room, transformed in a fashion from what had been a game room and an indoor bocci court. Its green and salmon decor is gussied up with floral curtains, fresh flowers and votive candles.

The fairly ambitious dinner menu is the kind that makes choices difficult. For starters ($4.50 to $7.50), how about sautéed escargots with sundried tomatoes over penne pasta, house-cured tuna on an artichoke puree with vegetable chips, or grilled shrimp glazed with red pepper jelly in a black-bean and fruit salsa? Or a salad ($2.95 to $4.95) of oriental field greens with Chinese noodles in a safflower dressing or another with Coach Farm goat cheese tossed with watercress and charred apples in a dijon vinaigrette.

A sous chef from Algeria has added a few dishes with Mediterranean and Thai overtones, including peanut pasta with black mushrooms, chestnuts and green beans in a Thai sauce of basil and coconut milk and grilled lamb chops on a roasted walnut-mint pesto with Mediterranean vegetable compote. Otherwise, most of the entrées ($12.95 to $17.95) are new American: grilled swordfish on a cool cucumber salad with a red-chile oil, sautéed medallions of pork with sundried-cherry sauce, grilled local quail with roasted shallots and black raspberries, and grilled filet mignon in an ancho-chile demi-glace with a medley of roasted peppers.

The pastry chef knows what she's doing. Terrific breads (pesto, raisin and nut, focaccia and cinnamon swirl) start the meal. Flaky apple pie spiced with cinnamon, raspberry-chocolate brûlée, carrot cake with apple/sweet-potato puree and chocolate/peanut-butter pound cake with caramelized bananas and banana crème anglaise are worthy endings.

New dimensions are given to the bar and grill's lunch menu with such offerings as oriental chicken salad with roasted almonds and Chinese noodles, a salmon gravlax BLT on pepper brioche and grilled ribeye steak with five-onion butter, pleasantly priced from $3.95 to $8.95.

Lunch, Monday-Friday 11:30 to 2; dinner nightly, 5 to 9 or 10:30.

The Inn at Osborne Hill, 150 Osborne Hill Road, Fishkill. (914) 897-3055.

Geese seem to be the theme at this country restaurant, from the sign outside to the simple but pretty decor inside. But the food is far from simple, and since Michele and Frank Nola set up business in 1988, their reputation has spread far and wide. Thomas Hoving, no less, wrote in Connoisseur magazine that they had created one of America's top restaurants. Both CIA grads, they'd had experience in Connecticut restaurants, he at Tapestries and she at Stonehenge. Along with devising a sophisticated menu, Frank, a native Californian, has built a 3,000-bottle wine cellar that earned the restaurant a three-page spread in Wine Spectator.

Except for the unexpectedly stale rolls, we were quite impressed with a weekday lunch. The blackboard menu ($6.50 to $8.95) yielded a superb linguini with rock shrimp, scallions, mushrooms and tomatoes in a lobster-cream sauce and a potent sweet-and-sour oriental pheasant soup, which we teamed with an appetizer of shrimp and crab cakes, small and precious with squiggles of sauce and flecks of herbs. The small appetizer left one of us hungry, so we shared the dessert sampler plate. It turned out on the bill to be a $7.95 indulgence of white-chocolate mousse on a designed bed of raspberry coulis, chocolate-pecan mousse cake, the specialty profiteroles and a couple of scoops of cassis and lemon-mint sorbet.

At night, appetizers range from $5.95 for baked brie with raspberry and ruby port to $14.95 for fresh American duck liver with pears and walnuts. Entrées ($12.95 to $21.95) include salmon napoleon, sea scallops niçoise, calves liver with pancetta and red onions, breast of pheasant with cranberries and green peppercorns, beef and kidney pie, and loin of veal with roasted chestnuts and sherry cream. They are accompanied by interesting starches like nut pilaf, minted barley or red bliss potatoes. The salad is a mix of exotic greens.

All this good eating takes place in two small beamed and wainscoted rooms with black lacquered chairs, white linens, votive candles and bare floors. The theme is one of "simple elegance," the owners say.

Frank and Michele Nola have won acclaim for their Inn at Osborne Hill.

As for his wines, Frank says his cellar features "my favorites, hard-to-find varieties or both."

Lunch, Monday to Friday, 11:30 to 2:30; dinner, Monday to Saturday from 5.

Cafe Tamayo, 89 Partition St., Saugerties. (914) 246-9371.

The dining scene on the west bank of the Hudson has been enhanced by this large, sprightly restaurant in a restored 1864 downtown tavern in the rustic riverfront village of Saugerties. James Tamayo, a CIA graduate who worked in New York at the Russian Tea Room, the Plaza and Green Street Cafe, sought a smaller venue of his own. He and his wife Rickie, who ran a theater in Woodstock, had summered in the area and "wanted a hometown." Their double storefront is a surprisingly large, somewhat theatrical space with bare floors, pine wainscoting, high molded ceilings, green trim and stenciling here and there. More than 100 patrons can spread out at well-spaced, white-linened tables facing the original massive walnut bar, a couple of rear dining sections, a more formal side dining room and an outdoor patio alongside.

Support from the local community was a long time coming, Rickie said. The couple survived with a contingent of regulars from New York, who liked to feast on such delicacies as pompano (obtained from the Fulton Fish Market and served with an herb vinaigrette and saffron rice), grilled swordfish with sundried-tomato vinaigrette, sautéed loin of rabbit, navarin of lamb and pan-roasted venison. The menu changes nightly, but the price of the main courses ($12.95 to $17.50) always includes a salad (red-leaf with balsamic vinaigrette) to appease the locals.

Of Mexican descent, James adds the spicy bite of chile peppers to such favorite dishes as cappellini tossed with tomato, garlic, gaeta olives and pecorino cheese or mussels in an olive-oil, garlic and tomato broth. Other starters ($3.75 to $6.50) could be polenta bolognese,, sautéed calamari with potatoes and an acclaimed grated-potato pancake encasing slivers of house-smoked salmon.

Among desserts are crème brûlée, chocolate-truffle cake with raspberry sauce, biscotti and homemade sorbets -- blackberry, pineapple and melon, when we were there. A small wine list is priced in the teens and twenties.

Dinner, Wednesday-Sunday 5:30 to 9 or 10; Sunday brunch, 11:30 to 3.

Le Pavillon, 230 Salt Point Tpke., Poughkeepsie. (914) 473-2525.

A Victorian, red brick structure on the outskirts of town houses an intimate, country-French restaurant run by chef-owner Claude Guermont, who was born in Normandy and apprenticed himself to a French chef at age 14. After a stint as an instructor at the CIA's Escoffier Restaurant, he opened Le Pavillon in 1980 against the prevailing wisdom that a fine restaurant would not survive in the area. In 1985, he wrote *The Norman Table* (Charles Scribner & Sons), an acclaimed cookbook of 200 regional recipes from his native land.

You enter through a vestibule lined with clippings ("Chef has never really left Normandy," exclaims one headline) into a brick and beamed bar. Dining is by candlelight in two intimate front dining rooms, each accommodating thirty. French posters and art, white service plates bearing a discreet Le Pavillon logo, black candles in small hurricane lamps and white linens create a charming setting.

The French menu is pleasantly priced. "I try to stay with local products, make everything here and try to be a little contemporary — but not entirely classic or nouvelle," Claude says. Dining is à la carte during the week and the same menu is available prix-fixe only ($28) on Saturday night.

Among appetizers ($6 to $6.50), his tortellini filled with crab meat, a crisp mushroom pancake and escargots baked in brandy-garlic sauce are highly rated. So are his Normandy-style onion soup and the shrimp bisque with sherry.

The dozen or so entrées run from $16.50 for chicken with walnut sauce to $19.50 for lobster with tri-color pasta or rack of lamb persillade. Salmon with two sauces, roast duck with honey-orange sauce, sweetbreads with port sauce in puff pastry, veal kidneys in mustard sauce and filet mignon forestière are other choices. New Zealand venison, quail au poivre, rabbit with mustard sauce and other game dishes are offered when available.

Desserts ($4 to $5) include hot soufflés and flaming crêpes au caramel, as well as French pastries, profiteroles and the like. Le Pavillon's wine list ranges widely from Hudson Valley vintages to French châteaux, priced from $14 to $125.

A blackboard menu offers cassoulet, grilled swordfish with pesto, pheasant sauté and other items in the $8.95 to $13.95 range for lunch.

Lunch, Tuesday-Friday noon to 2; dinner, Monday-Saturday 5:30 to 10.

Cascade Mountain Winery & Restaurant, Flint Hill Road, Amenia. (914) 373-9021.

Why is a winery listed under dining choices? Because this out-of-the-way place is a gem, known as much for its creative food prepared from local ingredients as for its award-winning wines and a funky, California kind of spirit. In fact, we almost felt we were on a Napa Valley hillside the sunny autumn day we lingered on the deck overlooking the apple orchards, enjoying a bottle of seyval blanc and some appealing luncheon fare.

The food is the work of chef Richard Reeve, who also prepares four-course wine-tasting dinners on Saturday nights in the winery's homey dining room to "show off our local wines and food products." The dinners are $45 prix-fixe for soup, appetizer, main course and dessert, with a recommended wine to go with each course, although the same items also may be ordered à la carte. The meal might begin with seafood bisque, cold strawberry soup, hot walnut-crusted local camembert on baby greens with raspberry vinaigrette, or potato-corn pancakes with smoked salmon and crème fraîche. Main courses ($14 to $18.50) could be spicy barbecued shrimp, penne with shrimp and sundried tomatoes, grilled quail

stuffed with liver mousse and served with cream scallion sauce and shoestring fries, and peppercorn-crusted filet mignon with a bourbon-molasses sauce and garlic mashed potatoes. For dessert, how about fresh berry napoleon with sabayon sauce, apple brown betty or a fruit and cheese plate, complemented by a glass of rich, gold-medal-winning vignoles wine?

At lunch, our party of four enjoyed the thick butternut-squash soup, the gingered carrot soup and the clear leek soup with roasted garlic (all $4). Then we dug into an excellent smoked-trout plate, a pâté and goat-cheese plate, a mustardy maple chicken salad with green and red grapes, and grilled chicken — grilled here on the deck — stuffed with herb and garlic goat cheese

Novelist-winemaker William Wetmore.

(all $7.50). An apple-pear crisp (the crisps or shortcake are always on the menu and incorporate whatever fruit is in season), spiced maple cheesecake with gingersnap crust and Hudson Valley mud cake ended a leisurely, memorable meal. The bill was written on the back of a wine label.

After lunch, we stepped gingerly around workmen to enter the main winery downstairs, an unexpectedly small and primitive affair, considering the merit of its output (it made the strongest showing of any winery east of the Rockies at a couple of wine competitions). The chief workman at our first visit turned out to be William Wetmore, owner-winemaker and author of four novels, a jack-of-all-trades who produces almost as many red wines as whites because of his grape-planting decisions two decades ago. Lately, William has semi-retired and the winery is run by his son Michael, whose seyval blanc won the only gold medal in its class at the 1993 International Eastern Wine Competition.

A couple of typewritten sheets inside cellophane wrappers point out salient facets of winemaking for self-guided tours. Visitors taste wines in the crowded and convivial downstairs setting, where no one takes things too seriously. How could they, at a place where a couple of favorite bottlings were called "Le Hamburger" and "Pardonnez-Moi," the latter billed as a dry red wine "for social emergencies" but also a play on the word chardonnay. The Wetmores named their latest beaujolais-style red release Coeur de Lion, meaning heart of the lion, after 60 Minutes documented the drinking of red wine as good for the heart.

Such is the homespun fun of Cascade Mountain Vineyards, a place full of integrity.

Lunch daily, noon to 3, April-December; dinner by reservation, Saturday 6 to 9, June-September. Tours and tastings daily, 10 to 6.

Other Dining Choices

Le Petit Bistro, 8 East Market St., Rhinebeck. (914) 876-7400.

Yvonne and Jean-Paul Croizer were at Auberge 32 in Kingston before they moved to Rhinebeck in 1986 to open an establishment held in high esteem by locals. The space used to be occupied by a Greek restaurant, and the Croizers didn't have to do much to the pine walls and floors to give it a country-French theme. Except for globe lamps inside wooden frames, the decor is simple and the atmosphere convivial and intimate. There are 40 seats in the dining room and a half-circle bar at the side.

From Jean-Paul's classic French menu, start with onion soup, pâté maison, smoked trout or escargots ($4.75 to $6.75). Entrées go from $14.50 for the chicken special that changes weekly to $19.75 for dover sole meunière. Sea scallops with crushed black peppercorns and cream sauce, duck with cherries, veal piccata, frog's legs, rack of lamb provençal and steak au poivre are other choices.

Desserts include crème caramel, mocha mousse, raspberry frappe and peach melba. "People tell me the lemon pie is the best around," says the chef. The fairly extensive wine list mixes French and domestic at prices from $12 to $85.

Dinner, Thursday-Monday 5 to 10, Sunday 4 to 9.

Green & Bresler, 29 West Market St., Red Hook. (914) 758-5992.

A small and snazzy cafe, Green & Bresler (named for the grandmothers of the owners) attracts a young, hip clientele. Partners Steve Weininger and Leo Comensoli share cooking duties with pastry chef Sally Frick. Lately, they've added more vegetarian items to their changing, contemporary American menu.

The popular Sunday brunch might include eggs sardou, apple pancakes, torta rustica, spanakopita, wild-mushroom and ham quiche, and open-face smoked trout with pesto and roasted peppers on grilled French bread, $5.95 to $8.50.

At lunch, inside or on a side deck, order from an array of delectable sandwiches (most in the $5 to $7 range), like Israeli falafel or roasted turkey and brie with honey mustard on mixed-grain bread. Soups, quiche, mushroom chili, chicken and spinach pie, and a salad sampler are other choices.

Dinnertime brings linen cloths to the ten or so small tables, candlelight and sweet music. You might start with potato, leek and mushroom pancakes with roasted garlic sauce, Louisiana gumbo, grilled swordfish and salmon skewers with two dipping sauces, or prosciutto and fresh mango served with reggiano parmesan ($3.75 to $4.50). Entrées ($11.50 to $16.95) could be Maryland crab cakes with homemade tartar sauce and scallion biscuits, lobster enchilada with green-tomato salsa, grilled tuna with avocado and tomato guacamole, Thai chicken breast with green curry sauce and fried plantains, and loin lamb chops with mixed fruit chutney and whole-grain coconut couscous.

Desserts ($3.50 to $4.25) are to groan over, perhaps pumpkin cheesecake, linzer torte, fallen almond soufflé cake or lime tart. Finish with espresso or Harvey's hunting port. All the offerings from a good little wine list are priced in the teens.

Lunch daily except Wednesday, 11 to 3; dinner, Friday and Saturday 5:30 to 9:30; Sunday brunch. Closed in January.

Allyn's Restaurant & Cafe, Route 44, Millbrook. (914) 677-5888.

Four miles east of Millbrook "in the heart of hunt country" is this renovated establishment, the pride of chef-owner Allan Katz and staff, all of them CIA grads. Just inside the entry of what appears to be a blue and white house is an elegant sun porch/sitting room with plush leather sofas and chairs. Beyond is an airy cafe with flagstone floor and windows onto horse country and a spacious bar-lounge. Hidden somewhat out of immediate sight is the high-ceilinged dining room, pretty in pink and white with horsy prints, two fireplaces, votive candles in old New York cabaret-style lamps and seats for 75 at well-spaced tables. This section was built 210 years ago as a church, and tables have been added lately in the former choir loft.

The cafe and outdoor patio are the most popular dining spots, and here you can order from a cafe menu plus the dinner menu (only the latter is available in the dining room). For a weekday lunch, we (and subsequent others) were left to fend for ourselves as no one could be found to seat -- much less greet -- patrons. The bartender eventually told us to take any available table in the cafe, of which there were many. A harried waiter finally turned up to take our orders and provide a basket of crackers and breads, including a very peppery melba. The Maryland crab cakes with tomato and corn relish ($10.95) were enlivened with a tarragon-laced tartar sauce and jalapeño cornbread. The cappellini ($9.50) was tossed with plum tomatoes, red onion, arugula, fontina and romano cheeses and a basil vinaigrette.

The dinner menu might list a dozen entrées starting at $14.50 for linguini with seasonal greens and shiitake and oyster mushrooms. Poached salmon fillet with tarragon crème fraîche, roast cornish game hen with smoked cajun sausage and papaya chutney, and grilled swordfish are other possibilities, topping off at $21.95 for California-style fish and seafood stew, steak au poivre, paupiettes of stuffed veal tenderloin and pan-seared tournedos of beef with chipotle peppers and oyster mushrooms. The day's special menu is as lengthy as many a small, serious restaurant's regular menu. Chocolate-bourbon cake, pumpkin pie, New York-style cheesecake and crème brûlée are among desserts. The wine list is extensive and pricey for the area.

Lunch, 11:30 to 3; cafe menu from 3; dinner, 5:30 to 9:30 or 10:30. Closed Tuesday.

Northern Spy Cafe, Route 213, High Falls. (914) 687-7298.

If long hours and a hands-on approach pay off, this new cafe should succeed where predecessors have failed. Chef Tim Celuch, a CIA grad, and host-bartender George Nagle were putting in twenty-hour days after opening in 1993, the former preparing and the latter serving lunch at our visit. Occupying a hilltop across the road from the falls that give the village its name, theirs is a rustic, rather whimsical place: an angular bar and a casual dining area with black and white tiled floor, bare windows in which dried herbs hang and simple wood tables, some painted with checkerboards and resting on saw horses.

This was the setting for an innovative fall lunch, which began with an unusual touch -- a gratis bowl of popcorn molé enlivened with chile powder and cocoa. One of us ordered the spicy mushroom and pumpkin soup, a huge portion in which both the bowl and the plate upon which it rested were speckled with herbs. Colorful "decoration" continued with the ample Northern Spy salad, an oversize plate bearing smoked chicken and apples and decked out with flecks of herbs and carrots, and spring rolls with peanut noodles, topped with squiggles of hot red sauce (both $5.95). A huge portion of plum sorbet ($2.50) supplied a refreshing ending to a fiery meal.

"International soul foods" is how Tim bills his fare. He applies creative touches to simple foods of different cultures. At dinner, you'll find such starters and light fare ($4.50 to $7.95) as pressed deep-fried tofu with ginger dipping sauce, fried calamari with roasted-garlic tomato sauce, grilled pizza with sundried tomatoes and red onions, spanakopita and aforementioned spring roll with peanut noodles. Main courses ($10.95 to $13.50) include falafel and roasted vegetables, pad Thai, shrimp risotto with arborio rice, roasted Moroccan-style chicken with ginger and cilantro, turkey pot pie, roasted duck with maple-walnut glaze, and chile- and garlic-rubbed steak with basil aioli. Desserts, besides great ice creams and sorbets, include a signature Northern Spy pie, named for the apples that Tim likes to cook with and that are picked in the orchard out back.

Dinner is available in the bar dining area, outside on the side terrace or in a main dining room somewhat more refined with a rust-colored stenciled floor, a candle chandelier and small swag curtains around the windows. The bar was billed as a coffee and juice bar, but a liquor license was pending.

Lunch, 11:30 to 3; dinner, 4:30 to 10, weekend brunch, 9 to 3. Closed Tuesdays.

Santa Fe, 52 Broadway, Tivoli. (914) 757-4100.

Margaritas are a claim to fame of this bright yellow building with lavender trim at the only intersection in the one-horse riverside hamlet of Tivoli. It's long been held in high regard by aficionados of serious Mexican fare. So much so that owners David Weiss and Valerie Nehez, who have traveled extensively in Mexico and know well its cuisine, have expanded into an adjacent liquor store and now offer three dining areas on the main floor and another upstairs. The decor is colorful: woven rugs adorn the salmon-colored walls and the ceiling has been painted blue. Votive candles flicker in brandy snifters.

Margaritas come by the glass or pitcher and in flavors from peach to raspberry to cuervo to blue curacao, served up with gusto from the ornate bar. Although they started with strictly authentic Mexican food made from scratch, as their reputation grew they "took some artistic license," in Valerie's words. "We've spent some time in Thailand, and found there's a lot of crossover between the two cuisines with their uses of coriander and garlic."

So at Santa Fe now you'll find the tried-and-true Mexican standbys supplemented by an appetizer of shrimp chimichanga, rolled up like a spring roll and served with a homemade Thai ginger broth, or a salad of calamari tossed with arugula, endive and other greens. Among entrées ($7.95 to $13.95), the Oaxican taco is a corn tortilla with chicken, cheddar, cilantro and homemade molé made with thirteen kinds of dried chiles. The spicy Baja shrimp satay comes with a Thai peanut sauce, sweet plantains and black beans. Catfish could be glazed with honey, pineapple and Thai chili. A Caribbean veggie cake comes with apple-raisin chutney, plantains and black beans. Save room for dessert, perhaps homemade flan, ginger crème brûlée or key lime pie.

In 1993, the partners opened the Tivoli Bread Company and Cafe Pongo, a retail bakery and cafe just down the street (see Gourmet Treats).

Dinner, Tuesday-Sunday 5 to 10. Closed in January.

The Texas Taco, Route 22, Patterson. (914) 878-9665.

Rosemary Jamison, who hails from Texas, began selling tacos in front of the Plaza Hotel in Manhattan in 1968 "before anyone even knew what they were," she says with a laugh. Within a week she had lines down the block. Moving to Patterson in 1971, she proceeded to fill her small house with flea-market objects and now not an inch is left uncovered and hardly a blade of grass outside, either.

Even the curbs, paving stones and driveways are painted in wild colors to match the exterior of the house.

Cooking from her old New York cart that's ensconced in what must have been

Rosemary Jamison at The Texas Taco.

a dining room off the kitchen, she serves tacos, burritos, tostadas, chili, guacamole and fiesta pups ($1.15 to $2.50), and that's it. "Very simple, and I don't have to do a lot of ordering," she explains. With a rhinestone on her front tooth and long green hair ("I change it to fit my mood"), Rosemary is someone you can't miss.

Tiny dining rooms are filled with small tables, with hundreds of business cards displayed under their glass tops. Old toys, Marilyn Monroe collectibles, posters, jewelry – there's so much to look at you can't begin to take it all in. The bathroom is unique -- Rosemary thinks it gives one a feeling of being in an aquarium, with a huge shark on the ceiling. On the front lawn are a bunch of pink flamingo statuettes and the most motley collection of lawn chairs we ever saw. Even Rosemary's pickup truck is decorated to the max with stickers and jewelry. The Patterson flea-market people understand her tastes and bring to her door things they know she'll buy. Now an icon in the area, she lives in the cellar and rarely goes out except to cater parties. "I have no family," she volunteers, "so this is my life."

Her place sure has character. We think her tacos are pretty dang good, too. Open 11:30 a.m. to 9 p.m. daily.

Food for Thought, 9 Mill St. (Route 9), Rhinebeck. (914) 876-2749.

Tiny and intimate, this is the casual, contemporary kind of place attractive to New Yorkers who want a taste of home when out in the country. Chef-owners Robin Roosa and James Lener, who had experience working in Manhattan restaurants, designed their own 28-seat venue to be "small and select – to do a few things well," in Robin's words. They started with lunch and Sunday brunch, and in 1993 began serving weekend dinners, too.

Their contemporary American menu features lunch items like warm oriental chicken salad with spicy Chinese sesame noodles, Southwestern chicken salad with black beans and spicy tomato salsa, vegetable burrito and omelet of the day, along with burgers (California and Tex-Mex, among them) and interesting sandwiches (Middle Eastern ratatouille, hummus in a whole-wheat pita, and sautéed catfish fillet with spicy cajun tartar sauce on a toasted bun). Everything is in the $4.95 to $6.25 range, except for a sandwich combining Coach Farm goat cheese with grilled eggplant, roasted red peppers and watercress ($7.50).

The "small and select" theme continues at dinner, when you might start with gazpacho or creamy butternut-squash soup, crisp seafood wontons or baked brie en croûte. Main dishes ($12.95 to $14.95) could be shrimp tempura with wasabi-soy dipping sauce and basmati rice, honey-roasted duck with orange-scented port wine sauce and mashed potatoes, and grilled leg of lamb with plum chutney. Desserts include pumpkin flan, raspberry tart and banana chocolate-chip cheesecake. There's an espresso machine, and beers and wines are available.

The storefront decor is spare, with blue-checked tablecloths, fresh flowers and candles. Colorful plates line a shelf along the wall.

Lunch daily except Tuesday, 11:30 to 3; dinner, Thursday-Sunday from 5:30; Sunday brunch, 11 to 3.

Bed and Board

Le Chambord, 2075 Route 52, Hopewell Junction 12533. (914) 221-1941.

Here, thanks to the eighteen-hour days of versatile innkeeper Roy Benich, is a distinguished restaurant, a shop and an expanding inn and conference center focused on a pillared, glistening white Georgian Colonial mansion with dark green shutters and an ornate statue on the front patio. The dining rooms are posh, the guest rooms quite European, and romance permeates every nook and cranny. "New Yorkers love this," says Roy, who was previously at the city's Tavern on the Green. "They're only an hour from downtown but way out in the country."

First things first. The contemporary French food, prepared by executive chef Henri Benveniste, is superb, from the duck pâté and green salad with all kinds of julienned vegetables that began our dinners to the almond pastry shell filled with whipped cream and luscious fresh raspberries that was the crowning touch.

A complimentary plate of small canapés (two like an egg salad and four of salmon mousse with golden caviar) and a small loaf of sourdough bread came with drinks. The continental menu, formerly written in French and quite exotic, has been Americanized and toned down a bit for the 1990s. For appetizers (most $7.95 but one at $12.95), expect such diverse treats as cold black-ink linguini tossed with baby octopus and sesame dressing, marinated salmon rolls filled with crabmeat and a bacon vinaigrette, fresh tuna cakes with a cajun rémoulade sauce, Coach Farm goat-cheese turnovers and stir-fry scallops served with an oriental black-bean sauce.

Among entrées ($18.95 to $22.95), the veal chop sautéed with diced onions and a touch of paprika was a standout. One of us tried the tasting menu, which changes weekly. It brought mesquite-smoked flank steak carpaccio with corn relish, sea scallops in puff pastry with ginger and oregano, medallions of pork in calvados sauce, steamed salmon with carrots, and breast of chicken with broccoli and fennel, plus a trio of chocolate desserts and excellent decaf coffee.

All this was served with polish in one of the two intimate dining rooms, where the tables for two were so large that we had to slide our chairs and place settings closer together to avoid shouting. Lighting is fairly bright from a crystal chandelier as well as candles, plus the lights illuminating each work in a collection of art worth quite a bundle, we were told. The wine list starts at $16 but rises rapidly to $3,000. Roy had recently sold for $4,100 an 1891 port from Portugal, one of the oldest available in the world and one of 30 ports he had obtained on trips to Portugal and Madeira and displays proudly on a hallway credenza. Our more modest Parducci chardonnay was poured into champagne flute glasses.

Rack of lamb for two ($49) is highly recommended; it may be topped with a coating of kiwi, grapefruit, honey and cumin, and served with a tarragon sauce. The fish course represents "a new creation every night," says Roy, and the sauce that accompanies the roast duck is ever-changing -- plum one night, tangerine

Innkeeper Roy Benich in front of patio at Le Chambord.

and vodka the next -- "to keep things exciting." Desserts range from chocolate mousse and tulipe aux framboise to soufflés and crêpes suzette ($14.95 for two).

Upstairs on the second and third floors are eight spacious guest rooms, each with private bath, television and telephone. They're furnished in different periods with European and American antiques.

Out back in a pillared Georgian Colonial structure that Roy had built and named Tara are sixteen large guest rooms with sitting areas and what he calls a "Gone with the Wind" theme. Imported tapestries adorn the sofas and chairs, the queensize beds include canopies and four-posters, and toiletries await on the faux-marble vanities in the large bathrooms. The mahogany furniture includes a European-style desk and a full-length, free-standing mirror in each room. An outdoor terrace with sitting area goes off the fireplaced lobby.

Newly ensconced in front of Le Chambord is Rajko's, the innkeeper's suave gourmet and gift shop (see Gourmet Treats).

Guests are served a complimentary continental breakfast (fruit, juices, and croissants and scones baked by the inn's two pastry chefs) in the main restaurant. Downstairs in the cozy Marine Bar at night, exotic coffees and cordials are offered in front of the fireplace.

Lunch, Monday-Friday 11:30 to 2:30; dinner, Monday-Saturday 6 to 10, Sunday 3 to 9. Doubles, $105.

Old Drovers Inn, Old Route 22, Dover Plains 12522. (914) 832-9311.

The sense of history is palpable in this out-of-the-way, white wood inn, built in 1750 to serve the cattle drovers traveling to New York City on the post roads. It's been in continuous operation ever since, but never so grandly as since it was acquired in 1989 by New York film producer Kemper Peacock and Nantucket restaurateur Alice Pitcher. Kemper had been coming here for 25 years and leapt at the chance to buy "my favorite place." Theirs was only the third deed transfer since 1750 — the Preston family had it until 1937, when they sold to hotelier James Potter's family, from whom the new innkeepers bought. "We're the four P's — Preston, Potter, Pitcher and Peacock," quips Kemper.

He and Alice have breathed new life into the old inn, refurbishing and lightening up the colors and making it more comfortable -- to the point where they became the world's smallest Relais & Châteaux property in 1993. "They call us their littlest angel," declares Alice.

Upstairs they offer four guest rooms with private baths (with two more in the planning stage on the third floor). Three have fireplaces and guests in each are provided with fluffy terrycloth robes. Largest is the Meeting Room, so-called because it served that function for the Town of Dover in the 19th century. Long and fairly wide, it boasts the only known barrel-shaped (rounded) ceiling in New York State. Two upholstered chairs face the fireplace and double beds flank the side walls. Nightly turndown service brings a plate with an apple, chocolate mints and truffles.

The museum-quality main floor houses a fireplaced parlor/TV room, a long reception hall and the grand Federal Room with five remarkable Edward Paine murals of local and valley scenes. This was the inn's original dining room (the drovers imbibed in the Tap Room downstairs). Now it's the romantic setting in which order a leisurely, substantial breakfast off a blackboard menu.

Few rooms anywhere feel more historic and romantic than the Tap Room, site of the inn's acclaimed restaurant. Forty-two diners can be seated in a stone and beamed room lit almost entirely by candles that fairly sparkle inside hurricane chimneys day and night . (An outdoor courtyard also is popular in summer.) Tables, dressed in gray and burgundy linens, are set with red and white service plates bearing pictures of the inn. More hurricane chimneys etched with eagles top the bar and brass utensils adorn the fireplace.

The level of the food has been elevated by chef Jeff Marquise, who worked with Jasper White in Boston. His is an updated American menu rooted firmly in the past, starting perhaps with wild-rice, lentil and parsnip broth, cheddar-cheese soup or a robiola-cheese salad with yellow beets and roasted peppers. Appetizers ($8 to $12) might include Maine crab meat in a potato crust with truffled oxtail, pumpkin risotto with duck confit and foie-gras terrine with lentil puree. These may be superfluous given the small squares of toasted black bread, the dishes of crudités and deviled eggs, and the hot popovers that arrive at every table.

The autumn menu listed entrées from $16.75 for a signature turkey hash with mustard sauce to $31 for black-angus cowboy steak with potato and celeriac galette. Possibilities included broiled skate, arctic char, lobster hash with corn sauce, lamb chops with tomato chutney, and grilled quail in sage pesto with tri-colored polenta.

Among desserts are key lime pie, lemon-soufflé cheesecake, chocolate decadence cake, raspberry sorbet doused with cassis and crème brûlée with fruit.

Turkey hash is a fixture at lunch. Other possibilities could be smoked-salmon omelet, homemade noodles with duck confit and sundried tomatoes, steak and kidney pie, and yellowfin tuna with olives, peppers and garlic, $9 to $15.

Lunch, Thursday-Monday noon to 3; dinner, 5:30 to 9, Saturday 3 to 10, Sunday noon to 8:30; closed Tuesday and Wednesday except October. Doubles, $120 to $170.

Beekman Arms, 4 Mill St. (Route 9), Rhinebeck 12572. (914) 876-7077.

Dating from 1766, America's oldest continuously operating inn now is decidedly up to date, from the new American cuisine emanating from its restaurant leased to famed New York chef Larry Forgione to its Delamater Courtyard rooms with color TV, air-conditioning and working fireplaces. In fact, from the outside, as

Tap Room has been in continuous use since 1750 at Old Drovers Inn.

you gaze upon the striking, contemporary greenhouse restaurant at the side of the main entrance, you might think history is deceiving.

But you can have your history and eat it, too, in the dark and beamed, low-ceilinged Tap Room, the Pewter Room and the Wine Cellar Room, with wooden tables and many private booths, all lit by candles, even at midday. Or you can feel more contemporary in the greenhouse room facing the center of town, which can be opened to the outside on nice days.

The restaurant, now named **The Beekman 1776 Tavern,** reopened to unprecedented fanfare after it was leased in 1991 to Forgione, the celebrated owner of An American Place in Manhattan, who was familiar with the area as a 1974 CIA graduate. The inn's owner of 35 years "wanted to pull back and this was the perfect match," said the manager -- "America's oldest inn and An American Place's country restaurant." Forgione, who since has opened a third restaurant in Miami Beach and seldom is in the kitchen here, directed an updating of the menu that incorporates American classics and regional ingredients.

A recent autumn menu listed such appetizers ($5.95 to $9.95) as local corn and Hudson Valley smoked-trout chowder with a warm buttery corn stick, crispy fried Point Judith calamari with spicy rémoulade sauce, Hudson valley camembert crisp with a cherry-gooseberry chutney and field greens, and adobo-style barbecued duck ravioli wrapped in black-bean pasta with poblano peppers, roasted corn and grilled red onions.

The trendy, American-to-the-max roster continues with such main courses ($16.95 to $24) as cedar-planked Atlantic salmon atop a soft corn pudding with a toasted pumpkin-seed vinaigrette, Montauk yellowfin tuna crusted with black sesame seeds (accessorized with a gingered sticky rice cake, a julienne of local vegetables and a soy dipping sauce), peanut-barbecued gulf shrimp with a jack-cheese grits cake, honey-glazed roast Adirondack free-range duck, braised lamb shank on a bed of rosemary whipped potatoes, and wood-grilled filet of beef with Iowa blue-cheese potatoes gratin, braised shallots and roasted baby carrots.

Desserts ($4.50 to $5.25) include old-fashioned double-chocolate pudding, banana betty, warm local fruit crisp of the day with vanilla custard sauce, homemade ice cream and sorbet of the day, and something endearingly called a campfire s'mores ice-cream sandwich, a throwback to one's youth but with *homemade* marshmallows and graham crackers.

Obviously, the menu implies excitement, many of the accompaniments are interesting and unusual, and the prices are happily far lower than they would be in Manhattan. But the anticipation may prove better than the reality. The execution is left to resident chefs (about whom there was an air of mystery at our visit), the local food community has had mixed reactions and we found the welcome less than warm.

Elsewhere in the main inn, history is palpable. We marveled over the glass-enclosed replica of an old tavern in the far main-floor parlor, an incredible table-top display complete with miniature glasses and liquor bottles behind the bar and the most intricate little chairs and bar stools we ever saw. Guest rooms upstairs are modest and historic, quite as you'd expect from their 18th-century heritage. More luxurious are those in the gingerbread-trimmed 1844 Delamater House, one of the few early examples of American Gothic residences still in existence, a long block away from the main inn. Television sets are hidden in the armoires of its eight rooms, sherry awaits in decanters, and front and rear porches are great for relaxing. Behind it are top-of-the-line rooms in the cathedral-ceilinged Carriage House and the Delamater Courtyard area. Altogether the inn's ten buildings offer 59 rooms, all with private baths and 22 with fireplaces.

Lunch, 11:30 to 3; dinner, 5:30 to 9 or 10; Sunday, brunch 10 to 2, dinner 3:30 to 9. Doubles, $70 to $110; two-night minimum most weekends.

Lodging

Inn at the Falls, 50 Red Oaks Mill Road, Poughkeepsie 12603. (914) 462-5770.

Hard to find but worth the effort is this elegant bed-and-breakfast hotel beside a picturesque stream in suburban Poughkeepsie.

Owners Arnold and Barbara Sheer, who previously ran a nearby motor inn, liked to visit New England inns and B&Bs, "but we didn't like bathrooms down the hall or sharing the house with its owners," Arnold explained. So they decided to create in their hometown a combination of what they felt were the best features of a hotel and a B&B.

An unusual architectural scheme, a Boston decorator and $3 million produced a curving, two-story, residential-style building following the path of the stream. Opened in 1985, it has 22 rooms and suites, beautifully decorated in seven themes from English country to oriental to contemporary. A California artist did the striking paintings that enhance the rooms. Our suite had a comfy sitting room with extra-high ceilings, good reading lights, a dining table and kitchen sink with wet bar, plus two TV sets, three telephones and a canopied kingsize bed. It also had one of the biggest bathrooms we've seen, with an oversize tub and a huge walk-in shower. Floor-to-ceiling mirrors, bottles of toiletries and a marble-topped sink added to the effect.

The marble floors of the lobby lead to a large living room with a soaring ceiling, a gigantic chandelier, luxurious seating areas and a wall of windows onto the stream. Here, cocktails are available at night and a complimentary continental

Breakfast room at Inn at the Falls looks out onto passing stream.

breakfast is waiting in the morning (you also can have it sent to your room). French doors open to a terrace, where chairs and tables are put out in summer.

The Sheers pamper guests with nightly turndown service, chocolate mints on the pillow and a mini-safe in every closet. They even provide a card with explicit written directions to each of their favorite restaurants.

Doubles, $105; suites, $115 to $150. Closed Dec. 24 to Jan. 6.

Bykenhulle House, 21 Bykenhulle Road, Hopewell Junction 12533. (914) 221-4182.

An imposing, fifteen-room Georgian manor house built in 1841 for a Dutch silversmith was opened as a B&B in 1990 by Florence Beausoleil. Listed on the National Register and located on six acres off an exurban residential street not far from Le Chambord, the house has six fireplaces and double living rooms that are decorated with imported crystal chandeliers. We were particularly impressed with the plant-filled side sun room with a marble floor, outfitted in chintz and wicker and yielding a view of the patio and vast lawn. Beyond the 20-by-40-foot swimming pool, a stone path edged with thyme leads through Florence's perennial gardens to a gazebo.

On the second floor are four large bedrooms with private baths. Four-poster beds and antique furniture are the rule. The third floor has two large new bedrooms with sitting areas and jacuzzi baths.

A full country breakfast is served on fine china in the formal dining room, the table set with crystal candelabra. The innkeeper serves things like cheese frittata, french toast, eggs benedict, apple pancakes, and other recipes from her studies at the Culinary Institute. On busy weekends, husband Bill, an IBM engineer, helps serve. They arrived at the house in 1972 with six children and ten Arabian horses, all now departed.

Doubles, $105 to $125. No smoking.

Captain Schoonmaker's B&B, Route 113, High Falls 12440. (914) 687-7946.

Seven-course breakfasts and early-evening wine parties are executed with flair and personality here by Sam and Julia Krieg, retired educators-turned-antiques dealers. The festivities, the antiques, interesting common spaces and an eclectic clutter more than compensate for a shortfall of private baths in this fourteen-bedroom operation scattered across four buildings.

Most activity evolves around the Kriegs' good-looking 1760 stone house, nestled along a hillside between the road and a creek. The couple's antique furnishings add to the early American ambiance throughout. A porcelain chandelier graces the entry hall. The guest living room displays quilts, old crocks, a wagon full of stuffed animals and a bunch of stuffed mice atop a cabinet. Baskets hang from the ceiling of the fireplaced sun room, furnished with wicker and warmed in season by a potbelly stove. The Kriegs offer local wines, cider, popcorn and cheeses from 6 to 8 in the evening here or, in summer, on the decks outside.

The heart of the house -- literally -- is the fireplaced dining room, through which guests generally pass to reach other areas. It holds a long antique table for twelve, where the Kriegs serve legendary breakfasts at 9 (a couple of tables in the living room are pressed into service when the house is full). One day's repast began with orange juice, poached pears with raspberry sauce and whipped cream, and homemade breads. The main event was spinach-cheese-dill soufflé, with sausage on the side. Blueberry-banana-walnut strudel and apricot-honey danish concluded ("we always have two desserts," explains Julia). Sam is known for his broccoli quiche that's like a frittata; another favorite is silver-dollar pancakes flavored with crème de cacao or amaretto. Julia, a former grade-school teacher, may lead guests in serenading birthday or anniversary celebrants.

The guest rooms seem almost secondary in the Kriegs' house-party atmosphere. First to be rented are four rooms sharing two baths in the cottage in the woods behind the main house. One with floor-to-ceiling windows opens onto a deck built around a tree beside the creek. Those upstairs have timbered walls and vaulted ceilings. They're outfitted with feather beds and hooked rugs. Six more rooms are rented in two guest houses in the nearby village. An 1870 Victorian house contains two large bedrooms with the only private baths. The 1840 Towpath House adds four large rooms with double and twin beds; they share two baths and one has a fireplace. Four small bedrooms upstairs in the main house share one bath and are rented last.

Doubles, $80 to $90.

Veranda House, 82 Montgomery St., Rhinebeck 12572. (914) 876-4133.

An attractive 1845 Federal house that started as a farmhouse and once was an Episcopal church parsonage took on a new life in 1993. Ward and Linda Stanley of Philadelphia bought the place to run as a B&B. They offer four guest rooms with private baths and a variety of beds, from four-poster Shaker queensize to antique brass and iron double or old-fashioned wood twin beds. Two bedrooms, one downstairs in what had been a dining room and the other above, are architecturally notable for their bay windows attached to a five-sided bay.

The Stanleys have outfitted the common areas with rather modern furniture from their Philadelphia home. The living room opens onto a breakfast room as well as a TV room/library. The original parquet floors and nice glassware are on display throughout. Ward hosts lively wine and cheese hours for guests on the wicker-filled front veranda on weekends (he commutes to Philadelphia where he continues a university job teaching the history of architecture and design).

Linda serves a full breakfast, starting with a fruit plate and a homemade pastry, perhaps sour-cream coffee cake. Sweet and savory crêpes -- ham and mushroom

Georgian Colonial built in 1841 now takes B&B guests as Bykenhulle House.

paired with ones filled with jam -- or scrambled eggs with bacon could be the main course. Apple or pecan strudel might follow. Linda says she gave out the recipe three times in the first month for her sausage and tomato tart, made with tomatoes from their garden.

Doubles, $85 to $90.

Wine Tastings

Millbrook Winery, Wing Road off Route 57, Millbrook. (914) 677-8383.

The Hudson Valley's first winery dedicated exclusively to the production of vinifera, Millbrook occupies 130 remote, hilly acres, somewhere in the back of beyond. It's blessed with dramatic views of vine-covered hillsides, a couple of ponds, a picnic area and an unparalleled vista toward the Catskill Mountains. Owner John Dyson, former New York agriculture and commerce commissioner, converted a former dairy barn into the winery.

He and winemaker John Graziano produce 7,000 cases of fine wine a year, including award-winning chardonnays, pinot noirs, cabernet sauvignons and merlots ($10.99 to $16.99) that some find as spectacular as the setting. Everything is state of the art, from the manmade ponds that help moderate temperatures to a patented "goblet" trellis system that lets his pinot noir grapes get more sun and air for better ripening. Dyson, who also has purchased two California vineyards, grows and experiments with about 25 European grape varieties, more than anyone in the East. By example he has proved two claims: that the Hudson Valley can produce world-class viniferas, and that grapes provide a better return for farmers than cows, hay or corn.

You can follow his interesting story during a twenty-minute winery tour. Sample the results in a small sales room holding literature and a tasting counter barely big enough for two. Open daily, noon to 5.

Benmarl Vineyards, Highland Avenue, Marlborough-on-Hudson. (914) 236-4265.

One of the first of the Hudson Valley's farm wineries, this is particularly interesting for its seasonal **Benmarl Bistro,** a rakish cafe that has served some

93

extraordinary lunches over the years, depending on circumstances and chefs, most from the Culinary Institute. At our latest visit we found a less exciting menu: french bean soup, a pesto burger and four entrées ($8.95), including barbecued ribs with cornbread and coleslaw, grilled chicken with scalloped potatoes, and fusilli pasta with sundried tomatoes and parmesan cheese. Sit inside or out at a table with a grand view of the Hudson as you sip a $7.50 bottle of seyval blanc.

Another distinction for the winery, founded in 1957 by artist Mark Miller, is that it also represents (and sells) wines from other farm wineries, two from Long Island and five from the Finger Lakes. On hand are nearly 35 varieties, from blush to cabernet. The winery operation seems to have been upstaged lately by its Gallery in a Vineyard, which displays Miller's collection of art.

Winery open weekdays 11 to 5, weekends noon to 5. Bistro open Friday-Sunday, 11:30 to 3:30.

Gourmet Treats

The Corner Bakery, 10 Charles Colman Blvd., Pawling, 855-3707. This is one of the new breed of bakeries, featured in a New York Times magazine article and described by Redbook magazine in 1993 as one of the five finest bakeries in America. Shannon McKinney and Brian Doyle, who studied with Swiss dean of pastry Albert Kumin, opened in smaller quarters in 1986 (they expanded in 1992 with the Fine Foods Cafe and a large takeout-food operation.) Using all natural ingredients, they bake exquisite cakes, pastries and pies (how about eggnog chiffon?), Irish soda bread that was written up in Food & Wine magazine, gingerbread houses and stollen. We can vouch for their blueberry muffins and a scone, which we enjoyed with a latte from the espresso bar. Their much-publicized World Class Collection at Christmas includes jalapeño cornbread, Belgian chocolate pound cake, Irish brown bread and a moist lemon-poppyseed tea cake, $24.95 for eight ounces each and a mail-order hit. They also bottle their own dijon herb dressing, English mint sauce and preserves made on site by Shannon's mother, and offer a large selection of soups, salads, appetizers and entrées to go. Open daily from 6:30 or 7 a.m.

Coach Farm, Mill Hill Road off Route 82, Pine Plains, 398-5325. America's premier producer of goat cheese, this is the brainchild of Miles and Lillian Cahn, who gave America the classic Coach leather handbags from their New York City factory. In 1984, the Cahns imported a French cheesemaker and a Californian who owned the nation's largest goat herd to their 300-acre farm in the remote town of Gallatin. Within three years, they had 400 goats, 26 employees and a goat cheese "that is the equal of any French chèvre sold in this country," according to the New York Times. Already they are the largest American producer, "though that doesn't mean much," Miles quips. The music of Bach plays during milking, from 4 to 5 daily, and the milk from each goat yields about one pound of cheese a day. Coach goat cheese comes plain or with herbs or pepper, and the farm also produces yogurt and Yo-Goat, a natural yogurt drink with no preservatives or sugar added. The farm shop is open occasionally in summer, and tours of the milking parlor during the milking may be arranged. Since he wasn't selling cheese on the premises at the time, Miles directed us to the nearby General Store in Ancramdale, where we bought Coach Farm yogurt and peppered chèvre.

Cafe Pongo and Tivoli Bread Co., 69 Broadway, Tivoli, 757-4403. This is the 1993 offshoot of the well-known Santa Fe restaurant. Owners Valerie Nehez and David Weiss joined David's sister Amy in the venture just down and across the street. The retail bakery makes up to ten kinds of organic breads from scratch as well as interesting pastries, everything form chocolate-espresso torte to cranberry-walnut tea bread to fresh focaccia incorporating goat's-milk ricotta. The cafe serves breakfasts both mundane (eggs or waffles) and exotic (scallion-potato fritters with smoked salmon) as well as a great Sunday brunch. Sandwiches ($3.75 to $5) on the bakery breads range from peanut butter and jelly to ratatouille, sardines with lemon and capers, chicken salad and Vermont ham. The owners applied for a beer and wine license and planned to open weekend evenings starting in the summer of 1994. Otherwise, it's open Tuesday-Sunday 8 to 6.

Rajko's at Le Chambord, 2075 Route 52, Hopewell Junction, 221-1941. Billed as the Hudson Valley's "most unique gift shop," this gem of a little store is a must stop in the area. It features a variety of Le Chambord's gourmet food products, from balsamic vinegar with capers ($10.50) to chocolate-covered raisins, plus a line of handmade gourmet pastas (lobster fettuccine, $8 a package). Also part of the repertoire are exquisite porcelain and ceramics, handmade jewelry from Greece, stunning Italian silk neckties designed by innkeeper Roy Benich, handpainted fused glass, island imports and more.

American Spoon Foods, 51 East Market St., Rhinebeck, 876-6463. This is the first branch outside Michigan of the specialty-food enterprise that New York chef Larry Forgione (also of the Beekman 1776 Tavern) co-founded in 1981 in Petosky, Mich. Here you'll find quite an array of preserves, jams, relishes, spoon fruits (no-sugar preserves), sundried Michigan cherries and other fruits, wild rice, salad dazzlers (no-oil dressings) and Forgione condiments, sauces and salsas. The jams are called spoon preserves because they're more suited to spooning than spreading with a knife.

Joyous Kitchen, 307 Wall St., Kingston, 339-2111. Here is the ultimate kitchen shop and a well-stocked gourmet store, where we admired fantastic teapots and a Ghirardelli concoction billed as the world's largest chocolate bar (five pounds, $40.95). We sat at the counter in the cafe along one side and breakfasted on latte, a glass of carrot-beet-ginger juice, a toasted bagel with scallion-cream cheese and an order of eggs with oven-roasted potatoes and toast, for a combined bill of $8.50. The gourmet-to-go deli case is full of salads, entrées and.baked goods. Interesting classes are offered in the evenings in the cooking studio.

La Deliziosa, 10 Mount Carmel Place, Poughkeepsie, 471-3636. "Delicious is part of our name," says Frank Cordaro Jr., proprietor of this Italian pastry shop in the ethnic Mount Carmel Square section. Culinary experts agree, awarding the shop first-place honors for breads, appetizers, pastries and desserts in the annual Taste of the Hudson Valley competition. The specialty cakes are sights to behold, but you'll also find peanut-butter-mousse brownies, chocolate and almond cigars, rugalach in various flavors, struffoli and homemade truffles. Colorful Italian butter cookies nestle under blown-up photos of Elvis Prestley and Marilyn Monroe.

Adams Fairacre Farms, 195 Dutchess Tpke. (Route 44), Poughkeepsie. (914) 454-4330. Geared up for its 75th anniversary in 1994, this is a farm market like no other we've experienced — really a one-stop supermarket sprawl of produce, gourmet foods and garden items. The produce section is bigger than many a grocery store, dwarfing even the Adams grocery section. There are a gift shop and a Pastry Garden bake shop, where the aromas fairly overwhelm. Fresh rabbit was $2.99 a pound at the Country Butcher shop when we were there. The country deli and cheese shop offers all kinds of interesting goodies. Ralph Adams and company recently opened a somewhat smaller branch along Route 9W just north of the Kingston-Rhinecliff bridge.

Keuka Lake provides backdrop for wines on Bluff Point.

Finger Lakes
The Pleasures of the Grape

Anyone who has indulged in the pleasures of the grape in the California wine country yearns to return, especially when the harvest is at its height. Easterners no longer have to go out West. Closer to home, the Finger Lakes region of upstate New York embraces a cluster of vineyards and wineries too little known or appreciated outside their locale.

Once dismissed for their grapey taste, New York wines have long been strong in champagnes, sherries and dessert offerings. In recent years, they have been invited to dinner as well.

Finger Lakes wineries now are producing some fledglings of international distinction. The New York Times headlined an article posted later at many a local winery: "Sorry, France. Too Bad, California. Some New York Wines Outshine Even Yours." At last count, three dozen wineries were located in an area about the size of Connecticut. It is a landscape of rolling hills, lakes and vineyard vistas that are not only the match of any in California but often exceed them because of their proximity to water.

The Finger Lakes wineries range from giant Taylor, which attracts upwards of 2,000 tourists on busy days, to tiny McGregor Vineyard, a boutique winery at the end of a gravel road. Most are clustered along the hillsides rising sharply from the southern ends of Cayuga, Seneca and Keuka lakes.

The wine boom has spawned related ventures, far beyond the winery visits that beckon more than 300,000 tourists annually to the Finger Lakes, most in the late summer and fall.

Foremost, of course, is the sale of grapes — pick-your-own or available by the basket or in juice for wine. Grape pie is a staple on traditional dessert menus, especially in Naples, where fire hydrants are painted purple during the annual Grape Festival in September.

New restaurants, most featuring Finger Lakes wines, have emerged, especially in the Ithaca area. So have a handful of new or refurbished inns and dozens of B&Bs.

Also emerging lately is a cottage food industry. "We're at the same point with foods today that we were ten years ago with wine," said Michael Turback, whose Ithaca restaurant celebrates upstate New York food ingredients. "It took time for people to understand the renaissance in winemaking, and it's going to take some time with the food, too." Particularly noteworthy is the local cheese industry. Ithaca was the site for the first annual meeting of the American Cheese Society, and the Ithaca Journal reported the Finger Lakes were "becoming known as the wine and cheese region of the country." In 1993, Ithaca's Farmers' Market -- known across the country as a model of its genre -- celebrated its 20th anniversary.

These days, a tour of the Finger Lakes wine country is much more than a one-day affair, and involves far more than simply touring a winery or two. On a leisurely trip, all the senses are at once heightened and lulled as you sample wines and indigenous foods on a sun-bathed deck overlooking one of the Finger Lakes, particularly in autumn when the hillsides are ablaze in color.

Tippling Through the Wineries

Canandaigua Wine Co. is the biggest, Taylor the best known, Widmer's the most picturesque, and Bully Hill Vineyards the most controversial of the larger Finger Lakes wineries.

But others are more interesting for visitors with some background in winemaking and an appreciation for finer wines, especially those who seek personalized, informal tours that follow the dictates not of the leader but of the led.

For orientation purposes, start at one of the larger wineries, whose guided tours offer a comprehensive if perfunctory overview of the winemaking process followed by a quick short course on the proper way to taste wines and a commercialized pitch to purchase your favorites on the way out. Then head for the smaller wineries, where the tours, if any, are intimate, the conversations spirited, the tastings more varied and the guide may be the winemaker or the owner. Since they tend to be clustered at the southern ends of three lakes, you can "do" the wineries along one lake each day. Locally available brochures group them under the Cayuga Wine Trail, Seneca Lake Wineries and the Keuka Lake Winery Route.

Because they are so central to the Finger Lakes and their appeal is so special, we begin this chapter with a guide to some of the best or most interesting.

Hermann J. Wiemer Vineyard, Route 14, Dundee. (607) 243-7971.

Hermann Wiemer, whose family has grown grapes and made wine for more than three centuries along the Mosel River in Germany, ranks as today's icon of Finger Lakes vintners. He makes wine only from viniferas -- a successful sequel to the effort by the late Dr. Konstantin Frank to promote European-style vinifera grapes in an area where native lambrusco and French-American hybrids had reigned.

Wiemer, then the winemaker for Walter Taylor (who championed the hybrid cause), acquired an abandoned soybean farm on a slope above Seneca Lake in 1973 and began planting both hybrids and viniferas. Fired by Taylor six years later as disloyal to the hybrid cause, Wiemer set up his own winery and never looked back. His soaring barn winery, renovated to state-of-the-art condition, is low-key and very serious, as befits a producer of award-winning chardonnays and rieslings that command top prices. Wiemer established a nursery that has become one of the country's most important sources for top-quality grapevines, a business that in its way dwarfs his vineyard and winery. He produces about 12,000 cases of wine annually, samples of which can be tasted in a rather forbidding tasting room where the solo visitor senses that the staff has other priorities. Prices range from $8 for a dry riesling to $16 for the reserve chardonnay. There are self-guided tours; private tours may be arranged by appointment.

Open Monday-Saturday 10 to 5, Sunday 11 to 5. Closed on winter weekends.

Glenora Wine Cellars, Glenora-on-Seneca, 5435 Route 14, Dundee. (607) 243-5511.

Among medium-size Finger Lakes wineries, this is a pace-setter with a commanding view from the west side of Seneca Lake. Glenora has been winning awards since it opened in 1977. Its 1992 johannisberg riesling was rated the best in America two years in a row, and its reserve chardonnay was served at President Bush's inauguration. Glenora long ago abandoned variety in order to concentrate on premium white viniferas and French-American varietals, plus premium sparkling wines. Wine Spectator magazine ranks it among the world's 70 top producers of fine wines.

Glenora's merger with the smaller Finger Lakes Wine Cellars of Branchport has doubled output to 60,000 cases a year. A large, two-story addition has expanded the production facility as well as the upstairs tasting area and added an impressive new showroom with an outdoor deck on the south end.

After viewing a twelve-minute audio-visual presentation, visitors sample up to five wines. Questioners who linger may get to try a few others, as is the case at most smaller wineries. Wines cost $8 to $15 a bottle. Glenora sponsors occasional Sunday afternoon jazz concerts on its lawn (Bela Fleck and the Flecktones kicked off the 1993 series). New at our latest visit was the Wine Garden on the deck, where you could purchase wines by the glass and buy a loaf of bread and some cheese or sandwiches ($4.95 for chicken salad, turkey or ham).

Open Monday-Saturday, 10 to 5; Sunday, 11 to 5, May-October, noon to 5, November-April.

Wagner Vineyards, 9322 Route 414, Lodi. (607) 582-6450.

This is another favorite among the larger estate wineries, thanks both to its fortuitous location overlooking Seneca Lake and to the myriad endeavors of owner Bill Wagner, a dairy farmer-turned grape grower-turned winemaker. One of the most appealing is his Ginny Lee Cafe (see below), but he's no doubt proudest that his also has been ranked among the world's top 70 wineries by Wine Spectator.

Wagner differs from some in that he grows all his grapes ("my philosophy is that good wine is made out in the vineyards, which makes winemakers shudder, but I like that full-time control over the grapes," says its owner), the amount of research ("more than the rest of the wineries put together"), and the proportion of red wines ("nearly 50-50, contrary to the rest, which are heavily white").

He and his staff host hundreds of visitors on busy weekends in the octagonal building he designed himself. After guided tours, visitors are offered a free tasting

Lamoreaux Landing Wine Cellars occupies striking building above Seneca Lake.

of eight wines, or a paid tasting of better vintages. We came home with a good gewürztraminer for $7.99.

Open daily 10 to 4:30, weekends to 5.

Lamoreaux Landing Wine Cellars, 9224 Route 414, Lodi. (607) 582-6011.

In its construction stage, passersby thought this striking structure atop a hill commanding a panoramic view of Seneca Lake was going to be a cathedral. It turned out to be, yes, another winery -- but one with a difference. What owner Mark Wagner calls "a neo-Greek Revival barn" houses an award-winning producer of a wide variety of premium viniferas. California architect Bruce Corson, a friend whose father was president of Cornell University, designed a four-level master-piece of open spaces, oak floors, floor-to-ceiling windows and cream-colored walls hung with changing art exhibits.

It's a stylish backdrop for the making of fine wines, including a 1991 riesling that won honors as the best at the 1993 New World International Wine Competition. Wagner, a distant cousin of Bill Wagner of the adjacent Wagner Vineyards, had been growing classic vinifera grapes on his 130 lakeside acres for other wineries before opening his own winery in 1992. His first eight wines included five medal winners in the 1992 New York State Fair commercial wine competition; prices range from $6.50 to $16 for reserve chardonnay and $25 for a riesling ice wine.

The initial 3,400 cases of wine will grow incrementally, with additions of merlot and cabernet sauvignon to the original chardonnays, rieslings and champagnes. Wagner explains that some of his wines may not be at their best as stand-alone tasting wines, "but I drink wines with food so those are the kind I'm producing here." He and winemaker Rob Thomas plan to remain small and aim for the ultra-premium market. Expansion plans include a wing on either side of the slender building for increased production space and eventually a concert pavilion with a hillside view of the lake.

Open Monday-Saturday 10 to 5, Sunday noon to 5.

Knapp Vineyards, 2770 County Road 128, Romulus. (607) 869-9271.

A vaguely California air pervades this winery, a growing family operation on 100 acres of a former chicken farm above Cayuga Lake. There's a large, airy tasting room with a California-like veranda, but the prize addition is the new Restaurant at Knapp Vineyards fashioned from a storeroom at the rear of the winery (see below). Winery owners Doug and Suzie Knapp have been joined in the venture by his daughter, Lori, the winemaker, and Suzie's son Jeff Adema, the chef.

The Knapps say theirs is one of the few wineries producing "methode champenoise" champagne. It also is one of the growing handful doing red viniferas, including pinot noir and cabernet sauvignon. Total production is 10,000 cases a year, and its late-harvest riesling is a gold-medal winner. Tours and tastings are offered for $1. Wines are priced from $5.95 to $17.99 (for the brut champagne). Eat at the restaurant, or pick up a Knapp-Sack picnic (pasta and grilled chicken salad, beverage and two white-chocolate-pecan cookies, $7.50, or a loaf of Jeff's bread, two cheeses and fruit, $5.50 for two).

Open Monday-Saturday 10 to 5, Sunday noon to 5.

McGregor Vineyard, 5503 Dutch St. off Route 54, Dundee. (607) 292-3999.

This 25-acre vineyard near the end of a dead-end gravel road high above the

east side of Keuka Lake is a small haven for premium wines and such adjuncts as wine jellies prepared by Marge McGregor. She says her retired Eastman Kodak engineer-husband Bob "was advised to plant anything but viniferas, but he said, hey, if he's going to plant he's going to do the kinds of wines he likes."

The result is several thousand gallons worth of varietals, ranging from prize-winning chardonnays and rieslings to pinot noirs.

Everything is done by the family and a couple of employees from a building the size of a four-car garage. "We do a lot of maneuvering," Marge McGregor pointed out, showing a portable heater blowing warm air on a bottle of pinot noir. "When you're small, you do things differently."

Tastings are $1 for three wines at tables on an enclosed deck overlooking Keuka Lake. Cheese and fruit plates are available.

Open Monday-Saturday 10 to 6, Sunday 11 to 6; winter, daily 11 to 5.

Keuka Lake, from McGregor Vineyard.

Chateau Lafayette Reneau, Route 414, Hector. (607) 546-2062.

Alabama computer businessman Richard Reno is nothing if not versatile. He and wife Betty moved into a brick house above Seneca Lake, took over 35 acres of vineyards, and opened a winery with a food and gift shop and a picnic deck with a view of the lake. He offers occasional weekend picnic suppers and hayrides through the vineyards, plus the odd Southern barbecue steak dinner with wine and "all the fixins" ($25). At our visit, he was about to open a B&B in a house with a deck overlooking the lake, just north of the winery. Two of the five bedrooms have private baths, and guests are served continental breakfast (doubles, $65 to $95). The sidelines may upstage the wines, although we were impressed with the 1992 dry riesling ($9.95). We also liked the gift shop stocking its own wine jellies, wine syrup, wine soaps, wine mulling spices and specialty foods. Wine tastings are three for $1, or $2.50 for all thirteen offerings.

Open Monday-Saturday 10 to 6, Sunday 11 to 6, April-October; to 4, rest of year.

Lakeshore Winery, 5132 Route 89, Romulus. (315) 549-8461.

In this personal, quirky barn with an antiques and crafts shop, owner Bill Brown tries to show people how to match wine with food, and calls his tasting a twenty-minute mini-course. "Instead of a winery tour," he intones, "we take you through a tour of wine and foods."

You learn that not swirling the wine properly is "like going to Thanksgiving dinner with a clothespin on your nose." Serving a bit of food with each wine, he tries to dispel clichés, such as the one that white wines must go with seafood and reds with meat. "Whole new vistas of wine with food open up," he says at the conclusion, and notes a 50 to 60 percent "success rate" with first-timers.

It certainly is a different experience and an effort to be praised. Lakeshore's 3,000 gallons of wine, sold exclusively on premises, go from $4.50 for Aunt Clara and Uncle Charlie to $16 for a reserve chardonnay.

Open Monday-Saturday 11 to 5, Sunday noon to 5, May-October; weekends only in November and December.

Other wineries worth a look-see, depending on time and interests:

Dr. Konstantin Frank/Vinifera Wine Cellars, Middle Road, Hammondsport, is the home and vineyard of the late Dr. Frank, who was the first to plant European vinifera grapes in the Finger Lakes. His son Willy continues the tradition of producing fine wines from the famed vineyard. Tastings daily from 9 to 5, Sunday 1 to 5. Willy also has opened **Chateau Frank** in the cellar of the Frank home for the making of methode-champenoise sparkling wines, including a brut in the French style that sells for $18.

Cayuga Ridge Estate Winery, 6800 Route 89, Ovid, established by the former head of the New York State Agricultural Experiment Station in Geneva, has been taken over by longtime Ontario winemaker Tom Challen. All the grapes for its award-winning wines are grown in its 35-acre vineyard, with juice and grapes left over for sale to other wineries. Visitors enjoy an audio-visual presentation in the barn's loft and may take a half-hour guided tour daily at 2:30. Susie Challen has set up part of the loft level as an art gallery and produces some of the goodies available for tasting along with the wines, priced from $4.95 to $10.95. Open daily, noon to 5, mid-May through mid-November; weekends, noon to 4, rest of year.

Hosmer Winery, 6999 Route 89, Ovid, serves popcorn as a change from the ubiquitous crackers at its tastings of five wines of the visitor's choice for $1. Cameron and Maren Hosmer feature wines from the cayuga grape, developed by the Experiment Station at Geneva to increase the yield and survive harsh winters; many of the offerings here are favored by those partial to sweeter wines. We liked the gift items and specialty foods, including wine jellies and wine biscuits that pack a peppery kick. Open Monday-Saturday 10 to 5, Sunday noon to 5, April-December.

Four Chimneys Farm Winery, Hall Road, Himrod-on-Seneca, was the first organic winery in the country. Walter Pederson, founder of the commune-type operation, says the grapes are grown organically to protect the customer from harmful chemical residues and to protect the environment. The chardonnay is first-rate and the Eye of the Bee rosé, a concord wine sweetened with raw honey from the winery's own beehives, is a best-seller. Four Chimneys submits its 1990 pinot noir, available for a whopping $34.95 a bottle, to be one of New York's finest. A deli offers snacks for picnics and sandwiches sometimes can be made on request. Gourmet dinners are served in conjunction with a chamber-music festival (see below). Tastings, Monday-Saturday 10 to 6, Sunday 1 to 6, May-October; open for sales year-round.

Special Winery Treats

The Restaurant at Knapp Vineyards, 2770 County Road 128, Romulus. (607) 869-9481.

Pair a chef trained at the Culinary Institute of America with a scenic winery setting and you have a culinary hit in the Finger Lakes area. Jeffrey Adema and his wife Louise joined his family's business in 1992, launching a full-service restaurant at the rear of the winery. It opens onto a trellised outdoor terrace where vines grow above, herb and flower gardens bloom beyond, vineyards spread out on three sides, you can see or hear wild turkeys and pheasants, and bluebirds fly all around. It's a delightful setting for some inspired meals. Assisted by sous chef Amy Schaefers, also a CIA grad ("we're the only restaurant around with two CIA chefs," says Jeffrey), he changes his dinner menu every two weeks and his lunch menu monthly to take advantage of local and seasonal ingredients.

Dinner at our visit produced a quartet of entrées ($13.95 to $18.95): grilled chicken with sautéed artichokes and onions, tri-colored tortellini with smoked salmon, roasted pork tenderloin with a black-currant-cabernet sauce and sautéed beef medallions rolled in crushed black pepper, topped with mushrooms and a pinot-noir cream sauce. Starters included clam and black-bean chowder, grilled jumbo shrimp and fresh rabbit sausage on a bed of stir-fried vegetables, and chicken satay with a Thai peanut sauce. Desserts were white-chocolate-mousse cake, fruit cobblers, peach ice cream and passion-fruit sorbet. Suggested wines are paired with each choice at the same prices charged at the winery.

Lunch time brings similar innovation at lower prices ($5.25 to $8.95). You might try a garlic pizza with sundried tomatoes, balsamic onions and mozzarella, served with a small salad, red-pepper penne pasta sautéed with herbs and vegetables, or cheese-filled-tortellini salad with poached shrimp and seasonal vegetables.

Pastel watercolors lend a bit of color to the interior dining room, fairly stylish in black and white. But we'd opt for the outdoor terrace, a summertime retreat for folks from Syracuse and Rochester who come for a leisurely dinner amid the peace and quiet.

Lunch, Monday-Saturday 11 to 3; dinner, Thursday-Saturday 5:30 to 8:30; no lunch Monday-Wednesday in April, November-December. Closed January-March.

Ginny Lee Cafe, Wagner Vineyards, 9322 Route 414, Lodi. (607) 582-6574.

With its reasonably priced wines and charming setting (a panoramic view of its vineyards and Seneca Lake), the Ginny Lee has long been a treat. The expansive deck formerly topped by a white and blue circus-type tent has been enclosed to better weather the elements and to extend the season. Now there's a vast space with cathedral ceiling, white walls and white garden-type furniture. A section of the outdoor deck remains. Although dinner no longer is served and

Glenora Wine Cellars' new Wine Garden dining deck overlooks Seneca Lake.

the cuisine is scaled down from its original heights, lunch here is a must on each of our visits.

Twenty-eight Wagner wines and Aurora grape juice by the bottle, half carafe and glass are available at winery prices at the cafe, the first at a Finger Lakes winery and named for the owner's then-infant granddaughter.

The menu has been expanded to include soups, salads, sandwiches, burgers, pizzas and entrées, with $7.25 the top price for house-smoked salmon in puff pastry or crab-meat salad. At various visits we've enjoyed the Greek salad, shrimp salad on a croissant, chicken salad on a kaiser roll and the Ginny Lee, an assortment of fruits, cheeses and French bread. On the children's menu is a peanut-butter and grape-jelly sandwich, and for dessert strawberry-amaretto torte, chocolate truffles or crème de vin, vanilla ice cream laced with ravat ice wine.

Lunch, Monday-Saturday 11 to 4; Sunday, brunch 10 to 2, lunch 2 to 4. Open mid-May through mid-October.

Four Chimneys Farm Winery, Hall Road, Himrod-on-Seneca. (607) 243-7502.

The Saturday wine tastings and dinners following the Seneca Lake Chamber Music Series concerts in July, August and September are special treats. After the 7 o'clock concerts in the converted barn that houses the winery, guests adjourn for a seven-course dinner accompanied by up to five wines.

Host Walter Pederson, his wife Dayle and several of the seven Pederson children present the meal in an organic and new American style. The menu changes weekly, but you might start with roquefort-pear tartlette and broiled mushroom caps with walnut butter. A sorbet of organically grown strawberries clears the palate for the main course, perhaps a choice of herbed salmon, monkfish in saffron sauce or turkey tenderloin stuffed with goat cheese and sundried tomatoes. Then come a mesclun salad with hazelnuts, a plate of regional cheeses and dessert, perhaps chocolate-hazelnut torte or white-chocolate mousse with raspberries. All the while you're sampling the fine Four Chimneys wines, from a stylish dry Eye of the Dove to a rich late-harvest vignoles dessert wine.

The price is $39 for a seven-course meal, $12 for the wine tasting and $5 for the concert. Saturdays at 7 in July, August and September

Castel Grisch Estate, 3380 County Route 28, Watkins Glen. (607) 535-9614.

An enormous wine cask at the entry -- with the Louis Pasteur quote, "Wine rejuvenates," emblazoned on the far end -- welcomes visitors to this winery-cum-restaurant and a B&B in the manor house. Tom and Barbara Malina carry on the traditions of the original Swiss owners, who sought to provide a touch of Europe in the Finger Lakes.

The restaurant setting is dynamite: two large dining rooms dressed in burgundy and pink with full-length windows onto a partly canopied, partly open deck strung with tiny white lights. Beyond is a view of Seneca Lake beneath steep hillsides.

Lunch is a casual affair, with interesting soups, salads, pizzas and sandwiches priced from $2.95 to $5.95. The winemaker's plate -- an assortment of pâtés, galantines, cheeses and fresh fruits -- costs $6.95. Castel Grisch wines are available by the glass or bottle at winery prices ($7.95 to $14.95).

The dinner fare gets more ambitious. Although purists of our acquaintance found it lacking, no one could fault the setting as they dine on wiener schnitzel, duck breast française, trout bonne femme, spaëtzle, filet mignon or lamb chops provided by a neighbor who has a sheep farm, priced from $9.95 to $17.95. Desserts include apple strudel, chocolate-raspberry mousse with chardonnay topping and perhaps "a liquid dessert," late-harvest johannisberg riesling or ice wine. The Malinas keep things hopping with Friday-night fish festivals, Sunday buffet brunches with complimentary wines, buggy and hay rides by appointment, harvest dinners and more.

The treats continue inside the nearby timbered and vine-covered Manor House, where the Malinas offer three bedrooms ($59 to $99) for overnight guests. The rooms are upstairs; the master room in shades of rose with its own little balcony overlooking the vineyards and the lake has a private bath and kingsize bed. The other two, one with twins and one with a queen, share a large bathroom with a double vanity. The octagonal living room has rattan furniture; the adjacent sun room needs work. Guests are welcomed with wine and cheese, and are served fresh fruit and muffins in the morning.

Lunch daily, 11 to 4:30; dinner nightly, 5 to 9; Sunday, brunch 11 to 2, dinner 2 to 9. Closed Mondays in April, November and December and no meals January-March.

Dining

The Best of the Best

Dano's on Cayuga, 113 South Cayuga St., Ithaca. (607) 277-8942.

Dano Hutnik had quite a background before opening in 1990 a small downtown-Ithaca restaurant that quickly became one of the area's best. Born in the Ukraine, he grew up in Czechoslovakia and was a ballet dancer for fifteen years in Vienna before embarking on a restaurant career in New York and San Francisco. A classified ad in the New York Times led him to Ithaca and this old space that he and his wife, artist Karen Gilman, transformed into a chic French-style bistro in peach and blue-gray. There's seating for 44 at white-linened tables topped with white paper against a backdrop of her artworks on the walls and a spotlit alcove showcasing the fabulous desserts.

Chef Dano (pronounced Dan-yo) changes his menu of contemporary central European, French and northern Italian fare daily. Those in the know go for such

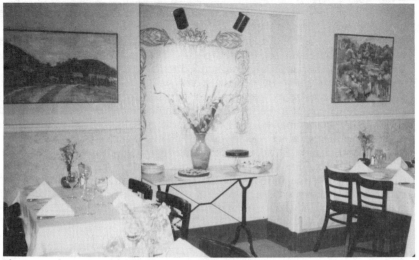

Flowers and pastries are displayed in niche at Dano's on Cayuga.

specialties as oxtail stew with black and green olives or veal sausage with braised red cabbage and spaëtzle. One autumn night, we sampled an appetizer of melted raclette with boiled potatoes, cornichons and pearl onions, the classic version and enough for two, and the house terrine of chicken, pork, duck, veal "and everything — a little cut here, a little there," according to the chef.

Among main courses ($10.95 to $18.95), we were delighted by the sautéed chicken breast with artichoke hearts and smoked mozzarella, served with incredibly good polenta sticks, and the linguini with shrimp, peas and scallions. Other tempters included baked Norwegian salmon in saffron sauce, grilled tuna with sundried tomato butter, grilled sirloin steak with shiitake mushrooms and osso buco. We also liked the Hermann J. Weimer dry riesling ($16), the only Finger Lakes choice on an excellent little wine list specializing in imported wines and rarely seen Californias. Crème brûlée and a bittersweet-chocolate gâteau with raspberry sauce were worthy endings to one of our better meals in a long time. The occasion was made more enjoyable as congenial chef Dano, table-hopping at night's end, proved to be quite the talker and philosopher.

Dinner, Tuesday-Saturday 5:30 to 10 or 11, Sunday 5 to 9.

Renée's Bistro, 202 East Falls St., Ithaca. (607) 272-0656.

The old Cafe des Amis was reopened in 1990 as an American bistro by Renée Senne, who had been sous chef at L'Auberge du Cochon Rouge and chef at the Greystone Inn, upon her return to Ithaca from studying at La Varenne in France and teaching in New York City.

Ficus trees and hanging plants thrive in the airy dining room and a small bar, both illuminated by a wall of windows across the front. It was in the former that we enjoyed a fine spring lunch: an excellent cream of onion soup, a slice of French bread topped with fresh mozzarella, sundried tomatoes and basil, and a special of fettuccine with grilled shrimp and garlic-cream sauce.

Alas, at our latest visit lunch was missing, a victim of the restaurant's success. Renée advised that she had spread herself too thin, so decided to concentrate on dinner. Dining is at tables dressed in white linens topped with butcher paper.

Innovative seafood preparations are highlighted on the short dinner menu supplemented by myriad specials, priced from $12.50 for lemon chicken served with couscous to $19.75 for lamb chops. You might find grilled salmon served with basil, tomatoes and roasted new potatoes; swordfish seared with garlic and olive oil resting on spinach linguini or grilled and served with shrimp-filled ravioli; soft-shell crabs meunière, or grilled halibut on steamed spinach with beurre blanc, garnished with roasted red peppers, pink peppercorns and basil.

Renée's repertoire includes such starters as shrimp and scallop vol-au-vent with saffron beurre blanc, smoked-salmon quesadilla, polenta with grilled vegetables, Mediterranean vegetables baked in phyllo, and shrimp cakes served with roasted-pepper sauce. How we'd like to graze through a couple of those, a salad of Goat Folks Farm chèvre and new potatoes served on greens, and one of the pasta dishes, perhaps cheese tortellini with sautéed walnuts, garlic and fresh basil. The owner's background as a pastry chef shows in the desserts, which run from mille-feuille to peach shortcake, and include lots of ices and granités.

Dinner, Monday-Saturday 5:30 to 10.

L'Auberge du Cochon Rouge, 1152 Danby Road, Ithaca. (607) 273-3464.

For some years, the best-known restaurant in the region has been ensconced in this yellow farmhouse on a hillside near a duck pond about a mile south of the Ithaca College campus, overlooking the Cayuga Lake valley. It's also associated with an adjacent inn of more recent vintage called La Tourelle (see Lodging). Proprietor Walter Wiggins and chef Tim Leonard have updated the classic French fare following the retirement of founding chef Etienne Merle.

There are two main dining rooms — one paneled, carpeted and clubby, and the other beamed with wide-board floors and a warming fireplace. But we like best for dining any time of year the small sun porch with white slatted blinds, wicker armchairs, and a green and white canopy that forms the ceiling. Each of the five white-linened tables has a copper stand holding a hurricane oil lamp, a salt cellar and pepper grinder, and fresh flowers in a square vase. The room is dimly lit, interesting art is on the walls and classical piano music plays softly in the background. As you look onto the spotlit grounds, the effect is entrancing.

"Apéritif or cocktail?" our Parisian-born waiter asked as we studied the menu, which is inscribed on each service plate. Among appetizers ranging from fresh asparagus with mango vinaigrette to goat cheese baked in puff pastry, we tried wild mushrooms in sorrel sauce, which was bitter but good, and an exceptional pâté served with tiny olives, cornichons and aspic. A zippy grapefruit granité in a frosted shot-glass affair cleared the palate for the main course.

Entrées run from $16.50 for penne Italienne to $24.50 for rack of lamb persillade. Sweetbreads in black butter with lemon and capers and sliced breast of goose with five kinds of peppercorns were magnificent. The latter was an ample plateful with rice and a mix of zucchini, corn and black olives.

The dessert trolley ($4.75) carried such treats as chocolate velvet cake with crème anglaise (the signature offering), peach cake with amaretto, fruit bavarians, and an exceptional chocolate and praline dacquoise. Strong French-roast coffee, served with petits fours and almond cookies, ended a memorable meal.

The expanded wine list offers the rarest of wines at prices to match (up to $1,500 for a 1919 Château D'Yquem). We managed to find a Château Ste. Michelle merlot from a selection of reasonably priced wines in the high teens and twenties. Our waiter said the Finger Lakes rieslings are especially popular here.

Dinner, Tuesday-Sunday 6 to 10; Sunday brunch, 11 to 2.

Entrance to L'Auberge du Cochon Rouge.

Tre Stelle, 120 Third St., Ithaca. (607) 273-8515.

New in 1993 was this striking Italian trattoria, home of wood-fired pizzas and a winning Mediterranean decor. The owners are designer-architects who did the sculptures in the corners of the dining room, rag-rolled the walls, designed the metal chairs and orchestrated the marble look on the bar. One also is a mushroom expert who picks the chanterelles that turn up in various dishes.

The printed menu is short but sweet: a couple of antipasti, five changing pizzas ($7.50 each), a couple of side dishes and four desserts. Chalkboard entrées ($8.50 to $11.50) might include herb and cheese lasagna, braciola (flank steak rolled around sausage and egg) and an acclaimed rabbit dish simmered in white wine and bearing a smoky taste from the wood oven. Most folks start with a platter of air-cured ham or the salad of fresh chanterelles on a bed of bibb lettuce, both served with focaccia. The favorite of the pizzas is the della casa (wild mushrooms with sundried tomatoes, caramelized onions and parmesan). Desserts include ricotta cheesecake with fresh blueberries, polenta cake served with whipped cream and cherry sauce, and almond biscotti.

Although prices are modest, some Ithacans complain that so are the portions. There's an excellent all-Italian wine list, priced mostly in the teens.

Dinner, Thursday-Monday 5 to 9:30 or 10:30.

Wildflower Cafe, 301 North Franklin St., Watkins Glen. (607) 535-9797.

Light, innovative food and an artsy menu with watercolors echoing the theme of a colorful painting on the barroom wall. These are hallmarks of this trendy little cafe that opened in 1990. Gourmet pizzas quickly became the rage, producing treats like a nine-inch honey crust topped with mozzarella and pesto. We can vouch for the California pizza special ($5.95), big enough that three shared it as an appetizer and still took part home in a doggy bag.

Among entrées ($12.95 to $22.95), we liked the salmon alfredo, enjoyed a special of fettuccine with anchovies and mushrooms, and wished the flame-roasted vegetables served with the charbroiled chicken hadn't been the same

107

kinds as those that had graced both the pizza and an appetizer of fresh vegetables with dip — a bit of veggie overkill. Vegetables are stressed here, however, and the menu offers four vegetarian entrées.

The Glenora Glen seyval blanc was a bargain and the apple crisp with whipped cream, the pear-almond tart and the chocolate-hazelnut ice cream were fine. The price was right, the atmosphere spirited and casual, and the menu more interesting than most in the area. Folks like the sautés of veal, pork and chicken, and the grills, among them halibut steak, pork anjou and strip steak.

Fifty patrons can be seated at a mix of booths and oak tables beside brick walls and beneath a pressed-tin ceiling.

Lunch daily, 11:30 to 4; dinner, 4 to 10 or 11.

Other Dining Choices

The Thai Cuisine, 501 South Meadow St., Ithaca. (607) 273-2031.

The best Thai food in New York State, including New York City — that's the opinion of many knowledgeable Thai-food lovers. It's served up in a serene, white and pink linened, L-shaped dining room in a commercial plaza by a Thai family in the kitchen and a mainly American staff out front. All is overseen by gregarious manager Sunit ("call me Lex") Chutintaranond. A large choice of soups, salads and appetizers at dinner ($2.50 to $9.95) includes shrimp chips with special house dip for the former price, and for the latter, Yum Ta-lay, a salad of shrimp, clams, scallops, squid, mint leaves and fresh chile peppers. There are six rice and noodle dishes; pad Thai is $8.50.

You'll have a hard time choosing among such entrées (all served with jasmine rice) as panang-neur, sliced tender beef simmered in panang sauce with sweet basil and pineapple, served with a side of pickled cauliflower, and gaeng-goong, shrimp simmered in Thai green curry with coconut milk, baby corn, straw mushrooms, chiles and kaffir lime. The selection is enormous, with eight shrimp dishes, for example. Nothing is over $12.95, except for a few of the chef's specials.

Lunch changes daily. Six main courses are served with soup or salad for $4.95 to $6.50. Sunday brunch is the Thai equivalent of a dim sum meal, offering more than 30 exotic little plates for $1.95 each. Thai Cuisine has a pretty good wine list and, of course, Thai beer.

Lunch, Tuesday-Friday 11:30 to 2; dinner nightly, 5 to 9:30 or 10, Sunday brunch, 11:30 to 2.

Just a Taste, 116 North Aurora St., Ithaca. (607) 277-9463.

A year after opening The Thai Cuisine, its owners branched out with Central New York's largest wine and tapas bar. Sleek in gray, black and white with black lacquered chairs, the downtown establishment also offers a tiny outdoor court-yard to the rear.

More than 50 wines are offered by the glass — in 2.5 ounce or 5-ounce sizes or by the "flight," which means a sampling of 1.5 ounces in a particular category, say five rieslings for $6 or a changing selection of cabernet sauvignons for $7.

We know folks who like to order a couple of flights and a selection of international tapas ($3.95 to $5.50) and while the night away here. We had to settle for a quick lunch, sharing a breaded oyster served on a bed of spinach, a chicken teriyaki kabob with an array of vegetables, and a pizza of smoked salmon and brie (the most expensive item at $5.95). The last was great; the other two were marred by the missing house sauce (so spicy when we finally got it that one of us wished we'd done without) and no semblance of the "array" of vegetables. Cappuccino and a terrific pineapple cheesecake served on a small black octagonal plate made up for the lapses.

Besides tapas and salads, the dinner hour brings entrées ($9.95 to $11.95) ranging from grilled sea bass with tomato-basil salsa to grilled lamb loin with spinach and a white-bean and tomato compote, served with fried polenta.

Open daily, 11:30 to 10, weekends to midnight.

Utage, 1749 Slaterville Road (Route 79), Ithaca. (607) 277-4417.

One of the premiere Japanese dining experiences in the East is offered at this rural restaurant of the old school. The setting in a small white house is nothing remarkable, although the hilly countryside is on view from the large rear windows. But the food is presented, as it usually is in Japanese restaurants, as if each plate were a picture. The kimono-clad waitresses are the only non-Orientals working in the family restaurant of Kenji Terao, who imports some of his fish from Japan by way of New York City.

Squid, eel, octopus and fiddlehead ferns are among the appetizer offerings ($2.50 to $8). We liked the sound of pink caviar (salmon roe with shredded radish), the Japanese-style pork dumplings and the chicken served with spinach in a wasabi sauce. One local innkeeper urges her customers to start with the gyoza ($5) and move on to the outstanding sushimi plate ($20). The freshest tuna and squid are also part of the sashimi presentation. Complete dinners, from fish consommé or soybean soup through ice cream and green tea, go for $12 to $23. The fifteen choices plus variations are a bonanza of yakitori, tempura, sukiyaki, teriyaki and mizutaki dishes. Sake, Kirin beer and plum wine go with.

Those in the know sometimes splurge for the $34 prix-fixe special, which varies with the chef's whim.

Dinner by reservation, Wednesday-Sunday 6 to 9. No smoking.

Moosewood Restaurant, 215 North Cayuga St., Ithaca. (607) 273-9610.

Small and plain, this establishment on the lower level of the Dewitt shopping mall is known to vegetarians around the country because of the *Moosewood Cookbook,* written by a former owner of the co-op operation, which had eighteen owners last we knew. The place closed for remodeling in 1993, reopening with a lighter look in blond pine, with yellow-sponged walls and wooden banquettes all around. It also offers a covered sidewalk cafe out front.

Original and natural-food cuisine is featured, although purists are skeptical. ("Beware," warns a printed vegan and vegetarian guide to the area. "This well-known vegetarian restaurant is no longer vegetarian and has virtually no vegan courses" -- a charge disputed by the restaurant, which says it always has a vegan entrée.)

"We're lazy about changing prices," one owner told us, and indeed they are quite modest, with lunch entrées at $5 and dinner between $8.50 and $10. Tofu burgers, pasta primavera and Hungarian vegetable soup are frequent choices — the menu changes twice daily to take advantage of what's fresh. A mushroom-cheese strudel, a plate of Middle Eastern salads, cauliflower-pea curry and flounder rollatini are regulars. The blackboard menu lists an imaginative selection of casseroles, curries, ragouts, salads and luscious homemade desserts like lemon-glazed gingerbread, peach trifle or a pear poached in wine with whipped cream. We liked the sound of tagine, a Moroccan vegetable stew simmered with lemon and saffron on couscous, at one visit, when folks were lined up in a row of chairs outside, waiting for tables at 1 o'clock. Also tempting was a Chesapeake platter -- baked catfish with old Bay seasoning, salt potatoes and stewed corn and tomatoes. The food is said to vary, depending on which of the rotating chefs is in the kitchen.

Fresh pasta is featured Wednesday or Thursday nights, fish is served Thursday through Sunday, and Sunday nights are devoted to varying ethnic or regional cuisines. Beer and wines are available.

Lunch, Monday-Saturday 11:30 to 2; dinner nightly, 5:30 to 8:30 or 9. No credit cards. No smoking.

Cabbagetown Cafe, 404 Eddy St., Ithaca. (607) 273-2847.

There are those who think this totally vegetarian restaurant at the edge of the Cornell University campus outshines Moosewood, especially lately -- although the local vegetarian flyer points out that "the staff may not speak 'vegan'"). It's a simple and endearing spot, with field flowers on the tables and a cabbage mural on the wall. The 25-member staff work cooperatively and split all tips.

From the "world's best" garlic bread to the falafel in pita, everything is cooked here. Try cashew chili, the enchilada of the day or the "wings of life" salad, with steamed broccoli, marinated tofu, toasted cashews and sunflower seeds, and sprouts. A choice of nine salad dressings includes yogurt-tahini, lemon-sesame and rugged garlic. Most dishes are in the $6.95 to $8.95 range at dinner, when the menu ranges around the world from North Africa and Italy to the Far East. Huevos rancheros and scrambled tofu are listed on the weekend brunch menu.

Lunch, Monday-Friday 11:30 to 4, dinner nightly, 4 to 9 or 10; Saturday and Sunday brunch, 10:30 to 2:30.

The Crow's Nest, 415 Boody's Hill Road, Geneva. (315) 781-0600.

Jackie Gleason's valet, who, legend has it, once ran the old Skin Divers Club as a restaurant, would never recognize its incarnation as a contemporary purveyor of food and drink, nicely situated beside the Barge Canal near its entrance to Seneca Lake.

Chip and Carol Smith of Waterloo took over what had turned into the old Riverside Inn, renovated, expanded and succeeded in a college town sadly lacking good, casual restaurants. The location alone would suffice: enormous, angled outdoor decks beside the canal and a marina with a state park and the lake in the background. It's a busy yet tranquil setting, not unlike similar places we've enjoyed along the Inter-Coastal Waterway in Florida.

The food, standard but quite good, is enhanced by the location. One afternoon, we lunched on a tuna salad and beer-boiled cold shrimp at an umbrella-covered table on the deck while watching a parade of homebound boats and ducks as storm clouds brewed over Seneca Lake and lightning crackled in the distance.

About 180 people can be served outside and another 90 inside in a starkly white room with vaulted ceiling and skylights, woven mats on butcher-block tables, caramel-colored vinyl chairs, Marimekko-type prints on the walls, and fishnetting and plants draped from the rafters. There's live music on the new raw-bar-style deck.

Dinner entrées range from broiled or fried haddock ($9.95) to the captain's seafood platter ($19.95). A few landlubber items are offered amid the seafood and, if you want both, go for surf and turf ($23.95). Desserts include Nana's homemade heavenly pie (like a lemon meringue), double-chocolate torte and New York cheesecake.

Open daily from 11 to 10. Closed Monday in winter.

Barge Canal and Seneca Lake are on view from deck at the Crow's Nest.

Fratelli's of New York, 481 Hamilton St., Geneva. (315) 789-5522.

When one of the original partners split, this Italian newcomer changed its name from Moretti's of San Francisco to Fratelli's of New York. There was no good reason, the remaining owner allowed, but it made for a good theme and did attract our eye when we were looking for a takeout dinner to enjoy back in our suite at Geneva on the Lake. Ensconced in a commercial strip center, the L-shaped restaurant has a mix of booths and tables separated by a divider from the bar.

We found the portions ample and the tastes fine for a casual dinner of Soho saltimbocca and Canal Street carbonara, accompanied by good salads, steak fries and homemade bread. Pastas are priced from $6.95 to $9.95, with entrées from $8.95 to $19.95 (for Manhattan filet stuffed with brie and topped with a sherry-mushroom sauce).

Favorite starters are the baked bulb of garlic served with warm brie and a baguette, the East Side greens (escarole and white beans sautéed in oil and garlic), and Fratelli's bread stuffed with sausage, spinach, pepperoni and provolone cheese, $5.95 for a half loaf. The restaurant claims the largest selection of New York State wines in the area.

Lunch, Monday-Friday from 11, Saturday from noon; dinner nightly, 4 to 10.

Room and Board

The Rose Inn, 813 Auburn Road, Box 6576, Ithaca 14851. (607) 533-7905.

Charles Rosemann, who had moved to Ithaca to manage the Cornell University hotel school's Statler Inn, gave it up to join his wife Sherry full-time in running their own inn. The large and classic Italianate mansion they bought in 1983, known locally as "The House with the Circular Staircase," was built around 1850 on twenty acres in the hilly countryside ten miles north of Ithaca.

Starting with five guest rooms and mostly shared baths, they have worked constantly to improve the guest quarters and now have ten rooms with private baths, plus five glamorous suites with fireplaces and jacuzzis for two. A parlor with a game table, a living room with Victorian furniture, TV, books and games, outdoor terraces and a rose garden also are available for guests' enjoyment.

In a short time, the Rosemanns have built the Rose Inn into New York State's only four-diamond, four-star country inn, as rated by AAA and Mobil, and one of the nation's ten best inns, according to Uncle Ben's. Those accolades tell only part of the story, for this is one great, friendly, personal place that's haute without being the least bit haughty. From the minute you enter (through the family kitchen, where dinner likely is being prepared) to your departure following an exceptional breakfast, you are in for a rare treat.

Rooms are individually decorated by Sherry, and those in a new two-story addition capture the classic flavor of the rest of the house. They are luxurious, with everything from lace curtains, ceiling fans and fresh flowers to luggage racks, terry robes, Vitabath and other amenities. In two, the bathroom fixtures (including a stretch-out tub) are from the Eastman House in Rochester. Folk art and antiques abound. Our rear suite came with a sunken jacuzzi in a garden-like space filled with plants off the bedroom, a majestic kingsize bed and antique furnishings in the bedroom, a large closet and a modern bath. Ever perfecting, the Rosemanns redid the original rooms in 1993. They took out the wall between two rooms to make a suite, complete with an 1860s fireplace and an early American Empire bed angled from a corner. Even Room 16, the smallest, is no slouch, with beautiful wall coverings and borders coordinated with the bedspread and the bathroom, an Empire desk and a plaster bust of King Tut on the wall. A new conference center in a restored carriage house at the side comes with its original walls and hand-hewn oak beams, a reception room, oriental rugs on the floors and ultra-elegant rest rooms.

Breakfast, served in the parlor, dining room or foyer with its beautiful parquet floors, is an event worthy of the rest of the inn experience. Rose mats are on the polished wood tables, as are white baskets filled with seasonal flowers. The juice glasses sport the Rosemann crest. Because fifteen varieties of apples are picked from their apple orchard, homemade cider is often poured. Also on the table are Charles's homemade jams and preserves — maybe black currant/red raspberry, mirabelle plum or gooseberry/red currant. Local fruit is served from early June to mid-September (we loved the raspberries), often with the Rosemanns' own crème fraîche. Sometimes the main dish will be an omelet with smoked salmon and croissants, sometimes cream cheese, bagels and lox. Charles's extra-specialty is his puffy Black Forest apple pancake, which we can attest is absolutely yummy. The coffee is his own blend of beans, including Kona from Hawaii.

The Rosemanns set an elegant dinner table as well, with candles, flowers, sterling silver and sparkling wine glasses. For $50 per person, they serve a many-course feast fit for a king. (The dinner is optional and must be booked in advance, but it could turn out to be your most memorable meal in the Finger Lakes area).

You might start as we did with smoked oysters in a puff pastry and hot artichoke strudel on a bed of pureed tomatoes. The colorful salad was a work of art: boston lettuce with snow peas, radicchio, watercress and sprouts, dotted with red and yellow peppers and red and yellow tomatoes, and enhanced with a raspberry-dijon vinaigrette. The rack of lamb (cooked on an outdoor grill, even in winter) or a veal chop with chanterelles might be garnished with baby ears of corn.

112

Sherry and Charles Rosemann in front of the Rose Inn.

Scampi Mediterranean style is served on a bed of acini, the sauce including a touch of curry and pinenuts on top. And the béarnaise sauce on the châteaubriand is first rate. Our favorite vegetable was the potato basket, which the Rosemanns do with every dinner. Individual grand-marnier soufflés with either chocolate or a foamy brandy sauce are a perfect end to the meal, but perhaps you'd prefer fresh raspberries with cointreau? The mostly French wine list is selective as well, with several dozen carefully-put-together choices priced from $14 to $150.

The Rosemanns' goal was to offer first-class lodging and an intimate dining experience. They have succeeded in spades.

Dinner by reservation, Tuesday-Saturday at 7. Doubles, $110 to $160; suites, $185 to $250. No smoking.

Geneva on the Lake, 1001 Lochland Road (Route 14), Box 929, Geneva 14456. (315) 789-7190 or (800) 343-6382.

If you want to pretend you are in a villa on an Italian lake, stay a night or two at this onetime monastery, now a European-style resort, which many consider the crème de la crème in the northern Finger Lakes area.

Built in 1910 as a replica of the Lancellotti Villa in Frascati outside Rome, with marble fireplaces and symmetrical gardens, the original Byron M. Nester estate was the home from 1949 to 1974 of Capuchin monks, who added a chapel, dormitory and dining room. Influenced by the Algonquin Hotel in New York, designer William J. Schickel of Ithaca turned it first into apartments and then into a deluxe resort with 29 rooms and suites in 1982.

Extra-large and sumptuously decorated bedrooms, suites with fireplaced living rooms and two-story townhouses are among the accommodations available. The bigger ones like the Landmark one-bedroom suite with kitchen and elegant living room could not be more luxurious. It made the small studio in which we first stayed (a combination living-bedroom with a fold-down queen bed and a small kitchenette) seem cramped and a bit dated; some of the dormitory vestiges inevitably remain.

Manicured grounds dotted with marble statues stretch to the swimming pool on a bluff at lake's edge. A trail leads down to the lake, where guests may swim, fish or boat. A colonnade provides a lovely shaded area for breakfast, lunch or cocktails on the rear terrace, which converts to a skating rink in winter.

Guests are treated to a complimentary bottle of wine in their room and, on Friday nights, a tasting of New York State wines and cheeses.

A light continental breakfast of fresh juice and a croissant is included in the rates. A full breakfast is available; the scrambled eggs with cream cheese and the shirred eggs with Canadian bacon are excellent.

Candlelight dinners with live music are offered to guests and the public Friday through Sunday at one or two seatings in the romantic Lancellotti Dining Room that could be in Rome; it's the former chapel with carved wood ceilings, marble fireplaces and tapestries. A 17th-century Mexican tin-crafted mirror and Italian chandeliered sconces are among its treasures.

A singer or a pianist entertain as guests partake of appetizers like dilled jumbo shrimp cocktail ($10.35, and featured in Bon Appétit magazine), and such entrées as veal scampi diane, mesquite-grilled tournedos béarnaise and chicken veronique ($19.50 to $36.80). We enjoyed a dinner of chicken Jacqueline in port wine and heavy cream with sliced apples and toasted almonds and the night's special shrimp dejonghe, both with crisp beans and mixed rice, followed by pumpkin cheesecake and a grand-marnier mousse. A $21.50 Hermann J. Wiemer riesling was one of the more affordable accompaniments from a pricey wine list.

New in 1993 was lunch daily on the terrace. The shaded Colonnade Pavilion is a fine setting for a leisurely meal, with prices ranging from $6.25 for a vegetarian delight to $11.95 for chicken provençal. We liked the garlicky and chunky vegetable gazpacho with a curried chicken and avocado plate, and the curried chicken in pita sandwich, followed by a cheesecake with blueberries and a delectable frozen grand-marnier coupe.

The resort is expensive, but worth it for perhaps a second or third honeymoon. Spring for a Landmark suite ($260) with a four-poster bed and a lovely view or a deluxe suite with fireplace and balcony ($227).

Lunch in summer, Monday-Saturday noon to 2; dinner, Friday and Saturday at 7 or 7:30, Sunday at 6:30 or 7. Sunday brunch, 9 to 11:30. Doubles, $196 to $419.

Morgan-Samuels Inn, 2920 Smith Road, Canandaigua 14424. (716) 394-9232.

Actor Judson Morgan, not J.P. Morgan as was first thought, built this rambling stone mansion in 1810, and eventually it became the home of industrialist Howard Samuels, who ran unsuccessfully for governor of New York a couple of decades ago. The house was acquired by Julie and John Sullivan, who left jobs in Geneseo to convert it into a very special inn in 1989. They named it the J.P. Morgan House, but later learned they were in error and, honest and perfectionist types that they are, they renamed it the Morgan-Samuels in 1993.

One fastidious innkeeper of our acquaintance said she had the best breakfast she'd ever had in this mansion on 46 private acres, run ever so personally by the Sullivans. Our breakfast certainly was a triumph, and so pretty we wished we'd brought along our camera for a color photograph.

The meal -- for some the highlight of a stay at this sophisticated and enchanting inn -- is taken in the beamed dining room, in a small breakfast-tea room, on a slate-floored screened porch or, our choice, out on the rear patio. We counted at least sixteen varieties on the fresh fruit platter, including local Irondequoit

Geneva on the Lake resort accommodates guests in a luxury villa.

platter was fresh orange juice served in delicate etched glasses. Following were huge and delicious carrot muffins and a choice of buckwheat pancakes with blackberries, blueberries or pecans (or all three), scrambled eggs with herbs, french toast or a double-cheese omelet. The last was one of the best breakfast treats we've had. It looked like a pizza with slices of tomato, scallions, red peppers, jalapeño peppers, mushrooms, herbs and parsley. Monterey jack, mozzarella, parmesan and blue cheeses were on top. spicy sausage patties and sunflower-seed toast accompanied this breakfast fit for a Morgan, as did hazelnut coffee.

John, who does most of the cooking, also serves dinner Thursday-Sunday by reservation. "I cook the way I like to cook," says John, who has had no formal training. He certainly cooks the way we like to eat. His prix-fixe dinner ($30 to $50) varies by the number and selection of courses. A typical dinner might begin with sashimi, clams casino, a shrimp cocktail for which Gourmet magazine requested the recipe, or chicken wings with a homemade hot sauce that, John says, "people always want to buy." Then comes a soup of homemade chicken or chilled apple-berry and a salad, usually spinach and romaine tossed with raspberry vinaigrette, cut strawberries and sliced granny smith apples or a mix of red-leaf lettuce, snow peas, artichoke hearts, hearts of palm, tomatoes and water chestnuts. A lemon shrub with cranberry and cherry juice precedes the main course, often a whole marinated tenderloin or lamb chops two and a half inches thick. Three to five vegetables and a basket of local breads accompany. Dessert could be cheesecake with berries, black-raspberry pie or cantaloupe with vanilla ice cream, sliced strawberries and chocolate sauce. Guests bring their own wine and enjoy togetherness in the dining room or porch, or privacy in five separate dining areas.

Although food is obviously a passion here, the seven guest rooms are hardly an afterthought. They range from the tiny single Thomas Jefferson Room with a built-in bed to the Morgan Suite with late 17th-century French furniture, a kingsize bed, an over-length loveseat in front of the TV and a new double jacuzzi in a corner of the bathroom, one of two jacuzzis in the house. All but the single have private baths and are dressed to the nines in exquisite taste by Julie. Our room

115

private baths and are dressed to the nines in exquisite taste by Julie. Our room on the third floor, small but exquisitely done, featured an interesting Gothic window and a kingsize bed awash with fourteen pillows.

Soft music plays and candles glow in the common rooms. There are a well-furnished living room, an intimate library with a TV and one of the mansion's eight fireplaces, a glass-enclosed tea room with a fireplace, a large screened porch where we were served iced tea in the afternoon and, outside, no fewer than four patios, a lily pond with fountain and a tennis court. Ducks and chickens and a heifer or two roam around in the distance. You could easily imagine you were at a house party in the country with *the* J.P. Morgan et al.

Dinner by reservation, Thursday-Sunday at 7 or 7:30. Doubles, $99 to $150. Suite, $195.

Belhurst Castle, Lochland Road (Route 14), Box 609, Geneva 14456. (315) 781-0201.

This red Medina stone structure built in Richardson Romanesque style in 1885 for half a million dollars on the shores of Seneca Lake really is a castle — from its ivy-covered, turreted entry to its porcelain Pierrots on top of the hall fireplace. Its storied past has also had it a gambling casino, speakeasy, restaurant and now a restaurant and inn. We first ate here in the late 1950s when its baronial splendor was as legendary as its flamboyant entrepreneur, Cornelius J. "Red" Dwyer.

Dining is in a variety of grand rooms and alcoves on the main floor, including a library, solarium and an oval garden room with windows on three sides. A luncheon buffet is popular. Evenings turn glamorous with a continental menu presented in a romantic setting. Appetizers include duck pâté, escargots bourguignonne, lobster ravioli and smoked salmon. Entrées run the gamut from chicken marsala ($15.95) to New Zealand rack of lamb with a rosemary-mustard sauce ($21.95). Prime rib has been a Belhurst specialty for 60 years, and the veal with shrimp over tomato fettuccine is always popular.

Geneva banker Duane Reeder, who acquired the inn in 1992, added a suite in the carriage house and a cozy loft bedroom with an efficiency kitchen in the ice house on the grounds behind the castle. They join eleven large guest rooms and suites with huge, modern bathrooms in the main building. All have antiques and oriental rugs, air-conditioning and television, and some have bidets, four-poster beds, working mosaic fireplaces, and stained-glass and leaded windows. On the second-floor landing, an original ice-water spigot dispenses complimentary wine for guests. Arrive early, or you'll have to tote your luggage through the entry foyer past dinner guests. Continental breakfast is complimentary in the off-season, and a full breakfast is available for guests.

Lunch, April-October, Monday-Saturday 11:30 to 2; dinner nightly, 5 to 9:30; Sunday, brunch 11 to 2, dinner 3 to 9. Doubles, $85 to $150; suites, $205 and $275.

The Statler Hotel, Cornell University, Ithaca 14853. (607) 257-2500 or (800) 541-2501.

Run by Cornell's famed School of Hotel Administration, most of the three-story Statler was razed and, like a phoenix, reborn. After an infusion of millions from the hotel industry, this is the nine-story monument to the Statler dream.

From the richly paneled lobby with bowls of dried flowers grown at Cornell Plantations to the 150 guest rooms, all is state of the art. Through the TV sets hidden in armoires, you can even order room service and settle your bill at check-out. Lord & Mayfair toiletries, Saratoga mineral water, minibars stocked

Bucolic landscape surrounds rambling Morgan-Samuels House.

with New York wines and local art enhance the rooms, the rear half of which afford stunning views over Cornell landmarks toward Cayuga Lake.

Banfi's is the luxurious, top-of-the-line dining room, offering a soup and salad luncheon buffet, a $10.95 Sunday brunch that is a Cornell tradition of long standing, and dinners overseen by a chef hired from Locke-Ober in Boston. The room couldn't be more serene and pleasant with damask linens on well-spaced tables, moss-green and black lacquered chairs and banquettes, and full-length windows onto a view of the campus. Half the staff are students.

The short dinner menu bears contemporary southern French overtones. Entrées run from $13.75 for shredded duck cassoulet to $17.50 for rack of lamb with roasted red-onion relish. Mushroom risotto, crisped sweeetbreads with balsamic sauce, and braised pheasant with oyster and sausage dressing and port sauce are other possibilities. Start with warm duck salad with ginger and raspberry vinaigrette (also an entrée possibility at lunch). Finish with one of the exotic house pastries.

Lunch, Monday-Friday 11:30 to 2:30; dinner, Monday-Saturday 5:30 to 10; Sunday brunch, 10 to 2. Doubles, $140; suites to $325.

Lodging

La Tourelle Country Inn, 1150 Danby Road (Route 96B), Ithaca 14850. (607) 273-2734 or (800) 765-1492.

A white stucco building trimmed in brown, this French-style country inn was opened in 1986 by Walter Wiggins, a partner of chef Etienne Merle in the acclaimed L'Auberge du Cochon Rouge restaurant next door. Set back from the road on a 75-acre property leading to Buttermilk Falls State Park, this is a place where you feel a world apart.

The entry is a glamorous, plant-filled lobby notable for colorful tiled floors. Three comfy sofas are in front of a stone fireplace, blazing in winter. Thirty-one spacious rooms and two executive suites, one with a fireplace, are handsomely appointed in country-French style with king or queen beds topped with quilts or comforters, color TVs, VCRs (movies are available at the front desk), tiled and marble bathrooms, and good art. A decanter of Spanish sherry is in each room.

Most memorable are the two round "romantic tower suites," each with a sunken circular waterbed, a double jacuzzi just behind it, a TV mounted over the door and a mirrored ceiling. These have to be seen to be believed.

The inn offers a walking map of the grounds with, incredibly, the points of interest listed in French.

An optional continental breakfast will be delivered to the room for $5.95 per person. Meals from the restaurant are available through room service.

Doubles, $75 to $110; suites, $110 to $125.

Hanshaw House B&B, 15 Sapsucker Woods Road, Ithaca 14850. (607) 273-8034.

Part of this farmhouse dates to 1830, but you'd hardly know it from the elegant restoration, the new second-story addition, and the sumptuous country decor offered by Helen Scoones in her B&B. Helen used to work for a decorator and did all the work herself.

Furnished with great flair and an eye to the comforts of home, Hanshaw House offers four air-conditioned guest rooms, all with private baths and two with sitting areas. We lucked into the second-floor suite, with a queensize feather bed, down comforter and pillows, antique furnishings, a modern bath and plenty of space to spread out. We didn't need all that space, however, for we had the run of the house — a classy living room outfitted in chintz and wicker with dhurries all over, a side room with TV, and a lovely yard backing up to a small pond and woods full of deer, woodchucks and other wildlife.

Helen greets guests with beverages in the afternoon and pampers early-risers with a choice of exotic coffees as she prepares a gourmet breakfast in a kitchen open to the original dining room. After fresh orange juice, we had an orange-banana-yogurt frappe and delectable Swedish pancakes puffed in the oven with peaches and crème fraîche. These were served on blue and white china on a lace-clothed table, topped with field flowers in stunning MacKenzie-Childs pottery from nearby Aurora. Other breakfasts at this special place could be quiche with cheddar cheese, dijon mustard and spanish olives (which Helen describes as more like a frittata), baked french toast with caramel sauce, baked eggs and heart-shaped waffles.

In 1993, Helen and her husband, an Ithaca College dean, were adding a wing in back for their own quarters, plus a formal dining room for guests' use beyond the TV room. That meant she could end her commute from their former house and spend more time pampering her guests.

Doubles, $72 to $98.

Buttermilk Falls B&B, 110 East Buttermilk Falls Road, Ithaca 14850. (607) 273-3947.

A huge painting of Buttermilk Falls is at the head of the stairs of this attractive, white brick 1825 house, which is the closest private building to the foot of Buttermilk Falls. Margie Rumsey came to the home of her late husband's grandfather as a bride in 1948. They ran it as a tourist home until they had children. When their youngest son graduated from Cornell in 1983, she reopened it as a B&B and has been improving it ever since.

Now all six guest rooms have private baths, though some are down the hall, and some retain a homey look (built-in cupboards like those one of us grew up with). But good art of Finger Lakes scenes, oriental rugs and early American antiques grace each room. The luxurious new downstairs bedroom in which we stayed has a wood-burning fireplace and a double jacuzzi surrounded by plants in the corner, from which we could glimpse Buttermilk Falls through the hedge.

Classical music plays throughout the public rooms. These include a parlor with games like chess and checkers, a plant-filled dining room notable for a long cherry table flanked by twelve different styles of windsor chairs made by Margie's son Ed, a large kitchen and a comfortable screened porch with a garden in one corner.

Breakfast is an event, starting perhaps with a frozen orange concoction that includes a whole banana and is spiced with fresh ginger. Margie invites guests to build "a cereal sundae" with a variety of fruit and nut toppings on her hot whole-grain cereal. Next might come a cheese soufflé with a hot local salsa, served with local Brown Cow yogurt to cool it down. "I never serve muffins; everyone else has them," says she. Instead she features toasted sourdough-rye bread or popovers, with intense peach-ginger, raspberry and rhubarb-raspberry jams that we found sensational. Guests in the dining room barter with those on the porch -- and vice-versa -- for exchanges on jams, seconds and what not, with loquacious Margie encouraging it all as she cooks up a storm in the kitchen in the midst of all the fun.

A rear carriage house includes a simple two-room cottage good for families. It's not far from the large maple tree up which the hostess sometimes climbs in good weather to sleep out in an open-air tree house.

Doubles, $88 to $125; jacuzzi room, $245. Smoking restricted.

The Red House Country Inn, Picnic Area Road, Burdett 14818. (607) 546-8566.

Innkeepers Joan Martin and Sandy Schmanke and their guests are the only humans in this preserve in the Finger Lakes National Forest, full of birds and wildlife. Leaving careers in Rochester, they opened their charming B&B inn in an 1844 farmhouse. The entourage now includes three dogs and four goats.

Five upstairs bedrooms, all lovingly furnished with antiques in a quaint country style, share four baths, two up and two down, nicely outfitted with perfumes, powders and soaps. Guests sip sherry by the fireplace in the old-fashioned parlor and sometimes play board games. A stunning scene of the area, hand-stitched with 60 kinds of material by a guest from Canada, graces the wall of the main dining room. Country items are offered in their good little gift shop. There are a kitchen for making drinks or snacks and a wicker-filled front veranda to relax on, as well as berries to be picked and miles of trails awaiting in the forest.

And not long ago, for her 50th birthday, Sandy treated herself and guests to a great new swimming pool, flanked by a patio and cabana where guests can lounge and barbecue. The last is a good thing, for otherwise it's a bit of a hike into Watkins Glen or Ithaca for dinner.

In the off-season from November through April, for an astonishingly low $18 a head, the owners will prepare country dinners for house guests with advance notice. Ours started with a great composed spinach salad, homemade rolls and a whole roasted chicken with a rice and pecan stuffing, green beans with mushrooms and delightful pattypan squash. Banana-cream pie capped a meal that was nicely paced and graciously served. Other entrée possibilities might be duck garnished with fresh raspberries in vodka and accompanied by wild rice or poached salmon steaks with dill sauce on the side. A frequent guest brings saffron to put in the rice pilafs and paellas. Meals often begin with Red House chowder, which has a potato and leek base and adds cream and fresh vegetables.

119

Warden tarts made with local warden grapes, butter-pecan-rum cake, chocolate-chestnut cake with kahlua-butter cream, and fruit pies and tarts are among desserts.

Breakfast, served in the main dining room with its pressed-oak chairs and lace cloths or in a smaller adjunct to the side, always includes juice and a fruit course, which in our case was a dish of peaches, blueberries and raspberries, garnished with mint from the owners' garden. Butter scones with black currants, pecan popovers, banana pancakes and cottage french toast are some of the goodies. We were quite happy with scrambled eggs, ham and toast.

"Our raspberries are as big as most strawberries," says Sandy. We know. She led us up the road to her favorite haunts to pick blueberries and black raspberries, and then directed us to a pick-your-own raspberry patch. We enjoyed assorted berries from the Finger Lakes for days afterward.

Doubles, $60 to $85. Smoking restricted.

Gourmet Treats

There's a growing awareness of what one booster calls the "foods of the Finger Lakes," a reference to the diversity of locally produced foods, from goat cheese to exotic produce. Having returned from California, where he had spent ten years in the food business, a restaurant manager in Ithaca contended that "some of the foods being produced here are as good if not better than their more publicized California counterparts."

A national model of its type now in its 21st year, the **Ithaca Farmers' Market** is a joy for fresh produce, local crafts and odds and ends (free kittens, bluegrass music, hand-stenciled shirts and such). Fresh egg rolls or falafel sandwiches washed down with homemade raspberry juice are one local innkeeper's Saturday lunch of choice. The market operates at Steamboat Landing off Route 13 north of downtown on Saturdays from 9 to 2 and Sundays from 10 to 2. A smaller version operates Tuesdays from 9 to 2 in Dewitt Park downtown at Buffalo and Cayuga streets. Another market is the **Windmill,** likened to the Pennsylvania farm markets (Mennonite foods are available), off Route 14 between Penn Yan and Dundee. Wineries are among the booths that operate Saturdays from 8 to 4 throughout summer and fall.

Ludgate Produce Farms, 1552 Hanshaw Road, Ithaca, is where you can get an idea of the variety and magnitude of the local food phenomenon. It is a produce stand without peer, as well as a purveyor of fresh herbs (eight kinds of mint; seven kinds of thyme), edible flowers for garnishes, wild game and a potpourri of specialty items. Linda Ludgate and her brother Michael started a decade ago with a card table along the road, selling fresh produce from their father's fields. Today, the stand is an enclosed store open 365 days a year. Local restaurateurs shop here for hard-to-find foods, exotic lettuces and rare vegetables.

For the best in baked goods, don't miss **Clever Hans Bakery,** a European-style kosher bakery at 701 West Buffalo St. next to a co-op food market. It boasts "the freshest coffee beans in Ithaca." The bakery opens at 7 a.m., and folks come in for the $1.29 breakfast of half a loaf of French bread, butter, jam and coffee. There are a couple of tables where you can sit — maybe with a sacher torte or an amaretto brownie?

Up by the Cornell campus is **Cafe Decadence** at 114 Dryden Road, also the home of **Finger Lakes Coffee Roasters,** so you know you can get a fine cup of coffee here. The cafe has a new branch at the Downtown Ithaca Commons.

The Brous and Mehaffey families have cornered a share of the specialty-food market in Ithaca since they bought **Collegetown Bagels** at 413 College Ave. in 1981. Now with a new branch downtown at 203 N. Aurora St., this is where local folks go for twelve varieties of bagels, baked fresh daily. Bagel sandwiches and a fourteen-foot-long salad, soup and baked-potato bar are attractions. A few years later they opened **CTB Appetizers,** which calls itself "Ithaca's ultimate gourmet takeout.," in Triphammer Mall. There are tables in back for enjoying the fare, from exotic salads to "outrageous sandwiches" to bagels to desserts like almond tarts. In 1989 they purchased the **Ithaca Bakery** at 400 North Meadow St. to create a flagship store with the best of all their operations in a single convenient location. Here is one gourmet paradise, where we've often found the makings for a fabulous picnic or a dinner at home. We have a tough time deciding between salads and roasted chicken items, but that's nothing compared to our dilemma in front of the pastry counter. The scope of the possibilities is unbelievable.

Now You're Cooking at 124 Cayuga St. carries unusual aprons, many regional and other cookbooks, dishes painted with colorful fruits and vegetables, fine flatware and napkins. Along with classic cookware are hard-to-find gadgets and an enormous collection of cookie cutters.

Northside Wine & Spirits boasts the largest selection of Finger Lakes wines in the world. It may be an idle boast, although the owner says he checked around. But the selection is mind-boggling and nicely priced. The toughest part is finding the place, which actually is on the south side of town in the Ithaca Shopping Plaza off Elmira Road, where the sign calls it Discount Beverage Center.

Some of the most exotic and best pizzas in town are served at **Christiano's Pizza,** a new downtown emporium at 106 North Aurora St. The place isn't much to look at, but they sure know how to bake pizzas.

A supermarket for gourmets? You bet, in Ithaca. In fact, there are two almost side by side on Route 13 south. Some folks like **Tops,** but we prefer **Wegmans,** which bears faint resemblance to the Wegmans markets we frequented when we lived in Rochester, its headquarters. The updated Wegmans in Ithaca, and to a lesser extent the one in Canandaigua, are heaven on earth for food lovers. The Ultimate Coffee Adventure, a coffee bar and shop at the entry, sets the stage for the wonders to come. We enjoyed a medium latte for $1.69 as we ogled pastry delectables and pondered the choices at the bakery and the gourmet salad bar (from broccoli slaw to caesar with shrimp or chicken), the deli quiche, chicken fajita and muffuletta pizzas, shrimp egg rolls and an array of chicken dishes (from herbed to fried to ribs to sweet and sour wings). With choices like these to eat here or to go, who'd ever cook at home? But if you want to, Wegmans will oblige. The 26 checkout counters at the front await.

In Watkins Glen, head for the **Glen Mountain Market** at 200 North Franklin St. for fine sandwiches ($3.50 to $6.25). The Blues Brother is turkey breast with sliced apples and blue cheese on homemade bread. Vegetarians will find a good selection of salads and sandwiches as well as a tofu burger. You can eat at one of the market's picnic tables. **Sullivan's** at 309 North Franklin is the place for homemade fudge, hand-dipped chocolates and butter crunch.

Along Seneca Lake, we like **Family Fare** on Route 414 in Burdett, where Joan Wickham of the former Wickham Vineyards offers gifts and gourmet foods (including her own pickles and salsas, which she has set out for tasting) in a delightful little house built by her husband's grandmother as a tea room and ice cream shop. Across the lake on Route 14 in Glenora is **Orchard Ovens,** a farm stand with the makings for a great picnic, run until 1993 by the founders of

Glenora Wine Cellars across the road. We couldn't resist the corn chowder and a piece of yummy grape pie.

Misty Meadow Hog Farm at 2828 Vineyard Road in Romulus is where you can take a 50-minute guided tour (adults $3.50, children $1.75) of the barns, hold baby pigs and feed the grownup pigs. We passed, thank you, but had lunch at the Misty Meadow Farm Kitchen, a screened-in structure that was rebuilt in a day in 1993 by neighborhood Amish in an old-fashioned barn-raising after it burned to the ground. We enjoyed a delicious barbecued pork sandwich for $4.25, including a visit to a buffet table holding baked beans, sauerkraut, potatoes and watermelon. Shortbread cookies in the shape of pigs are 90 cents, and there's a view of Cayuga Lake in the distance. In the Farm Shop you can pick up all kinds of pig-related items, plus the farm's lean pork packed to travel — chops, three kinds of sausage, sugar-cured ham and hickory-smoked barbecue. Tours conducted Tuesday-Saturday on the hour from 11 to 2 in summer; fewer hours Saturday only in June and September to mid-October.

You may have seen the fanciful hand-painted china of the **MacKenzie-Childs** studio in fine gift shops and department stores across the country. Be aware that their studio is in the area — a wonderful estate called Highbanks, a couple of miles north of Aurora. Two rooms of great fantasy in the Victorian home of Victoria and Richard MacKenzie-Childs show their furniture, china, painted floor rugs and trimmings. Tours of the factory are given weekdays at 2, and there is a shop where seconds are sold. The prices are expensive, however. The couple invite visitors to picnic on their beautiful grounds; there is even a pushcart where you can buy a hot dog, poppyseed cake or lemonade.

In Canandaigua, a must stop is **Sonnenberg Gardens and Mansion,** 151 Charlotte St. Restored in 1973 after 40 years of neglect, the Victorian gardens are recognized by the Smithsonian as some of the most magnificent ever created in America. The 50-acre garden estate around their 40-room summer home was planned at the turn of the century by Mary Clark Thompson, who traveled the world to create nine formal gardens, an arboretum, a greenhouse complex and more as a memorial to her husband. We were quite taken by the Japanese hill garden and tea house, the Pansy Garden in which even the bird bath is shaped like a pansy, and a rock garden with streams, waterfalls and pools fed by geysers and springs. Marvelous, too, are all the accompanying statues, gazebos, belvederes, arbors, a temple of Diana, a sitting Buddha and even a Roman bath. The mansion, a testament to the extravagances of the Gilded Age, has its own delights, among them the Lavender and Old Lace gift shop. The greenhouse in which Mrs. Thomas raised peaches and nectarines is now the Peach House, a jaunty little luncheon spot (open daily in season, 11:30 to 2) serving a limited menu. Stop here for a chef's or a shrimp salad or a turkey croissant ($5.50 to $7.50), accompanied by peach mineral water and dessert. Gardens and museum open daily, 9:30 to 5:30, mid-May to mid-October. Adults, $6.

Canandaigua has two special shops of interest to goumrets. **Renaissance — the Goodie II Shoppe** at 56 South Main St. stocks all the socially correct gifts, from jewelry to porcelain dolls, Port Merion china and lovely Christmas ornaments. Cookbooks (we picked up Linda McCarthy's for a vegetarian son) and nifty paper plates and napkins abound. At **Cat's in the Kitchen,** 367 West Ave., Laurel Wemett has collected, from tag sales and auctions, all the things our mothers and grandmothers used in the kitchen. She specializes in the Depression era to the 1960s, and it's fun to check the old canisters, cookie jars, china, pots and pans and more. New items are mixed in.

Roadside stands testify to nature's bounty all around Niagara fruit belt.

Niagara-on-the-Lake
Wine, Orchards and Shaw

We first met Niagara-on-the-Lake in the late 1960s when it was Sleepy Hollow, as Canadians sometimes called it.

With a set of parents in tow, we had driven over from our home in Rochester so a visiting father could see "The Devil's Disciple" by one of his favorite playwrights, George Bernard Shaw. After a matinee performance at the Courthouse theater, we browsed through the few shops worth browsing, ate dinner at the quaint Oban Inn and headed home under a full moon. It was the night man first landed on the moon, and that extra-terrestrial feat remained etched in our consciousness long after the Niagara outing had passed.

Now, many moons later, we regard Niagara-on-the-Lake much more fondly. This Sleepy Hollow has awakened, blossomed, spread its wings and come of age. The opening in 1973 of the Shaw Festival Theater sparked a renaissance in culture and tourism.

It wasn't always so for this charming, tree-lined town sited where the Niagara River meets Lake Ontario. The first capital of what was called Upper Canada, it played a pivotal role in the War of 1812 — still called "the war" in local circles today. But the capital was moved to safer ground in Toronto and business languished as the Welland Canal bypassed Niagara to the west.

Spared the onslaught that an economic boom can wreak, Niagara's Old Town was an architectural treasury of early buildings awaiting revival. The home-grown Shaw Festival provided that impetus, attracting a clientele that required good lodging, good food and good shopping. All of which Niagara-on-the-Lake now offers with charm and style.

Geography has afforded the area natural advantages. Old military reserves and farmlands provide a greenbelt around the town. The Niagara River Parkway cuts through 35 miles of the prettiest park lands and scenery you'll ever see. The Niagara fruit belt yields an abundance of fresh fruits and vegetables. And wineries have flourished in what Canadians call "the Napa of the North."

We were struck by the British ties of so many innkeepers and restaurateurs in this most English of Canadian towns, which traces its roots to the Empire Loyalists who fled to Canada during the American Revolution. It is appropriate that nearly every large inn and restaurant goes all-out for afternoon tea, a daily ritual here.

There are no chain stores or hotels, beyond a large Crabtree & Evelyn branch that seems very much at home. There is only one traffic light (at the edge of town). A clock tower in the middle of Queen Street is the dominant landmark of the flower-bedecked downtown. This is a sophisticated, affluent town appropriate for adult visitors; the few young children we saw in tow were obviously not thrilled to be here.

Come along and see why Niagara-on-the-Lake is such a choice getaway for the gourmet.

Dining

The Best of the Best

On the Twenty Restaurant & Wine Bar, 3638 Main St., Jordan. (905) 562-7313.

Ontario's first full-service winery restaurant quickly drew food lovers from miles around following its opening in 1993. Housed in the old Jordan Winery dating to 1870, the restaurant has an elegant country air and food to match.

"You can't imagine what it's like for a cook to come into an area like this," said young executive chef Michael Olson, who trained in Toronto and Ottawa restaurants. Upon arrival at the ambitious food and catering venture launched by the owner of the adjacent Cave Spring Cellars, Michael took off on his mountain bike to scout out local purveyors. His forays turned up growers who provide him with everything from mesclun to mushrooms. With Angelo Pavan, Cave Spring's winemaker, he set about matching wines and foods for adventuresome palates. He bottles his own vinegars and preserves, and bakes the gorgeous breads for the bake shop in front, where passersby can pick up pastries and picnics to go.

His lunch and dinner menus are the area's most innovative. Lunch might start with chilled potato and leek soup with fresh marjoram cream or warm brie with roasted garlic. Among entrées ($7.95 to $9.95), how about the cellar-master sandwich (roasted grain-fed chicken with bacon, lettuce, tomato and basil mayonnaise) or grilled sirloin with shallot-herb sauce and french fries?

At dinner, our party of four was impressed with both the tastes and presentation, especially the night's specials. A bruschetta of toasted sourdough bread with herbed tomatoes barely made it around the table, so good was each morsel. Among other starters ($3.25 to $6.95), the Hamilton Mountain mushroom bisque with chardonnay cream and sourdough croutons was a work of art and the salad of roasted sweet bell peppers on greens with baked olives and feta cheese was sensational. The pan-fried chicken livers with sour cherries atop greens and toasted pumpkin seeds was an interesting if not wholly successful combination, and the chilled cucumber soup with smoked trout and chives turned out a bit bland. For main courses ($11.95 to $15.95), we were delighted with the Pacific

Dining room at On the Twenty Restaurant & Wine Bar looks onto wooded ravine.

halibut with sweet-corn salsa, grilled trout with golden-plum and mint salsa, roasted lamb with red and black currants, and fresh spaghettini with roasted chicken, leeks and apricots in a riesling/olive-oil sauce. Each plate came with chef Michael's trademark decoration, squiggles of pureed beets blended with yogurt, as well as simple steamed vegetables that weren't as interesting as the rest of the meal.

The night's desserts included blueberry/sour-cream cake with maple hard sauce, chocolate-espresso torte with caramelized orange glaze and cardamom cream, and a selection of standard ice-cream flavors. All passed in favor of a sample of Cave Spring's riesling icewine, which winemaker Angelo correctly described as "dessert in a glass" -- a heavenly ending to a delightful meal.

Dining is at white-linened tables in a couple of airy rooms with sponged pale gold walls, floors and columns of travertine marble, striking art works and floor-to-ceiling windows onto the ravine shielding Twenty Mile Creek from view below. Cave Spring wines are featured at little markup, the restaurant has a full liquor license and carries the best of other local winery offerings. Upstairs beyond a planned banquet facility and an outdoor deck, winery owner Leonard Pennachetti expected to open a small B&B in 1994.

Open Tuesday-Sunday, lunch from 11:30; dinner, to 10.

In Piazza Pasta and Wine Bar, 3530 Schmond Pkwy., Thorold. (905) 984-8484.

Another winning newcomer in 1993 was this chic Italian establishment opened by award-winning chef Lino Collevecchio and sommelier Claudio Marchese in the new Embassy Suites Hotel, southeast of St. Catherines. Their soaring space at the base of the hotel's four-story atrium is at once airy and intimate, thanks to a billowing cloth canopy overhead. A table in the center showcases breads, vegetables and wines in the Italian style, and more wines are housed in free-standing wood cases around the dining room and behind the curving bar. Sleek green chairs with upholstered seats are at oversize tables, nicely spaced and dressed in white linens. More tables await on a canopied terrace outside.

125

Pastas and pizzettas are featured, $6.50 to $10.25 at both lunch and dinner. The gnocchi dumplings with four cheeses and the day's risotto, perhaps with fresh salmon and prawns, are standouts, as is the pizzetta with pancetta, goat cheese, tomato and chile oil. Also the same at lunch and dinner are the antipasti ($3.95 to $8.95), among them beef carpaccio paired with delicate greens drizzled with basil, smoked salmon with herbed mascarpone and cream-cheese beignet, and prosciutto with figs, sweet melons and, a nice contrast, rosemary crisps.

Food display at In Piazza.

At night, the menu expands to include principal plates ($14 to $17.50). We've heard great things about the medallions of beef tenderloin resting on a crisp potato cake and garnished with wild mushrooms and the mignon of veal accompanied by mushrooms and slices of eggplant marinated in wine. Desserts range from tirami su and espresso crème brûlée to Italian ices and gelatos with fruit or berries.

The expansive wine list is especially strong on Italian reds, one selling for the most un-Canadian-like price of $15 a bottle. A changing selection of wines is offered for $4.25 a glass.

Lunch daily, 11:30 to 3; dinner, 5:30 to 10; pizzas available until midnight.

The Queenston Heights Restaurant, Queenston Heights Park, Queenston. (905) 262-4274.

Operated by the Niagara Parks Commission, this restaurant is a cut above — in aspirations, as well as in location, commanding a panoramic view down the Niagara River toward Lake Ontario.

The menu stresses contemporary cuisine, though not necessarily at the heights we enjoyed at our fist visit. Then, everything on it appealed for a summertime lunch on the capacious outdoor terrace — until we were advised that the power had gone off and only cold meals were available.

Nonetheless, one of us made a lunch of two appetizers: a tomato and eggplant salad ($4.25), served on a black octagonal plate brightened by corn kernels and colorful bits of peppers, and smoked-salmon carpaccio ($7.50), garnished with shavings of romano cheese, herbs and tiny purple edible flowers. The other had to pass up what he wanted to order — charred and peppered steak salad on boston bibb and radicchio with horseradish-roquefort dressing ($10.95) — for smoked turkey with cranberry mayonnaise in a whole-wheat croissant ($7.95).

The Inniskillin brae blanc was a good wine choice. From the dessert cart we picked a super chocolate-strawberry charlotte with curls of chocolate as we savored the afternoon sunshine.

At our latest visit, the menu had been toned down a bit, although caesar salad with grilled chicken and a lamb burger enticed for lunch. At night, entrées run from $15.95 for rainbow trout with smoked salmon and a blue-cheese sauce to $18.95 for grilled strip steak with roasted-pepper relish. Atlantic salmon with

Niagara River lies far below dining terrace of Queenston Heights restaurant.

strawberry-champagne hollandaise and prime rib with Yorkshire pudding are other possibilities. The roast leg of lamb comes with a port-wine demi-glace and fiddlehead greens. One of the more interesting starters was a camembert spring roll with spicy fruit chutney. Desserts run to strawberry mousse, chocolate cheesecake and local peaches. The extensive wine list contains a page of Niagara whites and another of reds.

The formal main dining room is Tudor in feeling with a high timbered ceiling, armchairs at well-spaced tables and a painting of Niagara Falls above a huge stone fireplace. The view down the length of the river, while sitting at a table by the expansive windows, gives one the sense of being on an airplane.

Open mid-March through October, Monday-Saturday 11:30 to 9; tea, 3 to 5; Sunday brunch, 11 to 3.

Other Dining Choices

Fans Court, 135 Queen St., Niagara-on-the-Lake. (905) 468-4511.

"We serve gourmet Chinese food only — no chow mein," proclaims the sign at the door. In the opinion of local gourmets, this unpretentious Chinese restaurant shares top billing with the sleek, swanky Ristorante Giardino across the street as the town's best place to eat.

There's a pleasant outdoor patio for dining in front. Inside are a couple of nondescript rooms, where tables are set simply with silverware and chopsticks atop peach cloths. Oriental art and music provided a soothing backdrop as we nursed an Inniskillin brae blanc ($13.50) from a short list featuring Canadian wines and Chinese beers.

The menu advised that "sharing is one of the biggest enjoyments of a Chinese meal." Yet orders were not served in typical, help-yourself Chinese fashion, but rather on small dinner plates that made sharing difficult.

For starters, we chose deep-fried wontons ($2.80) and an intriguing-sounding radish and pork soup ($2.50) that arrived without much evidence of radish. For main courses ($9 to $16.80), we tried the shrimp and scallops in a phoenix (crisp noodle) nest and double-cooked pork tenderloin. Both were fine, but we were astounded that steamed rice (rice!) cost extra, as did tea — the first time we have encountered this in a Chinese restaurant. For that matter, there were no Chinese noodles and plum sauce to nibble on, as in most Chinese restaurants, and the service, while correct, was icy.

Open daily, noon to 9 or 10. Entire menu available for takeout.

The Buttery, 19 Queen St., Niagara-on-the-Lake. (905) 468-2564.

After the obligatory dinner at the Oban Inn, our second meal in town years ago was lunch at The Buttery. We were attracted by the casual menu and a conspicuous outdoor terrace fronting on the main street, perfect for watching the world go by.

Said tavern menu includes a trio of Colonial soups served with homemade bread, salads, sandwiches and such diverse fare as welsh rarebit, cornish pasties, salmagundi and croques monsieur. The tavern menu, served daily from 11, also includes crêpes, curries, steak and kidney pie, and spareribs, priced from $6.95 to $15.50 (for filet mignon).

Inside are a couple of dim dining rooms notable for pierced-copper tables. One is a banquet hall that hosts weekend medieval banquets, four-course theatrical events called Henry VIII feasts ($37.50 per person Friday, $38.50 on Saturday). The regular dinner menu is a mix of Canadian and continental entrées ranging from chicken chardonnay and lobster newburg to steak teriyaki and château-briand, priced from $15.95 to $21.

Tavern menu, daily from 11; afternoon tea, 2 to 5; dinner, Tuesday-Sunday 5:30 to 10; after-theater menu, Thursday-Sunday 10 to midnight.

The Wine Deck and Boardwalk Room, Vineland Estates Winery, 3620 Moyer Road, Vineland. (905) 562-7088.

Ontario liquor authorities finally allowed wineries to open on Sundays, accept credit cards and serve food on the premises starting in 1990. Vineland Estates, probably the area's most picturesque winery with a hilly country setting, was the first to oblige by enclosing the front porch of its original 1845 estate house and opening a bistro-style restaurant named for the wooden beams in the floor. In 1993, the side deck was vastly expanded to seat 100 under cover and outside, where on a clear day you can see the Toronto skyline through the grapevines.

The menu is short but select, perfect for sampling the winery's offerings. We lingered on the deck over a bottle of premium dry riesling ($11.45) as three of us shared platters of assorted cheeses ($8.95 for one) and assorted pâtés ($14.95 for two). The first yielded brie, cream cheese, cheddar and havarti with fruit, tomato and vegetable garnishes. The second contained garlic and red-wine pâté, shrimp and lobster mousse, and black-peppercorn and country pâtés, garnished with pickled mushrooms, vegetables and eggs. Both came in vine-basket trays decorated with asters and containing assorted breads and big soft pretzels. A fresh peach tart and steaming coffee were worthy endings.

The setting could not be more bucolic and, if you linger too long, you may want to stay the night. The dear little stucco cottage across the way is a B&B called **Wine 'n Recline.** It harbors a fully equipped kitchen, living room, bathroom and sleeping accommodations for four. There's a TV set for contact with the outside world, you can barbecue on the deck, and the refrigerator is stocked with a bottle of wine and the fixings for the next day's breakfast.

Lunch daily, 11 to 4; weekends only in winter; special barbecues by arrangement. B&B, $95.

Expansive windows bring outside in at Ristorante Giardino in Gate House Hotel.

The Epicurean, 84 Queen St., Niagara-on-the-Lake. (905) 468-3408.

Pick up your own food to take to the shaded patio or eat inside the colorful yellow and blue dining room. Soups like Mexican chicken or gazpacho are $2.95, or you might get eggplant pie or seafood in an avocado ($6.95). Salads made with the freshest of lettuces and sandwiches are available. Live jazz is scheduled Friday and Saturday nights from 10 to 12:30 in season.

Open daily, 11 a.m. to 11:30 p.m.

Bed and Board

Gate House Hotel, 142 Queen St., Niagara-on-the-Lake L0S 1J0. (905) 468-3263.

The simple, old Gate House Inn was gutted in 1988 and this sleek, mirrored hotel in black and white emerged — tastefully on the outside, thank goodness; contemporary Italian and showy on the inside.

Beyond bright red doors, a marble entry leads to the reception desk, where guests are directed to the two-tiered dining room (considered the fanciest in town) or upstairs to nine guest rooms on the second floor. We were shown a very modern room done in teal and black with two double beds, German and Italian furnishings, and a bathroom with double sinks, a bidet and Auberge toiletries. Rooms have TVs and all the usual amenities in contemporary European style. A continental breakfast is included.

But it is the hotel's **Ristorante Giardino** that is the talk of the town. Chef Tullio Calvello presents an exciting menu in a dining room that's at once ultra-chic, pristine and modern as can be. Huge windows look onto the gardens and lawns (and passersby look in as well). Generally well-spaced tables are set with black-edged service plates, white napkins rolled up in black paper rings, pink

129

carnations in heavy crystal vases, votive candles and two long-stemmed wine glasses at each place. All the plates and water glasses are octagonal. Masses of changing flowers (begonias at our visit) brighten the room's dividers, and good art hangs on the walls here and in the halls.

The menu is contemporary Italian and expensive (dinner entrées, $20 to $29; antipasti, $7.50 to $11, and desserts, $6 to $8). The possibilities range from braised snails with garlic and polenta, steamed shrimp with sweet and sour zucchini and mushroom terrine garnished with tomato concasse to pastas like penne sautéed with eggplant and tomato sauce or black ravioli stuffed with shellfish. Dover sole sautéed with radicchio, poached Atlantic salmon with pesto, roasted duck with grilled polenta in mustard-seed sauce and osso buco are main-course possibilities.

Not wishing to break the bank, we settled for lunch, which consisted of five prix-fixe offerings for $13 — all but one yielding soup or salad, entrée and dessert. A plate of crusty Italian bread arrived along with two glasses of the house Inniskillin wine (brae blanc and brae rouge). One of us started with an intensely flavored and silken shrimp bisque, followed by a rolled pasta with spinach and ricotta cheese. The other sampled the trio of Italian pastas: spaghetti with pancetta and parmesan-cream sauce, gnocchi with four cheeses, and fettuccine tossed with vegetables and herbs. All were good but their mainly white colors looked rather anemic — more colorful was the spinach fettuccine pesto we eyed at the next table. Dessert was a thin slice of carrot cake with vanilla ice cream and fresh strawberries — imported from California, which struck us as strange, given all the fresh peaches, pears and plums in season at the time around Niagara. Good cappuccino ($2.50) and coffee finished a memorable repast. The prix-fixe menu lately has been dropped in favor of à la carte selections: salads and pastas $6 to $8, main courses $10 to $15. The extensive wine list is especially strong on Niagara and Italian vintages.

Doubles, $125 to $145. Lunch daily, noon to 2:30; dinner nightly, 5 to 9. No lunch in off-season. Closed January-February.

Prince of Wales Hotel, 6 Picton St., Niagara-on-the-Lake LOS 1J0. (905) 468-3246 or (800) 263-2452.

When Henry Wiens took over a 127-year-old hostelry in the center of town in 1974, "it was a dive," recalls daughter Angelika Whitham, a partner in this family-run enterprise with her parents, brother and sister. Through property acquisitions and thoughtful restorations, they have expanded from the original sixteen rooms to 104 on three floors behind a meandering brick facade that looks more residential than commercial.

Period furnishings, brass beds and floral chintzes enhance all the guest rooms, which vary in size from standard double through deluxe and superior to the Windsor, an enormous suite with two television sets. High ceilings, minibar refrigerators and gleaming bathrooms with bidets and hair dryers are the norm.

The layout is enough of a maze that guests are given a floor plan to help find their rooms, the indoor pool, the basement health club, the paddle-tennis court on the second-floor roof and the rooftop sun deck.

Light fare is available in the **Three Feathers Cafe** and the **Queen's Royal Lounge,** the latter a sumptuous space with a fireplace on one side and a solarium in which to enjoy the $7.50 luncheon buffet.

Royals, the main dining room, is the showcase for Toronto-trained chef Mark Walpole's culinary talents. It's a study in restrained elegance, the walls covered in rusty-pumpkin suede-like fabric, the tables set with silver octagonal service

Meandering brick structure houses Prince of Wales Hotel.

plates, and full-length windows facing the hotel's lush flower beds and Simcoe Park.

During pre-theater dinner, countless well-heeled pedestrians passed outside our window table amid zillions of plants in the solarium, providing diversion and a reminder that this is a strolling town for pleasure-seekers.

A small salmon and spinach terrine, "compliments of the chef," preceded our appetizers, a good spinach salad with hot bacon dressing ($4) and an oversize portion of sliced smoked venison with English cucumbers, tomatoes and a roasted-garlic vinaigrette ($7). Among entrées ($18 to $25) were a superior roasted rabbit with prosciutto, spinach, garlic and tomato and a more ordinary dish of medallions of beef tenderloin bathed in a sauce of cream, cognac and peppercorns. Cauliflower, crisp green beans and potatoes au gratin accompanied.

Other entrée possibilities included baked halibut with garlic and sweet peppers, grilled pork tenderloin with spinach, radicchio and silver onions, and rack of lamb with mint noodles and roasted garlic.

The dessert list covered everything from macaroon-lemon cheesecake and a duet of frangelico and chocolate mousses to Bailey's ice-cream fudge cake and frozen neapolitan mille-feuille. A "regal sampler" of several costs $8. We shared a plate of raspberry sorbet with three ice creams (vanilla, pistachio and caramel), garnished with fresh blueberries and raspberries and plenty for two.

Doubles, $115 to $188; suites, $188 to $234.. Lunch daily, noon to 2; dinner nightly, 6 to 9 or 10; Sunday brunch, 11 to 2:30.

Queen's Landing Inn, 115 Byron St., Box 1180, Niagara-on-the-Lake L0S 1J0. (905) 468-2195.

The owner of the Pillar and Post, which started Niagara's inn boom in the 1970s, opened the town's largest hostelry in 1990. Its four-story Georgian facade appears

131

as if it's been around awhile, though local skeptics still consider its scale inappropriate for the town.

The rear of the hotel looks across the busy Niagara-on-the-Lake Sailing Club marina onto the river, but inside all is serene in classic Williamsburg style. A couple of shiny elevators take guests to their rooms, which have TVs, minibars, and tiled and marble bathrooms, each with an unusually large assortment of toiletries and some with jacuzzis. A few rooms have fireplaces. They are individually decorated in appealing colors, some in Wedgwood blue and others in raspberry and teal.

The lower floors, built into the side of a slope, offer conference rooms, a huge gift shop, a restaurant and lounge, a health facility and a light, airy indoor swimming pool area that includes a whirlpool and something we'd never seen before, a "swim-ex," a short pool that creates waves for resistance so you can swim in place.

The two-level dining room, with expansive windows toward marina and river, is pretty in powder blue with upholstered and Chippendale-type chairs in raspberry or teal. The setting is better than the food, according to the consensus of regional innkeepers who ate here, but the latter is said to be improving lately.

The dinner menu offers starters ($3.95 to $8.95) like scallop and cucumber ceviche, risotto with shrimp and wild mushrooms, and spicy chicken in phyllo toned down with apricots, yogurt and cilantro. Entrées range from $15.25 for linguini with shrimp, sundried tomatoes and essence of star anise to $24.95 for roasted rack of lamb presented on minted flageolets and tomato concasse. Choices include grilled Atlantic salmon on a tamarind and ginger sauce, sautéed pickerel meunière topped with mushrooms and lemon balm, sautéed sweetbreads with apple-cider-sage glaze and grilled beef tenderloin with a smoked three-onion sauce. Dessert could be a fruit flan, white-and-dark-chocolate mousse, amaretto ice cream and berries in brandy or a selection of homemade ice creams and sherbets. The extensive wine list features Canadian brands.

Light alternatives, such as caesar salad with grilled chicken, supplement the pricey lunch menu (entrées, $9.95 to $12.95). Some of the dining-room specialties as well as light fare turn up on the lounge menu, priced from $5.50 to $10.50.

Doubles, $145 to $350. Lunch daily, noon to 2; tea, 3 to 4:30; dinner, 6 to 9; lounge menu, 11 a.m. to 1 a.m.

The Oban Inn, 160 Front St., Box 94, Niagara-on-the-Lake L0S 1J0. (905) 468-2165.

This landmark facing Lake Ontario across a strip of golf course has been around since 1824 and looks it. Which is quite remarkable, given that it was destroyed by fire on Christmas Day 1992 and was rebuilt to its original specifications for reopening in November 1993. Owner Gary Burroughs was thrilled with the authenticity of the $2 million reconstruction, as was his loyal clientele.

Guests now have an elevator to reach the second and third floors, where rooms go off narrow corridors adorned with a multitude of ornate paintings. The best are those in front facing the lake; they are larger and have queen or twin beds, antique furnishings, gas fireplaces and plush armchairs or a loveseat facing a TV set. A large second-story balcony, outfitted with tables, chairs and many plants, goes off the rooms at the back of the Inn; it also may be used by all the house guests. Other rooms vary in size, but are all a little larger since there are now eighteen instead of twenty. They are decorated about as they used to be, but have been lightened up a bit. Vivid wallpapers, toiletries, a clock-radio and a

Gate posts mark entrance to Queen's Landing hotel and restaurant.

phone in each room are the rule. Guests enjoy a new library-sitting room upstairs with TV, gas fireplace and lots of books and games.

Besides rooms in the main house, the inn offers three that are highly prized in the adjacent Oban House.

The waiters and bartenders are in tartan plaids in the formal dining rooms and the ever-so-British **Shaw's Corner** piano bar full of Festival memorabilia. The place is abuzz day and night, for the bar, which miraculously has been rebuilt with exactly the same atmosphere, is a popular gathering place and the inn is considered the quintessential Niagara experience.

The dinner menu includes such English specialties as dover sole with tartar sauce and prime rib with Yorkshire pudding and horseradish. Among other entrées ($19 to $21) are Grand Banks flounder stuffed with shrimp and crab, pork medallions with calvados cream sauce, and twin filet mignons. Rack of lamb with a minted peach and garlic-cream sauce drew raves from friends, who also praised the caesar salad and were particularly impressed with the service.

For starters ($5 to $8) there are an assortment of smoked fish, potted shrimp (blended with spices and butter and served with toast points), and deep-fried camembert with English crackers and homemade red-pepper jelly. Desserts ($4.50) run from meringue chantilly and hot fudge sundae to English trifle and frozen grand-marnier soufflé.

Steak and kidney pie, fried salmon fish cakes, and cold pork pie with piccalilli relish, potato salad and sliced tomatoes are included on the lunch menu. These and other English specialties are featured on the lounge menu in winter.

Doubles, $120 to $155. Lunch daily, 11:30 to 2; tea, 3 to 5; dinner, 5:30 to 8:30.

The Pillar and Post, King and John Streets, Box 1011, Niagara-on-the-Lake L0S 1J0. (905) 468-2123.

This campus-like hostelry with 90 rooms, a restaurant and gift shop dates to the 1890s when it began life as a canning factory. Baskets later were manufactured here, but the building was converted in 1970 into a restaurant and crafts center, thus beginning former owner Doug McLeod's venture in the local hospitality business. (He later acquired the Royal Anchorage Motel and built the Queen's Landing Inn, before foreclosure set in. In 1993, the properties were acquired by a group of local investors).

The Pillar and Post wears its history well, from the bellboys in breeches and waitresses in period costumes to the deluxe queensize room we saw with a beamed ceiling, huge fireplace, a sofa and wing chairs, all dark and cozy. Other rooms are brighter and newer, in attached, motel-like buildings around a nicely landscaped courtyard and swimming pool (it's quite a hike from the lobby around what amounts to a square block to rooms on the far side). All rooms have private baths, toiletries and minibars, and many have canopied four-poster beds with patchwork quilts, hand-crafted pine furnishings and fireplaces. The Shaw Suite, done up in patchwork and wicker, has its own little garden patio.

The spacious Carriages restaurant off the lobby is full of bricks and beams, reflecting its factory heritage. Copper pots, a blazing fireplace and barnwood siding convey a Colonial feeling. Captain's chairs flank tables covered with beige linens and striking large white service plates — the plates and the wildflower placemats used for breakfast are for sale in the adjacent **Country Treasures** gift shop.

The dinner menu mixes a dollop of nouvelle cuisine amid such standbys as escargots provençal and prime rib with Yorkshire pudding. Among entrées ($13.95 to $23.95) are grilled swordfish with lime-ginger sauce, pork tenderloin braised in cider with red onions and apples, sweetbreads in port-cream sauce and grilled veal tenderloin served with red-pepper chutney.

Doubles, $138 to $205. Lunch daily, noon to 2:30; tea, 3 to 5:30; dinner, 5 to 9, winter 6 to 8.

Lodging

The Old Bank House, 10 Front St., Box 1708, Niagara-on-the-Lake L0S 1J0. (905) 468-7136.

The first Bank of Upper Canada branch was converted into the town's largest B&B, facing a lakefront park with a glimpse of Lake Ontario through the trees from the shady front veranda. Inside is a formal living room so spacious that tables can be set up to seat sixteen for breakfast with room to spare.

Rooms vary widely. Four upstairs with wash basins in the room share one bathroom with a separate w.c. We were ensconced in the Gallery Suite with its own entrance off the veranda, a double-bedded room containing the only private bathroom with combination shower-tub, a small sitting area and a dressing room that doubled as a kitchenette with a mini-fridge, an electric kettle, supplies of coffee and tea, and even a teapot with a tea cozy. Two other rooms also have private baths with showers and private entrances, and the Rose Suite has two bedrooms, a sitting room and "four-piece bathroom ensuite," as full private baths connected to the rooms are called in Ontario.

British-born innkeeper Marjorie Ironmonger prepares what she calls a hearty English country breakfast. One morning it started with fruit crisp and the next with mixed fresh fruit in crème fraîche. There's always a choice of orange and apple juice, as well as a basket of muffins and toast. One morning we had scrambled eggs, bacon, fried tomatoes and potatoes, and the next, crêpes filled with corned beef topped with cream sauce, accompanied by sautéed yellow and red peppers and sausage. Delicious! Raspberry and banana pancakes, cheese stratas, ratatouille and welsh rarebit are also in the repertoire. For the Sunday buffet breakfast, Marjorie often bakes a big ham and serves it with asparagus vinaigrette, new potatoes, scrambled eggs, homemade soda bread and more.

Doubles, $88 to $125; suite, $195.

Veranda at the Old Bank House.   **Dining room at Oban Inn.**

Moffatt Inn, 60 Picton St., Box 578, Niagara-on-the-Lake L0S 1J0. (905) 468-4116.

The 22 rooms here are individually decorated, up-to-date and arranged for privacy. Considering the in-town location and the amenities, they're a good value, too. Dating to 1834 and successively a private residence, house, offices and apartments, it was renovated in 1983 by Jim and Vena Johnstone, who have run it as an inn ever since. The two buildings flank a garden solarium that doubles as a guest lounge and as part of the **Coach and Horses Restaurant and English Pub,** a separate operation where breakfast and other meals are available.

Our room on the second floor front had a queen bed, a pleasant sitting area with TV and telephone, and a modern bath with Finesse toiletries and hair dryer. It was very quiet until our next-door neighbors showered in the morning, when it sounded as if they were in our room. We also liked the four rooms on the main floor sharing a side patio and garden. All rooms have private baths, queensize or two double beds, brass headboards and unusual carved wood doors.

What one of us felt was the most appealing room (the other disagreed) is kept for walk-ins. It's the downstairs conference room, which is convertible to an extra-spacious guest room with high windows and a murphy bed for $80. One couple so liked it that they stayed a week.

Doubles, $75 to $105.

The Kiely House Heritage Inn, 209 Queen St., Box 1642, Niagara-on-the-Lake L0S 1J0. (905) 468-4588.

Large verandas on two stories, front and back, dominate this imposing, pillared Georgian house built in 1832, set on an acre of lawns backing up to a golf course overlooking Lake Ontario. The rear veranda is so big it contains both a screened porch and an open porch facing spectacular gardens, where roses bloom into November and English ivy and other exotica grow as they do nowhere else in eastern Canada.

Innkeepers Heather and Ray Pettit took over in 1989 and converted a section of the main-floor double parlor into their private quarters. One large guest room with canopy bed is in the original kitchen; note the kitchen-size fireplace, the rich wood paneling and deep-toned wallpaper, and a loveseat looking out at the gardens. Room 8 upstairs is lighter with a 1930s art-deco look, a fireplace and a private veranda. The upstairs rear balcony slopes a bit — the better to catch the breeze off Lake Ontario, says Heather.

Of the thirteen guest rooms, five have fireplaces and all have private baths. The six smallest are in a wing at the side.

A cheery Victorian breakfast room with watercolors for sale on the walls is the setting for a continental-plus breakfast of juice, seasonal fruits, cereal, homebaked scones and muffins.

In 1994, the Pettits were working on plans to convert their living quarters and the breakfast room into a fine-dining restaurant serving lunch and dinner daily.

Doubles, $75 to $168.

South Landing Inn, Kent and Front Streets, Queenston L0S 1L0. (905) 262-4634.

Niagara's hilltop neighbor, Queenston, offers this pleasant inn and motel overlooking the Niagara River. Five rooms in the main house, built as an inn in the early 1800s and the town's oldest building, have private baths, are furnished in Canadian pine, and have TV and air-conditioning. The views from the inn's two front verandas are stunning.

Check out the remarkable needlepoint pictures done by Kathy Szabo, innkeeper with her husband Tony, in the second-floor foyer. Breakfast (not included in the rates) is available in a simple little restaurant on the main floor.

A motel-style annex across the street contains eighteen rooms and private baths on two floors. Four suites on either end are most prized, particularly Suite 102 with two double beds, a sofa, an armoire, a private veranda and a river view. The standard rooms have two double beds and fancy chairs in the Louis XV style covered in a tapestry-like material. Those on the second floor have ceiling fans, and one suite has a cathedral ceiling.

Upon our arrival after a long working day in the summer of 1993, the room we had booked here by credit card two weeks in advance turned up AWOL. The place was full, so there was little we could do but trundle off -- without even an apology from the owner – to the new Embassy Suites Hotel, which we'd seen earlier in the day a few miles west in Thorold. There we lucked into a luxurious two-room suite for $79 and everything turned out fine, after all.

Doubles, $80; suites, $95.

Villa McNab, 1356 McNab Road, Niagara-on-the-Lake L0S 1J0. (905) 934-6865.

Statuary and fountains on the lawns, a red roof, and a glass-covered atrium and swimming pool mark this Spanish-style villa west of town. Built eighteen years ago by a Dutch couple, it has been operated since 1990 by Bob and Beryl Owen from England, who ran a hotel there until their daughter married a Canadian and moved to Welland. "We visited, and fell in love with the area," says Beryl.

The Owens share the pool area, a jacuzzi room, a sauna, an ornate dining room with red velvet chairs and a fireplaced, Spanish-looking sitting room with their guests. Each of three spacious bedrooms has a private bath, antique queensize bed, TV with remote control, good reading lamps and two chairs (noteworthy because so many rooms in the area contain only one chair).

Amidst exotic plants in the pool area or in the dining room, the Owens serve an expanded continental breakfast of sliced fruits, cereal, cottage cheese, tomatoes, muffins and croissants. For an extra $5 Beryl will prepare what she calls a "cardiac arrest" breakfast (all of the above plus eggs, bacon, sausage, blood pudding and that English delight for some, fried bread).

The villa is surrounded by an acre of lawns and trees, and Lake Ontario is a short walk down the road. Guests also can walk up the road to McNab Anglican Church for tea served on summer afternoons in the church hall.

Doubles, $95.

Victoria Cottage, 178 Victoria St., Niagara-on-the-Lake L0S 1J0. (905) 468-2570.

The brochure advertises a "one-of-a-kind studio apartment" with bed-sitting room, kitchen and bathroom in a Victorian coach house.

This cottage happens to adjoin the home of Angie Strauss, local watercolorist and designer whose work is well-known in Canadian art and fashion circles. A private entrance leads into a courtyard rose garden. The small main floor has a kitchenette/dining area, where you can make your own breakfast or snacks. Upstairs over a two-car garage is an attic loft big enough for four with a kingsize bed, a sleeper sofa, TV and an oriental rug atop pink carpeting.

Best of all, you'll likely get to meet Angie and husband Hartley, who built the cottage himself six years ago, and maybe get a peek at their fabulous back-yard garden that you'd never guess was tucked in behind the Shaw Festival's Royal George Theatre right in the heart of town.

Rate, $120 per night for two or four. No smoking.

Aston House, 285 Victoria St., Box 1153, Niagara-on-the-Lake L0S 1J0. (905) 468-4880.

This glamorous home that would make a designer-magazine feature takes in guests in two bedrooms with private baths. It was built in 1987 to look Georgian and hides an unexpectedly large back yard.

The rooms are decorated to the hilt by Rosemary Norman, whose husband Keith oversees the stunning gardens shielded from view — as so many are in town.

"We fell into this when a neighbor overbooked her B&B and asked us to help out," recalls Rosemary. "To our surprise, we enjoyed it." Although guests don't really have a common area in which to sit, things get convivial over a breakfast of fresh fruit, cereals, bran muffins and such in the family kitchen.

Doubles, $85. Open late April through October.

Heron House, 356 Regent St., Box 249, Niagara-on-the-Lake L0S 1J0. (905) 468-4553.

Two spacious rooms with private baths are offered by Katherine Heron in the new coach house behind her pretty deep-blue house with a front veranda. The rooms are among the more elegant in town, with lacy linens and handsome furnishings. A continental-plus breakfast featuring home-baked goods is served in the sun room. Unlike many of the B&Bs that close with the Shaw Festival, this is open year-round.

Doubles, $95.

In addition to the establishments detailed here, some 65 bed-and-breakfast homes are registered with the local Chamber of Commerce. All are inspected and licensed, have three or fewer guest rooms, and the hosts live on the premises. Most do not have signs or brochures. Contact the Chamber at (905) 468-4263 and you will be matched to a B&B for a $5 booking fee.

Touring the Wineries

Geographically, one would not think of Canada as a wine-producing country. But the Niagara Peninsula has changed that thinking lately.

Shortly after New York's Finger Lakes region started proving that European viniferas could be grown in the Eastern climate, Niagara followed suit, scrapping acres of concord and niagara grapes in favor of chardonnays, rieslings and pinot noirs. Today, vineyards are everywhere around Niagara-on-the-Lake, interspersed among orchards of fruit trees. Both are the area's distinguishing feature, yielding mile after mile of beauty and bounty.

Vineyards have proliferated in the last few years to the point where Niagara-on-the-Lake boasted a Group of Seven, borrowing a well-known name from the Canadian art world. That became the Group of Seven Plus One with the opening of another winery in 1993, and still another was in the works for 1994.

The grape-growing region is wedged between Lake Ontario to the north, the Niagara River to the east and the picturesque Niagara Escarpment to the south. The escarpment — a long, tiered ridge shaped something like a bench — separates the flatlands along Lakes Erie and Ontario. (The land along the seat of the bench is considered the most fertile, giving rise to the local phenomenon of "the Bench," whose growers put down those in the flatlands below as "the Swamp.") The escarpment is responsible for making this so prolific a fruit belt, both in terms of the rich minerals eroded into its soil and the micro-climate created by its sheltering effect and the moderating influence of Lake Ontario.

Its location near the 43rd-degree latitude puts Niagara in the same position as such wine-growing regions as northern California, southern France and northern Italy. Some increasingly acclaimed wines, particularly rieslings, are the result. "For an area our size," says Cave Spring Cellars winemaker Angelo Pavan, "we probably win more awards in international competitions than any other region in the world."

The Niagara region also has become the world's leading maker of icewine (eiswein), a rare, sweet, almost chewy dessert wine whose miniscule production formerly was centered in Germany and Austria. Riesling and vidal grapes for icewine are left to freeze on the vine and are pressed frozen in winter to yield a wine that will age for ten or fifteen years. The limited supply fetches $25 to $46 a half bottle, and one wine writer predicted icewine could become "as Canadian as ice hockey."

Connoisseurs might like to spend a day touring the wineries in the flatlands around Niagara-on-the-Lake and another day touring those along the Bench.

Inniskillin Wines Inc., Line 3 Road off Niagara Parkway, Niagara-on-the-Lake. (905) 468-3554.

In 1975, Inniskillin was granted the first Ontario wine license since 1929 and became Ontario's first cottage winery, specializing in viniferas. Karl Kaiser, winemaker, and Don Ziraldo, promoter, are co-owners of what some consider

Inniskillin has grown far beyond its beginning as Ontario's first cottage winery.

to be Canada's finest winery, seller of 120,000 cases annually, nearly half from its own 60 acres of vineyards.

Visitors may take a new twenty-station self-guided tour or a 45-minute guided tour and taste wines in a 1930s barn, the ground floor of which has been transformed into a sparkling showroom. The large second floor remains more rustic, the better for changing art exhibits, sit-down "festival tastings," and four theme dinners a year at $75 per, including wine (the one prior to our visit was a Thai dinner). A menu at the door shows that Inniskillin's cabernet sauvignon reserve was served at Prime Minister Mulroney's 1993 dinner for Mikhail Gorbachev. Successive vintages of icewine made from vidal grapes won a record three gold medals in a row, culminating in the Grand Prix d'Honneur at Vinexpo in France. Tastings of three wines are free; others cost 50 cents an ounce.

Tours, daily at 10:30 and 2:30, June-October; weekends only rest of year. Showroom, daily 10 to 6, to 5 in winter.

Hillebrand Estates Winery, Highway 55, Niagara-on-the-Lake. (905) 468-7123.

Billed as Canada's most award-winning winery and top producer of varietals, this is the nation's largest estate winery, producing 288,000 cases a year and running more than 50 retail stores across Ontario. Only eight years old in the Niagara region, its heritage is linked to that of its sister wineries in Germany.

The frequent tours here are said to be the most lively and informative of any Niagara winery. Indeed, it's the only winery to give regular tours year-round and they last an hour or longer.

The large showroom looks like a wine store. Watercolorist Angie Strauss designed labels for new blush and rose wines. The superb Collector's Choice chardonnay and cabernet-merlot (both $13.95) bear the labels of some of Canada's famed Group of Seven artists. We coveted the poster of their labels, but left empty-handed because they sell faster than they can be produced.

Tours daily, 11, 1, 3 and 4; additional tours on weekends, in the summer and during fall harvest. Showroom, daily 10 to 6.

139

Château des Charmes, Four Mile Creek Road at Line 7, St. Davids. (905) 262-4219.

This was touted by a Finger Lakes winemaker as Niagara's "best of the bunch." It is known for its chardonnays, aged in oak barrels imported from France for $550 each. Its brut sparkling wine is widely considered to be Canada's best, and its recent cabernet and merlot releases are quite good. The winery was Canada's first to experiment with the French barrels, and its 60-acre vineyard was the first in Canada planted entirely with European vinifera vines. Another 85 acres have been planted lately.

Until lately, there wasn't much to see at the small, rather rundown winery. But owner Paul Bosc was building a $6 million French château to house the winery, a champagne cellar, a banquet facility and a reception area with a video presentation. It promised to be quite a showplace upon opening in 1994.

Tours, Tuesday-Sunday at 11, 1:30 and 3, May-September; showroom open daily 10 to 5.

Konzelmann Estate Winery, Lakeshore Road, Niagara-on-the-Lake. (905) 935-2866.

Wines in the German style are featured here by Herman Konzelmann, his wife and son, who returned from studying in Germany to join his parents as winemaker -- the fifth generation involved in a family winery founded in Germany in 1893. Rows and rows of grapes, all labeled, grow primly on 40 acres beside their expanding winery, which bottled its first harvest in 1986 and now produces 100,000 bottles a year. The dry riesling ($8.60) is especially good here, as is the gewürztraminer ($10.90), and Konzelmann's vidal icewine won the grand gold award at the VinItaly competition in 1993. A couple of pinot noirs and a gamay noir show Niagara's potential in red wines as well.

Winery tours, Saturday at 2. Showroom, Monday-Saturday 10 to 6, Sunday 12:30 to 5:30, May-December; Wednesday-Saturday 10 to 6, rest of year.

Vineland Estates, 3620 Moyer Road, Vineland. (905) 562-7088.

This small, personal winery is Niagara's most picturesque — situated in the rolling countryside along the Bench, with a view of Lake Ontario to the northwest. Lots of trees and hills make for a pleasant break from the sameness of the flatlands scenery below (follow Route 81 and the Niagara Winery Route along the Bench and you may think you're in the upper vales of California's Napa Valley).

German wine grower Hermann Weis had to prove to skeptical Canadian growers that his riesling grapes could be cultivated so far north, so he established a vineyard of his own here. Today, his original 45 acres produce 12,000 cases annually of mostly riesling and some chardonnay. They have put the expanding operation, now owned by Hamilton wine connoisseur John Howard, in the forefront of Bench wineries. The new owner acquired 50 more acres, planting fifteen in 1993 with merlot and pinot noir vines and planning to double production to 25,000 cases. He vastly expanded the wine deck and patio off the original 1845 estate house and opened a rear carriage house for craft shows, art auctions and a series of monthly theme dinners pairing the food of area chefs and Vineland Estates wines. Winemaker Allan Schmidt's premium dry rieslings ($8.50) are decisive proof that Niagara rieslings are "better than anything outside the Rhine-Mosel axis itself," one writer proclaimed. He's also known for his gewürztraminers, pinot noirs and icewines.

Showroom open daily, 11 to 5; tours at 11, 1 and 3; weekends only in winter.

Cave Spring Cellars, 3836 Main St., Jordan. (905) 562-3581.

Serious, prize-winning wines from vinifera grapes are the specialty of this new boutique winery on the Bench, housed in a lineup of buildings that comprised the defunct Jordan Winery, Ontario's oldest winemaking facility. There's an elegant, small wine-tasting and sales room that's as stylish as the On the Twenty restaurant at the other end of the complex.

Chardonnays and rieslings are featured here, the elegant and oaky 1990 chardonnay reserve selling for a cool $17.95 and the smooth, award-winning 1991 riesling icewine commanding $46.45 a half bottle. The venture headed by Leonard Pennachetti also produces rosé, cabernet-merlot and gamay noir varietals among its 15,000 cases annually in an effort to put Cave Spring in the vanguard of small North American wineries.

Open Monday-Saturday 10 to 5, Sunday noon to 5. Tours on weekends.

Other wineries worth a visit:

Reif Winery, Niagara Parkway, Niagara-on-the-Lake, the closest to town and river, opened in 1983 and is known for wines in the German style. All North American grapes were uprooted in favor of European vinifera and premium French hybrids on the 130-acre estate behind the winery. Klaus W. Reif, 13th generation of a wine growing family in Germany, still selects only the best 40 percent of the harvest for his own wines, selling the rest to other wineries. The dry riesling ($7.95) and gewürztraminer ($12.80) are standouts here. A new Artvine Gallery features the works of Canadian artists. Tours daily at 1:30, May-August; showroom, daily 10 to 6, to 5 in winter.

Henry of Pelham, 1469 Pelham Road, St. Catherines, has a small new winery with quite a history. Located in the heart of the Bench, the vineyard celebrates its 200th anniversary in 1994. A single family has owned the hilly property since Henry Smith planted the first grapes in 1794. We sampled a variety from the Loyalist house red ($5.50) to a reserve chardonnay for $13.40 in the stone basement of an inn dating from 1842. Its chardonnays, rieslings and icewines are considered some of the best in Ontario, but the winemaker held out promise for red wines in the future. Open daily, 10 to 5.

Pillitteri Estates Winery, 1696 Highway 55, Niagara-on-the-Lake, opened in 1993, adding wines to owner Gary Pillitteri's traditional farm and fruit offerings. The 14,000-square-foot winery also houses a farm market known for good values and a bakery where we were pleased to find real butter tarts for 45 cents -- half the cost of fake butter tarts we'd bought earlier at another market. A trellised **Wine Garden** overlooking a cherry orchard offers a daily special, perhaps tuna salad on a fresh croissant with cheese, olives and a glass of wine for $5.95. The wine labels picture a stylized Sicilian donkey cart, the original of which stands amid a gallery of art works in the winery's reception area and has been in the family for generations. The winery's initial production included a couple of rieslings and chardonnays, plus pinot noir, merlot and cabernet sauvignon, priced from $6.45 to $16.95. Open daily, 10 to 8, to 6 in winter.

Fruit Stands

In harvest season, the fruit fairly drops off the trees, evidence of how prolific the Niagara orchards are. They represent 90 percent of the fruit raised in Ontario, and Niagara is a major fruit bowl for much of Canada. Country markets, some of them run by local Mennonites, stand chock-a-block between orchards along every road. Prices naturally are lower the farther you get from the Queen Elizabeth Way and population centers. Some of the best are around Niagara-on-the-Lake.

Rempel's Farm and Flower Market, 1651 Lakeshore Road, is a favorite with locals and markets its own fruits and vegetables grown on a 50-acre farm. The selection is limited and choice. A sign said the peaches were "washed and defuzzed, so you can eat them right away," and the radishes were the biggest we ever saw. Debbie Rempel's bakery produces great strudels (maybe apricot), cappuccino nanaimo bars and raspberry squares (99 cents); we took home a rempelberry pie ($6.95) baked with raspberries, blackberries, rhubarb and apples and a sample of Mennonite platz. New at our latest visit were frozen yogurts (even a rempelberry) made with their own fruits, especially popular at Rempel's new downtown bakery and frozen-yogurt outlet on Queen Street. Out back is a huge greenhouse where roses are grown for cutting year-round.

Harvest Barn Country Market, Highway 55 at East-West Line, is a large country market selling everything from fresh produce to home-baked breads, pies, cornish pasties, and steak and kidney pies ($1.89); two of the last made a good dinner back home. We also made a lunch picnic out of the fantastic salad bar ($3.19 a pound, supermarket style), with ever-so-fresh ingredients set out on ice in about 50 separate dishes.

Kurtz Orchards Family Market, Niagara Parkway at East-West Line, is the biggest and most commercial market, but don't be fazed by the tour buses out front. Jean and Ed Kurtz started 25 years ago with one table under an umbrella and still maintain the family touch. There are varieties of jams, honeys and plum butter with crackers for sampling, a Candy Shack, many specialty foods, baked goods like almond-raisin bread (a local specialty with marzipan in the middle) and huge cookies, drinks like cherry cider and peach nectar, and a new sundae bar and Hillebrand Estates wine section. The Kurtzes hire two Japanese staffers to cater to Japanese customers, the biggest segment of their tourist and mail-order business, and they even have signs in Japanese on many of their gift items.

Gourmet Treats

Angie Strauss, 125 Queen St., has become the town's best-known shopping destination for with-it visitors, thanks to the artist's watercolors and her vibrant floral designs. They're on everything from high-fashion sweatshirts in the $50 range to gifts, cards, wine labels and kitchen accessories, among them placemats, coasters, bibs and oven mitts. We acquired a couple of refrigerator magnets and a large print at a fraction of the cost of one of her lovely originals ($2,000), and thus qualified for a pair of free sweat pants at the **Last Few** outlet store at 183 Victoria St., where discontinued patterns are sold. Angie's is quite a story — previously a potter, she injured her left elbow in a roller-skating accident and started dabbling in watercolors with her good right arm, painting the flowers that husband Hartley brought her each week. People admired her paintings, asked to buy them and the rest, since the early 1980s, is history. All the designs are Angie's, created in the back-yard studio and stunning gardens behind her house on Victoria Street. But the copies and products are the work of 25 Mennonite women whom Angie employs around town.

Imagine an entire downtown store in a prime corner location devoted to jams. **Greaves Jams & Marmalades,** 55 Queen St., looks just as it must have 50 years ago. This is where the Greaves family retails its jams, marmalades and preserves. Bins of jams, shelves of jams, boysenberry, peach, raspberry, red and black currant — you name it, they have it, and they use no pectin, preservatives or coloring. We picked up six mini-jars for $6, as well as some special mustards (these they don't make).

Niagara is known for its fudge, and **Niagara Fudge** at 92 Picton St. is where you can choose from 35 kinds, including chocolate-ginger studded with chunks of fresh ginger. It's $7.98 a pound, and produced right there on the marble table. Irish cream is the most popular flavor.

The **Niagara Home Bakery** at 66 Queen St., the oldest business is town, operates as it did half a century ago. The bread is still baked in an old stone oven and the Easter chocolate is made by hand. Scones, tea biscuits, almond tarts, sausage rolls, quiches and more are for sale.

Taylors at 69 Queen is a good place to stock up for a picnic. You could get a submarine for $3.95, but why not try a sausage roll, a cornish pastie or a pizza pretzel? Sandwiches come on a choice of breads or "balm" cakes, which are large rolls, and there's a fixings bar to add stuff on. Have a date square or an Empire biscuit for dessert, or one of the 21 flavors of ice cream, including Laurentian vanilla. Almost next door, **Donna's Old Towne Ice Cream Shoppe** also has frozen yogurt like orange-pineapple punch plus old-fashioned milk shakes, sodas and floats. Why not spring for a super sundae? The Canadian mint starts with chocolate-mint and mint-chocolate-chip ice creams with chocolate sauce, whipped cream and chocolate wafers, and is topped with a cherry soaked in crème de menthe. Would you pay $6.95 for it?

Yes, Niagara keeps up with the times. **Monika's Coffees,** a new coffee and pastry shop at 126 Queen St., sells espresso, cappuccino, caffe mocha and caffe latte, along with strudels, muffins, broccoli-cheese puffs, spinach pies and, a new one on us, smoked-salmon cheesecake.

Its name is a mouthful, but the products sure are good. The new **Rempel's Farm and Flower Market Bakery & Frozen Yogurt** on Queen Street offers many flavors of frozen yogurt (only 150 calories, $2.29 a cup), made with fruit from its farm. Real fruit and fiber is evidenced in its mango, kiwi, banana and raspberry flavors, to name a few. Pecan tarts, little pizzas, quiches and salads are also available.

In the back of **McCrary Hall Gifts & English Tea Room,** you can get a meat pie with chile sauce or scone with English cream and jam for $2.95, and a choice of several teas for $1.95. The shaded patio is pleasant. Victoria's Tea at 108 Queen has a large collection of teas like blueberry, honey and grape. A glass of fruit-blend iced tea is $1.

No report on Niagara-on-the-Lake would be complete without mention of the **Shaw Festival.** Nine productions of George Bernard Shaw and his contemporaries are staged in three theaters from April through October. Artistic director Christopher Newton and one of the world's largest permanent ensembles of actors explores classic plays in a modern way for contemporary audiences. The 861-seat Festival Theater, built in 1973, contains the larger epic works. The 345-seat Court House Theater presents smaller Shaw works and the more intimate American and European dramas of the period. The 353-seat Royal George Theater in 1993 housed the musical "Gentlemen Prefer Blondes." Regular ticket prices range from $30 to $50. For information, contact the Shaw Festival Box Office, Box 774, Niagara-on-the-Lake L0S 1J0, or call (905) 468-2172 or (800) 724-2934 (U.S.) or (800) 267-4759 (Canada).

Saratoga Springs
The Sheen Shines Silver Now

The sheen is less tarnished these days on that grand old dowager of American resorts, Saratoga Springs. The town that mineral springs, horse racing and society summers made famous had nearly died in the 1950s and 1960s. It re-emerged slowly in the 1970s and came full steam into its own in the 1980s.

A phenomenon described locally as a renaissance for gourmets has added dimension to what U.S. News and World Report termed "the August delirium of Saratoga, for generations America's symbol of high living."

The result is a uniquely Saratoga spirit and panache, one that gives it an odd parochialism as if encased in its own cocoon with a north-south focus on Albany and New York, oblivious to points east and west.

The romance of the old Saratoga was evident in its grand, long-gone hotels with their sprawling porches. Herbert A. Chesbrough, executive director of the Saratoga Performing Arts Center, which was instrumental in the city's rejuvenation, says "the romance of the new Saratoga is in the small cafes, unusual restaurants and the boutiques that have opened in some of the community's oldest buildings."

Food has become a big — and expensive — business in Saratoga lately, and some restaurants stay open until 3 a.m. in August to accommodate the after-the-concert or after-the-race crowds. In fact, scoffs one former restaurateur, "even the clothing stores sell food. Everything and anything becomes a restaurant for two months." In a bit of Saratoga hyperbole, she claims the town has more restaurants and bars per capita than any other in the United States.

Most of the year, Saratoga is "very low key," says Linda G. Toohey, former Daily Saratogian publisher who became executive vice president of the local Chamber of Commerce. "We think we're the best-kept secret in the world."

But come August, the crowds converge for Saratoga's storied racing season and the Philadelphia Orchestra series at the Saratoga Performing Arts Center. Prices double and even triple, but many are the people who are willing to pay them.

Where else would a Holiday Inn change from a range of $64 to $82 for eleven months to a base of $185 in August?

That's Saratoga for you, a curious anomaly of a world-class resort with a shining silver sheen and a hand out for the big bucks. Especially in season.

Dining

Serving days and meal hours vary widely in Saratoga, especially   season. To avoid disappointment, check ahead.

The Best of the Best

Eartha's, 60 Court St., Saratoga Springs. (518) 583-0602.

This small grill and wine bar has headed everyone's list of best restaurants since it was opened in 1985 by Selma Nemer, who trained with Jean Morel at L'Hostellerie Bressane in Hillsdale. She moved here from a cramped space on Phila Street and ultimately sold Eartha's Kitchen in 1990 to her young chef, Kevin Morrill, who maintained the culinary tradition he had helped establish.

This is Saratoga food at its most interesting and assertive. The surroundings are

Dining room at Eartha's features wood-stove grill specialties.

stylish and congenial, and the background jazz or classical music is played at just the right volume. It's easy to understand why Eartha's has such a loyal following.

The name, incidentally, derives not from the chef but from the six-foot wood stove the founder called Eartha. From it come eight or nine entrées, mostly grilled but with an occasional sautéed dish, as in shrimp and scallops with citrus-chive sauce over pasta or escalopes of veal with wild-mushroom-marsala sauce. The menu changes frequently.

When we were there, the huge wood stove was ready for mesquite, charcoal and apple wood. It produced a super grilled mahi-mahi with avocado mousseline and a remarkable grilled catfish with pickled ginger and a mango glaze, among entrées from $14.50 to $20. They were accompanied by good rice and the best zucchini we've tasted in a long time. Another occasion yielded grilled breast of chicken with melted brie and apple-cranberry chutney and roasted rack of lamb.

Preceding these were appetizers of salmon roulade with horseradish-cream sauce and grilled belgian endive with basil aioli, served on nasturtium leaves. Other starters ($5.50 to $6.75) might be baked brie in phyllo with fresh fruit purees, fried spicy pork wontons with dipping sauce, and grilled quail with hunter sauce and wild rice pancake. The soup might be sweet-pepper and leek bisque, cold curried apple, scallop and salmon gumbo, or watercress-mushroom bisque.

Desserts ($4) are to sigh over: cinnamon bread pudding with sabayon, orange-sherry butter-cream cake and chocolate pâté with strawberry puree. We enjoyed a creamy cheesecake with strawberry puree on top.

A choice, expensive wine list harbored a fine Hidden Cellars sauvignon blanc ($18), served in delicate pink-stemmed glasses and stored in a lucite bucket.

Chef Kevin is even more into grilling than was his predecessor. At our last visit, one salad was grilled endive with wild mushrooms and a sherry vinaigrette. The soup was also called "grilled" — everything in it was grilled, Kevin explained. We simply had to try the grilled pâté, a man-size slab surrounded by garnishes, chutneys and toast rounds.

The decor is upscale bistro — white tablecloths and china, fresh flowers in carafes, bentwood chairs, wood wainscoting, and local art on the walls.

Dinner nightly in summer, 6 to 9 or 10; closed Sunday and Monday in off-season.

43 Phila Bistro, 43 Phila St., Saratoga Springs. (518) 584-2720.

A worthy new contender for top honors in Saratoga is this suave American cafe-bistro opened in 1993 by Michael Lenza, an ex-South Jersey chef who cooked locally at Sperry's before launching his own venture. "I might as well own a place if I'm working so hard," he explained.

Hard work (sixteen-hour days) has paid off for Michael, who spent eight months gutting and remodeling the former Mother Goldsmith's cafe. He and a kitchen staff of four earned rave reviews for their contemporary fare served with finesse. His wife Patricia oversees the 50-seat dining room, lovely in peach and terra cotta. The bar and banquettes are custom-made of bird's-eye and tiger's-eye maple. Caricatures of local businessmen brighten one wall. Tables, some rather close together, are covered with white linens topped with paper mats bearing the 43 Phila logo (a curious but attractive touch that we far prefer to glass). Atop each are fresh flowers, a lucite pepper grinder and a bottle of red wine -- a different label at each table.

Arriving almost as we were seated was a dish of assorted spicy olives marinated in olive oil, the oil useful for soaking the accompanying bread from Michael London's Rock Hill Bakery, an area institution (with a new retail shop in South Glens Falls). Among starters ($5.50 to $9) were a smooth chicken-liver pâté served with crostini and cornichons, a terrific trio of smoked seafood (with capers in a little carrot flowerette and roasted red-pepper crème fraîche) and an enormous pizzetta on Italian bruschetta, a meal in itself.

Had we eaten more than a sliver of the pizzetta we never would have made it through the main courses, a choice of four pastas ($12 to $15) and eight entrées ($15.50 to $24), each with a house salad of curly endive. The Tuscan chicken pasta with roasted peppers, olives and white beans was a lusty autumn dish; the fillet of sole en parchment on a bed of julienned vegetables and rice, a signature item, turned out a bit bland. Other possibilities included chicken caponata, pan-seared salmon, veal chop milanese (topped with a warm salad of endive, arugula and radicchio and finished with crab meat) and grilled lamb chops in an Asian marinade and garnished with toasted sesame seeds and chutney. A $15 bottle of our favorite Hogue Cellars fumé blanc accompanied from a varied, well-chosen wine list.

Culinary Institute-trained pastry chef Amy Coleman is known for her distinctive desserts, including a nationally acclaimed 43 Phila violet torte, banana bread pudding, maple mousse with molasses cookies, apple-walnut crumb pie and poached pear on a puff-pastry square with pear butter and caramel sauce. We settled for a dish of plum-port sorbet, a refreshing ending to an uncommonly good meal.

Not content with his existing work schedule and sensing a need, Michael planned to open for lunch shortly after our visit.

Lunch, Monday-Friday 11:30 to 2:30; dinner, nightly 5 to 10 or 11, Sunday to 9.

The Wheat Fields, 440 Broadway, Saratoga Springs. (518) 587-0534.

A pasta machine in the front window attracts passersby to this restaurant, which features "unique pasta dining."

New York advertising exec Joseph Loiacono and his wife Isabella opened the place in 1989. She decorated the two long, narrow storefront rooms with taste and pretty wallpaper accented with baskets of wheat. Glass-topped (oh, how we wish all the glass on all the glass-topped tables everywhere would clank itself into oblivion) tables in one room and white linens over pale mauve in the other,

Artworks are backdrop for diners at 43 Phila Bistro.

modern blond tweedy chairs and Saratoga mineral water bottles filled with dried pasta topped with dried flowers complete the decor.

Every dish contains pasta and all the pasta is made by Joseph, according to his advertising — allowing for some license that goes with the trade, given that every time we've been there a young staffer was working at the pasta machine.

The 30 pasta dishes are priced at night from $7.95 for spaghetti and meatballs to $16.95 for sliced Tuscan flank steak on a bed of spinach and egg fettuccine with a tomato-mushroom sauce. The chicken breast stuffed with asparagus mousse is served over tomato fettuccine, while the shrimp and mushrooms with fresh snow peas comes on a bed of linguini. Starters include a hearty soup of pasta and beans, stuffed pasta sticks with dipping sauce and a sampler of three special pastas and sauces of the day. Even the quiche of the day has a unique angel-hair pasta crust, topped with imported cheeses.

At lunch, one of us tried the cream of artichoke soup (delicious) and the fiesta Italiano — chilled pasta salad, garnished with edible nasturtiums. The other chose the pasta sampler ($7.25), an uninteresting cavetelli with house sauce, a better spinach fettuccine with herb butter and a tasty tomato-basil rotelle with sweet-basil cream. Good, chewy bread with a sesame-seed crust and a generous glass of the house chardonnay accompanied. The sugar that came with coffee was flavored with anise, a new one on us.

Pumpkin-pecan cheesecake, a killer chocolate cake described as like fudge, and cappuccino pie are favored desserts.

Lunch, Monday-Saturday 11:30 to 3; dinner, Monday-Saturday 5 to 9, 10 or 11, Sunday 4:30 to 9.

Sperry's, 30 Caroline St., Saratoga Springs. (518) 584-9618.
Only in Saratoga could what "looks like a gin mill" (a local booster's words) pass itself off as a good restaurant. Everyone we talked with, from top chefs to hotel desk clerks, mentioned Sperry's as one of their favorites.

It's certainly not for the decor — after one peek you might not venture inside.

A long bar with a black and white linoleum floor takes up about half the space. At either end of the room are dark old booths and tables covered with blue and white checked cloths. Beyond is a covered patio for additional seating in season.

Chef-owner Ridge Qua is known for consistently good food at reasonable prices. The menu rarely changes, but some of the preparations do.

For lunch, one of us enjoyed a great grilled duck-breast salad with citrus vinaigrette ($7) and the other a cup of potato-leek soup with an enormous open-face dill-havarti-tomato sandwich ($5.25), served with a side salad for overkill. Service on a slow day, unfortunately, was so slow as to be disinterested. We had to go to the bar to request -- and later to pay -- the bill.

At night, when we assume service must be better, the short menu runs from $12.95 for jambalaya to $17.95 for steak au poivre. Fillet of sole sautéed with English malt vinegar, an extra-garlicky shrimp scampi, grilled salmon with orange-dill glaze, grilled swordfish with roasted peppers and garlic, and veal medallions with wild mushrooms and port sauce were choices at our latest visit. The day's pasta was sautéed rock shrimp, scallops, tomatoes and radicchio over tagliatelle.

Appetizers like escargots, pâté du jour, wasabi shrimp and mushroom caps with seafood stuffing are better than run-of-the-gin-mill offerings ($5.50 to $6.95). Desserts include tortes, cheesecakes, seasonal fruit tarts, crème caramel, and lemon and chocolate mousses.

The wine list is reasonably priced, a further attraction for locals who gravitate here when outsiders take over their other favorites.

Lunch in season, Tuesday-Saturday 11:30 to 4; dinner nightly, 5 to 10 or 11.

Beverly's Specialty Foods, 47 Phila St., Saratoga Springs. (518) 583-2755.

Baskets on the ceilings, shelves full of gourmet foods, a deli case and a handful of tables typify this cafe and catering service that serves up some of the more assertive food in town. We were steered this way by several regulars, and it wasn't until halfway through lunch that we realized we were back in the original quarters of Eartha's Kitchen.

Beverly Cone took over the small space vacated when Eartha's moved to Court Street. Catering, baked goods and specialty foods comprise the bulk of her business, but there's space for half a dozen tables that are filled day and night.

Stop in for breakfast — anything from cinnamon buns and croissants to omelets, french toast, belgian waffles and gingerbread pancakes with lemon sauce.

Sandwiches, salads, platters and specials like New Mexican chili (with green peppers), chicken stuffed with prosciutto and ricotta, and pork medallions with rosemary, sherry and onions are featured at lunch. We enjoyed a fall vegetable soup with a Greek salad ($6.25) and a salad platter bringing a choice of three (pasta with tuna and pesto, curried chicken, and sesame snow peas, very good but very niggardly for $6.95). The sandwiches, served on the Rock Hill breads made by Michael London, looked to be much more filling.

Table touches like a lemon slice in the water glass, asters in Saratoga Water bottles, sea salt and malabar black pepper show that Beverly knows what she's doing. She's at her best, probably, with dinners. Her handwritten menu varies widely: perhaps eight choices ($11.50 to $19.95) like sole sautéed with bananas, sesame-crusted salmon with lime crème fraîche and salmon caviar, grilled veal chop with sundried-tomato pesto and pan-seared flank steak with bourbon-green peppercorn sauce.

Bailey's Irish Cream cheesecake, chocolate-chambord torte, carrot cake with cream-cheese frosting and apple-bourbon cake with bourbon sauce are among the desserts, which Beverly prepares for customers here and at other restaurants.

Open Monday-Friday 7 to 6:30, Saturday 8 to 6:30, Sunday 8 to 3; dinner nightly in August, 5 to 10.

Grist Mill, River Street, Warrensburg. (518) 623-3949.

This is a bit out of the way, but Saratoga gourmets don't mind the drive, up the Northway to Warrensburg and an 1824 grist mill along the Schroon River.

The interior is a stunner, properly historic in front and dramatically modern in a main-floor dining addition built over the rapids in back. One table for eight,

with a lazy susan in the middle, is right over the water, and soaring windows throughout take full advantage of the view. Stunning hand-painted wood service plates grace the white-clothed tables. The cozy, dark bar with timbered ceiling and fireplace in the basement and the spacious, second-floor dining area are both full of farm implements and all the original grindstones and mill workings.

As if the atmosphere and scenery weren't enough, chef-owner Shane Newell is a brilliant cook with national awards to prove it. A stickler for purity and quality, he specializes in innovative regional cuisine, what he calls "American heritage cooking."

Dinner at our latest visit consisted of a choice of eight entrées, priced from $16 for chicken breast with andouille sausage, red bell peppers, diced shrimp and sweet peas to $24 for thyme-roasted loin

Riverside dining room at Grist Mill.

of lamb over sautéed greens, served with a vegetable demi-glace. The pan-fried catfish with crayfish tails, green onions and creole sauce and the charbroiled beef tenderloins served with estouffade sauce and charred bermuda onions also sounded terrific.

Appealing starters ($4.50 to $7.50) include pan-fried salmon cake with dill mayonnaise, barbecued shrimp with grilled orange and spinach, and pan-seared beef tenderloin slices with fennel spices and tomatoes, served chilled with anchovy sauce. Desserts could be assorted cheesecakes, three-mousse torte, bread pudding with whiskey sauce or tirami su.

The changing chef's menu sampler is a six-course meal for $38 per person.

Dinner nightly in summer, 5 to 10, Sunday 4 to 9. Closed Monday and Tuesday, Columbus Day to Memorial Day.

Bayberry Corners Restaurant, Route 149 at Bay Road, Queensbury. (518) 796-6492.

Also out of the way but worth the trek for some creative food, especially exotic game, is this former truck stop, now a family-owned roadhouse run by Devereaux and Georgia Priest and their chef-son, Scott.

Saratoga innkeepers raved about the food at our last visit, so we dropped in to see what the fuss was about. We found the lunch menu fairly standard (sandwiches, soup and burgers in the $4.50 to $6.95 range). Ditto for the dinner menu (entrées like broiled scrod or scallops, teriyaki steak and veal marsala, $10.95 to $17.95).

It is in his many specials that chef Scott surprises, as in baked stuffed quail with toasted-almond glaze, braid of salmon and sole with noisette sauce, and alligator sautéed with sherry-mushroom sauce. His hot popovers with strawberry butter are to die for, we hear, and his vegetables always interesting, like red bliss potatoes carved to look like mushrooms. Prawns "the size of lobsters," mallard duck, pheasant and beefalo are other favorites of this versatile chef, and we hear the presentation of the plates is impressive.

For dessert you might find warm bread pudding, homemade pies, low-fat ice cream or strawberries with warmed English cream. All wines are under $16.50, and there's an extensive list of beers, many from micro-breweries. The two dining rooms are dark paneled and unremarkable but comfortable.

Lunch daily in summer, 11:30 to 2; dinner, 4:30 to 9 or 10. Closed Monday rest of year.

Other Dining Choices

The Inn at Saratoga, 231 Broadway, Saratoga Springs 12866. (518) 583-1890.

The dining room at this up-and-coming inn has had its ups and downs, depending on the vagaries of a succession of chefs. It was up in 1993 following the arrival of chef David K. Martin, a Culinary Institute of America grad, who had been at the Mansion Hill Inn in Albany.

His opening menu was very short but very good, according to reports. There were only two appetizers ($5.95 and $6.95), braised wild mushrooms with Texas toast and beer-steamed shrimp with ancho-chile cocktail sauce and Chinese noodle salad, unless you counted the lobster bisque, the "chef's soup created just for today" or a couple of pastas that shared double duty as main dishes.

Among entrées ($12.95 to $19.95) were North Atlantic salmon baked in phyllo with mushroom duxelles and mousseline, gulf shrimp with Jamaican jerked seasonings and mango coulis, grilled chicken with apple-cider sauce and sweet-potato cakes, New York strip steak with crispy fried onions and, unexpectedly, grilled chops of wild boar, infused with spices and served with an apple glaze.

Desserts ($3.50) were sophisticated as well: black and white bread pudding with butterscotch-caramel sauce, chocolate-chiffon cake topped with peanut-butter mousse and coated with dark chocolate, and linzer torte with vanilla crème and raspberry coulis.

The Sunday brunch buffet ($14.95) with a lavish spread and live jazz groups has attracted a loyal following.

The main dining room is formal Victorian in pink and black. Drinks are offered at bamboo club chairs or at the marble bar in the adjacent Ascot Lounge with walls of glass. A small garden courtyard is also available for dining.

Dinner nightly from 5; Sunday brunch, 10 to 2.

The Olde Bryan Inn, 123 Maple Ave., Saratoga Springs. (518) 587-9741.

All gray stone and flanked by tubs full of geraniums and white petunias, this is the oldest building in Saratoga (1773). It's jammed day and night, no doubt because of its moderate prices (the same menu is served all day) and fare that is considered better than average. Inside is a pleasant atmosphere of brick, brass

150

and booths. There's also a covered outdoor terrace that we found torridly uncomfortable on a sunny day.

For lunch, try a grilled-chicken BLT ($6.25) or a cajun burger ($4.50), or perhaps one of the six salads ($5.95 to $7.95) served with a homemade nut muffin or garlic bread.

Dinner could be a burger or a light entrée, perhaps chili, scallops florentine, hot turkey sandwich with mashed potatoes and gravy, stir-fried chicken maui or petite sirloin. Heartier dishes range from an old-fashioned turkey dinner for $10.95 to blackened steak or New York sirloin for $16.95, with plenty of options in between. Chocolate oblivion, a dense, fudge-like creation topped with whipped cream and resting on a pool of raspberry sauce, is the signature dessert.

The atmosphere is as casual as the menu, but locals consider the food outstanding. And success spawns success: the owner has opened another restaurant, the **Old Homestead,** on Route 50 in nearby Burnt Hills — same format, same menu.

Open daily, 11:30 a.m. to midnight.

Caunterbury Restaurant, Route 9P and Union Avenue, Saratoga Springs. (518) 587-9653.

You have to see this to believe it: from the outside it's huge horse and cow barns joined together and from the inside it's pure Disney World. Gone is the lagoon in the middle with tables for two beside — "a lady fell in, so we covered it and use it for banquet space," owner Margaret Farone advised. There still are several dining rooms on several levels in sort of a house set around what was the lagoon — it's impossible to describe, but folks love it. The Waterfall Room has a wooden footbridge across a pond full of goldfish; there's a wicker table for two near a waterfall, and it's all very tropical. Other rooms in five "village houses" are smaller and more standard. The posh, two-story lounge with lofts is favored in winter. Here, lights twinkling on trees and vines are reflected in the mirrors on the angled roof, a fire blazes in the enormous hearth, and all is cozy and romantic. All told, the place seats 425.

The food, once secondary to the atmosphere, is now considered to be its equal. A new hickory grill produces such treats as pork chops with apple chutney, chicken with fresh salsa, swordfish with greens, shiitake mushrooms and a red-pepper aioli, and a mixed grill of beef tenderloin, chicken and sea scallops. Other entrées ($12.95 to $20.95) include Maryland crab cakes, grilled scampi over basmati rice, tournedos Henry IV, steak au poivre, beef wellington and veal sautéed with shrimp, sundried tomatoes, brandy, brie and cream. The eight appetizers embrace all the standards from French onion soup ($3) to shrimp cocktail ($8.95), plus such contemporary fillips as bruschetta and a grilled garlic-cilantro crêpe filled with hummus, feta cheese, roasted red peppers and pinenuts. Desserts include tollhouse pie, trifle and English toffee cheesecake.

The extensive wine list is nicely priced, with some of our favorites in the mid teens. So you know a night out here won't break the bank, even if it will make your eyes pop.

Dinner nightly in summer, 5:30 to 10, Sunday 4 to 9. Closed Wednesday rest of year.

Scallions, 404 Broadway, Saratoga Springs. (518) 584-0192.

What started as a gourmet takeout with a few tables has grown like topsy. Now it has doubled in size, with a multitude of jaunty, peach-over-white-under-glass-covered tables for dining, and Saratoga's most attractive deli case displaying food to go. Breakfast fare has been abandoned in favor of extended dinner hours.

"We pack a lot of picnics on a busy day," says owner James Morris, who oversees the kitchen with his wife Kerry. Gourmet picnic selections include vegetarian pitas and hearty sandwiches ($10.95 and $11.95) and the Parisian, an indulgence of pâtés, all-butter croissants and shrimp salad ($16.95).

Chilled peach soup — a secret recipe — is a refreshing starter, as are gazpacho and one of the hot soups of the day. Besides sandwiches and salads, light meals such as curried chicken and rice casserole, spanakopita, spinach lasagna and quiche with soup or salad are available ($8.75 to $10.95) for lunch. Dinner brings more of the same plus additions like wild-mushroom chicken and grilled shrimp with linguini, $9.25 to $11.95. The combination salad plate along with a sampling of pâtés turned our late supper at home into a special occasion.

Wine, beer, cappuccino and espresso are available.

Open daily in summer, 11 to 10; rest of year, Monday-Saturday 11 to 9, Sunday noon to 5.

The Gideon Putnam Hotel, Saratoga Spa State Park, Saratoga Springs. (518) 584-3000.

The huge, red-brick and white-columned Gideon Putnam Hotel, its front outdoor cafe almost walled in by colorful hanging plants and window boxes, is owned by the state, operated by a new concessionaire and on its way up.

The lodging is much improved, and the Sunday buffet brunch ($14.95 each, $17.95 with unlimited bloody marys) draws mobs of people. We wish we could be more enthusiastic about it, but scrambled eggs, bacon, ham, sausage, french toast, green beans and carrots, scrod and chicken just don't make it at brunch in these days of creative cookery. We will put in a good word for the broiled bananas and the sylvan setting, however, and noted at our last visit that more salads, pastas and carved round of beef had been added to the buffet spread.

We know local food connoisseurs who go here regularly for lunch, savoring the quiet and majestic setting, the sensitive refurbishing and the restored murals in the main dining room, the old-fashioned food and service by "real" waitresses. Chicken pot pie, seafood crêpes, broiled scrod, welsh rarebit and moussaka are on the docket, $5.95 to $9.75.

At night, longtime chef Otto Korner's menu goes continental, offering chicken piccata, Long Island duckling, frog's legs provençal, shrimp and scallops primavera, veal marsala and filet mignon for $15.50 to $21.50. Three four-course dinners are good values at $16.95.

Lunch daily, noon to 2; dinner, 6 to 9 or 10; Sunday brunch, 11 to 2. No smoking.

Bruno's, 237 Union Ave., Saratoga Springs. (518) 583-3333.

Hubba, hubba, ding, ding — Bruno's has everything. What's more jivey at this restaurant transformed from a roadhouse — the pastas, salads, burgers and gourmet pizzas, or all the reminders of the 1950s?

Bruno's, cooked up in 1987 by local school teachers Peter and Carol Kurto before such things became all the rage, has been such a hit that it has opened a clone in the Albany suburb of Colonie. And why not? The Kurtos play their food and fifties theme to the hilt.

While Bruno (Peter) is sometimes in back flipping pizza dough in the air, you may find Rosie (Carol) out front in sneakers and a pink circle skirt, her husband's class ring dangling on a chain around her neck. Old license plates, posters and

In midst of Saratoga Spa State Park is Georgian brick Gideon Putnam Hotel.

pennants cover the walls (one entire wall is given over to Elvis), and a jukebox grinds out all the oldies.

Covers of '50s magazines are under glass over white cloths on the tables, where the cutlery has red handles and candle wax drips from chianti bottles. Old milk bottles are used for carafes of wine.

"People say the pizzas are as good as any they've had in this country," enthuses Rosie (oops Carol), not immodestly. Bruno (née Peter) once owned the Union Coach House restaurant but now is having a gas tending his open, wood-fired brick oven, which turns dough to pizzas in six minutes. Try the Twiggy (white mushrooms, spinach, sliced tomatoes and mozzarella cheese, approximately 475 calories — the only one so listed – $8.95), the Marilyn Monroe (zucchini, tomatoes, snow peas, spinach, broccoli, mushrooms, mozzarella and smoked gouda cheese, $9.50) or the Brando (cajun spiced shrimp, tomato sauce, scallions and mozzarella, $9.50).

Salads are socko. The Twist has chicken with pesto, shrimp, salami, cheeses, cavetelli and countless vegetables with mixed greens ($7.95). Most of the pastas are named after old cars. We'd toot the horn for the Studebaker ($9.50), penne with tomato sauce, zucchini, mushrooms and snow peas.

Strawberry flan, french silk pie and toll house pie are among the desserts.

Open daily from 11 a.m. to 10, 11 or midnight.

Hattie's, 45 Phila St., Saratoga Springs. (518) 584-4790.

After 55 years as Hattie's Chicken Shack, this well-known institution changed hands and shortened its name in 1993. Hattie Austin, still doing the baking here at age 93, sold to Christel Baker, a 33-year-old Wall Street investment banker. "We're old friends," explained Christel. "Our families go way back."

Christel, who was making apple butter in the kitchen at our visit, retained Hattie's chef and staff. She broadened the emphasis from soul food to Southern home cooking, but kept the homey, cozy red-and-white-checked-tablecloth

153

decor. She also expanded the hours and applied for a liquor license, planning to feature Southern drinks like mint juleps.

The food, according to local consensus, is better than ever, the legend having surpassed the reality in recent years. Such traditional favorites as collard greens, dirty rice, and turkey and rice soup have yielded to things like broiled lamb chops and prime rib, although regulars still go for the crispy fried chicken and barbecued spare ribs ($11.25 to $15). Dinners are served with hot biscuits, two Southern accompaniments and green salad. Starters and light fare include cornbread, catfish fingers with salsa, sautéed chicken livers on toast and a vegetarian sampler. Sandwiches and a chicken-salad plate are available for lunch.

Among desserts are peach cobbler, berry pies, puddings and cakes.

Open daily in summer, 7 a.m. to midnight; rest of year, lunch daily 11:30 to 5, dinner 5 to 9 or 10.

Hobo's, 423 Broadway, Saratoga Springs. (518) 487-7764.

With hobo signs depicted on the menu, this newcomer is a plain restaurant, which gets a bit fancier at night with black tablecloths. Billing itself as "an American restaurant and deli," it serves breakfast on Sundays (two eggs, corned beef and toast, $5.25) and deli-type sandwiches for lunch, in the $2.65 (egg salad) to $4.50 (shrimp salad) range. Combination sandwiches and triple-deckers are $4.75 and $5.50.

But there are some twists. The day's four or five soups always include a gumbo, fries are seasoned with garlic and basil, and hot sauce and tabasco adorn each table. At night, the roast pork is served with oyster dressing and eggplant gravy, the chicken breast Vermont is brushed with maple syrup and dredged in seasoned pecan flour, and there's panéed rabbit and fettuccine in a cheese sauce. Entrées run from $9.95 for pasta marinara to $14.75 for steak diane, and if you want jambalaya, it's $1 extra. Cajun bread pudding ($2.85) is the dessert of choice.

Open daily, 11 a.m. to midnight; Sunday, 8:30 a.m. to 10:30 p.m.

Lodging

Gideon Putnam Hotel and Conference Center, Saratoga Springs 12866. (518) 584-3000 or (800) 732-1560.

You head deep into Saratoga Spa State Park past verdant golf-course fairways barely visible through the trees along the glorious Avenue of the Pines. Around the corner is this impressive, five-story Georgian brick structure that looks as if it's been there forever. A long green awning extends out from the entry between Corinthian columns to a circular drive upon which carriages and limousines once arrived (and still do). The marbled, chandeliered lobby leads to three dining rooms and countless lounges.

This is a state-owned resort of the old school — lately upgraded by the state and a new concessionaire, TW Recreational Services of Chicago, which also runs the national-park lodges at Yellowstone, Bryce and Zion, and was enhancing this as a year-round facility.

About $3 million was invested in the hotel over a three-year period. Improvements include new and renovated bathrooms, better air-conditioning and heating, and new carpeting and lighting. TW Services also was awarded the contract to manage and redo the nearby Roosevelt Baths.

Each of the 132 guest rooms has at least a glimpse of part of the 1,500-acre park. Rooms are furnished in Colonial reproductions and wicker in rose or blue

Lobby of Hotel Adelphi, with Cafe Adelphi beyond, is notable for Victorian frills.

color schemes. Because two double beds didn't fit well, most rooms have one queensize and an extra-long twin bed. All have enormous closets, television sets and telephones. Guests who spend the season usually snap up the six parlor and six porch suites; the latter come with large screened porches furnished in bamboo overlooking a forest.

Doubles, $120, EP; suites, $145 or $165. August, doubles, $245; suites, $400 and up.

The Adelphi Hotel, 365 Broadway, Saratoga Springs 12855. (518) 587-4688.

Built in 1877, the Adelphi had been closed for four years when Gregg Siefker and Sheila Parkert bought it in 1978 and started its ongoing restoration into a fantasy of Victoriana. "It was a complete wreck, but we were lucky because it was never modernized," said Sheila, who made the curtains, sought out the antiques and now arranges the beautiful flowers for the seasonal Cafe Adelphi.

Thirty-four air-conditioned rooms and suites with private baths, telephones and television are available from May through November for overnight guests. All are spacious and feature lofty ceilings, ornate woodwork, antiques, rich wallpapers and lavish doses of Victoriana. We've never seen quite so much lace or so many crazy quilts all around. Check out the Adirondack Mission Room with its twig furniture, a sitting room in Stickley arts and crafts style, and a bathroom paneled in dark wood slats. Across the hall is a suite furnished in French country style.

Spectacular towering floral arrangements grace the elaborate Victorian lobby, as well as Cafe Adelphi, a Victorian cafe and bar incorporated into the rear of the lobby and extending beyond to a back porch and courtyard garden. The Adelphi's latest amenity is a small landscaped swimming pool in the courtyard.

Complimentary continental breakfast is served in bed, on the second floor in the High Victorian Parlor or outside on the Grand Piazza, the geranium-bedecked porch overlooking Broadway.

Doubles, $90 to $130; suites, $125 to $175. August: doubles, $130 to $205; suites, $210 to $290.

The Mansion, Route 29, Box 77, Rock City Falls 12863. (518) 885-1607.

About seven miles west of Saratoga in an old mill town is a 23-room Venetian, villa-style mansion that has been carefully turned into a fine Victorian B&B. Built as a summer home in 1866 by self-made industrialist George West, known as the Paper Bag King for his invention of the folded paper bag, the imposing white Victorian house with cupola on top was acquired in 1986 by Tom Clark, a former college president who had restored four other houses in Saratoga.

He and partner Alan Churchill opened the house for guests, who luxuriate in grand parlors, four bedrooms and a suite amid priceless Victoriana, and enjoy four acres of landscaped grounds across from the mills. Off the central hall with its deep green rug and an unsigned Tiffany chandelier is a double parlor with recessed pocket doors and an old hand pump organ. One parlor is furnished in Empire furniture and the other in Eastlake.

Upstairs is a small, plant-filled area, where you can sit on bentwood rockers and admire the river and falls across the road, plus four spacious guest rooms, all with air-conditioning, private baths and the original inside shutters. Armoires, wing chairs and puffy comforters are among the furnishings. A selection of hard candies is in each room, as are fresh flowers and plants that attest to Alan's green thumb as well as his talent for arranging the results in his collection of 200 vases. A suite on the main floor has a sitting room with a Victorian couch from Saratoga's old Grand Union Hotel, parquet floors, marble fireplaces and a pink marble sink.

Classical music from Alan's extensive collection of tapes plays in the front library, a fascinating room with a life-size carved wood statue of St. Francis in a window area and so full of coffee-table books and magazines that one of us could hardly be pried away for breakfast.

The gourmet feast quickly tempered any reluctance. A bowl of exotic fruits centered by an alstroemeria blossom was followed by fresh orange or grapefruit juice. Next came a platter with half a dozen breads: lemon, zucchini, banana-bran, pumpkin, applesauce and six-grain toast. Cooked to order was a hot dish of one's choice. We relished a masterful eggs benedict and a vegetable omelet with a slice of ham. Chocolate-almond coffee was poured throughout at individual linen-covered tables topped with fresh roses and tulips (this in January). A flame flickered from an Aladdin's lamp in front of the mirror on the fireplace mantel.

The innkeepers are known to serve picnic brunches (cold soups and seafood salads) on the side porch, and a glass of wine or milk with cookies in the afternoon. The cupola is open for a rooftop drink, if you'd like.

The house is full of striking details, like the six fireplaces with massive mantelpieces, brass and copper chandeliers with Waterford glass shades, etched-glass doors, parquet floors of three woods, and Currier and Ives prints. Brass doorknobs detailed with classical heads — including a dog with one paw outstretched -- greet you at the front door.

Doubles, $95, $160 in August; suite, $115, $175 in August. No credit cards.

The Westchester House, 102 Lincoln Ave., Box 944, Saratoga Springs 12866. (518) 587-7613.

One of Saratoga's oldest guest houses, this Queen Anne Victorian structure has been taking in guests for more than 100 years. But never so lovingly as since Bob and Stephanie Melvin of Washington, D.C., realized a dream by restoring the abandoned house into an elegant yet welcoming B&B.

Double parlor is a feature of The Mansion, once an industrialist's summer home.

All seven guest rooms have handsomely tiled private baths and four have queensize beds. Each is attractively (and intriguingly) furnished to the period. On the chest of drawers you'll find fresh flowers and chocolates embossed with the raised Westchester House logo. Handsome woodwork, blue tiles, two elaborate fireplaces and distinctive wainscoting are all original. "We just had to clean up the house and update the systems," says Bob, in something of an understatement, given this couple's ongoing improvements and embellishments. He makes the stained glass and both collect antiques, which are scattered throughout the house, along with "old" art and modern art.

Guests gather on the wraparound porch overlooking old-fashioned gardens for tea and cookies or wine and cheese. The side and rear gardens contain five distinct sitting areas, where guests also can relax. Or they can enjoy two main-floor parlors, one with a great suede sofa and a grand piano (upon which Stephanie practices, when no guests are around, for her continuing performances as an opera singer).

The Melvins serve a continental breakfast stylishly and with lively conversation amid fine linens, china, crystal mugs and stemmed glasses in the dining room or on the porch. Juice, fresh fruit salad, baked goods from the nearby Bread Basket and sometimes cheese are the fare, enhanced by Stephanie's homemade peach butter and apple preserves. After breakfast, Bob snaps photos of guests, which are forwarded with a thank-you note to remind them of their stay.

Doubles, $80 to $150; $170 to $250 in August. No smoking.

Saratoga Bed & Breakfast, 434 Church St., Saratoga Springs 12866. (518) 584-0920.

Possibly Saratoga's most luxurious B&B accommodations are offered by Noel and Kathleen Smith in their newly opened 1850 House. The four sumptuous suites there are a far cry from the simpler 1860 farmhouse in which they got their start as Saratoga's first B&B, or their basic motel that gives them an unusually broad range of accommodations and prices.

Let Kathy lead a tour of her pride and joy, the brick Federal structure whose modest facade belies its plush interior. First comes the President Grant Suite, named for her husband's distant cousin, who died not far from here, which harbors a partial-canopy kingsize bed and beautiful oriental rugs. Next is the Roberts Room, done up in 1920s masculine style. Beyond is the McKinley Room, where one of the accessories is an Irish cradle in which Kathy first saw the world, her mother having brought it from Ireland. To the rear and upstairs is the Irish Cottage Suite, very quiet and private with two queensize beds and two curved loveseats facing the TV and fireplace. The Waverly Sweet Violets fabrics match the curtains and wallpaper; even the clawfoot tub is painted violet. One man who stayed here claimed it was like "waking up in a Bonwit Teller shopping bag," reports Kathy. All the suites have gas fireplaces, splashy coordinated fabrics, walnut and mahogany antique furniture, glistening hardwood floors, TVs and bottles of Saratoga water. There are a main-floor sitting room that Kathy calls "a work in progress" and an enclosed side porch, where breakfast is served at tables for four and eight in the summer.

The four lodgings in the farmhouse where the Smiths' B&B got its start vary from a couple of small rooms with double beds and maple and oak furniture to two larger rooms with fireplaces, wicker furniture and queensize beds topped by colorful quilts made by local church women. All have private baths.

Breakfast is an event, staged on the porch in season and in the farmhouse in winter. Noel handles the cooking while Kathy converses with guests. The fare might be blueberry-walnut pancakes one day and cream-cheese omelets with bacon the next. Juice, fresh fruit and corn muffins or toast accompany.

Doubles, $65 to $95, $85 to $125 in August; suites, $95 to $125; $150 to $195 in August.

Union Gables, 53 Union Ave., Saratoga Springs 12866. (518) 584-1558 or (800) 398-1558.

One of Saratoga's grand old homes, a circa 1901 Queen Anne Victorian with a corner turret and wraparound veranda, was restored and opened as its largest B&B in 1992. Local realtor Tom Roohan, his wife Jody and their family, who live in the rear of the well-kept house, offer twelve bedrooms with private baths in the main house and a renovated carriage house.

The rooms – spacious, airy and uncluttered – have been professionally decorated with partial-canopy beds and colorful fabrics. Each is named for one of the couple's brothers or sisters. Annie, a front-corner turret room, has a painted sideboard, an interesting periwinkle glaze paint and a white floor painted with ribbons, a kingsize bed and a single wicker chair. Edward also has a king canopy bed, two armchairs and a bay window awash in pillows. Kate's room is dark and horsy; a horse's collar is wrapped around the mirror in the bath, and a great wreath hangs above the kingsize bed. All rooms come with air-conditioning, television, telephone and mini-refrigerator.

Rich paneling abounds throughout the house, especially in the large foyer and the huge living room/dining area. The Roohans put out a continental breakfast of fresh fruits, yogurt, cereals and pastries from the Bread Basket in the morning. It can be taken at a table for eight or outside on the great veranda.

Doubles, $90; August, $200.

Turreted Queen Anne Victorian has been converted into Union Gables, a B&B.

The Wayside Inn, 104 Wilton Road, Greenfield 12833. (518) 893-2884.

There's a lot to recommend this rural B&B north of town, an 18th-century farmhouse with an international and artsy flavor. World travelers Karen and Dale Shook offer four bedrooms and a two-bedroom suite, all with private baths and furnished with exotica from places where they have lived. They also show some of the occupants of their big blue barn (the largest in Saratoga County), including four sheep, a donkey, thirty chickens, ten cats and two dogs. Another section of the barn houses the Wayside Inn's "arts in the country" center, home to award-winning potter John Visser and a resident candle-maker and a display showcase for other local artisans.

The Shooks lived around the world while Dale taught on military bases before he moved to Saratoga in 1987 as a professor of international business at Skidmore College. The stage is set in the large fireplaced living room, where an oriental screen and a shelf display of collections hint at things to come. Upstairs, Canadiana is featured in the Captain St. John Room. Furniture from China and Korea is shown to advantage in the Madame Butterfly Room, where an incredible screen frames an equally incredible chair in the corner. Puppets are pinned to the curtains in the Toy Room, and clothes worn by Saudi Arabians are displayed in the third-floor Scheherazade Suite. The Maria Theresa Room provides reminders of the Shooks' stays in Holland, Belgium, Germany and Italy.

Karen has compiled a good little cookbook of her breakfast menus and recipes. Typical fare could be layered granola and strawberries, Mexican eggs, potatoes with onions and cheese, and pineapple upside-down cake, along with juices (guava and passion fruit), yogurt, cereal, fruit, pastries and bagels. The feast is served in the formal dining room, at rattan tables on a sun porch or at a couple of tables in the entryway off the kitchen. After breakfast, guests like to adjourn to the barn to look at the animals and to watch the potter's demonstration.

Doubles, $70 to $105; racing, $85 to $125. No smoking. Arts center open daily.

The Six Sisters Bed & Breakfast, 149 Union Ave., Saratoga Springs 12866. (518) 583-1173.

Verandas on the first and second floor mark this 1890 Victorian facing busy Union Avenue, the main route to the racetrack. Kate Benton and her husband, Steve Ramirez, named it for her six sisters.

The four air-conditioned guest rooms, all with private baths, are quite large (two have kingsize beds, one a queen and one two doubles) and furnished in different styles. The master-bedroom suite comes with a small sun room and a private front porch. Wicker and floral prints mark the Hawaiian room, furnished in the style the couple enjoyed when they met in Hawaii. The rear suite has a living room and a kitchen.

Known for his breakfasts, Steve serves a family-style feast in the large dining room. Fresh fruit and baked apples might be followed by vegetable quiche or frittata, a side plate of bacon or sausage, and zucchini or nut breads. Kona macadamia-nut coffee accompanies.

The pleasant front parlor harbors considerable local information, plus Steve's chatty little offbeat guide to Saratoga dining. Ever the B&B promoter, Steve had just been elected president of the New York State Bed & Breakfast Association and was the proud father of the couple's first-born.

Doubles, $60 to $105; August, $195 to $225. No smoking.

The Inn at Saratoga, 231 Broadway, Saratoga Springs 12866. (518) 583-1890.

The old Coachman's Inn has given way to the Inn at Saratoga, a Clarion Carriage House Inn that's an all-things-to-everyone blend of inn, motel, hotel and meeting center with an equestrian and English theme. The New York Times touted it in 1993 as "the liveliest hotel in town" for its Sunday jazz brunch, theme weekends, and lunch and dinner theaters.

Redone from top to bottom, the 38 former motel rooms go off a wide hall in back. All with private baths, telephones and TV, they are comfortably furnished in inn style in a mix of color schemes with fancy wallpapers, heavy draperies and comforters. A bottle of Saratoga water is in each room.

Breakfast and dinner are offered in a Victorian dining room.

Doubles, $105 to $125; $195 to $245 in August; suites, $125 to $145; $240 to $340 in August.

Gourmet Treats

New Skete Farms, Cambridge 12816. (518) 677-3928.

The smoked chicken we noticed on several area menus prompted us to ask where it came from. "The monks at New Skete," we were told.

We learned that the monastery east of Cambridge near the Vermont border had a gift shop, and on our next trip — with cooler and ice in the trunk — we set out to find it. You take East Main Street (Route 67) out of Cambridge and drive about five miles to a dirt road, where you turn right after you see the monks' distinctive sign of white with a red cross. Up and up a road you go until 1,500 feet up, you finally arrive at the Russian Orthodox Monastery.

We were there on a Sunday morning when services, open to the public, were just ending. The only sounds we could hear were the birds and the mixed choir of monks and nuns singing.

Besides smoking bacon, sausage and hams and making many flavors of

Russian Orthodox monastery at New Skete.

cheddar-cheese spread, the monks paint icons and the traditional Easter eggs, which they also sell. Their main source of income, however, is the breeding of German shepherds — a story told in their well-known book called *How to Be Your Dog's Best Friend* — and the training and boarding of all dogs.

They also sell maple syrup and acclaimed cheesecakes made by the nuns who live five miles away. The cheesecakes appear on the tables of some first-rate restaurants, in flavors of amaretto and cream, chocolate and kahlua.

We departed with a few pounds of chicken, smoked over apple and hickory wood, and some delicious horseradish-cheese spread that we served at a gathering a few days later. The memories of an utterly peaceful place lingered long afterward.

Breakfast is a Saratoga tradition, from the buffet at the thoroughbred race track to brunch at the Gideon Putnam Hotel. At the track, watch the horses as you sip the Saratoga Sunrise — a concoction of vodka, orange and cranberry juices, and a slice of melon — and pick your way through a standard selection of breakfast items (the tab includes admission to the grandstand).

Bagels with "custom" cream-cheese spreads are available at **Bruegger's Bagel Bakery,** 453 Broadway, which has tables inside and out.

The Bread Basket at 65 Spring St. is where many innkeepers in town obtain their breakfast breads. Proprietor Joan Tallman bakes daily "from scratch -- no mixes used" in a basement bakery beneath her retail showroom. There's also a little front room with help-yourself coffee, tables and chairs. Besides at least 30 varieties of breads, Joan offers muffins, walnut sticky buns, coffee cakes, coconut-apricot dessert bars, raspberry mousse brownies, assorted cookies and a triple-layer chocolate cheesecake that's to die for. There's an off-price bin for "yesterday's temptations." Plus -- would you believe? -- dog biscuits.

Saratoga Sweets, 480 Broadway, offers sandwiches and snacks. But if you get the idea that the food plays second fiddle to the coffees and confections, that's because "we're the candy people in town," says owner Michael Fitzgerald. He makes all the candies in his new Clifton Park store. Fudge and truffles are his forte, made with twenty percent less sugar than usual, and his apple-walnut fudge is shipped far and wide. He changes flavors with the season, using raspberry and peach in the summer, and at Christmas makes hard-candy peppermint pigs — a symbol of good fortune in Saratoga in days gone by. Saratoga chews, incorporating brown sugar and caramel with pecans, are "probably the best thing in the world," says Mike.

Wonderful coffees and pastries are featured at **Uncommon Grounds,** 402 Broadway, an uncommonly long cavern of a room with bags of coffee beans inside the entrance and lots of bulk coffees and teas. Pick out a cranberry-orange muffin or a slice of English toffee cheesecake or peanut-butter-mousse pie to go with a café au lait and enjoy with the day's newspapers at one of the many tables.

Two more downtown places worth knowing about: **WineSellers,** 358 Broadway, stocks a great selection of exotic wines. The new generation of owners at **D'Andrea's,** a block off Broadway at 33 Caroline St., offers deep-dish pizzas, stuffed breads (one is chicken cacciatore, $4 a loaf), and hot and cold foccacia sandwiches in a colorful old paint store that was standing-room-only -- literally, a vast space with no seats -- at our visit.

Caffè Lena, 47 Phila St., (518) 584-9789. This coffeehouse par excellence, the first of its type in the country, was run from 1960 until her death in 1989 by Lena Spencer, and friends have continued the tradition since. Her legacy remains in the small upstairs room full of atmosphere as patrons enjoy the music along with good coffees, teas and homemade pastries (no alcohol served). Many are the name folk singers and cabaret singers who have entertained here. Open Thursday-Sunday evenings.

Sutton's Country Store and Cafe, Route 9, Glens Falls, is our favorite gourmet shop hereabouts. It's just north of Glens Falls on the road to Lake George, and has an abundant selection of Crabtree & Evelyn gourmet foods and bath items, handmade chocolates (even a chocolate sheep with a white-chocolate bow), delectable baked goods, produce, zillions of cookbooks, a line of Adirondack coffee cups that look as though they're made of birch bark, and all kinds of fine gifts and accessories. Hearty, homemade food is served in the large, contemporary cafe at down-to-earth prices and attracts people from miles around. Sometimes when we're on our way to Montreal we take out a couple of Sutton's hefty sandwiches ($3.50 to $4.95) for a picnic. Breakfast, 7 to 11:30 (noon on Sunday); lunch, 11:30 to 3.

The Roosevelt Mineral Baths, Saratoga Spa State Park, (518) 584-2011. The Roosevelt 1 Bathhouse is a great place in which to relax after over-indulging in Saratoga's good life. Stress and pain float away as you sink into a deep tub of hot, bubbly, brown mineral water in a private room, $14 for twenty minutes; for $26 more, a masseur will wrap you in hot sheets and massage you from head to toe before you nap for a half hour. This and the other two architecturally grand mineral baths that drew thousands to Saratoga in years past for the cure are being upgraded by the state's new concessionaire. The Roosevelt 2 Bathhouse is now a health spa, and the Lincoln Bathhouse a visitor center. Roosevelt 1 Bathhouse is open from 8:30 to 5 Wednesday-Sunday year-round, also Tuesday in summer; make reservations several weeks in advance in summer.

Sidewalk cafes enliven street scene in Montreal's Duluth-Prince Arthur section.

Montreal
A Tale of Two Cities

What can one say that hasn't already been said about Montreal, that changing, cosmopolitan slice of the continent just north of the Canadian border?

It's the city and the heritage in which one of us was raised, and it's been a home away from home ever since. But it's very different from the Montreal we once knew, the French-Canadian majority having asserted itself to give the city and the province in which it is located a singular, strong sense of place.

More than any other, Montreal is a city of duality. Which side one sees depends on the eye of the beholder.

The reigning duality is, of course, the "French fact." After Paris, Montreal is the world's second largest French-speaking city, and Canadian bilingualism translates in Quebec into French, down to the street names, signs and menus.

Its English heritage has given parts of Montreal a British character. The mix of British and French in North America makes Montreal unique — solid, sedate and sophisticated but also surging, swinging and, yes, sensual.

We do not aspire here to give a definitive guide to Montreal, which has been well defined since it hosted two international extravaganzas, the Expo 67 World's Fair and the 1976 Summer Olympics. Instead, we share our personal observations of a city that always surprises our friends as being so near, yet so far — never more than a six-hour drive or an hour's flight from where we've lived but a world apart from the one most Americans know.

As a mecca for fine dining for every taste and pocketbook, Montreal takes a back seat to no city in North America. Haute cuisine competes side by side with more casual fare in thousands of cafes and bistros. The ethnic enclaves span the spectrum of the world's cuisines. There's also a taste of the hearty regional Quebeçois fare.

To the casual visitor along the main streets, all Montreal appears to be one vast emporium of food and drink, from boucherie to bistro. There are four principal concentrations of restaurants: for urban sophisticates, the downtown hotels and the Crescent-Mountain street area south of Sherbrooke Street West; for tourists, the mixed bag of haute and honky-tonk that is Old Montreal, most of which we omit here; for the young and young at heart, the swinging Left Bank bistro row along Rue St.-Denis, St. Laurent Boulevard and the Duluth-Prince Arthur section east of downtown, and for the real thing, the enclave of chic spots in Outremont, where the more affluent French-Montrealers go.

Be advised: you don't need to know French (almost everyone can speak some English), but it certainly helps — if only in the reading of visitor brochures and menus. In the mysteries of translation, "essence de col-vert en surprise" in the Sheraton Centre Hotel dining room becomes "duckling consommé."

Be advised also that prices in Montreal, as elsewhere, run the gamut from bargain to rip-off (liquor and wine prices are unduly high). When the currency exchange rate is in Americans' favor, as it has been in recent years, food items can be cheap — American money stretches about twenty percent farther than the Canadian prices quoted here. Much of that difference may be negated by Canada's wide-ranging Goods and Services Tax, however.

Finally, be advised to look beyond the Basilica-Wax Museum-calèche on Mount Royal tourist circuit of the Montreal of yore. Look beyond the glittering skyscrapers, shiny shopping concourses, the underground city and subways that are the monuments of new Montreal.

Savor the spirit and style of the real Montreal, the joie de vivre that makes it so special. Especially when it comes to culinary pleasures.

Dining

Most restaurants offer many-course, table-d'hôte meals that are good values compared with the à-la-carte prices if ordered separately. On Montreal menus, "entrées" are appetizers, "pâtes" are pastas and "plats" are main courses. The barbecued chicken you'll find at a host of places is some of the best in the world, and the brochetteries offer marvelous meals on a skewer.

The Best of the Best

Les Mignardises, 2037 St. Denis St. (514) 842-1151.

In French, the word means the extra touches. And at Les Mignardises, from the moment you sit down at dinner to a complimentary hors d'oeuvre (perhaps salmon or rabbit pâté) to the final silver compote tray of miniature sweets that makes the dessert you just ate seem superfluous, you will feel extra-pampered.

Along a busy stretch of St. Denis Street, you descend a few stairs to a reception area, then climb to a serene and spacious dining room, understated in its simplicity. Some of the walls are brick, dotted with copper pans. Wood paneling and trim, scenic pictures of the province and brass chandeliers add to the expensive ambiance. Large tables, spaced well apart, are topped with crisp white linens, heavy silver cutlery and flowers in small white vases.

Food, decor and service are in perfect harmony here in what many consider to be Montreal's best restaurant. It was opened in 1986 by Jean-Pierre Monnet, who for fifteen years after he had left his native Montmorency was chef at Montreal's famed Les Halles.

Service is extraordinarily polished. Cutlery, whether used or not, is removed and replenished between courses. The atmosphere is so refined that at lunch one could almost hear a napkin drop. But it is not at all intimidating or overbearing.

Chef Jean-Pierre describes his as French country cooking in an elegant style. "I look for the plate at the table to be simple and clean," he explained, but he

Dining room is serene and spacious at Les Mignardises.

likes some decoration and wants each dish to have personality. His is nouvelle cooking without conceit, defined by straightforward English translations on the menu.

We found lunch to be a relative bargain, considering the $58.50 tab for a six-course patron's dinner from a changing menu or the $68.50 price for the chef's menu dégustation, recited nightly.

One of us chose the three-course, table-d'hôte luncheon for $15. A delicious timbale of salmon and monkfish was followed by a puff pastry enclosing a seafood mousse on a light butter sauce and a fabulous chocolate-praline cake on a raspberry coulis. The other ordered à la carte: a velvety potato-leek soup filled with strips of fall vegetables ($3.25) and a main course of medallions of rabbit ($10.50) garnished with sliced pears. Mixed vegetables and gutsy potatoes lyonnaise came in two small copper saucepans — a delightful touch. Good crusty French bread and strong French-roast coffee also were served.

Of the two wine lists, one is much more extensive and expensive, offering perhaps 30 red bordeaux up to $399. Our $25 white côtes du rhônes was properly chilled in an ice bucket. In another ice bucket was a bottle of Vitel water, from which our water glasses were unobtrusively replenished.

At night, you can select from an à-la-carte menu. Lobster salad with raspberries and lime, sautéed quails in pear-vinegar sauce and smoked trout with its mousseline sauce are among the appetizers for $8.95 to $14.95. Fillet of grouper with lobster sauce, veal sweetbreads in a rhubarb compote, rabbit in marjoram sauce, sliced veal with leeks and onions, and roasted rack of lamb with fine herbs are possible main courses, $18.50 to $28.95.

The $58.50 patron menu, offering a couple of choices for each of the six courses, might start with grilled scallops in lime butter and go on to roasted veal sweetbreads with sauternes sauce or saddle of rabbit with preserved rhubarb. After a granité, you could order roasted veal medallions in chive sauce or sliced venison with shallot-herb sauce. A salad and cheese plate precedes desserts, perhaps frozen soufflé with fruit in armagnac and apricot sauce or chocolate cake with orange sauce. Those delightful little aforementioned sweets with coffee are the final pampering touch.

A large selection of tea bags, presented in a wooden box (for one awful moment we thought the waiter was offering cigars), is available. Check out the brandy cart, containing what the owners say is the best cognac in the world, a 30-year-old Louis XIII that sells for $90 a snifter.

Lunch, Tuesday-Friday 11:45 to 2; dinner, Monday-Saturday 6 to 10:30.

Au Tournant de la Rivière, 5070 Salaberry, Carignan. (514) 658-7372.

You're ensconced in Montreal, with its hundreds of fine restaurants. Why on earth would you choose to get in a car or taxi and travel half an hour east on the Eastern Townships Autoroute to a hard-to-find restaurant in a former snowmobile barn in a windswept and rather godforsaken (at least in winter) landscape? Because you might just have the best dining experience of your trip, that's why.

We did, and that was before the country charmer of a barn went upscale with a renovation that transformed it into a stunningly sophisticated place. Add the glimpse of the passing river beyond and you have a real winner.

When Au Tournant was opened in 1977 by Louise and Jacques Robert — he under 30 and an amateur but enthusiastic chef — it had room for only six tables. A glass addition in 1982 opened up the barn considerably, but gave no indication of what was to come six years later: an expansion of more than twice the size, a flagstone lobby with an array of plants in a copper island, a spacious lounge on one side and on the other an airy dining room (still embracing the glassed addition) that is the ultimate in dramatic good taste. Fifty people can be seated on plush Caribbean-style bamboo chairs with plump floral cushions at tables set with stunning black and copper-colored service plates on peach linens. The lights resemble flying saucers and on the walls is a museum-quality collection of Canadian art.

Jacques Robert is one of the once-famous Group of Six restaurateurs who launched nouvelle cuisine in Quebec. His menu has no English translations and some of the staff cannot muster up much English, so you should have a smattering of French if you dine here. Each time we've been the only English-speakers in the room; we did not feel out of place, however, and had fun translating.

Dinner is served three ways: à la carte (entrées, $25 to $31), table d'hôte (four courses for $25 to $40, priced according to the choice of nine entrées) and the eight-course menu dégustation, which changes nightly, for $65. Although you are served three appetizers, a campari and grapefruit sorbet, salad, cheeses and dessert, the main dish involves only two choices — almost always duck and beef. At our visit these were mallard duck with gooseberries and filet mignon with red currants. Since we were four and knew we could taste around the table, we chose the table d'hôte and were served more food than we could possibly eat.

A plate of small canapés sustained us while we deciphered the menu. So did the best French bread we have had, a round loaf that, where it met, had several slices of crisp melba tucked in, served with sweet butter from a small copper pan.

Almost everything that was to come was superlative and arranged delicately with the hand of an artist. Oysters in flaky puff pastry dotted with red-pepper butter, a cream of tomato soup with langoustines, a consommé with goat-cheese raviolis, and tender shrimp with fresh tomato and lime all disappeared in no time.

A main course of slices of rabbit, garnished with bright green pea pods and red cranberries, was the epitome of a colorful close-to-Christmas meal. Other choices were lobster and sweetbreads sautéed in a port-laced sauce, an escalope of salmon with a confit of garlic and honey, and a knockout plate of noisettes

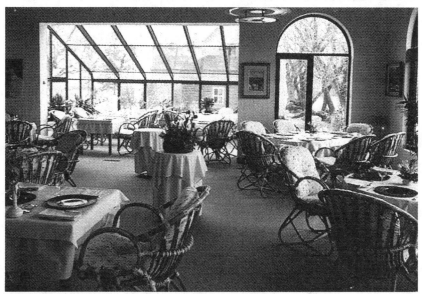
Windows offer glimpse of passing river from Au Tournant de la Rivière.

of lamb, arranged in a circle in the middle of which was a small mound of chopped lamb kidneys topped with chanterelles. These were accompanied by a dish of chopped potatoes, onions, garlic and mushrooms cooked in fat — rather peasant like for such delicate main courses, but wonderful nonetheless.

The wine list was formidable, and formidably expensive (many in the $100s), with only a few Chilean and Australian entries in the $20s. For instance, there are seven vintages of Domaine de la Romanée-Conti, from $150 to $600. Wines are available by the glass, however, and a selection of half-bottles starts at $15.

Desserts were pretty and refreshing: a cake soaked in cointreau, decorated with kiwi fruit and slices of orange; a charlotte au chocolate, an assortment of mousses served around ice cream, and, the pièce de résistance, a selection of tiny cups of sorbets and ice creams of every conceivable hue, including grape and licorice. The only one we didn't like looked and tasted like butternut squash.

At a subsequent Sunday brunch, three of us got to try more of the chef's offerings — an interesting leek salad cut like coleslaw, lobster mousseline and cream of watercress soup for starters; noisettes of lamb, emince de boeuf and wild hare for main courses, and desserts of fanned grapefruit slices with campari, peach and mango sorbets, and a panache of miniature sorbets and tarts.

If we lived in Montreal, this would be our "special occasion" restaurant for sure. The combination of sophisticated and surprising food plus the deluxe decor and country setting has great appeal.

Dinner, Wednesday-Sunday 6:30 to 9:30; Sunday brunch, 11 to 2.

Les Halles, 1450 Crescent St. (514) 844-2328.

Following the departure of its longtime chef and one of the original partners, Les Halles slipped a trifle since the lofty years when it was universally acclaimed the best restaurant in Montreal. But lately it has remodeled and repositioned itself for the mid-1990s and still ranks right up there. How high may depend on who you are and who you know.

167

Although we were on time for our 8:45 reservation (the earliest we could get three days ahead for a Saturday night), we were ushered to the intimate bar at the rear of this two-story lineup of rooms patterned after the old market in Paris. There were facsimiles of market signs, murals depicting French vineyards and enormous bottles of the house Reserve Macon burgundy — "methusalems," the friendly Portuguese bartender told us. As we nursed our drinks, others arrived, were greeted jovially and were seated.

Two inquiries and 45 minutes later, we were shown to a table in one of two main-floor dining rooms, not far from the working boucherie/charcuterie/pâtis-serie that is a focal point of the room with its colorful awnings and smack against another twosome. The rooms are small and bright, and the tables so close together that a friend says you can eavesdrop and hear everything going on in Montreal, if you understand French. But the French-Canadian joie de vivre raises the noise level to just the right pitch where you neither have to whisper or shout.

The menu is extensive, expensive (appetizers, $10.70 to $16.95) and somewhat intimidating. So was our waiter, who rattled off the daily specials at some length from memory until the female half of our party interrupted to ask the price of the duck. "Twenty-five dollars," he could barely let out through his clenched lips, affronted by both the question and its source. He then condensed the rest of his recital and departed. We were left wanting to know more about the specials, which are reputed to be the high points of the kitchen, and their prices, which are usually several dollars more than dishes on the regular menu. Having asked, however, it was not to be.

For appetizers, one of us settled for the cold assortment of cochonouilles and terrines from the menu ($9.95), a lunch-size plate of salamis and three pâtés from the boucherie. The other tried a special appetizer, St. Peter's fish — an entrée-size portion of rather boring European white fish in a superior sorrel sauce and garnished with green beans (later priced on our bill at $14). These were preceded by a basket of French bread and ends of melba toast.

For main courses ($19.95 to $31), we had sliced breast of chicken in crayfish sauce, artfully arranged in a swirl with carrots, beans and turnips, and sweetbreads in a raspberry-vinegar sauce (a special, $23), with the same vegetables plus cauliflower. Both were sensational.

With our meal we had the cheapest bottle we could find on the lengthy wine list, $29 for a smooth Château Mondetour bordeaux. Prices are mainly in the three figures and we noticed that the wines of those more selective than we were poured in extra-large balloon glasses. (We all got the same white Les Halles bags on departure; we had thought they were doggie bags, but they contained an apple and an orange to go.)

Desserts are fairly classic French ($4.95 to $6.75, except $18 for peppered strawberries for two). We shared a plate of homemade sorbets — orange, raspberry and pear, served with kiwi, tangerine, fresh mint and a red sauce notable for its herbs, including rosemary. The waiter, who by this time had become more friendly, even offered two plates without our asking. We finished with coffee "ordinaire" ($1.40 and excellent). forgoing the double espresso ($2.50) and the house special ($7.35).

After dinner, we looked upstairs at three other dining rooms, which were more formal and quiet, lacking the market flavor. There we happened to bump into owner Jacques Landurier, who said he usually makes the rounds to talk with his diners. He and a partner opened Les Halles in 1972. The partner left in 1986 to enter politics, but Jacques and his wife Ita are maintaining the tradition.

Le Mitoyen occupies century-old gray house in suburban Laval.

As we departed, we could understand why most Montrealers consider Les Halles among the best. We could only ask, the best for whom? For unknown visitors who have the audacity to ask prices, the atmosphere is rather more chilly than we appreciate, especially when we are spending more than $150 for dinner for two.

Next time, we'd skip the specials and stick to the limited table-d'hôte menus, $27.50 or $39.95 at dinner. Or we'd follow the Landuriers' suggestion and try the $59 menu gastronomique, which includes two substantial appetizers, a sorbet, a small main course, dessert, coffee and sweets. Unlike many such feasts, the chef ensures that each person at the table has a different dish for each course and that most of his specialties are presented. Either way, we'd get a good taste of Les Halles and wouldn't break the bank or the waiter's demeanor.

Lunch, Tuesday-Friday 11:45 to 2:30; dinner, Monday-Saturday 6 to 11.

Le Mitoyen, 652 Place Publique, Ste.-Dorothée, Laval. (514) 689-2977.
A 100-year-old gray house with bright red roof and white trim facing the town square in this typical French-Canadian village north of Montreal has dispensed some of the region's best food since 1977. In fact, Le Mitoyen was the highest rated Montreal restaurant in the Zagat survey, scoring a near-perfect 29 for cuisine.

Dining is at widely spaced tables in five small rooms on two floors. Tile floors, fireplaces, white chairs with cane seats at crisp-linened tables, votive candles and chef-owner Richard Bastien's stunning dried-flower arrangements convey a simple, country-French setting. He and partner Carole Lèger work in a grand, sparkling kitchen that's as big as the restaurant.

The menu offers three choices: à la carte (entrées, $22.50 to $27.50), three-course table d'hôte with three choices ($25) and a seven-course dégustation menu ($52) that's favored by regulars. At our visit it started with a rilette of rabbit, salmon with an olive-oil sauce and cabbage stuffed with sweetbreads and mushroom sauce. A chicken bouillon or a sorbet of pear and red wine prepared the palate for the main course, lamb with mushrooms and puree of l'antella with onions. A mixed salad followed. Desserts involved a choice of chocolate mousse, pecan cake with butterscotch sauce and homemade vanilla ice cream, a tartelette of strawberries or dates stuffed with white-chocolate mousse and mocha sauce.

If you're not up to such a feast, the table-d'hôte meal -- soup or salad and perhaps chicken with fennel, leg of lamb or stuffed shrimp oriental, plus dessert -- represents good value. The short wine list is priced from $23 to $105.

Dinner, Tuesday-Sunday 6 to 10 or 11.

La Maison de Chavignol, 3 Avenue des Terrasses, Ste.-Rose, Laval. (514) 628-0161.

Knowing Montrealers think this suburban haunt ranks among the best in the region, a belief confirmed by an official provincial rating in 1993 called *Repertoire de Bonne Tables au Quebec.* French-born chef Bruno Manlhiot and his wife, Josée, met at the famed Hélène de Champlain restaurant on Montreal's St. Helen's Island, where he was a cook and she a student. They decided to open their own place in her native Laval in 1986 and imbued their 19th-century house with great character and charm.

Bruno oversees the kitchen, while his wife handles the front of the house. The five-person kitchen staff is rather labor intensive for a dining room that seats only 40.

The à-la-carte menu, written in French, ranges from $24.50 to $32.50. The nightly gastronomique menu ($42), which changes every two months, focuses on a region of France. The theme at our visit was Sologne. The meal in-

Corner table at La Maison de Chavignol.

cluded a starter of stuffed partridge, a main course of wild rabbit with a cornet of petite raviolis, and a choice of cheeses or a puff-pastry tart with rum mousse.

More treats were available through three dégustation menus, $48, $58 and $64, each yielding seven courses and each more complex than the last. Among the possibilities: marinated scallops with leeks and black truffles, a mille-feuille of salmon with green lentils and tomato confit, noisettes of lamb with fresh herbs, and barbary duck with honey vinegar and coulis of foie gras. And more tasting platters for dessert: a dégustation plate with a little bit of everything, we were told, plus a sorbet plate and a plate of chocolates. The extensive, all-French wine list is priced from the thirties to $135.

The candlelit dining room, outfitted in white and apricot colors, is elegant country French.

Dinner, Tuesday-Saturday 6 to 10.

Les Chenets, 2075 Bishop St. (514) 844-1842.

This relative old-timer, with an awesome wine cellar and a collection of copper that's out of this world, also is one of the coziest, warmest restaurants we've seen.

It's doubly so on a wintry Yuletide afternoon, when the copper pots and pans that cover every available bit of wall space reflect the glow of candles and even the Christmas tree behind the reception table is trimmed mostly in copper.

Chef-owner Michel Gillet, a Frenchman who opened the restaurant in 1973 after a stint at Le Chambord in Westport, Conn., employs one person full-time just to keep all that copper gleaming. Copper service plates top the white-linened tables in two dining rooms, and there's a mix of semi-circular banquettes and chairs upholstered in velvet.

Wine connoisseurs marvel at two weighty tomes of wine selections mounted on a bookstand behind the reception table. They list 1,200 choices representing 30,000 bottles at prices up to $15,000 for an 1890 Château Lafite-Rothschild. The pricier bottles are too old to drink, our waiter advised; instead, they are sold as collector's items. He led us upstairs (yes, up) to the wine cellar on the second floor, where he hoisted himself to the top shelf to retrieve the 1890 Lafite, which, we must say, looked much like any other. Michel, who's partial to white wines himself, also has an outstanding collection of cognacs — 103 kinds, we're told.

His menu is quite traditional, but the preparation is innovative. The soup du jour might be a delicate cream of watercress swirled with crème fraîche and centered with croutons. The seafood feuillete comes in puff pastry shaped like a little fish; the terrine of rabbit is enhanced by anisette. House specialties are fish with two sauces (salmon with beurre blanc and halibut with hollandaise and a dollop of caviar, the two separated by a puree of broccoli over slivered carrots), pheasant with morels (accompanied by a pastry barque filled with beans, carrots and potato sticks), and filet mignon with goose liver.

Dinner appetizers are priced from $5.50 to $12 (for goose-liver pâté) and main courses from $19.50 (chicken in wine sauce) to $28.50 (scampi with garlic). The best bet may be the table-d'hôte menu, a quite lengthy choice of four courses for $35. That includes such desserts as grand-marnier parfait, pears hélène and raspberry-mousse cake.

Although this is considered a place for a splurge (the noontime four-course gastronomique menu is $35), you also can find good value. The special $14.50 lunch is said to be one of the best bargains in the city.

Lunch, Monday-Friday noon to 3; dinner nightly, 5:30 to 11.

Chez la Mère Michel, 1209 Guy St. (514) 934-0473.

For more than 25 years we've been directing friends heading for Montreal to this intimate downtown restaurant we first visited during the summer of Expo 67, shortly after it opened. None has been disappointed, nor have we on subsequent trips. And given all the glitzy and trendy Montreal eateries, it is a comfort to know that this has hardly changed.

Inside a typical Montreal graystone townhouse are three small dining rooms, plus a massive downstairs wine cellar and a skylit courtyard that's exceptionally pleasant for dining year-round.

Decor is elegantly rustic: high ceilings with dark beams and stuccoed arches, shiny hardwood floors, colorful stained-glass windows, ladderback chairs and copper pots here, there and everywhere. Bright red linens and lovely arrangements of roses and lilies grace the tables, and candles inside graters cast fascinating shadows. Brilliant enamel paintings add to an already colorful scene.

The crowning glory is the atrium courtyard, lovely with banquettes and high-back chairs, antique tables, a Delft-tiled fireplace and a sixteen-foot enamel mural.

Seasonal and contemporary specialties enhance the traditional fare from the kitchen of Micheline Delbuquet, who bestowed her childhood nickname Michel on her "little house" in the city and her French Riviera restaurant background on her cuisine.

Over the years, we've enjoyed, among other appetizers ($5.50 to $10), a pâté en croûte with pistachios, leek and potato soup, baked pheasant and mushrooms au gratin, and asparagus and sweetbreads in puff pastry. Each of the dozen or so entrées ($19.50 to $24, except $29.50 for grilled scampi) comes with garnishes and vegetables — purees of celery root and carrot on one visit, brussels sprouts and carrots with rosettes of potatoes, whipped and then sautéed on another. At dinner, dishes are finished tableside and served on piping-hot plates.

The veal kidneys flamed in armagnac, which we've always recommended, are as good as when we first had them in the 1960s. We've also liked sweetbreads with wild mushrooms en croûte, noisettes of lamb with tarragon sauce and lobster soufflé nantua.

At lunch, when a three-course meal runs from $13.50 to $16, we've enjoyed a wonderful vegetable terrine that was a mosaic of colors, a tender noisette of beef with bordelaise sauce, chicken with coconut sauce and an interesting special of skate fish.

Such desserts as strawberry puff pastry, grand-marnier parfait, fresh fruits with kirsch and black-currant sorbet are refreshing endings. The chocolate delice with grand marnier, kiwi and raspberry sauce is a work of art. So is a whole poached pear, its cavity filled with black-currant sorbet and served atop an almond tuile.

A special five-course dégustation menu is offered nightly for $35.

The wine list is handsome and extensive, as you'd guess when you look at Micheline's husband René's wine cellar, which he ranks among the four or five best in the city. We were pleased to find a $22 muscadet and a $25 beaujolais interspersed among more expensive vintages.

Micheline and René, a photographer, consider this their baby. They've had only two chefs in twenty years, and maître-d Hans welcomes returning customers by name. The cozy French provincial ambiance, consistently fine food and value combine to make La Mère Michel a good bet for visitors in this city where more trendy establishments can be pricey, pretentious and perhaps short-lived.

Lunch, Tuesday-Friday noon to 2:30; dinner, Monday-Saturday 5:30 to 10:30.

Claude Postel, 443 St. Vincent St. (514) 875-5067.

This elegant restaurant in Old Montreal doesn't advertise and is not widely known, but three of the city's leading restaurateurs tipped us off to its existence. It's owned by Claude Postel, a chef from Chartres who had made Bonaparte one of the best restaurants in the old city.

Here he makes the rounds to describe for early patrons the day's selections before he gets too busy in the kitchen. He'll likely recommend the salmon and scallops from his own smokehouse, the salad of mesclun and beet roots, the grilled scallops in Acacia honey, salmon steaks au muscat, the paupiette of lobster and scallops with fresh grapes, or the loin of lamb roasted with ginger. Entrées on the all-day menu are priced from $19.50 for scallops with ginger glaze to $29.50 for prawns in puff pastry. The emphasis is on seafood (rack of monkfish from the Grenadine Islands, tapenade red-porgy fillet, oriental sea-perch fillet, wheat-wrapped Atlantic salmon with fresh herbs), although you'll also find things like maget of barbary duck with green peppercorns or caribou garnished with marrow. There's a three-course, seven-item, table-d'hôte menu, priced from

Wine cellar is well stocked at Chez la Mère Michel.

$19.95 to $25.95 at dinner, about $5 less at lunch. Three dégustation menus are available at $48 each for two. The pastry cart is known for its lemon-meringue tart and a chocolate-hazelnut-cream cake.

Dining is in two masculine-looking rooms with dark wainscoting, high beamed ceilings, wrought-iron light fixtures, deep-set windows with fresh flowers on each sill, small framed posters from La Belle Epoch, a copper bar and flowers in gleaming copper planters. The structure was built in 1861 as the Hotel Richelieu, in which actress Sarah Bernhardt once stayed, and later served as a morgue before it was transformed by Claude Postel.

Lunch, Monday-Friday 11:30 to 3; dinner nightly, 5:30 to 11.

Le Latini, 1130 Jeanne Mance St. (514) 861-3166.

From a modest beginning in 1979, Moreno de Marchi and two partners have built quite a culinary empire. They recently rebuilt this original with a spectacular, two-story glass addition and an incredible wine cellar. Down the street at 205 Viger St. is a newer complex of Italian eateries. On the main floor is **L'Altro Più,** an exceptional market of Italian gourmet foods, from antipasti to pastas to salads to main courses and desserts, perfect for lunch, takeout dinners or picnics. Adjacent is **Pane e Vino,** a wine bistro, and upstairs is a fancy yet moderately priced restaurant called **L'Altro.**

Ebullient Moreno gave us a tour of Le Latini, which is indescribably handsome with pillars, arches, four kinds of custom-made chairs and damask-covered tables, each with a bottle of Manciuti extra-virgin olive oil as a centerpiece. We were mighty impressed by the dining rooms up and down with views from soaring windows, the canopied dining patio, the three fireplaces, the entry facing antipasto counters and display shelves for fruits, cheeses and more. To say nothing of the 85,000-bottle wine cellar, with a table for sixteen set up with seven glasses at each place for a wine-tasting dinner (the all-Italian cellar is one of the biggest of its kind in North America, with prices starting in the mid-twenties). Or of the gleaming kitchen, where seven chefs man the stations at every meal "and they all can do everything." A stickler for detail, Moreno imports bread from his hometown in Italy — "I'm crazy, they say."

As for the food, he showed his computer, which itemized 154 hors d'oeuvre, 231 pasta dishes, 121 beef and veal dishes and 99 fish entrées. He changes 75 items on the menu twice daily. Appetizers were priced from $6.25 for mozzarella alla caprese to $13.75 for scampi with tomatoes and mangos; pastas from $12.50 for pennini all'arrabiata to $21 for fedelini with mushrooms and truffles, and "plats de résistance" from $18 for veal piccata to $34 for grilled veal cutlet. Shrimp fra diavolo, roast quail, sweetbreads and pepper steak were other possibilities. The table-d'hôte dinner has six choices, from grilled salmon ($22) to entrecôte ($30.25); appetizer and dessert come with.

Unlike most Montreal restaurants, Le Latini posts no reviews at the entry — except for one in French, which is accompanied by Moreno's typewritten reply in French. It seems he disagreed with what was said. But the Montreal Gazette reviewer hailed its "spectacular makeover and superb food," and an Outremont restaurateur praised this as a knockout place.

Lunch, Monday-Friday 11:30 to 3; dinner, Monday-Saturday 5:30 to 11:45.

Vent Vert, 2105 Mountain St. (514) 842-2482.

Young French-born chef-owners Patrick Vesnoc and Denis Genero have a press kit full of clippings, a gold medal from the provincial government for the best regional cuisine "gastronomique," and a winning philosophy of work. The two alternate who is chef and who runs the front of the house every couple of weeks, thus avoiding kitchen disputes and each getting to know customers' desires. Patrick's specialty is game and game birds, while Denis concentrates on seafood.

Theirs is a handsome restaurant: a glassed-in front solarium that opens to the street in season and remains summer-like all year, a small main dining room that is artfully angled with niches for privacy (and mirrors that reflect everything going on), two recessed booths that can be fully enclosed, and a cozy bar with tables for overflow. Cane and chrome chairs or green banquettes flank gray and white tables amid mirrors, stone walls, large flower arrangements, cactus and track lighting.

Local critics consider the food exceptionally good, sometimes inspired, and reasonably priced. Four table-d'hôte dinners are priced from $14.95 to $18.25. Favored dinner appetizers ($5.95 to $12.75), according to the mâitre-d, are a shrimp mousse with a touch of smoked salmon and fresh poached scallops with lobster sauce and braised endive. Among entrées ($16.95 to $23.75), he recommends rack of lamb in a mild garlic sauce or veal tenderloin with goat cheese and rosemary sauce, and for dessert ($4.95 to $7.75), a frozen soufflé of three chocolates or a picture-perfect poached pear presented on bavarian-almond cream patterned with raspberry sauce.

Five of the eleven table-d'hôte items at lunch are under $10, and prices top off at $16.95 for quail with cassis. After munching on good, crusty rolls that assuaged our hunger prior to a winter lunch in the solarium, we liked the suave, velvety carrot soup and the small endive and onion salad for starters. Our main courses of veal kidneys with mustard sauce and a tender escalope of salmon with carrot butter came with cauliflower and potatoes dauphine separated by broccoli. Coconut-bavarois mousse on a raspberry coulis garnished with a sprig of mint

Interior dining room at Le Latini.   **Outside porch dining at Le Latini.**

and a house sorbet were the dessert choices. From a horrendously expensive wine list, we lucked out on a half carafe of the house white (the price not listed, but showing up at $9.50 on the bill).

Lunch, Monday-Saturday 11 to 3; dinner nightly, 5:30 to 11.

Laloux, 250 Pine St. East. (514) 287-9127.

A high-ceilinged storefront formally done up in striking black and white and an inspired, reasonably priced menu recommend this restaurant run by chef André Besson, who trained with Paul Bocuse and proclaims his membership in the Academie Culinaire de France.

The decor is modern Parisian bistro, simple and stark: bare floors, white linens, black banquettes, hanging globe lamps and a wall of mirrors — not even flowers to intrude on the black and white. The customers and food provide color, we guess.

The cuisine is nouvelle and the chef's reach far-ranging. Changing three-course, table-d'hôte dinners are priced from $24.50 for quail with two sauces to $26.50 for magret of duck with petite vegetables. Ordered à la carte, the dozen main courses at our latest dinner ranged from $9 for cinnamon black pudding with apples and $9.95 for fried angel-hair pasta with shiitakes oriental style to $19.50 for filet mignon with wild mushrooms. Other choices were yellow-pike fillet with gin and fresh tomatoes, supreme of red snapper with sweet peppers, veal sweetbreads in a port-wine sauce, and lamb filet with eggplant marmalade and sweet peppers.

Appetizers run from $3.75 for soup du jour (seafood, at our visit) to $11.75 for beef carpaccio with fresh mint and mango. The sweet-and-sour crab dumpling and mushroom ravioli with a tomato-herb puree intrigued. Salads might be papaya and watercress, beet root and purslane, or "toutes vertes" (all greens).

Desserts looked delectable: genoise with pralines, chocolate and crème anglaise; an acclaimed chocolate mousse topped with coconut, ginger and choco-

175

late shavings; candied pear on grand-marnier ice cream, and crêpes with pralines. André suggests the grand dessert ($8.50), a selection of three and "better to share." He's also proud of his plates of assorted French cheeses for $7 and $10.

Many wines are available by the glass. The wine list is comprehensive and somewhat pricey, but starts at $20 for a Tunisian entry.

Lunch, Monday-Friday 11 to 2:30; dinner nightly, 6 to 10:30 or 11:30.

Other Dining Choices

Henri II, 1175A Crescent St. (514) 395-8730.

Henri Miguet-Sage moved from St. Lawrence Boulevard to smaller quarters near downtown hotels and both he and his clientele like the change. The pretty little room seats only 30 people, but a wall of mirrors makes the space appear twice its size. Decor is striking (pale gray walls hung with interesting art, burgundy lacquered chairs, and burgundy napkins rolled into twin peaks and standing tall in the wine glasses).

Although there is a modest table-d'hôte sheet (four choices from $19 for pork medallions in red wine sauce to $25 for duck legs with port-wine sauce), this is one of the city's few restaurants where the day's specials make it best to order à la carte. The fare consists of classic French bourgeois dishes, prepared in the modern idiom.

The night we visited, the three choices for appetizers on the special menu — the best bet — were a "salade gourmande" of warm oyster mushrooms in a walnut vinaigrette, sweetbreads with wild mushrooms and sautéed scallops with shrimp sauce ($7.50 to $9.75). Between courses comes a complimentary "trou normande," a green apple and calvados sorbet. Special entrées were steamed salmon with lobster-bisque sauce ($19.25) and roasted lamb filet with tarragon-mustard sauce ($19.75). If those didn't entice, the regular menu offered fillet of doré with sesame seeds, dover sole meunière, coq au vin, veal kidneys in mustard sauce and steak au poivre, $13.75 to $25. A medley of unusual vegetables is served on the side. The wine list starts in the $20s.

Save room for dessert. Partner Anne-Marie Meley's brother is a pastry chef in a downtown hotel and makes about ten specials here daily. The choice might include mango mousse cake with raspberry coulis and garnishes of mint, frozen nougatine cake, chocolate and pear charlotte on a hot chocolate sauce, and a marquise that chocolate lovers die for. Small homemade chocolates come with the bill.

Dinner, Monday-Saturday 5:30 to 10.

Les Mas des Oliviers, 1216 Bishop St. (514) 861-6733.

This long-established restaurant (since 1966) has a corner on the lunch business. It's jammed nearly every noontime, except the blizzardy Christmas Eve a few years ago when we had the place to ourselves for lunch. We'll never forget the warm welcome, the cozy room or the great fish soup with a garlicky rouquine, the house specialty for $6.25.

Now doubled in size to 120 seats, the restaurant has an unassuming facade that belies its charming interior of stucco walls, brick and flagstone floors, massive beams and wrought-iron wall sconces. A striking copper burst adorns the rear brick wall. Green upholstered ladderback chairs at widely spaced tables covered in pistachio green recreate the feeling of Southern France, in the words of owner Jacques Muller.

Here's an old-fashioned, comfort restaurant for people who like comfort food.

"Forget nouvelle," Jacques advised at one visit. "Everybody's going back to basics." He never gave up on substantial, traditional cuisine, even while being influenced by nouvelle trends in terms of light sauces and appealing presentations. Over the years, only the prices have changed on the basic menu, which is the same at lunch and dinner.

Table-d'hôte prices at lunch range from $10 for omelet basquaise to $18 for entrecôte with pepper sauce. Do try the fish soup at any meal, and from the à-la-carte menu, such entrées ($18.50 to $22) as sweetbreads braised in port, roast rabbit with herbs, duckling with green pepper, steak sauvage or rack of lamb provençal. Crisp snow peas, broccoli, sliced carrots and fried potatoes accompanied at our holiday meal. Except for crêpes suzette and sabayon à la mandarin for two, desserts are $3.85 to $5.50 for crème caramel, tarts, profiteroles and such.

The wine list is pleasantly priced for Montreal, with a number of choices in the twenties.

Lunch, Monday-Friday noon to 3; dinner nightly, 6 to 11.

Les Primeurs, 295 St. Paul St. East. (514) 861-5337.

This airy and gracious dining room is a cut above its Old Montreal neighbors that cater to the common denominator as envisioned by tourists. Opened in 1992, the restaurant is a beauty, located on the main floor of the restored Rasco Hotel in which Charles Dickens stayed in 1842. The tables, set with white linens and white china, are well spaced, and there's dining al fresco on a terrace in back.

The dinner menu is short and straightforward (with English translations, for those tourists who do choose the spot). Starters ($4.75 to $9.75) include lobster bisque perfumed with thyme, leek and goat-cheese ravioli, smoked salmon and artichoke hearts with scallops.

Main courses are priced from $12.75 for French-cut beefsteak with candied shallots to $19.75 for lobster with vanilla-cream sauce on a flaky pastry. Others include scallops with braised endives in a lemon sauce, breast of grain-fed chicken stuffed with lobster, and roast rack of lamb with fine herbs and mustard. Dessert could be mille-feuille au chocolat, praline biscuit, orange cake or assorted sorbets.

Two three-course, table-d'hôte menus are offered for $17 and $26.

Open Monday-Friday 11:30 to 10, Saturday 5 to 11, Sunday 5 to 10.

Toqué! 3842 St. Denis St. (514) 499-2084.

Young local chef Normand Laprise gained quite a following at the former Citrus restaurant on St. Laurent Boulevard. He created more of a stir when he and his former sous-chef, Christine Lamarche, opened their own place in the heart of the St. Denis restaurant row in 1993. The place is suave and stylish, with an open kitchen beside the front entry, a curved bar and two side-by-side, long and narrow dining areas separated by a wall upholstered in red velvet, with banquettes against white brick walls and tables rather too close together.

The name, loosely translated, means crazy or nuts, Christine advised. We don't know whether it refers to the spirit or the food, but our lunch was one of the nuttier we've had -- pricey, oddball and not at all what we had expected having perused the dinner menu a few weeks earlier. One of us settled for a tomato soup with olive oil, which tasted like Campbell's without the salt, and a terrine of goat cheese, which turned out to be not a terrine, bland and such a small portion as to be laughable. Ditto for the glass of house rosé wine, the teeniest ounce we've seen for $5 (and they forgot to serve it until we finally asked again), selected from an expensive wine list priced from $24 to $125. The other chose the confit of duck with mashed potatoes on top ($9), which proved to be just that and was totally unembellished. Serv-ice was slow and distant, while attention was lavished on a rear table where Nor-mand was lunching with young cronies. The high point was a huge basket of toasted melbas and sliced french bread. We also liked the panache of three in-tense sorbets (a tulipe bearing six little scoops of mango, blueberry and straw-berry, garnished with exotic berries and currants, a downright bargain at $3).

The restaurant critic in the next day's Montreal Gazette waxed rhapsodic in a rave review that echoed the tips of our informants. Dinner here, we guess, is a better bet, for the reviewer agonized over the kinds of choices that we had felt inappropriate for lunch. The short menu changes nightly, but offers original main courses ($16 to $23) like grilled salmon with a ragout of red beans and peppers, grilled halibut served with mushroom risotto and a confit of cabbage, peas and

Mod dining area at Toqué!

tomatoes, and chilled foie gras of Quebec duck, thick tender liver topped with slices of duck breast, resting on caramelized eggplant caviar and topped by crisp, fried rice noodles. Unlike us, the reviewer found nothing wanting.

Lunch, Monday-Friday 11:30 to 2; dinner, Monday-Saturday 6 to 11.

Ginger, 1271 Amherst St. (514) 526-4940.

Very much to our liking was a memorable lunch at this showy little restaurant with a vivid red facade and a couple of potted palm trees out front. Inside the 1992 newcomer are yellow walls and swagged mauve draperies, a brick-red ceiling, crystal chandeliers and sconces, fringed lamps, a mix of tables and booths, colorful floral mats and mismatched china, a bird cage and a fish bowl holding cups and a tea pot on the bar.

The name? Chef-owner Yves Dion likes ginger and the decor is reminiscent of Ginger Rogers, our waitress informed. Haunting, wild music played as we sampled a couple of gingery treats. One of us found the cream of yam, ginger, corn and jalapeño ($3.50) one of the best soups she'd ever tasted, accompanied by a composed salad with greens and shreds of zucchini, and an order of the house french fries served with mayonnaise. The other liked the andalusian gazpacho and a chicken salad with figs and ginger ($8.95), accompanied by a skewer of peppers, tomatoes and cauliflower. The signature pureed ginger pie, rather like a sugar pie and quite wonderful, was served on a bed of four fruit sauces.

The all-day menu is supplemented by specials for lunch and dinner. Main courses ($12.50 to $18) could be Atlantic salmon, rabbit with mustard and white wine, rack of lamb and venison in season. Exotic vegetables, including perhaps okra sliced to resemble a desert cactus standing in a slice of grilled eggplant, accompany. Besides the ginger pie, desserts include chocolate fondue, margarita gâteau and honey cheesecake topped with almonds and bananas on a kiwi coulis. Lunch, Monday-Friday 11:30 to 2:30; dinner, Tuesday-Sunday 5:30 to 10 or 11.

Le Bouchon Lyonnaise, 1595 St. Denis St. (514) 842-1502.

The ground floor holds La Brioche Lyonnaise, a pâtisserie of considerable renown. Here pastry chef Guy Lafont serves a receptive clientele in a jaunty cafe open to a delightful terrace in back. Upstairs is a somewhat fancier bistro called Le Bouchon, with a separate kitchen but the same owner and the same desserts. There are a pleasant, brick-walled dining room and bar, and tables along a narrow balcony overlooking the terrace. A good wine list focuses on regions near Lyons.

The cafe menu is a trove of salads, quiches, sandwiches, pâtés and such, nicely priced and perfect for grazing. The heart of the matter lies in the pastries -- page after page of les tarts, les ganaches, les glacés, les crèmes, les mousselines, everything your sweet tooth could desire.

The same desserts are available upstairs, where you could feast more substantially on main dishes priced from $9.50 to $15. The table-d'hôte meals of the day ($16.95 to $17.95) represent good value for an appetizer, a main course like sweetbreads à l'orange, fillet of arctic char with anise butter or filet of veal flamande, and beverage.

Lunch, Monday-Friday 11:30 to 2; dinner nightly, 6 to 10.

Witloof, 3619 St. Denis St. (514) 281-0100.

Here is a bistro with a Belgian flavor -- the name is Flemish for endive -- and a decidedly New Orleans look about it. It's Galatoire's up north: a black and white marble floor, an etched-glass divider between the room-length bar and dining area, a wall of mirrors, globe lights, coat hooks on the walls and white tablecloths covered with paper. Inset into the walls are black squares labeling the dishes served, and to the rear, beyond a shelf of European magazines, is a small room with a skylight.

Witloof is known for the best mussels in a city that adores mussels. Try the mussel soup ($5.50), the cassolette of mussels in garlic appetizer ($5.75), or eight versions of mussels as entrées ($13.50 to $15).

Other choices on the wide-ranging menu vary from terrine of rabbit with Belgian beer for $5.50 to salmon tartare for $9.25 as appetizers, from Flemish waterzoi for $13.75 to lamb stuffed with duxelles for $18.50 as entrées. Most are served with Belgian french fries — the best anywhere. Among fresh tartares is cheval (horse) for $12.75, which owner Gilbert Marciano said is eaten in Belgium like beef. Desserts include mille-feuille and fresh fruits, profiteroles and crêpes au praline.

Eight Belgian beers are listed on the menu. The cheese selection is excellent. Open Monday-Friday 11:30 to midnight, Sunday 5 to 11.

Le Bouchon, 4448 St. Laurent Blvd. (514) 985-2232.,

Witloof owner Gilbert Marciano's new bistro received high marks upon opening in 1992. It's rather expansive for a bistro, with high ceilings, tall windows in front and along one side, rich wood walls, leather banquettes, polished tables and a side terrace that's popular in season.

The menu here is up-to-date, simple and affordable, priced from $12.50 for seafood sausage or grilled sausage Toulouse with tarragon and fries to $17.95 for grilled entrecôte béarnaise. Grilled salmon with sauce choron, sweetbreads, confit of duck, quail with apricot sauce, calves liver with raspberries, chicken pot au feu and lamb chops with fine herbs are among the possibilities. For starters ($5.50 to $9.95), try the Marseilles fish soup with rouille, salmon tartare, leek tartlette with melted goat cheese, the house terrine or salad niçoise. Save room for dessert, perhaps a charlotte of two chocolates, nougat glacé, tarte tatin, assorted sorbets or those staples of contemporary sweets, crème brûlée and tirami su.

Open Monday-Friday 11:30 a.m. to 1 a.m., Saturday and Sunday 5 to 1, Sunday brunch.

Outremont Restaurants

When in Montreal, do as the knowing Montrealers do — which is to say, the with-it French-Canadian gourmets emulating Parisian style in their own neighborhood. Head around Mount Royal for Outremont, the residential bastion of French chic, with its changing array of bistros, outdoor cafes and serious small restaurants. Be forewarned: you may be the only English-speaker in the crowd.

Bagatelle, 4806 Park Ave. (514) 273-4088.

You almost would think you were in Paris at this popular bistro, opened in 1987 by Pascal Gellé, one of the "Group of Six" chefs and former owner of Montreal's much-acclaimed La Chamade. The kitchen, with a neon sign over the opening that says "Café Restaurant Bagatelle," is open to view at the back of the long, narrow space. On the left is a bar that stretches almost the length of the room; one can eat here as well as across the divider at marble tables in a wood-floor dining area. The walls are covered with mirrors and handsome paneling, there are hooks on the walls to hang your coats upon, and the animated clientele is young, with-it and French.

At night, all appetizers are $4.75 and entrées, $8.75 to $13.75. Fish is the specialty, including dishes like whitefish with watercress sauce, doré with saffron cream, grouper with beer sauce, salmon with roquefort-cream sauce and shark with three peppers. Our party of three enjoyed a special kir ($4.75) made with sparkling wine, and devoured appetizers of mussels with almond butter, a mussel and zucchini gratin glazed with crayfish-bisque sauce, and a chicory salad adorned with croutons topped with warm goat cheese. The usual good French bread — you really can't get bad French bread in Montreal — was great for mopping up the sauces.

Two entrées of quenelles Val de Loire were light and airy and in a delicious sauce, but were served with bland rice, which did nothing much for the quenelles. Leg of lamb with a garlic confit was rare and tender. It was nicely garnished with a mound of zucchini and eggplant, grated and cooked together, and, for rather a surfeit of vegetables, a side plate of cauliflower, julienned vegetables and a marvelous potato tart.

We were pleased with an Australian chardonnay, one of the least expensive on a wine list that was mostly $25 and up. There is also an excellent selection of beers, many of which we'd never heard of.

The short menu changes often, but a couple of other appetizers that you usually find are a terrine of smoked salmon, a duck-liver mousse, a ragout of snails and a fish soup with rouille.

For dessert ($4.75), we had heavenly chestnut ice cream over a hot chocolate sauce, a "gâteau des crêpes" (layers of crêpes and hazelnut mousse), and a dish of passion-fruit and raspberry sorbets. With cappuccino and espresso to finish, we felt we'd had a terrific bistro meal.

At lunch, the table d'hôte is $8.75 to $13.75 for soup, salad or terrine and a main dish. Most of the evening dishes are available then.

Lunch, Monday-Friday 11 to 2; dinner, Monday-Saturday 5 to 11.

Christophe, 1231 Lajoie St., Outremont. (514) 277-6775.

Chef Christophe Geffray has impeccable credentials for his pint-size eatery that occupies the former L'Auvergnat, once our favorite Outremont haunt. He was chef for French president Mitterand and was sous chef at two prominent restaurants in France. Here, in partnership with mâitre-d' Michel Deslauriers, he features "cuisine réfléchie." That translates to considered or thoughtful cooking and one of Montreal's more inventive menus, which changes weekly.

Christophe offers a six-course dégustation menu for $45, but most patrons opt for the three-course table d'hôte, $19.75 to $24.75 for soup, salad or "l'appétit" (whatever strikes the chef's fancy) and main course. Our dinner began with a complimentary rabbit pâté, served with good sourdough French bread. The l'appétit was a masterpiece: two purses of savoy-cabbage leaves wrapped around shrimp mousse. The salad, julienned strips of endive and cantaloupe with a walnut-oil dressing, was unusual but good. A surcharge yielded a lobster terrine that looked like a mosaic, topped with a sauce of tiny caviar eggs. Main courses were medallions of rabbit with rosemary-wine sauce and a mound of sweetbreads with wild mushrooms, the latter unfortunately lacking rice or anything to complement (and to soak up) the marvelous sauce. A $24 bottle of bordeaux, one of the more affordable on the wine list, accompanied. There was an odd choice of two desserts: a chocolate "omelet" soufflé with bananas, which didn't taste very eggy, and a chilled melon soup with mint and blackberries, curiously refreshing. With the bill came four more little dessert treats, including a candied orange peel and a chocolate-covered cherry.

Service, was cordial but slow, our meal taking 2 hours on a Saturday night. The small dining room is intimate yet comfortable, the tables positioned so we weren't seated right next to someone else. However, we found the cigarette smoke from the next table most annoying -- a too-frequent situation in Montreal. There's not much in the way of decor: lace curtains on the windows, fringed lamps overhead, white tablecloths; no flowers, no candles, no salt. The food is the star here.

Lunch, Tuesday-Friday 11:30 to 2; dinner, Tuesday-Saturday 6 to 10.

Elysée Mandarin, 1203 Bernard Ave. West. (514) 277-3889.

Exotic Thai cuisine is featured at this branch of one of Montreal's first Szechuan restaurants, which has been ensconced for years downtown on Mackay Street.

Occupying the premises of the late French restaurant Le Flore, it consists of a canopied sidewalk terrace and two dining rooms with red velvet banquettes, art-deco lamps and sconces on mirrored and paneled walls, and blue ceilings, linens and carpeting. One look at the menu and we knew that here was an inspired kitchen: hot-and-sour shrimp soup, Thai-style fillet of sole with green curry, beef with basil leaves, seafood salad with pineapple, and scallops sautéed with Thai peppers and bordered with deep-fried spinach leaves, water chestnuts and baby corn cobs. The à-la-carte menu is priced from $8.50 to $13.50. The place is particularly inviting for lunch, when interesting salads are in the $7.50 range and six table-d'hôte meals with soup, rice and dessert are $5.95 to $10.50.

Lunch, Monday-Friday noon to 2:30; dinner nightly, 6 to 10:30 or 11:30.

La Moulerie, 1249 Bernard Ave. West. (514) 273-8132.

Mussels done every way imaginable, served with french fries and mustardy mayonnaise, is the theme of this high-tech bistro with an all-glass front and a color scheme of black, gray and moss green. Water trickles down a marble wall in one corner. Starting small, La Moulerie doubled its size in 1989 and added 40 more seats in 1991. In summer there are 150 more seats outside on what the manager called "the nicest and busiest terrace in town."

Mussel out on mussel soup with saffron ($5.25), hot mussels with garlic cream ($5.75) or any of twelve varieties of main courses ($12.95 to $14.95), from mussels Madagascar, Italian or Indian style (with ginger and coriander) to mussels roquefort and jardinière. No, there are no mussel desserts, but there are plenty of pies, cakes, profiteroles, sorbets and dessert-coffees. Six shrimp dishes, steak tartare, pastas and a handful of other items are offered in a section of the menu with a drawing of a glowering character exclaiming "I hate mussels!"

Open daily, 11:30 a.m. to midnight.

La Lucarne, 1030 Laurier West. (514) 279-7355.

This warm and inviting French auberge is formally decked out in Louis XVI style. The standard French menu has been diversified lately, offering a variety of table-d'hôte options from "le petit classique" ($14.95) to "du jour" ($8.25 to $18.50) to "des cuisiniers" ($13.50 to $23) to "bombance du chef" ($26.90) to menu of the month ($28.50) and "menu du ripailleur" ($38.50).

Each has its adherents, but the adventuresome might go for the menu of the month: one, called the Marriage of Diana and Neptune, included salad of foie gras of Quebec duck, caribou with sauce poivrade and an apple-filled crêpe perfumed with grand marnier. The "ripailleur" paired fresh malpeque oysters with filet mignon in perigueux foie-gras sauce and a tuile with three sorbets. Otherwise, go for the classics, perhaps Atlantic salmon with sorrel sauce, shrimp with two lemon sauces, sweetbreads with truffles, stuffed saddle of rabbit or peppered filet mignon, most of which turn up on the nightly "bombance" menu. Chocolate marquise, crème caramel and fruit tarts are favored desserts.

Pierre and Patricia Leveque, who have owned La Lucarne more than twenty years, have opened two more restaurants. But traditionalists cherish the original, with its beamed ceiling and shiny copper pots festooning walls and mirrors. Upstairs is a dining salon that's made for tête-à-têtes.

Lunch, Monday-Friday 11:30 to 3; dinner nightly, 5:30 to 10 or 11.

Eduardo-Laurier, 1014 Laurier Ave. West, Outremont. (514) 948-1826.

This large offshoot of Eduardo on Duluth features Italian food at affordable prices, according to its owner. Dining is on two floors facing a soaring, three-story glass front, with walls of brick and 18th-century English wood.

The emphasis is on pastas ($6.75 to $10.95), most of which also are available in the new gourmet Italian food shop downstairs. You'll also find thirteen veal and five seafood dishes, priced from $9.95 to $13.95.

Open daily, 11 to 11 or midnight.

Two relatively new, nearby establishments indicate the range of specialty restaurants in Montreal. **Spaghettata,** 399 Laurier, is a large and cheery two-level melange of a place serving pasta and veal. Offered are fifteen varieties of spaghetti, fettuccine, ravioli and such ($9.90 to $14.25), a dollar or two less as appetizers, and eleven versions of veal ($13 to $15.95). Across Hutchison Street is **Restaurant La Pizzaiolle,** a designer pizzeria ("pizza for the upper crust," it

The Ritz Garden is a traditional favorite for dining at the Ritz-Carlton.

used to advertise, before the provincial language law barred signs in English) with a magnificent open wood-burning oven and the world's best pizza, according to another Outremont restaurateur. Twenty-two kinds of pizza by the numbers are $4.95 to $11.50 (for seafood); they're complemented by wines and all kinds of fancy desserts. A second La Pizzaiolle has opened downtown at 1446 Crescent St.

Hotel Dining

In the European tradition, Montreal is a city in which the hotel dining rooms are among the foremost. The best:

Ritz-Carlton Kempinski, 1228 Sherbrooke St. West. (514) 842-4212.

In a city that becomes more French every year, the Ritz is a tradition to be treasured. It is a nostalgic reminder of the days when Sherbrooke Street West was a bastion of English institutions and tastes, although we must say we were a bit taken aback at our latest visit to find the Ritz to have been taken over by a German hotel chain.

Its restaurants have been favorites of Montrealers for years. One of us remembers having the businessman's lunch in the Ritz Café for about $3.95 for three courses back in the 1950s; it was there she was introduced to such unfamiliar dishes (because her mother certainly never cooked them) as calves brains in black butter.

The adjacent **Ritz Garden** has been the scene of family celebrations. Tables on a covered terrace on two sides of a courtyard look out over an oasis of lawns, flowers and a duck pond.

At night, the extensive menu for the **Café de Paris** offers an entire page of caviars, including two dégustation options of beluga, ossetra and sevruga, $174 for 30 grams each and $288 for 50 grams. Dinner appetizers ($6.50 to $13.25) mix the classic and the trendy: consommé or seafood taboulleh with artichoke, tomatoes and grilled scallops; shrimp cocktail or tuna sashimi and beef carpaccio with arugula salad, wasabi and Japanese vinaigrette. Main courses are priced

183

from $18.50 for pan-fried noisettes of piglet with spicy satay sauce to $38 for Canadian rack of lamb riviera. Chef Michel Lanot has moved the fare into the vanguard with things like chicken kabob yakitori with crisp noodle cake and shiitake mushrooms, roast leg of rabbit florentine with tomato concasse, and sautéed mignons of veal with tamarillo and a fondue of endives with mango. Dover sole is still offered here "as you prefer it." That's in deference to the Ritz's now-closed Maritime Bar, where it used to be served fifteen different ways, just as at Wheeler's in London. Try it poached in beer with braised endives or poached in fish stock, glazed and garnished with shrimp and mussels. Sample some Canadian Oka cheese for dessert with a glass of vintage port, or try some of the marvelous French pastries.

Lighter, more casual fare is available in the **Ritz Bar.** A pianist entertains in the **Grand Prix** piano bar.

Afternoon tea from 3:30 to 5 is an event at the Ritz. A dozen loose-leaf teas are offered (Russian Caravan, Prince of Wales and Green Gunpowder are some). "English style" finds your tea presented with tea sandwiches, scones with devonshire cream, petits fours and sweets ($12.50); or you can order individually from the sweets table. Sunday brunch is also an event, as it should be for $38.

Lunch daily, noon to 2:30; dinner, 6 to 10; Sunday brunch, 11:30 to 2. Jackets required.

Le Quatre Saisons (Four Seasons Hotel), 1050 Sherbrooke St. West. (514) 284-1110.

Since the Pierre de Coubertin was converted into a banquet facility, the main dining room at what arguably is Montreal's most luxurious hotel has gone downscale or, should we say, avant-garde. Located two floors below in the basement, it was called simply Le Restaurant, a source of consternation to local dining critics who thought it implied either extreme modesty or extreme arrogance, until it was rechristened **Le Cercle**.

No matter. The circular room is très mod — a stage set with a raised Roman rotunda in the middle, pillars, marble floors, chain-mesh curtains shielding some tables and fringed sofas fronting on others, and palm trees all around. The chef claims inspiration from the colors of California and the basics of Italian cuisine. He offers alternative cuisine for the health-conscious, among entrées ($19 to $26) like grilled Atlantic salmon on a bed of vegetables with ginger and yogurt-dill sauce, grilled sea bass with tomato and coriander sauce, and veal chop with port wine and roquefort sauce. Many dinner items are offered at lunch, when you also can order sandwiches, salads, pastas and specials like a salad of quail and roasted red bell peppers with a warm mustard-thyme dressing ($13.50).

Zen, the first North American venture for the Zen restaurant chain originating in Hong Kong and London, operates in the depths of the hotel. The two-tier, circular space is dramatic in white and black. It has a curved bar, an elliptical pit in the center and raised tables bearing stunning oriental floral service plates all around. Chopsticks and soup spoons are ready for exotic fare. The lengthy menu makes for fascinating reading. You'll want to peruse the entire epistle, unless you decide on some of the delicacies from three pages of 40 signature dishes from all the Zen restaurants. Called "the Zen experience," it was an incredible bargain for $19.95 – a dinner that would cost at least triple that on its regular menu – and you could choose as many items as you liked. The menu reflects chefs from China, Thailand, Malaya and Indonesia as well as Montreal. The regular à-la-carte offerings ($9.50 to $16.50) run from sweet-and-sour pork filet to Szechuan crispy

Raised Roman rotunda is in center of Le Cercle restaurant at Four Seasons Hotel.

shredded beef with chiles. Or splurge on one of Zen's specialties: perhaps double-boiled and braised fluffy supreme shark's fin ($70 for two), braised whole abalone ($60 for two) or roasted Peking duck ($32 for two). Or settle on chargrilled fillet of doré with coriander ($16.50) or tofu and minced meat in hot sauce ($8.50). The choices — 63, plus variations — are yours.

Le Cercle, lunch daily, 11 to 3; dinner, 6 to 11. Zen, 11:30 to 3 and 5:30 to 11.

Société Café, Hotel Vogue, 1415 Mountain St. (514) 987-8168.

The main dining room of this luxury hotel that opened in 1991 quickly won acclaim in a city of more fine restaurants than anyone could ever get to in a lifetime. Executive chef is Philippe Mollé, who had made a name for himself at St. Honoré, the stylish restaurant behind Le Faubourg.

His travels to Tahiti (where he owned a restaurant), Africa and Japan have manifested themselves in his cuisine, which the staff calls Eurasian, as in bass fillet with carrot and saffron sauce, pasta with cuttlefish ink and squid sauce, and mahi-mahi with curry sauce and coconut milk.

At dinner, you might start with a carpaccio of smoked lamb, mussels cooked in white wine with seaweed and Chinese noodles or, a regional treat, tartare of bison from Quebec's Eastern Townships, served with homemade french fries. Main courses ($19 to $21) include a torte of Moroccan-style rabbit, chicken and duck in phyllo pastry; sweetbreads with scallops and marrow in port wine sauce, grilled duck with sweet-and-sour honey sauce, braised suckling pig with tamarind and ginger, and horsemeat filet mignon with juniper berries and star anise.

The stunning, split-level room includes lots of stainless steel with electric blue accents, white tablecloths with pink napkins, and a rich carpet in apricot and terra-cotta hues.

Open daily, 7 a.m. to midnight.

Champs Elysées, 1800 Sherbrooke St. West. (514) 939-1212.

Former Ritz-Carlton chef Christian Leveque teamed with Germain Villeneuve, a Cornell University Hotel School graduate, to launch this highly regarded restaurant in the Versailles Tower, the hotel opened by Germain's parents. The gray and peach room seats 120 in Louis XV chairs so comfortable that you might never want to get up. Tables are generally well-spaced; for the view, we like the deuces along the long side window better than those against the wall.

The straightforward menu is priced from $14.50 for chicken with sesame seeds and sweet-and-sour ginger sauce to $24 for lobster and shrimp with puree of mango in puff pastry. In between are scallops and salmon with foie gras, filet of veal with pinenuts and roquefort sauce, and port-flavored beef tournedos with a fricassee of morels. The presentations are artful, and the sauces exceptional.

Start with the house-smoked salmon, fried frog's legs with watercress or a terrine of foie gras in crawfish aspic ($6.50 to $19.50). Finish with the terrine of chocolate and orange, pistachio-flavored nougat ice, or such down-home offerings as warm apple pie, baked cinnamon apples or a "soupe" of pineapple and red fruits.

Lunch, Monday-Friday noon to 2:30; dinner, Monday-Saturday 6 to 10.

Lodging

Of the multitude of hotels and motels in this metropolis, we suggest a few with special appeal:

Ritz-Carlton Kempinski, 1228 Sherbrooke St. West, Montreal H3G 1H6. (514) 842-4212.

Splendidly posh and comfortable in the Old World sense, Montreal's oldest hotel is still chosen by many knowledgeable travelers over the more glitzy newcomers. "The grand dame of Sherbrooke Street" is the city's symbol of elegance and service, with 230 high-ceilinged guest rooms and suites, a lobby that is refreshingly clubby and old-line Montreal, and noted restaurants (although, lamentably, the Maritime Bar has been closed for good). Renovated and grandly updated over the years, the hotel has preserved much of its cherished interior. Twenty rooms contain fireplaces and many have original moldings, embossed ceilings and chandeliers.

Doubles, $220 to $250.

Le Quatre Saisons (Four Seasons Hotel), 1040 Sherbrooke St. West, Montreal H3A 2R6. (514) 284-1110.

If the Ritz is Montreal's grand, understated hotel, the Four Seasons is its most sumptuous high-rise (and one of the rare hotels with a five-diamond AAA rating). Built for the Summer Olympics in 1976, it has 300 large, tastefully appointed rooms and suites, an indoor-outdoor pool, saunas and an exercise room full of Universal equipment. Each guest room has a stocked minibar, most have sitting areas with sofas, and the bathrooms offer bidets, hair dryers and terrycloth robes.

Doubles, $205 to $280.

Hotel Vogue, 1425 Mountain St., Montreal H3G 1Z3. (514) 285-5555.

This new boutique-style downtown hotel is the ultimate in luxury. It's geared toward the business traveler (with a fax machine in every room), but tourists will find it an exceptional place to stay, too. Each of the 126 rooms, done in soft greens, creams and pinks, and sixteen suites has a king or queen bed, dressed in duvet comforters and pillows, and in each bathroom there are a TV, telephone, whirlpool bath and separate shower. Minibars, electronic safes and multi-line telephones are other pluses. The suites, in deep jewel tones, are decorated in late Empire style by internationally renowned Stanley J. Friedman.

186

Of course, there are a 24-hour concierge, room service and turndown service, and a workout room with exercise equipment is on the ninth floor. The **Opera Bar** in the intimate and stylish lobby atrium is the place for afternoon tea and desserts for post-theater snacking. Hotel Vogue's location is terrific, just off St. Catherine Street and across from our favorite department store, Ogilvy's.

Doubles, $255 to $305.

Hotel Château Versailles & Tower, 1659 Sherbrooke St. West, Montreal H3H 1E3. (514) 933-3611 or (800) 361-3664 in U.S., 361-7199 in Canada.

Starting as newlyweds with one house and 23 rooms in 1957, André and Mary-Louise Villeneuve have developed a choice for those who value small, European-style inns and hotels. The château has 70 comfortable rooms fashioned from four old four-story graystone townhouses on the western edge of downtown. Exteriors have been restored, the only change being an illuminated yellow sign bearing the hotel's name. The once-humble pension now has antique furnishings, walls that look like those in an art gallery, halls dotted with sofas, and a small, manicured yard. All rooms come with private baths and cable TV; one deluxe room with windows onto Sherbrooke Street has a large velvet sofa, two armchairs, a non-working fireplace and an armoire.

Lately, the Villeneuves invested $5 million in a fourteen-story apartment building across the street, turning it into a 107-room hotel called the Tower. Twenty-two corner rooms have jacuzzis, microwaves and wet bars; all have mini-refrigerators, full-size work tables and computerized safes. Rooms are light and airy, with big windows screened by roman blinds; "when the blinds come down at night," says Mary-Louise, who did the decorating, "they become the art." Italian marble is plentiful in the bathrooms. All the toiletries are custom-made; Mary-Louise found the soap at a health-food store, had it reproduced for her hotel and puts it out in soap dishes crafted by a Laurentian potter. Even the luggage racks here match the furniture.

The difference between the château and the tower is the difference between old-world charm and state-of-the-art sophistication.

Doubles, $115 to $155 in chateau, $135 to $155 in tower.

L'Hôtel de la Montagne, 1430 Mountain St., Montreal H3G 1Z5. (514) 288-5656 or (800) 361-6262.

Backing up to Ogilvy's, an historic enclave of anglo merchandising, this apartment building-turned-hotel represents another part of the diverse spectrum that is Montreal. It caters to business people, couples and singles, most of them French. Welcoming guests in the lobby is a prominent nude sculpture with stained-glass butterfly wings, perched atop a gurgling fountain. The 136 rooms and suites on nineteen floors are decorated in five styles. They contain original art, bathrobes and fruit baskets, and beds are turned down nightly at sundown.

That's when the action really picks up in **Le Lutecia,** the hotel's Greco-Roman-Victorian dining room bedecked in palms, sofas and table lamps. We know English Montrealers who take their maiden aunts there for lunch, despite (or because of?) hotelier Bernard Ragueneau's claim that his restaurant is "a place for intrigue." So is the rooftop cafe and outdoor swimming pool, where some of the lithesome sunbathers go topless. A tunnel from the hotel leads to a multi-level ramble of disco and drink, plants and people called **Thursday's,** part of an evolving enterprise that includes a club called **Crocodile.**

Doubles, $119 to $139; suites, $195 to 225.

A Country Retreat

Hostellerie Les Trois Tilleuls, 290 Rue Richelieu, St. Marc sur Richelieu, J0L 2E0. (514) 584-2231.

About a 20-minute drive southeast of Montreal is this Relais & Châteaux property, a delightful refuge beside the quiet Richelieu River, situated at a particularly scenic spot where the river seems to go in three directions. "It's a calm retreat for Relais & Châteaux types" who want to be close to Montreal, but not all the time, advised a manager.

It takes its name from the three gnarled linden trees at the entrance. Although the front is smack up against the road, the hotel is oriented to the rear to take advantage of the riverside setting.

We first came here for a luncheon outing. The hotel's lovely restaurant spills across several different areas with large picture windows looking onto an outdoor dining patio, a gazebo and the tree-lined river. The rooms were notable for Canadian art on the barnwood walls, comfy chairs that looked handcrafted, pink linens and handsome pottery plates.

The table-d'hôte lunch cost $16.75 each, but with three glasses of wine, coffee, taxes and tip the tab came to about $70 for two. The springtime splurge started with a lovely cream of celery soup, a large salad of fresh boston lettuce with roquefort cheese, and great melba toasts and French breads. One of us had poached halibut with wine-sabayon sauce; the other enjoyed calves liver with a brown sauce and chanterelles. Both came with roast potatoes, cauliflower, carrots and snow peas. A divine chocolate-mousse cake was a worthy ending. Service verging on the supercilious and some tarnished silverware were the only negatives.

Dinner for the public is à la carte, except on Friday when only a six-course gastronomique menu for $42.50 is offered. Guests normally dine table d'hôte. A typical dinner involves a choice among three soups, an appetizer like wild-boar terrine with its port jelly or a combination of marinated lamb tenderloin and smoked bison and a tequila and lime sorbet. The main course could be a duo of salmon and halibut with watercress sauce, medallions of veal with cambozola sauce and caramelized pear, or filet mignon with three varieties of mushrooms. Desserts include chocolate marquise, cheese crêpes with fruit sauce and profiteroles with caramelized maple sauce.

Between meals, overnight guests swim in the pool, play tennis or simply relax in Adirondack chairs beside the gardens. The setting proved so appealing that we asked to see the overnight accommodations.

The 24 guest rooms are spread out on three floors, and each has a patio or balcony looking onto the river. Decorated in what could be described as Quebec rustic style, they are outfitted with handcrafted, custom-made furniture, queen or kingsize beds, two swivel chairs, thick carpeting, TV and telephone. Bathrooms come with hair dryers, terrycloth robes and lots of amenities. The enormous Royal Suite is breathtaking, what with loveseats on all sides of a central fireplace, a sofabed beside a TV, a kingsize canopied bed and a dining area in the solarium. Its bath contains a sauna and a whirlpool for four, which is almost big enough for swimming.

Among the hotel's offerings is a gastronomical package, including room, six-course dinner and breakfast for two, a good deal for $185 to $233, including tax and service.

Restaurant open daily, 7:30 to 10 and noon to 10. Doubles, $110; MAP, $222.

Rooftop cafe at L'Hotel de la Montagne.   **Food hall at Le Faubourg Ste.-Catherine.**

Gourmet Treats

More than any place we know, all Montreal seems to be into eating. In such a city where there is a bakery or charcuterie or cafe issuing forth delectable aromas at almost every corner, we can do no more than cite a few favorites.

Le Faubourg Ste.-Catherine, 1600 St. Catherine St. West. This is the ultimate food hall, a block-long stretch of stalls, markets and eateries on two floors, with some of the eating areas on floors suspended between. The $40 million renovation of a downtown block is a frenchified version of Boston's Faneuil Hall Marketplace. You can find places like Le Hamburger, Crêpes Maison, Le Wok, La Creole, Pasta Villa, Istanbul Express and Sushi Plus. After scouting the selections, one of us settled on a filling (but mediocre) lunch of steak teriyaki with salad and rice for $3.99.

If you find Le Faubourg rather dizzying, cross Guy Street to our favorite Montreal store, **Ogilvy's,** the born-again department store, spiffed up with boutiques and specialty shops (including Crabtree & Evelyn and Godiva). In the basement are a small kitchen shop offering jams and relishes, a pâtisserie and the sprightly **Café Ogilvy,** which dispenses quiche, sandwiches, salads and such from $5.25 to $8.95.

Lest you miss it, we should point out a food court of staggering proportions farther east on St. Catherine Street at **Les Promenades de la Cathédrale,** deep in the bowels of an underground complex that had Christ Church Cathedral overhead on stilts as it was being built a few years ago.

La Tulipe Noir, 2100 Stanley St., is part of the Maison Alcan complex. At a neat cafe, chocolaterie, pâtisserie and food store, you can have a snack or a meal on premises or to go. Rather art deco, with colors of soft browns and mauve and white wrought-iron chairs, the cafe dispenses everything from a croissant to a burger to Mexican chili salsa fresca to Viennese coffee at moderate prices. Wine by the glass is $3.95. The food shop carries all kinds of oils and vinegars from

France, a good selection of Belgian chocolates, Elsenham preserves from England and fantastic pastries.

Optimum, 630 Sherbrooke St. East at Union, is billed as Montreal's largest all-natural supermarket and department store. It's full of a wondrous variety of natural foods, a takeout counter, vitamins, minerals, healthware appliances, juicers and such -- the biggest selection we've seen in Canada.

There is probably not a Montrealer who hasn't at some time in his or her life had a smoked meat sandwich at **Bens Delicatessen,** 990 Maisonneuve Blvd. West. Although it has expanded and now has a liquor license, it hasn't changed much since one of us, who attended nearby McGill University in the 1950s, would stop in late at night after parties to sit with other students under dreadful fluorescent lights that made faces green and nosh on the inch-high smoked meat creation (now $3.70). The Kravitz family have operated this institution since 1908, and one of them is always around to keep an eye on things. Also on the menu are wonderful potato latkes, blintzes, corned beef and cabbage, borscht, Bens famous strawberry cheesecake and — would you believe? — smoked-meat egg rolls with plum sauce. Bens opens at 7 a.m. for breakfast and stays open until 4 or 5 a.m.

Just to make your smoked-meat choice more difficult, our Canadian nieces say Bens is passé, left behind by **Schwartz's Hebrew Delicatessen** at 3895 St., Laurent Blvd., a favorite of the younger generation.

For the authentic French experience, tour the shops along Laurier Street in Outremont. **Le Nôtre** at 1050, one of the franchise operations of Gaston Le Nôtre, France's master of desserts, is heaven for chocolate lovers. Given the dazzling array of gorgeous pastries and cakes, tiny pizzas, baguettes, pâtés, salads, jams and such, you'll have trouble leaving. You can smell the coffees at **Cafe GVH (Gerard Van Houtte)** at 1042 Laurier, a large grocery store specializing in coffees, health foods, gourmet items and cookware; it also has a bakery and a cafe. The tiny smoked-salmon rolls and kiwi cakes are delicious. There are GVH cafes all over Montreal. **Anjou Quebec** at 1025 is about the best charcuterie/boucherie we've seen, a paradise of terrines, wild mushrooms, exotic fruits and more. The tiny haricots verts are flown in from France. **La Maison d'Emile** at 1073 is a good kitchen and bath shop. **La Pâtisserie Belge** at 1075 has display cases full of pastries. Around the corner on Park Avenue is **L'Herbier du Midi,** which offers hundreds of herbs and spices, salad seasonings, soaps and creams from France, potpourri and everything for tea time.

Best all-around is **Les 5 Saisons,** in Outremont at 1180 Bernard St. and, a bit anglicized, in Westmount at 1250 Greene Ave. We've shopped both, but are partial to the Outremont store for exotic vegetables, fresh salmon pies, pastas, beautiful steaks and seafood, a salad bar with hot soups and café filtre, a charcuterie with fantastic pâtés, and a pastry shop with adorable animals made out of marzipan. Here is the ultimate gourmet paradise.

If you'd simply like a glass of wine and a nibble of cheese in your hotel room, drop into 550 President Kennedy Ave. The **Maison des Vins** has the best selection of wines in the city. Across the lobby is **The Cheese Shoppe,** where John Porter, an irrepressible Irishman, purveys port-soaked stilton, creamy brie and sharp cheddar that he has aged for five years. Every Canadian and imported cheese you can imagine is here, as are impeccably smoked salmon, Malossol caviar, pâté de foie gras, cornichons, capers, the finest imported preserves and much more. Check out the scales on the counter. They are more than 220 years old and still in use.

Burlington's Church Street Marketplace is a smorgasbord of carts and cafes.

Burlington
A Culinary Sense of Place

Few areas exude such strong feelings of pride and place as Vermont, and nowhere are these more pronounced than in Burlington, the state's Queen City, poised on a slope above Lake Champlain. From a university town that once had little more than college hangouts and greasy spoons, Burlington has blossomed into the culinary mecca of northern New England.

A dozen restaurants of distinction have opened in the last decade in the city, as well as south along the lake toward Shelburne. "They seem to spring up every other day here," reports the manager of one of the better ones, the Daily Planet. "This town is ripe."

At the edge of downtown Burlington, one small block of Church Street has a lineup of side-by-side eateries that run the gamut from Tex-Mex to Pacific Rim, including vegetarian and gourmet pizza. Countless more are within a block or two of this culinary centerpiece.

The main shopping area, the Church Street Marketplace pedestrian mall, is a smorgasbord of carts and cafes dispensing everything from chicken wings to chimichangas to egg rolls. Coffee à la Carte pours espressos and lattes as long as the temperature is above 20 degrees.

Ben & Jerry, the gurus of fancy ice cream, got their start in Burlington in 1978. Since 1979, the New England Culinary Institute in nearby Montpelier has focused attention on regional cuisine, and moved closer to the action when it opened restaurants in the new Inn at Essex outside Burlington.

In Shelburne, the Webb family's Shelburne Museum is renowned as a remark-

191

able "collection of collections" of Americana. Another part of the Webb family has reopened Shelburne Farms, which is known for its farm programs and cheddar cheeses, and lately has received national recognition for its majestic Shelburne House inn and restaurant. The area claims the Lake Champlain Chocolates factory, New England's largest cheese and wine outlet, the Harrington Ham Company and Champ's Chips, plus countless gourmet food shops and growers or producers of Vermont-made products.

Almost every restaurant in the Burlington area offers outdoor dining in season, and tables spill onto sidewalks and decks at every turn. This is a casual, outdoors city, where people go for interesting food, simply prepared, and with a Vermont-made theme.

Dining

The Best of the Best

Cafe Shelburne, Route 7, Shelburne. (802) 985-3939.

This prize among small provincial French restaurants has been going strong since 1969, but never better than under chef-owner Patrick Grangien, who trained with Paul Bocuse and came to Vermont as part of Gerard's Haute Cuisine enterprise in Fairfax.

Talk about happy circumstance: after twenty years, owners André and Daniele Ducrot offered the cafe for sale in 1988, Patrick was available, and he and his wife Christine bought it and moved in upstairs. Knowing diners seeking inspired food and good value have been drawn to the place ever since.

The copper bar and the dining areas with their black bentwood chairs and white-linened tables topped with tiny lamps retain much of the Ducrot ambiance. Patrick covered and screened the rear patio, a beauty with lattice ceiling and grapevines all around — a good choice for dinner on a pleasant evening.

Patrick calls his cuisine "more bistro style than nouvelle." Seafood is his forte (he won the National Seafood Challenge in 1988 and was elected best seafood chef of the year). Try his prize-winning fillet of lotte on a bed of spinach and mushrooms in a shrimp sauce (a fixture on the menu), fillet of Atlantic salmon with sundried tomato sauce and a broccoli mousse, shelled lobster with home-made linguini in basil-butter sauce or fillet of dover sole with saffron sauce and celery root. Other entrées ($16.50 to $19.50) include roasted pork tenderloin served with polenta, Vermont farm-raised partridge with savoy cabbage, duck breast with lentils from Le Puy, tournedos au poivre and filet mignon tartare.

Any of the five soups — among them creamy lobster, baked duck and vegetable topped with puff pastry, and vegetable-lentil served with a pheasant mousse — are triumphs. Tempting appetizers ($4.50 to $6.50) are carpaccio of tuna, sliced rabbit on top of sautéed mushrooms, baked crab and wild-rice cake wrapped in phyllo dough, and warm oysters and baby vegetables in a champagne sauce.

Crème brûlée is the favorite dessert. Others from the changing but always delectable repertoire in the $4.50 range include frozen caramelized hazelnut mousse with hazelnut crème anglaise, marquise au chocolat, fresh fruit gratin with maple syrup and raspberry sauce, and a trio of chocolate ice creams -- semi-sweet, white and cacao.

The wine list, priced from the high teens to $320 for 1986 Château Leoville, harbors considerable variety. Quite a few are available by the half bottle.

Dinner, Tuesday-Sunday 6 to 9:30.

Chef-owner Patrick Grangien at entrance to Cafe Shelburne.

Pauline's Cafe & Restaurant, 1834 Shelburne Road, South Burlington. (802) 862-1081.

One of the earliest of the Burlington area's fine restaurants (née Pauline's Kitchen in the 1970s), this unlikely-looking place with twinkling white lights framing the front windows year-round has been expanded under the ownership of Robert Fuller.

The original downstairs dining room is now an exceptionally attractive cafe paneled in cherry and oak. Here you can make a mighty good meal of appetizers and light entrées, $5.50 to $9.95 for the likes of salads, pastas, crab cakes, tropical grilled tuna, chicken with Shelburne Farms cheddar-cream sauce and seafood mixed grill.

The original upstairs lounge has been transformed into a ramble of small dining rooms. All is serene and white from the heavy lace curtains obscuring the view from the windows of busy Route 7 to the nicely spaced tables topped with small lamps or hurricane candles and, at our spring visit, vases of tulips.

The printed menu, which changes nightly, is the kind upon which everything appeals. Entrée prices typically run from $12.95 to $19.95. You might start with roasted garlic soup or a sauté of exotic mushrooms and move on to baked Atlantic salmon with a roasted-pepper and cucumber relish or roasted pheasant with apple-hazelnut stuffing.

Our spring dinner began with remarkably good appetizers of morels and local fiddleheads in a rich madeira sauce and a sprightly dish of shrimp and scallops in ginger, garnished with snow peas and cherry tomatoes. A basket of oh-so-good steaming popovers and so-so bread accompanied, as did salads with zippy cream dressings and homemade croutons that redeemed the tough curly endive lettuce.

The entrées were superior: three strips of lamb wrapped around goat cheese,

193

and a thick filet mignon, served with spring vegetables and boiled new potatoes. The glasses bearing the house Père Patriarche white wine, generous and good, were whisked away for the proper globes when it came time for a Rutherford Hill merlot. A honey-chocolate mousse from Pauline's acclaimed assortment of desserts (Bon Appétit magazine requested the recipe for the bananas foster) and a special coffee with cointreau and apricot brandy ended a fine meal.

The pleasant little side patio ensconced in the evergreens is popular during warm weather.

Lunch daily, 11:30 to 2:30; cafe menu, 2:30 to closing; dinner, 5:30 to 10; Sunday brunch, 10:30 to 2.

Déjà Vu Cafe & Grill, 185 Pearl St., Burlington. (802) 864-7917.

Déjà Vu has evolved, too, since its start as a glamorous, richly paneled spread of rooms on several levels featuring a crêpe-oriented menu. It now has the city's most unusual outdoor cafe, an appealing New Orleans-style Spanish courtyard serving 30 for lunch or dinner. Candles in glass bulbs arch from the stucco walls out over the tables, which are topped with cloths and ceramic baskets of fresh flowers.

The courtyard setting is as enchanting as the dimly lit, cathedral-ceilinged interior is dramatic. It's full of rich wood and a variety of lamps, some wonderful glass ones fluted like lilies, and the biggest copper containers we ever saw, up on a hoist and filled with plants. Owner Robert Fuller (of Pauline's) transformed a storage area into the formal Wright Room, inspired by a salon in a Frank Lloyd Wright-designed home in Minnesota. It's now a showplace for private parties.

Déjà Vu still has an all-day menu incorporating five of its popular crêpes (we enjoyed one filled with sweetbreads and chicken), soups like soupe au pistou, salads, grilled flatbread pizzas and bistro plates ($7.50 to $12.95) such as Chinese chicken with soba noodles, shrimp modena and New York strip steak. A lengthy list of lunch and dinner specials changes daily.

The expanded dinner menu bears some of the regional American touches from Pauline's. Among the choices might be grilled monkfish with tangerine sauce, grilled tuna with a smoked-tomato coulis, rainbow trout meunière, grilled pork tenderloin with peach gastrique, and grilled lamb chop with rosemary-port wine sauce and Vermont goat cheese ($14.95 to $18.50).

Champagne sorbet with fruit and biscotti, apple-cranberry crisp, chocolate-raspberry crêpe, lemon-lime tart and maple-walnut bread pudding are among the award-winning desserts. An $11.95 sampler offers a tasting of several. The comprehensive wine list offers carafes for $8.95.

Lunch daily, 11:30 to 2:30; dinner, 5:30 to 10; Sunday brunch, 11 to 2:30.

The Daily Planet, 15 Center St., Burlington. (802) 862-9647.

Celestial food at down-to-earth prices is the forte of this quirky place, advertised in the alternative press as an "inner city playground."

The name reflects its "global fare — ethnic and eclectic," in the words of the staff. Casual, innovative and a favorite local watering hole among knowledgeable noshers, it has a large bar with a pressed-tin ceiling, a solarium filled with cactus and jade plants plus a jukebox, and a lofty, sun-splashed dining room where the pipes are exposed, the walls are covered with works of local artists, and the oilcloth table coverings at noon are changed to white linens at night.

The chefs, most trained at the Culinary Institute of America or the California Culinary Academy, are known for turning out the most imaginative fare in town.

Spanish courtyard is popular in summer at Déjà Vu Cafe.

For lunch, how about Vietnamese shrimp or cobb salad, cold and spicy Chinese noodles, a choice of four wok dishes with four sauces, an oversize grilled eggplant sandwich or an artichoke-parmesan spread with apple wedges and crackers (all under $5.95)?

At night, the Daily Planet sparkles with appetizers and light entrées like Korean vegetable pancake with spicy dipping sauce, smoked-salmon flatbread pizza, Vermont cheddar quesadilla, Japanese chicken salad, and corn cakes with black-bean and chipotle salsa and cilantro crème fraîche. Entrées ($9.95 to $15.50) might include Thai seafood stew, pink sea bass with spicy crust and fresh pineapple salsa, grilled Yucatan-style pork, grilled breast and roast leg of duck, Asian garlic lamb sauté and grilled medallions of beef with red-pepper/garlic butter and caramelized onions. When was the last time you saw grilled lamb loin for $14, with a roasted-vegetable/goat-cheese tart, no less? Have you even heard of pork vindaloo, an Indian hot and sour pork loin sautéed with tomatoes and chick peas and served with a scallion flatbread?

Desserts that change daily intrigue as well. Some are pear-blueberry pie, white-chocolate/apricot cheesecake, Southern nut cake with bourbon crème anglaise, fresh plum ice cream, and baked apples with figs and cranberries, $3 to $4.

As you might expect, the wine list, though small, is well-chosen and offers incredible steals. So does the bar menu, upon which nothing is priced over $4.95.

Lunch, Monday-Saturday 11:30 to 3; dinner nightly, 5 to 10:30 or 11; Saturday and Sunday brunch, 11 to 3.

Five Spice Cafe, 175 Church St., Burlington. (802) 864-4505.

This spicy little prize occupies two floors of a former counter-culture restaurant at the edge of downtown. Since 1985, chef Jerry Weinberg has won a host of followers for his multi-Asian menu of unusual, tantalizing dishes from India, Thailand, Vietnam, Indonesia and China.

We had the upstairs dining room almost to ourselves for a Wednesday lunch, but our waitress said it would be packed that night.

And what a lunch it was! It began with a bowl of hot and sour soup that was extra hot and a house sampler ($8.50) of appetizers, among them smoked shrimp, Siu Mai dumplings, Hunan noodles, Szechuan escargots and spicy cucumbers. The less adventurous among us passed up the Thai red snapper in black-bean sauce for a blackboard special of mock duck stir-fry in peanut sauce (the vegetarian dish really does taste like duck, just as, we were assured, the mock abalone really tastes like abalone). Sated as we were, we had to share the ginger-tangerine cheesecake, which proved denser and more subtly flavored than we had expected.

Chef Weinberg's wizardry in the downstairs kitchen is apparent on a chatty, wide-ranging dinner menu that boasts, quite endearingly, that some of the items and spices have been imitated locally but never matched. Prices of the main courses run from $7.95 for spicy Hunan noodles to $13.95 for a couple of shrimp dishes, one an eye-opener called Thai fire shrimp ("until this dish, we had a three-star heat rating. Now there are four").

A drunken chocolate mousse laced with liqueurs and a blackout cake drenched with triple sec are among favored desserts. The ginger-tangerine cheesecake won Jerry a first prize somewhere, and the ginger-honeydew sorbet is extra-appealing. A dessert sampler teams the chocolate mousse with three other desserts for $10.75.

The Dim Sum brunch on weekends offers fifteen dumplings, including a dessert, for $1.25 and $2.25 a plate. A sampler of four dumplings, noodles and spicy cabbage is $7.95.

The setting does nothing to detract from the food. Oil lamps flicker on each table even at noon. Beige cloths and flowers in green vases comprise the decor. Above the serving sideboard is a collection of Five Spice T-shirts emblazoned with fire-breathing dragons and the saying, "Some Like It Hot." Yes, indeed.

Lunch, Tuesday-Sunday 11:30 to 2:30; dinner nightly, 5 to 9, 10 or 11; Dim Sum brunch, Saturday and Sunday 11 to 3. No smoking upstairs.

Isabel's on the Waterfront, 112 Lake St., Burlington. (802) 865-2522.

This cafe with a canopied terrace not far from Lake Champlain is one of a kind. Started as a catering business and cooking school, it began serving lunch and brunch, and now offers weekend dinners with great panache. About 50 diners can be seated in the high-ceilinged room, and perhaps 50 more on the outdoor terrace overlooking the lake.

Isabel's is the happy brainchild of Beverly Watson, who ran a catering service out of her home for nine years before moving in 1987 to the Waterfront Place complex of offices fashioned from an old lumber yard. Isabel is her middle name, and good food her raison d'être.

The spaciousness of the room surprises the first-time visitor, as do the well-spaced, cloth-covered tables and the bouquets of field flowers. In the rear is a short blackboard menu, a self-service counter upon which samples of the lunchtime offerings are displayed on show plates (which makes the choice really rending), and a small, open kitchen.

The blackboard menu changes daily, but you can be assured that everything is superb. We enjoyed a piquant platter of shrimp and snow peas oriental with egg fettuccine, plus a build-your-own salad with the biggest fresh croutons ever and a choice of four dressings. We also were enticed by the Mexican pizza, a

Canopied terrace offers outdoor dining at Isabel's on the Waterfront.

luscious-looking pan-fried pork with maple-mustard sauce, the heart-healthy dish (dijon chicken), an omelet with olives, onions and artichokes, and a grilled turkey sandwich with cheddar and apples. Prices are not inexpensive ($5.75 to $7.95, with salad), but the value is received.

At night, the short menu changes weekly and the price of main courses ($9.95 to $14.95) includes soup or salad. Among the possibilities might be herb-crusted Atlantic salmon on a roasted red-pepper coulis, breast of chicken with pineapple and walnuts in a pesto-cream sauce, sautéed lamb with a red wine and shiitake mushroom sauce, and filet of beef with a mustard-thyme sauce. Starters could be Maine crab cakes with sweet tomato salsa, caesar salad, chicken quesadilla or baked brie topped with almonds and homemade cranberry-apple chutney, served with a sliced baguette.

For brunch, try the banana and walnut pancakes, the broccoli benedict or "Old MacDonald Goes to France," a croissant topped with two poached eggs, sausage patties, mushrooms, brie and hollandaise ($7.95).

Lunch, Monday-Friday 11 to 2; dinner, Thursday-Saturday 5:30 to 9; Sunday brunch, 11 to 2.

Gerard's Restaurant & Lounge, Radisson Hotel, Burlington. (802) 864-5005.

Subtitled "Windows on the Lake," this restaurant has been nicely relocated from a window-less area of the Burlington Radisson Hotel to a former disco on the hotel's lakeside second floor, where tall windows and tiered levels take full advantage of the view. The mix of banquettes and tables is sophisticated, the service urbane, the presentation artistic and the food sometimes controversial, though generally highly regarded.

The controversy stems from owner Gerard Rubaud's use of vacuum-packed gourmet food prepared at his Gerard's Haute Cuisine enterprise in nearby Fairfax. Gerard, the former president of Rossignol Ski Co., and three partners created the ultimate convenience food, some of which has found its way onto the plates at Gerard's over the years.

Now an independently owned and operated restaurant in the main dining room at the Radisson, Gerard's has embellished its menu, adding a section of regional cuisine to the "classic" specialties. Prices run from $12 for Canadian turkey breast in puff pastry to $20 for filet mignon béarnaise. Among the options are grilled or poached Norwegian salmon with leeks and basil fettuccine, grilled striped bass with green lentils, grilled Vermont trout with angel-hair pasta, Mediterranean fillet of snapper, Louisiana seafood stew, roasted duck with bordelaise sauce and scalloped potatoes, Thai red curry chicken with soba noodles, roasted pork tenderloin in port wine sauce, and roasted rack of lamb with brown garlic sauce and scalloped potatoes. The dishes are nicely presented, and much ado is made over the sauces.

Starters ($4.90 to $7.90) could be soba noodles with vegetable stir-fry, escargots with wild mushrooms, smoked-salmon ravioli, and roasted crab cakes served with julienned vegetables. Or try one of the acclaimed soups, perhaps lobster bisque or Mediterranean fish. Desserts from the cart could be anything from orange terrine with chocolate mousse to a white-chocolate entremet.

The lunch menu is similar but abbreviated in length and price ($5.90 to $8.90). Both menus are available at the new outdoor cafe, from which the Adirondacks are on bold display across the lake. A gourmet brunch is served for $14.95. A five-course tasting dinner is offered for a prix-fixe $29.

Lunch daily, 11:30 to 2; dinner, 5:30 to 9:30 or 10; Sunday brunch, 9 to 3.

Chaz Restaurant & Cafe, 1016 Shelburne Road, South Burlington. (802) 658-2325.

Long at the cutting edge of culinary affairs in the Burlington area, chef Chaz Sternberg finally opened a restaurant of his own in 1992 in the front of the Best Western Redwood Inn. His name is emblazoned in neon out front, and it takes a sense of bravado to do so -- in association with a motor inn and with a name that's not exactly recognized, at least with the motoring public. Chaz distances himself as far as possible from the motel image, though part of his agreement calls for serving breakfast, which he does with typical flair.

He offers a main-floor cafe, lounge and espresso bar and a dramatic, L-shaped dining room upstairs. It's pretty in pale pink with sponged rose walls and windows onto a view of Lake Champlain and the Adirondacks. A trompe-l'oeil mural of french doors opening onto a garden graces the landing of the stairway between the two sections.

Chaz, who's a stickler for healthy eating, uses no eggs, butter or cream in his cooking and sautées with olive oil. He starts every diner off with a complimentary Spanish tapenade of minced black olives, capers, tomatoes and roasted garlic to go with the French bread. The night's soup could be duck, red cabbage and white bean. Among appetizers ($4.50 to $6.95) are light clam fritters with a green herb sauce, smoked-salmon carpaccio, mozzarella with Miskell organic tomatoes and his trademark caesar salad, embellished with crispy deep-fried oysters and croutons. A sampler of four appetizers is $7.95 for two.

Dinner entrées ($12.75 to $14.95) change frequently. Expect treats like sea scallops niçoise served over black pasta, braised salmon fillet served with a two-bean compote and saffron pasta, New England seafood stew with saffron-rice pilaf, potato-encrusted shrimp in a soy-sesame dressing with wild and saffron rice, pan-seared duck breast with roasted garlic-dijon vinaigrette and beet pasta, Vermont lamb chops with a mushroom and spinach polenta, and seared sirloin steak with pecans and a tri-pepper and corn ragout.

Tiered dining room at Gerard's affords view of Lake Champlain.

"Sweet rewards" feature fruits, as in homemade strawberry shortcake, English trifle with fresh raspberries, angel food cake with raspberry mousse, and chocolate torte with raspberries. Or treat yourself to a long-standing Chaz specialty, hot cheesecake that's as light as a lemon soufflé. The short wine list, priced in the teens and twenties, is heavy on Australian and Hungarian offerings "because I like them," says wife Kathy, who handles the front of the house.

Breakfast specials at our latest visit included herbed duck with poached eggs and french toast stuffed with raspberry compote and pecans.

Breakfast, Monday-Friday 7 to 10:30; Saturday 8 to noon, Sunday 8 to 2; dinner, Tuesday-Saturday 4 to 9:30 or 10. No smoking upstairs.

Other Dining Choices

The Village Pumphouse Restaurant, On the Green, Shelburne. (802) 985-3728.

The hand-written menu changes frequently at this little restaurant, with 35 seats in two intimate dining rooms and an enclosed porch.

Assisted by his sister in the prep department, chef David Webster prepares some exciting fare. Dinners, served with soup and a green salad, run from $17.75 to $21.50. One night's offerings were Thai shrimp sautéed with scallions and ginger, poached Norwegian salmon with orange-hollandaise sauce, red snapper baked with a topping of crab meat and bread crumbs, veal madeira with shiitake mushrooms and dried cherries, and sautéed loin of lamb finished with port and shallots. Four "suppers," with salad only, produced yellowfin tuna, crab cakes, stuffed pork loin and broiled New York sirloin for $14.50 to $15.75.

Start with mussels baked with swiss cheese and bacon, chicken satay with peanut sauce or a tomato, basil and ricotta tart. Finish with a raspberry-peach crisp, chocolate-hazelnut meringue tart, maple crème caramel or cream-cheese crêpes with apricot sauce.

Decor is country simple, with a stress on the simple, according to David. Most of the assorted oak and maple chairs came from his parents' barn.

David's partner, host-bartender David Miner, is responsible for the large beer list. It's as lengthy as the wine list, and includes seven on draft.

Dinner, Tuesday-Saturday 5:30 to 9:30 or 10.

199

Sakura, 2 Church St., Burlington. (802) 863-1988.

The urbane City-Side restaurant in Richardson Place didn't last long. Its successor since 1987, the city's first Japanese restaurant, has fared better.

The Japanese owner was more interested in showing us his sparkling kitchen than describing elements of the decor, which is minimal. Bare blond wood tables are set with chopsticks tucked inside peach napkins. Cranes in flight painted on the walls look like shadows. Along one side is a sushi bar. In the center is a raised tatami room with two tables at which you sit on cushions and take your shoes off.

More than two dozen appetizers are featured on the dinner menu, written in English with straightforward descriptions. They range from sashimi to California maki to bean curd cooked in seaweed-flavored soup. The sushi bar offers ten choices from $9.50 to $29.50 (for something called Sushi Heaven). All the other Japanese treats are available, individually in a wide range of prices or in combination dinners for $19.95. The only desserts are fresh fruit, yokan, and Japanese and tempura ice creams.

The Sakura lunch box, served with soup, salad, rice and fruit, contains a California maki roll, assorted tempura and chicken teriyaki for $9.75.

Kirin beer, sake and plum wine are among choices from the well-stocked bar.

Lunch, Monday-Friday 11:30 to 2; dinner, Monday-Saturday 5 to 9:30 or 10:30, Sunday 5 to 9.

Sweet Tomatoes Trattoria, 83 Church St., Burlington. (802) 660-9533.

Borrowing a page from their smash-success restaurant of the same name in Lebanon, N.H., Robert Meyers and James Reiman opened a carbon copy here in 1992

From Burlington's first wood-fired brick oven come zesty pizzas like the namesake sweet tomato pie, a combination of tomato, basil, mozzarella and olive oil ($7.75). From the rest of the open kitchen that runs along the side of the surprisingly large downstairs space emerge earthy pastas, grills and entrées at wallet-pleasing prices — $9.95 is the highest for a mixed grill or skewers of lamb. For a quick dinner, we were quite impressed with the cavateppi with spit-roasted chicken ($8.75). Less impressive was a special of linguini infused with olive oil and mushrooms ($7.75), rather bland and desperately in need of more pecorino romano cheese, the container of which the waitress sprinkled less than liberally and guarded as if with her life until we finally asked for (and received) our own container full to rescue the dish. A huge salad topped with romano, a basket of bread for dipping in the house olive oil and a $14 bottle of Orvieto accompanied.

The stark decor in white and black is offset by brick arches and stone walls with a neon strip over the kitchen. It's a convivial and noisy setting for what Robert calls "strictly ethnic Italian cooking, as prepared in a home kitchen." The sidewalk cafe in front would likely be a quieter setting in season.

Lunch, Monday-Saturday 11:30 to 2; dinner, 5 to 9:30 or 10, Sunday to 9.

Trattoria Delia, 152 St. Paul St., Burlington. (802) 864-5253.

New in 1993 and well-received was this Italian establishment with something of an old-world ambiance and an updated menu. Tom Daley, who used to cook at Mr. Up's in Middlebury, and his wife Lori took over the old What's Your Beef steakhouse and transformed it into a trattoria. The beamed and timbered room is comfortable and good-looking in deep red and green, with a long bar along one side.

Pastas are featured as primi dishes ($6.95 to $10.95). Tagliatelle with wood-grilled mushrooms and gnocchi with a ragout of sausage, veal meatballs and rabbit are favorites. Among secondi ($9.95 to $14.50) are wood-grilled fish of the day with a garlic-pepper sauce, salt cod simmered with raisins in a sweet tomato sauce, rabbit cacciatore, grilled free-range Tuscan chicken, wild boar braised in barolo wine and served on a bed of saffron risotto, veal saltimbocca, osso buco and wood-grilled angus sirloin finished with sage and olive oil.

Antipasti ($3.50 to $5.95) include bruschetta, deep-fried calamari, veal carpaccio, wild-boar sausage on a bed of sautéed spinach and the traditional sampling of imported Italian meats, cheeses and roasted vegetables. Among desserts are tirami su, profiteroles filled with gelati and homemade crème caramel with golden raisins and Vino Santo.

The all-Italian wine list is extensive and fairly priced. Digestives at the end of the dinner menu include sweet Italian dessert wines. Also offered are cappuccino and caffe latte.

Dinner nightly, 5 to 10.

Coastal City Grill, 207 College St., Burlington. (802) 862-6278.

Leave it to Burlington to come up with as trendy a little tropical seafood eatery as you'd find north of Boston or New York. And in such an unlikely place: a storefront adjacent to and opening into the funky City Market, a bakery cafe with a vegetarian accent.

A former chef from the Daily Planet was responsible for the global cuisine at the market's upscale offshoot. The menu details such treats ($10.50 to $14.95) as grilled swordfish with mango-pistachio chutney, grilled halibut served with coconut milk and green-chile sauce and garnished with a citrus relish, sautéed marlin au poivre garnished with papaya-chile sauce and finished with a lime-rum vinaigrette and grilled shrimp kabobs with Indonesian banana-coconut chutney. Fish can be grilled plain "for the plain folk." Available for the non-fish eaters are grilled free-range chicken of the Indies with hot apricot chutney, grilled Yucatan chicken with salsa of the day, grilled tofu and vegetarian stir-fry.

Entrées come with a spinach salad tossed with a ginger-honey-mustard dressing, Cuban black-bean salad and a choice of angel-hair pasta or rice. But do try one of the exotic appetizers ($4.95 to $5.95), perhaps conch fritters, scallops seviche, seafood tacos, salmon gravlax with lime and cilantro, or grilled oysters with a spicy mignonette sauce. Desserts include a really limey key lime pie, Caribbean angel cake with a lime mousse, chocolate-zucchini cake and ricotta-cheese pie.

All this is served up in an airy but understated tropical interior dressed in pastel hues. The food takes precedence over decor here.

Dinner nightly, 5 to 10. No smoking.

Coyotes Tex-Mex Cafe, 161 Church St., Burlington. (802) 865-3632.

Another newcomer of particular appeal to the younger set is this venture fashioned from a rundown arcade. Brothers Eric and Jeff Lipkin from Kennebunkport, Me., teamed with Jim Glatz of Philadelphia to produce as authentic a Tex-Mex menu as possible (considering the far northern location) in a very authentic setting. The place is striking for its inlaid tile tables imported from Mexico, walls sponged burnt orange and shelves of pottery from the famed Goose Rocks Pottery owned by the brothers' parents. Rattlesnake beer and "ultimate" margaritas are served at a long bar converted from a bowling lane.

Texas Hellfire sauce is on each table to add heat to the already hot fare offered on the all-day menu: things like fried jalapeños stuffed with cheese, three-bean chipotle chili, blackened chicken fingers, a basket of corn fritters and fajitas. Main-course prices run from $4.25 for a Texas burger topped with chili to $11.95 for cowboy steak blackened in cajun spices and served on a sizzling platter with onions and peppers. The tortilla chips, crisp and light, come with a zesty salsa that's addictive. We also liked the black-bean soup, again with its own kick, served in a heavy custom-made pottery bowl and big enough to share. The Amarillo appetizer sampler (five changing choices, $5.95) was less successful, and a taco chicken salad ($4.95) proved far too much to eat for lunch. Next time we'd try the tequila chicken ($7.95), served with rice and sautéed vegetables.

Lunch daily, 11:30 to 4; dinner, 11:30 to 10; late-night menu to 12:30.

Ice House Restaurant, 171 Battery St., Burlington. (802) 864-1800.

Two open-air decks, an oyster bar, a wine bar and a classic menu with an emphasis on North Atlantic seafood are attractions at Burlington's first restaurant restoration (circa 1976) and, though some in the culinary vanguard scoff, still as popular as ever.

At the entrance is a charming Brueghel-like sign depicting ice skaters on the lake. Inside the massive stone building that really was an ice house are a large upstairs lounge and dining room with huge rough beams and plush sofas and a downstairs dining room with fieldstone walls and nicely separated tables. Beyond the lounge is an open deck with a view of the waterfront across the sheds of a boat yard. Beneath that is a covered deck for shade on a hot day.

We enjoyed grilled marinated lamb on a skewer and mussels Tuscan style prior to a dinner of poached scallops with julienned vegetables in a wine and cheese sauce and stuffed chicken breast with leeks, wild mushrooms, balsamic vinegar and red wine sauce. Other entrées ($14.50 to $20.95) include braised sea bass topped with asparagus and leeks, mesquite-grilled swordfish with an avocado-cilantro-lime butter, steak, cioppino, grilled salmon with hollandaise or smoked-tomato butter, veal scaloppine hunter style, filet mignon oscar and roast rack of lamb with a pommery-sesame crust. Desserts might be chocolate-toffee torte, bourbon-pecan pie and caramel-vanilla boats in crème anglaise.

Broiled scrod, a platter of backfin crabs with spiced prawns and a pork sandwich with horseradish were blackboard specials for lunch at a recent visit.

The wine list is good, but has more of a price markup than most Burlington restaurants.

Lunch, Monday-Saturday 11 to 11; dinner nightly, 5 to 10; Sunday brunch, 10:30 to 2:30.

Leunig's, 115 Church St., Burlington. (802) 863-3759.

The garage doors go up in the summer to open this funky, "old world cafe" and bar to the sidewalk. The sign advertises pastries, hors d'oeuvre and espresso, but that's not the half of it. People pack its tables day and night, sipping drinks, espresso and what the New York Times called the best cup of coffee in town.

Go here for a memorable breakfast or brunch. The breakfast special is really special -- eggs benedict and cappuccino, for a bargain $4.95. Or settle perhaps for crumpets, a croissant with blackberry cream cheese, Wolferman's English muffins or a popover with maple butter.

The deceptively simple all-day menu lists salads and sandwiches plus appetizers like salmon mousse, pesto vegetable pâté, an addictive hot black-bean dip with chips, wild mushrooms with grilled polenta and Sicilian antipasti ($4.95 to $5.95).

Towered and turreted mansion is open for dining and lodging as Shelburne House.

Entrées include mussels bouillabaisse and steak frites (the most expensive items at $7.95, except for dinner specials up to $11.95), croque monsieur, quiche with salad, lobster tostada and baked kielbasa with sweet potatoes. Mocha cheesecake, bread pudding and chocolate-truffle cake are favored desserts. All wines are priced at $15 a bottle.

European music adds to the cafe setting. "It's a meeting place, where all types of people stop by to see their friends," says owner Laura Thompson.

Open Monday-Friday 7:30 a.m. to 2 a.m., Saturday 9 to 1 a.m., Sunday 9 to 2 a.m.

Bed and Board

Shelburne House, Shelburne Farms, Shelburne 05482. (802) 985-8498 (late May to mid-October); 985-8686 (mid-October to May).

It's hard to imagine a more luxurious inn, albeit in an old-school way, or a more spectacular setting than the summer mansion built by Dr. William Seward Webb and his wife, Lila Vanderbilt Webb, high on a promontory surrounded on three sides by Lake Champlain.

Their 1,000-acre agricultural estate was planned by Frederick Law Olmsted, the landscape architect who designed New York's Central Park. The focal point is their incomparable summer home, a lakeside landmark built in 1899 for $10 million and converted in 1987 into an inn and restaurant of distinction.

The rambling, towered and turreted, Queen Anne-style mansion has 24 bedrooms and suites, seventeen with private baths. It retains the original furnishings, although Old Deerfield Fabrics created for the inn a Shelburne House line of fabrics and wall coverings reproduced from original designs dating to the turn of the century.

Most guest rooms on the second and third floors are awesome in size, some with three windows onto the water and non-working fireplaces. Each is done in its own style, but four-poster beds, armoires, settees, lavishly carved chairs, writing tables and such barely begin to fill the space. Fresh flowers adorn the bathrooms, mostly original and some with skylights. Guests' names are on the doors and bowls of fruit in the rooms upon arrival.

For their spaciousness and aura of royalty, we would choose to stay in Lila Webb's south corner room with its twin pencil-post beds and a fine view of forests and lake from mullioned windows, or Dr. Webb's room with a two-story bathroom and stairs up to his valet's quarters (now the White Room full of wicker and containing one of the inn's few queensize beds). Other choices would be the master bedroom in between, or the Rose Room with a canopy bed and a view of sunsets over mountains and lake that defies description. Although they represent good value, we would not want to stay in some of the smaller rooms with shared baths and hard-to-climb-in double beds up against the wall.

The main floor is a living museum reflecting the graciousness of another era. There are porches full of wicker, a library with 6,000 volumes, several sitting rooms (one for afternoon tea and pastries), a dark and masculine game room harboring an 1886 billiards table, and a formal dining room in which breakfast and dinner are served. Telephones in the guest rooms, TV sets on request and a tennis court are among the few concessions to modernity.

Meals are quiet and formal at twelve tables dressed with Villeroy & Boch china and white napkins in the spacious Marble Room, quite stunning with its walls covered in red silk damask fabric and black and white tiled floors.

The public may join house guests by reservation, paying $6.50 to $8 for appetizers, $16.50 to $23.50 for entrées, and $5.50 to $6 for desserts.

Chef Matt Larson, who trained at La Varenne in France, summers here and winters at Snowbird ski resort in Utah. He revises his menu daily to incorporate the freshest of local ingredients. Complimentary canapés, perhaps truffle mousse or salami with Shelburne Farms cheddar, begin the meal. Then there could be a choice of roasted-pumpkin bisque with braised Vermont rabbit and cheddar, wild-mushroom ravioli with marinated sweet peppers and wilted local greens, or smoked salmon terrine with Shelburne Farms grain mustard and Vermont crème fraîche. Salads could be Miskell tomato with warm Vermont chèvre and grilled red onion, or local romaine and spinach with hickory-smoked trout, black olives and citrus vinaigrette.

For main courses, how about pan-seared halibut served on a wild-mushroom and fennel sauce, loin of pork with apple-cranberry-black-currant chutney, Wylie Hill pheasant with smoked Vermont bacon and wild mushrooms, and filet of beef with warm Vermont brie and green-peppercorn butter? The rack of Yankee Shepherd lamb comes with Shelburne Farms honey and a rosemary-thyme glaze.

Exotic desserts might be lemon-ginger cheesecake prepared with Vermont mascarpone and baked on a rosemary-shortbread crust, maple-pecan-chocolate torte with chocolate ganache on raspberry coulis, or raspberry marquise with white and dark Belgian chocolate mousse on hazelnut pastry.

Breakfast for guests is à la carte, starting at $4.50 for continental and rising to $8.50 for poached eggs with tomatoes on English muffins with rosemary and red-pepper home fries.

Guests can walk the grounds, enjoy the superb gardens, swim at a small beach, play croquet on a manicured lawn and hike up Lone Tree Hill for a 360-degree view of the lake and mountains, says Alec Webb, general manager of Shelburne Farms and great-grandson of the original owners. The quiet and sense of privacy are overwhelming.

The house was opened as an inn "to preserve the structure and generate revenues," adds Alec, who spent summers in the house as a teenager before his father bequeathed it to a non-profit foundation. "It's an appropriate use since it was basically a guest house originally."

Dinner nightly, 6 to 9. Doubles, $100 to $250, EP. No smoking except in game room. Two-night minimum stay on weekends. Open mid-May to mid-October.

The Inn at Essex, 70 Essex Way, Essex Junction 05452. (802) 878-1100 or (800) 727-4295.

It's a surprise to find an inn of this elegance — with restaurants of distinction — in the midst of a large field on the commercial outskirts of Essex Junction. The location was an early drawback, one that made the task of filling the new inn's 97 rooms challenging, to say the least. That was alleviated in 1994 with the opening of the I-289 circumferential highway with an exit near the inn's entrance.

Conceived by the Hawk Mountain Corp. and now run by Eurowest Inns of California, the white three-story structure looks and feels like an inn, despite its odd surroundings. Furnishings and wallpapers in each room are different, and decor varies from Shaker to Queen Anne, from canopy to pencil-post to brass beds. In each room is a sitting area with comfortable upholstered chairs, a TV hidden in the armoire and a modern bath. Thirty have working fireplaces. An indoor pool and a whirlpool are among the facilities.

The inn has earned accolades for its restaurants, for this is the Burlington-area home of the New England Culinary Institute out of Montpelier. There's considerable creativity in the enormous professional kitchen, thanks to executive chef Robert Barral (a native of France who was executive chef at the Four Seasons Hotel in Boston), fifteen teaching chefs and a hundred student assistants.

There are two restaurants: the formal, 50-seat **Butler's** with a vaguely Georgian look, upholstered Queen Anne chairs, heavy white china and windows draped in chintz, and the more casual **Birch Tree Cafe,** where woven mats on bare tables, dark green wainscoting and small lamps with gilt shades create a Vermont country setting.

The cafe was where we had a fine Christmastime lunch: sundried-tomato fettuccine with scallops and a wedge of pheasant pie with a salad of mixed greens, among entrées from $5 to $6.50. Although the portions were small and the service slow, we saw signs of inspiration, on the menu as well as in a dessert of chocolate medallions with mousseline and blueberries in a pool of raspberry-swirled crème fraîche, presented like a work of art. Two pieces of biscotti came with the bill, a very reasonable tab. Interesting meals and theme dinners at bargain prices are served in the cafe at night.

Dinner in Butler's, NECI's temple to haute cuisine, is a study in trendy food. The menu changes daily, but you might start with a soup ($3.50) of braised spinach and grilled artichoke or smoked pumpkin and green apple with sweet currants. Appetizers ($3.50 to $4.25) could be shrimp Hawaiian with seared pineapple and mango chutney or mille-feuille of tomato and cayenne pasta with a roasted-garlic and chèvre mousse. A champagne or kiwi sorbet refreshes the palate for the main course ($14 to $20), perhaps red snapper sautéed with eggplant and artichokes with chick peas and pesto, grilled salmon with warm vegetable relish and curried butternut sauce, smoked duck on saffron and wild rice with snow peas and baby carrots, or roasted rack of lamb with minted-oil and balsamic vinaigrette, asiago risotto and haricots verts. For dessert ($3.50), how about a caramelized phyllo napoleon with warm apples, sour cream and a green-grape sorbet; flourless dark chocolate cake with raspberry sorbet and a splash of apricot brandy, or frozen margarita parfait with oranges, lemon and black-currant sauce?

Butler's, dinner, Monday-Saturday 6 to 10; no smoking. Birch Tree Cafe, lunch, Monday-Saturday 11:30 to 1:30; dinner nightly, 5:30 to 9:30; Sunday brunch, 11 to 2. Doubles, $99 to $160.

Lodging

Radisson Burlington Hotel, 60 Battery St., Burlington 05401. (802) 658-6500.

When it opened in the late 1970s as part of the Burlington Square office/commercial complex, it was billed as northern New England's most urbane hotel (it's still urbane, but the competition is increasing). The seven-story, 256-room hotel occupies a choice piece of real estate between downtown and the lakefront, and the most desirable rooms, of course, are those that face the water.

The lobby is a bit austere by Burlington standards, but our room was spacious and subtly decorated in golds and browns. The seventh-floor Plaza Club has concierge service, a complimentary continental breakfast, afternoon wine and other amenities. There's a great jacuzzi on one side of the indoor swimming pool, which is surrounded by fourteen poolside cabanas.

In addition to **Gerard's** restaurant (see above), the **Village Green Cafe** offers three meals a day at moderate prices.

Doubles, $95 to $135

Sheraton-Burlington Hotel and Conference Center, 870 Williston Road, South Burlington 05401. (802) 862-6576.

This started as a "Sheraton Inn," a gray and white shingled structure topped by five cupolas built around a 150-year-old barn. In 1987, it was vastly expanded into a hotel and conference center, to the point where you need a map to find your room and to get around the campus-like, Disneyesque complex. Enclosed pedestrian bridges and directional signs help. Some of the 309 rooms flank an interior courtyard open to the sky. Others face the indoor atrium, some of those with sliding doors onto a garden-style restaurant with an L-shaped indoor pool and fitness center beyond. The rooms we saw were stylish, with comfortable armchairs and remote-control TVs tucked away in cabinets.

Lunch is served at G's, aforementioned garden restaurant in the four-story-high "summerhouse" atrium (the name reflects the first initial of the two owners). Drinks and light meals are available nearby in **Tuckaway's,** a lounge with a sun deck on the roof. Out front, **Baxter's** serves an appealing and varied menu for dinner (from $11.95 for chicken teriyaki to $16.75 for veal and shrimp scampi).

Doubles, $79 to $137.

The Inn at Charlotte, 1188 State Park Road, Charlotte 05445. (802) 425-2934 or (800) 425-2934.

The immediate Burlington area is lacking in good B&Bs, but this newcomer is a good bet to the south of town. Located just off Route 7 near the foot of Mount Philo, it started as a boutique in an old schoolhouse with the owner's living quarters behind. You'd never know it today, such is the transformation into a rambling, contemporary, chalet-style house with six guest rooms, four with private baths. Most also have private entrances via sliding doors onto a tiered

Inn at Essex is home of two New England Culinary Institute restaurants.

rear garden around a swimming pool and tennis court. We're partial to the two rooms at the far end, one with a kingsize bed and full bath and the other with twin four-posters and a closet-size shower. Another favorite is a detached cottage with two twin beds. A thermos of Vermont spring water is in every bedroom.

Besides the pool and garden area, guests enjoy a large and comfortable living room and a dining room in which owner Letty Ellinger, a caterer, serves dinner to guests by reservation (she was making delectable-smelling Chinese egg rolls at our visit). A typical $25 prix-fixe meal might involve oriental soup or green salad, chicken teriyaki or New York strip sirloin (grilled outside on the barbecue), a homemade pie, a glass of wine and gourmet coffee.

She serves a full breakfast in the morning, perhaps ham and eggs, quiche, french toast or blueberry pancakes.

Doubles, $65 to $85.

Thomas Mott Homestead, Blue Rock Road, Alburg 05440. (802) 796-3736 or (800) 348-0843.

This lakeside prize at the top of the Champlain Islands north of Burlington is one of our favorite B&Bs anywhere. Ex-California wine distributor Pat Schallert transformed an 1838 farmhouse into a homey B&B with five spacious guest rooms and a secluded lakeside location with panoramic water and mountain views that won't quit. Three porches invite lounging, the fireplaced living room is stocked with books and magazines, and a massive collection of cookbooks and wine books flanks the stairway. Each of the five guest rooms with private baths is furnished with antiques and quilts from different states. The ultimate is Ransom's Rest, nestled beneath a cathedral ceiling with a queen bed, two chairs in front of a fireplace and a balcony looking across Ransom's Bay to Mount Mansfield.

Pat cooks up a hearty breakfast, perhaps raspberry or blackberry pancakes, crab or shrimp omelets, or french toast spread with cream cheese and five kinds of nuts. Prix-fixe dinners that are quite a bargain are served by area caterers Joli Fare by prior arrangement. Other special touches that make this place a winner: a stash of Ben & Jerry's ice cream in the refrigerator, a lakeside gazebo, a barnyard pen where Pat raises quail and a patch of what he calls "stealing" raspberries. We were surprised they were still producing in late September 1993 and gladly would have picked a few quarts to take home -- but that would have been stealing!

Doubles, $55 to $70. No smoking.

Gourmet Treats

Shelburne Museum and Heritage Park, Route 7, Shelburne. (802) 985-3344. The incredible collections of Electra Havemeyer Webb, wife of a Vanderbilt heir, became the Shelburne Museum in 1947, and the resulting 37 structures spread across a 45-acre heritage park fascinate young and old. The almost overwhelming display of Americana, unrivaled in New England, spans three centuries and a multitude of interests. People into things culinary will enjoy the kitchens in four restored homes, each with large open hearths full of gadgets that our ancestors used. The Weed House has a remarkable collection of pewter and glass, and the dining-room tables in the side-wheeler Ticonderoga are set with Syracuse china. A free shuttle tram transports visitors from the new visitor center to the far ends of the grounds every fifteen minutes. Open daily, mid-May to mid-October, 9 to 5; rest of year, guided tours, daily at 1. Adults, $15; second consecutive day free.

Shelburne Farms, the 1,000-acre agricultural estate of Dr. William Seward Webb and Lila Vanderbilt Webb, has been open to the public since 1984. Blessed with one of the more spectacular lakeside-mountain settings in the Northeast, Shelburne Farms combines an active dairy and cheesemaking operation, a bakery, a market garden and other leased enterprises in a working-farm setting that has a Camelot-like quality. Guided tours leave every 90 minutes from the Visitor Center after a free multi-media slide introduction. You board a bus to view the enormous Farm Barn, the Dairy Barn, the formal gardens and the exterior of the Shelburne House. You may see grazing along the way the fine herd of Brown Swiss cows, descended from stock raised for cheesemaking in Switzerland. Their Shelburne Farms farmhouse cheddar (some of the best cheddar we have ever tasted) is sold in the Visitor Center, where a fine shop also stocks other Vermont farm products and crafts and is open daily year-round. Tours, late May to mid-October, daily at 9:30, 11, 12:30, 2 and 3:30. Adults, $5.50.

In Burlington, **Lake Champlain Chocolates** at 431 Pine St. produces some of the best chocolates anywhere. It's an outgrowth of Jim Lampman's Ice House restaurant, where partner Richard Spurgeon was the baker and produced truffles that generated such demand that they branched into the chocolate enterprise in 1983. Although tours are no longer offered, you can view the production area from the windows of a small showroom that smells like chocolate heaven. Richard starts with Belgian chocolate but the addition of Vermont heavy cream and sweet butter and intense natural flavoring puts their creations "on a par with the best in the world," according to Cuisine magazine. Among the latest treats are Vermints, and factory seconds are offered at 40 percent off.

Across the street, the **Cheese Outlet** at 400 Pine St. is touted as northern New England's largest cheese and wine warehouse, with an excellent selection of pâtés and cheeses, quiches and cheesecakes at bargain prices. We often buy a couple of quiches on our way to Montreal at Christmastime.

"Custom-built coffees" are the trademark of **Speeder & Earl's,** a high-tech, high-ceilinged space in black and white at 412 Pine St. Its roastery and a cafe are located here, while a store and cafe are situated downtown at 104 Church St. What are custom-built coffees? The menu answers: "Simply put, if you want hazelnut Italian syrup in a nonfat latte, with nonfat whipped cream topping, sprinkled with mint-flavored sugar, don't be shy. Just ask." Ask also for teas, Italian sodas, biscotti and pastries.

Nearby at Pine Square, 266 Pine St., a long warehouse holds **Champ's Chips,** home of the "Vermont old-fashion potato chip" and other all-natural snack foods. You can watch potato chips being made and buy them here.

Desserts and pastries that turn up at the best parties in town come from **Mirabelles,** 198 Main St., a terrific bakery and deli created by Alison Fox and Andrew Silva and named for the golden plums grown on the Continent, where both had worked. Sandwiches are inspired, perhaps black forest ham and brie or goat cheese with Mediterranean tapenade and fresh vegetables on a baguette for $3.95 ($2.50 for a half). The ploughman's lunch ($5.95) is a sampling of cheeses, breads, fruits and a sweet. Finish with a raspberry butter tart, raspberry dacquoise or a slice of cappuccino-truffle cake.

Sebastian's Gourmet Pizzeria & Deli, 179 Church St., serves up some of the best pizzas around from a maplewood oven. We liked one with jerked chicken and mango salsa and another with grilled shrimp and pesto, chosen from a roster of eighteen priced from $7.95 to $9.50, except $4.95 for a peanut butter and jelly pizza ("don't laugh until you try it!" advises the menu).

Freddy's Say Healthy, 171 Church St., is the East's first vegetarian fast-food restaurant, according to owner Fred Solomon. Veggie burgers, veggie hot dogs, veggie sandwiches and subs, soups and chilis are available at the counter, McDonald's style. We liked the vegetarian chili just fine, but found the falafel sandwich to be a crumbling mix of pita and marble-hard falafel that couldn't be rescued even with a knife and fork.

Pepper's Memphis Barbecue at 1110 Shelburne Road, South Burlington, is a must-stop for those into Memphis music and barbecue. There's a lot to look at and listen to in the old diner section, where huge glasses of iced tea are the drink of choice at lunch time, and in a small, memorabilia-filled dining room, where musical instruments and photos of jazz musicians line the walls. Legendary BBQ chef Robert Moye came from Memphis to prepare the real thing. We liked his signature pulled pork sandwich ($4.95) topped with zippy coleslaw and the corned-beef brisket. The pork shoulder is smoked for fourteen hours in a closet-size rotisserie, yielding such treats as dry ribs ($8.95) and a sampler platter ($11.25). There are a few munchies and salads to go with.

Shelburne is home to the **Shelburne Country Store,** opposite the village green. It still sells penny candy but now also offers an upscale assortment of country things, accessories, Vermont cow items, homemade fudge and specialty foods, including its own line of chowders and finnan haddie.

"The world's best ham sandwich" ($4.75) is advertised at **Harrington's,** Route 7 next to Cafe Shelburne. Headquartered in nearby Richmond, this has a cafe as well as everything for the kitchen from cookbooks to Cuisinarts. It sells a panoply of gourmet foods, including every kind of cracker imaginable.

MIDDLE BRIDGE — WOODSTOCK VERMONT

Woodstock and Hanover

Quintessential New England

Woodstock, which has been called one of America's prettiest towns by National Geographic, is the quintessential New England village. Across the New Hampshire state line is Hanover, the quintessential New England college town.

Put them together and you have an extraordinary destination area for purists who seek the real New England, relatively unspoiled, even if highly sophisticated. Happily, both towns have escaped the commercial trappings that so often accompany tourism — Woodstock even to the point where the utility wires in the center have been buried underground. Both also exude an aura of culture and class that appeals to moneyed residents and visitors, but which tends to be viewed askance by down-home natives and back-to-the-earth newcomers.

The attraction of the area is epitomized by historic Woodstock, where America's first ski tow was installed 60 years ago, propelling it into a winter sports mecca called "the St. Moritz of the East — without the Ritz."

There's still no Ritz, although the Woodstock Inn and Resort built in 1969 by Laurance Rockefeller interests and the new Twin Farms luxury hideaway that emerged in 1993 could qualify.

The Rockefeller connection with Woodstock began in 1934 when he married Mary Billings French, the granddaughter of railroad magnate Frederick Billings. Now the town's largest landowner and employer, he lives about two months of the year in the mansion north of town that was once the home of George Perkins Marsh, the 19th-century ambassador and a founder of the Smithsonian. Just as Rockefeller money has saved and enhanced much of Woodstock, the Rockefellers are preserving the family heritage — and that of Vermont — in their Billings Farm Museum with its thousands of 19th-century farm implements.

Woodstock is known as the town with three covered bridges, the cradle of

210

winter sports, the town with four Paul Revere bells, and the picture-perfect Currier and Ives village. It's a place for all seasons. In the charming downtown area in summer, colorful flowers cascade from boxes once used for gathering maple syrup; in winter, large white Christmas lights bedeck the store facades; in autumn, the fiery foliage provides color aplenty.

Accompanying the influx of tourists and new residents has been a proliferation of restaurants and inns.

A generation ago, chowders, boiled dinners and pumpkin pies were the fare served at the White Cupboard Inn — which closed in 1967 — and at the Woodstock Inn, a decaying predecessor that was razed to make the new showplace. "Had a patron requested chocolate mousse he probably would have been told that the pharmacy didn't carry those but they did have maple sugar candies shaped like Indians," according to a local magazine.

Today, the Woodstock and Hanover region abounds with fine restaurants of diverse backgrounds. The area also has more than its share of casual restaurants serving up creative fare at down-to-earth prices.

Dining

The Best of the Best

D'Artagnan, 13 Dartmouth College Highway, Lyme, N.H. (603) 795-2137.

Through all our travels, certain dining establishments stand out in memory like beacons. D'Artagnan is such a place.

It's not necessarily for the atmosphere, which is most pleasant. Or for the service, which is friendly and flawless. Or for the prices, which represent good value. It's primarily for the food, which is extraordinary.

This exceptional dining experience — one that we as well as several leading restaurateurs of our acquaintance readily drive many miles for — is provided by Peter Gaylor, a French-trained chef, and his wife, Rebecca Cunningham. Theirs is a pristine, pretty dining room in the brick and beamed basement of the reconstructed 18th-century Ambrose Publick House, nestled beside Hewes Brook in a small complex of restored offices and buildings ten miles north of Hanover.

Both had extensive training with noted chef Yannick Cam in Washington, D.C. They had been seeking a place of their own in New England when the developer called. "In six months we went from nothing to opening our doors," Peter remembers.

That was in 1981, and D'Artagnan has quietly built a regional following that would do justice to the couple's mentor, at whose restaurant Peter served as sous chef. At D'Artagnan, he does the cooking and his wife oversees the baking and the front of the house. Two others help in the kitchen, and four waitresses serve the 60 lucky diners who can be seated at tables in the spacious dining room with windows onto the stream.

Dinners are $38 prix-fixe for four courses ($43 with an additional appetizer or dessert), and the typewritten menu changes nightly. For a few extra dollars by special arrangement, a tasting menu provides a pre-determined sampling of this innovative team's work, which they often vary and embellish upon request.

A changing amuse-gueule, perhaps local chèvre or smoked salmon on cucumber, is served with generous drinks in heavy glasses. Very hot rolls with butter in small ramekins precede the appetizers.

We chose the tasting menu, the appetizers being selected by the chef: an outstanding mussel soup with saffron and garlic, superb hot oysters on a bed of rock salt, a salad of rabbit fillet with endive and hazelnut oil, a shrimp mousseline with carrot, leek and watercress sauce, and a subtle duck pâté with armagnac and madeira. All were as intriguing to look at as they were to taste.

A granité of white wine with juniper berry and orange rind cleared the palate for the main course, pan-roasted loin of lamb with a shallot and fresh lime sauce, served with broccoli. The only disappointment was that the tasting menu did not allow a sampling of the night's other entrées: escalope of salmon with asparagus and mushrooms, boneless fillets of trout with smoked-salmon mousse and cucumbers in crème-fraîche/vermouth sauce and golden caviar, sautéed medallions of beef with a green-peppercorn and cabernet sauce, breast of Vermont pheasant with sautéed fennel, and pan-roasted leg and fillet of rabbit with mustard-cream sauce, snow peas and mushrooms. A salad of ruby lettuce and slivered carrots with hazelnut-oil dressing followed the entrées.

Everyone saves room for Rebecca's glorious sweets, which are in such demand that she wholesales to area inns. You couldn't ask for better than her chocolate medley of chocolate mousse on chocolate meringue, pistachio-chocolate torte and orange-milk-chocolate ice cream; her raspberry tartlets in a pool of crème anglaise with raspberry coulis; her sliced strawberries on a marmalade of cortland apples and red-wine/vanilla-bean sauce; her pear trio of pear-caramel custard, pear-ginger sorbet and pear tartlet; her orange crème caramel with grand marnier and creme chantilly, and her three sorbets of grapefruit, strawberry-banana and lime. To gild the lily, two truffles in any number of flavors come with the bill.

The wine list is one of New Hampshire's best, at prices from $17 to $82. It includes maps showing regions from which the wines come, the owners believing maps to be more effective than labels in guiding patrons to their favorites.

The dining room is a study in simplicity, with a handful of art works and fencing swords hung on the stenciled walls, a few oriental rugs on the wide-board floors, and bentwood and upholstered chairs around tables dressed in white napery. A single white rose and candles in silver candlesticks grace each table.

Rebecca added new Pierre Deux draperies to give "more color for the advent of spring" before our latest visit. She and Peter also added a new "little tasting" menu featuring two appetizers, dessert and beverage for $22 on Wednesday, Thursday and Sunday evenings in the off-season. Together they added infant daughter Nicole, who "eats here more often than a lot of people," says Peter. "She loves fish and her first green vegetable was asparagus."

Peter espouses the spirit of nouvelle cuisine in theory as well as in practice. He and his three brothers were fencers, and the restaurant is named for his hero in Dumas's *The Three Musketeers.* "The spirit with which he leaps into his adventures seemed to capture best that feeling we had upon starting this restaurant," reads the explanation on the menu. His patrons are the luckier for this spirit.

Dinner, Wednesday-Sunday 6 to 10; Sunday lunch (a lighter meal, $19 or $22), noon to 1:15. Reservations required.

Barnard Inn, Route 12, Barnard, Vt. (802) 234-9961.

Its red-brick facade accented by four white pillars and surrounded by mighty trees, the Barnard Inn is a handsome two-story structure dating back to 1796.

It really is out in the country, ten miles north of Woodstock almost at the "back of beyond." But fans of Sepp Schenker, the Swiss chef-owner who lives with his wife and children upstairs, consider the distance a trifle to be put up with when they anticipate one of the fine meals he has been offering since 1975 at a restaurant that some tout as the best in Vermont.

Peter Gaylor and Rebecca Cunningham provide culinary inspiration at D'Artagnan.

Inside is an elegant, late-Colonial inn with dark beamed ceilings, wide-plank floors, white ruffled curtains, brass sconces casting shadows on the white stucco walls, and a few select baskets hanging here and there. In the biggest of four small dining rooms, a fire blazes in the hearth and the fireplace mantel is hung with old black tools and topped with two brass ducks. Round tables are spaced nicely apart and covered with white linens, heavy silver, fresh flowers in tiny porcelain vases and white candles in big hurricane lamps.

To accompany generous drinks, a nippy spread of cheddar cheese, sour cream, minced onion and celery, worcestershire sauce and sherry is served with crackers. We'd choose one of Sepp's special soups — mulligatawny, cream of leek, peasant, cold fiddlehead or shrimp bisque — over an appetizer (smoked rainbow trout, raviolis florentine, sausage en croûte or poached shrimp with a trio of sauces, though the last are plump and unusually tasty), since meals here are quite hearty and you ought to save room for dessert. His Bermuda fish chowder, thick and spicy and served with the island's famous hot pepper-sherry sauce, evolves from his experience as chef at the Cambridge Beaches resort in Somerset. We found the curried pumpkin soup absolutely delicious.

Hot crunchy rolls and a house salad of mixed greens (including lamb's lettuce from Sepp's garden), fresh morels, slivers of carrot and red cabbage, topped with a creamy Swiss or Italian dressing, come with the meals.

Entrées ($21.50 to $29) are heavy on the beef and veal side, with a few choices of chicken, duck and seafood. We chose the tournedo Adriano, a center cut of fork-tender tenderloin with a rich sauce of heavy cream, brandy and green peppercorns, and the suprêmes de poulet à l'estragon, the chicken breast sautéed in garlic butter with a wine, cream and tarragon sauce. Another occasion produced the crisp roast duck, which many regulars consider to be the inn's specialty. Barely steamed broccoli stems cut like match sticks, glazed carrots and one of the inn's trademarks — a potato shaped and coated to look like a pear with a clove at the bottom and a pear stem on top — made a hefty plateful. Another favorite vegetable is hubbard squash baked and pureed with maple syrup and piped onto a slice of sweet potato with a cranberry on top.

The reasonable prices on the wine list were a pleasant surprise. There are a couple of Swiss wines and we tried an interesting Torresella merlot from Spain, which was served in large, delicate globes.

The dessert cart is laden with caloric wonders. One cake was decorated with whipped cream and candied violets. Sepp is partial to his apple charlotte with raspberry topping, a mille-feuille with hazelnut nougat, and cinnamon ice cream with apricot-apple topping. A refreshing choice was a dish of fresh fruit laced with kirsch — would that more restaurants had desserts like this for those who need a thousand more calories like a hole in the head.

Attentive, unobtrusive service is provided by women in white blouses and long black skirts.

Besides growing his own herbs and planting new beds of lamb's lettuce each month, Sepp gathers his own fiddleheads (270 pounds a year) and morels, and picks wild grapes that make a colorful sauce for his roasted duck.

Dinner, nightly 6 to 9 or 9:30 in fall, Tuesday-Sunday in summer, Wednesday-Saturday in winter. Closed mid-November to mid-December and month of April.

Hemingway's, Route 4, Killington, Vt. (802) 422-3886.

The restored, 19th-century Asa Briggs farmhouse has been earning culinary accolades since Linda and Ted Fondulas moved over from Annabelle's in Stockbridge in 1981.

Antiques, locally crafted furniture, fresh flowers from Linda's gardens and original oil paintings, watercolors and sculpture enhance the decor of each of three dining rooms. A European feeling is effected in the formal dining room with velvet chairs and chandeliers, a garden room done up in white and pink with brick floors and pierced lamps on the walls, and a charming wine cellar with stone walls, lace tablecloths and elaborate candlesticks.

These are the diverse settings for ever-changing food that made Hemingway's the first four-star, four-diamond dining room in northern New England. An added accolade came in 1992 when Food & Wine magazine ranked it among the top 25 restaurants in America. Hemingway's also is known for its monthly food and wine tastings featuring wine experts as guest speakers. The Fondulases stock more than 150 selections, at prices from the teens to $150.

Dinner is prix-fixe, available in three formats: $42 for three courses, plus hors d'oeuvre, coffee and confection; $58 for four tasting portions served with four glasses of selected wines, and $42 for a four-course vegetarian menu.

About six choices are available in each category for the first option. For starters you might find hand-rolled lobster and shrimp ravioli with cilantro and mint, scallop and crab cake with tomato and mango, and grilled quail with wild mushrooms and parmesan. Main courses include pan-roasted swordfish with crispy potato basket, West Antillian sauté of shrimp and crab, wood-roasted chicken with grilled cheddar polenta and Vermont lamb with roasted eggplant.

Desserts could be three frozen fruit mousses, lime and ginger crème brûlée, chocolate-hazelnut torte with white-chocolate mousse, coconut ice cream under a caramel cage with mango and banana, or "local anything," says Linda, whose husband oversees the kitchen. Chef Francis Clogston gets his herbs from a garden out back, and scented geraniums might turn up as a garnish.

Dinner, Wednesday-Sunday 6 to 10. Closed Easter to mid-May.

Swiss chef-owner Sepp Schenker offers fine dining at Barnard Inn.

The Prince and the Pauper, 24 Elm St., Woodstock, Vt. (802) 457-1818.

Walk up the brick walkway alongside one of the area's oldest buildings, open the green door, pass the pubby bar and enter the L-shaped dining room. You're in what is considered to be the best restaurant in Woodstock proper.

Oil lamps cast shadows on beamed ceilings and tables are surrounded by Hitchcock chairs or tucked away in high, dark wood booths, the ultimate in privacy. Old prints decorate the white walls, one of which has a shelf of old books. Tables are covered with rich brown napkins and white cloths, oil lanterns and a single flower in a clear vase.

Chef-owner Chris Balcer calls his cuisine "creative continental." The prix-fixe menu ($28, for appetizer, salad and main course) changes nightly. His pasta of the day could be with scallops, shrimp and sundried tomatoes; his soup, charred carrot garnished with crème fraîche, and his pâté of Vermont pheasant teamed with orange chutney. Vietnamese spring rolls, smoked coho salmon and toasted brioche with goat cheese and tomato concasse might be other appetizers.

Entrées at our last visit were grilled swordfish with Japanese-style pickled ginger, veal rib chop madeira, grilled breast of duck with a sauce of fresh raspberries, grilled delmonico steak with porcini-cream sauce and the house specialty, boneless rack of lamb baked in puff pastry with spinach and duxelles.

Spend some time reviewing the interesting wine list (strong on California chardonnays and cabernets), priced from the teens to more than $100 for Château Lafite. But save room for dessert — maybe a fabulous raspberry tart with white-chocolate mousse served with raspberry-cabernet wine sauce, pumpkin cheesecake with pecan topping, walnut-apricot linzer torte or a homemade sorbet like Jack Daniels chocolate-chip. Finish with espresso, cappuccino or an international coffee.

A bistro menu is available in the elegant bar. It offers half a dozen entrées (including perhaps delmonico steak, grilled leg of lamb and sautéed crab cakes) for $11.95 to $13.50. Also served here are five kinds of hearth-baked pizzas for $9.95.

Dinner nightly, 6 to 9 or 9:30; bistro menu to 10 or 11.

215

Simon Pearce Restaurant, The Mill, Quechee, Vt. (802) 295-1470.

Irish glass-blower Simon Pearce's intriguing mill complex includes an exceptional restaurant with Irish and regional Vermont specialties in a smashing setting beside the Ottauquechee River. We think the covered outdoor terrace almost over the waterfall is great for lunch, and the Pennsylvania friends to whom we recommended it liked it so much they took relatives back the next day. Countless others have been directed here and, captivated by the magic of a special place, now make it a point to eat here whenever they're in the vicinity.

The interior dining areas, vastly expanded since its opening, reflect the exquisite taste of the rest of the complex. Sturdy ash chairs are at well-spaced wood tables outfitted with small woven mats by day and dressed with white linens at night. The heavy glassware and the deep brown and white china are made by Simon Pearce and his family at the mill. Plants, dried flowers in baskets and antique quilts lend a soft counterpoint to the brick walls, bare floors and expansive windows. That popular covered terrace has recently been enclosed. Its full-length windows open in summer, but diners now can feel as if they're eating outside beside the waterfall in other seasons as well.

The chefs train at Ballymaloe in Ireland, and they import flour from Ireland to make their great Irish soda bread and Ballymaloe brown bread. They change the menu periodically, but there are always specialties like beef and Guinness stew (which we tried at lunch — for $9.25, a generous serving of fork-tender beef and vegetables, plus a small side salad of julienned vegetables). We also liked a pasta salad ($7.75) heaped with vegetables and a superior basil-parmesan dressing. We often order the smoked salmon, which is sensational here. The famed walnut-meringue cake with strawberry sauce and a mountain of whipped cream is the crowning glory; it's a menu fixture, crisp and crunchy, and melts in the mouth. Cappuccino cheesecake is another possibility.

Candlelight dinners might start with spicy grilled shrimp, marinated grilled chicken with a spicy peanut sauce or coho salmon, hickory-smoked at the mill. Entrées run from $14.50 for the beef and Guinness stew to $22.50 for grilled beef tenderloin with fresh mint béarnaise. Other choices might be sesame-crusted tuna with noodle cakes, wasabi and pickled ginger; grilled Cavendish quail with fresh plum sauce; roasted duck with mango chutney. and grilled leg of lamb with garlic, rosemary and balsamic vinaigrette

The wine list printed on the menus, short but choice, is supplemented by a longer list priced from $16 to $48. Naturally, you can get beers and ales from the British Isles.

Lunch daily, 11:30 to 2:45; dinner nightly, 6 to 9. No smoking.

La Poule à Dents, Main and Carpenter Streets, Norwich, Vt. (802) 649-2922.

Texas chef Barry Snyder and his wife Claire gave up an innkeeping stint at the nearby Parker House in Quechee to open their own restaurant. When the former Carpenter Street Restaurant became available in 1990, they jumped at the chance. Knowing diners applauded their move as well.

Both Culinary Institute of America graduates, the Snyders say they cook in the classic French style and change their short, contemporary menu every few weeks. Main courses ($17.50 to $22.50) could include grilled tuna with aioli and scallion pasta, noisettes of pork with french lentils and morels, grilled venison with a sauce of dried cherries and merlot wine, and roasted beef tenderloin with herb spaëtzle and bordelaise. For starters, try salmon and curry chowder, lobster and shrimp in risotto with spinach, or confit of Peking duck grilled with red onions.

Arched windows give diners view of waterfall outside Simon Pearce Restaurant.

With Texas bravado, Barry calls his wife's dessert tarts the best around. Other possibilities are poached plums with Vermont mascarpone cheese and cinnamon cookies, and chocolate mousse inside little meringue cookies with raspberries.

All this is served in two dining rooms. A beautiful oak bar flanks a more casual, post and beam, cafe-style dining area with mismatched chairs. Lately the side dining room has been papered and painted, royal purple swags and jabots have been hung, and, the Snyders proclaim, "finally our decor starts to catch up to the food, service and wine." This elegant room, lit by candles in hurricane lamps, has a couple of recessed alcoves, barely big enough for two.

We got a taste of this talented pair's work a few years ago at lunch, which since has been discontinued. Three of us enjoyed various soups — a velvety puree of butternut squash with dill chantilly, an intense wild-mushroom broth with porcini and shiitakes, and the winner, a hearty zuppa di pasta e fagioli. Then we tackled a charcuterie plate with pâté and goat cheese, breaded salmon anglaise with herb vinaigrette, and estockificada, a bouillabaisse of shrimp, scallops and mahi-mahi on a plate with saffron sauce and a bowl of broth topped by garlic toast on the side. Perfect salads of exotic greens followed, a bit spare but painstakingly prepared. The meal whetted our appetites to return for dinner.

Oh yes, the French name? Loosely translated, Barry says, it means "chicken with teeth," an obscure takeoff on the saying "as scarce as hen's teeth."

Dinner, nightly from 6; Sunday brunch, 11 to 1.

The Middlebrook Restaurant, Middlebrook Road, Fairlee, Vt. (802) 333-4240.
Folks from Hanover, Woodstock and beyond trek north to the Lake Fairlee countryside for an unusual dining experience. Surprise: the young owners built their restaurant inside a house inside a barn, they grow much of their food, and their changing menu is far more inspired than you'd expect in such rural surroundings.

Partners John Quimby and Michael O'Donnell "dreamed of opening a restaurant

217

where we could grow the food and make it seasonal," in John's words. "We knew there would be people who would appreciate this." They fulfilled the dream in 1992, rebuilding a barn and building a clapboard house inside "to fit into the agricultural environment" behind their farmhouse.

The result is an architecturally intriguing, quirky place with high ceilings, huge windows onto the hilly countryside and a contemporary atmosphere. Each of the several dining rooms is outfitted with colorful mismatched chairs, tables covered with cloths from the 1930s and old dish towels for use as napkins. Candles of different colors are in assorted candlesticks. None of the salt and peppers match, nor do the vases holding various kinds of flowers. The effect is thoroughly charming.

And the cooking measures up. Each of the partners has restaurant experience, Michael at the late Cafe la Fraise in Hanover and John at the New Prospect Cafe in Brooklyn. Here they employ herbs and vegetables from their prolific gardens just outside the restaurant. They change their menu nightly to offer such starters ($3.25 to $6.75) as gazpacho with fresh corn, red-potato and leek soup with caraway, tomatoes and smoked mozzarella with pesto vinaigrette, crab cakes with corn, peppers and cumin/sour-cream sauce, and smoked yellowfin tuna with jicama, ginger and sesame. The night's main courses ($12.75 to $16.25) could be grilled swordfish with tomato jalapeño relish, black-bean and corn salad; curry- and sesame-glazed fillet of halibut with gingered cucumber salad; maple-lemon duck breast with curried basmati-rice salad, and sirloin steak with caramelized onions, brandy and black pepper. The wine list is short but sweet and eminently affordable.

Desserts ($3.75) could be fresh peach pie, blueberry crisp with vanilla sauce, milk chocolate mousse with chocolate-almond biscotti or fresh apple cake with caramel sauce.

Dining areas at Middlebrook Restaurant.

Sunday brunch at this special place is a treat as well. The menu varies from sourdough french toast with melon and poached eggs with smoked salmon to a salad of poached salmon and greens or grilled swordfish with rosemary and lemon.

Dinner, Wednesday-Sunday 5 to 9; Sunday brunch, 10 to 2. Closed November-April.

Other Dining Choices

Sweet Tomatoes Trattoria, 1 Court St., Lebanon, N.H. (603) 448-1711.

This sleek but casual, New Yorkish place that opened in 1990 added a breath of fresh air to the area's dining scene and remains what several area foodies call "the restaurant sensation of the Upper Valley." Pizzas from a wood-burning oven, pastas and entrées from a wood and charcoal grill at wallet-pleasing prices pack in the crowds, despite an unlikely location fronting the green in oft-overlooked Lebanon.

Occupying the key front-corner space of a new downtown commercial complex, this is the brainchild of James Reiman, who was formerly at the Prince and the Pauper and opened Spooner's in Woodstock, and Robert Meyers, a builder whose experience was pivotal in putting the space together. And it's quite a space. Seats for 100 are at tables placed well apart under mod California spotlights, their neon-like rims echoing the neon encircling the exposed metal grid beneath a high black ceiling. A black and white tiled floor, a few indoor trees, a mural along one wall, a tin mobile and plants hanging on pillars complete the minimalist decor.

Excitement is provided by the totally open kitchen, where the owners may join the cooks at the grills, wood-burning oven and counters amidst garlic ropes hanging from on high. Theirs is what Robert calls "strictly ethnic Italian cooking, priced for the 1990s." You'll find pastas ($6.75 to $9.75) like linguini with sautéed shrimp in horseradish-tomato-basil sauce or ravioli with plum tomatoes, and pizzas ($7.75) from the namesake sweet tomato pie to fresh clams and olive oil, all liberally accessorized with mozzarella and garlic.

Entrées (8.75 to $11.95) include grilled chicken with herbs, skewers of marinated lamb, mixed grill, rainbow trout stuffed with bay shrimp and crab meat, and, our choice, grilled swordfish with basil pesto, served with a side salad of red potatoes, sweet peas, leeks, garlic and extra-virgin olive oil.

You can sample most of the menu at lunch time, when prices are in the rock-bottom $4 to $6 range. We thoroughly enjoyed the cavatappi with roasted chicken, plum tomatoes and arugula, a memorable concoction served with two slices of herbed sourdough bread and cheese sprinkled liberally from a hand grater. The enormous clam pizza, its thin crackly crust weighted down with clams and mozzarella, proved too much to eat. Lamentably, we had to forego the delectable desserts, which included chocolate-espresso cake, cannolis, tirami su and dacquoise. There's no bar service, but a short beer and wine list is available.

Success here led the partners to open a carbon copy in 1992 in Burlington, Vt.

Lunch, Monday-Friday 11:30 to 2; dinner, Tuesday-Sunday 5 to 9 or 9:30.

Cafe Buon Gustaio, 72 South Main St., Hanover, N.H. (603) 643-5711.

The owners of Peter Christian's restaurants (Hanover and New London) teamed up with a chef from Harvest in Cambridge to open this engaging Italian bistro in 1990.

Murray and Karen Washburn transformed a decrepit eatery into a picture-pretty room of intimate tables outfitted with white linens, carafes of alstroemeria and votive candles. A bottle of extra-virgin olive oil is on every table, ready to pour into a saucer for dipping the crusty Tuscan bread. Walls are covered with a warm orange-peach fabric, candles flicker in the wall sconces and the place positively glows in the evening. Tiny white lights twinkle on the beams in the adjacent bar.

The restaurant lives up to its name, which means "good eats." The menu changes nightly and is categorized by appetizers, salads, pastas, pizzettas, entrées and even bread.

You might start with cioppino, rabbit stew or grilled calamari with greens, roasted peppers and olives. Pizzettas ($8 to $10) could include sundried tomatoes with roasted peppers and brie or grilled chicken with cilantro pesto and button mushrooms. How about a calzone of salami, spinach, tomatoes, provolone and cheddar?

Typical entrées ($17 to $19) are seared yellowfin tuna with leeks, tomatoes and mussels; grilled loin of pork with madeira-peppercorn sauce and polenta, and sautéed veal medallions with porcini-marsala cream and ravioli. Desserts are made by the pastry chef at Peter Christian's, who runs over with such treats as a toffee-lime tart, napoleons and chocolate lover's cake topped with chocolate-dipped strawberries.

Dinner, Tuesday-Saturday 5:30 to 9:30 or 10.

Bentleys Restaurant, 3 Elm St., Woodstock, Vt. (802) 457-3232.

A rather funky and casual spot at the prime corner in Woodstock, Bentley's caters to every taste at every hour. It serves lunch, dinner and Sunday brunch, has dancing on weekends, and has a great bar to visit in cold weather for a hot buttered rum or a Bentley burner (hot apple cider, ginger, cinnamon and brandy).

On two levels with bentwood chairs, jungles of plants and cozy alcoves with Victorian sofas, it offers at lunch all kinds of burgers, sandwiches (some in croissants), chili, Mexican dishes and salads in the $5.75 to $8.95 range. We enjoyed torta rustica, a hot Italian puff pastry filled with prosciutto, imported ham, mozzarella and marinated vegetables, and a fluffy quiche with turkey, mushrooms and snow peas, both accompanied by side salads. For dessert, a delicate chocolate-mousse cake with layers of meringue was served with good Green Mountain coffee in clear glass cups.

At brunch, try a bellini (champagne with the essence of peaches) before eggs benedict, Italian frittata or salade niçoise.

Dinners go up to $18.95 for Jack Daniels strip steak, flamed tableside, with hand-cut french fries. Entrées include maple-mustard chicken, champagne-poached salmon with a cucumber and dill salad, pan-seared local trout topped with a roasted red-pepper coulis and medallions of lamb with a fig and cherry compote.

Partners Bill Decklebaum and David Creech also run **Rosalita's,** billed as a Southwestern bar and grill, in Waterman Place at Quechee, full of Mexican atmosphere with adobe-type walls, bare wood tables and skylights. At lunch, we found the food to be standard Tex-Mex rather than Southwestern, and the taco salad ($5.50) was nothing to write home about.

Lunch, daily 11:30 to 3 (late lunch menu, 3 to 5); dinner, 5 to 9:30 or 10; Sunday brunch, 11 to 3.

Chez Françoise, 44-48 South Main St., Hanover, N.H. (603) 643-4448.

"A taste of France in Hanover" is the billing for this nifty patisserie. Françoise Duffy, a native of Paris, arrived in Hanover with her new husband when he became director of the C. Everett Koop Institute at Dartmouth, after she had taught for many years at the University of Montreal. Struck by the need for epicurean delights in her new town ("I was appalled," she sighs), Françoise took a course in pastry making at the Ritz in Paris and opened a bakery in the rear of a new bank building. Here she offers such delights as paris-brest, croissants, baguettes, palmiers, lady fingers, cappuccino biscotti and fancy cakes to a receptive clientele. She bakes bread twice a day, "just like they do in France with the steam injection." Wonderful French salads (the dressing for the tuna is "totally French -- no mayo") and croissant sandwiches make good lunch-time fare.

Barely opened when we stopped by, she planned soon to offer gelati and "all the things we can find in Europe." Eventually, she hoped to open a full-fledged French cafe in town -- "a mid-priced French restaurant, not necessarily fancy."

Open Monday-Saturday 7:30 to 7, Sunday 8 to 3.

Chandeliers and two fireplaces enhance dining room at Twin Farms.

Bed and Board

Twin Farms, Barnard, Vt. 05031. (802) 234-9999 or (800) 894-6327.

The crème de la crème of small, luxury country resorts has arrived in New England in the unlikely Vermont hamlet of Barnard. The secluded farm once owned by writers Sinclair Lewis and Dorothy Thompson was converted to the tune of $11 million into the East's most sumptuous inn in 1993. One of a kind, it offers nine-going-on-sixteen rooms and cottages, superb dining and a full-time staff of 27 to pamper 18-going-on-36 guests. The tab? A cool $700 to $1,500 a night for two, including meals, drinks and recreational activities, but not the tax and fifteen percent service charge. The clientele? A moneyed international crowd that likes to travel. Twin Farms is deluxe, of course, but understated and not at all ostentatious -- not nearly as drop-dead showy as one might expect. "The idea is you're a guest at somebody's country estate for the weekend," says Beverley Matthews, innkeeper with her husband Shaun, both of whom are British and who come with impeccable resort-management credentials.

The idea evolved after the Twigg-Smith family of Honolulu acquired the estate's main Sonnenberg Haus and ski area as a vacation home in 1974 when chef Sepp Schenker left to open his nearby Barnard Inn. In 1989, Laila and Thurston Twigg-Smith acquired the other half of Twin Farms from Sinclair Lewis's grandchildren, returning the estate to its original 235 acres. Son Thurston (Koke) Twigg-Smith Jr. and his wife Andrea, twenty-year residents of Barnard, managed the development phase of Twin Farms. Andrea and Ibby Jenkins of Woodstock. Koke's sister, assisted Laila with the interior design and product selection.

Their resources and taste show throughout the property, from the electronically operated gates at the entrance to the fully equipped fitness center and separate Japanese furo soaking tubs beneath a creekside pub reached by a covered bridge. In the main house, three living rooms, each bigger than the last, unfold as the innkeepers welcome their guests. One with a vaulted ceiling opens onto a neat little library loft and soaring windows gazing onto a 30-mile view toward Mount Ascutney. Decor is elegantly rustic and utterly comfortable.

Upstairs are four bedrooms bearing some of the Twin Farms trademarks: plump

221

kingsize feather beds, tiled fireplaces, comfortable sitting areas, fabulous folk art and contemporary paintings, TV-VCR-stereos, tea trays with a coffee press and Kona coffees from the family-owned corporation, twin sinks in the bathrooms, baskets of all-natural toiletries, terrycloth robes, and unbleached and undyed cotton towels. They impart a feeling of elegant antiquity, but come with every convenience of the perfect home away from home.

Less antiquity and even more convenience are found in the newly built stone and wood guest cottages, each with at least one fireplace, a screened porch or terrace, and its own private place in the landscape. The Perch, for instance, is situated above a small stream and beaver pond. It harbors luxuriant seating around the fireplace, a desk, a dining area, a refrigerator with ice maker, a bed recessed in an alcove and shielded by a hand-carved arch of wooden roping, a wicker-filled porch where a wood sculpture of a shark hangs overhead, and a bathroom with a copper tub the size of a small pool and a separate shower stall, both with windows to the outdoors.

Good food and drink (from well-stocked, help-yourself bars) are among Twin Farms strong points. Guests meet at 7 o'clock for cocktails in a changing venue -- perhaps the wine cellar, one of the living rooms or, the night before our visit, in the Studio, the largest cottage. A set, four-course dinner is served at 8 in a baronial dining hall. The two chestnut tables for eight are flanked by Indiana hickory chairs with leather cane seats and seem strangely dwarfed by the vaulted ceilings and the fieldstone fireplaces at either end. Although the hefty 32-page, four-color book that serves as the inn's brochure says guests "are often inspired to dress for dinner," the reality is that more casual attire is encouraged.

The talented chef is Neil Wigglesworth, who came from The Point on Saranac Lake in the Adirondacks, a smaller but similarly grand inn that has perhaps been upstaged by Twin Farms. A typical dinner might start with medallions of lobster with avocado relish and angel-hair pasta, followed by warm red-cabbage salad with slices of smoked chicken. The main course could be veal mignon with timbales of wild rice and xeres sauce, and dessert, fresh figs with beummes de venese ice cream and peach-caramel sauce. Coffee, cheeses and a glass of aged port might round out the evening. One or the other of the Matthewses hosts the dinner each night.

A visit to the glittering new professional kitchen is instructive -- and Neil says he likes to have guests in to "talk and dabble." We enjoyed seeing the three different patterns of Wedgwood china (one each for breakfast, lunch and dinner), the pantry wall of table linens in every color and material -- there were about 25 sets of placemats and it was like being inside a well-stocked linen shop, the fiestaware used exclusively for picnics, the fine sterling-silver pieces and the glassware from Simon Pearce.

Breakfast is continental if taken in the guest rooms and cooked to order in the dining room from a small menu -- raspberry pancakes or eggs benedict with lobster the day we visited. The property is a registered American natural organic farm, and Neil and his kitchen staff of five make their own oils, vinegars, breads and preserves. some from the family of raspberry bushes planted by Dorothy Thompson 60 years earlier.

Lunch is a movable feast, depending on the day and guests' inclinations. It could be a sit-down meal in the dining room, a picnic anywhere, or a barbecue beside the inn's seven-acre Copper Pond or at its own ski area, where there's never a lineup for the pomalift. Afternoon tea is a presentation worthy of the

Ritz, complete, perhaps, with little gold leaves on one of the five kinds of tea pastries.

The pub, incidentally, is nearly a museum piece with its collection of beer bottles from around the world. Beer-bottle caps cover the light shades over the billiards table, outline the mirror and sconces above the fireplace, and cover the candlesticks on the mantel. Even a pub chair is dressed in beer caps -- a dramatic piece of pop art from the Twigg-Smiths' renowned art collection. Such are some of the delights and surprises encountered by guests at Twin Farms.

Doubles, $700 and $850; cottages, $850, $1,050 and $1,500. All-inclusive, except for 15 percent service charge and 8 percent state tax. Two-night minimum on weekends, three nights on holidays.

Woodstock Inn and Resort, 14 The Green, Woodstock, Vt. 05091. (802) 457-1100 or (800) 448-7900.

Sitting majestically back from the village green, the three-story, Vermont-white Woodstock Inn built by Rockresorts in 1969 replaces an older inn that was torn down. The lobby is warmed by a ten-foot-high stone fireplace, where in chilly weather guests congregate on sofas in front of the always-burning fire. Renovations and additions in 1989 and 1990 created a number of other cozy sitting areas, including an inviting library for card-playing and a rear wicker room where afternoon tea and cookies are served.

The 146 luxurious guest rooms are among the most comfortable in which we have stayed, with peppy color schemes, handmade quilts on the beds, upholstered chairs, TV sets, three-way reading lights, and large bathrooms and closets. Nightly turndown service brings chocolates and fresh, fluffy towels. Paintings and photographs of local scenes decorate the walls. The latest addition is the Tavern Wing, designed as three attached townhouses. It features 34 deluxe rooms with built-in bookcases and desks, fine cabinet work, mini-refrigerators, safes and double marble vanities in the bathrooms. Many come with fireplaces, and three have sitting-room porches overlooking the putting green.

Besides an eighteen-hole golf course, ten tennis courts, an outdoor pool and an indoor sports center, hundreds of acres of forests managed by the inn are available to guests for hiking, horseback riding and cross-country skiing. The woods also contain troves of fiddlehead ferns, morels and wild leeks, which the chef incorporates into his menus in season.

The glamorous main dining room is characterized by pillars, graceful curves and large windows onto a spacious outdoor terrace overlooking the putting green and gardens. Vases of lavish flowers, wine glasses and the inn's own monogrammed, green-rimmed china sparkle on crisp white linens. Off each side of the main room are smaller, more intimate dining areas.

Dinner entrées are priced from $18.25 for seared breast of capon with chanterelles to $22 for baked apple-smoked rack of lamb. Choices range from poached Atlantic salmon with asparagus and fennel salad and truffled potato pancakes to grilled veal chop with Maine crab meat, parmesan-cheese polenta and tomato fondue. Seasonal specialties include an appetizer of Green Mountain fiddlehead terrine, entrées of sautéed veal with Vermont cheddar cheese and fresh morels or roast loin of pork glazed in maple syrup with apple-prune stuffing, and a dessert of flambéed pineapple with maple syrup.

The elaborate Sunday buffet brunch for $16.95 is enormously popular and a good value.

You can dine quite reasonably in the **Eagle Cafe,** transformed from the old coffee shop and more attractive than most in both decor and fare. At lunch, we've enjoyed interesting salads — chef's, chilled bouillabaisse and seared tuna with wild rice, among them. Dinner entrées ($9 to $12) run from baked scrod to seared pork medallions oscar.

Linger with an after-dinner drink in the sophisticated **Richardson's Tavern**, as urbane a night spot as you'll find in Vermont. The inn's gift shop offers all kinds of suave country things.

Doubles, $135 to $255, EP; $205 to $325, MAP. Lunch, 11:30 to 2; dinner, 6 to 9; Sunday brunch, 11 to 1:30. Jackets required in dining room for dinner in season.

The Hanover Inn, Main Street, Box 151, Hanover, N.H. 03755. (603) 643-4300 or (800) 443-7024.

As its advertising claims, this venerable inn is really a "small, fine hotel." Facing the Dartmouth College green, the five-story, 19th-century brick structure has 92 Colonial-style rooms decorated with period furniture, handmade lampshades and eiderdown comforters.

The older East Wing has been remodeled to make the rooms larger and more comfortable, like those of the West Wing. An expanded lobby and a new front entrance are the latest in a continuing series of renovations that have helped make the inn the only four-diamond hotel and restaurant in New Hampshire.

Dining is in the formal Daniel Webster Room or the more intimate **Ivy Grill,** a most New Yorkish-looking spot. The two-level grill has a trendy and contemporary style with sleek lacquered chairs, track lighting, four murals of seasonal

Daniel Webster Room at Hanover Inn.

Dartmouth scenes, huge clay pots spilling over with ivy and Vermont-made hanging lamps.

Executive chef Michael Gray, whose credentials include Rarities in Cambridge and Seasons in Boston, oversees a menu of contemporary American cuisine, described as "simply prepared but with adventurous twists."

For dinner in the Ivy Grill, start with steamed dim sum with Thai peanut sauce, tuna carpaccio with angel-hair pasta and lime or crisp falafel with grilled pineapple and cucumber salad. Entrées ($11 to $16.50) include grilled yellowfin tuna with wontons and panzu sauce, lobster and crab ravioli with roasted-garlic butter, grilled veal chop with wild mushrooms and lemon-tarragon risotto, and grilled delmonico steak with vidalia onions and Sam Adams stout. Desserts could be white-chocolate/cashew cheesecake and apple crisp with whipped cream.

More formal meals are served in the gracious, gray and mauve **Daniel Webster Room,** a vast space in the Georgian style with potted palms, brass chandeliers and changing food displays at the entry. Standouts among dinner entrées ($17.75 to $21) are halibut wrapped in phyllo with scallop-herb mousse; grilled sweetbreads with arugula, hazelnuts and chick peas; roast duckling with currants, port and orange risotto; olive-crusted rack of lamb with roma tomatoes and garlic whipped potatoes, and grilled medallions of venison with a wild-rice cake.

Honored by Wine Spectator, the wine list is among New Hampshire's more extensive. The room also hosts a series of wine dinners with visiting chefs every other month.

In summer, meals from both restaurants are available on a shady outdoor terrace overlooking the Dartmouth green. Canvas umbrellas, planters and tiny white lights in the trees make it a most engaging spot.

Daniel Webster Room, lunch, Monday-Friday 11:30 to 1:30, dinner Tuesday-- Saturday 6 to 9; Sunday, brunch 11 to 1:30, buffet dinner, 5 to 8. Ivy Grill, open Monday-Saturday 11:30 to 10, Sunday 1:30 to 10. Doubles, $174; suites, $224.

The Quechee Inn at Marshland Farm, Clubhouse Road, Quechee, Vt. 05059. (802) 295-3133 or (800) 235-3133.

This handsomely situated, rambling white Vermont farmhouse was built in 1793 as the home of Vermont's first lieutenant governor. Since 1978 it has been an inn of comfort and distinction, renovated with care and attention to detail but providing comforts like modern baths and color TV in all 24 spacious, elegantly appointed rooms. Reproduction Queen Anne furniture, wing chairs, hooked rugs and several queensize canopy beds convey the feeling of an earlier age. So does the beamed and barnwood main living room with a fireplace and lounge area, lately expanded and a center of inn activity.

The main dining room in the original house is the essence of old Vermont with pegged floors, beamed ceiling, wood stove and lovely stenciled borders on the walls — a pattern repeated on the menu. White china, pink linens and three wine glasses at each place setting lend sophistication.

The changing menu might start with mussel chowder or cream of potato and watercress soup, smoked tuna loin on toasted baguette slices with roasted-pepper relish, artichoke and cheese raviolis on mixed greens or grilled Texas boar ribs marinated in maple-mango barbecue sauce. Entrées ($15 to $21) could be grilled free-range chicken with a crisp shiitake-mushroom and potato gallette, sautéed orange roughy, smoked pork chops with cannellini beans, roasted red peppers and corn, and roast rack of lamb served with butter flageolets and thyme. Fiddleheads and okra are featured vegetables in season.

French silk pie is the signature dessert. Other favorites are tirami su, bittersweet-chocolate terrine and frozen fruit soufflé. The lengthy wine list is reasonably priced and notable for its narrative descriptions.

Overnight guests help themselves to a full breakfast buffet in the main dining room. Coffee, tea and fruit breads are offered in the afternoon.

Dinner nightly, 6 to 9. Doubles, $148 to $198, MAP.

Lodging

The Jackson House at Woodstock, 37 Route 4 West, Woodstock 05091. (802) 457-2065.

It's hard to tell what we like best about the Jackson House: the marvelous guest rooms worthy of coverage in an antiques magazine, the sumptuous breakfasts, or the wine and champagne with fancy hors d'oeuvre in the early evenings.

No matter. You get them all when you stay in this three-story Victorian house, lovingly run by innkeepers Jack Foster and Bruce McIlveen, on three acres of grounds west of the village. Nine rooms and two suites, all with private baths, vary from French Empire to British Oriental to old New England. Each is eclectically furnished with such delights as an 1860 cannonball post bed, a

Casablanca ceiling fan, antique brass lamps on either side of the bathroom mirror, a marble-topped bedside table, a night table fashioned from an old sewing stand of tiger maple, steam radiators painted gold and handmade afghans coordinated to each room's colors.

Most prized are two new third-floor suites, about twice the size of the other rooms. Both contain queensize cherry sleigh beds, Italian marble baths and french doors onto a rear deck overlooking the new English gardens in back. We found plenty of room here to spread out, what with a leather sofa and an upholstered wing chair, plus two lounge chairs on the deck beyond. The mirrored, marble bathroom was absolutely sparkling as if it had never before been used -- an attribute that fellow guests agreed was characteristic of this special place.

The floors in each room are of different woods because the house was built by a sawmill owner — upon arrival you may be given fuzzy brown slippers so your shoes won't mar the floors. A lovely celadon collection is shown in a lighted stand at the top of the polished cherry staircase.

A harpist sometimes entertains as guests gather at 6 in the elegant parlor for champagne or wine and a buffet of hors d'oeuvre: in our case, homemade chicken-liver pâté with cognac, shrimp mousse and cambozola cheese.

In the morning, breakfast is served in the formal dining room around a Jacobean gate-leg table obtained from an English pub. Preliminaries are fresh juices and a choice of first courses, perhaps a melon plate with exotic fruits or bananas and cream with toasted almonds in summer, or a baked apple stuffed with mincemeat in a wine, rum and cream sauce in winter. The main event changes daily: the poached eggs on dill biscuits with smoked salmon and hollandaise sauce was the highlight of one of our best breakfasts ever. Other possibilities are zucchini omelets with Vermont cheddar, peppers, onions and mushrooms; french toast Santa Fe, deep-fried and puffed and served with whipped cream; chicken in champagne sauce with a poached egg on top; eggs grisante, scrambled with spinach and garlic and served in a ramekin with a cheese blintz, and a creole dish of fried eggplant with poached egg in a hot sauce. Always available are croissants, muffins and scones, and a big bowl of whipped cream sweetened with maple syrup — "cholesterol city," Jack calls it.

If, after all this, you can't move, settle into a deep wing chair in the adjacent library, shut the door, pick out an English classic to read and listen to the 1937 Zenith radio. You may still be there at dinner time, which is why the innkeepers hope eventually to offer gourmet dinners to house guests.

Doubles, $125 to $150; suites, $175 and $225. No smoking.

The Charleston House, 21 Pleasant St., Woodstock, Vt. 05091. (802) 457-3843.

Barbara and Bill Hough from Maryland run this handsome, 1835 Greek Revival townhouse, named for the hometown of its former owner. Although it's listed in the National Register of Historic Places and is elegantly furnished with period antiques and an extensive selection of art and oriental rugs, the Houghs don't consider this B&B a museum piece. Barbara, a former flight attendant, and Bill, a sales and marketing executive, are quite outgoing, and their absence is noted when they are out on one of their not-infrequent sailing cruises. An innkeeper runs their seven-room **Canterbury House** at 43 Pleasant St.

Stunning floral arrangements and grand needlepoint pillows adorn the dining room and the comfortable living room. All seven guest rooms have private baths and most have four-poster queensize beds. The rear Gables room, which holds

Sideboard is laden with goodies at Jackson House at Woodstock.

Barbara's childhood furniture, is the most popular, though honeymooners favor the Summer Kitchen room, downstairs in back with a private entrance.

Breakfasts here are such an attraction that Barbara put together a cookbook of her recipes, called *Breakfast at Charleston House* and available for $10. Among her specialties are puffed pancakes, "sort of like a popover and filled with fruit," a cheese and grits soufflé, and Charleston strata, an egg dish with sausage and apples. Other favorites are chipped-beef eggs, California omelet, and macadamia-nut waffles with papaya and strawberries.

Bill laughs when he tells the story of a new B&B owner on Cape Cod. She was frantic about what to serve for breakfast until a guest gave her Barbara's cookbook. Now, he says, her breakfasts are the talk of the Cape.

Doubles, $110 to $145. No smoking.

Quechee Bed & Breakfast, Route 4, Quechee, Vt. 05059. (802) 295-1776.

The front of this 1795 Colonial is smack up against the road. You'd never guess that the back is atop a cliff looking down onto the Ottauquechee River, with a wide sloping side lawn and a wraparound veranda taking full advantage. Susan and Ken Kaduboski, transplanted Boston accountants, converted it into a luxurious B&B, offering eight spacious, air-conditioned bedrooms with private baths.

Guests congregate in a large living/dining area with sofas gathered around a huge brick and granite fireplace, a television set and individual breakfast tables topped with dusky rose clothes and potted flowers. An interesting art collection is on display, and a large cactus stands in one corner.

A smaller parlor leads through heavy doors into the original house, where the guest quarters are nicely secluded and private. Three rooms are on the first floor and five on the second, including two with beamed, vaulted ceilings. Each is nicely furnished with king or queensize beds (one has twin mahogany sleigh beds), antique dressers, two wing chairs, large baths with colorful towels, and decorative touches like swags and stenciled lamp shades.

Susan serves a full breakfast starting with juices, baked apple or broiled grapefruit, and homemade Swedish breads with different jams. The main dish could be herbed scrambled eggs, apple pancakes or french toast stuffed with cream cheese and walnuts.

Doubles, $85 to $125. No smoking.

Gourmet Treats

The Woodstock area has a couple of good bakeries as well as two excellent farm markets. **Dunham Hill Bakery,** 61 Central St., is where local folks go for sensational baked goods -- anything from mocha torte to ganache cake to apple turnovers. You also can get a few breakfast and lunch items, the latter priced from $3.75 to $5.75. The sandwiches are fine, but the bowl of cream of potato and leek soup was so lukewarm we had to ask that it be reheated. **Chumley's Bakery** at 9 Main St., Quechee, right across the street from Simon Pierce, is a good place to pick up a sandwich. We liked one of lemon-pepper chicken and hickory ham with melted provolone and tomato, served on a basil roll with tomato and pepper-parmesan dressing. Or you could get a chocolate-almond croissant, a raspberry bear claw, or some of the colorful icebox cookies. There are a few tables where you can eat, or, better still, take out to have by the Quechee River.

Bet you've never heard the strains of Vivaldi's "Four Seasons" emanating from a farm stand. We did at **The Green Market,** Route 4, Quechee, a farm stand extraordinaire. Here is a trove of produce, coffee beans, specialty foods, breads, cheeses, clay pots and bird houses, to name a few.

Woodstock is chock full of elegant stores — just stroll along Central or Elm streets. The most fun shop of all is **F.H. Gillingham & Co.** at 16 Elm, a general store owned by the same family for more than a century and reputed to have been a favorite of Robert Frost's. It's now run by Jireh Swift Billings, great-grandson of the founder. His is an incredibly sophisticated and varied emporium, with everything from Lake Champlain chocolates to trapunto aprons (embroidered with blue jays, rabbits or squirrels). Fresh fruits (even baskets of lichee nuts) and vegetables, wines, cooking equipment, Vermont cheeses, Bennington pottery, dozens of mustards, cloudberry preserves from Scandinavia, Black Jewel American sturgeon caviar — you want to cook with it? They probably have it.

Next door is **The Village Butcher** with wines, a deli and gourmet items. Across the street is **Bentleys Coffee Bar and Florist Shop,** which has lovely flowers and twelve flavors of cappuccino, which you can drink at little marble tables amid the plants. **Aubergine,** a good kitchenware shop, is a few doors away. You'll probably find a thermos of the day's coffee flavor to sample, as well as a whole lineup of jams, relishes and salsas to try on various crackers. We particularly like the majolica pottery here. Another store not to miss is **Log Cabin Quilts,** where we fell in love with a calico hen on a wooden egg in a straw-filled coop. If you're looking for natural foods, head for **18 Carrots,** a market with deli at 47 Pleasant St.

The old mill built in Quechee has been turned into a nationally known glass blowing center and shop known as **Simon Pearce.** Simon Pearce, the Irish glass maker, moved here in 1981. It's worth a visit just to see how space is used in his tremendous mill, but it's also fascinating to watch the glass blowers by the fiery furnaces on the ground floor. You can see the water roar over the dam outside from a floor-to-ceiling window on the second floor, and you can buy seconds of the beautiful glass pieces (still expensive), pottery and woolens from Ireland. The table settings are to be admired. Shop is open daily, 9 to 9.

Pristine white facade of The Equinox is symbolic of Southern Vermont.

Southern Vermont
Old Inns, New Style

As verdant as the Green Mountains and as New England as they come. That's the area from Dover to Dorset, names that have an English ring to them, but that are the heart of old New England — or is it old New England, new style?

The fairly broad area embraces such storybook Vermont towns as Wilmington, Newfane, Weston and Manchester. It ranges from unspoiled Dorset, a hamlet almost too quaint for words, to changing West Dover, where condominiums and resorts thrive in the shadow of Mount Snow ski area.

This is a land of mountains and lakes, ski and summer resorts and, because of its fortuitous location for four-season enjoyment within weekend commuting distance of major metropolitan areas, a center for fine inns and restaurants.

The food is far more than Vermont cheddar cheese and maple syrup, as adventuresome diners have known for the last fifteen years or so. Some of the East's leading inns were established here before people elsewhere even thought of the idea. In an era in which new inns and B&Bs are popping up all over, many of those featured here have been around a while, the better to have established themselves in the vanguard of lodging and culinary success.

Two inns have set the standards for dining in Southern Vermont. They are at opposite ends of the area this chapter covers — The Inn at Sawmill Farm in West Dover and The Dorset Inn in Dorset.

In between are all kinds of interesting inns and chic country restaurants. The opportunities for good eating are legion.

Bed and Board

The Inn at Sawmill Farm, Route 100, Box 367, West Dover 05356. (802) 464-8131.

For a country inn, the Inn at Sawmill Farm is one of the most posh, sophisticated and luxurious, not to mention quiet and pretty, that we have seen. Owned by architect Rodney Williams, his interior-decorator wife Ione and their son Brill, who is the talented chef, it is the epitome of country elegance and a worthy member of Relais & Châteaux.

Admiring the old barn and farmhouse during ski expeditions to Mount Snow, the Williamses bought the property in 1967 and spent the next few years turning it into a decorator's dream.

The rates here are MAP and such that, for many, this is a special-occasion destination: up to $310 for a master bedroom in the inn and $310 to $350 for gorgeous suites with fireplaces in the outlying cottages. However, the value received in any of the 21 rooms is considerable — queen and kingsize beds, comfortable upholstered chairs with good reading lights, little gold boxes of Lake Champlain and Godiva chocolates, wonderful dinners, incredible breakfasts, even afternoon tea with nutbread and ginger cookies by the fire in the living room.

The large brick fireplace in the cathedral-ceilinged living room, festooned all around with copper pots and utensils, is the focal point for guests who gather on comfortable chintz-covered sofas and wing chairs and read magazines that are spread out on a gigantic copper table. Other groupings are near the huge windows, through which you get a perfect view of Mount Snow. Upstairs in a loft room are more sofas, an entire wall of books and the lone television set in the inn, which does not seem often to be in use. Anyway, the bedrooms are so cheery and deluxe that you may not want to leave such private, comfortable surroundings.

The three dining rooms are equally attractive and display the owners' collection of folk art. One, off the living room, also has a cathedral ceiling, with large wrought-iron chandeliers and Queen Anne-style chairs contrasting delightfully with barnwood and fabric walls. We like best the Greenhouse Room in back, with its indoor garden and rose-papered and beamed ceiling. In winter, you almost think you're outside; in summer, it opens onto the pool area.

You can pop into the small and cozy bar between the dining rooms for a drink before dinner; crackers and cheese are set out then. The dining rooms at night are dim and romantic: tables are set with heavy silver, candles inside hurricane chimneys, napkins in silver napkin rings, fresh flowers and delicate, pink-edged floral china. The waitresses are in long peasant-style dresses that match the wallpaper.

A large selection of appetizers and entrées awaits you. For non-house guests, the former are priced from $7.50 to $15 for delicacies like salmon terrine with fresh fruit and cucumber sauce, lobster savannah, stuffed quail with game sauce and beer-battered shrimp in pungent fruit sauce. The fifteen entrées are priced from $24 for chicken breasts française to $35 for loin of venison with poivrade sauce.

Guests are served a dish of celery and black and green olives on ice to begin (it seems an age since we've seen that) and a basket of good hot rolls and crisp homemade melba toast. That will hold you while you pick a wine from Brill Williams's remarkable and quite costly wine list (selected annually by Wine Spectator as one of the 100 best in the country and ranked in the top five in 1992 as winner of its Grand Award). The house wine is French, bottled specially for the inn, and the côtes du rhône rouge we tried has been acclaimed better than many a châteauneuf du pape. Prices rise steeply, with only a few in the high teens and low twenties. Those with a special interest can descend to the newly expanded wine cellars, where about 900 selections and 36,000 bottles reside. Brill says he does this "more as a hobby than a business," but manages to sell $4,000 to $6,000 worth of wine a week.

We liked an appetizer of thinly sliced raw sirloin with a shallot and mustard sauce and enjoyed the salads of crisp lettuce topped with blue cheese. Fresh

Main dining room at the Inn at Sawmill Farm is country elegant.

rabbit chasseur and sautéed sweetbreads were hearty autumn dishes, and the garnish of french-fried parsley on the sweetbreads was both unusual and delicious. Creamed salsify and onion with sautéed cucumber, squash stuffed with pinenuts and maple syrup, and wild-mushroom or spinach and tomato timbales might accompany the entrées, every presentation being different.

Game specialties -- of which Brill says he and co-chef James Hadley are doing more than in the past -- include pheasant, partridge and venison with a foie-gras sauce. A game consommé with diced smoked goose and marrow is sometimes on the fall soup list. Among seafood items are dover sole and poached halibut on a bed of leeks.

Dessert lovers will appreciate chocolate-whiskey cake with grand-marnier sauce, fresh raspberry tart, bananas romanoff, coconut cake and ice cream with chocolate-butternut sauce. Coffee lovers will like the strong espresso or better-than-usual decaffeinated coffee served in a silver pot.

Breakfast lovers will be in their glory in the sun-drenched greenhouse, watching chickadees at the bird feeders and choosing from all kinds of fruits, oatmeal and fancy egg dishes (eggs buckingham is a wonderful mix of eggs, sautéed red and green peppers, onions and bacon seasoned with dijon mustard and worcester-shire sauce, placed on an English muffin and topped with Vermont cheddar cheese and baked). Scrambled eggs might come with golden caviar, and poached eggs with grilled trout. The Vermont breakfast includes poached eggs and apples baked in maple syrup served over smoked ham. Don't pass up the homemade tomato juice; thick and spicy, it serves as a base for the inn's peppy bloody marys.

Dinner nightly by reservation, 6 to 9. Jackets required. Doubles, $290 to $350, MAP. Closed Thanksgiving to mid-December.

The Dorset Inn, Church and Main Streets, Dorset 05251. (802) 867-5500.

Built in 1796 and the oldest continually operating inn in Vermont, The Dorset Inn has been nicely upgraded in both lodging and meals by innkeepers Sissy Hicks and Gretchen Schmidt.

All 35 rooms on the two upper floors have been redone with wall-to-wall carpeting, modern baths with wood washstands, lovely print wallpapers and antique furnishings. A handsome collection of blue glass is displayed in lighted cases at the top of the stairway.

Dressed-up bears in the lobby greet guests, who have use of a sitting room with comfortable furniture around a fireplace. Vermont-woven mats top wood tables in a cheery breakfast room, its green floral curtains framing small-paned windows that extend to the floor. Out back is a pleasant tavern with a large oak bar and a pub menu that is favored by locals.

The main dining room has been redecorated in hunter green with white trim and wainscoting. A focal point is a spotlit glass cabinet displaying cups and horse figurines along one wall. It's an elegant setting for what Gretchen calls "a very serious new menu." Chef Sissy, a practitioner of the new American cuisine, has joined the previously separate tavern and dining-room menus into one that serves both areas. Now you'll find a classic burger ($7.50) on the same menu as veal medallions with lemon-lime-cilantro brown sauce, potato and vegetables ($18.50), to say nothing of spicy chicken wings and crisp potato skins with the "original warm chicken tenderloin salad." Five vegetarian items, including garbanzo croquettes and wild-mushroom sandwich, also are available.

Folks who remember the traditional experience in the dining room may not love the change, for the perception of fine dining has been diminished. Those who found the tavern too noisy, however, like to be able to order light fare in the more tranquil dining room.

We found the smoked-trout mousse with avocado sauce and a few slices of melba toast a fine appetizer, big enough for two to share. Other choices include warm Vermont goat cheese on a bed of wilted spinach with sundried-tomato toast and steamed mussels in a garlic-leek-wine broth with garlic toast.

How could we pass up the calves liver ($14.50), which we'd heard was the best anywhere? Served rare with crisp bacon and slightly underdone slices of onion, it was superb. The fresh trout ($15.50), deboned but served with its skin still on, was laden with braised leeks and mushrooms. These came with a medley of vegetables, including red-skin potatoes with a dollop of sour cream and crisp cauliflower, broccoli and yellow squash.

Among delectable desserts are fruit pies, bread pudding with whiskey sauce, white-chocolate cheesecake with raspberry sauce and -- when did you last see this on a menu? -- tapioca with whipped cream. We chose a kiwi sorbet, wonderfully deep flavored and with the consistency of ice cream, accompanied by a big sugar cookie.

The inn serves a hearty, prix-fixe breakfast and interesting lunches -- tuna and herb bruschetta, welsh rarebit, baked eggplant crêpes and apple-smoked chicken ($6 to $9.50), with enough selection to appeal one fall day a few years ago to all in our party of seven youngsters and adults.

Lunch daily in summer and fall, 11:30 to 2; dinner nightly, 5:30 to 9. Doubles, $130 to $175, MAP.

The Reluctant Panther, West Road, Box 678, Manchester Village 05254. (802) 362-2568 or (800) 822-2331.

Creature comforts. Fine food. Urbane atmosphere. Intimate setting.

Innkeepers Robert and Maye Bachofen have made the most of these attributes, parlaying the venerable Reluctant Panther into one of the great small inns of the Northeast since they took over in 1988.

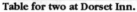

Table for two at Dorset Inn.   **Dining area at Reluctant Panther.**

Creature comforts they provide aplenty in twelve rooms in the main inn, striking for its purple facade with yellow trim, and in four suites in the stark-white Mary Porter House next door. All rooms have air-conditioning, private baths, TVs and telephones. Ten come with fireplaces and all but two with twins have king or queensize beds. During our tenure in the Seminary Suite we were enveloped in privacy and comfort, although we would have liked to have been able to open some of the windows on all sides to let in that fresh Vermont air and we rued the lack of good reading lights in the places we wanted to read, namely the sofa and the armchair. The bathroom was deluxe, though not quite as showy as the one we'd observed earlier in a suite downstairs. That has a double jacuzzi in the center of one of the largest bathrooms we've seen, with a fireplace opposite, two pedestal sinks and a separate shower. "If you ever find another room like this, you tell me," Maye said proudly -- and we haven't. Sparkly Maye, who hails from Peru, has redecorated most of the rooms in a mix of styles, each with splashy wallpapers, fabrics and window treatments, and goose down comforters on the beds.

Guests find a half-bottle of Robert Mondavi red wine in their room upon arrival. That's a mere preliminary to what's to come in the attractive dining room, crisply dressed in white linens and fine china, and harboring a solarium at one end. Chef John McMillan changes his ambitious menu daily. His fare is so highly regarded that fully two-thirds of the diners, on average, are not house guests.

The room was full and pleasantly vibrant the Monday night we were there. An amuse-gueule -- lobster salad in a hollowed-out cucumber slice -- preceded our appetizers, an excellent terrine of pheasant with sundried-cherry chutney and an assertive caesar salad topped with three spicy grilled shrimp. For main courses ($14.95 to $22), we enjoyed the medallions of New Zealand venison finished with green peppercorns and Beefeater gin and, one of the chef's favorites, the fricassee of Vermont rabbit with local chanterelles and pearl onions -- good but rather rich and too much to eat. An array of new potatoes, sautéed baby carrots, broccoli and zucchini accompanied. Among the delectable desserts ($4.95) were a fan of fresh berries in sparkling wine around homemade apricot sherbet and fresh plums baked in a light cointreau custard. Innkeeper Robert, who is Swiss and who has extensive background in the food and beverage business, expertly oversees a dining room in which the ambiance is sophisticated and the service friendly but flawless. He has put together an exceptional, and quite reasonable, wine list.

Robert and Maye serve breakfast at round marble tables topped with floral mats in a fireplaced breakfast room. Fresh orange juice, a baked apple stuffed with nuts and raisins, and corn muffins preceded a plate of blueberry pancakes topped with powdered sugar and garnished with blueberries, blackberries and raspberries.

We left feeling well fed and well taken care of. The New Yorkers who make up much of the inn's clientele consider the experience quite a bargain.

Dinner, Thursday-Monday from 6; weekends only in off-season. Doubles, $175 to $195, MAP; suites, $210 to $250, MAP.

The Four Columns Inn, 230 West St. on the Common, Box 278, Newfane 05345. (802) 365-7713.

From a restauraeuring family in Manhattan and New Jersey, Jacques Allembert has taken to rural Vermont and this venerable inn with enthusiasm. His head chef, Gregory Parks, sous chef under former owner Rene Chardain, has had free rein in the kitchen since the beginning and has a reputation for inventiveness.

The dining room is in a white building behind the white clapboard structure containing guest rooms and the four pillars that give the inn its name. With beamed ceilings and a huge fireplace, the dining room is country charming and full of antiques and folk art. Fresh white organdy curtains and pink tablecloths topped with white overcloths add to the country look. Each table bears different flowers and different service plates.

Behind the dining room is a super lounge, with an old French pewter bar, decorated with things like calico hens. Cider was simmering in a crock pot here on one autumn visit. An armoire displays wines.

The dinner menu is supplemented by blackboard specials. "Greg's an artist," says Jacques of his chef, "so the menu is constantly changing."

Starters ($5.50 to $9) might include smoked-salmon and horseradish mousse served cold with sliced smoked salmon, grilled sweetbreads and artichoke bottoms with fried polenta and chipotle mayonnaise, and lobster raviolette with sundried tomato, olive oil and parmesan. Seasonal soups could be leek and onion with herbed biscuits or potato and spinach with shrimp and green-chile salsa.

Entrées run from $19 for grilled chicken breast and spicy Tuscan sausage with roasted garlic and goat cheese to $24 for filet mignon with bourbon-peppercorn cream sauce or loin of venison with juniper and mushroom demi-glace. Others could be bouillabaisse, broiled salmon with ginger and soy or curried shrimp with white basmati rice, warm greens and pineapple yogurt.

Jacques's wife Pam, who does the changing desserts, has become known for her chocolate pâté. Other favorites are apple-spice cake with cappuccino ice cream and caramel sauce, hazelnut layer cake with mocha cream, tirami su, and homemade sorbets and ice creams. You can stop in the lounge to enjoy one from the cart, even if you haven't dined at the inn.

All fifteen guest rooms have private baths, most have king or queensize beds, and all are decorated colorfully with hooked rugs, handmade afghans and quilts. Room 3, with a four-poster bed, comes with a jacuzzi for two in a marble

French country look prevails at Four Columns Inn in Newfane.

bathroom that's larger than the bedroom. Another favorite is the third-floor hideaway, with trim of old wood and Laura Ashley fabrics in shades of deep rusts. It has a canopied bed set into an alcove, plush beige carpeting and a sitting room with a private porch overlooking the Newfane green. A center chimney that divides the room gives it unusual spaces.

The Allemberts put out what he calls "a healthy, new age, country breakfast" for overnight guests. The buffet table contains lots of fresh fruit, yogurt, homemade granola, hot oatmeal in winter and an assortment of homemade muffins, scones and datenut breads. The inn also has a swimming pool, trout pond, lovely gardens and spacious lawns on which to relax in "real country-auberge style," says Jacques.

Dinner nightly except Tuesday, 6 to 9. Doubles, $100 to $120; suites, $140 to $175. No smoking.

Windham Hill Inn, West Townshend 05359. (802) 874-4080 or (800) 944-4080.

Gourmet dining is a major part of the appeal of this elegant but remote inn out in the middle of nowhere on a hill overlooking the West River Valley. Once there, you tend to stay there, which is why new innkeepers Griggs and Pat Markham go out of their way to make their guests' stays satisfying.

Six-course dinners are served nightly at 7 to guests and, increasingly, the public, as the new innkeepers put to best use their new Colorado-trained chef, Mark Martin, and plan to expand the dining room. Guests gather first for hors d'oeuvre and drinks with the innkeepers in the parlor. Then they adjourn to large tables in the main dining room or to tables for two in the Frog Pond Room looking onto the pond and lawns.

Dinner at our latest visit began with a sauté of smoked game hen and pasta, chilled peach bisque, cilantro-dill spice bread and a salad of mixed greens with blue-cheese vinaigrette. An orange sorbet over raspberry sauce preceded the main course, broiled halibut with smoked mussel and sweet-pepper cream sauce,

235

paired with forest-mushroom risotto, snap peas and sweet corn. A dessert of fresh figs, mangos and raspberries with grand marnier finished the leisurely meal.

The chef's repertoire for entrées that week included roast stuffed quail with spinach and mushrooms, coconut sole amandine, roast loin of venison with Indian pudding, fillet of salmon with beurre rouge and hazelnut-encrusted rack of lamb. With a pending expansion of the dining room, the owners were thinking about adding more selections to the menu and extending the dinner hours.

Griggs is proud of his wine selection, about 35 good choices, and mixes drinks in his small service-bar area, which has a victrola. A pleasant back room with wicker furniture offers a wood stove, television and a game table, as well as wonderful views of the surrounding hills.

Small decanters of sherry are in each of the fifteen spacious guest rooms, all with private baths. They're furnished with a panache that merited a six-page photo spread in Country Decorating magazine. Among the most popular are the five rooms fashioned from nooks and alcoves in the White Barn annex, particularly the two sharing a large deck overlooking the mountains.

Full breakfasts are served amid a background of taped chamber music, antique silver and crystal: fresh orange juice in champagne flutes, breakfast breads and fresh fruits, and a main dish like french toast, eggs mornay or griddle cakes shaped like little doughnuts, made of winter wheat and cornmeal.

Neighbor Taffy Morgan offers gourmet picnics. She picks guests up in a horse-drawn buggy and takes them into the forest where the picnic of their choice awaits (for about $75 a couple).

Doubles, $160 to $180, MAP. No smoking.

The Barrows House, Route 30, Dorset 05251. (802) 867-4455.

After six years of upgrading by the previous owners, Jim and Linda McGinnis took over a going concern when they acquired this well-regarded hostelry in 1993.

The dining room is country-pretty with Pierre Deux wallpaper and tables set with white Mountain Weavers cloths over country-checked rust undercloths. We're partial to the lower greenhouse addition that makes you feel you're almost outdoors. Ken Paquin, former executive chef at The Equinox in Manchester, moved to the kitchen here in the fall of 1993. He retained the inn's culinary style, particularly the emphasis on vegetables for which the Barrows House has long been known, although he did introduce lighter and fruitier sauces.

Our dinner began with smoked tuna with caper and red-onion crème fraîche and a tartelette of smoked scallops and mussels with scallions and red peppers, both excellent. Maine crab cakes and a smoked-chicken and garlic flan with roasted peppers and shiitake mushrooms on tomato coulis were other choices. A small loaf of bread and a garden salad with a honey-mustard dressing came next.

Among eight entrées ($14.95 to $19.95), we liked the sirloin of beef with four-peppercorn sauce and the calves liver with caramelized onions and smoked bacon. They were accompanied by a platter of vegetables served family style, on this occasion spaghetti-squash creole, lemon-scented broccoli, carrot puree with maple syrup, and risotto with fennel and red peppers. Grilled swordfish on sweet-pea puree, pan-roasted Norwegian salmon in a hazelnut-mustard crust, pork tenderloin with oranges and raisins, and grilled quail on peanut fried brown rice could be on the summer menu.

A huckleberry tart and wonderful cappuccino ice cream were winners from the changing dessert list, which also included triple-chocolate cake with strawberry/grand-marnier sauce, walnut lace cup with orange mousse and cantaloupe sorbet.

Off the dining room is a cozy tavern dressed in white and hunter green, its trompe-l'oeil walls of books so real you think you're in a library. The light menu in the $8.75 to $12 range is supplemented by specials like blackened salmon with yellow-pepper butter.

Besides the dining room and tavern, the 200-year-old main house has a fireplaced living room and six upstairs guest rooms. Scattered about eleven acres of park-like grounds (with swimming pool, tennis courts and gazebo) are twenty-two more rooms and suites in eight outbuildings, five with sitting rooms and five with fireplaces. All are filled with nice touches like ruffled pillows and the attractive patchcraft hangings of local artist Joan Stewart Neave.

Dinner nightly, 6 to 9 (no tavern menu on Saturday). No smoking in dining room. Doubles, $170 to $230, MAP.

The Hermitage, Coldbrook Road, Wilmington 05365. (802) 464-3511.

You arrive atop a hill via a dirt road past Haystack Mountain ski area. You hear the quacking of ducks and the squawking of geese as you enter the inn. You can fish in the trout pond, watch a lively group of game birds in their pens, visit the wine and gift shop, and study the bottles that comprise New England's largest wine list (more than 2,000 selections).

This is the Hermitage, an expanded restaurant-turned-inn that reflects the diverse inclinations of its owner, Jim McGovern. The renowned restaurant was almost overshadowed by Jim's other pursuits — from the raising of game birds and English setters to the making of maple syrup and jams to the selling of rare wines (as well as a bathtub full of tiny Riunite bottles for 75 cents). That is, it ran the risk of being overshadowed until he built an enormous addition that now houses the main dining room, luxurious with upholstered and wing chairs around well-spaced tables set with white linens and blue overcloths, fresh flowers, heavy silver and white china. High ceilings, shelves of hand-carved decoys, a grand piano and walls covered with the prints of Michel Delacroix complete the scene. A wreath made of corks graces one wall of the adjacent lounge, where the innkeeper presides in a party atmosphere. Decoys are everywhere (filling a new gallery at the entrance), and be advised that some of the fifteen setters may be underfoot, even in the dining room.

A special treat is the Hermitage's weekend brunch. We were seated on the sun porch, an intimate room with white wrought-iron chairs at five tables looking onto a marble patio, enjoying the view of the pond and distant hills. The award-winning wine list, a black-bound, typeset affair, details more than 500 varieties. The choice is staggering: eleven pages of California cabernets, six of chardonnays. Prices start in the teens and many are in the triple figures.

Although we were sorry that the Hermitage's famed game-bird entrées were lacking on the brunch menu, we made do with a rich game pâté on toast triangles as well as a house specialty, four mushroom caps stuffed with caviar and garnished with a pimento slice and chopped raw onion on a bed of ruby lettuce ($6 and $6.50 respectively as appetizers). The highlight was a chicken salad ($7.95), an ample plateful colorfully and deliciously surrounded by a melange of sliced oranges, apples, green melon, strawberries, grapes and tomatoes on a bed of bibb lettuce. Other choices include eggs benedict, trout and eggs, hunters stew, and schinken und spiegelei ($7 to $14.95). The portions were substantial enough that we passed up the desserts — a hot Indian pudding that a couple at the next table pronounced the best they'd had, a maple parfait made with Hermitage syrup and, surprisingly for a fall day, fresh strawberries on a homemade shortcake.

At night, the limited, unchanging and dated menu is supplemented by game specialties. The nine entrées include boneless trout supreme, shrimp, frog's legs provençal, chicken amandine, wiener schnitzel and steak, priced from $14 to $25. Understated on the menu, the presentation can be superb, though some recent diners report the kitchen is slipping.

The same criticism, we've heard, may apply to the housekeeping in the fifteen guest rooms in the main 18th-century farmhouse, the converted carriage house and the new Wine House. All have private baths, telephones and working fireplaces. Rooms are generally large and modern, and furnished with antiques.

Men in particular appreciate the Hermitage experience, and that's what it is. To know it, you have only to view the maple-syrup shed, in which Jim McGovern also produces more than 10,000 jars of preserves (one of them an unusual maple jelly), and the outdoor pens — an aviary of wild turkeys, ducks and peacocks reflecting every color of the rainbow.

Dinner nightly, 5 to 11; weekend brunch, 11 to 3 in winter, Sunday only rest of year. Doubles, $200 to $225, MAP.

The Red Shutter Inn, Route 9, Box 636, Wilmington. (802) 464-3768 or (800) 845-7548.

This hostelry nicely blends the old and new: a main Colonial house and adjacent carriage house dating to 1894, a homey restaurant, and contemporary rooms and amenities.

The blend was achieved by Max and Carolyn Hopkins, who took over in 1987 and began three years of upgrading. The five rooms in the main house have queen or kingsize beds with private baths. The burgundy showing through a crocheted white bedspread is repeated in the wallpaper in one of the handsomely decorated rooms. We like best the rear two-room suite with fireplaced sitting room, vaulted ceiling and bay window, its bedroom with queensize brass bed and full-length windows opening onto a private deck.

Also impressive are the four rooms in the reborn carriage house, especially the fireplaced suite with queensize bed, sitting room with loveseat and armchair, and a bathroom with two-person jacuzzi beneath a skylight. A vintage radio here is juxtaposed beside a new color TV.

Comfortable as the accommodations are, it is dining for which the Red Shutter is best known, thanks to chef Kevin Howard. He has worked alone in the inn's small, homey kitchen since 1983 through three sets of innkeepers, preparing up to 80 dinners on busy nights. The pine-paneled main dining room is appropriately Vermonty with shelves of books, caneback chairs, cloth mats and candlelight. Tables in the narrow back room sport floral cloths, and there's a canopied outdoor dining deck in front.

The changing blackboard menu lists entrées from $13 for scrod au gratin to $23 for prime black-angus filet mignon. Among the dozen possibilities might be grilled Norwegian salmon with dill butter, trout meunière, chicken marsala, loin lamb chops with mint jelly and, on Saturday nights, prime rib. Accompaniments the night we were there were broccoli with cheese sauce, oven-roasted potatoes and butternut squash (so good that a guest from Texas phoned afterward for the recipe). Guests design their own salads by checking off ingredients on a note

Table for two at the Hermitage.   Dining area at Four Chimneys.

pad. The sweet-and-sour house dressing was requested so frequently that the inn has started bottling it for sale.

Appetizers are limited, perhaps french onion or celery soup, shrimp cocktail, cajun shrimp and mushroom caps stuffed with crab meat. The same for desserts: apple crisp, blueberry and apple cobbler, Ben & Jerry's ice cream. The 60-bottle wine list is Max Hopkins's pride and joy, and the bar off the cozy living room operates on the honor system.

Inn guests partake of a hearty breakfast, including scrambled eggs with choice of meat and homefries, french toast or apple pancakes.

Dinner, Tuesday-Sunday 6 to 9, July-September; Wednesday-Saturday in winter. Doubles, $95; suites, $108 to $165. Closed April and most of May.

The Four Chimneys Inn and Restaurant, 21 West Road (Route 9), Old Bennington 05201. (802) 447-3500.

Thanks to Alex Koks, one of Southern Vermont's premier chefs, the Four Chimneys has been restored to its heyday of the 1950s and 1960s. At our latest visit, he had all the necessary zoning permits for a long-planned expansion of overnight facilities and a contraction of the dining facility.

One of the two former dining rooms was being converted into two handicapped-accessible suites. Four more deluxe rooms, all but one with a fireplace and all with jacuzzis, were being fashioned from two outbuildings on the ten-acre property. That would raise the total to twelve guest rooms, and make this as much an inn as a restaurant. The six commodious guest rooms we saw were bright and airy in off-white and rose colors, three with fireplaces and porches and two with jacuzzis. Continental breakfast is delivered on a tray to one's room or served in the restaurant.

Alex planned to reduce the seating from 160 to 96, concentrating dining in the

239

old lounge which was to be expanded and moving the bar into a second former dining room, where the west porch opens onto restored gardens. The rooms are beautifully appointed in shades of pale mauve, pink and rose, from the velvet seats of the chairs to the brocade draperies and matching panels on the walls, the heavy linens and the carnations on the mantel above the fireplace. Flickering oil lamps in hurricane globes and classical background music complete the romantic, formal atmosphere for what Alex calls "estate dining in a park-like setting."

Even the scaled-down restaurant facility remains bigger than the Village Auberge, his former hostelry in Dorset. But Dutch-born Alex and his partner, Andra Erickson, are up to the challenge.

A weekday lunch showed chef Alex at his best. The creamed spinach soup and an order of home-cured gravlax were simple and superb, while the roast quail came with a complex brown game sauce, wild rice and a side dish of asparagus scented with nutmeg. Hazelnut-praline mousse in a chocolate shell and a trio of refreshing sorbets (raspberry, blueberry and strawberry) ended a memorable lunch for two for under $30.

The French fare with a touch of nouvelle continues at dinner, when entrées run from $14.50 for sautéed spicy sirloin with red-onion preserve to $21.50 for rack of lamb, the chef's specialty. Other choices could be poached salmon with an herb sauce, veal chop with morels, roast duckling with amarena cherries and beef wellington for two. Good sourdough bread and salad with a champagne vinaigrette come with. Creamed fennel and celery root with rice or a creamy swirl of pureed and rebaked potato might accompany.

Dinner is preceded by complimentary cheese fritters, a Koks trademark. To begin, go for Alex's oft-requested cream of mustard soup, duck pâté with cognac in puff pastry or duck salad. A new section of the menu labeled "lighter fare" includes shrimp and fettuccine, chicken julienne and salmon quenelles with scallops, $9.25 to $12.50. A chocolate marquise with raspberry sauce, peach cheesecake, frozen chocolate-mocha parfait torte, Bailey's Irish Cream cake and those sparkling sorbets are among desserts ($4.50).

Lunch, July-October, Tuesday-Saturday noon to 2; dinner, Monday-Saturday from 5; Sunday, brunch noon to 2, dinner 2 to 9. Doubles, $100 to $175.

The Equinox, Route 7A, Manchester Village 05254. (802) 362-4700 or (800) 362-4747.

In a class by itself is the grand old Equinox, a resort hotel dating to 1769 and renovated to the tune of $20 million in 1985 and another $12 million in 1992. The last finishing touches were applied by a partnership whose majority owner is Guinness, the beer company that owns the noted Gleneagles Hotel in Scotland. The hotel was closed for three months in 1992 to correct shortcomings in the previous renovation. This one, which really made a difference, involved all 141 guest rooms and eleven suites, a new lobby, a vastly expanded Marsh Tavern and the formal Colonnade dining room.

The classic, columned white hotel now opens into a world of lush comfort, starting with a dramatic, two-story lobby with a view of Mount Equinox, converted from what had been nine guest rooms. All bedrooms have been winterized, equipped with modern baths, TVs and telephones, and dressed in light pine furniture, new carpeting, and coordinated bedspreads and draperies. Rooms come in four sizes (standard, superior, deluxe and premium), and anything less than deluxe may be a letdown.

The former lobby gave way to the **Marsh Tavern,** now rich and attractive in dark green, red and black. The tavern is four times as big as before with a handsome bar and well-spaced tables flanked by windsor and wing chairs and loveseats. We found it too bright one winter's night with lights right over our heads, although the hostess said that was a new one on her -- most folks thought the place too dark. We also found the dinner menu rather pricey and lacking in depth, given that it was the only restaurant open in the hotel that evening. Witness a caesar salad with a few baby shrimp for $7, a simple tossed salad for $5, a good lamb stew with potato gratin for $10 (it was called shepherd's pie but wasn't) and a small roasted cornish game hen for $13.50. With a shared cranberry-walnut torte and a bottle of Hawk's Crest cabernet for $21, a simple supper for two turned into something of an extravagance for $70. Our reaction, we should point out, does not seem to be shared by the loyal clientele, who sing the plaudits of the tavern and its food priced from $8 for a burger to $16 for planked salmon.

The barrel-vaulted ceiling in the enormous **Colonnade** dining room was stenciled by hand by a latter-day Michelangelo who lay on his back on scaffolding for days on end. It's suitably formal for those who like to dress for dinner and pay $18.50 to $24 for the likes of veal ribeye steak with wild-mushroom sauce and garlic mashed potatoes or roasted Vermont pheasant with mushroom compote and turnips. The short menu details such appetizers as essence of lobster soup, chilled smoked-seafood assiette and a warm terrine of lobster and sweetbreads with leek and cucumber relish. Desserts include chocolate/grand-marnier cake, a trio of cheesecakes with berries and raspberry-lemon pavé with coconut anglaise.

Work off the calories at the spa in an adjacent building, which contains a pool, steam rooms, an exercise room with Nautilus equipment, massage therapy, aerobics programs, the works -- and spa packages to match. The challenging Gleneagles Golf Course has been improved as well, and we're told there's no better setting for a summer's lunch than the Dormy Grill in the clubhouse.

"Stately" is the word that comes to mind every time we visit this imposing hotel. The golfers and conventioneers who seem to frequent it most certainly like it.

Marsh Tavern: Lunch, Monday-Saturday noon to 2; dinner nightly, 6 to 9:30. Colonnade: Dinner nightly at peak periods, 6 to 9:30; weekends only, rest of year; Sunday brunch, 11 to 2:30. Doubles, $145 to $260, EP; suites, $325 to $475. Add $50 per person for MAP, $70 per person for full AP.

Wilburton Inn, River Road, Manchester 05254. (802) 362-2500 or (800) 648-4944.

A winding drive past stone walls leads up a hillside to the imposing porte cochere of this baronial red-brick mansion, billed as a "grand country estate — 1902." Away from the hubbub, the setting overlooking the Battenkill Valley could not be more serene. Under the auspices of owners Georgette and Albert Levis, the inn has become a year-round resort with a good dining room.

The rich, dark decor of carved mahogany paneling, moldings, beamed ceilings, fancy brass doorknobs and leaded windows is enhanced by oriental rugs and fine art. Many of the ten rooms in the main inn are spacious and of the old school with enormous bathrooms and walk-in closets. Georgette has redecorated in contemporary peach and teal tones some of the 25 rooms in outlying buildings that she calls villas. A local artist painted the murals that enliven two of the bathrooms in one eight-room cottage. The twenty acres include a heated swimming pool, hiking trails and tennis courts.

Sliding doors off the entry hall on the mansion's main floor lead to an enormous living room, with seating areas for enjoying all the magazines, the wood-burning stove in front of the fireplace and piano music on weekends. Breakfast is served in the summery Terrace Room with wrought-iron tables on a tile floor. A stone terrace just beyond is where you can sit and look over a spectacular view of valley and mountains.

One small dining room has a blue tiled fireplace and cabbage rose wallpaper. The larger Billiard Room evokes an English clubby feel with its green leather chairs, dark paneling and crisp white linens.

For appetizers ($3.75 to $7.25), we enjoyed the house pâté and escargots with sambuca and garlic on a bed of spinach. Next came a selection of breads, including date and sourdough (but not focaccia, which we expected from the menu listing), and a green salad with choice of five dressings, good creamy sweet red pepper and garlic-cracked peppercorn among them.

Entrées range from $15.75 for sautéed chicken with fine herbs to $26 for braised veal chop with morel demi-glace. The breast of local smoked duckling served with maple-glazed apple slices tasted amazingly like ham. It was delicious, as was the roast rack of lamb in a romano-breadcrumb crust, served with a mint-pesto sauce. Both were surrounded by unusually interesting vegetables: green beans with almonds, carrots, creamy potatoes and stuffed tomatoes.

The kitchen also has a way with desserts, including a wonderful apple crisp with ginger ice cream, melon or raspberry sorbet, chocolate-walnut pie and profiteroles. The wine list, heavy on Californias, is attractively priced.

A complimentary full breakfast is served to inn guests. The menu lists all the usual dishes, plus corned-beef hash with poached egg. Afternoon tea is served from 4 to 5.

Although this is a gracious inn with a tranquil sense of grandeur, Georgette does not want it to be too formal or uptight. She curtailed the traditional jackets-only policy after 5 p.m. and aimed for an affordable price structure.

Dinner nightly, 6 to 9. Doubles, $95 to $155.

The Inn at Long Last, Main Street, Box 589, Chester 05143. (802) 875-2444.

The route to Jack Coleman's "inn at long last" was circuitous. The former president of Haverford College and of a New York charitable foundation, he caused a stir when his book, *Blue Collar Journal,* traced his experiences as a garbage man, short-order cook and ditch digger. He later worked on a Southern chain gang, served as a voluntary inmate in five prisons and as a guard in two others, and lived with the homeless in Manhattan during a record cold spell. He finds that running an inn is the most difficult challenge he has encountered so far.

Patrons at the 30-room hostelry he opened in 1986 in the abandoned Chester Inn facing the village green would never guess. "The inn displays the story of my life," remarked the man who always wanted an inn and tirelessly transformed a rundown building into a showcase for his personality and memorabilia. "My son told me, 'Dad, this is just your apartment made larger.'"

Indeed, the furnishings from his New York apartment have plenty of room to spread out in the three-story inn. All the rooms are named for either an aspect of Jack Coleman's life, authors he admires or famous Vermont personages. They are decorated accordingly, from the Fair Winds Farm Room reflecting his best friends in his native Ontario to the Grand Opera Room in which framed opera programs adorn the walls. They vary considerably, but all are endearingly charming and all have private baths.

Green Mountains provide scenic backdrop for Wilburton Inn.

Cocktails are served in a fireplaced parlor that holds Jack's personal library, including a collection of travel magazines shelved as in a periodical room and "the largest collection of books on prisons of any inn in Vermont," he quips. The main living room houses illuminated shelves of miniature soldiers, mostly marching bands, arranged in a dozen European scenes.

The mirrored back of a twelve-foot-long bar obtained from a razed Maine hotel is the focal point of the dining room, in which a changing menu of regional American cuisine is offered by adventuresome chef Michael Williams, whose reach includes the offbeat.

The dinner menu changes seasonally. It began at our summer visit with beef bouillon with fresh peas and aioli crouton and chilled gazpacho with cilantro cream and tortilla sticks. Other starters ($4 to $7) were smoked-salmon mousse wrapped in a dill crêpe with chive beurre blanc, spicy lamb and goat cheese baked in phyllo with minted yogurt, and Gulf shrimp and pancetta with grilled pineapple relish and black mignonette.

The seven entrées are $12.50 to $18.50 for the likes of catfish with black bean sauce and corn-okra relish, hazelnut-crusted pork loin chop with papaya and tangerine, veal roulades with sundried tomatoes and enoki mushrooms, and grilled ribeye steak with roasted shallot-garlic ragout. The Vermont lamb might be roasted with fresh thyme and Vermont goat cheese or grilled with caramelized pistachios. A green salad with a secret dressing, sourdough rolls and vegetables accompany.

Banana or pumpkin-ginger cheesecake, Williamsburg orange cake, blueberry pie and almond-pecan tarts are among the luscious desserts. The innkeeper's favorite, although he cannot always prevail upon the chef, remains a Shaker lemon pie made with whole lemons. The short wine list is affordably priced.

Jack prepares the breakfasts, taken in a sunny room overlooking the tranquil rear lawn and garden. The fare when we visited included his own six-grain hot cereal following juice and cantaloupe, apple and anise muffins, oatmeal scones with apricots, and a choice of scrambled eggs with corn-cob-smoked ham and sharp cheddar cheese, fresh strawberry pancakes and shirred eggs ("like Portuguese, but without the anchovies," says Jack). He has compiled favorite recipes, each accompanied by a morning reflection, in a good little cookbook called *Breakfast...At Long Last* (for sale at the front desk for $7.50).

To go with these gourmet feasts, the inn decorates for the season: a Christmas tree decked out with guests' personal greetings and a collection of 96 Santas helped the inn win the town's Yuletide decoration contest in 1992 — a fitting reward for a special place.

Dinner, Tuesday-Sunday 6 to 8 or 9. Doubles, $160, MAP. Closed in early November and month of April.

The Inn at Weston, Route 100, Weston 05161. (802) 824-5804.

Jeanne and Bob Wilder have expanded the dining room and spiffed up the guest rooms of this much-admired inn fashioned from an 1848 farmhouse. An airy new dining room, quite chic with skylights, small hurricane lamps, floral wallpaper and beige-over-white linens, supplements the older dining room with barn siding and a convivial pub with a fireplace.

Veteran chef Jay McCoy trained at the Culinary Institute of America. His entrées run from $14.95 for chicken paillard served with a sweet-pepper salad to $22.50 for steak au poivre. Other choices could be scampi with olives and goat cheese over linguini, blackened pork medallions topped with goat cheese and jalapeño jelly, and confit of duck leg and roasted duck breast with a raspberry-peppercorn sauce.

Start with homemade soup (the duck with Chinese cabbage is a favorite), smoked salmon or scallop and sole ceviche with roasted peppers and chiles. The dessert tray offers cheesecakes, fruit-filled cakes and tarts, and an abundance of chocolate items. Bob Wilder oversees the excellent, reasonably priced wine list.

Tuesday, the head chef's night off, is Vermont Night, when four-course dinners with a local twist are available for $12.95. English tea and pastries are served in the dining room seasonally from 4 to 5.

Wreaths are on the doors of the main inn's thirteen redecorated guest rooms, which are fairly small. Seven have private baths; the others have sinks in the rooms. Guests here enjoy a comfy parlor with cozy chairs and a wood stove.

The Wilders acquired an 1830 farmhouse across the road and renovated it to make a living room and six more guest rooms, most with queensize beds and all with private baths and telephones. They come with well-worn oriental rugs, sturdy reproduction furniture and a decor that some find a bit cheerless. Guests are served a full breakfast, including different kinds of pancakes and eggs any style.

Dinner nightly, 5:30 to 8:30. No smoking. Doubles, $110 to $155, MAP.

Dining

Chantecleer, Route 7, Manchester Center. (802) 362-1616.

Ask anyone the best restaurants in the Manchester area and the Chantecleer traditionally heads the list -- absolutely tops, says an innkeeper whose taste we respect. One of Swiss chef Michel Baumann's strengths is consistency, ever since he opened his contemporary-style restaurant in an old dairy barn north of town in 1981. The rough wood beams and barn siding remain, but fresh flowers, oil lamps, good art, hanging quilts, shelves of bric-a-brac, and navy and white china atop white-over-blue calico tablecloths lend elegance to the rusticity. A pig tureen decorates the massive fireplace.

The contemporary continental menu has Swiss and American touches and changes bi-weekly except for staples like rack of lamb.

Our party of four sampled a number of offerings, starting with a classic baked onion soup, penne with smoked salmon, potato pancakes with sautéed crab meat

Country decor at Chantecleer.   Airy dining room at Inn at Weston.

and a heavenly lime-butter sauce, and bundnerfleisch, the Swiss air-dried beef, fanned out in little coronets with pearl onions, cornichons and melba rounds. Seafood gumbo, Swiss sausage plate, shrimp calypso and Maine crab cakes are other favorites among appetizers (most $7.95).

Entrées are priced from $16.95 for chicken breast sautéed with sundried apricots and toasted almonds to $25 for whole dover sole. We savored the specialty rack of lamb roasted with fine herbs, veal sweetbreads morel, sautéed quail stuffed with duxelles and the night's special of boneless local pheasant, served with smoked bacon and grapes. Fabulous roësti potatoes upstaged the other accompaniments, puree of winter squash, snow peas and strands of celery.

Grand-marnier layer cake, bananas foster, Swiss tobler chocolate mousse and trifle were memorable endings to a rich, expensive meal. A number of Swiss wines are included on the reasonably priced wine list, and Swiss yodeling may be heard on tape as background music.

Dinner by reservation, Wednesday-Sunday 6 to 10.

Mistral's at Tollgate, Tollgate Road, Manchester Center. (802) 362-1779.

The old Toll Gate Lodge was a classic French restaurant of the old school, one of Vermont's original Travel-Holiday award winners with a tuxedoed staff and lofty prices. Brown with bright blue trim and looking a bit like grandmother's cottage out in the woods, it was reborn in 1988 by young chef-owners Dana and Cheryl Markey, who live upstairs and have given it a personal, less formal touch. Both local, they met as teenagers at the Sirloin Saloon and worked their way through area restaurants before buying the Toll Gate.

Although the dining room is country pretty with dark woods, lace curtains, blue and white linens, and gold-edged white china, it is the views through picture windows looking onto the flume of Bromley Brook that are compelling. At night, when the brook and woods, accented by purple petunias and brilliant impatiens are illuminated, the setting is magical.

245

The menu offers a choice of about ten appetizers and fourteen entrées, most classic French with some nouvelle and northern Italian touches. Tempting starters include crab cakes grenobloise, lobster spinach roulade, smoked-salmon mousse with golden caviar and smoked trout with Beefeater sauce.

Main courses ($13.75 to $19) include sweetbreads dijonnaise, grilled swordfish with fresh tomato grenobloise, salmon stuffed with scallop mousse and champagne sauce, medallions of veal with lobster béarnaise, grilled duck with green-peppercorn sauce and rack of lamb or châteaubriand for two. Homemade bread and salad with a choice of dressings accompany.

For dessert, how about a hot soufflé, linzer torte, fruit sorbet or, the best seller, coupe mistral (coffee ice cream rolled in hazelnuts with hot fudge sauce and frangelico)?

While Dana is in the kitchen, Cheryl oversees the front of the house and a decent wine list, which starts in the mid-teens.

Dinner, Thursday-Sunday from 6, nightly during holiday periods. Jackets preferred.

The Black Swan, Route 7A, Manchester Village. (802) 362-3807.

Richard Whisenhunt, a classically trained French chef who acquired a California touch in Sausalito, and his wife Kathy opened their own restaurant in an 18th-century farmhouse almost in front of the Jelly Mill complex. Lately they have added a formal, fireplaced dining room with a country look in the rear, converting one of the small front rooms into a lounge and another into **The Mucky Duck,** a casual bistro.

The bistro is a welcome addition, where you can get soups, salads and sandwiches like those we enjoyed at lunch a few years back. Lunch is no longer offered, and the bistro adds heartier fare like chili, escargots with julienned vegetables and garlic sauce, sautéed trout with lemon-garlic butter, and grilled pork chop with sundried-tomato and scallion butter in the $5 to $9 range.

Dinner in the Munson Room is more ambitious, starting perhaps with chilled strawberry soup, shrimp Portuguese, oriental spring rolls with plum sauce or smoked pheasant served on mesclun greens ($4.75 to $8). Billi-bi and cream of tomato-basil are other specialty soups.

Entrées ($15 to $19.75) include sautéed salmon topped with tomatoes and mushrooms, garlic-stuffed roast game hen, sweetbreads with fresh vegetables in puff pastry, herb-crusted roast loin of pork with red-onion marmalade and grilled veal chop with a brandied-fig compote.

The dessert choice might include white-chocolate mousse with raspberry-melba sauce, walnut torte, and poached pears in brandy and triple sec with cinnamon.

Dinner from 5:30 (closed Tuesday and Wednesday except peak periods); Mucky Duck, Sunday-Friday from 5:30.

Brush Hill, Route 100, West Wardsboro. (802) 896-6100.

"Contemporary American Cuisine," says the suave roadside sign marking this rustic, rural restaurant that used to be the Old Barn. Chef-owner Michael Sylva studied at the New England Culinary Institute in Montpelier, where he met his wife Lee, a waitress at the Elm Street Cafe. He then trained at Jasper's in Boston with Jasper White, whose autographed best wishes are framed in the foyer of this personal gem of a place that the couple opened in 1989. Their card says that he's the chef-proprietor and Lee is "everything else."

An open, twelve-foot-wide brick fireplace is the central feature of the candlelit dining room, which seats 25 at tables cloaked in pink and white amid a backdrop of artworks on the walls and oriental rugs on old pine floors.

Lee writes the short monthly menu in her distinctive cursive. One of the three appetizers might be a gutsy "nu-wave antipasto" ($6.95 for a selection of roasted and grilled items, such as artichoke, asiago cheese and a small open-face sandwich on sourdough bread doused with freshly pressed olive oil topped with a slice of scamorza cheese, roasted red peppers, half a head of roasted garlic and black olives). Whew! Others might be eggplant timbale with basil, spicy smoked hoisin spare ribs, black-bean and goat-cheese terrine or vegetable samosas with tamarind relish. The salad could be tomato with avocado and endive or grilled leek and red bliss potato.

From a kitchen the size of a shoe box come a handful of entrées priced from $16.25 to $22.50. At our latest visit they were smoked shrimp with ginger and scallions, Thai sweet-and-sour trout, stir-fried chicken with cashews and oyster sauce, roast pork loin with lobster/black-bean sauce, beef tenderloin with yogurt and cardamom sauce, and saddle of lamb with mint essence. Michael obviously likes to experiment and his plates bear considerable visual interest. Lee prepares such desserts as black bottom pie, fresh fruit tarts and frozen zabaglione with chocolate and espresso.

She also put together the wine list, which specializes in small châteaux of good value and quality, most in the $15 to $30 price range. The wine details are handwritten in a photo album, interspersed among pictures of the chef's relatives.

Dinner, Wednesday-Sunday 6 to 10. No smoking.

Two Tannery Road, 2 Tannery Road, West Dover. (802) 464-2707.

The first frame house in the town of Dover has quite a history. Built in the late 1700s and moved "stick by stick" from Marlborough, Mass., it was the summer home in the early 1900s of President Theodore Roosevelt's son and daughter-in-law, and the president is said to have visited. In the early 1940s it was moved again to its present location, the site of a former sawmill and tannery. It became the first lodge for nearby Mount Snow and finally a restaurant in 1982.

Along the way it also has been transformed into a place of great attractiveness, especially the main Garden Room with its vaulted ceiling, a many-windowed space so filled with plants and so open that you almost don't know where the inside ends and the outside begins. A wall of windows looks onto the Garden Room from the Fireplace Room, which along with two smaller interior dining rooms has beamed ceilings, barnwood walls and wide-plank floors dotted with oriental-patterned rugs. Charming stenciling and folk art are everywhere. A pleasant lounge contains part of the original bar from the Waldorf-Astoria.

Long-time chef Brian Reynolds stayed on when Karen and Steve Steinfeldt took ownership. Dinners start with a hot or cold soup du jour (hot cauliflower and cold cucumber with dill the night we were there) and more than a dozen appetizers ($5 to $8.50). Chilled duck breast with ginger and lingonberries, calamari and tomato salad, and Acadian pepper shrimp are popular, and we enjoyed duck livers with onions in a terrific sauce.

Seventeen entrées plus nightly specials range from $16.50 for two chicken dishes to $23 for filet mignon. Veal is a specialty, so we tried veal granonico in a basil sauce as well as grilled New Mexican chicken with chiles, herbs and special salsa, accompanied by a goodly array of vegetables — broccoli, carrots, parsley and boiled new potatoes in one case, rice pilaf in the other. Shrimp bangkok, mixed grill and grilled lamb medallions with sour cream, cucumber and horseradish sauce are other frequent choices on the changing menu.

A four-layer grand-marnier cake with strawberries was enough for two to share and testified to the kitchen's prowess with desserts. Among them are a renowned mud pie, frozen white-chocolate mousse, fudge-pecan pie and homemade peanut-butter ice cream.

Colombian-blend coffee and espresso end a pleasant, reasonably priced meal. And if the dining room is a wondrous garden retreat with rabbits running around the lawn in summer, think how lovely it must be with snow outside in winter.

Dinner nightly except Monday, 6 to 10.

Le Petit Chef, Route 100, Wilmington. (802) 464-8437.

Although the renovated 1850 Cutler Homestead looks tiny from the outside, it is surprisingly roomy inside, with three dining rooms and an inviting lounge. The chef is Betty Hillman, whose mother Libby is the noted cookbook author and food writer. Betty studied in France for a year and her menu is rather classic.

Appetizers ($5.75 to $8.50) include Swiss onion tart, marinated goat cheese en croûte and ragout of escargots and shiitake mushrooms. Among entrées ($16.50 to $22), you might find fillet of salmon baked in a crust of potato, crab cakes on a julienne of leeks and carrots, shrimp in black-bean sauce, chicken baked with pinenuts and grapes, and loin of venison with fruit chutney and red-currant sauce.

Homemade lemon sorbet and ice creams, fresh fruit tarts, apple cake, crunchy meringue and chocolate torte are among desserts.

Tables are covered with white linens, blue napkins, handsome and heavy white china and cutlery, and oil lamps. Oriental rugs, grapevine wreaths and cabinets filled with antique china and glass are accents.

Dinner nightly except Tuesday, 6 to 9 or 10.

Casa del Sol, Main Street, Putney. (802) 387-5318.

Here is a place purer than Ivory Snow, with prices from never-never land, which never advertises and which fills up through word of mouth. We only found out about it when we read a small article in a local weekly. It's owned by Susana and Richard Ramsay -- she, the cook, from Mexico City and he, an anthropologist, who grew up in Georgia and who met her in Peru.

From her small kitchen, Susana turns out some of the best Mexican food we have ever tasted, from her tortilla soup to her flan de leche. The tostada sampler, five small tostadas with toppings of tinga, molé, picadillo, cochinita pibil and refried beans, makes a superb lunch for $4.50. A taco with a choice of toppings (maybe steamed green beans and guacamole or sautéed green peppers with corn and sour cream) is only $2. And the suizas, a chicken casserole with green tomatillo sauce, sour cream and cheese, served with refried beans, would satisfy the heartiest of eaters for $5.95.

Complete dinners, including soup or salad, two tostadas of refried beans, Mexican rice, vegetable and tortillas will set you back only $9.85. We took home pork tenderloin in salsa verde and pollo en molé rojo and savored every bite.

The small dining room with its cathedral ceiling is decorated with fine Mexican crafts (some are for sale in a little gift shop). It contains only a dozen or so tables but there are quite a few picnic tables in a garden outside. Bring your own beer or have a bottle of Penafiel, the Mexican mineral water, and end with one of Richard's plates of pecan balls, chocolate-walnut squares and lemon curd ($2.25). If you've indulged in the mixiotes (barbecued lamb in a very hot chile guajillo), you might like some non-fat frozen yogurt with fresh berries.

A lazy susan on the table holds five of Susana's homemade salsas, pickled jalapeños, serrano chiles and marinated onions. This food is dynamite!

Bistro decor at Main Street Cafe.   **Table for two at Le Petit Chef.**

Lunch, Tuesday-Friday 11:30 to 2; dinner, Tuesday-Friday 4 to 8, Saturday and Sunday, 11:30 to 8. BYOB.

T.J. Buckley's, 132 Elliot St., Brattleboro. (802) 257-4922.

"Uptown dining" along a side street in Brattleboro is how chef-owner Michael Fuller bills this choice little black, red and silver diner with tables for up to twenty lucky patrons. The setting is charming and the food creative and widely regarded. Amazingly, the city slicker from Cleveland, who came to Vermont eighteen years ago to ski and to apprentice with Rene Chardain at the Four Columns, does everything here himself, except for some of the prep work and serving.

He usually offers four entrées a night at a fixed price of $20, which he's quick to point out includes rolls, vegetable and a zippy salad of four lettuces, endive, radicchio and marinated peppers dressed with the house vinaigrette. At our latest winter visit, Michael was preparing a neat-sounding shrimp and clam dish with a puree of roasted plum tomatoes and dill oil with shaved fennel and slices of reggiano, to be served with polenta. Other choices were poached Norwegian salmon topped with a puree of Maine rock shrimp and coriander, roasted chicken coated with goat cheese and sundried tomatoes on a bed of fennel and Italian sausage, and grilled beef tenderloin with portobello mushrooms and red wine.

Typical appetizers include a country pâté of veal and pork, and a four-cheese tart that resembles a pizza. For dessert, look for a lime-macadamia tart that's very tart and a rich but not terribly sweet chocolate-hazelnut torte. Only beers and wines are served, the latter priced from $19 to $58.

Red roses grace the linen-covered tables in wintertime, and other flowers the rest of the year. They add a touch of elegance to this charming place.

Dinner, Tuesday-Sunday 6 to 10. Beer and wine only.

Main Street Cafe, 1 Prospect St., North Bennington. (802) 442-3210.

This tiny storefront cafe has attracted quite a coterie of devotees since it opened in 1989. Spruced up with sponged peach walls under a deep burgundy pressed-tin

249

ceiling, it is charming with its cafe lights, one hanging over each table, casting a flattering glow.

Owner Jeff Ben-David, who used to be at the late great Sam's Place diner in Saratoga Springs, handles the cooking chores. His wife Peggy takes care of the perfect dried-flower arrangements. Each table sports bottles of red and white house wine that you may open and pour as much or as little as you like into delicate, pink-stemmed glasses (and be charged only for what you drink). It's all quite jolly and "like coming to our home," says Jeff.

Tuxedo-clad waiters serve the northern Italian fare, which might begin with antipasti, stuffed eggplant or spinach-ricotta soufflé for two. Pastas (most $10.95) may be split for appetizers. They include rigatoni tossed with romano and parmesan cheeses, broccoli and sausage, and fettuccine topped with prosciutto, basil, onion, tomato and garlic. Entrées ($13.95 to $18.95) might be swordfish with smoked salmon in horseradish-dijon sauce over steamed spinach, broiled snapper with rock shrimp and Caribbean sauce over angel-hair pasta, medallions of chicken in a wine-lemon sauce with chanterelles and oyster mushrooms, filet mignon and, at our latest visit, several dishes involving rock shrimp.

Among desserts are Italian lemon sponge cake, chocolate-kahlua cheesecake and tirami su with tia maria and Myers's dark rum. The wine list is nicely priced from $12 to $40, with half in the teens.

Dinner nightly from 6; closed Sunday in winter.

Alldays & Onions, 519 Main St., Bennington. (802) 447-0043.

This trendy restaurant and deli was named for an obscure manufacturer of early British cars, and it sums up the free-wheeling spirit and style of young owners Matthew and Maureen Forlenza.

The style is evident from the racks of choice specialty foods to the deli case full of intriguing salads to the lucite pepper grinders with colored peppercorns on the cafe-style tables, which are set with black octagonal plates and coordinated white octagonal cups. The spirit shone in a weekday lunch that included a delicate cream of golden squash soup and a delightful dish of nachos made with organic blue corn chips, all kinds of chopped vegetables (happily, no refried beans), spicy salsa and melted jack cheese. Another winner was a trio of salads: fettuccine with smoked chicken, tortellini with basil and red potato.

Things get even better at night. Black, white and pink linens dress the tables and tall black halogen lamps provide soft lighting. Matthew, who cooked at the old Village Auberge and the Barrows House in Dorset, prepares dynamite dinners like grilled swordfish with pesto butter, peppered salmon with sweet-cilantro salsa, sautéed sweetbreads with shiitake mushrooms, sirloin steak with garlic and beaujolais sauce, and rack of lamb with honey-rosemary sauce (the changing entrées are in the $12.95 to $20.95 range). Appetizers could be grilled spicy shrimp, farfalle with tomato and bacon, or smoked salmon and brie with honeycup mustard. Among desserts are double diablo, a chocolate lover's dream with a warm bittersweet ganache, fresh peach or raspberry pie, coffee ice cream and oatmeal-fudge bars (for which Gourmet magazine requested the recipe, but the Forlenzas wouldn't give it out). The interesting wine list harbors good values.

Deli-cafe, Monday-Saturday 7 to 5; dinner, Thursday-Saturday 6 to 8.

Brasserie, 324 County St., Bennington. (802) 447-7922.

A cafe with quite a European flair and an expansive, shaded outdoor terrace paved in marble, Brasserie was opened in the 1960s by the late great chef, Dionne

Lucas, and still bears her mark under Sheela Harden, who took over in the early 1970s.

Airy and bright, the restaurant has quarry tiles on the floors and plain white walls and ceilings (even the old rough beams have been painted white). Tables are set with Bennington pottery from the Potter's Yard next door.

The all-day menu was innovative ahead of its time. Our favorite item — something we seldom see in New England — is pissaladière ($5.95), a Provence snack of sweet onions cooked until they are almost jam, topping thick French bread, with anchovies and oil-cured olives forming a pattern on top.

Another fine lunch is the Yard special ($6.50), a crock of Danish pâté sealed with clarified butter, with French bread and a salad of delicate boston lettuce with a fabulous dressing of olive oil, tarragon vinegar, garlic, lemon juice, dijon mustard and a pinch of salt, bound with eggs.

A friend says she never orders anything here but the baked onion soup, considering it the best anywhere. We liked the soup of the day, cream of watercress and potato, as well as the house quiches, lorraine and spinach, both of the melt-in-the-mouth variety. A relatively new item is called "the best and simplest," a slab of Coach Farm goat cheese, a small loaf of whole-wheat/sun-flower-seed bread, and the house tomato salad with kalamata olives ($6.95).

Nine omelets, salads, pâtés and antipasto plates are offered daily, as are changing specials for heartier appetites, among them grilled duck salad, sautéed chicken breast with a sauce of exotic mushrooms and grilled mako shark served with corn, organic baby potatoes, beans and cherry tomatoes ($9.95 to $12.95).

Favored desserts ($3.25) are roulade leontine, a sponge roll filled with chocolate soufflé and topped with ice cream, and an Austrian nut roll — except for the chunks of nuts, this could have floated away, it was so light and good. The "virtuous chocolate and apricot torte" is said to have less than two milligrams of cholesterol. Brasserie has a full license but a disappointing wine selection. The beers and ales are more interesting.

Open daily, 11:30 to 8 or 8:30, Sunday 10:30 to 8.

Lodging

Cornucopia of Dorset, Route 30, Dorset 05251. (802) 867-5751.

The personality and hospitality of effervescent innkeepers Bill and Linda Ley fairly sparkle at this, one of the more deluxe and comfortable B&Bs we've encountered.

The four guest rooms in the main house, each with private bath, are large and handsomely outfitted with poster or canopy beds, ranging in size from twins to kingsize. The Scallop Room has a working fireplace in the corner. We found the Mother Myrick Room particularly comfortable with a kingsize bed against a wall of shelves containing books and family photos. All rooms are lusciously decorated with down comforters and pillows and merino wool mattress pads, chairs with good reading lights, artworks and pieces from the Leys' assorted collections (check the lovers' bench that really isn't). Bowls of fresh fruit, terrycloth robes and Crabtree & Evelyn toiletries are standard equipment. A rear cottage suite with cathedral-ceilinged living room, fireplace, kitchenette and a loft bedroom is a private retreat. Champagne is served at check-in and a decanter of brandy is ready to be poured in the upstairs hall. Upon your return from dinner, you'll find your bed turned down, the lights off and an oil lamp flickering, and perhaps that yummy buttercrunch from Mother Myrick's Confectionery on the pillow.

Delightful as the bedrooms are, they are nearly overshadowed by the common rooms. The Leys turn over the entire first floor of the house to guests. The small front parlor has bare wide-plank floors, a leather chair with hassock and a built-in backgammon board. The fireplaced living room holds overstuffed sofas and a Tracker organ. The large dining room has a family-style table on a huge oriental rug and opens onto a contemporary sun room with bird feeders attached to the windows and comfy seating where we'd gladly while away the hours. More than 100 movies are available for the VCR here. Outside are lounge chairs on Dorset's obligatory marble patio, set near the colorful gardens.

The Leys pamper their guests with everything from scrapbooks displaying mounted restaurant menus to lavish breakfasts, the menu for which is detailed on a personalized card left in your room the night before. The meal starts with a fruit course, perhaps warm spiced applesauce topped with granola, toasted almonds and crème fraîche; a melon boat filled with berries; blackberry-raspberry cobbler, or kiwi, sliced bananas and blueberries arranged on a strawberry-raspberry sauce. Berry and pecan muffins follow. For main courses, how about apple-cinnamon pancakes with sausage, baked french toast with ham, cream-cheese blintzes with warm fruit topping and sour cream, quiche lorraine with tomato and dill, or baked ham and egg cup with Vermont cheddar served with a petite croissant? The baked raspberry pancakes were so good that we asked Linda for the recipe.

You won't leave the table hungry or the Cornucopia unimpressed.

Doubles, $100 to $130; suite, $175. No smoking.

1811 House, Route 7A, Manchester Village 05254. (802) 362-1811.

Bowls of popcorn and no fewer than 26 single-malt scotches -- the biggest selection in Vermont, they say -- are available in the intimate pub of this elegant B&B full of antiques, oriental rugs and charm. The pub (open nightly from 5:30 to 8) is where owners Marnie and Bruce Duff offer McEwan's ale on draught or one of their rare scotches, $4 to $7 a shot or three for $10 for a wee dram of each, if you're into testing. Although it's supposed to be a reproduction of an early American tavern, it looks just like a Scottish pub with its McDuff tartan seats and horse brasses. Nearby are the elegant yet comfortable parlor and library with stenciled flowers of the British Isles (the thistle, shamrock, rose and daffodil), dark wood paneling, fine paintings and porcelains.

All eleven guest rooms are spacious, air-conditioned and, with the exception of two, come with private baths. Three have fireplaces, and a corner suite has a kingsize canopy four-poster and a fireplace. The fabrics in the draperies and bedspreads are exceptionally tasteful. The bedroom of Mary Lincoln Isham (Abraham Lincoln's granddaughter, who lived here for a short time) contains a marble enclosure for the bathtub that she had put in. An addition in a rear cottage produced three deluxe rooms with kingsize beds, fireplaces and private baths.

In the big kitchen with a commercial stove, Marnie Duff whips up hearty English breakfasts, perhaps including fresh scones, fried tomatoes, eggs any style or special french toast soaked overnight with pecans. Guests partake in the dining room or pub amid Villeroy & Boch china and the family sterling.

Doubles, $110 (two smaller rooms with double beds) to $180.

The Inn at Ormsby Hill, Route 7A, RR2, Box 3264, Manchester Center 05255. (802) 362-1163.

A welcoming atmosphere, plush accommodations and leisurely breakfasts of

Luxurious accommodations are offered at Cornucopia of Dorset.

distinction are the hallmarks of this new B&B backing up to Robert Todd Lincoln's Hildene estate.

The welcome is extended by owners Nancy and Don Burd, talented and gregarious New Jersey transplants who moved in 1991 to the sprawling manor house long owned by Edward Isham, an Illinois state legislator and senior partner in a Chicago law firm with Abraham Lincoln's son, whom he entertained here. The foyer leads to a front parlor furnished with antiques from both sides of the Burd family. From here one looks to the rear through a spacious fireplaced library into a conservatory dining room extending 40 feet back. At first glance, the total depth, in what is a strikingly wide house, takes the breath away. So does the view across terrace, back yard, gardens and Hildene to mountains through the many-paned windows. Beyond two large dining tables are a couple of facing loveseats at one end of the conservatory.

The Burds offer five comfortable guest rooms, four with whirlpool baths and separate showers. All contain oversize canopy or four-poster beds, plush armchairs, antique chests, artworks and oriental rugs. Some like best the main-floor library room, beamed and dark. Romantics are partial to the upstairs Taft Suite, where the Burds will serve a tête-à-tête breakfast for two in a cozy little room at the top of a private staircase. We like the rear Hildene Room, light and airy in yellow and white, where ivy is twined around the bed canopy.

Breakfast at 9 often becomes a two-hour feast, as guests linger and then pose for snapshots with each other and their hosts. At a summer visit, we enjoyed the fresh strawberries and blueberries in a light sauce of vanilla yogurt, the coffee cake with a cinnamon swirl, and the herbed scrambled eggs with bacon and toast. "Breakfast is Don's part of the bargain," says Nancy, who bakes the pastries and serves. His specialties include oven-baked french toast with cinnamon-crumb topping and blueberries, baked pancakes with raspberries, and a vegetable "tata" incorporating his own garden vegetables and eggs, baked with parmesan cheese and topped with ham slices and new red potatoes. "We try never to repeat a meal for guests on long stays," says Don. That includes the table settings, which Nancy changes five times a week.

In the afternoon, these hospitable innkeepers offer iced tea or lemonade with cookies in summer, hot mulled cider or sherry in winter. Their welcome is appreciated by guests, who gush in their room diaries: "You both make us feel so comfortable -- a home away from home."

Doubles, $90 to $160. No smoking.

Inn Victoria, On the Green, Box 788, Chester 05143. (802) 875-4288 or (800) 732-4288.

Most elegant of the B&Bs that are sprouting all over Chester is this 1850 yellow brick house with lavender shutters. The interior is a showcase of Victoriana, from the rugs ("so nice that if I had them I wouldn't let guests walk on them," says Jack Coleman of the nearby Inn at Long Last) to the period antiques throughout.

Upstairs are seven guest rooms, three with private baths. And what baths they are! The one off the pink room has moiré wallpaper, a huge jacuzzi with bubble baths and votive candles beside, a separate shower, and a wicker chair with ottoman. "Somebody asked if I had a bathroom fetish," said innkeeper K.C. (for Kathleen Cummings) Lanagan, "and I think maybe I have." The other two private baths with jacuzzis are similarly impressive. Beds are awash with pillows and Chinese linens. All rooms are lavishly furnished in different periods of Victoriana by K.C., who was an antiques dealer in Princeton, N.J.

She and husband Tom serve a hearty breakfast, perhaps a choice of eggs benedict or fancy french toast with maple butter, at an oval table with chevron armchairs beneath antique crystal chandeliers in the formal dining room. A lavish high tea with scones and devonshire cream and sherry is served afternoons in a niche between the dining room and the parlor with its 1820 melodeon. Next door is the charming little **Tea Pot Shop,** where K.C. sells tea pots and accessories.

The Lanagans also present "dinner parties" to guests and the public by reservation Saturdays at 7:30. The prix-fixe dinner ($29) might begin with drunken tomato soup or stromboli with horseradish. Tossed salad with sweet and sour dressing follows the main course, perhaps filet mignon with peppercorn sauce or lobster tail. Tom's cheese course precedes a dessert of brandied fruit and cream or coffee profiteroles with chocolate sauce and whipped cream.

Doubles, $85 to $150.

Gourmet Treats

Halfway up a mountain, the **Garden Cafe** at the Southern Vermont Art Center in Manchester is a great place for lunch with a view of the sculpture garden as well as birch trees, valleys and hills. Dine inside or on the outdoor terrace on ice-cream parlor chairs, perhaps choosing a skewer of chicken with peanut sauce and salad. We remember a fantastic tomato-orange soup and a good chicken salad with snow peas. Desserts run to fresh fruit tarts and pastries. The menu ($6.25 to $11.50) is identical to that at the Four Chimneys in Bennington, since the cafe is run by innkeeper Alex Koks. His sous chef preps at the inn and cooks at the cafe. It's open Tuesday-Sunday from 11:30 to 2, June to mid-October (he was considering staying open with the art center in the winter).

Another good place for lunch is the **Buttery at the Jelly Mill** on Route 7A just south of Manchester Center, a fun collection of shops selling gourmet foods and kitchenware, among other things. Open from 11 to 4 (3 in winter), it offers many sandwiches, including smoked salmon on a toasted croissant with capers. The Buttery special is ham, cheese, artichoke hearts and hollandaise on toasted rye. Snacks like nachos, soups, salads and specials such as a tomato, bacon and cheddar quiche are listed, and you can end with neapolitan mousse torte or amaretto bread pudding. Weekend brunches are served from 10 to 1.

More exotic sandwiches and salads are available at **The Village Store,** Union Street, Manchester Village, which is mainly foods -- specialty and deli. Guests at the nearby Equinox resort take a break from high living to lunch on a grilled turkey sandwich with broccoli, cheddar and raspberry mayonnaise on whole wheat or Vermont ham and cheddar with applesauce and tangy mustard on farm bread. Both are listed at $4.95 on the blackboard, which supplements the regular $3.95 sandwiches. Salad plates ($5.50) might be tuna, chicken tarragon, seafood or chef's. Open Monday-Saturday 9 to 5:30, Sunday 9 to 3.

Up for Breakfast, Main Street, Manchester Center, is just what its name says: upstairs above a storefront, and open for breakfast only (weekdays except Tuesday 6 to noon, weekends 7 to 1). You'll find sourdough pancakes, cajun frittata, huevos rancheros and belgian waffles in the $5 to $7 range. We chose "one of each" -- one eggs benedict and one eggs argyle (with smoked salmon). These proved hearty dishes for Vermont appetites, as did the heavy Irish scone, both garnished with chunks of pineapple and watermelon. Only after we'd eaten did we see the blackboard menu around the side, listing some rather exotic specials like rainbow trout with eggs or mango-cranberry-nutmeg pancakes.

For superior fresh mozzarella, drop into **Al Ducci's Italian Pantry,** Elm Street, Manchester Center, and meet Al Scheps, who has been making his own since he was eight years old. The name of the little Italian grocery is a takeoff on Balducci's in Manhattan. "We have a lot of fun here," says Al, who jokes back and forth with his customers. A one-pound ball of mozzarella is $3.99 and, as Al suggests, it is delicious cut into cubes and mixed with ripe tomatoes, red onions, fruity olive oil, balsamic vinegar and cubes of homemade Italian bread, all of which he sells. Good sandwiches ($3.50, or $5.50 for combos) are also made on the bread; you can have additions like grated carrots, sundried tomatoes. roasted peppers and fresh basil. Homemade sausage, cannoli, and sfogliatelle (a flaky pastry with ricotta cheese) are other goodies. Open daily 9 to 6, Sunday to 4.

Peltier's Market on the Green in Dorset has been the center of Dorset life since the early 1800s. A true country store with all the staples, it also caters to the upscale. You might pick up a sandwich from the refrigerator -- perhaps smoked salmon or avocado, cheese and tomato. Caviar, good wines, Vermont products like cheese from Shelburne Farms, exotic vegetables and prime meats can be found here. So can worms and night crawlers, close by the pesto and sundried tomatoes in the chilled produce case.

Two large stores in tiny Weston are well worth a visit. Almost across the street from each other, the **Vermont Country Store** and the **Weston Village Store** are chock full of those wonderful Vermont items we all love to shop for. The Country Store is far more upscale in three buildings, including the new West River Jewelry Company and Bandstand Books & Art. Check the candy counter at the Country Store for a fantastic selection of old-fashioned candy. How about a log cabin made of maple sugar? The Village Store is an old-fashioned, jumbled-up emporium from yesteryear. It has a good selection of Vermont cheeses.

The essence of Vermont, in food as well as decor, is served up at **The Bryant House Restaurant,** part of the Vermont Country Store complex. Here you can get a grilled Vermont cheddar sandwich plate with shoestring french fries or, a Vermont standby from days gone by, Vermont Common crackers and milk with a hunk of cheddar cheese, eaten with a spoon from a bowl. Except for that, most lunch items are in the $6 to $7 range. Or stop in the **Ice Cream Parlor** for Indian pudding, a root-beer float, ice-cream sodas or an Ovaltine milk frappe ($2.75).

As if Weston visitors needed more food, the **Grafton Village Apple Co.** moved from Grafton in 1992 into the thick of the Weston action. "Come taste Vermont," it beckons. Indeed you can. All kinds of Vermont foods are for sale and you get to sample anything or everything, including seven salsas, horseradish-pepper jelly, vinegars, apple butter, mustards, cheeses and biscuits. There were oodles of kitchen gadgets, but no apples -- we were there before apple season.

Bennington Potters at 324 County St., Bennington, is the place to head for a great selection of pottery at discount prices. Also part of the Bennington Potters Yard complex is **Cinnamons,** specializing in kitchen ware.

Partridge Feathers at Tollgate Village, Route 100, West Dover, is where well-known chef Brill Williams of The Inn at Saw Mill Farm hangs his hat by day. It's an interesting new pottery and woodenware shop where he stocks a few choice and expensive lines, among them Simon Pearce glass, Monroe Salt Works stoneware, Woodbury Woodenware and colorful modern majolica from Deruta of Italy.

Fine produce, fruit, plants and more are featured at **Dutton Farm Stands,** a fixture along Route 30 in Newfane and with an expanded second location along Routes 11-30 in Manchester Center. Wendy and Paul Dutton grow the produce on their 105-acre Newfane farm and apples on a 30-acre orchard in Brattleboro.

We've left the best for last. **Mother Myrick's Confectionery and Ice Cream Parlor** on Route 7A in Manchester Center is paradise for anyone with a sweet tooth. Jacki Baker and Ron Mancini have operated Mother Myrick's (named for a famous midwife) for a dozen years and their chocolates and candy are known across the East. It's fun to watch the confections being made. Using old-fashioned equipment wherever possible (like the two-foot cream beater from the 1940s for fondant), they make a myriad of chocolates, truffles, fudge, apricots hand-dipped in dark chocolate, fancy molds and their most popular candy, buttercrunch, rolled in roasted almonds and cashews, $16 a pound and worth every penny, and now available in dark chocolate. The best fudge sauce we have tasted (even better than mom's) comes out of the kitchen here. Several flavors of ice cream changing by the season (Irish coffee, bittersweet-pumpkin and raspberry at our latest fall visit), cheesecake and much more are for sale. Lately the couple have been experimenting with scones; the coffee-hazelnut-chocolate chip is delicious. Stop by for blueberry-raspberry or sour cream-chocolate chunk coffee cake and superior cappuccino in the morning or anytime for a myrtle (their kind of turtle) or a piece of grand-marnier truffle cake, $4.25 a slice. This is served to go or to have in the charmingly art-deco cafe or outside on the front deck. You can send for Mother Myrick's little newsletter and catalog, The Scoop (Box 1142, Manchester Center 05255) and order some of these things by mail. Open daily 10 to 6, weekends to 9.

Grapevines screen Monument Mountain from porch of Chesterwood in Berkshires.

The Tri-State Berkshires

A Tradition of High Tastes

Country inns may seem more historic in Vermont, but they have reached their pinnacle in the Berkshires, an area whose name is inseparably linked with country inns and summer tradition in the national perception.

That may be a result of Norman Rockwell's depiction of the Red Lion Inn and Main Street in Stockbridge, a scene that has come to epitomize the essence of New England for anyone west of the Hudson River.

Indeed, when friends from Switzerland visited us one foliage season and asked to "see" New England in a day, we headed off to the Berkshires and Stockbridge so they could sense what New England is all about. They shot two rolls of color film before departing for Texas.

Had their visit been in the summer, we would have taken them to Tanglewood in Lenox, where the elaborate picnics complete with tablecloths and candelabra on the lawns beside the Music Shed are as delightful a tradition in which to partake (and observe) as the Boston Symphony Orchestra is to hear.

The inns in the Berkshires are keeping up with the times, both in quality and in numbers. And although the area has had good restaurants longer than most

257

resort regions, thanks to its early and traditional status as a destination for summer visitors, new restaurants pop up every year.

As with the inns, the dining situation reflects the sophisticated tastes and often the prices of a noted resort and cultural area close to metropolitan centers.

But there also are rural, rustic charms to be discovered amid the luxury of Lenox or Lakeville and the sophistication of Stockbridge or Salisbury. Seek them out as well, to savor the total Berkshire experience.

Bed and Board

The Berkshires are such a popular destination that three-night (and even four-night) stays are the minimum for weekends in summer and foliage season at many inns. Prices quoted here are for peak weekends; mid-week and off-season often are considerably lower. Restaurant hours generally vary from daily in summer and fall to part-time the rest of the year.

The Old Inn on the Green and Gedney Farm, Route 57, New Marlborough, Mass. 01230. (413) 229-3131.

Bradford Wagstaff bought this abandoned 1760 inn on the old Hartford-Albany stage route in 1973 and it took ten years to get it back into shape. The result was a six-room B&B and a dining room of distinction. He's since opened eleven luxurious rooms and suites in a great Normandy-style barn called Gedney Farm down the road, and in 1993 added a sculpture park and farm gallery, with a cafe for lunch that's positively idyllic.

Brad's wife, Leslie Miller, a baker who used to supply area restaurants, and chef Christopher Capstick oversee gourmet dinners served totally by candlelight in as historic a setting as can be conceived. About 50 people are seated in the tavern room, a formal parlor or at the harvest table in the dining room. In each, the original wainscoting, stenciling, antiques and windows draped in velvet are shown to advantage. Pamela Hardcastle's unique, handmade wreaths using branches and bark are fascinating, the large mural of cows grazing on the New Marlborough green is wonderful to see, and it's easy to imagine yourself transported back a couple of centuries for the evening.

While the inn traditionally served only prix-fixe dinners on weekends, it now offers à-la-carte menus weeknights on the canopied outdoor terrace in summer or in the tavern the rest of the year, as well as lunches in that great new Gallery Cafe or outside overlooking the sculpture park. Even with its bold new contemporary dimensions, its culinary claim to fame continues to be the Saturday prix-fixe dinners ($45) with a set menu except for a choice from two entrées and two desserts. Arranged three months in advance for mailing to 2,000 regulars, the quarterly menu makes for delicious reading and is guaranteed to make you think about getting yourself to New Marlborough pronto.

Chèvre and almond puff-pastry sticks accompany drinks, served in delicate stemmed glasses. From a mushroom and herb soup that is the essence of mushroom to the final cappuccino with shredded chocolate on top, things go from great to greater. We can't say enough for either the food or the experience. A summer meal might start with grilled rabbit sausage with sweet-corn cakes, wilted dandelion greens and creole mustard sauce. The main dish could be cured pork loin with sautéed pancetta, gremolata and arugula-dijon sauce or grilled marinated swordfish with kalamata olive tapenade and zucchini flan. Dessert could be mocha mousse in tuiles or key lime and pink-grapefruit pie.

Besides Leslie's breads and desserts, the couple's specialties are lamb and veal

New Gallery Cafe at Gedney Farm.   **Table for two at Old Inn on the Green.**

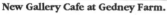

raised on their Willow Creek Farm. Brad's wine list is extensive and expensive, with most bottles $30 and up.

The candlelit bar area and the canopied brick terrace in the rear are popular for casual dining. The terrace/fireside à-la-carte menu is short but appealing, from smoked-salmon napoleon with sorrel mousse or red snapper and roasted-corn fishcake with cayenne pepper sauce to sautéed shrimp with roasted-garlic/shallot sauce or roasted baby pheasant with green-peppercorn sauce and braised lentils. Appetizers are in the $7 range and entrées, $16 to $19.50.

Upstairs are six rather spare guest rooms, two with private baths, authentically furnished with old armoires, hooked rugs and crewel bedspreads. The second-floor veranda across the front of the inn is a serene spot from which to view the passing scene. A generous continental breakfast -- including fresh fruits, cereals, pastries, coffee cake, croissants and homemade preserves -- is served on the terrace or in the tavern.

The Gedney Farm restoration is a sight to behold. Beneath the barn's soaring, 30-foot ceiling is a lineup of six guest rooms and five two-level suites, their second floors fashioned from the old hayloft and reached by private staircases. Most have fireplaced sitting rooms. The modern baths are outfitted with Neutrogena amenities; some have deep, two-person whirlpool tubs under glass ceilings open to the roof structure. Leslie has decorated each room with panache in styles from French provincial to Moroccan. Oriental and kilim rugs are on the floors, woven or fabric coverlets are on the beds, and Pamela Hardcastle's exotic wreaths adorn the walls.

And now, crowning glory, comes the Gedney Farm Gallery in a restored Normandy horse barn. Some fantastic paintings, sculptures, furniture and other artworks are displayed against the white painted interior walls. The barn door is open onto a trellised stone terrace and the green fields, where the outdoor sculptures are strategically placed for viewing. White-clothed tables are set here and there for lunch in the **Gallery Cafe.** From the abbreviated menu we liked the sound of the Gedney Farm salad with mesclun, roasted peppers and

259

house-made ricotta. Start with toasted-corn and shellfish soup. Continue with grilled sirloin steak au poivre with sautéed mushrooms on a crispy sourdough baguette, torta rustica or a vegetable brioche ($7 to $11). After a piece of fruit pie or a refreshing sorbet in that pastoral setting, you may be lulled into buying some art to remember the place by.

Lunch, Thursday-Sunday 11 to 4, summer-foliage. Dinner by reservation, prix-fixe, Saturday 6 to 9; à la carte Sunday-Friday 5:30 to 9, closed Monday-Wednesday in winter. Doubles, $90 to $140 in inn; $160 to $240 at Gedney Farm.

L'Hostellerie Bressane, Routes 22 and 23, Hillsdale, N.Y. 12529. (518) 325-3412.

Chef Jean Morel has won all kinds of awards for his cooking, but he seems most proud of the wall just inside the entrance to his acclaimed restaurant, which is covered with letters from happy customers. A large and jovial man, he is the epitome of what a French chef should be. And L'Hostellerie, named after his native Bresse, has a relaxed and cozy air about it, though the food is classic and the service quite formal.

The rosy brick inn, in the Dutch Colonial style, was built in 1783 by a Revolutionary War soldier. A Victorian addition (1850) of red wood with white gingerbread trim houses the bar.

Four smallish, fireplaced dining rooms are candlelit at night. Fresh flowers, pots of azaleas, pretty wallpapers and curtains, and ladderback or round-backed velvet chairs in a sienna color add to the French country charm. A few tables are set up for the Saturday overflow in the lounge with its copper bar.

The inn has been owned since 1971 by Morel and his chic wife Madeleine — who is the "directrice" and keeps things running. It has an established and comfortable feel to it. Many customers are regulars and are greeted with affection by the longtime staff.

Possibly the best value around is the four-course prix-fixe dinner for $21.50, served nightly except Saturday to supplement the à-la-carte items.

Chef Morel says he has "a small menu, but I love to play with it." Although he admits to little in the way of trendiness, and that mostly in fish dishes, we found his food presentations on large Villeroy & Boch plates (four different patterns) to be as pretty as a picture. A dish of scallops with saffron butter (one of the night's specials, $21.50) was laid out like a wheel with julienned vegetables in several colors; the same for the sweetbreads with chestnuts in old port ($23). Both had the most delicious sauces imaginable.

Before that, generous drinks were served, followed by bread, which we enjoyed with the coarse and garlicky pâté of the week, surrounded by cornichons. Other appetizers ($6 to $8) include snails in puff pastry with burgundy and brandy, flourless chicken-liver soufflé with a touch of garlic, and potato pancakes with smoked salmon and aigrelette sauce. Soups (perhaps onion with madeira and cognac, or pea soup with sorrel) are served from a silver tureen at tableside.

Entrées are in the $17.50 to $24 range, the former price for fillets of trout with red-pepper coulis, coq au vin or calves liver lyonnaise. The higher range is for mignonettes of beef with green peppercorns and roquefort sauce or filet of lamb with tarragon sauce. Vegetables garnish all dishes but special vegetables are extra; we fell for crêpes Bressane, three ethereally light potato pancakes.

The wine list is basically French, with a nod to California and New York State. Rare wines command up to $800 and many incredible ports go up to $195, but a very decent muscadet and beaujolais can be had for less than $20.

Jean Morel at L'Hostellerie Bressane.   **Dining room at Blantyre.**

The most special desserts are the soufflés, hot or cold. "I did 68 soufflés last Saturday night, all made to order," the chef said after we tried his frozen coffee soufflé with kirsch, ringed by figs and candied chestnuts.

He showed us his immaculate kitchen, unusually large and well organized. He also showed the men's room, its walls papered entirely with wine labels. Lately turned 60, he bicycles 30 miles almost every morning to keep in shape.

The inn has four plain but comfortable guest rooms, sharing two large bathrooms, on the second floor. On the third are two luxurious bedrooms with private baths. One is done in soft lavenders with a queensize bed and one is in coral shades with twins. Breakfast is available for $7.50 from 8:30 to 9:30. We can't think of a nicer way to spend an evening than to savor one of Jean Morel's sensational meals and then, instead of driving home, wend our way upstairs to the Lavender Room.

Dinner, Tuesday-Saturday 6 to 9, Sunday 5 to 8:30; also closed Tuesday, September-June. Closed March and April. No credit cards. Doubles, $75 to $95.

Blantyre, Route 20 and East Street, Lenox, Mass. 01240. (413) 637-3556 (November-April, 298-3806).

Past a gatekeeper and up a long, curving driveway in the midst of 85 country acres appears the castle of your dreams. In fact, the 1902 Tudor-style brick manor built as a summer cottage for a millionaire in the turpentine business as an authentic replica of the Hall of Blantyre in Scotland used to be called a castle. It's full of hand-carved wood ornamentation, high-beamed ceilings, crystal chandeliers and spacious public rooms, plus turrets, gargoyles and carved friezes -- just as in the English country-house hotels that innkeeper Roderick Anderson seeks to emulate.

Faithfully restored by owner Jane Fitzpatrick of the Red Lion Inn in nearby Stockbridge, Blantyre houses guests in eight elegant rooms and suites in the mansion, twelve more contemporary quarters in a distant carriage house, two in the "winter palace," and three scattered about the property in small cottages.

The public rooms and guest rooms are so luxurious in a castle kind of way as to defy description — take our word or that of those who pay up to $550 a night for the Paterson Suite with a fireplaced living room (complete with a crystal chandelier over a lace-covered table in the middle of the room), two bathrooms and a large bedroom with a kingsize four-poster bed. A typical bathroom has a scale, a wooden valet, heated towel racks, embroidered curtains and more toiletries than you'd ever hoped to see. With newly handpainted tile bathrooms, rooms in the carriage house have balconies or decks and wet bars. Some have lofts or sitting rooms, and all are near the pool.

A continental breakfast of fresh croissants and muffins is served in a sunny conservatory. Tables topped with mustard jars full of flowers are set beside windows overlooking gnarled trees and golf-course-like lawns. Additional breakfast items can be ordered for a charge.

Country-house cuisine, lately lightened up in style, is available to house guests and the public in the formal dining room or two smaller rooms. The tables are set with different themes, the china and crystal changing frequently as Jane Fitzpatrick adds more to the collection. Investing in its kitchen, Blantyre has added a barbecue for grilling purposes and new and adventurous dishes for what chef David Lawson, formerly of the Old Inn on the Green in New Marlborough, calls a "remarkably savvy clientele with such a high level of expectation." David runs "a very European-style kitchen," he and his staff of seven putting in 70-hour work weeks. Dinner is prix-fixe, $65 for three courses with many choices. A seven-course tasting menu ($90) ranges farther afield, rather than offering smaller portions of existing dishes.

A typical dinner starts with a "surprise," perhaps foie gras or veal sweetbreads with sauternes and carrot sauce. Just a couple of bites to whet the appetite for what's to come -- perhaps avocado and tomatillo soup, a bouillabaisse terrine with saffron vinaigrette and rouille croutons, or house-cured gravlax on potato pancakes with horseradish and black caviar. Main courses could include sauté of monkfish and lobster with a leek flan, pan-roasted halibut au poivre with white-bean puree and fried shallots, breast of range chicken with foie gras and wild-rice risotto, and sautéed veal medallions on pappardelle with black olives and fried sage. An array of steamed vegetables might contain turnips, squash, carrots and haricots verts.

For dessert, how about a light tirami su with imported Italian mascarpone, a trio of filled beignets (caramelized apples, poached cherries and bittersweet chocolate on a pool of raspberry, strawberry and mango coulis), a bittersweet-chocolate torte with macadamia-nut crust or a trilogy of three mousses? The wine list is exceptionally strong on California chardonnays and cabernets and French regionals, priced up to $220. After dinner, guests like to adjourn to the Music Room for coffee and cordials, this being a convivial country-house atmosphere.

Lunch on the terrace ($12 to $23) is a sybaritic indulgence. Walk it off around the gorgeous property. Play tennis on one of four Har-Tru courts or croquet on the only bent-grass tournament lawn in Massachusetts. The oversize guest book in the main hall is full of superlatives. The consensus: "Perfect. We'll be back."

Lunch in July and August, 12:30 to 1:45; dinner by reservation, Tuesday-Sunday 6 to 9. Doubles, $220 to $370; suites, $250 to $550. Closed November-April.

Wheatleigh, West Hawthorne Road, Lenox, Mass. 01240. (413) 637-0610.

"Wheatleigh is singular and stands alone," proclaims the most elaborate brochure of any Berkshires resort.

People who expect the height of luxury are partial to this Italian palazzo built in 1893 as a wedding gift for the Countess de Heredia. It's romantic, extravagant, dramatic and ornate. Its food ranks with the best in the Berkshires, and the area food cognoscenti covet the experience, if not the expense.

The imposing (some might say intimidating) entrance of the honey-colored brick building framed in wrought iron leads into an immense lobby with a striking sitting area at one end, a majestic staircase rising to the second floor, parquet floors and fine art all around. For its centennial year in 1993, innkeepers Susan and Linwood Simon redecorated the entire place, "bringing in antiques we've been collecting for years," in Susan's words. Window treatments now match the bed canopies, and bathrooms sport new tiles and fixtures. All seventeen air-conditioned guest rooms are different. Seven are huge, two merely large, two medium and the rest, frankly, small. Nine have fireplaces and some have terraces or balconies. Each comes with a telephone, but no TV. Susan's aim was to be "true to the period of the house and its architectural style" (it took her five years to find the right pattern of English axminster for the carpeting in the halls). The period can be austere; some guests think the larger rooms could use more furniture and more of a cozy feeling. Having seen a variety of rooms, we urge would-be guests to go for the best; the small rooms seem claustrophobic in comparison. Outside are the joys of a 22-acre property within walking distance of Tanglewood, a tennis court and a swimming pool hidden away in a glade.

Like the French châteaux, says Linwood, the pride of Wheatleigh is its main-floor restaurant. It includes two pretty chandeliered dining rooms and a large enclosed porch, their tables set with white linens, service plates in three patterns, a white candle in a pewter holder and delicate wine glasses. We especially like the antique tiled pictures of scenes in Italy and Portugal.

Prix-fixe dinners are $65 (with a number of surcharges) for three courses involving numerous choices. A special dégustation menu allows a sampling of nine courses for $90; participation by the entire table is required.

Executive chef Peter Platt, a 1980 Williams College history graduate, trained at the Cordon Bleu in London and worked under Jasper White and Lydia Shire at the Parker House in Boston before moving to Wheatleigh in 1986. Lean and lanky, he's articulate and as down-to-earth as his food prices and aspirations are lofty. He oversees a cooking staff of fourteen, some of whose foreign backgrounds give an international flavor to what he calls "new French classic cuisine."

His changing menu might begin with a choice of roasted red and yellow bell-pepper soup with a lobster flan, sautéed medallion of New York duck foie gras and French green lentils, or roasted California squab with sweet-corn pancakes and black truffle sauce.

Main courses could be monkfish and lobster enrobed in savoy cabbage with saffron sauce, pan-roasted salmon with leek-mushroom sauce and littleneck clams, sautéed breast of muscovy duck and honey-roasted thigh with Canadian wild rice and elderberry sauce, and roasted loin of wild Texas antelope with dauphinoise potatoes and elderberry sauce.

Before dessert, pause perhaps for a salad of seasonal lettuces with balsamic vinaigrette or an assortment of cheeses with walnut bread (both $8 extra) or a warm chèvre salad with white truffle oil ($11).

Desserts are as exciting as the rest of the meal. The framboise-scented Monterey goat cheese layered with raspberries in a delicate pastry is a signature triumph. Others might be pear and hazelnut cream gâteau with mascarpone parfait, apple baba with vanilla ice cream and bourbon sabayon, a trilogy of chocolates or a tasting of homemade sorbets: chocolate, crabapple, passion fruit, raspberry, grapefruit and cider, apple, blueberry and raspberry.

A wine list complete with table of contents presents selections worthy of the feast. It starts at $34 — "that's the level that begins to fit in with our food," the maître-d informed — and goes to $1,150. To all but connoisseurs, the prices are exorbitant.

Even the biggest of Wheatleigh's big spenders may tire of the ritual. A smaller, à-la-carte menu priced to appeal to mere mortals or those booked for long stays ($15.50 to $24) is offered nightly in the **Grill Room** from May to October.

Lunch in summer, noon to 1:30; dinner nightly by reservation, 6 to 9; Grill Room, 5 to 9 or 9:30. No smoking. Doubles, $175 to $465, EP.

Mayflower Inn, Route 47, Washington, Conn. 06793. (203) 868-9466.

"Stately" is the word to describe this renovated and expanded inn, as styled by new owners Robert and Adriana Mnuchin of New York and innkeeper Donald Meginley. They took a venerable inn, once owned by The Gunnery school and hidden away on 28 wooded acres, and -- with a Midas touch -- reopened it in 1992 as one of the premier English-style country hotels in America.

No expense was spared in producing 25 guest rooms and suites that are the ultimate in good taste. Fifteen rooms are upstairs on the second and third floors of the expanded main inn. Ten more are in two guest houses astride a hill beside a magnificent tiered rose garden rising toward a swimming pool.

Fine British, French and American antiques and accessories, prized artworks and elegant touches of whimsy — like the four ancient trunks stashed in a corner of the second-floor hallway — dignify public and private rooms alike. Opening off the lobby, an intimate parlor with plush leather sofas leads into the ever-so-British gentleman's library. Across the back of the inn are three dining rooms and along one side is an English-style bar.

Chef John Farnsworth, tapped as one of America's top ten chefs by Food and Wine magazine when he was at RockResorts' Lodge at Keole in Hawaii, presents a changing menu that has received mixed reviews. The night's main courses ($15.50 to $24) might include roasted monkfish on corn polenta with lobster rouille, breast of guinea hen with apple-pear sauce and mashed potatoes and grilled veal chop with stone-ground mustard sauce and dauphinoise potatoes. Starters ($5.75 to $9) range from pizza with roasted shallots, mozzarella and taleggio or cream of lobster soup with armagnac to chicken-liver terrine with brandied figs and arugula salad with chicken confit, Coach Farm chèvre and roasted peppers. And dessert? Perhaps pear-custard tart with caramel-apple ice cream, double-chocolate cake with English cream or melon, orange or raspberry ice. Work it off in the fitness club and sauna on the lower garden level.

The setting for meals is exceptional, especially the outdoor terrace with its sylvan view of manicured lawns and imported specimen trees. But not all is glowing. Our party of four found the surroundings more impressive than the food at a birthday lunch that none remembers as remarkable. We also know affluent guests who, after staying in a $350 suite, were stunned to be charged an extra $25 for continental breakfast in the morning.

Each guest room, however, is a sight to behold and some are almost the ultimate in glamour. We like Room 24 with a kingsize canopied four-poster feather bed awash in pillows, embroidered linens and a chenille throw. An angled loveseat faces the fireplace and oversize wicker rockers await on the balcony. Books and magazines are spread out on the coffee table, the armoire contains a TV and

Mayflower Inn is known for stylish accommodations and dining.

there's a walk-in closet. The paneled bathroom, bigger than most bedrooms, has marble floors, a double vanity opposite a glistening tub, a separate toilet area and a walk-in shower big enough for an army. Even all that didn't prepare us for a second-floor corner suite with a large living room straight out of Country Life magazine, a dining-conference room, a lavatory, a bedroom with a kingsize canopied four-poster and a second bathroom, plus a porch overlooking the sylvan scene. The rear balconies and decks off the rooms in the guest houses face the woods and are particularly private.

Lunch daily, noon to 2:30; dinner nightly, 6 to 9. Doubles, $225 to $300, EP; suites, $325 to $495.

The Boulders Inn, Route 45, New Preston, Conn. 06777. (203) 868-0541.

This handsome stone and shingled inn, set astride a knoll overlooking Lake Waramaug, lives up to its billing as "a very special country retreat," and a stay here doesn't require drawing on your equity line of credit. Kees and Ulla Adema, he originally a ship's broker from Holland and she born in Germany, took it over in 1988 as a retirement venture and have upgraded both the accommodations and the dining room.

The latter, an intimate room with walls of boulders plus a seven-sided addition that's seemingly all windows with views of woods and lake, has provided us some memorable meals over the years. New French chef Claude Chassagne has trimmed the dinner menu a bit, preferring to add more nightly specials.

Among appetizers ($6 to $8), you might find duck and oxtail terrine with grilled wild-mushroom salad and mustard vinaigrette, fresh pumpkin ravioli in a savory mint broth, smoked duck on a bed of greens with roasted-beet vinaigrette or grilled boneless quail with foie gras and braised leeks. For main courses ($17.50 to $22), how about seared Atlantic salmon and mussels in an "oceanic" bouillon with melted celery and fennel, roasted smoked-pork tenderloin with sweet-potato gratin and corn relish, or herb-roasted loin of lamb with grilled-vegetable lasagna and glazed pearl onions. Dessert could be raspberry amandine, bartlett-pear charlotte, a trio of Callebaut Belgian chocolate concoctions, or apple-cider mousse with vanilla biscuit and fresh berries.

The Ademas have made fine improvements to the four comfortable guest rooms and two suites in the inn as well as the eight more contemporary rooms in four outlying duplex guest houses scattered along the hillside behind the inn. The latter are in great demand because they're like small private country houses, all with refrigerators and groupings of sofas and chairs around free-standing fireplaces. Each has a deck with a view of the lake. A rear carriage house adds three choice, carpeted guest rooms with plush chintz seating in front of stone fireplaces.

Back in the inn, a basement game room offers ping-pong and skittles, and a library has been added to a small den with a color TV. The paneled living room, its picture windows overlooking the lake (binoculars are provided), is a lovely mix of antiques and groupings of sofas and wing chairs in reds, blues and chintz prints. In one corner are book shelves and a stereo with many tapes. More active types enjoy swimming, sailing and canoeing from the beach house in summer.

A full breakfast is served by the windows in the Lake Dining Room. A help-yourself cold buffet is set up with fresh fruit and juices, cereals and coffee cake. Eggs any style, omelets, french toast and pecan, apple or blueberry pancakes with bacon, sausage or ham can be ordered and are accompanied by English muffins or homemade whole wheat toast.

Dinner nightly except Tuesday in summer, 6 to 9, Thursday-Saturday in winter; Sunday brunch, noon to 2. Doubles, $225 MAP; B&B available midweek, $175.

White Hart Inn, Route 44 & Route 41, Salisbury, Conn. 06039. (203) 435-0030.

A wide white porch full of wicker and chintz provides the entry to the venerable White Hart Inn, now grandly restored by Terry and Juliet Moore, owners of our favorite Old Mill restaurant in South Egremont, Mass. The Moores, who said they couldn't bear to see the century-old Salisbury landmark vanish from the scene, acquired the property at a foreclosure auction and poured big bucks into its renovation.

Given their track record, we knew the food would be first-rate, which it is. But the overnight accommodations turned out first-rate as well. The Moores reduced the original 33 rooms on the second and third floors to 26, all with private baths, pedestal sinks and new plumbing. Vivid floral wallpapers with matching comforters are their trademark. Mahogany reproduction furniture, TV sets in armoires and canopy four-poster beds are featured.

The porch and main-floor public rooms are showplaces. Flowers are hand-painted on the pillars on the porch; the floor is stenciled and curtains -- yes, curtains -- are swagged. Off the lobby on one side is the clubby Hunt Room for functions. On the other side is the convivial Tap Room, full of dark wood with green curtains and print wallpaper. Breakfast and lunch are offered in the airy **Garden Court,** where upholstered rattan chairs flank white faux-marble tables.

The Moores commissioned a South Egremont friend to do the paintings of fruits and vegetables that grace the tangerine and green walls of **Julie's New American Sea Grille,** the pristine main dining room; they tie in with the tapestry fabric from Italy. Splendid floral arrangements provide colorful accents to an L-shaped room serene with white over mint linens, floral upholstered chairs and banquettes, and generally widely spaced tables seating a total of 80.

Chef Thomas Stone, with a background of credits in California, New York and Connecticut, changes his menus seasonally and stresses seafood. You might start with oysters on the half shell, locally smoked salmon with horseradish oil, or grilled duck and jalapeño sausage with spiced green lentils and frisée. Entrées ($16 to $23) could be grilled tuna on risotto cake with tapenade sauce,

Handpainted flowers, curtains and wicker grace porch at White Hart Inn.

Moroccan-spiced salmon with pistachio couscous and red-pepper coulis, grilled mahi-mahi with mango-papaya salsa, pecan-crusted chicken with gorgonzola sauce and broccoli rabe, or Tuscan-grilled strip steak with braised leeks and cocotte potatoes. Desserts ($5) are exotic and unusual: clichy cake (chocolate genoise and ganache with coffee buttercream, crème anglaise and raspberry coulis), ladyfinger and mascarpone terrine with espresso sauce, buttermilk and vanilla-bean brûlée, and ricotta-lemon tart with honey-fig-caramel sauce. The primarily American wine list starts in the $15 range.

The evening **Tap Room** menu is similar to the lunchtime fare, bringing salads, sandwiches, gourmet pizzas and entrées from $10 to $14 (for Maine crab cakes or New York steak on garlic toast, both served with shoestring fries).

Lunch daily, 11:30 to 2:30, all day on weekends; dinner in Grill, Wednesday-Sunday 5:30 to 9 or 10, nightly in summer; Tap Room, nightly 5 to 9:30 or 10:30. Doubles, $145 to $165, EP; suites, $180.

Simmons' Way Village Inn, 33 Main St., Millerton, N.Y. 12546. (518) 789-6235.

An emerging area of quirky chic, Millerton got a full-service inn in 1985 and, upon being pictured on the cover of New York magazine, the success of this cream-colored Victorian mansion dating to 1854 was assured. Innkeepers Richard and Nancy Carter, formerly of Westport, Conn., have modeled it after European inns they have cherished in their travels.

The nine guest rooms, all with private baths, are outfitted with antiques, draped canopy beds (most queensize), down pillows and fancy sheets. Some have private porches, working fireplaces and attractive sitting areas. The local weekly newspaper awaits on every bed.

The inn's own blended teas or cappuccino are served in the afternoon in a front tea room and cappuccino bar or, on warm days, on the outdoor veranda with its beige wicker furniture. Guests take a continental breakfast of fruit, cereal, muffins and croissants in an airy breakfast room.

In back is the main dining room with an angled ceiling, gathered curtains in the lower windows, sturdy wood chairs and a dozen tables, two of them tucked into niches. Oil lamps and wall sconces illuminate the white and beige decor. The Carters are particularly proud of their antique silver service platters from England's Highland Regiment.

Chef Michael Myers changes his short menu frequently and provides many tableside flourishes. Dinner might begin with appetizers ($4.25 to $6.95) like smoked trout and avocado with honey-horseradish sauce, vegetable terrine with pimento coulis and watercress sauce or, a house specialty, sundried tomato and brie soup. Main courses are much more expensive: from $19.95 for sautéed coho salmon with lime and walnuts to $26.95 for breast of pheasant with bacon and gorgonzola sauce. Lobster savannah, bluefin tuna with ginger-scallion butter and filet mignon with five-peppercorn sauce are among the possibilities.

Simmons' Way Village Inn dining room.

Desserts could be Dutch apple cake with bavarian cream, lemon trifle, plum torte, cappuccino-mousse cake or the signature white-chocolate-mousse cake. Richard had fun putting together the wine list (both affordable and rare), "thinking of all the good times we had on my travels with the U.N."

Dinner, Wednesday-Sunday 6 to 8, Friday and Saturday 5:30 to 9:30; Sunday brunch, 11:30 to 2:30. No smoking. Doubles, $125 to $150.

Williamsville Inn, Route 41, West Stockbridge, Mass. 01266. (413) 274-6118.

Gail Ryan, a chef from New York, and her mother Kathleen have taken over this quiet and remote country inn, built in 1797 but feeling considerably newer. "We ate here and it was exactly the inn we wanted to buy," said energetic Gail. "It was 18th century, a farmhouse, out in the country but still close to Lenox and Stockbridge."

Ten acres of nicely landscaped grounds stretching toward Tom Ball Mountain include a swimming pool, a clay tennis court and a sculpture garden. Fifteen rooms with private baths are in the main inn, a remodeled barn and two cottages. The spacious rooms are air-conditioned and furnished in period decor. Two armchairs are in front of the fireplace in one with a queen canopy bed; newer rooms on the third floor have skylights.

A tavern off the front entry is most inviting, with a copper hood over the fireplace, stenciled walls and colorful fabrics on the chairs. Guests also relax in a sitting area by the dining room.

With her cooking background, Gail takes special interest in the inn's four pretty, candlelit dining rooms. Her mother's dining-room table graces the fireplaced party room for twelve in the rear, where, Gail says, "you feel like you're dining in a home, not a restaurant." The fireplaced library, where we once ate, has tables on old sewing-machine bases and walls of books. We're also partial to the garden room, with windows on three sides. It's perfect for breakfast, and thus the site for a continental-plus buffet of homemade muffins, pastries, fresh fruit, cheeses, and quiche or a casserole for house guests.

Although Gail might cook up a holiday dessert treat, she leaves the kitchen chores to chef Dennis Powell, who opened the former Wendell House Bistro in Pittsfield after a career at the Culinary Institute of America. You might find some of his Southern/Cajun favorites among the entrées ($12.95 to $19.95), perhaps barbecued shortribs of beef with three-bean salsa or grilled marinated quail served with sweet-potato gaufrette and roasted garlic. Other choices range from chicken pie and grilled breast of duck with orange-fig sauce to wild-mushroom stroganoff with brown basmati rice, spinach pasta with rock shrimp and sautéed beef tournedos with rosemary and extra-virgin olive oil.

Appetizers ($4.50 to $6.25) include vegetable terrine, escargots bordelaise and wild mushrooms gratin. Homemade desserts could be crème brûlée, chocolate-mocha torte or warm apricot crêpe. The good little wine list is affordably priced, with many in the teens.

Dinner nightly in summer, 6 to 9, Thursday-Sunday rest of year. Doubles, $115 to $150; suites, $165.

The Red Lion Inn, Main Street, Stockbridge, Mass. 01262. (413) 298-5545.

As far as one of our relatives from Montreal is concerned, there is only one place to stay and dine when he's on business or pleasure in the Berkshires. It's the Red Lion, the quintessential New England inn that is a mecca for visitors from near and far.

For more than two centuries, it has dominated Stockbridge's Main Street, its guests rocking on the front porch or sipping cocktails in the parlor. Antique furniture and china fill the public rooms, and the Pink Kitty gift shop is just the ticket for selective browsers. The 91 rooms and seventeen suites in the rambling inn, its four outbuildings and its Stevens House (formerly the Berkshire Thistle Inn) are furnished in period decor. All have telephones and air-conditioning, 80 have private baths and some have color TV.

Dining is formal in the bright and spacious main dining room, where New England favorites are featured on a continental-American menu. Entrées range from $16.50 for grilled chicken or trout amandine to $24.50 for prime rib or filet mignon with béarnaise sauce. They run the gamut from turkey with the trimmings to roast Long Island duckling and veal saltimbocca. Start with marinated herring or shrimp cocktail and finish with Indian pudding or apple pie with ice cream or cheddar cheese for a meal out of yesteryear.

More intimate dining takes place in the dark-paneled Widow Bingham Tavern, everyone's idea of what a Colonial pub should look like. In season, the popular outdoor courtyard lined with spectacular impatiens is a colorful and cool retreat for a drink, lunch or dinner. The same menu is served inside and out. A smaller menu is available downstairs in the Lion's Den, which offers entertainment at night.

For lunch ($7.50 to $10.50), you can order almost anything from welsh rarebit or corn fritters and sausage to finnan haddie or creamed chicken over puff pastry. The aforementioned relative always orders the chef's salad, which he thinks is terrific.

Lunch daily, noon to 2; dinner, 6 to 9 (summer, 5:30 to 9:30), Sunday, noon to 9. Doubles, $125 to $155, EP; suites, $235.

Dining

The Best of the Best

West Street Grill, 43 West St., Litchfield, Conn. (203) 567-3885.

Two of the best meals we've ever had were served at this jaunty newcomer, which, we think, offers the most exciting food in Connecticut. It's the subject of universal adulation from food reviewers and the perfect foil for the Litchfield Hills trendoids who make this their own at lunch and dinner seven days a week. The two dining rooms were full the winter Saturday we lunched here, and the manager rattled off the names of half a dozen celebrities who had reserved for that evening.

Lunch began with a rich butternut-squash and pumpkin bisque ($3.95) and the signature grilled peasant bread with parmesan aioli that was absolutely divine ($4.95). Main dishes were an appetizer of grilled country bread with a brandade of white beans and marinated artichokes ($5.50) and a special of grilled smoked-pork tenderloin with spicy Christmas limas ($8.95). The latter arrived on an oversize white plate, nicely presented but looking miniscule and needing a few of the tossed greens that accompanied the brandade. Among the highly touted desserts, we succumbed to an ethereal crème brûlée and a key lime tart that was really tart. With two generous glasses of wine ($3.75 each), the total bill for lunch for two came to a rather New Yorkish $50.

That was nothing, however, compared to the special tasting dinner that Irish owner James O'Shea presented in 1993 to showcase chef Matthew Fahrer's summer menu. The meal began with beet-green soup, grilled peasant bread with parmesan aioli and roasted tomato and goat cheese, corn cakes with crème fraîche and chives, roasted-beet and goat-cheese napoleons with a composed salad, and nori-wrapped salmon with marinated daikon, cucumbers and seaweed. A passion-fruit sorbet followed. By then we felt that we had already dined well, but no, on came the entrées: tasting portions -- which we shared back and forth -- of pan-seared halibut with a beet pappardelle, spicy shrimp cake with ragout of black beans and corn, grilled ginger chicken with polenta and ginger chips, and grilled leg of lamb with a ragout of lentils, spicy curried vegetables and fried greens, including flat-leaf spinach. A little bit here, a little there, and next we knew came a parade of desserts: a plum tart in a pastry so tender as not to be believed, a frozen passion-fruit soufflé, a hazelnut torte with caramel ice cream and a sampling of sorbets (raspberry, white peach and blackberry). How could we be anything but convinced, if ever there were a question, of West Street's incredible culinary prowess? The results easily merit the prices ($6.95 to $10.95 for appetizers, $14.95 to $21.95 for pastas and main courses).

Although the food is foremost, the decor is no slouch. The long, narrow dining room is sleek in black and white, with a row of low booths up the middle, tables and mirrors on either side, and a back room with trompe-l'oeil curtains on the walls. Lavish floral arrangements add splashes of color.

Lunch daily, 11:30 to 3, weekends to 4; dinner nightly, 5:30 to 9 or 10.

John Andrew's, Route 23, South Egremont, Mass. (413) 528-3469.

"Innovative and spectacular." These are words that area chefs and innkeepers frequently employ when describing this real comer, which has evolved nicely from the former Sebastian's restaurant. Chef-owner Dan Smith and his wife Susan

Sponged walls and tiled fireplace add warmth to John Andrew's.

have given the decor a dramatic upgrade and the food is considered some of the most creative in the Berkshires.

The sponged walls are a romantic red, the ceiling green and the striking chairs that came from the Copacabana in New York have been reupholstered and repainted green. Metal wall sconces and a tiled fireplace add warmth. At night, the walls "positively glow -- like copper," says Susan. The enclosed rear porch is mod in cane and chrome, artfully decorated with black and white runners flowing from the roof out toward an outdoor dining deck.

The Smiths, who came here in 1990 from the Ragamont Inn and Freshfields in northwest Connecticut, met in Florida when he was cooking at the Ritz-Carlton in Naples. She wanted to return to her native Berkshires and named their acquisition after her grandfather, John Andrew Bianchi.

Dan favors Northern Italian and Mediterranean cuisine on his straightforward menu, which changes seasonally and represents good value. You might start with white-cornmeal pizza with hickory-smoked salmon and mascarpone; peasant bread with roasted garlic, goat cheese, sundried tomatoes and black olives; pan-fried oysters with baby greens and anchovy-mustard vinaigrette, or grilled tequila-marinated shrimp with black-bean sauce and mango-cilantro salsa ($5.75 to $7). The homemade pastas ($11 to $11.75) might pair fettuccine with shiitake and porcini mushrooms, spinach, pinenuts and cream, or saffron pasta with prosciutto, arugula and roasted peppers.

Entrées start at $14.50 for grilled leg of lamb with straw-potato pancake and grilled vegetables or grilled pork chop with cumin, tomatillo and corn salsa and sweet-potato gratin. Top price is $17.50 for pan-seared veal steak with hazelnuts, wild mushrooms and thyme. In between are monkfish with roasted red-pepper coulis and couscous, grilled swordfish with braised fennel and black olives, and crisp duck with garlic mashed potatoes.

Desserts ($4) include frangelico crème caramel, plum and vanilla tart, chocolate-hazelnut torta with hazelnut ice cream, pear crisp with vanilla ice cream and caramelized-apple tart with cider crème anglaise. The wine list, heavily American with a few Italian and French selections, is priced from $17 to $79.

Some of the appetizers turn up on the Sunday brunch menu ($6.50 to $9.50). We were particularly taken by the fried eggs over roasted asparagus and shaved parmesan and a salad of chicken, watercress, scallions, pears and hazelnuts with a cider-maple vinaigrette.

Dinner nightly, 5 to 10; Sunday brunch, 11:30 to 5.

Church Street Cafe, 69 Church St., Lenox, Mass. (413) 637-2745.

This is the casual, creative kind of American bistro to which we return time and again for an interesting meal whenever we're in Lenox. Owners Linda Forman and Clayton Hambrick, once Ethel Kennedy's chef, specialize in light, fresh cafe food, served inside by a ficus tree and outside on two decks.

Blackboard specials supplement the seasonal menus. Clayton once worked at a creole restaurant in Washington, a background that shows in his Louisiana gumbo ($7.95 at lunch, $5.95 as an appetizer at dinner) and a special of blackened redfish. Dinners might start with fried corn cake with refried black beans and chipotle-chile sauce or spicy jalapeño tortilla with goat cheese, roasted chiles and salsa ($4.95 to $6.50). Entrées ($13.95 to $17.50) include Southwestern vegetable stew with butternut squash, hominy and chiles; cassoulet of white beans, duck confit and garlic sausage; grilled salmon with smoked-salmon butter and potato-leek pancakes; bouillabaisse with roasted-pepper rouille; sautéed Maine crab cakes with dilled rémoulade sauce, and grilled oriental peppered lamb loin with ginger sauce, sautéed greens and szechuan eggplant. One of the four pasta dishes ($13.95 to $14.95) incorporates arugula, chickpeas, potatoes, tomatoes and asiago cheese over orecchiette.

A recent lunch included a super black-bean tostada and the Church Street salad, a colorful array of mixed greens, goat cheese, chick peas, eggs and red pepper, with a zippy balsamic vinaigrette dressing on the side. The whole-wheat/sunflower-seed rolls were so good that we accepted seconds. The ten lunch offerings are in the $6.50 to $7.95 range.

For dessert, try the chilled cranberry soufflé topped with whipped cream, if it's available. Frozen rum-raisin mousse, white-chocolate crème brûlée and bittersweet-chocolate/espresso torte with vanilla crème anglaise are other possibilities. The house Georges Duboeuf wine is $11.50 a bottle; two dozen other wines are priced in the teens and twenties.

There are fresh flowers on the white-linened tables and changing artworks on the ragged salmon walls above dark wine-colored wainscoting. The stools at the small bar are charmingly painted with farm animals.

Lunch, Monday-Saturday 11 to 2; dinner nightly, 5:30 to 9; Sunday brunch in summer. Closed Monday and Tuesday in winter. No smoking.

La Bruschetta, 1 Harris St., West Stockbridge, Mass. (413) 232-7141.

Steven and Catherine Taub -- both young alumni of Wheatleigh and Blantyre, where he last was executive chef and she pastry chef -- opened their own winner of a place in 1992 in the quarters where Truc Orient Express got its start. They

Steven and Catherine Taub in dining room at La Bruschetta.

offer contemporary and traditional Italian cuisine at down-to-earth prices to an appreciative clientele.

It's a Mom and Pop operation, Steve and Catherine being the only ones in the kitchen the afternoon we stopped by. They were busy preparing everything for the night's meals from scratch. Their short menu features pastas ($11 to $14.95), perhaps tagliatelle bolognese, rigatoni with roasted chicken and braised escarole, and spinach fettuccine with wild and domestic mushrooms.

Main courses ($11 to $15.75) could be pan-roasted trout stuffed with a duxelles of mushrooms and olives, pan-roasted fillet of salmon with salsa verde, cioppino, breast of duckling cured in herbs and spices with a cabernet sauce, and a signature grilled breast of free-range chicken redolent of oils, herbs and spices. Heartier meat dishes like beef and lamb were conspicuously missing at our visit, although grilled New York strip with gorgonzola polenta was offered on an earlier menu.

The namesake bruschetta ($4.15) might come with chèvre, grilled radicchio and basil-olive oil. Other starters ($4.50 to $7.75) include warm duck salad with apples and toasted pinenuts, radicchio and endive; rollatini of marinated eggplant filled with sundried tomatoes and chèvre; roasted quail stuffed with risotto and pancetta; house-cured salmon with a Mediterranean vegetable relish, crostini and olivada, and prosciutto of venison smoked with ripe pears and provolone.

By all means save room for one of Catherine's incredible desserts, perhaps chocolate-hazelnut cake, walnut jam tart made of fruits cooked in wine, a rich chocolate-orange crème served with caramel-liqueur sauce. tirami su or assorted gelati. The Taubs also have fun with their wine list, which is layered in sheets with "our latest finds" on top, starting at $11.

The decor in two small rooms remains much as when it was Truc's: white linens, upholstered rattan chairs, lovely glass vases full of fresh flowers and sheer French curtains draped over the windows. Two big wine globes are part of every setting.

Dinner nightly except Wednesday, 6 to 8:30 or 9, Sunday 5:30 to 8:30. No smoking.

The Old Mill, Route 23, South Egremont, Mass. (413) 528-1421.

In the charming and oft-overlooked hamlet of South Egremont, the Old Mill (which really is an old gristmill and blacksmith shop) has been impressing diners since 1978. The atmosphere is a cross between a simple Colonial tavern and a European wayside inn, warm and friendly, yet sophisticated.

The large, L-shaped main dining room has wide-planked and stenciled floors, beamed ceilings, pewter cutlery and bottles of olive oil as centerpieces on the nicely spaced tables, and a collection of old mincing tools on the cream-colored walls. Reflections of candles sparkle in the small-paned windows. An addition to a sunken rear dining room provides large windows onto Hubbard Brook.

A few nightly specials supplement the dozen entrées on the seasonal menu. They start at a bargain $12 for penne with ragout of ground beef and pork. The bulk are in the $16 range, and the most expensive at $23 are broiled veal chop with porcini butter or New York steak with green-peppercorn/mustard sauce. All come with vegetables and house salad.

The black-bean soup ($3.50) is a treat — hot, thick with pieces of spicy sausage and garnished with scallions. Other starters ($5 to $6.50) might be country-style pâté, house-cured gravlax with mustard-dill sauce, grilled shrimp over black-bean cake with tomato-lime salsa and red-pepper ravioli filled with goat cheese. Three kinds of rolls are served in a handsome basket. The salad is a mixture of greens, tomatoes and sliced mushrooms with a creamy, tangy oil and vinegar dressing.

Of the entrées, which always include the freshest of fish, we have enjoyed broiled red snapper, fillet of gray sole, and baked bluefish with ginger and scallions. Veal piccata with a lemony sauce was sensational, and calves liver with apple-smoked bacon was superior. Other possibilities include grilled salmon with orange-fennel salsa, herb-crusted pork chop with peach-blueberry chutney and sweet-potato chips, and medallions of venison with chanterelles.

The interesting wine list, reasonably priced, is split in origin between California and France, with nods to Italy and Australia. There's a cozy parlor bar for drinks while you wait for a table, a likely occurrence since reservations are not taken for less than five and the throngs arrive early on weekends.

Of the desserts, we think the mocha torte and the meringue glacé with cointreau and strawberries are most heavenly. Others include profiteroles au chocolat, crème brûlée, apricot charlotte and flourless chocolate cake.

Owners Terry and Juliet Moore — he is British and trained as a chef on the Cunard Line ships — have reopened the White Hart Inn in Salisbury, Conn., where they now make their home and spend a good bit of their time. But the Old Mill carries on, and its 65 seats may turn over four times on busy nights.

Dinner nightly, 5:30 to 9:30 or 10:30; Sunday brunch, 11 to 3. Closed Monday or Tuesday in off-season.

Castle Street Cafe, 10 Castle St., Great Barrington, Mass. (413) 528-5244.

The locals cheered when Michael Ballon, who used to cook at the Williamsville Inn in West Stockbridge, returned to the Berkshires to open his own cafe in 1989 after several years at upscale restaurants in New York City.

Other restaurants have not had much luck in this space beside the movie theater, but Michael succeeds with his bistro, especially on nights the theater is busy. Artworks are hung on the brick walls of the long narrow room with white-linened tables and windsor chairs. The bar at the rear, where Michael puts out goodies like pâté and cheese, is the only place where smoking is allowed. The wine bar dispenses a number of select choices by the glass.

With appetizers ($4 to $6) like grilled shiitake mushrooms with garlic and herbs, spinach and goat-cheese salad and a plate of the good local Merrimac smoked salmon and entrées like a Castle burger with straw potatoes ($9) or eggplant

Chef-owner Michael Ballon at Castle Street Cafe.

roulade stuffed with three cheeses ($12), there is something for every vegetarian and carnivore. Other main courses ($15 to $18) include grilled salmon with coriander salsa, bouillabaisse, braised chicken with black olives and garlic, grilled filet of lamb with cannellini-bean salad and steak au poivre with straw potatoes.

The dessert list is headed by the world's best chocolate-mousse cake (according to New York Newsday). Others include crème brûlée, warm apple crisp with vanilla ice cream and frozen lemon soufflé.

Michael makes a point of buying from Berkshire farmers and purveyors, whom he nicely acknowledges on the back of his menu.

Dinner, Wednesday-Monday 5 to 9:30 or 10:30.

Boiler Room Cafe, 405 Stockbridge Road (Route 7), Great Barrington, Mass. (413) 528-4280.

Michelle Miller, once a chef at Alice's Restaurant of Arlo Guthrie fame and founder of Suchele Bakers, moved her restaurant and catering service from an old boiler room at the out-of-the-way Southfield Outlet and Craft Center in 1993 into the thick of things along Route 7 in Great Barrington. She transformed an old farmhouse into three colorful rooms -- one red, one beige and one olive green -- joined by arched doorways. Mismatched chairs are at tables covered with white cloths. Twiggy branches are arranged artfully here and there, as are wood sculptures by Michele's husband, Peter Murkett. Although she has turned cooking chores over to chef Susan Donaghey, Michele still does some of the baking, which is fortunate, for her dacquoise is about the best we've tasted.

Michelle contends the food here is not very fancy — "we tread a line between comfortable and sophisticated." Instead of being categorized, everything on the changing menu is lumped together roughly in the sequence you would expect to order. The menu might start, for instance, with gazpacho toledano and creamy mussel and saffron soup in the $4.50 to $5 range. The list continues with things like sorrel and red-onion tart, lamb sausage with white-bean and sage ragout, fried Maine crab cakes with homemade tartar sauce, Vietnamese-style shrimp with cellophane noodles and cilantro, and creamy polenta with grilled leeks, fennel and crimini mushrooms (these in the $6 to $12 range). Next in order are what other menus would consider main courses ($17 to $21), perhaps grilled curry-crusted lamb kabob with minted couscous, paella valenciana, grilled tuna tapenade, oven-roasted salmon with ruby chard and corn pudding, and Puerto Rican roast chicken with black beans and cornbread. Vegetables like garlic mashed potatoes and eggplant and tomato tian are add-ons.

Desserts are on a separate list, as they should be, given the repertoire of their creator. You might find apple-blackberry crumb pie, toasted-pecan cheesecake, chocolate pots de crème with concord grapes and cookies, and "drowned" vanilla ice cream with scotch and espresso. Interesting wines and beers are offered.

A casualty of the restaurant's move is the elimination of lunches, which used to make a great little intermission during shopping forays at the outlet center. The dinner hours have been expanded to compensate.

Dinner, Wednesday-Sunday from 5:30. No smoking.

Doc's, Flirtation Avenue at Route 45, New Preston, Conn. (203) 868-9415.

Just about everybody's favorite restaurant in Connecticut's Northwest Corner seems to be this roadside stand gone upscale across the street from Lake Waramaug. Adam Riess, a Californian fresh out of the University of Pennsylvania, opened the Italian cafe, pizzeria and bakery in 1989 to immediate success.

He leased it in 1992 to his Palestinian chef, Riad Aamar, while he pursued cooking and graduate studies in New York. But the tradition continues: dynamite pizzas in the $7 range, super pastas from $9.75 to $13.75 and a smattering of robust entrées ($13.75 to $16.75), among them sautéed salmon with pesto, chicken roasted with shallots and crimini mushrooms, and rack of lamb roasted with white beans, shiitake mushrooms and black olives.

You might start with an appetizer of fried polenta with gorgonzola or goat cheese with roasted peppers on arugula with pesto vinaigrette. But most opt for one of the new-wave pizzas, perhaps the cipolla (caramelized onions, gorgonzola and fresh rosemary) or the pomidoro secchi (sundried tomatoes, mozzarella and basil). Pastas could be handmade fettuccine with smoked trout, tomato, garlic and olive oil or farfalle with salmon, garlic and cream sauce. Desserts could be ricotta cheesecake, torta di chocolate or tirami su.

The ever-so-rustic rustic dining room contains chairs painted pea green, spartan tables bearing butcher paper, votive candles and big bottles of extra-virgin olive oil (plus metal containers that the menu notes contain salt, not cheese), and a handful of posters and plants for accents.

The name? Adam was thinking of naming it Adamo's, but ended up naming it for his grandfather, a physician who has summered on the lake for 40 years.

Lunch, Friday-Sunday noon to 2; dinner, Wednesday-Sunday 5 to 10. BYOB.

Other Dining Choices

Cafe Lucia, 90 Church St., Lenox, Mass. (413) 637-2640.

Authentic northern Italian cuisine is served up by Jim Lucie at this serious little cafe, which has evolved from its days as an art gallery with a cafe. Jim opened up the kitchen so patrons could glimpse the culinary proceedings and lately replaced the artworks with family photos on the exposed brick walls. A spiral staircase remains the focal point of the main dining room. Especially popular in season are the outdoor cafe and garden bar, their tables topped with umbrellas.

An antipasto table with the day's offerings ($7.95) is showcased at the entry. Fans praise the carpaccio with mustard and caper sauce ($3.95), pastas like imported linguini with shrimp and sundried tomatoes ($14.95), and such entrées ($11.95 to $17.95) as chicken scarapello, baked calamari Genoa style, veal milanese and a signature osso buco with risotto, so distinguished that it draws New Yorkers back annually.

Desserts include tirami su, fresh fruit tarts, flourless chocolate torte and gelatos. Those desserts, a fine port or brandy, and cappuccino can be taken on warm evenings on the flower-bedecked patio. A few Californias augment the basically Italian wine list.

Dinner nightly from 5; closed Sunday and Monday in winter. No smoking.

La Tomate, 293 Main St., Great Barrington, Mass. (413) 528-3003.

Born in the south of France, Jean Claude Vierne had his fill of New York restaurants (La Caravelle and La Côte Basque, among others) when he and his family moved to his wife's native territory. "She showed me the Berkshires — it looked like France," he said. And the rest is La Tomate, a lively bistro serving earthy, French provincial food at down-to-earth prices.

Jean Claude uses lots of fresh herbs, garlic and tomatoes in his cooking, and says he can barely keep up with orders for his basic chicken broiled in a 700-degree oven.

Among the hearty little appetizers are onion tart, grilled garlic sausage with warm potato salad, tuna tapenade and steamed mussels in saffron sauce ($3.50 to $11). There are interesting soups and salads, plus six pasta dishes ($9 to $10), among them fusilli with shrimp and scallops in a lobster cream sauce.

The ten main courses range from $16 for the signature half broiled chicken or scallops and shrimp cardinale to $22 for lobster bouillabaisse or grilled lamb chops with mild olive butter.

Desserts include crème caramel, chocolate mousse, fruit tarts and raspberry/chocolate-truffle torte. The wine list is pleasantly priced.

Two side-by-side dining rooms contain tables covered with white butcher paper over linens. Adorning some of the walls are the framed prints of Jean Claude's wife, photographer Nikki Hayes, who also oversees the front of the house.

Lunch, May-October, Tuesday-Saturday noon to 2; dinner, Tuesday-Sunday 5 to 10 or 11; Sunday brunch, 11:30 to 3.

Truc Orient Express, Harris Street, West Stockbridge, Mass. (413) 232-4204.

This enchanting place is run by Trai Thi Buong, who is from Vietnam by way of Truc's restaurant in Hartford, and has done so well that she opened La Truc, a Vietnamese restaurant in Boca Raton, Fla. It also testifies to the successful saga of a courageous family starting anew and reunited after fleeing Saigon in 1975. A fascinating scrapbook at the entrance contains press accounts of their six-year-long effort to retrieve their oldest son from Saigon.

Trai and her husband Luy first leased a restored 1841 house in West Stockbridge for takeout and patio dining and commuted from Hartford. Eventually they were able to purchase the house, expand it, and offer both patio and indoor dining amid chic oriental decor. They had to close the house to diners in 1990 because of too expensive a town sewerage assessment, Luy lamented, but they managed to lease it later to La Bruschetta.

Now they concentrate their dining on two floors of an adjacent building, acquired in 1988 and linked to the original by an umbrellaed outdoor deck. In this ultra-sleek space there's seating for 110 on lacquered burgundy and black chairs at tables topped with white linens. The polished wide-board floors are dotted with beautiful oriental rugs, and there are gorgeous screens and huge black vases inlaid with mother of pearl. An open staircase leads past lovely stained-glass windows to more dining areas beneath vaulted ceilings and skylights on the second floor.

Vietnamese music plays in the background, and haunting aromas waft from the kitchen. While Luy and his family are congenial hosts, an occasional communications gap is bridged by pointing to the numbers of the 65 items on the menu.

Dishes are perfectly prepared, not too spicy, and prices are moderate (about $8 at lunch, $11.50 to $17 at dinner). We love the Vietnamese egg rolls, the best crispy happy pancakes ever, roast pork sautéed with cashews and vegetables, the shrimp sautéed with snow peas in lemon grass, "singing chicken" and Mongolian hot pot (dinner only, $24 for two), washed down with one of the good beers. Luy takes great pride in pointing out new specialties like the crispy duck with lemon grass, the very spicy "seafood delight" sautéed in garlic and tomato sauce, and the "very, very special beef in four dishes" dinner, from sliced beef soup to shaking beef salad to Vietnamese beef fondue, $45 for two.

Flan, a very lemony lemon mousse, and lichee nuts on ice make worthy endings.

Lunch daily, 11 to 3; dinner, 5:30 to 9 or 10. Closed Monday in winter.

Bronze Dog Cafe, Great Barrington Railroad Station, Great Barrington, Mass. (413) 528-5678.

It had to be serendipitous. The first time we encountered this laid-back new eatery shortly after it opened in 1993 in the Great Barrington railroad station it was billed as serving healthful gourmet food from a California-style menu. A month or so later, we stopped in for lunch. The menu was markedly different

Trai Thi Buong and husband Luy Nguyen at Truc Orient Express.

and a little notice indicated that Miss Ruby was back. Could it be? One of our favorite Berkshires chefs, Ruby Bronz, who'd moved on to New York, unexpectedly turned up in the Bronze Cafe kitchen as chef. "We had no idea when we named it," said Heather Austin, one of the owners. "It must have been cosmic."

Until Ruby Bronz was there, the only things bronze were the two bronze dogs at the door. A few Turkish rugs on the walls and hanging plants from the ceiling add color to the small cavern of a train-station room, spare as spare can be with shiny bare wood tables and floors. There's seasonal dining at little tables outside on the railroad platform.

As Heather declared, Miss Ruby's love is cooking. That was quickly re-confirmed for us at lunch. One of us tried the soup of the day, cabbage and beet ($2.95), and an inspired appetizer of corn-batter cakes with black beans and grapefruit salsa. The other sampled the piping-hot quiche made with green chiles and monterey jack ($5.75), served with a good mixed-green salad. French bread came with a crock of butter but no side plate, making eating a bit messy before our meals arrived. A slice of fresh peach and raspberry pie and a cup of cappuccino from the showy espresso machine on the bar ended a happy reunion.

The menus are perfect for mixing and matching, from great egg dishes for brunch or lunch to inspired salads, main dishes and desserts. Dinner appetizers ($3.25 to $5.95) are as diverse as spicy broiled tofu, smoked bluefish pâté and a roasted-garlic plate with fresh mozzarella and sundried tomatoes. Salads ($2.95 to $3.50) could involve peppery greens with roasted pecans, blue cheese and sherry vinaigrette; warm salad with watercress, steamed Chinese greens and miso-plum vinaigrette; curried brown lentils with cucumber-yogurt sauce, and tofu, cucumber and soba noodles with ponza sauce.

Entrées run from $6.95 for pinto-bean tostada with guacamole to $13.95 for marinated leg of lamb with chèvre-stuffed onions. In between are the likes of grilled polenta with wild mushrooms and spicy greens, warm scallops with blueberry vinaigrette, seared salmon with coriander sauce and papaya salsa, and szechuan chicken with hot peppers, Chinese vegetables, peanuts and a medley of grains.

Desserts vary from Miss Ruby's Houston Junior League fudge pie to tarte tatin with whipped cream. An interesting little French and California wine list is priced from $11 to $31.

Lunch, Tuesday-Friday noon to 2:30; brunch, Saturday and Sunday, 10 to 2; dinner, Thursday-Sunday 5:30 to 9:30 or 10.

Zampano's, 579 Pittsfield-Lenox Road, Lenox. (413) 448-8600.

"We can cook" is the motto at this appealing and casual eatery. And they sure can, based on a couple of summertime lunches on the trellised deck, fortunately screened off from busy Route 7. With rolls came a sweet red-pepper and cheddar soup and a spicy gazpacho, chosen from an array that included potato and garlic, black bean and ginger-pear-nectarine. These were followed by a trip to the salad bar ($6.50 at lunch, $7.99 at dinner), an experience that wins over even those of us who turn up their noses at salad bars. It's a gourmet (and all-vegetarian) layout of twenty treats that looks like a deli spread at Dean & DeLuca, from three kinds of potato salad to wild mushrooms, noodles, chick peas, black beans, lentils and rice, with balsamic vinegar, extra-virgin olive oil and raspberry vinaigrette among the dressings. Everything appealed, so one of us went back to the salad bar for a dessert of fresh fruits and a whole poached pear in cinnamon sauce.

On another occasion we found the grilled chicken sandwich on a sesame roll, served with a small salad, very tasty and exceptionally priced at $3.99. Ditto for a pasta special called Nantucket Bay parmesano ($5.95), a sensational dish of scallops and fettuccine.

The same menu is available at dinner, when you also can order entrées and blackboard specials ($12.95 to $14.95) like oyster stew, shrimp scampi, scallops with pesto and broccoli, grilled swordfish and chargrilled steak à la grecque. The daily specials "are where we have our fun," says Culinary Institute-trained chef-owner Chris Masiero, who with his brother Matt runs the nearby Guido's Freshmarket Place. Desserts are up to the rest of the fare, perhaps black-raspberry cheesecake, chocolate-mousse pie with walnuts and bread pudding with maple sauce. There's a good, attractively priced beer and wine selection as well.

Lunch daily, 11:30 to 4; dinner nightly, from 5.

New Yorker, Route 44, Millerton, N.Y. (518) 789-6293.

What's this? A sleek, sizable establishment with something of the look of a Southern-style house called the New Yorker? With a French chef and a French-American menu?

The confusion arises because Gerard Gaspel, who used to run L'Auberge de France across the state line in Lakeville, Conn., took over the trendy New Yorker in 1989 from a management that had specialized in prime angus beef. From an intimate auberge to a sprawling place with a large lounge, four dining rooms and a dining porch, Gerard seems to have made the transition well — better perhaps than some regulars from either place who say they suffer from schizophrenia.

At the New Yorker, he's mixed specialties that we've enjoyed from L'Auberge, such as beef wellington, calves-liver sauté with raspberry sauce, magret of barbary duck with peaches and wild rice, rack of lamb provençal and cassoulet with confit of duck, with American items like crab cakes with orange-pecan sauce, catfish veracruz and chicken breast with goat cheese and sundried tomatoes. Black angus beef continues to be featured. Entrées run from $16.95 to $24.95.

Equally broad in scope are the appetizers ($6.95 to $8.95), from a mousseline of avocado and smoked salmon on a tomato-basil coulis to frog's legs provençal and a seafood combo yielding oysters rockefeller, clams casino and mussels provençal. Desserts range from chocolate-truffle cake to soufflé grand marnier. A lengthy cafe menu -- from sandwiches and salads to pastas, main courses and vegetarian dishes -- is priced from $9.95 to $13.95.

Dining is in the airy pub, on a big porch or in a series of more formal rooms, furnished with comfortable armchairs and white linens. Flickering oil lamps and small glass vases bearing slender anemones graced the tables at our visit.

Lunch daily, 11:30 to 3; dinner nightly, 3 to 9.

Lodging

Cliffwood Inn, 25 Cliffwood St., Lenox, Mass. 01240. (413) 637-3330.

Joy and Scottie Farrelly walked in the door of this gorgeous Belle Epoque mansion built in 1904 in the Stanford White style for a former ambassador to France and said, "this is it." The executive of Ralston Purina Co. and his wife had been looking for a retirement activity and a place to house the furnishings they had collected while living in Montreal, Brussels, Paris and Italy. Cliffwood was the perfect find.

Seven luxurious guest rooms (all with private baths and six with fireplaces, one of them in the bathroom) are beautifully furnished with the fruits of the Farrellys'

Former ambassador's Belle Epoque mansion takes in guests as Cliffwood Inn.

travels. Each is named for one of their ancestors, and a scrapbook describing the particular ancestor is on the bed — an illustrious lot they were. Joy had a bookcase and hutch designed and built in Vermont to fill a space in the second-floor hall and to pick up the pattern of the rounded windows nearby. It holds books from sixteen different countries. A gaily painted lunch pail is a decorative accent in one room; Joy has done folk-art boxes for Kleenex in the others. The Farrellys also are dealers in Eldred Wheeler 18th-Century American furniture and 27 of the prized pieces are in the rooms (and for sale). Notable at our latest visit were the queensize canopy Sheraton field bed and side tables in the Nathanial Foote room, lately enlarged by removing a wall between two rooms and boasting two wing chairs in front of the fireplace.

Guests gather in the magnificent living room, foyer and dining room, much as they would as house guests in a mansion. A full-length back porch overlooks a lap swimming pool with hammocks nearby. Wine and hors d'oeuvre — things like marinated olives, cheeses and a hot artichoke dip — are served in the late afternoon. "Dinners in a party atmosphere" are offered occasionally in the spring. "Sharing our house is a great way to keep busy and have fun," Joy explains.

A buffet-style continental breakfast in the elegant dining room brings home-made breads, popovers and muffins, homemade granola for which Joy shares the recipe, and a special hot fruit compote with crème fraîche.

Doubles, $105 to $180. No smoking.

The Gables Inn, 103 Walker St., Lenox 01240. (413) 637-3416.

Frank Newton, a former banker and sometime pianist, and his wife Mary operated the Gables as a restaurant before converting their banquet hall into lodging and making this a deluxe inn. Built in the Queen Anne style, the century-old classic Berkshire "cottage" was the home of Edith Wharton at the turn of the century while she was building her permanent edifice, the Mount. Her upstairs room is particularly alluring with its illustrious heritage, the four-poster bed canopied in a pink and white print, a beautiful patterned rug and a deep plum sofa by the fireplace. The Newtons will happily show you the famous eight-sided library where she once wrote some of her short stories.

Also full of flair and Victorian warmth are the other seventeen guest rooms and suites, all with private baths and many with wood-burning fireplaces. The Jockey Club Suite offers a brass bed in a niche, an ample sitting area with two sofas facing a big-screen TV and a private entrance from the back-yard pool area. Also in demand are two large second-floor suites built out over a former roof. Both have cathedral ceilings, high windows, swagged draperies, fireplaces and TVs.

The Show Business Room is full of signed photos of old stars and a library of showbiz volumes, with which to curl up on the chintz loveseat in front of the fireplace. Aptly named, the Presidents' Room contains one of the largest collections of presidential photos, autographs and memoirs in Massachusetts.

The breakfast room is spectacular with one long table in the center and, along the sides, six round tables for two skirted in pink, green and white. Sour-cream cake, bran muffins and pumpkin, lemon-almond and banana breads are typical fare. Pancakes and french toast are added in the summer.

In the back yard, the Newtons have planted pretty gardens. They also put in a tennis court and an enclosed, solar-heated swimming pool with a jacuzzi.

Doubles, $70 to $145; suites, $195.

The Inn at Stockbridge, Route 7, Box 618, Stockbridge, Mass. 01262. (413) 298-3337.

A lovely pillared house on twelve acres set far back from the road is a special destination for gourmets. New Jersey businessman Don Weitz and his wife Lee converted it in 1982 into a sumptuous bed-and-breakfast inn with eight guest rooms, all with private baths. "We try to make people comfortable in an elegant style," says Lee, the vivacious innkeeper whose husband commuted weekends until he "retired" to go into the inn business full-time.

In the formal dining room set with the family's fine Wedgwood and silver serving pieces, this former food-service management instructor has been known to serve grand dinners (including wine) as part of holiday packages and to groups by reservation. The inn's New Year's Eve weekend package traditionally culminates in a black-tie dinner with live music.

A house-party atmosphere prevails as the Weitzes serve wine and cheese in the afternoons to guests, who play the stereo in one of the luxurious sitting rooms or use the large outdoor pool in season. A fancy breakfast (baked french toast topped with grand-marnier butter and fresh fruit, soufflés or coffee cake with New Jersey blueberries) is served in the dining room or on the back patio.

Guest rooms are expensively and handsomely furnished; most have kingsize beds. There are fans over the bed in the Chinese Room with its oriental wallpaper, and two posh chairs all in rose and green in the Rose Room. The main-floor Terrace Room has a rear deck and private entrance overlooking the pool. Very spacious, it has three chairs, a small TV, a kingsize bed whose vivid floral spread matches the curtains, and a bathroom with a circular whirlpool tub. The toiletries bear the inn's private label.

Doubles, $115 to $225.

Merrell Tavern Inn, Route 102, Box 318, South Lee, Mass. 01260. (413) 243-1794 or (800) 243-1794.

History buffs particularly like this elegantly restored inn, one of the first properties in the Berkshires to be listed in the National Register of Historic Places. Saved early in the century by Mabel Choate of Naumkeag in Stockbridge, the 1800 building a mile east of Stockbridge was acquired by Faith and Charles Reynolds of Rochester, N.Y., who carefully created nine guest rooms on three floors in 1981 and poured several hundred thousand dollars into a complete redecoration a dozen years later.

All with private baths and some with fireplaces, the bedrooms are furnished

Circular Colonial bar is feature of breakfast room at Merrell Tavern Inn.

with canopy or four-poster beds and antiques the couple have collected over 35 years. They have been upscaled lately with telephones, Gilbert & Soames toiletries, tiled floors in the bathrooms, comfy sitting areas, fancy window treatments, and color-coordinated linens and towels. The owners even ignored the period to furnish a couple of bedrooms in fancy Victorian style, based upon customer requests. An air of luxury is created by decorator fabrics and oriental rugs throughout as well as prized possessions like an 1800 grandfather's clock. Guests register in the old tap room at the birdcage bar, the only surviving circular Colonial bar still intact. They relax over lemonade or hot cider in a guest parlor with a beehive oven, fashioned from the old keeping room. A small room adjacent, formerly a guest bedroom, has been converted into a TV room.

The tap room is where Faith serves breakfast of the guest's choice, remarkably cooked to order by Chuck in what he calls the world's smallest kitchen. The room is a beauty, with pale yellow tablecloths, handmade Bennington pottery, well-aged woodwork and a fireplace of Count Rumford design. Chuck decorates each breakfast plate -- a mushroom and cheese omelet, blueberry-walnut pancakes, french toast with raspberry syrup or whatever -- with parsley and johnny jump-ups from his garden. He also painted the incredible murals in the front hall, and built the screened gazebo down by the Housatonic River in the deep back yard.

Doubles, $95 to $155. No smoking.

Applegate Bed & Breakfast, 279 West Park St., RR 1, Box 576, Lee 01238. (413) 243-4451.

A pillared porte cochere hints of Tara at this majestic, sparkling white Georgian Colonial, built by a New York surgeon in the 1920s as a weekend retreat. Surrounding it are six tranquil acres bearing venerable apple trees, towering pines, flower gardens and a beckoning swimming pool. Inside are elegant common rooms, six guest rooms with private baths and an effervescent welcome by Nancy and Rick Cannata, she an airline flight attendant and he a pilot, who decided to alight here in 1990 and convert their large home into a B&B. They plan their flight schedules so at least one of them is always on hand,

Off a grand entry foyer are a fireplaced dining room, its three tables each set for breakfast for four, and an uncommonly large living room equipped with a grand piano. To the side of the living room is a sun porch, newly enclosed for use as a reading and TV room. Off the dining room is a screened back porch facing the pool and gardens.

A carved staircase leads to the four main guest rooms, one the master suite with a kingsize poster bed, family photos on the mantel above the working fireplace, a sitting area with a sofabed and two chairs, and a great steam shower. "What a treat to sit in there and steam away," advises Nancy. The other rooms are slightly less grand in scale, holding queensize beds. One has Shaker-style pine furniture, another a walnut sleigh bed and a third an antique white iron bed and white and blue wicker furnishings. At our visit, Rick was redoing two rooms in a far wing of the house. One is a corner space swathed in pale lavenders and greens with a tiger-maple four-poster, a sitting area and the best view of the grounds. The other is a smaller room done up in Victorian style with an antique bed and matching marble-topped dresser and a hat rack holding an opera cape and granny hats. A rear carriage house has been renovated into a two-bedroom, condo-style apartment, available for $330 a night, three-night minimum.

Godiva chocolates and decanters of brandy are in each room. The Cannatas offer wine and cheese around 5 p.m. The continental-plus breakfast, including cereal and yogurt, is served amid stemware and antique cups and saucers.

Doubles, $110 to $195.

The Roeder House, Route 183, Box 525, Stockbridge 01262. (413) 298-4015.

Their antiques and art business in Stockbridge helps explain the furnishings and decorative flair that Diane and Vernon Reuss have endowed on their restored 1856 farmhouse in rural Glendale. But it was sheer chance that led Diane to open a B&B when a daughter left for college. An innkeeper-friend begged for an extra room for one weekend's overflow. The next thing she knew she was opening three rooms – "we even rented our bed" – and breakfast was becoming a production. "We needed a bigger kitchen," so they doubled the house's size to add quarters for the family. The result is an interesting blend of old and new, a 40-foot-long professional kitchen, and six guest rooms with queensize poster beds and private baths.

The kitchen has become the focal point of the house, and the elaborate breakfast – served family style at 9 (Sundays at 9:30) – is the day's social hour. Coffee is put out at 8 in a big informal breakfast room, notable for a row of teddy bears on an antique bench and a lovely oriental carpet. Diane and her guests linger over fruit, juice, blueberry muffins, cranberry upside-down cake and perhaps buttermilk waffles, sourdough grand-marnier bread pudding, ricotta torte or frittata. These are served on English china and silver beneath a brass chandelier at a walnut table for twelve in the formal dining room or, in summer, at two tables for six on a wraparound screened porch full of wicker and chintz, overlooking the rear patio, gazebo, lavish flower gardens and swimming pool. The Reusses planned to enclose a side patio for another sitting room or a shop. Guests already enjoy a front porch and a small living room in what was the original kitchen.

Huge stone fireplace is feature of living room at Manor House.

Diane has furnished both common rooms and guest rooms with English chintz and antiques from the late 1700s to the 1840s. Also in evidence are some of Vernon's complete set of Audubon prints. Of the bedrooms, says Diane, "everyone fights over Nell's Room," such is its aura of refinement with a Stickley rice-carved bed. upscale linens, original artworks, a loveseat and wing chair, and a double vanity in the bath. Another favorite is the Red Bird Room, named for the pattern of its Deerfield paper -- Diane calls it "my Thomas Jefferson room with more spiff to it."

Iced tea and wine, fruit and cheese are served from 5 to 7. Diane stresses, however, that the real social hour comes with breakfast the next morning.

Doubles, $150 to $195. No smoking.

Manor House, Maple Avenue, Box 447, Norfolk, Conn. 06058. (203) 542-5690.

One of the grander estates in a town of many has been turned into an elegant Victorian B&B by Diane and Henry Tremblay, self-styled "corporate graduates" from the Hartford insurance world. Theirs is an eighteen-room, Tudor-style manor home built on five acres in 1898 by Charles Spofford, architect of London's subway system and the son of Abraham Lincoln's Librarian of Congress.

The eight guest rooms on the second and third floors come with private baths, one with a double jacuzzi and another with a double soaking tub. All are decorated to the period with antique sleigh, spindle, canopy or four-poster beds covered with duvet comforters. The Lincoln Room contains a reclining couch and a carved walnut sleigh bed that belonged to Diane's great-grandmother. Other rooms have such interesting features as Vanity Fair Bazaar wallpaper, an antique china wash basin and a bathroom with pink fixtures. The Spofford Room boasts a queensize canopy bed and a fireplaced sitting area. A Victorian wedding dress with Diane's wedding hat is in the upstairs hall.

The original Tiffany and leaded-glass windows, cherry paneling and stone fireplaces enhance the main floor, where guests can spread out in a small library, a baronial living room with a gigantic stone fireplace and a view onto the back gardens, a sun porch with a wood stove, a little barroom with stereo and TV, and two dining rooms, where the Tiffany windows represent fish on one side and fowl on the other.

In the afternoons, Diane puts out popcorn, cheese and crackers, and serves tea from her collection of teapots. In the morning, the unusually good coffee is laced with cinnamon. The Tremblays cook a couple of breakfast entrées each day, among them scrambled eggs, blueberry pancakes, french toast stuffed with raspberries, orange waffles with honey and maple syrup, and poached eggs with a sauce of lemon, butter and chives on muffins. The honey comes from their beehives and the herbs from their garden.

Doubles, $85 to $150.

Gourmet Treats

This entire area is a hotbed of food activity, with Great Barrington increasingly the focal point. Its railroad station is the site of a new farmers' market Saturday mornings in season.

Owner John Campanale didn't realize it at the time, but he came to "smoked fish heaven" when he moved his **Merrimac Smoked Fish** wholesale and retail operation in 1992 from eastern Massachusetts to 955 South Main St., Great Barrington. Seafood is smoked on the premises, resulting in superior Scotch-style Atlantic salmon, Idaho rainbow trout, mussels, bluefish, catfish and sea scallops, among others. Smoked fish is popular for takeout (we enjoyed the salmon at a Tanglewood picnic) and turns up on many a local restaurant menu. It also complements the H&H Bagels, imported from New York City and baked on the premises (with cream cheese and smoked salmon, $4.75). You'll find exotica from chanterelles to Russian caviar here, too.

Locke, Stock and Barrel, just north of Great Barrington along Stockbridge Road (Route 7), is more than a large natural-foods store with a nifty name. Sophisticated as all get-out, it supplies a great selection of English cheeses, exotic salsas and the Wolfgang Puck Spago frozen pizzas that we can't seem to find in our supermarkets at home. We never saw so many kinds of honey, including some eucalyptus honey from New Zealand.

The **Berkshire Co-op Market** doubled its size with a 1993 move to the old Grainery at 37 Rosseter St., Great Barrington. Besides the usual natural foodstuffs, we were impressed with some of the deli offerings: shiitake and chive quiche, jambalaya, cold plum soup and frozen cheesecake dipped in chocolate on a stick, to name a few.

The Market Place at 2 State Road, Great Barrington (along Route 7 next to the Housatonic River bridge), is a specialty-foods and gourmet-takeout shop par excellence. Two former New York chefs who met at the White Hart Inn, Kevin Schmitz and David Renner, left in 1993 to open their stylish establishment. It's fun to browse, but you'll likely be persuaded to take home some of their terrific breads (the olive bread is sensational), salads, quiches, dinner entrées and desserts. We couldn't resist picking up a special of lamb rolled with pinenuts and spinach, new potatoes with dill and grilled vegetables for a fancy dinner at home.

The Baker's Wife at 312 Main St., Great Barrington, has a good selection of breads, pastries and desserts. Raymond and Colleen Simo are known for their Berkshire Hills cake of light and dark chocolate mousse. They also make fabulous truffles, florentines, marzipan fruits and countless other desserts and cookies. Their breads like Tex-Mex corn and sprouted buckwheat are renowned — the ten-grain bread is studded with sunflower and sesame seeds. Upstairs is **Resources,** a good kitchen shop, where we particularly admired the picnic items, glassware and cookbooks.

Around the corner, the **Daily Bread Bakery** at 17 Railroad St. has a fine selection of natural breads, muffins, cakes and cookies. Sourdough and Irish soda breads are the specialty. At a little counter with four stools, you can enjoy a Devonshire scone (50 cents) or a cup of soup like golden broccoli and cheese with French bread ($1.75). A black-bottom cupcake would make a good ending. **The Berkshire Coffee Roasting Co.** at 286 Main St., offers all the right coffees, teas, fresh juice, muffins and croissants at a handful of tables or to go. It's under the same ownership as the new Kintaro Japanese restaurant and sushi bar next door. Breakfast is served all day at **Martin's Restaurant,** an L-shaped storefront at 49 Railroad St., where former Waldorf-Astoria chef Martin Lewis whips up incredible omelets along with luncheon salads and sandwiches.

For an authentic taste of Texas, head to **Hickory Bill's Bar-B-Que** at 403 Stockbridge Road, Great Barrington. "The best barbecue north of the Mason-Dixon" is typical of comments in the guest book at this fun place. Genial proprietor William C. Ross Jr., a former social worker, and staff sport red shirts as they turn out pork, chicken, brisket and ribs from the special indoor Oyler hickory-wood barbecue pit in the kitchen. Barbecue platters ($7.75 to $9.50) like spareribs or fancy brisket are served with a choice of two side dishes, perhaps collard greens and baked beans, along with the delicious Mexican cornbread, dotted with jalapeños. Mrs. Evelyn's sweet potato pie is a fitting dessert. Partake in the no-frills, luncheonette-style dining room or at picnic tables out back.

In South Egremont are two old-fashioned cafes of special appeal to city-dwellers. After its longtime owner sold in 1990, the **Gaslight Store** lost some of its personal touch and charm, according to locals. But it remains popular with visitors, who jam its tables on weekends for breakfast, lunch and ice cream, and pick out penny candies at the cash register. Next to Popeye's Convenience Store, home of the former Gourmet Cottage and Cheese Shop, is **Mom's Country Cafe,** where the tables are bases of old sewing machines and the windows open onto a deck overlooking the rushing brook in back. It serves breakfast all day, lunch and dinner. The menu is predictable, from ham steak and eggs with homefries and toast for $4.95 to Mom's burger with mushrooms and swiss cheese, $4.25. At night, the menu adds zillions of Italian-style entrées from $4.95 for spaghetti to $12.95 for swordfish or shrimp fra diavolo.

Considerably more contemporary is the **Berkshire Place** across the street, a cafe and bakery with a cappuccino and espresso bar. There's nothing old-fashioned about this establishment, unless it's the old-fashioned crumb cake resting next to the whiskey cake in the pastry case. Besides baked goods that are to die for, proprietor Dayne Edwin Kelly offers terrific soups, salads, sandwiches and such that are available to eat here or take out.

Establishments in quaint West Stockbridge seem to come and go. One we hope will last is **Caffe Pomo D'Oro** in the old train station at 6 Depot St.. It's been nicely transformed into an airy, high-ceilinged space with a quarry tile floor. There are specialty foods, a cappuccino bar and a handful of tables for enjoying some of the sandwiches, salads and antipasti tendered by proprietor Scott Edward Cole. You might find a triple-layer vegetable terrine served with baguette slices, an organically grown salad of mixed field greens with a fresh herb vinaigrette or a sandwich ($6.50) of prosciutto, chèvre and tomato on toasted farm bread, served with a side salad.

What was years ago the home of the famed Alice's Restaurant is now **Naji's,** down an alley behind 40 Main St., Stockbridge. Along with "outrageous" pizzas and overstuffed calzones, you'll find some delicious Mideast food like baba ghanoush and tabbouleh to take out or eat at one of the few little tables. We loved the Lebanese potato salad here. Picnic baskets are $13.50 to $17.50; the Lenox contains chicken curry with veggies, broiled eggplant with pinenuts, artichoke salad, cheese and crackers, and fruit and cookies -- surely enough for the hungriest of Tanglewood-goers.

Some of the best parties and picnics in town are catered by **Crosby's,** 62 Church St., Lenox. New proprietors Helen Hayes and Jeannette McCullough have reinstated the great takeout shop, where you might put together your own picnic of, say, carrot-ginger soup, black-bean and grilled corn salad, cold poached salmon with dill sauce and sour-cream chocolate cake.

Mary Stuart Collections, 81 Church St., Lenox, carries fine china and glass, exquisite accessories for bed and bath, hand-woven rugs, imported needlepoint designs, potpourris and fragrances, adorable things for babies, beautifully smocked dresses for little girls and hand-painted stools. Locally produced gourmet foods and solid cookware and dinnerware for the country chef are dispensed nearby at **Berkshire Cottage.**

Bev's Homemade Ice Cream, 38 Housatonic St., Lenox, is the place to head for an ice-cream fix. Ex-Californian Beverly Mazursky opened this establishment after graduating from the Culinary Institute of America in 1989. She and sons Dan and Jeff make all the wonderful flavors in two machines behind the counter. They're well-known for their raspberry/chocolate-chip and their margarita sorbet, served in sugar cones ($1.60 and $2.40). You can order gelatos, frappes, smoothies, sherbet coolers and even a banana split ($5.50), as well as espresso, cappuccino and cafe latte. Soups and sandwiches are available except in summer, when their popular Jamaican patties (different kinds of Caribbean breads with such fillings as beef, mixed veggies and broccoli-cheese) are about the only things that get in the way of the ice cream.

Guido's Freshmarket Place on Route 7 at the Pittsfield-Lenox line is a fascinating market complex. It offers pristine produce from the long-standing Guido's produce market, a deli where you can buy huge sandwiches, a bakery, fresh pasta, seafood, desserts from Berger's Specialty Foods, eggs from Otis and a great array of cookbooks. Overhead is a vast selection of baskets and dried flowers. Guido's planned to open a similar market in 1994 along Route 7 just south of Great Barrington.

The Store at Five Corners, an 18th-century general store gone upscale, is worth the extra jaunt to the junction of Routes 7 and 43 south of Williamstown. Ex-New Yorkers Stuart Shatken and his wife Andy offer select lines of specialty foods. Rather than carry 30 lines of jam, for instance, they stock a couple of their favorites. "We sell as many French St. Dalfour as we do jams from the lady down the street," says Stuart. You'll find Mendocino pastas, Epicurean spices, interesting wines, homemade fudge and Italian biscotti along with an espresso bar, baked goods from the store's bakery, "real NYC bagels," and an assortment of breakfast and lunch items from the deli.

Chaiwalla, a well-known tea house, has moved across the street to larger quarters at 1 Main St. in Salisbury, Conn. Now Mary O'Brien has six gate-leg tables with mismatched chairs in her charming dining room and a three-seat counter facing the open kitchen and a window seat overflowing with pillows. There's a pretty rock garden in back. Mary serves morning fare ("offered whenever it is 'morning' for you"), tiffin (midday fare) and tea. A stunning selection of perfectly brewed teas, using local spring water, is served in clear glass pots on warmers and poured into clear glass mugs. You also may try Chaiwalla's own granola, eggs en cocotte, fruit-filled french toast, perhaps a soup like corn chowder or tomato-kale, Mary's famous tomato pie, pot stickers or a sandwich like "scholar's delight," roast beef with watercress and homemade herb mayonnaise, all in the $3.50 to $6 range. At tea time, Scottish shortbread, crumpets and scones with lemon curd are among the goodies. When we stopped in, plum kuchen and three-berry cobbler were a couple of the desserts, and Mary's mother's whiskey cake is generally on the docket. The finest teas from across the world are available for $5.75 to $12 a pound, as are tea-making accessories.

Tea seems to be a claim to fame for Salisbury. The town also is home to **Harney & Sons,** located in a house facing the village green. Master blender John Harney, former innkeeper at the White Hart Inn across the street, is concentrating now on what used to be a sideline. Loose teas, flavored iced teas and tea bags -- ordered through a catalog by discriminating customers and famed hotels across the country – are on display along with jams, local maple syrup and lots of information about tea, including the Harneys' new book on tea leaf reading. Stunning ornaments and other must-have Christmas things are on display with decorative accessories and toys at **Garlande,** a fabulous shop nearby. Everything from cappuccino and espresso to soups, sandwiches and imported chocolates is available at **Four Seasons Foods,** a gourmet shop and deli in nearby Lakeville.

Of special interest in Norfolk, Conn., is **Nobody Eats Parsley,** an enchanting barn shop specializing in herbs. It's run by Valerie Craig, who named it thus because her children said that nobody eats that stuff and "they thought we would starve." Herbs (ten kinds of thyme, for instance,) chive-blossom vinegar, jellies like orange-ginger ("we sell about 8,000 jars a year," says Val), catnip mice, Mountain Meadows potpourri, dried-flower wreaths and all kinds and sizes of clay pots and planters are among her wares.

Does every single place in the Berkshires serve cappuccino? It seems so -- even **McArthur's Smoke House,** the venerable establishment for smoked meat , fish and cheeses in Millerton, N.Y., has a machine. It also offers soup like white-bean provençal, sandwiches ($4.25) like smoked turkey with cranberry chutney, and walnut and dill chicken salad. There's a good selection of pastas and sauces and many other specialty foods. Smoked bangers, duck breast, spiral party hams, pork chops and turkey are among the goodies from the smoker.

Two Northwest Connecticut wineries are of interest to visitors. At **Hopkins Vineyard** on Hopkins Road next to the renowned Hopkins Inn in New Preston, Bill and Judy Hopkins produce a superior seyval blanc, which has won many awards, among nine varieties from their twenty acres of French-American hybrid grapes. The Hayloft Art Gallery upstairs has changing exhibitions and the much-expanded shop sells wine-related items like stemware and grapevine wreaths. Yankee Cider is available in fall for those who like the hard stuff. You can picnic with a bottle of chardonnay or Vineyard reserve white and bask in the view of Lake Waramaug below. The winery is open daily from 10 to 5 May-December, Friday-Sunday rest of year. **Haight Vineyards and Winery,** the first farm winery in New England's biggest wine-producing state, is Connecticut's largest since moving into a Tudor-style building outside Litchfield. The Haight family take pride in their covertside white and red award-winners as well as their chardonnay and riesling labels. There's an informative vineyard walk and guided tours are available in the winery, which is open daily 10:30 to 5 year-round.

Rural pond with swan and geese is an attraction at Stonehenge.

Ridgefield
An Enclave of Elegant Eateries

For its size, no town in Connecticut — perhaps even in all New England — enjoys the reputation that Ridgefield has for fine dining. "Some people think that Ridgefield was put on the map by our restaurant," claims the brochure for Stonehenge. The same could be said by a couple of other restaurants after the rural charm of Ridgefield was discovered by New Yorkers in the post-war era.

For three decades or so, Stonehenge, the Inn at Ridgefield and The Elms had things pretty much to themselves. In the last few years, more first-rate restaurants have sprouted in Ridgefield and just to the west across the New York State line.

That there is such a concentration of great establishments in one small area does not surprise the restaurateurs. "It's like opening a fine shoe store," said one. "You don't want to be the only good store around."

Lately, the early emphasis on haute has been superseded by a proliferation of bistros and cafes that specialize in everything from Southwest fare to natural foods. "This town has really taken to gourmet takeout," says Lynelle Faircloth, proprietor of the Ridgefield General Store, whose cafe caters to the luncheon crowd as well as the takeout phenomenon.

That trend was noted by the folks from Hay Day, the Westport-based, country-chic farm market, as they opened a new market with an extensive takeout section, a coffee bar and a cafe in Ridgefield in 1991. Successful beyond expectations, it served as a prototype two years later for the expanded Westport operation and its new and larger cafe.

The Hay Day concept was tailor-made for Ridgefield. This is, after all, a town where a sidewalk vendor dispenses gourmet hot dogs and a store called Canine Cuisine advertises gourmet treats for pets.

The burgeoning of the restaurant business extends beyond to the lodging, with a fine B&B next to the Inn at Ridgefield, suavely upgraded and expanded accommodations at Stonehenge and The Elms, and a majestic new B&B.

But food remains foremost in Ridgefield, an enclave of creative cuisine.

Dining

The Best of the Best

Stonehenge, Route 7, Ridgefield. (203) 438-6511.

The famed Swiss chef Albert Stockli of Restaurant Associates in New York put Stonehenge on the culinary map back in the 1960s. Since his death, Douglas Seville has continued the tradition, adding a variety of settings for dining as well as upgrading and expanding the overnight accommodations. And, following a disastrous fire in 1988, the new Stonehenge has risen like a phoenix reborn, better than ever.

The rebuilt restaurant could not be more sophisticated in a country way. Slightly smaller than the original early 19th-century, Colonial white edifice upon which it is modeled, it has a new side entrance and a layout that gives almost every table a view of the property's tranquil pond. The main dining room is light and airy in a peachy coral, green and white color scheme. Fresh flowers and small lamps are on the widely spaced tables flanked by upholstered Chippendale-style chairs. Handsome swagged draperies frame the large end window onto the pond, and french doors open onto a flagstone cocktail terrace. More masculine is the cozy tavern in hunter green, where English sporting prints cover the walls and the sconces are made from hunting horns.

The ambiance is sheer luxury, but not one whit pretentious. "Stonehenge has left no stone unturned," a fellow restaurateur pointed out, no pun intended. "Everything is perfection."

Chef William Keating loves to cook and his food reflects it, both in taste and presentation. He adapts the traditional menu to changing times. You'll find Stonehenge's famed beer-batter shrimp as an appetizer on the Saturday menu, but you'll also find a nightly spa plate with broiled fish and natural vegetables.

Dinner is prix-fixe at $45 for four courses on Saturday and à la carte the rest of the week. Except for the substitution of beer-batter shrimp for the regular pâté of foie gras and smoked chicken, the menu is the same in both cases, and a couple of specials are offered nightly. There's also a four-course Sunday brunch for $24, the interesting menu changing weekly.

Generous drinks are served in pretty, long-stemmed goblets. They come with a couple of complimentary canapés, a miniature asparagus spear wrapped in prosciutto and a tiny new potato stuffed with caviar and sour cream at one visit. The predominantly American wine list is comprehensive and somewhat pricey, offering eleven chardonnays from $28 to $44. A page of rare vintages is priced from $150 to $1,200, for a magnum of 1970 Château Latour.

Among dinner appetizers ($8 to $11.50), we found mushroom crêpes with a mornay sauce and gruyère cheese out of this world and the renowned shrimp in beer batter with pungent fruit sauce seems to get better all the time. Although the menu changes, keep an eye out for the house-smoked sausage, served sizzling with an extraordinary mustard-wine sauce and garnished with grapes. Two favorites are seared pepper-crusted tuna with a wasabi-horseradish cream, tomato-chive relish and sesame-noodle crisps, and a terrine of lobster, shrimp and new potatoes, wrapped in smoked Scotch salmon and served with a dill crème fraîche.

Other specialties are a roast baby suckling pig (five days' notice required), saddle of venison with chanterelles in port-wine sauce, crisp Long Island duckling with wild rice and orange sauce, and rack of lamb with dijon mustard in a potato crust. Among other entrées ($18 to $27), we can vouch for the veal scallops with morels and cream and the broiled Atlantic salmon with ginger-chive beurre blanc.

The salad of leaf lettuces ($4.50) is a fresh mixture of greens, gleaming with a coat of mustardy vinaigrette. A more exotic salad choice for $7 brings arugula, endive and watercress in a balsamic vinaigrette. A basket of crusty French bread comes with a crock of sweet butter.

Vegetables are crisp and of the season, perhaps caramelized carrots, green beans wrapped in red pepper, and tiny potato balls dusted with parsley from the chef's herb garden. All are artfully arranged on white plates amidst swirls of herbs painted in interesting designs by the chef, using a woodworker's glue squeeze bottle he converted for the purpose.

Service is formal, quiet and efficient, with many dishes heated on and served from rolling carts.

The selection of desserts ($7.50) is luscious-looking. House favorites are a terrine of chocolate and sour cherries with a pistachio crème anglaise and an extravagant, creamy cheesecake with a white- and dark-chocolate sauce. Ours was a strawberry tart with an abundance of fresh berries on a shortcake crust and topped with a shiny glaze. We're also partial to the grand-marnier cheesecake and the raspberry crème brûlée with a vanilla brown-sugar crust. Requests for Stonehenge's chocolate recipes arrive almost weekly from across the country. Such is the stature of this extraordinary establishment.

Dinner nightly except Monday, 6 to 9; Sunday, brunch 11:30 to 2:30, dinner 4 to 8.

The Inn at Ridgefield, 20 West Lane (Route 35), Ridgefield. (203) 438-8282.

Masses of azaleas and rhododendrons in spring brighten the canopied entrance to this good-looking restaurant founded in 1947, the same year as Stonehenge. The entrance is lined with the sides of wine crates from across the world. Inside are a small cocktail lounge, three fireplaced dining rooms and a piano bar where a pianist entertains. There's a lovely new summer garden cafe, where lunch and dinner are served on the side lawn.

The main dining room, with the grand piano at the entrance, is our favorite. Some tables have window views of surrounding lawns and all focus on a huge spotlit painting of Monte Carlo. The upholstered chairs are comfortable, tables are well spaced, and the eye-catching pewter service plates are emblazoned with a picture of the inn.

Partners Ray Kuhnt and Johannes Brugger cater to the wants of a regular clientele. The ambitious, oversize dinner menu is prix-fixe at $42 for one side that favors the new French cuisine and à la carte for the traditional continental

Chippendale-style chairs and formally dressed tables enhance dining at Stonehenge.

side. It's supplemented by a variety of specials listed on a white board. Dinner is totally prix-fixe, $41 to $44, on Saturday nights.

Chef Brugger has maintained the inn's traditional dishes, among them smoked eel with dill sauce and Peruvian shrimp cocktail as appetizers ($7.95 to $12.95). Entrées run from $19.50 for fillet of sole normande to $26 for dover sole meunière, excluding flambéed roast duckling, châteaubriand and rack of lamb, $39 to $49 for two.

On the prix-fixe side, you might start with a pâté of salmon, sole and lobster with a fresh basil sauce, move on to filet mignon with pistachio and truffle sauce or sliced duck with green peppercorns and sweet and sour sauce, and finish with one of the acclaimed desserts, perhaps a chocolate mousse cake or an almond tart with raspberries and marzipan. The basic menu seldom changes, since that's the way the regulars like it.

The lunch menu has a smattering of the dinner offerings, priced from $9.25 for an omelet to $19.50 for chilled seafood salad. There also are steak tartare, shrimp in beer batter, a fresh vegetarian plate with a poached egg, and (doesn't *this* sound archaic?) "for my lady — blinis à la Reine," petite crêpes with mixed green salad, $9.50. The Sunday brunch is $21.

Lunch, Monday-Saturday noon to 2; dinner nightly, 6 to 9:30 or 10:30; Sunday, brunch noon to 3, dinner 3 to 8.

Hay Day Cafe, 21 Governor St., Ridgefield. (203) 438-2344.

This is an adjunct to the fabulous Hay Day Market, and reflects its culinary flair. The menus are exciting and the ambiance appealing. If you had unlimited means and an adventuresome palate, you might want to eat here every day.

Off to one side of the market with a separate entrance, the 58-seat cafe is quiet and refined. The decor is the ultimate in country Victoriana: bare wood floor, dark wainscoting, lacy curtains on tall windows beneath a high pressed-tin ceiling. The tables are handsomely set with fresh flowers and a lineup of one wine glass for white and another for red at each place setting.

A recommended wine or beer, priced both by the glass and the bottle, accompanies each item on the alluring dinner menu, which is new American and politically correct. It has a section labeled pasta and vegetable yielding vegetable

293

lasagna with grilled portobello mushrooms ($12.95) and a steamed vegetable platter with honey-mustard-yogurt sauce ($10.95). Those with more traditional tastes could start with smoked duck breast with warm camembert and cranberries, calamari rings with sweet bell-pepper preserve, a salad of poached pears and maytag blue cheese with pecans on bitter greens or a grilled eggplant, mozzarella and tomato croquette, priced from $6.95 to $8.95.

Main dishes ($14.95 to $18.95) could be smoked salmon and shrimp over angel-hair pasta, Maryland crab cakes with crisp sweet potatoes and rémoulade sauce, escalopes of salmon with a leek-potato puree and shiitake-mushroom vinaigrette, French lamb stew with buttered noodles or grilled tenderloin with glazed acorn squash, crisp potato cakes and wild-mushroom sauce. Because the cafe is right next door to an abundance of fresh produce, meat and fish, the food is impeccably fresh and billed as "top of the market." Everything is made on the premises, and accompanied by the Hay Day sauces and preserves that connoisseurs stock from the market. The interesting wines come from the adjacent Hay Day Wine Shop and are fairly priced.

Among desserts ($3.95 to $4.95) are french apple tart with cinnamon-apple ice cream, chocolate indiscretion cake, fruit cobbler with "wickedly rich ice cream" and Hay Day's frozen yogurt with granola bars.

If you're here during the day, take a shopping break for lunch: perhaps a cheese and charcuterie chef's salad, New England cobb salad, caesar salad with rotisserie chicken or smoked salmon, a grilled salmon BLT sandwich, moussaka with eggplant-caper sauce or tenderloin tips with barley/wild-mushroom salad ($6.95 to $12.95). Some of the lunch and dinner items are combined on the Sunday brunch menu, along with such breakfast treats as apricot-walnut pancakes and poached eggs on corn cakes with tenderloin tips and poblano and papaya salsa.

The cafe frequently stages special dinners, like the four-course game dinners with wine for a bargain $29.95 at our visit.

Lunch, Monday-Saturday 11:30 to 2:30; dinner nightly, 5:30 to 9 or 9:30; Sunday brunch. No smoking.

Sam's Grill, 3 Big Shop Lane, Ridgefield. (203) 438-1946.

The decor is whimsical. The service is without pretension. And the food is innovative and represents real value.

The place is a most worthy 1990s successor to Le Coq Hardi, an unfortunate victim of the end of the go-go 1980s. It's named for owner Louise Davis, who's called Sam by her husband David, former co-owner of Stonehenge. Louise, a professional decorator, has lightened up the formerly cave-like space, accenting the prevailing white of the stone walls and the beamed ceiling with rust-stenciled wallpaper, splashy bouquets of flowers, baskets of plants and colorful pottery here and there.

It's a bright, with-it backdrop for appealing international and Pacific Rim fare. We enjoyed one of our better lunches in a long time here: a salad sampler ($7.95) of steak and ginger, shrimp and cucumbers, and chicken with cinnamon and apples, accompanied by peasant bread and assertive herbed butter, and the Vermonter sandwich, an open-face BLT with Vermont cheddar on grilled peasant bread, which came with a great mustardy potato salad, coleslaw and enough garnishes to be almost a salad plate in itself (and quite a bargain for $4.95). We would gladly have tried any of the seven salads (the Arizona, the cobb and the Pacific Rim sounded particularly good), the Italian or California club sandwiches,

See-through divider at Hay Day Cafe.   **Dining area at Sam's Grill.**

the Texas-style chili, the turnover of seafood and grilled vegetables, or the three pizzettas from a wide-ranging menu priced from $4.95 to $8.50.

The dinner fare is equally inspired. From the grill come such treats ($11.95 to $17.50) as Norwegian salmon with macadamia-nut pesto and mango salsa, marinated shrimp kabobs with lemon-lime sauce, lime-marinated skirt steak with jalapeño butter and black-bean salad, chicken breast with Thai peanut sauce and cucumber relish, and twin lamb chops with chilled mint relish. Or you could try one of the fresh pastas ($8.50 to $14.75), perhaps a creamy black-pepper fettuccine with mozzarella, parmesan and fontina cheeses or shrimp, lobster and scallops over linguini. Or make a meal of appetizers (how about Indonesian chicken satay, crostini or steamed mussels with a Thai red curry and coconut sauce?), the provençal or ragin' cajun pizzettas or the shrimp and grilled seafood sausage over arugula salad with a lime-mint vinaigrette.

Desserts ($3.75) could be key lime pie, chocolate mousse, crème brûlée, ice-cream gâteau or a fresh fruit plate with a granité and champagne mist. The wine list is as well chosen as the rest of the fare.

Lunch, Monday-Friday noon to 2:30; dinner, Monday-Saturday, 5 to 9:30 or 10.

Auberge Maxime, Ridgefield Road, North Salem, N.Y. (914) 669-5450.

The charming white Normandy-style house at the intersection of Routes 116 and 121 is named for Westchester chef Maxime Ribera, who opened it in 1977 and sold a couple of years later to Bernard Le Bris, who arrived in this country from France in 1976. Bernard, a practitioner of the new French cuisine, is thoroughly at home in this picture-perfect French provincial restaurant and doing quite nicely, thank you.

Dinners are $49 prix-fixe, and tables in the 45-seat main dining room are booked far in advance on weekends. A pleasant new room in the walk-out lower level takes care of overflow. It looks out onto a patio where lunch and cocktails are served beside tranquil fields and hillsides.

You enter through a small lounge graced with a mass of fresh and silk flowers, and panels of etched glass depicting a bevy of ducks over the bar. The rectangular dining room has a mirrored rear wall that makes it seem larger. Chairs upholstered in a striped fabric, chintz draperies, dark paneling, candles in tall silver candlesticks, custom-designed white china from France bearing the restaurant's logo, and gleaming table settings present an elegant country flair. Carved ducks handpainted by a woman from Sherman, Conn., grace each table and are available for purchase ($110 each).

Duck is the specialty of the house, served in five versions from traditional l'orange to roasted with ginger or green peppercorns or whole red currants. Pressed duck à la Tour d'Argent is available with 48 hours' notice.

The six or seven other entrées on a seasonal menu might include grilled salmon in a warm vinaigrette, roast squab with dates, roast veal with mustard sauce and mushrooms, and grilled lamb steak with rosemary-garlic sauce.

Meals begin with appetizers like a trio of salmon (smoked, marinated and mousse), grilled lamb sausage on a bed of pasta, terrine of vegetables with goat cheese and sautéed foie gras with braised red cabbage in sesame oil. Salads of endive or mixed greens with a tarragon-vinegar dressing are served with a cheese of the day.

Chef Bernard offers nightly specials — soft-shell crabs with saffron, baby pheasant with wild mushrooms and a heavenly sounding blueberry soufflé one spring evening we visited. Although soufflés are the specialty, other worthy desserts include banana mousse crêpe with walnut and rum ice cream, three-flavored ice-cream cake, and white and dark chocolate-mousse cake.

His wine list, strong on champagnes, runs from $20 to $680 and is notable for its grid chart signifying the year. The chef makes his own vinegars and cherries in vodka and gives small bottles to regular customers at Christmas. He also will prepare a dégustation menu for two or more with 48 hours' notice. It's priced at about $60 and includes "foie gras, lobster and all that fancy stuff," says Bernard.

Lunch patrons like to start with the special house cocktail, a glass of champagne with passion-fruit liqueur, a dash of campari and a scoop of sorbet. Then they might try soup or one of the evening's appetizers, an omelet ($10.50) or entrée ($14.50 to $16.50) like confit of duck or entrecôte au poivre, and finish with one of those marvelous soufflés.

Lunch, weekdays noon to 3; dinner, 6 to 9; Sunday, noon to 3 and 3 to 9. Closed Wednesday.

Le Château, Route 35 at Route 123, South Salem, N.Y. (914) 533-6631.

Drive through the gate and up the winding, dogwood-lined road to the baronial stone mansion built by J. Pierpont Morgan on a hilltop in 1907 for his former minister and you'll get one of the most majestic views of any restaurant — a sylvan panorama across the northern Westchester valley. The entry hall is paneled in rare chestnut, hand-hewn and held together by butterfly pieces. Dining is in high-ceilinged rooms, a couple facing onto the garden patio and all with expansive views. No wonder Le Château does such a lively wedding business.

Despite the numbers, dining is correct and quiet. It's well regarded locally, a credit to Joseph Jaffre, son-in-law of the original owners who came here from Le Coq au Vin in New York in 1974, and his longtime staff. The fabulous array of appetizers and desserts, on display buffet-style on either side of the entry foyer, are enough to make the most diet-conscious succumb.

A $45 prix-fixe dinner changes nightly. Otherwise, entrées go from $22 for

Window table at Le Chateau.   **Bernard Le Bris at Auberge Maxime.**

roasted chicken with artichokes and mushrooms to $28 for lobster ragout in court bouillon. Shrimp provençal, salmon pommery, sweetbreads flamed with cognac, muscovy duck with sweet and sour sauce, rack of lamb with curry-herb sauce and baby pheasant with foie gras and truffle sauce are among the classic continental offerings. Appetizers range from $7.50 for vegetable terrine with horseradish sauce to $18 for fresh foie gras. Desserts include Paris-brest and soufflés. The wine list is well-chosen and rather expensive, although the price-conscious can find a few in the $20s.

The extensive menu for lunch, which taken here becomes a major meal, is similar to the dinner. Entrées are priced from $15.50 to $20.50. With soup or salad and dessert, you'll likely not need dinner that night. It's idyllic in summer to have cocktails on the lawn, enclosed by gray stone walls as in a castle. And it's great any time to tarry at the bar, its windows offering the best view around.

Lunch, Thursday and Friday noon to 2; dinner, Tuesday-Friday 6 to 9, Saturday to 11, Sunday 2 to 9. Closed Monday.

L'Europe, Route 123, South Salem, N.Y. (914) 533-2570.

With the demise of a couple of French restaurants and the slippage of others, this sprightly establishment has found a niche in the Vista section southwest of Ridgefield. Beautiful gardens flank the front entrance of a small gray house converted in 1988 by Rui Toska of Danbury from what he described as a gin mill. Lovely moss-green rugs, nicely spaced tables set with white damask and pots of flowers beautify the interior as well. A New York Times reviewer said a meal here is like dining in a private club.

Chef Kirtus Westhaver took over in the kitchen in 1990 after having shared the chef duties at Pot au Feu, one of our favorite restaurants in Providence, R.I., since its founding in the early 1980s.

Dinner entrées ($22.50 to $28) include fillet of sole rolled in salmon mousse, ragout of lobster and scallops, braised sweetbreads with wild mushrooms, roasted baby chicken with morel sauce, filet au poivre and escalope of veal with parma ham, cheese and madeira sauce. Specials could be salmon with saffron-dill cream garnished with cucumbers and salmon roe, quail stuffed with veal and goose liver and served with chestnut sauce in puff pastry, and venison medallions with game sauce and juniper berries.

Among appetizers ($7.50 to $13) are escargots in puff pastry, duck salad with raspberry vinaigrette and smoked salmon, trout and bluefish with Scandinavian garnishes. Beluga caviar with imported vodka is $45.

Soufflés ($8) are the dessert forte, always grand marnier and chocolate and often a seasonal special like raspberry. Lemon cheesecake, chocolate bombe, crème brûlée and walnut parfait are other favorites. The wine list is primarily French, starting at $18 for a beaujolais and rising rapidly into the hundreds.

Lunch is an abbreviated version of the dinner menu (entrées from $12 for pasta of the day to $19 for grilled lamb), augmented by a couple of salads like the duck with raspberry vinaigrette.

Lunch, Tuesday-Saturday noon to 2:30; dinner, 6 to 9:30, weekends to midnight; Sunday brunch, noon to 3. Closed Monday.

Other Dining Choices

The Elms, 500 Main St., Ridgefield. (203) 438-2541.

This is Ridgefield's oldest operating inn (1799), and in earlier days was considered one of the town's Big Three. Oldtimers still favor it for lunch on the enclosed front porch or dinner in one of the older, redecorated dining rooms. Robert Scala has continued the reputation for solid American and continental cuisine built by his father, John, a former master chef at the St. Regis in New York. Robert says his aim is "to remain traditional in a world of change," although lately he's modernized and lightened up the lunch menu.

Gone are the traditional consommé and lamb chops. In their place are lunchy items ($7.25 to $14.25) like duck salad, a Norwegian salmon sandwich plate, roast pork sandwich with carrot and fennel salad, sautéed wild mushrooms over polenta, spinach ravioli with tomato concasse and, for the diehards, fillet of sole meunière and chicken normande.

At night, the traditional table-d'hôte dinners have been discontinued and the à-la-carte menu has shrunk a bit. Appetizers range from $4.25 for pâté maison to $10 for scampi romani. Four pastas may be ordered in appetizer portions. Other entrées ($15.75 to $29.50) include such standbys as sole victoria, pork forestière, veal madeira, duckling bigarade and tournedos au poivre. Shrimp stuffed with snow crab, grilled swordfish salmoriglio, medallions of venison and rack of lamb are other possibilities.

Among desserts are Paris-brest, pears with grappa, chestnut cake and tirami su.

Robert Scala is proud of his wine cellar of 6,000 bottles — some are nicely displayed on a table in the main foyer, which is attractive with murals on the walls and antique chairs and seats. At our latest visit a canopied side patio was being added for outdoor dining.

Lunch, noon to 2:30; dinner, 6 to 9:30 or 10:30; Sunday brunch, 11:30 to 2:30. Closed Wednesday.

Spagone Ristorante, Copps Hill Common, Ridgefield. (203) 438-5518.

Another food establishment was added to the mix at this upscale shopping complex in 1993. Chef-owner Adriano DiMario opened what he called a macho-looking place to reflect his hearty, contemporary Italian fare. It's a striking space in Tuscan red, designed by a local architect who raised the ceiling and added arches to make it look airy. There are three booth areas with tables along one wall. Otherwise seating is at black cane chairs at well-spaced tables with beige cloths.

The early reviews were highly favorable for Adriano's cuisine. His short menu begins with the usual suspects like bruschetta and crostini, plus surprises like

Arches accent Spagone dining room.

chicken livers and portobello mushrooms served over sliced fennel or baked shrimp with prosciutto, roasted peppers and mozzarella. Five interesting pasta dishes are available as appetizers or main courses.

For entrées ($14.50 to $18.95), how about grilled chicken with wild mushrooms, vegetables, lamb's lettuce and warm goat cheese; Tuscan-style pork loin with warm apple puree; fillet of salmon baked in parchment with spring vegetables, or grilled lamb chops with tomatoes and thyme? The signature roasted veal with porcini mushrooms is $34.95 for two. Italian music plays in the background as patrons linger over a bottle of Italian wine, priced from $18 to $58. Tirami su is the dessert of choice.

Adriano, who lived in Mexico for a time and cooked for the president of Mexico, also runs Piccolo Mondo, a Mexican-Italian restaurant in Newtown. He was about to open a third establishment, the Bridge Cafe in Westport.

Dinner, Monday-Saturday 5:30 to 9:30 or 10:30.

Amadeo's Ristorante, 3 Bailey Ave., Ridgefield. (203) 438-3737.

While the owner of Spagone was branching out to Westport, the owners of Amadeo's in Westport branched out to Ridgefield in 1993. They took over the space formerly occupied by Scrimshaw's, an American seafood eatery, and turned it into a showcase of Mediterranean decor in white, terra cotta and hunter green. An artist was at work for months, transforming the entrance into a simulated Italian courtyard and painting garlands of leaves, flowers and grapes on the terra-cotta walls. A remarkable mural of two birds in a cage adorns a wall in the sunny front dining room, where a tableside cart awaits the preparation of caesar salads.

The chef here is known for unusual combinations of foods. Among entrées ($14.95 to $19.95) he pairs fillet of sole with spinach, baked salmon and scallops with spinach and leeks, grilled chicken with arugula, veal with artichoke hearts and capers, and rack of lamb with black olives and prosciutto. Starters ($4.95 to $8.95) could be bruschetta pomodoro, rolled eggplant with ricotta and mozzarella, beef carpaccio or a three-colored salad of endive, radicchio and arugula with gorgonzola and balsamic dressing. The fettuccine with smoked salmon and cognac is a house favorite. The mostly Italian wine list starts at $20.

Among the tableside preparations is bananas foster for two. Or finish with chocolate-ganache layer cake, tartuffo or tirami su.

Lunch, Tuesday-Friday noon to 2:30; dinner, Tuesday-Saturday 6 to 10.

Sacco, 50 Danbury Road, Ridgefield. (203) 438-2183.

Owner Brian Maitland-Smith is as British as can be, but his chef is Italian and so is the menu at his sleek little restaurant in a shopping strip.

All the traditional pastas are served and then some: rigatoni with wild mushrooms and fennel sausage, smoked salmon ravioli in a lemon brandy sauce and fettuccine with plum tomatoes, sweet cream, parmesan cheese and vodka. Prices at dinner range from $8.75 for spaghetti with meatballs in fresh tomato sauce to $15.95 for seafood over fettuccine.

Individual pizzas are around $6.25 to $7.50; salads like gorgonzola or caesar, $4.25 to $5.95, and you could start with marinated peppers with goat cheese. Entrées run the gamut from baked sole and chicken cacciatore to grilled sirloin steak and five versions of veal, $11.95 to $17.95. Two of the more unusual are orange roughy and jumbo shrimp stuffed with provolone and wrapped in prosciutto. Each is baked in a parchment bag. The wrapped meal is cut open with scissors at the table, giving off an intense aroma and tastes that put many a recipient in seventh heaven.

Tartuffo and Normandy apple cake are a couple of the good desserts. The wine list is heavy on Italian vintages, from the teens to the low $30s.

Sunday is music day, with a highly regarded jazz brunch in the afternoon and occasionally a classical guitarist playing in the evening. But Sacco remains best known for its 32 presentations of pasta. Those and the striking decor: framed drawings of jazz musicians on the walls, unique hanging lights with shades made of goat skins, and chrome and black-leather chairs at glass-topped tables very close together. A wall of wine bottles hides the small bar.

Lunch, Monday-Friday 11:30 to 2:30; dinner nightly, 5:30 to 10:30 or 11; Sunday, brunch 11:30 to 2:30 (October-June), dinner 5 to 10.

Ridgefield General Store Cafe, Copps Hill Common, 103 Danbury Road, Ridgefield. (203) 438-1984.

In the basement of a marvelous country store is this cafe, redecorated in English tearoom style by store owner Lynelle Faircloth, an interior designer. Although the whole store is her bailiwick, the cafe with its demonstration kitchen is her baby. In it her staff serves everything from Sunday brunch through creative lunches to formal English tea.

The blackboard lists soups, salads, sandwiches, quiches and desserts, to eat at one of the 36 seats or to take out. Everything's made fresh on the premises and is oh-so-good, from deep-dish chicken pie and Maryland crab cakes to desserts like chocolate velvet cake, pumpkin-spice cheesecake, raspberry pie and fresh fruit tarts, $2.50 to $4.50. The sliced turkey, pear and melted brie is her most popular sandwich, Lynelle says, although she seems to add a new twist to the menu every day.

The British tea involves three courses ($8.50) — scones and sandwiches, crumpets and sweets. It comes on doilies atop Portuguese floral pottery, the presentation being done with as much flair here as the food.

Lunch, Monday-Saturday 11:30 to 3; British tea, 3 to 5; Sunday brunch, 11 to 5.

Chez Lenard, Main Street, Ridgefield.

We can't give you a proper address for this operation, which he officially calls "Les Delices Culinaires de la Voiture," but it's usually near the corner of Prospect Street. Anywhere else but in Ridgefield it would be a hot dog cart, but this one has chutzpah, or should we say its pusher, Michael Soetbeer, who changes his hats with the seasons, has? Year-round on even the chilliest days, the "voiture" dispenses le hot dog, le hot dog supreme, le hot dog choucroute alsacienne, le hot dog garniture Suisse (topped with cheese fondue), and le hot dog facon Mexicain, $1.25 to $3.

Michael says he has "the first gourmet hot dog rolls in the world," made for him at Martin's Bakery with semolina flour and potato water. We thought le hot dog supreme with the works ($1.75) was the best we'd ever had. Beverages to go with these elegant hot dogs are cold sodas Americaines ($1) and Perrier with lime (de rigeur in the area), $1.25. For dessert, chocolate-chip cookies from O'Carmody's ("out of this world — they would put Famous Amos out of business," says the proprietor) are 75 cents.

Michael Soetbeer at Chez Lenard.

Open year-round, Monday-Saturday 11 to 4, sometimes later and sometimes on Sunday.

Gail's Station House II, 378 Main St., Ridgefield. (203) 438-9775.

One of the hottest places in Ridgefield is this offshoot of Gail's Station House in nearby West Redding. Partners Gail Dudek and Nancy Broughton converted the old Brunetti's Market into a lively, casual arena for good, basic food at affordable prices.

Gail's is known for its baked goods, and all the baking for both establishments is done downstairs at the new location. It's also known for its breakfasts, featuring a variety of pancakes and omelets in the $3.50 to $4.75 range (for corn and cheddar or banana-pecan pancakes). The skillet specials are something else: Texas Pink combines red-skinned hash browns, jalapeño peppers, scrambled eggs topped with salsa and sour cream, and a wedge of pink grapefruit for $5.75; Leo's brings scrambled eggs, Nova Scotia lox, green onions, hash browns and a bagel with cream cheese for $7.75.

At lunch time, burgers range from $3.50 to $6.95, depending on size and accessories. Standard sandwiches, salads, veggie casseroles and blackboard specials are in the $3.95 to $6.75 range.

The dinner menu changes weekly, offering entrées ($8.95 to $14.95) like vegetable lasagna, rainforest stir-fry (vegetables and tropical nuts), chicken enchiladas, shepherd's pie, shrimp creole, angel-hair pasta tossed with smoked salmon and New York steak with brandy-peppercorn sauce. Strawberry pie, coconut-apple pie and marble cheesecake are some of the good desserts.

The place is a mix of baked-goods displays, a counter with stools, and mismatched chairs at tables dressed up with floral cloths under glass at night. Assorted hats decorate one wall. A small rear dining room (once the market's store room) is perked up with a huge window and floral wallpaper above the wainscoting. Three layers of linoleum were removed to expose the original wood

301

floors, and the partners posted a Brunetti's sign in the rear hall because, Nancy said, "we loved the building and the store." They also put in an upright piano where Nancy's brother, a professional entertainer, performs when he's not playing a gig.

Breakfast, Monday-Friday 6 a.m. to 3 p.m., Saturday 7 to 3, Sunday 8 to 3; lunch daily, noon to 3; dinner, Wednesday-Sunday 5:30 to 9:30.

Southwest Cafe, 109 Danbury Road at Copps Hill Common, Ridgefield. (203) 431-3398.

A simple cafe with black and white tile floors and seven tables is where Barbara Nevins dishes up lunch and dinner and lots of takeout business. Her former partner, who owned a restaurant called the Chili Connection in Taos, N.M., won an award there for her green-chile sauce. It's the base for a hearty green-chile stew of carrots, celery and new potatoes, topped with melted cheese and served with a warm flour tortilla. Barbara also employs the sauce in many of the dinner dishes, such as cheese, chicken, seafood or beef enchiladas (the last layered New Mexican style and topped with a fried egg), chicken or beef chimichangas, chalupas, shrimp tostadas, quesadillas and huevos rancheros, all $9.95 or under. It's not often you find huevos on both lunch and dinner menus, or Colorado tostadas with chicken or shredded beef and New Mexican red-chile sauce, for that matter.

Much the same menu is available at lunch, as are sandwiches ($4.50) and salads ($6.95), varying from chicken and artichoke to shrimp and vegetables. Southwest dishes include a bowl of Cheryl's green chili ($2.95) and green-chile chicken, vegetable or beef stew, $6.95. Start with tortilla or split-pea soup. End with Mexican flan or kahlua-pecan pie. Mexican beers and Spanish wines are featured.

Lunch daily, 11 to 4; dinner nightly, 4 to 9:30 or 10.

Steve's Bagels, 483 Main St., Ridgefield. (203) 438-6506.

Ex-Vermont restaurateur Steven Grover saw a need for a good bagel shop in his new hometown. He went to New York and "tasted all the bagels in Manhattan. When I found the ones I liked, they said to cut the sugar and increase the malt. So I did." The rest is history. Steve's bagels took the town by storm. Opening in June 1993, he already was expanding, both in space and offerings.

The bagels (45 cents) are the foundation, upon which his friendly crew builds sandwiches. They range from $3.75 to $5.75 (for smoked salmon, cream cheese and onions) and include tuna, hummus, turkey, chicken salad and roast beef with watercress and horseradish. Or you can have said sandwiches on Steve's caraway rye or whole-wheat breads. There are vegetarian sandwiches (sundried tomatoes with brie; hummus with cucumbers and sprouts) as well. Accompany with one of the soups, the daily vegetarian, chicken and beef or sweet potato and kielbasa.

Steve's CIA-trained baker is also the chef, overseeing production of wonderful pastries, oversize cookies, pecan squares and the like. The deli case displays salads to go. There are tables at which to eat in this spare but spiffy place, or you may take out.

Is there life after bagels? "We're toying with the idea of gourmet pizzas in the evenings," said Steve, "to fill out the other side of the day."

Open daily, 5:30 a.m. to 8 p.m. No smoking.

Early 1800s residence now houses West Lane Inn in Ridgefield.

Lodging

Stonehenge, Route 7, Box 667, Ridgefield 06877. (203) 438-6511.

Instead of a country inn, this is now a fine inn in the country, stresses owner Douglas Seville of the "new" Stonehenge, southwestern Connecticut's grand old inn. He was showing some of the sixteen redecorated guest rooms — six in the inn, six in the Guest Cottage and the rest in a large new outbuilding called the Guest House — and a grand job has been done indeed.

Fashioned in 1947 from a country farmhouse into an English inn by a World War II veteran who had been stationed on the Salisbury Plain near the ancient monument of the same name, Stonehenge has been synonymous with fine food for years. Since the guest rooms were refurnished and more were added in 1984, it has been a place for country getaways as well.

Each room has its own style, from the corner Windsor Room in the inn with a bookcase, antique dresser, wing chairs and fireplace to the spacious bridal suite with large living room and kitchenette in the Guest House. The three master bedrooms and two suites can sleep four, and are particularly sumptuous and comfortable. All rooms have private baths, air-conditioning, telephones and TV.

A picnic hamper containing continental breakfast and the New York Times is delivered to the rooms each morning. In season, guests like to take it to the pond to watch the antics of the geese, ducks and swans. Guests also can use a swimming pool and the cozy, fireplaced parlor in the main inn, full of the latest magazines and books.

Doubles, $120 to $160; suites, $200.

West Lane Inn, 22 West Lane, Ridgefield 06877. (203) 438-7323.

Right beside the Inn at Ridgefield restaurant, this quiet inn is much favored by corporate types moving into the area or visiting on business. The rooms in the early 1800s home are exceptionally comfortable and decorated in soft colors, two with working fireplaces. All have two queensize or a kingsize bed, upholstered wing chairs and-or sofas, private baths, telephones and TVs; the sheets are 100 percent cotton and there are scales in the bathrooms.

Fourteen rooms are in the main inn; six more are out back in a converted garage named "The Cottage on the Hill." Each has a kitchenette and a private rear balcony looking onto emerald-green lawns. Three suites have been fashioned from the former home of innkeeper Maureen Mayer, hidden behind green plantings and a redwood fence between the inn and the restaurant.

Off the inn's rich, oak-paneled lobby is a cheery breakfast room for continental breakfast (fresh juice, danish and beverage). You can choose to have it in summer on the wide front porch with its inviting wicker furniture.

Doubles, $120 to $165.

The Elms, 500 Main St., Ridgefield 06877. (203) 438-2541.

At Ridgefield's oldest operating inn, parts of the original 1760 structure including the tap room look appropriately ancient, but the adjacent inn, totally refurbished in 1983, couldn't be more up to date.

Fifteen rooms and five suites on three floors are spacious, carpeted and outfitted with television and telephones; many of the bathrooms have dressing areas. Antique furnishings, a few four-poster beds and striking wallpapers add a feeling of tradition and luxury. Four rooms upstairs in the original inn are newly redecorated but retain their historic look, even to sloping floors. Two have stenciled bluebirds on the walls.

"The annex had reached the point where we either had to knock it down or build it up," said innkeeper Violet Scala, who is justifiably proud of the results. "For years we had been investing in our restaurant and now it was time for our lodging."

A continental breakfast with fresh croissants is served in guests' rooms.

Doubles, $99 to $110; suites, $125.

Windover Estate Bed & Breakfast, 194 West Lane, Ridgefield. (203) 438-2594.

"It's like being in the pages of Architectural Digest magazine," enthused one couple in the guest book after staying at Windover Estate. Francoise Harkavy, who made it her family's home for eighteen years, opened it as a B&B in 1992, to the delight of appreciative visitors. "It represents our tastes and our collectibles," says Francoise. "Fortunately, our guests seem to enjoy it."

Who wouldn't? The turn-of-the-century summer home built by the founding editor of Life magazine is a fourteen-room stunner situated in a residential section on three park-like acres. The hostess, an interior designer, has decorated with great flair and a predilection for scarlet-red walls. "This red is so easy to live with," says she of the high-gloss living-room walls. "It doesn't turn orange by day or bloody by night." It's a vivid backdrop for her many antiques, both nouveau and deco, her paintings and oriental rugs side by side with an extravagant contemporary rug.

You'll be impressed with the comfortable living room, the cozy fireplaced inglenook sitting area, the sun room with windows onto the gardens and woods, the swimming pool and pergola, the gazebo and bocci court. Not to mention the dining room, with a long table for six, a smaller table in the windowed tea alcove and a player piano at the other end. Here is where Francoise serves a substantial continental breakfast: fresh orange juice, fresh fruit, and croissants with strawberry butter, blueberry muffins, homemade banana bread with cream cheese and chocolate-chip scones – the day's goodies all detailed on a blackboard menu. Wine or tea and finger foods are offered in the afternoon.

Upstairs are three guest rooms with luxuriously comfortable queensize beds

Turn-of-the-century summer home has been converted into Windover Estate B&B.

and private baths and a master suite, where a sleigh bed of Italian tapestry is set against a wall of mirrors. It faces a TV/VCR hidden behind the wall on a built-in shelf. Antique jewelry and accessories are shown in a display closet. Beyond is a huge bath with dressing room, tub, separate shower and oodles of toiletries with which to indulge. Down comforters, terry robes, embroidered linens and fine lace are the norm in the bedrooms. The upstairs also harbors a large library with TV, decorated in dark brown right up to and including the ceiling.

Doubles, $125 and $135; suite, $175.

Gourmet Treats

Hay Day, The Country Farm Market, 21 Governor St., Ridgefield. (203) 431-4400. Hidden away behind Main Street in the old Grand Central supermarket is this branch of the Westport-based market par excellence. When it opened in 1991, it was the biggest and most diverse of the Hay Days with a "real marketplace atmosphere," in the words of vice president Christina Baxter. The 10,000-square-foot facility -- which became the model for a 1993 relocation and expansion of the original 1977 Westport store -- is a food lover's paradise of produce, bakery, fish store, butcher shop, charcuterie, gourmet shelf items and a deli to end all delis, plus a wine shop, a coffee-espresso bar and the **Hay Day Cafe,** which has gone decidedly upscale since its casual bistro beginnings. Best of all for noshers: you can sample your way through the store, tasting perhaps a spicy corn chowder and an addictive chunky clam and bacon dip at the deli, exotic cheeses at the cheese shop, hot mulled cider and Connecticut macoun apples, and there's French vanilla coffee at the door. Hay Day conducts cooking classes, publishes a monthly newspaper chock full of recipes and food tips that formed the nucleus of the wonderful *Hay Day Cookbook,* and does an extensive mail-order business. Open daily, 8 to 7, Sunday to 6.

The Ridgefield General Store in Copps Hill Common, 103 Danbury Road, is a nifty contemporary place full of all kinds of gourmet goodies, from exotic vinegars and its own line of jellies to good-looking china and cooking paraphernalia. Owner Lynelle Faircloth calls hers "a mini-department store" with fifteen departments stocking antiques and "gifts for all reasons." A large area of children's toys and a great selection of paper items from cards and wrapping to invitations are attractions.

Nearby is **The Ridgefield Food Company,** a good caterer that offers some of its specialties for picnics and to go.

Some think the best ice cream around is served at **Mr. Shane's Homemade Parlour Ice Cream,** 409 Main St. Energetic John Ghitman bought the former branch of Dr. Mike's, a well-known Bethel operation, where he learned how to make ice cream. Now he serves up dozens of flavors, from a rich chocolate ("very powerful," says John) to spiced apple, pumpkin and eggnog. We can vouch for his pralines 'n cream (cones, $1.70, 2.30 and $2.97), as well as his new mud ice cream "that's been flying out the door." To forestall questions, a sign detailed its ingredients: coffee ice cream, chocolate fudge, oreo cookies and almonds (and is it ever good). John also offers frappes (milkshakes, to those not familiar with the Massachusetts variety), brown cows (root beer with two scoops of ice cream) and frozen yogurt he doctors up from Columbo.

A large selection of gourmet foods, a coffee bar with great cappuccino, English tea with clotted cream and preserves, and more. That's what you'll find at **Thyme for Change,** Routes 116 and 124, North Salem Center, N.Y. The store is run with panache by Antony Ballard from England and his wife Sharon, a former Miss West Virginia. There are seven little tables with ice-cream-parlor chairs where you can partake of some of the gorgeous salads displayed in the case, or perhaps cream of cauliflower soup and a sandwich of turkey, sprouts, avocado and tomato. Depending on the day, there might be Thai lamb salad or crab cakes with salsa, stilton-cheese soup or bacon and leek quiche.

Consider the Cook, Route 35, Cross River, N.Y., is an excellent kitchen shop in the interesting Yellow Monkey village shopping complex west of Ridgefield. Quimper plates, fabulous table settings and all the latest gourmet foodstuffs are among the offerings. The village with many antique stores also contains **Susan Lawrence Gourmet Foods & Eatery,** a tiny place with five tables inside (and a few more outside in summer), which purveys coffee and espresso, soups, salads, quiches and sandwiches made with bread baked at its main Chappaqua store, as well as gourmet items to go. The garlic-gruyère and spinach-tomato twist breads and the chicken and mushroom sandwich with melted provolone on English oatmeal ($5.75) enticed at one visit. Another time we acquired a quarter pound of haricots verts with sundried tomatoes and olives ($3.25) to go with a couple of chicken pot pies and a grilled-vegetable potpourri from Hay Day for a late dinner back home.

The Silo, 44 Upland Road (off Route 202), New Milford. (203) 355-0300. Although a bit farther afield, no report on culinary affairs in this section of Connecticut would be complete without mention of the fabulous cookery shop and cooking instruction classes offered by Ruth and Skitch Henderson. In former stables and dairy barns are displayed everything from oversize Mexican pottery planters in shapes of rams and hens to a sizable collection of cookbooks interspersed among cooking equipment and jars and bottles of the most wonderful jams, sauces and herbs. The Gallery features changing exhibitions of Connecticut artists and craftspersons. Well-known cooking teachers give classes here; many chefs from area restaurants do as well, and there are two-week seminars and interesting one-session courses — for example, "Decadent Do-Ahead Desserts", "Healthy Cooking for Busy People," "Two in a Tuscan Kitchen," "My First Dinner Party" (ages 8 and up) and "Healthy Holiday Gift Temptations." The 200-acre Hunt Hill Farm, set among rolling hills and flower gardens where kittens tumble around and horses and cows are pastured nearby, is a destination in itself.

Seagull and sailboat are part of typical scene viewed from Dock & Dine restaurant.

Southeastern Connecticut
Down the River and Along the Shore

For reasons not entirely evident, many of Connecticut's better restaurants have clustered through the years along the lower Connecticut River and the shore of Long Island Sound.

Perhaps it is the natural affinity of restaurants for water locations. Perhaps it is the reputation for the good life that accompanies people of affluence with demanding palates and high tastes. Perhaps it is the busy but low-key resort status of the shore, summer home to thousands of inland Connecticut and Massachusetts residents.

Some of Southern New England's top innkeepers and restaurateurs put the area on the dining map in the 1970s. Several fine French restaurants followed, and in the last few years, more inns of distinction and restaurants have joined the scene.

"We've found this area full of people with discriminating tastes," says Bob Nelson, a New Jersey corporate dropout who has given new life to the old Bee and Thistle Inn in Old Lyme.

Except for Mystic, the Connecticut shore has been discovered relatively lately by most tourists. "Californians love this area," say promoters of the Norwich Inn, which has been reincarnated by the owner of the Sonoma Mission Inn and Spa. "It's sophisticated, yet close to the water and has plenty of rural charm."

The area this chapter covers has no large cities. Rather, it harbors remote, quaint villages like Chester and Stonington, affluent enclaves like Essex and Old Lyme, and resort sections like Mystic and Old Saybrook. (It also has the growing and widely touted Foxwoods casino and entertainment center, which quickly has become the most profitable casino in the hemisphere for its owners, the Pequot Indians.)

Because this is our home territory, we cover our favorites in a broad sweep down the Connecticut, Thames and Mystic rivers and along the shore of Long Island Sound.

Bed and Board

Bee and Thistle Inn, 100 Lyme St., Old Lyme 06371. (203) 434-1667 or (800) 622-4946.

When Bob and Penny Nelson decided to leave corporate life in northern New Jersey and buy a New England inn, little did they think of southern Connecticut or the Bee and Thistle. But on their rounds they took one look at this tranquil yellow house with its center entrance hall and graceful staircase, parlors on either side and three dining rooms, and said, "this is it."

That was in 1982. The Nelsons since have refurbished the inn's eleven guest rooms and public rooms, added a riverside cottage and have upgraded the dining situation.

Head chef Francis Brooke-Smith, who trained at the Ritz in London, delights in innovative touches and presentations, including garnishes of edible flowers and fresh herbs grown hydroponically year-round. He has help in the kitchen from the Nelsons' son Jeff, a CIA grad who trained at the 21 Club in New York and the Ritz-Carlton in Boston.

Dinner entrées range from $17.95 for summer chicken (combined with leeks, basil and lime, and served on radicchio with parmesan gnocchi) to $25.95 for rack of lamb with roasted garlic mousse. Other tempters are grilled shrimp on a curried apple coulis with basmati and golden-raisin rice, pan-fried rainbow trout on a coriander crème fraîche with a chile-pepper relish, roast loin of pork served on a plum-cabernet sauce with a corn and chive brioche, and roasted filet mignon with a tomato-horseradish salsa served with corn and scallion pancakes.

Meals might start with smoked seafood and smoked salmon mousse, wild mushrooms with mozzarella on grilled bruschetta, and baked goat cheese served

on a bed of frisée with roasted garlic, oysters and tomatoes ($6.95 to $8.95). Bread pudding, white-chocolate mousse with black-currant and cassis sauce, chocolate-caramel squares with frozen banana mousse and an apricot puree, bourbon fruit cake and fresh fruit sorbets are among the luscious desserts.

Bob Nelson, who studied wines at the Cornell University Hotel School, put together the wine list with an eye to price "so people can afford a good bottle."

A harpist plays on Saturday and a guitar duo sings love songs on Friday in this "inn designed for people to get away from their stresses and to relate to each other," in the words of Penny Nelson.

Lunch overlooking the lawns on the enclosed side porches — one with loads of plants hanging from the ceiling and the other full of Penny's collection of

Dining porch at Bee and Thistle Inn.

Mirror reflects tables in perfect formation in Old Lyme Inn dining room.

baskets — is a delight. Choices run from $7.95 for a stilton-cheese sandwich with thyme-potato salad to $11.95 for grilled lamb chops. The duck and orange salad, crab and corn cakes, and salmon lasagna are favorites.

A fairly extensive breakfast at modest extra cost may be enjoyed by guests in their rooms, on the cheery sun porches with their floral tablecloths or mats and ladderback chairs, or in one of the parlors beside a fire. The Bee and Thistle popover filled with scrambled eggs, bacon and cheese ($4.75) and the beef and bacon hash with eggs ($5.25) draw the public as well as overnighters. So do the finger sandwiches and scones served with preserves and whipped cream at English tea ($8.95) in the parlor from 3:30 to 5 on Monday, Wednesday and Thursday from November to April.

Sunday brunch ($10.95 to $14.95) features sticky buns and the chef's potatoes with such entrées as chicken hash, fillet of sole with tomato and leeks, french toast stuffed with semi-sweet chocolate on apricot puree, shrimp napoleon and pork oscar.

Games and books are on the two stairway landings leading to guest rooms on the second and third floors. Rooms vary from large with queensize canopy beds and a loveseat to small with twin beds. Nine come with private baths and all have antique, country-style furnishings. The cottage offers a riverside deck off the bedroom wrapping around to the fireplaced reading room, a TV room and a kitchen; its rates include continental breakfast.

Breakfast daily, 8 to 10, Sunday to 9:30; lunch, daily except Tuesday 11:30 to 2; dinner, nightly except Tuesday from 6; Sunday brunch, 11 to 2. Doubles, $69 to $125, EP; cottage, $195.

Old Lyme Inn, Lyme Street, Old Lyme 06371. (203) 434-2600.

In contrast to the antique clutter and charm of the Bee and Thistle across the street, the Old Lyme Inn is pristine and chic, quietly sedate in royal blue and

309

white. Inside a beautifully restored 1850s mansion is a formal restaurant with inventive French cuisine and seating for more than 200, as well as thirteen guest rooms upstairs and in a newer wing.

The setting in the main dining room is elegant if a bit austere — very tall and formally draped windows, walls papered in a gold pattern and chairs upholstered in deep blue velvet at tables angled in perfect formation. A single rose in a crystal vase is on each large, white-linened table, and tapestries and oil paintings (appropriately, some by the famed Lyme Impressionists) in elaborate frames adorn the walls. Beyond are two more dining rooms, one with an intimate windowed alcove embracing a table for four.

Under the aegis of owner Diana Field Atwood, the inn's restaurant has been awarded top ratings three times by the New York Times and its desserts were featured in successive issues of Bon Appétit magazine. Chef Stuart London oversees an ambitious dinner menu. Among main courses ($19.50 to $28) might be pan-seared tuna steak with a spicy fruit salsa, sautéed lobster meat over saffron pasta, sweetbreads dijonnaise in puff pastry, grilled duck breast with almond-cherry sauce, medallions of quail served on mesclun greens with a currant-cassis sauce, osso buco and broiled filet mignon forestière.

Appetizers ($7.25 to $10.50) include Irish smoked salmon, a smoked salmon-caviar-mascarpone torte served with rye bread, native bluefin crab cake with sweet pepper relish and caper-tartar sauce, carpaccio of filet mignon and pâté of Connecticut pheasant with apples and walnuts. The soup might be crab and parsnip bisque; the salad, duck confit with spicy pecans on a bed of field greens.

For dessert, try the award-winning chocolate-truffle tart, pumpkin cheesecake with cranberries, or layered gingerbread with buttercream, peaches and raspberries. Homemade ice creams include caramel and eggnog. We can vouch for a chocolate-truffle cake with mandarin-flavored pastry cream topped with a layer of sponge cake soaked in cointreau, and a fruit tart with an apricot glaze and kiwi and strawberries on top. Cafe Diana with chambord and chocolate liqueurs is a fitting finale.

The wine list is unusual in range and scope, from two Australian chardonnays for $13 to fine Bordeaux up to $450.

A light supper menu is available in the stylish bar-lounge, perhaps chicken with oysters in tarragon cream or a German sausage and sauerkraut platter, in the $14 to $15 range.

Luncheon brings some of the dinner appetizers, plus salads like curried turkey and wild rice or spinach with grilled chicken and feta, and entrées ($7.95 to $9.50) like venison chili, fresh buffalo burger, seafood brochette and grilled pizza. The Sunday brunch menu ($9.95 to $14.95) includes such exotic fare as zucchini pancakes with smoked ham, sundried-tomato waffles, sole and crab meat au gratin, cheese blintzes, and smoked salmon with eggs and onions.

The eight newer guest rooms in the north wing are decorated in plush Victorian style. Marblehead mints are perched atop the oversize pillows on the canopy and four-poster beds, comfortable sofas or chairs are grouped around marble-top tables, and gleaming white bathrooms are outfitted with herbal shampoos and Dickenson's Witch Hazel made in nearby Essex. The smaller rooms in the older part of the inn are not as elegant.

Homemade croissants and granola are served for continental breakfast in the Rose Room.

Lunch, Tuesday-Saturday noon to 2; dinner, Tuesday-Saturday 6 to 9; Sunday, brunch 11 to 3, dinner 4 to 9. Doubles, $98 to $144.

Twisted napkins look like candles in Georgian Room at Cooper Beech Inn.

Copper Beech Inn, Main Street, Ivoryton 06442. (203) 767-0330.

After slipping a bit from its lofty perch as one of Connecticut's premier dining spots in the 1970s, this imposing mansion shaded by the oldest copper beech tree in Connecticut is back on top. Owners Eldon and Sally Senner, he formerly with the World Bank in Washington and she an interior designer, have upgraded the accommodations and restored the dining experience to that of its glory days.

The Senners offer four period guest rooms upstairs, as well as nine deluxe guest rooms in an old carriage house behind the inn. Each of the latter has a jacuzzi, and french doors onto an outdoor deck or balcony overlooking the gardens; second-floor rooms have cathedral ceilings. Mahogany queensize beds and TVs are the rule. The Senners have added their own antiques and 19th-century art to the inn, and offer fine oriental porcelain in a small second-floor gallery, open by appointment.

They also have added an elegant Victorian sun room in the front of the inn, replacing a rear greenhouse that was inaccessible except in summer. Guests find it a pleasant and quiet retreat in which to relax.

A continental breakfast buffet of fresh fruit, cereals, breads and two kinds of French pastries is served in the clubby blue Cooper Beech Room, where tables are spaced well apart and the windows afford views of the great tree outside.

Dining is in several lovely rooms, including the striking rose and beige Georgian Room, where twisted napkins stand tall in the water glasses, looking like candles from afar. The dark, paneled Comstock Room with a beamed ceiling retains the look of the billiards parlor that it once was. Between the two is a pretty little garden porch with intricate wicker chairs at four tables for two amidst the plants.

The Senners credit the rise in the inn's dining fortunes to executive chef Robert Chiovoloni, a Culinary Institute grad who holds a master's degree in English literature. He was executive sous-chef at the Montpelier Room of Washington's Madison Hotel, which they considered the city's best restaurant at the time. Here he seeks out the best ingredients, importing, for instance, snails and wild huckleberries from Washington state.

His fare is country French, light but highly sophisticated. Witness such appetizers as warm lobster in a tawny-port and cream sauce, roasted oysters garnished with salmon caviar, terrine of foie gras with a toasted brioche, a ragout of wild mushrooms and escargots, and blinis with ossetra caviar. Pricey ($7.95 to $25.25), but worth it to connoisseurs.

Main courses ($22.50 to $25.25) include bouillabaisse, sautéed fillet of salmon served with saffron sauce on a cushion of crisp straw potatoes and lump crab meat, roasted saddle of lamb with a warm tomato coulis, roasted pheasant (under glass, no less), grilled filet mignon chasseur and roasted venison with currants and chestnut mousse.

Heady stuff this, and it continues through the desserts ($5.75 to $6.95). Tarte tatin, croustade of fresh fruit, white-chocolate mousse with praline-custard sauce, charlotte au chocolat and ice cream bombe with different sauces are to groan over. A plate of almond-studded tuiles may come with coffee. Linger over a liquered coffee or a glass of port and savor a meal worthy of a special occasion.

Dinner, Tuesday-Saturday 6 to 9, Sunday 1 to 8; closed Tuesday in winter. Doubles, $100 to $160.

The Inn at Chester, 318 West Main St., Chester 06412. (203) 526-9541 and (800) 949-7829.

One of our favorite inns and dining rooms -- unfortunately closed for a few years due to financial problems -- reopened in 1992 and is better than ever, thanks to energetic innkeeper Deborah Moore and talented chef Daniel McManamy.

They are a fortuitous fit. Deborah returned home after touring the world as a second mate in the Merchant Marine to run the inn her father had just purchased. Daniel, who had lost his lease for his great little Daniel's Table restaurant at the Ivoryton Inn, was ready and willing to take over the kitchen.

Most of the inn had been built in 1983 around the 1776 John B. Parmelee House, on twelve rural areas west of town. Deborah and her parents took six months to restore the place and redo the layout. They added a comfortable lobby and a gift shop where her mother sells the works of local artists on consignment, put in a skylit tavern on the site of the former patio and relaid the patio beyond, carpeted the dining room and reopened the downstairs game room with fireplace and billiards table. Deborah found the 43 guest rooms in two wings of modern construction rather spartan, so is gradually adding wallpaper, artworks, accessories, more comfortable chairs, kingsize beds and such. Most rooms are outfitted with queens, doubles or twin beds and Eldred Wheeler reproduction furniture, and come with TVs and telephones. Deborah's mother delivers baskets of candy to the guest rooms.

A 30-foot granite fireplace soars into the rafters between the new tavern, where light dinners are available, and **The Post and Beam** dining room, whose name describes its interior construction. The latter is a high-ceilinged room with barnwood walls, a fieldstone fireplace, two wrought-iron chandeliers, candle sconces and a plant-filled conservatory. The setting is serene with white tablecloths, white china and fresh flowers in bud vases.

Our latest dinner here began with a complimentary spread of duck-liver pâté that arrived with hot, crusty rolls, a perfect match. A hearty butternut-apple bisque hinted of curry and an appetizer of crabmeat flauta, a tortilla laden with crab meat, exploded with flavors from the ancho-chile sauce and a garnish of

Inn at Chester's Post and Beam dining room looks onto plant-filled conservatory.

coriander-lime aioli. Among other starters ($4.75 to $7.50) were a timbale of smoked seafoods with crème fraîche, Thai shrimp with a pineapple-mango relish, littleneck clams in a saffron broth with tomatoes and leeks. and warm duck salad with crispy fried potatoes and walnut dressing.

Huge green salads with mustardy vinaigrettes preceded our main dishes, veal sweetbreads simmered with madeira and exotic mushrooms, served with fresh fettuccine and snap peas, and grilled filet of beef with portobello mushrooms and dauphinoise potatoes. A Brown Brothers shiraz for $16 was the perfect choice from a fairly extensive wine list ranging up to $75. Other entrées were priced from $18 for chicken breast stuffed with sundried tomatoes and gorgonzola to $23 for medallions of lamb with a chardonnay sauce.

Plums with cinnamon and orange crème brûlée were worthy endings to a memorable meal.

Many of the appetizers and salads turn up on the lunch menu, which offers a good range from a grilled eggplant sandwich ($6) to bouillabaisse ($9.50). The Spanish omelet and smoked-salmon benedict are favorites at brunch. Continental breakfast is complimentary for house guests.

Incidentally, the inn is known for romance and has an award to show for it. Deborah should know. She became friendly with a businessman who frequently stayed at the inn and they were married in October 1993.

Lunch, Monday-Saturday 11:30 to 2; dinner, Monday-Saturday 5:30 to 9; Sunday, brunch 11:30 to 2:30, dinner 3:30 to 7:30. Doubles, $95 to $130, suites, $175 and $205.

The Griswold Inn, Main Street, Essex. (203) 767-1776.

"This place hasn't changed a bit in 40 years, Arnie," said one elderly man to another as they waited in line at the Gris, as this 200-plus-year-old inn is affectionately known.

Although we are not particularly drawn by the food (we'd eat here when we

313

had visiting parents in tow — it's the kind of place they love), it is perfectly adequate, especially for the simple fish and meat dishes on the standard menu (dinner entrées, $16.95 to $22.50), running the gamut from a mixed grill of the Griswold's trademark-registered 1776 sausages and barbecued ribs to broiled scrod, grilled veal steak and prime rib.

And you have to hand it to innkeeper Bill Winterer and crew — when the original kitchen was closed and a new one built in 1989, the Gris staff managed to keep serving food from an abbreviated menu every day. We also were impressed that this venerable inn has been in the vanguard every winter in the 1990s, offering a special four-course menu of Connecticut bounty for $15.95 on weeknights.

Like everyone else, we *are* drawn by the always-crowded Tap Room, the social center of town. It's a happy hubbub of banjo players or singers of sea chanteys, table-hopping, noisy conversation and fun, and has about the best New England atmosphere of any bar we know. Baskets of popcorn from the old-fashioned machine and cheese spread with crackers are complimentary at happy hour.

The several dining rooms display one of the nation's largest collections of marine art and are a veritable museum of Currier and Ives prints, steamboat memorabilia and, in the Gun Room, a noted collection of firearms, some as old as the 15th century.

The famed Hunt Breakfast on Sundays ($12.95) includes chicken livers, grits and cheddar-cheese soufflé and creamed chipped beef.

The floors in some of the 23 guest rooms list to port or starboard, which is to be expected of an inn built in 1776 as Connecticut's first three-story structure.

Lunch daily, noon to 2:30, Saturday from 11:30; dinner, 5:30 to 9 or 10; Sunday, hunt breakfast 11 to 2:30, dinner 4:30 to 9. Doubles, including continental breakfast, $90 to $95; suites, $105 to $175.

Water's Edge Inn & Resort, 1525 Boston Post Road, Box 938, Westbrook 06498. (203) 399-5901 or (800) 222-5901.

Anyone familiar with the legendary Bill Hahn's resort of the post-war era would scarcely recognize its multi-million-dollar successor, winner of three architectural awards bestowed the year it opened. Perched above Long Island Sound on fifteen acres with an unencumbered waterfront view, the resort commands arguably the best location of any such facility in Connecticut.

The main inn and nearby library building house twenty guest rooms and twelve suites, all with TVs and phones. (Thirty-six condos and an equal number of time-share units occupy low-slung buildings tiptoeing down to water's edge on either side.) Rooms are spiffily decorated in celadon green tones, their kingsize beds turned down with two foil-wrapped chocolates resting on the pillows and their private balconies furnished with a table and two chairs. The bathrooms are sparkling white, right down to the mats and shower curtains.

Facilities include a pool, tennis courts, an outdoor terrace and grill, an inviting bar, and a health spa with an indoor pool and exercise room.

Chef Dennis Brake Jr. offers a select new American menu in a glamorous, three-tiered dining room. The most choice section has a soaring ceiling, double-deck windows topped with balloon curtains, and upholstered armchairs at tables appointed in pink and gray, with alstroemeria in gray vases and spectacular flower arrangements all around.

At lunch, good country rolls were served with a generous glass of the day's Beringer chardonnay ($4.50). If we hadn't had to work that afternoon, we might

Outdoor diners have view of Long Island Sound from terrace at Water's Edge.

have indulged in a bottle of Château St. Michelle riesling for $14 from a good wine selection priced up to $60.

A spinach salad ($7.75) combined smoked scallops, toasted almonds and apples in a walnut-lemon dressing. The linguini with mussels, garlic and sweet butter ($8.95) was a zesty dish, garnished with mussels in their shells and two large croutons for dipping in the broth. Dessert was an excellent pear-cranberry tart with a strong almond flavoring.

At night, the moonlight reflecting off the Sound complements the light from tiny peach-colored, frosted-glass oil lamps on the tables and small brass lanterns on the walls. Entrées are priced from $17.50 for chicken with roasted garlic, thyme and lentils to $26 for grilled veal chop with roasted root vegetables. Halibut au poivre with braised savoy cabbage and vanilla-saffron sauce, seared salmon with steamed escarole and grilled rack of lamb with tequila sauce and black-bean and corn relish are among the possibilities.

Start with escargots fra diavolo, smoked-salmon mousseline, grilled portobello mushrooms on a pillow of endive, radicchio and arugula, or crab cakes with sour cream and caviar, $5.50 to $9.50. A cranberry sorbet is served before the main course. The dessert list might yield chocolate midnight cake, bourbon-pecan pie, brandysnap baskets, poached pears in wine and fuzzy navel peach pie.

A flutist and a pianist entertain on most evenings. In summer, meals are sometimes cooked on a large grill on the attractive outdoor patio.

Lunch, Monday-Saturday 11:30 to 2:30; dinner, 5:30 to 9:30 or 10; Sunday, brunch 10:30 to 3, dinner 6:30 to 9. Doubles, $150 to $200; suites and villas, $175 to $275.

Randall's Ordinary, Route 2, Box 243, North Stonington 06359. (203) 599-4540.
Here's where you can hearken back to pre-Revolutionary War times, enjoying hearthside dinners and historic accommodations in a rural farmhouse dating to 1685, sequestered in the midst of 27 acres at the end of a dirt road. Or you can

bask in the modern comforts of new guest rooms in a restored 1819 barn dismantled and moved to the property from Richmondville, N.Y.

Bill and Cindy Clark transformed a hobby of cooking dinners for friends and private parties over an open hearth at their former home in South Salem, N.Y., into a unique Colonial restaurant and inn in their native Connecticut.

Using antique iron pots and utensils and cooking in reflector ovens and an immense open hearth, they serve food from the Colonial era to patrons in a thoroughly authentic 18th-century setting. Up to 75 diners gather at 7 in a small taproom where they pick up a drink along with popcorn, crackers, and cheese. They are then shown through the house, after which they watch the cooks in Colonial costumes preparing their meals on the open hearth.

Seating in beamed dining rooms is at old tables with hand-loomed placemats, Bennington black and white pottery, flatware with pistol-grip knives and three-tined forks, and such unusual accessories as a salt plate and a sugar scoop.

The $30 prix-fixe dinner offers a choice of up to five entrées — roast capon with wild rice stuffing, roast ribeye beef, roast pork loin, hearth-grilled salmon, and Nantucket scallops with scallions and butter when we were there. The meal includes soup (country onion or Shaker herb, perhaps), whole-wheat walnut or spider corn bread, a conserve of red cabbage and apples, squash pudding, and carrot cake, apple crisp or Indian pudding. Choose a house Napa Ridge chardonnay or côtes du rhone from the small wine list to complement your meal.

Lunch is à la carte. We know local innkeepers who go here once a month and consider it the best value in the area. Start perhaps with parsnip and apple soup or Brunswick stew with spider bread. Try a hearth-roasted chicken sandwich with maple mustard, beefsteak pudding or broiled lamb chops with boiled red potatoes and cranberry conserve for $4.95 to $8.50.

Now the restaurant offers breakfast to the public, perhaps maple toast with fried apples and Shaker apple salad or johnnycakes. All are in the $4 range, except for the "Ordinary breakfast" bringing the works for $8.95.

Three guest rooms in the main house have working fireplaces and queensize four-poster beds with handloomed coverlets as well as modern baths with whirlpool jets in the tubs. Twelve new rooms and suites are located to the rear in the old-style English barn with open bays, to which a milking shed and a silo have been attached. The framing was left exposed, random pine floors are covered with scatter rugs, and rooms are furnished to the period, though they strike some as rather spartan. With modern baths, built-in sofas, phones and TVs, they are quite contemporary. Two have lofts with skylights and spiral staircases, and the new Silo Suite is enormous.

Breakfast daily, 7 to 11; lunch, noon to 3; dinner, Sunday-Friday at 7; Saturday 5 and 7:30. Doubles, $85 to $135; suites, $135 and $175.

The Mystic Hilton, Coogan Boulevard, Mystic 06355. (203) 572-0731 or (800) 826-8699.

This newish hotel boasts one of the area's premier restaurants, which earned a top rating from the New York Times. **The Mooring** is a comfortable, three-level affair with armchairs and banquettes in deep blue, rich wood accents and an array of canoe paddles artistically arranged as art on the walls. The airy room overlooks an outdoor courtyard centered with a sculpture of a dolphin.

The menu has been toned down a bit lately in concept, if not in execution. Some locals complain that the portions leave them hungry, but we were satisfied after our dinners of roast rack of lamb — four pink little chops accompanied by

316

Chef cooks hearthside dinner at Randall's Ordinary.

new potatoes, grilled yellow squash, zucchini and eggplant, and half a broiled tomato — and medallions of venison with a sauce of port wine, sage and chanterelles, plus green beans and carrots. Good crunchy French bread and salads of mixed greens and radicchio preceded. For dessert, the almond lace cookie filled with chocolate mousse and liqueur was enough for two.

The dinner menu ranges widely in scope and price, from $10.95 for charbroiled pesto chicken or fish and chips to $24.95 for the rack of lamb. Among the possibilities are roasted monkfish with lobster homefries, grilled swordfish with tomato-leek chutney, seared pepper-crusted salmon served on a bed of greens with grilled asparagus and wild mushrooms, roast duck with apple-cider sauce and grilled filet mignon with wild-mushroom demi-glace.

Start with duck strudel with oriental vegetables, seafood burrito or grilled quail salad ($5.50 to $7.95). For dessert, how about black forest layer cake, hazelnut-torte mousse cake or the signature hand-molded chocolate bag filled with chocolate mousse? The primarily American wine list is priced from $15 to $100.

The hotel is appropriate to the setting, its low red-brick exterior and peaked roofs emulating the look of 19th-century mills and warehouses. The 184 guest rooms are decorated in rose and green, each bearing two large prints of Mystic Seaport scenes commissioned from artist Sally Caldwell Fisher. The meandering, angled layout puts some rooms an inordinate distance from the elevators, but also contributes to peace and quiet.

Lunch, Monday-Saturday 11:30 to 2:30; dinner, 6 to 9:30 or 10. Doubles, $129 to $175.

Norwich Inn & Spa, Route 32, Norwich 06360. (203) 886-2401 or (800) 275-4772.
The stately, red-brick Norwich Inn was refurbished in 1983 and its long-awaited spa was opened three years later by Edward J. Safdie, author of the books "Spa

Food" and "New Spa Food" and founder of the luxury Sonoma Mission Inn and Spa in California.

At almost every turn, the inn shows the results of the Safdie style and money. It is a smashingly decorated showplace, from the copper lanterns flanking the corner entrance to the rear dining terrace, a sea of white against the surrounding greenery.

The spacious lobby in shades of pale green, rose and pink and lots of chintz is centered by a large, handcrafted dovecote, the home of Mexican fantail lovey doves Pat and Mike. To one side are the Hunt Room for private parties and the club-like Prince of Wales Bar.

A long, narrow sun porch, facing the spa building, leads to the dining room and outdoor deck. It is a scene straight out of the old South with peach walls and green wicker furniture, whirling overhead fans, and huge clay pots full of ferns and palms.

The spa, which resembles the Sonoma Mission spa, has a Western feeling. Here is the penultimate bathhouse with lap pool, whirlpool, sauna, fitness facilities, massage rooms and such. You can get anything from a full-body massage ($60) or a four-layer facial mask ($65) to a one-day revitalizer ($230), a three-day rejuvenator ($820) or a full five-day program with room and spa meals ($1,350 to $2,300).

Sixty-five guest rooms on three floors reached by graceful staircases are in pleasant shades of Nantucket blue and cinnamon or deep turquoise and pink. The refurbished Country Rooms have chintz-covered chairs, chintz comforters on the queensize four-poster beds and matching chintz draped around the windows. Dried or grapevine wreaths hang above every bed, rooms are carpeted and some TVs are hidden in armoires.

The inn's small, intimate dining room, **The Prince of Wales,** attracts those into luxury dining, including spa cuisine. Rich mauve silk on the walls and green wainscoting create a pleasant backdrop for white-linened tables flanked by high-back chairs of light pine. Behind the dining room, the large outdoor deck with white garden furniture and pots of red geraniums overlooking the Norwich Golf Course and distant hills is a grand setting for summer meals.

The short menu changes seasonally, and the spa selections nightly. Dinner might start with a terrine of smoked salmon and fresh salmon, country-style pâté of veal and pork, or a salad of baked goat cheese and roasted red peppers on baby greens ($7.95 to $11.95). Entrées ($16.50 to $21.95) include chargrilled swordfish in a tomato-soya marinade; fricassee of monkfish and button mushrooms with orzo pasta, snap peas and saffron cream; hoisin roast duck breasts on brown and wild rice pilaf, and sautéed veal medallions with a salpicon of lobster and morels. Spa specials could be Indonesian chicken satay with peanut sauce or vegetable lasagna.

For dessert, how about a hazelnut-chocolate torte, chocolate-mousse cake, New York-style cheesecake, Tuscan torte with profiteroles or assorted gelati? A good wine list, with a natural emphasis on Californias, is fairly priced.

Tea is served on weekends from 3 to 5 in front of the fireplace in the lobby, complete with tea sandwiches, scones and sometimes layer cake. The new Spa Bar on the terrace features non-alcoholic frozen drinks, served Saturday and Sunday afternoons.

Lunch, Monday-Friday noon to 2, Saturday to 3; dinner, 6 or 6:30 to 9:30 or 10:30, jackets required; Sunday brunch, noon to 3. Doubles, $140 to $215, EP.

Chef-owner Steve Wilkinson is known for inspired cooking at Fine Bouche.

Dining

The Best of the Best

Fine Bouche, 78 Main St., Centerbrook. (203) 767-1277.

The personal tastes and background of creative chef-owner Steven Wilkinson, an unpretentious man who apprenticed in London and San Francisco, are reflected in the small French restaurant and pâtisserie he opened in a lattice-trimmed Victorian house in 1979.

You enter through the former pâtisserie (lately moved to larger quarters in the rear), pass the handsome, dark wood service bar and head into a reception parlor, where two lighted, glassed-in shelves hold bottles of rare wine and memorabilia of the owner's career.

The two inner dining rooms are small and comfortable. One has pictures of grapes and vines on cream-colored walls; the other, pretty dark green and flowered wallpaper hung with old French prints. We're partial to the cafe-style wraparound porch, a picture of pristine cheer with white, not quite sheer full-length draperies hiding the view of the parking lot, peach-colored walls, arched lattice work over the windows and handsome rattan chairs with seats covered in dark green chintz dotted with exotic lilies.

Known as one of the top chefs in the state, Steve Wilkinson changes his menu seasonally. A prix-fixe dinner is $38 for five courses, or you may order many of the same items à la carte (appetizers, $6 to $7.50; entrées, $17.50 to $23).

Lobster gâteau (lobster and corn "lasagna" with saffron pasta and a chile-pepper dressing), a terrine of smoked salmon and smoked mackerel with peach-onion marmalade, and country terrine with pommery mustard and pickled cherries make good beginnings. Don't overlook the velvety lobster bisque with cognac or chilled blueberry-peach swirl soup.

You will nearly always find entrées of duck, lamb, beef and veal in different preparations. Sliced duck with port and figs, rack of lamb with roasted garlic and anise, tournedos with armagnac cream and choron sauce, and veal loin with leeks, shiitake mushrooms and ginger are among our favorites. Grilled salmon with fresh mango salsa and grilled swordfish with pesto ravioli are other winners. Seasonal dishes might include a dish of sea urchins, oysters and scallops in summer and sautéed breast of pheasant with fresh raspberries and framboise in winter.

Desserts are superlative, particularly the almond-hazelnut dacquoise, a light but intense chocolate cake with chocolate chantilly; and the marjolaine, a heavenly combination of almond praline, hazelnut meringue, crème fraîche and bitter Belgian chocolate. Those with more resistance than we can order a fruit sorbet.

Steve Wilkinson hosts many wine-tasting events at Fine Bouche, and his interest shows in the wine list, winner of Wine Spectator's grand award. The 450 selections, well balanced between French and California, are fairly priced.

Dinner, Tuesday-Saturday 6 to 9.

Restaurant du Village, 59 Main St., Chester. (203) 526-5301.

Of all the Southern New England restaurants in which we've dined, we think this is the most like what you would find in a French village. Its blue wood facade — with specially grown ivy geraniums spilling out of window boxes and the bottom half of the large windows curtained in an almost sheer white fabric — is smack on the main street of tiny Chester, but one enters by walking up a brick path attractively bordered with potted geraniums to a side door.

Alsatian chef Michel Keller and his Culinary Institute-trained American wife Cynthia run their highly rated establishment very personally. A third-generation pastry chef, Michel spends his time in the kitchen and bakes the breads and desserts. Cynthia does the soups and some of the fish dishes, but is in the front of the house to welcome guests in the evening.

Through the small bar-lounge, decorated with country-plump piggies (the logo of the restaurant) with a few tables for overflow, you reach the small square dining room. Along one wall, two sets of french doors open onto the brick walk for welcome breezes on warm nights. A sideboard between the doors contains the night's desserts and a large floral arrangement. A few lighted oil paintings adorn the stucco-type walls; a high shelf over the front windows displays antique plates.

The air of charming simplicity is enhanced at the thirteen tables by white cloths and napkins, carafes of flowers, votive candles, open salt and pepper dishes, and blue sprigged service plates.

What may be the best French bread you will taste in this country is brought to the table with generous cocktails. Crunchy and chewy, made of Hecker's unbleached flour that gives it a darker color, the baguette is cut into thick chunks. Each diner is served an individual crock of sweet butter. If you get near the last piece of bread — and most of us do — the basket is whisked away and refilled, which could be fatal. On one visit it came back three times.

Of the six appetizers ($6.25 to $8.50), standouts are the cassolette, a small copper casserole filled with sautéed shrimp in a light curry sauce; the croustade with grilled vegetables, and escargots with shiitake mushrooms in puff pastry. We also like the baked French goat cheese on herbed salad greens with garlic croutons. The soup changes daily, but often is a puree of vegetables or, on one summer night we dined, a cold cucumber and dill.

The ten or so entrées ($21 to $26) might include scrod with potato-shell scallops on a bed of leeks with tarragon sauce, steamed salmon pot au feu with a tomato

Dining room decor is country French at Restaurant du Village.

and basil coulis, roast duckling with cranberry chutney, pan-seared veal cutlet with a flan of wild mushrooms obtained by a local purveyor from nearby woods, roast leg of herb-marinated lamb with French green kidney beans, and Cynthia's specialty, a stew of veal, lamb and pork with leeks and potatoes. These are accompanied by treats like dauphinoise potatoes with melted gruyère, julienned carrots, and yellow squash and zucchini with a sherry-vinegar-shallot flavor. The salad of exotic greens is tossed with a creamy mustard dressing that packs a wallop.

The well-chosen, mostly French wine list is priced from $16 to $95 and features some vintages from Alsace.

Desserts change daily and are notable as well. At our latest visit, Michel was preparing an open fruit tart with blueberries and peaches in almond cream, a gratin of passion fruit and paris-brest in addition to his usual napoleons, soufflé glacé and crème brûlée.

Dinner, Tuesday-Saturday 5:30 to 9, Sunday 5 to 9. Closed Tuesday in winter.

Aleia's, 1353 Boston Post Road, Westbrook. (203) 399-5050.

Given their backgrounds (both Culinary Institute of America graduates), sisters Michelle Tine and Kimberly Snow raised many an expectation when they opened their long-awaited restaurant in a renovated 1872 white house with green shutters just off the town green. Michelle, who has cooked in such big-name Manhattan kitchens as Le Cirque and TriBeCa Grill, and Kimberly, who runs the acclaimed Kimberly's Limited bakery in Middletown, did not disappoint. Their unexpectedly large and somewhat formal restaurant has drawn nothing but raves since it bowed in 1993.

Michelle is in the kitchen and Kimberly commutes back and forth from her bakery, where she creates such treats as banana gâteau with layers of maple-nut mousse, cappuccino cheesecake with espresso crème anglaise, and bittersweet-chocolate torte with raspberry coulis accented with sweet whipped cream. That the dessert treats are so good is no surprise after you've sampled the basket of breads -- including a wonderful tomato-basil -- that arrives at the table as you order.

Lunch was more elaborate than we had expected, both in terms of menu offerings and setting. No cafe this, although a bar menu doubles as a deck menu in summer. Lunch appetizers are about the same as those at dinner, and priced accordingly ($5.25 for a salad of mesclun greens to $6.95 for fried calamari with house tartar on roasted tomato sauce). And there are no sandwiches, other than a grilled sirloin cheeseburger, at $6.95 the cheapest item except for capellini tossed in a roasted tomato-basil sauce ($6.25). So we were left to splurge on a menu priced up to $11.95: an elegant (how else to describe it?) lobster club sandwich with warm potato salad ($8.75) and grilled chicken with sautéed artichokes, roasted tomatoes and grilled baby eggplant, served over couscous ($7.95). Two little hazelnut cookies came with the bill.

The dinner menu yields similar Mediterranean-inspired treats, at prices that don't seem out of line. Main courses are $13.95 to $17.25, except $19.95 for seared veal chop with a wild-mushroom reduction sauce. The fresh flounder paired with couscous is surrounded by a starburst of sautéed artichokes and grilled baby eggplant, kalamata olives and chunks of oven-roasted tomatoes. The grilled tuna medallion is drizzled with sherry vinaigrette and accessorized with grilled vegetables. The sautéed salmon fillet arrives with a dijon-lime vinaigrette and black-pepper fettuccine. Six interesting pasta dishes are offered as well, including a linguini with Gulf shrimp seasoned in a lobster essence ($12.95). The good little wine list is priced mostly in the teens and twenties.

All this is served up at well-spaced tables and booths in white and deep green. A local artist painted the clay pots filled with vegetables and vines on the walls above dark stained wainscoting. Ribbed glass lamps hang overhead and votive candles cast shadows on the white-clothed tables.

The sisters' families are much involved in the operation, which bears their mother's maiden name.

Lunch, Tuesday-Friday 11:30 to 1:30; dinner, Tuesday-Sunday 5:30 to 9 or 10.

J.P. Daniels, Route 184, Old Mystic. (203) 572-9564.

Off the beaten path — as are many of the Mystic area's treasures — is this old, high-ceilinged dairy barn, handsomely restored and elegantly appointed. Tables on two floors are set with white cloths and fresh flowers; the subdued lighting is by oil lamps and lanterns on the rustic wood walls. A pianist or harpist entertains some evenings, and the atmosphere is quite enchanting.

The menu, formerly continental, has been broadened to include regional American and ethnic influences. Prices also have been lowered lately.

Appetizers ($2.95 to $6.95) run the gamut from pork tenderloin teriyaki and clams bienville to Chesapeake Bay crab cakes and grilled mussels. Main courses go from $8.95 for smoked chicken breast topped with cranberry chutney to $18.95 for bouillabaisse. There are four veal and four beef dishes, and a tempting new concoction called Mirlton Porro, a pear-shaped Southwestern vegetable with a squash-like flavor, filled with jumbo shrimp, lobster, scallops and andouille sausage in cajun spices and topped with béarnaise sauce. A specialty that remains is boneless duck stuffed with seasonal fruits and sauced with apricot brandy. And we applaud the idea of offering half portions of several entrées for half price.

Desserts include rum crisp, chocolate mousse, peach melba and chocolate-raspberry torte. The wine list contains an explanation of all the selections, which start in the low teens and top off at $155 for a 1978 Château Lafite Rothschild.

A casual dining menu is served in the barnwood lounge every day but Saturday from 4 to 9:30. The lounge is separated from the dining rooms on upper levels by a divider and a "limerick on chains," a hanging sign depicting the three owners.

Lunch, Monday-Friday 11:30 to 2; dinner nightly, 5 to 9:30 or 10; Sunday brunch, 11 to 2. No smoking.

Flood Tide, Route 1, Mystic. (203) 536-9604.

With a new porte cochere, entrance and lobby and a good continental menu, this has become Mystic's most glamorous restaurant. Part of the Inn at Mystic complex, it has an outdoor deck and an airy lounge with a piano, plush leather chairs and a wine bar, plus a spacious two-level dining room in elegant Colonial decor with handsome patterned wallpaper, brass chandeliers, captain's chairs and large windows onto Pequotsepos Cove. Tables are appointed with white linens, etched-glass lamps, hammered silverware and small vases holding a single rose each.

Executive chef Robert Tripp is known for his wine list and a popular Sunday brunch. We certainly liked the $10.95 luncheon buffet, which contained everything from seviche, caviar and seafood salad through eggs benedict, beef stroganoff, seafood crêpes and fettuccine with lobster alfredo, to kiwi tarts and bread pudding. You also can order dishes like curried chicken salad and baked fillet of sole with lobster and béarnaise sauce, à la carte from $7.95 to $19.95.

At night, start with the chef's special baked escargots with mushrooms and garlic in puff pastry, brie and leek soufflé, smoked-salmon rosettes or a crêpe filled with lobster madeira ($5.95 to $8.95). Herbed mushroom soup is a house specialty. Entrées ($16.95 to $23.95) run the gamut from rainbow trout with toasted nuts and amaretto cream, shrimp and artichokes provençal, roast duckling with peach glaze and medallions of veal aux poivres to such tableside classics as whole roast pheasant, beef wellington, rack of lamb and châteaubriand, $48 to $52 for two.

Bananas foster, strawberries romanoff, raspberry-kiwi parfait, cheese strudel topped with fruits, chocolate/peanut-butter mousse torte, cinnamon cheesecake, raspberry fudge cake and chocolate fondue are among the renowned desserts.

A smaller menu, featuring some of the house specialties as well as lighter fare, is offered in the **Crystal Swan Lounge.**

Lunch, Monday-Saturday 11:30 to 2:30; dinner, 5:30 to 9:30 or 10; Sunday brunch, 11 to 3.

The Harborview, Water Street at Cannon Square, Stonington. (203) 535-2720.

A pot-bellied stove warms the pub on chilly days and candles in the hurricane lamps in the dining room are lit even at noon in this dark and glamorous restaurant that set a standard for dining along the shore back in the 1970s and continues to shine, even with the departure of the original owners.

All is pink and dark blue in the large dining space conveying a charming, quasi-Victorian atmosphere of dark-paneled drawing room by the sea.

The format rarely changes, owner Terrance McTeague continuing the tradition that has made the Harborview such a success -- although the dinner menu contained a section called lighter fare ($8.95 to $13.95) at our latest visit. The extensive regular French menu ($12.50 to $19.95) includes a savory marseillaise

323

bouillabaisse, sautéed shrimp and scallops with pea pods and ginger butter, roast duckling with brandy-maple-mustard-morel sauce, and veal prepared three ways. We are partial to the veal sweetbreads and crayfish tails in basil cream sauce with orange-ginger linguini and the veal in a light calvados cream sauce, a portion large enough for two, served with julienned vegetables and tiny new potatoes, still in their jackets and swimming in butter.

Among the many appetizers ($4.50 to $7.95), we especially liked the crevettes rémoulade, a menu fixture bringing a dinner plate full of five huge shrimp on a bed of tender lettuce covered with a piquant sauce, and a sensational billi-bi soup, creamy, mussel-filled and redolent of herbs.

Grasshopper pie is among the better desserts. The wine list contains all the labels above good descriptions of the offerings, which are fairly priced.

Most of the dinner items are available at lunch, when entrées are $7.50 to $11.50. A more casual menu is served all day in the always-crowded pub.

The lavish Sunday brunch buffet ($14.95) in the main dining room has unusually interesting hot dishes and enough food to stave off hunger for a couple of days.

In season, we're drawn as well to the Harborview's adjunct, the **Skipper's Dock,** a casual place behind the main restaurant with a jaunty deck and a couple of interior dining rooms beside the water. The short menu here is equally appealing (Portuguese fishermen's stew, grilled mussels, and poached salmon with pineapple and ginger) and the deck setting is salubrious. We'll never forget an exhilarating lunch outside by the harbor on a warm day in early November.

Harborview, lunch 11:30 to 3, dinner 5 to 10, Sunday brunch 11 to 3; closed Tuesday in winter. Skipper's Dock, lunch daily 11:30 to 4, dinner, 4 to 10; closed in winter.

The Golden Lamb Buttery, Hillandale Farm, Bush Hill Road (off Route 169), Brooklyn. (203) 774-4423.

We first fell in love with this rural restaurant in 1978 and every time we go back, we are smitten again. It's a Constable landscape, a working farm, a hayride, folk music and much more.

It's also the home of Bob and Jimmie (for Virginia) Booth, who set the stage for the most magical evening imaginable. Bob is the genial host who makes wonderful drinks (the manhattan is garnished with a fresh cherry because the Booths don't like to use preservatives) and oversees the dining rooms. Jimmie does most of the cooking with originality, love and energy.

The evening begins around 7 with cocktails in summer on a deck off the barn overlooking a farm pond or on a wagon drawn by a tractor over fields while you sit — with drink in hand — on bales of hay, listening to the fresh voice of Susan Smith Lamb, who accompanies herself on the guitar. Before you set off on this adventure, your gingham-clad (and sometimes pigtailed) waitress takes your order from the four or five entrées written on the blackboard.

Dinner ($60 complete) starts with a choice of about four hot or cold soups: we have never tasted one that wasn't wonderful. Using herbs and vegetables from the farm's gardens, Jimmie Booth makes soups like cold lovage bisque, a green vegetable one using "every green vegetable you can name," raspberry puree, scotch barley, cold cucumber and an unusually good cabbage soup made with duck stock.

Almost always on the menu are duck (a crispy half, done with many different sauces), a châteaubriand for one and a fish (perhaps salmon or swordfish), cooked over applewood on the farm's smoker. Lately, Jimmie has added the

Energetic owners Jimmie and Bob Booth relax at entrance to Golden Lamb Buttery.

occasional pasta entrée. Salt is not used, but many herbs, and essences of lemons and limes, are. The only starch is crisp and thinly sliced onion bagels.

What we always remember best are the vegetables — six to eight an evening brought around in large crocks and wooden bowls and served family style (yes, you can have seconds). They could be almost anything, but always there are marinated mushrooms and nearly always cold minted peas. Tomatoes with basil, celery braised with fennel, carrots with orange rind and raisins, a casserole of zucchini and summer squash with mornay sauce — they depend on the season and the garden.

From a choice of five or six desserts, the coffee mousse, raspberry cream sherbet, heavy butter cake with fresh berries, pies (made by neighborhood women) and a chocolate roll using Belgian chocolate, topped with chocolate sauce and fruit, are fitting endings.

During all this, you are seated in a dining room in the barn or in the attached building with a loft that once was a studio used by writers. The old wood of the walls and raftered ceilings glows with the patina of age, as do the bare dark wood tables in the flickering candlelight. The singer strolls from table to table taking song requests.

It's all so subtly theatrical, yet with a feeling of honest simplicity, that you feel part of a midsummer night's dream.

Lunch, with entrées in the $9.50 to $14 range, might be oyster stew, or the delicious Hillandale hash or seafood crêpes. It might not be as romantic as dinner, but you get to see the surroundings better. And in summer the Northeast Repertory Theater, a local amateur group, presents musicals and plays in the barn on Wednesday and Thursday nights, with the Booths providing a picnic supper. Folks reserve a year in advance for the December dinners, when a group of renaissance singers wanders the dining rooms singing carols and pork tenderloin is the main course.

Although we have had more interesting entrées on our wanderings, we never have had such a satisfying total dining experience. It's not inexpensive, but what price can you put on total enchantment?

Lunch, Tuesday-Saturday noon to 2:30; dinner, Friday and Saturday, one seating from 7. Dinner reservations required far in advance. Closed January-May. No credit cards.

Other Dining Choices

Fiddler's Seafood Restaurant, 4 Water St., Chester. (203) 526-3210.

Paul McMahon of Old Lyme, who started in the business washing dishes at the old Black Swan when he was 16 and spent five years with the Chart House operation, named this restaurant for the boat of his father, who was his backer. His two dining rooms seat 60 in a cheerful cafe atmosphere (blue and white checked cafe curtains, cane and bentwood chairs, pictures of sailing ships on cream-colored walls, and tables with pedestals of old gears), all enhanced at night by white linens and flickering candlelight.

He serves interesting seafood creations, rarely changing the menu or the prices. Three or four kinds of fresh fish can be ordered pan-sautéed, poached or mesquite-grilled. At lunch, when these are in the $6 to $8 range, he also serves a cream-style crab soup with sherry, a lobster roll with steak fries or rice pilaf, and mussels in puff pastry with salad.

In the evening, entrées are $11.95 to $17.95 for the likes of baked stuffed fillet of sole with hollandaise sauce, oysters imperial, bouillabaisse, scallops niçoise, shrimp provençal and a few chicken and beef dishes. A lobster dish with peaches, peach brandy, shallots and mushrooms is a favorite. Garlic bread comes with aioli dip, and different julienned vegetables are served daily. The house salads (tossed or spinach) have a choice of honey-celery seed, creamy dill, blue cheese and vinaigrette dressings. Conch fritters and oysters rockefeller are among the appetizers ($4.75 to $7.25).

Chocolate-mousse terrine with lingonberries, lime mousse and chocolate-pecan ganache torte are featured desserts. The house wines are Californias, and the other wines are very reasonable.

Lunch, Tuesday-Saturday 11:30 to 2; dinner, 5:30 to 9 or 10, Sunday 4 to 10.

Mad Hatter, 16 Main St., Chester. (203) 526-2156.

Anglophile Maureen Higgins was a bond analyst in Manhattan when she shucked the yuppie life in 1988 to develop a tea catering company in New York and, eventually, this little bakery and tearoom with a low profile and high hopes in downtown Chester. Although her background was in specialty teas in New York, she started here in 1992 with a bakery, "so now I do things that go with bread." That includes a thriving retail bakery business, of course. It also means great sandwiches ($6), the blackboard listing the likes of chicken-almond, herbed tuna salad and grilled chicken with cranberry chutney on sourdough baguettes, each served with two side salads. She offers soups (white bean and ham, lentil or butternut squash and onion, $3.25), salad plates (with produce from her garden), chili, chicken tagine (spicy Moroccan stew), frittata and a charcuterie plate, priced up to $6.

Besides lunch, Maureen serves occasional five-course teas Sundays at 3:30 by reservation ($15) and regular Saturday theme dinners. The latter are based on menus from her world travels and vary from $25 to $40 per person, depending on the menu. A Mexican dinner yielded chips with black-bean dip and salsa cruda, white gazpacho, shrimp in coconut sauce with fruit salsa and spice rice, a salad of native corn and cilantro in tomato vinaigrette, a granita and flan with Mexican wedding cookies. Maureen also serves a dynamite french toast with challah bread, apples and almonds at Sunday brunch. There is a handful of tables inside and outside on the front porch at this charming place that takes its name from the owner's passion for tea parties and hats.

Lunch, Wednesday-Saturday noon to 3; dinner on Saturday, Sunday brunch, 11 to 3. Bakery open Wednesday-Sunday 11 to 5 or 6.

Restaurant Bravo Bravo, 20 East Main St., Mystic. (203) 536-3228.

Well-known area chefs Robert Sader and Carol Kanabis produce contemporary Italian fare at this new restaurant on the main floor of the Whaler's Inn, with a sidewalk cafe off to the side.

For dinner, sirloin carpaccio, grilled shrimp wrapped in prosciutto with skewered artichokes, chilled oysters wrapped in spinach and leeks, and interesting salads (one pairs chilled roast lamb and grilled eggplant with mixed greens and radicchio) make good starters in the $3.50 to $7.95 range. Creative pastas are priced from $8.95 to $14.95, the latter for lobster ravioli or tomato fettuccine tossed with lobster, scallops, mussels, tomatoes and asparagus in a tarragon-lobster cream sauce. Entrées ($11.95 to $19.95) might include Maryland crab cakes topped with lobster-chive sauce, garlic shrimp sautéed with pancetta and artichokes on a bed of escarole, seafood stew, roast duck with peach and pink-peppercorn sauce, and lamb chops with a mint and mango chutney sauce. The lengthy dessert roster includes the obligatory tirami su as well as tartuffo, raisin-walnut bread pudding, ricotta cheesecake with grand-marnier sauce and cognac-pumpkin cheesecake. The mainly Italian wine list is one of the area's more affordable, with all but two offerings in the teens and most under $15.

The down sides are the service, sometimes aloof and rushed, and the atmosphere. Dining is in a spare, noisy and rather cheerless room at tables quite close together. Much more appealing, we think, is the canopy-covered terrace with white molded furniture. The outdoor **Cafe Bravo** menu features brick-oven pizzas (we like the one with pesto, sundried tomatoes and goat cheese for $11.95), pastas and entrées from $8.95 to $13.95.

Lunch seasonally (October-May), 11:30 to 3; dinner, Tuesday-Sunday 5 to 9 or 10. Cafe, open May-October for lunch, 11:30 to 3; dinner, 5 to 9 or 10.

Boatyard Cafe, 194 Water St., Stonington. (203) 535-1381.

Some folks so like chef-owner Deborah Jensen's scones that they are calling the borough "Sconington," and her breakfasts are so popular that a section of the lunch menu now lists "eggs all day."

The tiny cafe in the Dodson Boatyard, with a great outdoor deck beside the harbor, is off to an auspicious start. Deborah, a former New York restaurateur and cooking school instructor, offers kicky "combination scrambles" like the Soho — eggs with sundried tomatoes and goat cheese — with oven fries and toast for $4.95 at breakfast, $5.95 the rest of the day. The lunch menu adds bobolis, a signature grilled chicken sandwich, an oyster po'boy and some trendy salads. We were impressed with the chef's sampler, taken on an umbrellaed table on the outdoor deck. The sampler ($6.95) changes with every plate, our waitress advised. This one yielded tastes of chicken-tarragon and tuna salads, a mellow pâté, spinach-mushroom quiche, roast turkey, bacon sprinkled with gorgonzola cheese, potato salad, cucumber salad and marinated red bell peppers. "The sampler is truly whimsical," the chef agreed afterward. "Some people order it every day, so we have to keep changing."

Fresh Stonington flounder takes top billing at dinner, prepared four ways for $10.95 to $12.95. Other possibilities ($10.95 to $18.95) include sherried chicken and mushrooms, spicy sea scallops Nantucket style, lobster sauté, grilled ribeye steak and spaghetti (with ham, mushrooms, roasted red peppers and sherry). Start with smoked salmon and capers ($5.95); finish with plum pie or key lime cheesecake. Everything's made here from scratch and oh-so-good. And there's no better place for eating it than on the waterside deck.

Breakfast , 8 to 11:30; lunch, 11:30 to 2:30; dinner, Wednesday-Sunday 6 to 8:30. Closed Tuesday in off-season. BYOB.

Abbott's Lobster in the Rough, 117 Pearl St., Noank. (203) 536-7719.

Gourmet it's not, but it's the closest thing to a Down East lobster pound this side of Maine. We've been Abbott's fans for years, drawn by the rocky setting where the Mystic River opens into Fishers Island Sound, thus providing a parade of interesting craft to watch. And when our children were little, they could keep occupied finding briny treasures on the rocks.

You can eat inside at Abbott's, but it's much more fun outdoors at the brightly painted picnic tables set on mashed-up clam shells. The menu is fairly limited and the wait for a lobster can be long — we bring along a cooler with drinks and snacks for sustenance.

A 1-pound lobster is about $13.95, including coleslaw and potato chips, while a New England feast goes for $18.95. Ram Island oysters are served on the half shell. Clam chowder or steamed clams, shrimp in the rough, lobster or crab rolls, steamed mussels and clams are other offerings; the only non-seafood item is a hot dog. Desserts are New York cheesecake and Yankee berry crisp.

Beside the restaurant operation are the large lobster tanks that youngsters like to look at and a retail store. Here you may purchase a couple of lobsters or some cans of Abbott's clam chowder to take home.

Open daily, noon to 9, May-October. No credit cards. BYOB.

Kitchen Little, Route 27, Mystic. (203) 536-2122.

People line up for breakfast on hottest summer and coldest winter days at this little gem beside the Mystic River. We waited our turn in the January chill for a dynamite breakfast of scrambled eggs with crab meat and cream cheese ($4.95), served with raisin toast, and a spicy scrambled-egg dish with jalapeño cheese on grilled corned-beef hash ($4.50), accompanied by toasted dill-rye.

At another visit, we were too late to get the day's specials: baked stuffed potato topped with scrambled eggs, cream cheese, scallions, sour cream and bacon, and a chicken-filled french toast sandwich with cranberry sauce and cheese.

The coffee flows endlessly into the red mugs, the folks occupying the nine tables and seats at the counter are convivial, and you can eat outside at a few picnic tables in season. Florence Brochu's open kitchen certainly is little (she says the entire establishment measures nineteen feet square). But it doesn't prevent her from putting out some remarkable omelets and breakfasts "like Momma didn't used to make" with a creativity and prices ($2.95 to $4.95) that put most bigger restaurants to shame. She also serves weekday lunches, and now has another restaurant serving the same menu in slightly larger quarters at 142 Water St. in Stonington.

Open Monday-Friday 6:30 to 2, weekends 6:30 to 1.

Lodging

Riverwind, 209 Main St., Deep River 06417. (203) 526-2014.

Her contractor didn't blanch when Barbara Barlow said in 1987 that she wanted to build an addition 100 years older than her existing 1850 inn. The result is a skillful blend of old and new, embracing eight guest rooms with private baths and an equal number of common rooms that afford space for mingling or privacy. An unexpected but happy side result: the innkeeper married the contractor, and Barbara and Bob Bucknall are now Riverwind's joint innkeepers.

Antiques from Barbara's former shop, wooden and stuffed animals in all guises (especially pigs), folk art, hand-stenciling, and tasteful knickknacks and memorabilia are all around. Each bedroom has thick robes in colorful patterns, some matching the decor. Poland Spring water and candies are put out in each.

The Hearts and Flowers Room has flowers on the bedroom wallpaper, hearts on the bathroom wallpaper and a specially made, heart-filled, stained-glass window. Every room is charming, but the ultimate is the Champagne and Roses Room with a private balcony, a wonderfully decadent (according to Barbara) bathroom with a shower and a Japanese steeping tub, a bottle of champagne cooling on a table between two wing chairs, and a fishnet canopy bed too lacy and frilly for words.

Barbara grew up in Smithfield, Va., where her father is a hog farmer. Naturally, she serves slices of red, salty Smithfield ham for breakfast every morning at a table for twelve in the new dining room and at a smaller table in the adjacent room. She may offer coffee cake, Southern biscuits, fresh fruit in summer and hot curried fruit in winter, as well as homemade jams and preserves. Lately she has added more breakfast casseroles to her repertoire. One that particularly appeals is like a quiche and incorporates swiss cheese, eggs, asparagus, mushrooms, cream sauce and french-fried onion rings.

Besides a delightful living room with fireplace, a library and a trophy room for games, guests enjoy a keeping room with a huge fireplace in which Barbara was cooking stews, chili and soups at one of our winter visits. Guests also make quite a to-do over the lifesize mounted moose, a century-old antique sited smack dab in the center of the living room -- staring head-on at the decanter of sherry, which is always at the ready in this hospitable B&B.

Doubles, $88 to $148.

Bishopsgate Inn, Goodspeed Landing, East Haddam 06423. (203) 873-1677.

Bountiful breakfasts and romantic candlelight dinners served in front of the fireplace in your room are attractions in this 1818 house built by an Essex shipbuilder and once occupied by a Goodspeed. Now it's lovingly tended by innkeepers Molly and Dan Swartz, for whom food is a passion.

Upon request, Molly prepares and Dan serves traditional American or northern Italian dinners to guests in their rooms for $15 each (BYOB). A typical meal might be sautéed artichokes, veal and sage stew or fusilli with zucchini and basil, salad and baked pears in cream.

A full breakfast could include cornmeal blueberry pancakes or french toast stuffed with cream cheese, currants and sliced almonds, served by the fireplace in the keeping room.

Six bedrooms with private baths are decorated with character and four have working fireplaces. The most dramatic is the Director's Suite, with a cathedral ceiling, its own balcony and a dressing area off a theatrical bathroom with lights around the mirror and its own sauna. Guests enjoy a cozy parlor downstairs with an electric piano, or a sitting area on the upstairs landing with television.

Doubles, $75 to $85; suite, $100.

Hidden Meadow, 40 Blood St., Lyme 06371. (203) 434-8360.

The Connecticut shore area gained this badly needed country house of a B&B when the family homestead gradually emptied as Karen Brossard's four daughters went off to college. It's a beauty of a home on four rural acres, dating to 1760. Subsequent additions (some by Broadway actor Henry Hull in the mid-1930s) produced a rambling, pale yellow Colonial Revival with circular driveway, Georgian entry, a number of stone terraces, iron railings and a reflecting pool.

The Brossards offer three guest rooms with private baths. Each is nicely outfitted with family furnishings and queensize or king/twin beds. Guests enjoy a living room with fireplace and original beehive oven, a library with TV and a fireplaced dining room with a table set for eight ("we sometimes have extra visitors for breakfast," explains Karen, an engaging hostess who likes a good party). Breakfast in summer is served on an unusual curved slate porch overlooking the reflecting pool. Beyond are a large swimming pool, a raspberry patch, stables and riding trails. Karen keeps four horses, and she teaches her pony club here three days a week.

Breakfast is an event. The fare might be baked eggs with brie, basil and heavy cream; orange-flavored french toast with brandy, or gingerbread pancakes with fruit sauce. Fruits, homemade muffins and zucchini bread accompany.

Doubles, $90 to $110.

Steamboat Inn, 73 Steamboat Wharf, Mystic 06355. (203) 536-8300.

This fairly new inn, transformed from a vacant restaurant along the Mystic River, offers ten luxurious guest rooms right beside the water in the heart of downtown Mystic.

Named after ships built in Mystic, all have jacuzzis, telephones and televisions hidden in cupboards or armoires and seven have fireplaced sitting areas facing the river. A local decorator outfitted them in lavish style: mounds of pillows and designer sheets on the queensize canopy or twin beds; loveseats or sofas with a plush armchair in front of the fireplaces. Mantels and cabinet work make these rooms look right at home.

Our favorites are the second-floor rooms at either end, brighter and more airy with bigger windows onto the water, a couple with half-cathedral ceilings. Rooms in the middle are darker in both decor and daylight. Rooms on the ground floor are suite-size in proportion, but suffer from being on view to the constant stream of passersby on the wharf. Each room is distinctively different and has its own merits; "one couple stayed here four times in the first month and worked their way around the inn, staying in different rooms," reports co-owner John McGee.

Guests have little reason to leave their rooms, but there's a common room with all the right magazines and glass tables for continental breakfast. The innkeeper puts out homemade breads and muffins each morning.

Doubles, $165 to $250.

The Palmer Inn, 25 Church St., Noank 06340. (203) 572-9000.

Behind a twenty-foot-high hedge is this pillared, turn-of-the-century mansion built by Palmer Shipyard craftsmen for Robert Palmer Jr. Its widow's walk yields a panoramic view of the quaint seafaring hamlet of Noank and of Long Island

Veranda at Inn at Mystic has sweeping view across hilltop toward Long Island Sound.

Sound. Until 1984 a private home, it has been restored by Patricia White Cornish into an attractive B&B.

From an impressive main hall with thirteen-foot-high ceilings, a mahogany staircase curves past stained-glass windows to six guest rooms on the second and third floors (all with private baths, a couple with balconies and a distant view of the water, and one with a fireplace). Rooms are furnished with family heirlooms and antiques as well as such contemporary amenities as hair dryers, makeup mirrors, Crabtree & Evelyn toiletries, designer sheets and plush towels.

Depending on the season, guests find iced or hot tea, mulled cider, sherry or sparkling water each afternoon. They scour Pat's scrapbooks on area attractions and restaurants in the comfortable parlor, or play checkers in the library. A continental-plus breakfast of fresh fruit, juice, homemade granola and muffins is served in the morning.

Doubles, $105 to $175.

The Inn at Mystic, Route 1, Mystic 06355. (203) 536-9604 or (800) 237-2415.

This is the crown jewel of the Mystic Motor Inn, the area's nicest motel and inn complex. Above the motor inn (which also boasts deluxe inn-style rooms in its East Wing) is an eight-acre hilltop estate with a white-pillared Colonial revival mansion and gatehouse offering sumptuous bedrooms — spacious, full of antiques, and with whirlpool-soaking tubs and spas in the bathrooms.

On one side of the house is an orchard. Laid out in the English style, the gardens are gorgeous. You can sit on the wide front porch overlooking the rock and water gardens and see Long Island Sound.

As a guest in one of the five rooms in the mansion, you may feel like a country squire soaking in your private spa, relaxing on a chintz-covered sofa by the fire in the drawing room with its 17th-century pin pine paneling, or rocking on the wicker-filled veranda. Behind the inn, the fireplaced guest rooms in the secluded

Gatehouse (redone with Ralph Lauren sheets and coverlets) could have come straight out of England.

Guests take breakfast in winter at the mansion (where it is said that Lauren Bacall and Humphrey Bogart spent their honeymoon). Complimentary tea and pastries are served from 4 to 5 at the inn's Flood Tide restaurant.

Sisters Jody Dyer and Nancy Gray, whose father started this as Mystic's first motor inn of size in 1963, have revamped the twelve rooms in the motor inn's East Wing, all with Federal-style furniture, queensize canopy beds, wing chairs and fireplaces, plus balconies or patios with views of the water. Six rooms here have huge jacuzzis in the bathrooms with mirrors all around.

Doubles, $100 to $195 in motor inn, $165 to $225 in inn and East Wing, $155 to $225 in Gatehouse.

Antiques & Accommodations, 32 Main St., North Stonington, Conn. 06359. (203) 535-1736 or (800) 554-7829.

Ann and Thomas Gray, who are into cooking, almost enrolled in the Johnson & Wales culinary program but decided to open a B&B instead. Their 1861 yellow house with the gingerbread trim of its era became the focal point for a complex that includes nine guest rooms, an antique shop in the barn and terrific breakfasts.

Tom puts his cooking skills to the test with a four-course English breakfast, served by candlelight at 8:30 or 9:30 in the formal dining room or on the flower-bedecked front porch. It always includes fresh fruit in an antique crystal bowl, perhaps melon with a yogurt, honey and mint sauce or hot plum-apple-sauce. Main courses could be eggs benedict, an egg soufflé with homemade salsa and basil, a stilton and aquavit omelet with dill sauce, cornmeal pancakes made with corn ("it sounds terrible but is delicious," according to Ann), an apple-rum puff garnished with strawberries and a signature sweet bread pudding laced with dried apricots and cream sherry. "Breakfast goes on for hours," says Ann, who was still serving at 11 the December weekday we last called in. These hospitable hosts also have been known to dispense wine late into the evening while everyone lingers on the front patio.

Memories of traveling in England inspired the Grays to furnish their home in the Georgian manner with formal antique furniture and accessories. Six rooms come with private baths, and all have canopied beds, fresh flowers and decanters of sherry. Besides a parlor with TV, the main house offers a downstairs bedroom with a working fireplace and a stereo system. Upstairs are two bedrooms, one a bridal room filled with photographs of honeymooners who have stayed there.

Families and couples traveling together also go for suites in the 1820 Garden Cottage, a two-story affair beside landscaped gardens in back. Rooms here contain some remarkable stenciling, sponge-painted furniture, marbelized dressers and floral curtains, along with the antiques that characterize the rest of the establishment, most of them early American and country. One bedroom is furnished by Whitmore of Middletown, and the contents are for sale. "You can sleep in the canopy bed and take it home," advises Ann.

Doubles, $125 to $185; cottage, $225 to $350. No smoking.

Gourmet Treats

Dorothea Cashman makes everything herself at **Our Daily Bread,** a small bakery and food shop at 32 Main St., East Haddam. Her stuffed croissants (maybe broccoli-mushroom-cheddar) and a wide variety of whole grain breads are renowned. Four kinds of muffins and five kinds of bagels, including spinach-garlic, are offered each morning. Quiches, soups (perhaps tomato florentine or cream of asparagus), cranberry or blueberry scones and sandwiches in the $3.50 range are among the treats. Dottie's honey-mustard vinaigrette is billed as "a brazen dressing for voluptuous salads," and her relishes sell as fast as she makes them.

Wheatmarket at 4 Water St., Chester, is a large and well-stocked specialty-foods store where you can order a prepared picnic (the Lovers' includes orange passion-fruit sodas, bliss potato salad and chocolate kisses!) or eat at one of the small tables in the front. Nineteen sandwiches ($3.19 to $4.99) include country pâté with sweet and rough mustard, turkey breast with cranberry conserve and cheddar, and roast beef with garlic and herb cheese. Also on the docket are salads, soups, stews, a handful of hot entrées (all under $5) and deep-dish pizzas (the chicken with artichoke and the eggplant with sundried tomatoes are especially popular). Owner Dennis Welch also does low-calorie dishes. A specialty is custard-filled cornbread (obviously not low-calorie). Browse among the racks for Belgian butter-almond cookies, Coryell's Crossing jams, Guiltless Gourmet dips, Beluga caviar, saffron and such.

Pasta Unlimited at 159 Main St., Deep River, is where to get the freshest pasta imaginable. Michelle St. Marie's pasta machine is in the window, and nothing gets cut until a customer orders it. Available types include spinach, pumpkin, tomato, lemon-dill and a dynamite black-peppercorn pasta that we tried with Michelle's good clam sauce. On our latest visit, we took home pumpkin pasta and topped it with the Raphael sauce (artichoke hearts, plum tomatoes and romano cheese) — oh, so good. The little shop also has cookware and gourmet items. Sandwiches ($3.50 to $4.50) include one with roast beef, Vermont cheddar, red onions and beer mustard. Soups, salads and desserts like key lime zest or black and white espresso cake are on display. The fantasy rice salad includes snow peas, scallions, radishes, water chestnuts, almonds, sesame seeds and more.

If, like us, you won't eat roast beef unless horseradish accompanies, check out where it's made. Almost behind Pasta Unlimited but reached from River Street is **Pinder's Pure Horseradish Co.,** 155 Main St. Here former meat cutter Michael Cormier works non-stop for three weeks a month chopping 300 pounds of horseradish root (watch and you'll see it's quite an art), blending in a converted meat grinder and bottling up to 80 jars a minute; the other week he's on the road selling to commercial accounts across Connecticut. His horseradish retails for $1.50 a bottle here. He also makes and sells horseradish mustard, seafood sauce and two kinds of salsas.

Sweet Sarah's is Steve Wilkinson's good pâtisserie and takeout shop behind his Fine Bouche restaurant at 78 Main St., Centerbrook. Available to go are delectable desserts, from mocha-hazelnut torte to almond and hazelnut dacquoise with mocha buttercream, napoleons, profiteroles, fruit tarts, plus cookies and Belgian chocolates. The tangerine sherbet with a linzer square made a good mid-afternoon pick-me-up.

Fromage at 1400 Boston Post Road, Old Saybrook, is an upscale shop where Christine Chesanek purveys wonderful cheeses, fine foods and coffees. She even stocks six kinds of olives, like french black olives in sunflower-seed oil and roasted garlic. Aged chèvre, her own cheese spreads, Harney & Sons teas, pâtés, pastas and more are on the docket. Christine even has an Italian machine that makes a good cup of latte, $2.

CIA grads and ex-restaurant chefs David Courant and Lissa Loucks team up at **Vanderbrooke Bakers and Caterers,** 65 Main St., Old Saybrook. They produce dynamite breads, pastries, salads, sandwiches and hot entrées, available at their retail shop or from their deli to eat in or take out. Among David's bread repertoire are country french, flanders (a Belgian white with oats), squaw, mustard-tarragon, sourdough, and gorgonzola and roasted red pepper, about eight changing varieties each day. The pastry case is full of delights. The deli also impresses with sandwiches (roast beef and brie or genoa salami, capicola and roasted peppers, all $3.95), salads (Moroccan chicken, minty barley, ginger coleslaw in the $2.50 range), soups like shrimp and corn chowder and the day's entrées (flank steak stuffed with spinach and mozzarella, zucchini and corn fritters with red onion confit. sausage and tomato quiche, and crab cakes rémoulade, all in the $3 range).

A mural of her new bake shop and cafe -- with owner Marie Beard at the cappuccino machine -- is painted on the wall at her suave black-and-white **Cappuccino Cafe** at 62 Halls Road, Old Lyme. We're told her espresso is the best anywhere. We liked the looks of the Italian desserts, the sandwiches ($4.75 to $5.50) and the wall of changing artworks dedicated to all the artists in town.

We've seldom seen so many unusual flavors as at **Mystic Drawbridge Gourmet Ice Cream Cafe,** 2 West Main St., Mystic. Rod Desmarais and his wife Cheryl, a pastry chef, say they get their ideas from their travels. Among the 25 changing choices, you might find praline-pecan, southern peach, spiked apple pie (with a touch of rum), ginger white-chocolate chunk, pumpkin pie ("sorry, no crust") and the perennial favorite, Mystic mud -- chocolate ice cream and anything else in the store, from truffles to apple pie. With less air overrun than usual, Mystic ice creams are creamier and richer than most. Shakes, sundaes, gourmet coffees and pastries are also served. Check out the mural on the wall: it's an endearing picture of Mystic, to which staff and customers keep adding local folks and landmarks.

Chamard Vineyards, 115 Cow Hill Road, Clinton, (203) 664-0299 or (800) 371-1609. The owner of this money-is-no-object winery is Bill Chaney, chairman and CEO of Tiffany & Co., so you know things are done with class. And classy

all the way is Chamard, reached via an unremarkable residential street off Exit 63 of I-95. Overlooking a farm pond, the winery occupies a gray shingled house built in 1988 as "a New England château" near the front entrance to the 40-acre property that is half planted with vines. Wines are tasted with crackers and cheese in a richly furnished living room with vaulted ceiling, a fieldstone fireplace and the air of a deluxe hunting lodge. Although Larry McCulloch is the active winemaker, Bill and Carolyn Chaney remain involved on weekends, from planting and picking to leading tours and pouring wines. Eighty per cent of the 6,000-case annual output is white wines, primarily a premium chardonnay that sells here for $10.99. About 150 cases of cabernet and 75 of pinot noir sell out as quickly as they are released, at $14.99 and $12.99 a bottle respectively. Bill Chaney acknowledges that his connections helped place his chardonnay in some of New York's finest restaurants, but merit keeps them there. Chamard's emerging chardonnay style is more European than Californian, and wine writers have ranked it among the best wines produced in this country. Tours and tastings, Wednesday-Saturday 11 to 4.

Commodore's Room at the Black Pearl looks onto the waterfront.

Newport, R.I.
In Pursuit of Pleasures

Few cities its size can match in quality or quantity the astonishing variety of restaurants of Newport, R.I.

Little wonder. Newport has been a symbol of high living since the Victorian era when America's affluent built summer "cottages" that now form the nation's most imposing collection of mansions in one place. Visitors from around the world have come to view the mansions as well as the restorations of some of America's oldest buildings. And, of course, sailing and tennis have given modern Newport a sporty face.

With all the tourists come the trappings. Restaurants, inns, B&Bs and shops are part of a tourist/building boom that has transformed Rhode Island's most visited city in the last few years.

It was not until the early 1970s that Newport's restaurants became known for much more than fresh seafood, served to the masses on venerable waterfront wharves. An immensely popular establishment called The Black Pearl changed that. The first of the town's innovative restaurants, it blended elegant cuisine with more casual fare in a mix that triggered a trend.

Now Newport is home to a notable small classic French restaurant, the nation's oldest continuously operating tavern, a couple of small eateries with pace-setting chefs, contemporary seafood houses, assorted ethnic spots and sidewalk cafes everywhere in a growing smorgasbord of fine and fast food. "The best of the lot here match the best restaurants in Boston," said the mâitre-d' at the Clarke Cooke House, whose owner also owns Locke-Ober in Boston.

Summers and weekends in Newport are pricey and crowded; dinner reservations a week in advance are the alternative to two-hour waits. It's best to visit mid-week or in the off-season, though many restaurants close for a few weeks in January and/or February.

The myriad pleasures of this small historic city will surprise you. So will the numbers of people pursuing them. On a sunny day, it may seem as if the whole world has come to Newport and its restaurants.

Dining

The Best of the Best

The Black Pearl, Bannister's Wharf, Newport. (401) 846-5264.

Since this rambling establishment opened in 1972 as the first of Newport's innovative restaurants, it's been one of our favorites, serving a staggering 1,500 meals a day in summer from what owner Tom Cullen calls "the world's smallest kitchen."

Outside under the Cinzano umbrellas, you can sit and watch the world go by as you enjoy what we think is Newport's best clam chowder — creamy, chock full of clams and laced with dill, served piping hot with a huge soda cracker ($2.50 a cup or $4.50 a bowl). You also can get a Pearlburger with mint salad served in pita bread for $5.95, and a variety of sandwiches or stew of the day.

Inside, the tavern is informal, hectic, noisy and fun, offering much the same fare as the outdoor cafe plus a few heartier offerings (grey sole, calves liver, petite tenderloin, $12 to $15.75) that can serve as lunch or dinner. In fact, after a bowl of chowder, the crab benedict with french fries ($7.50) was almost too much to finish. You also can get several desserts — we remember a delectable brandy-cream cake — and espresso as strong as it should be, plus cappuccino Black Pearl, enhanced with courvoisier and kahlua.

The pride of the Pearl is the **Commodore Room,** pristinely pretty with white linens, dark walls, low ceiling, ladderback chairs and a view of the harbor through small-paned windows.

Chef Dan Knerr's dinner appetizers run from $6.25 for fried brie or charred peppers with sundried tomatoes to $9.25 for Scotch smoked salmon. Start, perhaps, with oysters warmed with leeks and champagne beurre blanc or a salad of boston lettuce, radicchio, apples and walnuts. Entrées ($16.50 to $26) range from salmon steak with mustard-dill hollandaise to mallard duck with green-peppercorn sauce, breast of pheasant with perigueux sauce, and rack of lamb with roasted garlic and rosemary.

It's an ambitious menu, the more so considering the size of the kitchen. But the Black Pearl can expand or contract its service with the season and the crowds. While others have come and gone, it's been a pearl on the Newport scene for more than two decades.

Tavern and outdoor cafe open daily from 11, dinner in Commodore Room, 6 to 11. Closed early January to mid-February.

The Place, 28 Washington Square, Newport. (401) 847-0116.

This wine bar and grill has Newport foodies abuzz with its exciting cuisine. An adjunct to Yesterday's, a pubby downtown institution, it was opened in 1991 by owners Maria and Richard Korn as a showcase for their chef of thirteen years, Alex Daglis. Alex moved to a separate kitchen, hired a staff and devised a

Framed vaudeville curtain is dominant decorative piece along wall at The Place.

contemporary American menu with a European flair that, Richard says, "expands and challenges your tastes."

We'd happily order anything on his changing dinner menu. Everyone raves about the entrées, priced from $15.95 for Jamaican jerked chicken served with a sweet red banana and guava ketchup to $22.95 for the Place's highfalutin version of surf and turf: lobster sauté with sweet peppers and wild mushrooms, paired with grilled tenderloin topped with a sweet-bread herb crust on a cabernet sauce. Moroccan halibut served with couscous, a goat-cheese and yellow-tomato tart and a grilled vegetable kabob and Southwestern grilled lamb chops with sweet red-pepper and jalapeño preserve, served with a corn tamale, also entice.

But we never got beyond the appetizers ($5.95 to $7.95), which were so tantalizing that we shared and made a meal of five. The shrimp and corn tamales, terrific scallops with cranberries and ginger, the gratin of wild mushrooms, and raviolis of smoked chicken and goat cheese were warm-ups for a salad of smoked pheasant with poached pears and hazelnuts that was out of this world. Each was gorgeously presented on black octagonal plates. A strawberry margarita sorbet with fresh fruit and a warm apple crêpe with apple fries and apple sorbet were worthy endings to a fantastic meal.

To accompany, 33 wines are offered by the glass and 128 by the bottle. "Flights" offer a tasting of up to five wines for $9.50 to $13.50.

All this is stylishly served at white-clothed tables on two levels of a long, narrow dining room with brass rails, oil lamps and sconces. A vaudeville curtain from a New Bedford theater, framed and back lit on one wall, dominates the decor.

Dinner nightly, 5:30 to 10 or 11. Closed Sunday in November and December.

Pronto, 464 Thames St., Newport. (401) 847-5251.

Some of the most innovative cooking in the city emanates from the partially open kitchen of this dark and cozy cocoon of Victorian romance. Chef Ted Gidley's specials are particularly interesting here. So is owner Janne Osean's vintage decor: a melange of gilt mirrors, heavy dark draperies, potted palms, crystal chandeliers (a different one over almost every table), pressed-in walls and ceiling, oriental rugs on the floors and, horrors, ashtrays on each table. One innkeeper calls it the most romantic dining spot in the city, but we find the tables too close for comfort, let alone romance.

Soft jazz played as we lunched, fortunately nearly alone, here one winter weekday. The vegetable soup ($3.25) was hearty and the wild-mushroom crostini

Vintage decor at Pronto.

($4.75) quite tasty. Truly terrific was a special of chicken breast encrusted in pistachios and walnuts ($6.75), served on a bed of many greens with red and yellow pepper vinaigrette, the plate colorfully decorated with flecks of parsley and squiggles of vinaigrette. It was so good we asked the chef afterward how he prepared it. We also could understand how Newporters felt their favorite haunt, once perceived as quite reasonable, had become more expensive. Bread was extra (50 cents for half a loaf). A masterful apple tart with praline ice cream (razor-thin apple slices flecked with cinnamon and fanned around the perimeter of a dinner-size plate) turned out to be $6 on the bill. Add a couple of glasses of the house Sicilian wine for $3.75 and our luncheon tab escalated to $35 for two.

Yet we'd gladly go back (on an uncrowded night) for a dinner repertoire that yields some wonderful (and reasonable, $8.50 to $12.50) pastas and specials ($15 to $20), treats like fillet of sole niçoise, pan-seared breast of duck normande and grilled ribeye steak with madagascar green-peppercorn sauce and caramelized onions. Start with sesame-seared rare tuna with wasabi and pickled ginger or mesclun salad with marinated flank steak. Finish with key lime pie or white and dark chocolate mousse. Be prepared to be smitten by the specials, and to pay the piper. It should be worth it.

Lunch, Monday-Saturday 11:30 to 4, Sunday noon to 4; dinner, 5 to 10:30 or 11; Sunday breakfast, 8 to noon.

White Horse Tavern, corner of Marlborough and Farewell Streets, Newport. (401) 849-3600.

Claiming to be the oldest operating tavern in the United States, established in 1673, the tavern was restored by the Newport Preservation Society and opened as a restaurant in 1957. Lately, it's been known for some of the best — albeit expensive — food in town.

The White Horse is a lovely, deep red Colonial building, most appealing for cozy cold-weather dining, with its dark interior, wide-plank floors, beamed ceilings, huge fireplace and classical music. The dark rose and white draperies complement the handsome burgundy and off-white china and the winter arrangements of silk flowers and dried berries. Brass candlesticks with Colonial candles inside large clear hurricane chimneys are on each table.

Service is formal and even at lunch, some of the salads and all the entrées are in the $9 to $16 range, though you could order a burger or a club sandwich for $7.50. Chef David Deen is known for his soups, among them roasted chestnut, grilled chicken and black bean, and West African peanut soup with tomatoes and

Decor is elegant Colonial at historic White Horse Tavern.

chicken. At a springtime lunch, we tried the day's soup, an interesting chilled mixture of yogurt, cucumber, dill and walnuts. Baked marinated montrachet with baked garlic puree and herbed croutons was a delicious appetizer. The fish of the day, halibut in a sauce with grapefruit pieces and a hint of brandy, was excellent. The chicken salad resting in a half avocado was bland.

Wines are, as you would imagine, expensive, but many are available by the glass. The old bar room in one corner of the building is atmospheric as can be.

At night, appetizers are $7 to $9 for snails in puff pastry, baked oysters with wilted spinach and roasted-garlic vinaigrette, a ragout of wild mushrooms, and warmed goat-cheese and black-pepper polenta. roasted red-pepper terrine, mushroom ratatouille, and baked oysters with sesame and soy. Entrées start at $22 for baked chicken breast stuffed with parmesan and spinach, served with grilled endive and tomato fettuccine, and top off at $28 for individual beef wellington. Others include grilled Atlantic salmon with a sweet-pea and chive coulis, baked fillet of sole stuffed with salmon mousse and asparagus, and grilled veal tenderloin served in a potato nest with fresh arugula. Add five bucks for a salad of field greens sprinkled with goat cheese.

You might like to finish with a triple silk torte on a bed of raspberry-melba sauce. It's not exactly Colonial fare or prices, but well-heeled folks who like good food and formal ambiance keep the White Horse busy.

Lunch, daily except Tuesday noon to 3; dinner nightly, 6 to 10; Sunday brunch, noon to 3.

La Petite Auberge, 19 Charles St., Newport. (401) 849-6669.

Dining on classic French cuisine in the historic Stephen Decatur House has been a fairly serious matter since chef-owner Roger Putier opened his small, charming restaurant in 1975. He has lightened up with a new courtyard/bistro menu, however.

The dark green house, warmed by roses climbing fenceposts and trellises, is typical of many in old Newport, smack up against the sidewalk.

Inside in two main-floor dining rooms, each with a handful of tables, the atmosphere is convivial and intimate — not for naught is this called petite. To the side and rear are a cozy bar with a sofa in front of a fireplace and a courtyard with five tables for outdoor dining. Up steep stairs are three more small dining rooms. Elegant lace tablecloths are layered over blue or gold linens, and the large menu is in French with English translations. The printed menu rarely changes, but is supplemented by many nightly specials.

The only description for the sauces is heavenly — from the escargots with cèpes ($7.50), a house specialty (the heavily garlicked sauce fairly cries out to be sopped up with the crusty French bread) to our entrées of veal with morels and cream sauce and two tender pink lamb chops, also with cèpes and a rich brown sauce.

Appetizers and soups are $5.75 to $8.50 (for smoked salmon). They include a fish soup Marseilles style, goose-liver pate, mussels in a light cream sauce, and duck pâté.

Entrées, including vegetables (crisp green beans and creamy sliced potatoes topped with cheese at our visit), are priced from $19 for frog's legs provençal to $25.75 for beef wellington with truffle sauce. Other choices are salmon in cream sauce with pink peppercorns, trout with hazelnuts, duck with raspberry sauce and four presentations of beef.

Service by black-suited women is efficient. Most dishes were finished at tableside, even the tossed salad with choice of dressings.

We ended with strawberries romanoff, one of the old favorites. The desserts are mostly classics like crêpes suzette, pear hélène and cherries jubilee. The excellent wine list is mainly French and reasonably priced.

The bistro menu, served on the trellised courtyard or in the charming rear bar, is short and to the point. Start perhaps with fish soup, crab cakes, or a charcuterie assortment of pâtés and dry-cured sausage. Move on to swordfish with citrus-chile butter, sirloin strip steak, grilled quail or grilled lobster with fresh herbs ($10.95 to $14.95). Finish with chambord cheesecake or amaretto tartuffo.

Dinner, Monday-Saturday 6 to 10 (courtyard to 11), Sunday 5 to 9.

The Clarke Cooke House, Bannister's Wharf, Newport. (401) 849-2900.

Dining is on several levels and a breezy yet formal upper deck in this 1790-vintage Colonial house, another venerable Newport establishment.

Downstairs, the expanded **Candy Store Cafe** and Porch, opened up for a view of the water, and the main-floor **Bistro** serve the same casual menu in quite different settings. We can vouch for a lunch dish of eggs benedict, salad vinaigrette and great french fries ($6.25), and a wonderfully thick and creamy cup of clam chowder ($3.25) — one of the best we've had lately — with a juicy hamburger on an onion roll ($5.50), again with those addictive french fries. At night, the menu runs from $10.95 for oven-roasted chicken or baked New England cod to $16.95 for grilled sirloin steak or lamb chops.

The food is considerably more expensive, the service more polished and the atmosphere more haute (some call it haughty, and we've never found it welcoming) in the **Skybar.** Here is a formal dining room in green and white, with high beamed ceiling, green high-back chairs and green banquettes awash with pillows. The doors open onto a canopied deck with a splendid view of the harbor. Here hurricane lamps enclose silver candlesticks, and fresh flowers and ornate silver top the white-linened tables.

Chef Chris Hawver offers a short, contemporary French menu. Among appetizers ($9 to $11) are timbale of smoked salmon with caviar garnish, baked oysters with a star anise glaze and smoked-pheasant ravioli with chanterelles cream.

Entrées are priced from $22 for grilled swordfish over a crisp risotto cake to $28 for rack of New Zealand venison with sweet-potato puree. Others include

Waterfront is on view from upper dining deck at Clarke Cooke House.

baked salmon with lemon grass confit, veal tenderloin en croûte and napoleon of aged sirloin layered between potato cakes.

Among desserts are cinnamon bread pudding with whiskey sauce, gingerbread cake with fresh applesauce, derby pie with whipped cream, bittersweet chocolate torte with espresso cream, and Indian pudding à la mode — the last a fixture at Locke-Ober, the Boston institution also owned by proprietor David Ray.

The wine list ranks as the city's priciest, with many in the triple digits.

Decide before you leave if you wish to have an after-dinner drink in the upstairs bar, which the management treats as a private preserve. A foursome of our acquaintance was refused re-entry upon their return after dropping $300 for dinner.

Dinner nightly in season, 6 to 10 or 10:30, weekends in off-season. Cafe and bistro daily, 11:30 to 11 in summer; lunch on weekends and dinner Wednesday-Sunday in winter.

Le Bistro, Bowen's Wharf, Newport. (401) 849-7778.

The French provincial menu has been greatly expanded since Le Bistro moved from its small upstairs dining room on Thames Street to its two-story location (with a view of the harbor) on the wharf. Since its acquisition by the owner of the Wharf Deli below, it's had its ups and downs in the estimation of locals, but remains beloved by tourists. Chef John Philcox continues in the kitchen.

White linens and china, bow chairs and a beamed ceiling set a mood of country elegance on the second floor. The convivial third-floor bar serves light fare and is seemingly popular all day — and all evening.

For lunch, from a menu on which everything sounds (and later looks) good, we've enjoyed a fine salade niçoise ($6.95) and a classic bouillabaisse ($9.95), which is worth going back for. Our latest visit with visitors from Europe produced a delicious sausage with warm potato salad, codfish cakes with curry sauce, a warm salad with goat cheese and sundried tomatoes, and a warm duck salad with walnuts.

On a winter's night, the atmosphere is enchanting as you gaze from a window table onto the wharf, its historic buildings shining under street lights as passersby stroll from restaurant to restaurant. Hot oysters with golden caviar and a special

341

pheasant pâté were tasty appetizers ($5.50 to $8.50). Entrées range from $9.95 for Burgundian sausages with hot potato salad to $29.95 for a special of lobster sauté with tomato and basil. We enjoyed the veal kidneys in port and mushroom sauce and a hefty plate of roast duck in a red cream sauce with endives; we could have passed up the side dish of bland cauliflower, carrots, turnips and red potatoes.

A dessert tart of green grapes in puff pastry with whipped cream was a fine ending, as was Irish coffee. Creole bread pudding with bourbon sauce is always on the dessert menu, and you might find Ivory Coast cake, a rum-flavored chocolate cake with chocolate chantilly cream.

Lunch daily, 11:30 to 5; dinner nightly, 5 to 11; Sunday brunch, 11:30 to 2:30.

Other Dining Choices

Scales and Shells, 527 Thames St., Newport. (401) 846-3474.

This is perhaps the epitome of the Newport restaurant phenomenon. Opened in 1988, it was standing-room-only in its first week without so much as a word of advertising.

Plain and exotic seafood — simply prepared and presented in casual surroundings — is offered by retired sea captain Andy Ackerman and his wife Debra. Andy cooks up a storm in an open kitchen near the door, as fast as the seafood can be unloaded from the docks out back.

The delicious aromas almost overpowered as we read the blackboard menu with an immense range but nary a non-fish item in sight. Start with calamari salad, grilled clam pizza, Sicilian mussels or mesquite-grilled shrimp from the list of appetizers. From this you could make a meal and, Andy says, many people do, ordering Chinese style. Monkfish, scallops, shrimp, swordfish, snapper, scrod — you name it, it comes in many variations as entrées ($8.95 to $16.50). Lobster fra diavolo ($36.95 for two) and clams fra diavolo are served right in their own steaming-hot pans, as are several other dishes. Entrées come with a simple green salad or a pasta.

Tabasco, red pepper and parmesan cheese are on the tables, which are covered with black and white cloths. The floors are bare, and the decor is pretty much nil except for models of fish on the walls.

Italian gelatos (apricot and hazelnut are a couple) and tarts comprise the dessert selection. The short list of Italian and California wines is most affordably priced.

Dinner, Monday-Saturday 5 to 9 or 10, Sunday 4 to 9. No credit cards.

Elizabeth's, Brown and Howard Wharf, Newport. (401) 846-6862.

Only in Newport. And only Elizabeth Burley. The combination emerged when Welsh-born Elizabeth, a New York film producer, came to Newport in February 1991 to sit by the water and watch the boats come in. She fell in love with the town, likening it in winter to the Wales of her childhood. She decided to move to Newport to open a tea room "and play restaurant." Taking a ten-year lease on a building off Lower Thames Street, she started furnishing and decorating with gusto. Nine weeks later she was ready to open, but realized she couldn't survive on tea and scones. Her strategy: a restaurant in a living room, with a two-for-one pricing concept and everything for the same price ("my math is awful!").

The result is an idiosyncratic, somewhat theatrical experience. It's "like dining in my home," says Elizabeth, although the room is considerably larger than you might expect and there's a delightful outdoor terrace in the summer. The decor is a cross between Victorian living room and dining room, with high-back pews amid assorted wood chairs at round tables covered in dark green paisley fabric, mismatched plates, antique furnishings, assorted candles and baskets hanging from the ceiling. Elizabeth's culinary concept is "platters," $49.95 for two. The first course is always a salad platter and herbed toast for two, served family style. The main course involves a choice of bouillabaisse, steak, stuffed swordfish, salmon, chicken and sausage parmesan, scallop and shrimp parmesan, shrimp and piselli, barbecue feast and stuffed chicken breast marsala.

The platters are huge and rather unusual. Her signature bouillabaisse, for instance, combines scallops, shrimp, mussels and steamers, browned with mozzarella cheese and placed in a loaf of sourdough bread, served over ziti with sides of grilled zucchini, mushrooms, steamed broccoli and stuffed vegetable-cheese-garlic bread. Consider the steak platter: two honey-barbecued spare ribs, sweet-potato and marshmallow pie, baked beans and apples, roasted potatoes, onions and sourdough bread topped with sliced London broil with mushrooms and onions. The portions are enormous and the samples we tried quite tasty. Few have room for one of the four rich desserts (maybe dark chocolate cake filled with caramel topped with a white-milk-chocolate icing, or homemade noodle pudding.)

Elizabeth, a jack of all trades, says she does all the prepping and cooking, although assistants prepare the orders and serve while she works the dining room. She also sings jazz and opera upon whim or request. She cooks without butter, salt and preservatives, and guards her "secret" recipes. An aura of mystery surrounds her. "I'm not a chef or a cook," she opines. "I'm a creator of flavors and textures. Oh, I don't really know what I am."

She's apparently onto something good. She has raised her prices $10 a year from $29.95 to $49.95. The only credit card she accepts is American Express because that's what "matches the image." She plans to add more platters (she started with four and was up to nine at our visit) and wants to open clones in big cities. And she certainly talks a good game.

Dinner, Wednesday-Saturday 5 to 9:30 or 10. BYOB. More hours in summer.

International Cafe, 677 Thames St., Newport. (401) 847-1033.

Favored by the lower Thames Street crowd is this informal neighborhood bistro, run simply but appealingly by chef-caterer Fred Almanzor and his wife Lynn. It features foods from around the world at remarkably low prices (every entrée is available in regular or petite sizes).

Clams casino is only $3.75, but we'd opt for Fred's special appetizer combination of pancit behon (Philippine noodles sautéed with vegetables, garlic and chicken or pork), lumpia (Philippine egg rolls) or mushrooms stuffed with almonds ($3.50). Or try his sampler of pancit, lumpia and chicken wings for $4.

The two dozen entrées are priced from $6.75 for fish and chips to $12.75 for baked stuffed shrimp, unless you spring for sirloin steak served petite, regular and large ($14.75). Possibilities include Polynesian fried shrimp, scallops parisienne, Chinese chicken with vegetables, Hungarian chicken strudel and oriental pasta with shrimp, and come with a salad with homemade dressing. Szechuan crustacean deluxe is lobster meat, shrimp and oriental vegetables in a spicy sauce served on a sizzling platter. Lynn makes the desserts, including caramel flan (a traditional Philippine dessert), chocolate-truffle mousse cake, pumpkin cheesecake and walnut-cream pie.

Dinner, Wednesday-Sunday 4:30 to 9 or 10. Closed in February. BYOB. No credit cards.

The Hammett Room, 505 Thames St., Newport. (401) 848-0428.

Occupying part of the main floor of the new Hammett House Inn, a newly restored three-story Georgian built in 1785, is this elegant tea room done up in teals and burgundies. Partake of the $8.50 tea at a choice of small or large tables, set up as though in a private home. It includes four kinds of tea sandwiches, scones with homemade strawberry jam and thick cream, and a dessert like raspberry tart or mini-eclair. Owner Diane Beaver also offers weekend brunch and light dinners. Brunch ($4.75 to $6.75) includes eggs copenhagen and curried chicken or seafood crêpes. For dinner (entrées $8 to $13.75) you might find veal with sorrel butter or red-pepper angel-hair pasta with scallops, snow peas and sundried tomatoes. Sit on one of the bar stools covered in a teal velvet at the handsome carved wood bar for a cocktail or cordial.

Tea, Thursday-Monday 3 to 5:30; dinner, Monday, Friday and Saturday 5:30 to 9:30; brunch, Saturday and Sunday 11 to 3. Closed Tuesday and Wednesday.

Trattoria Simpatico, 13 Narragansett Ave., Jamestown. (401) 423-3731.

The dining sensation in 1993 was not in Newport but across the bridge in Jamestown. Acclaimed Italian food, reasonable prices and a receptive clientele produced instant success for Phyllis Bedard, a former restaurant manager for whom this was her first solo venture. The name "implies goodness, which is very important to me," says Phyllis.

Goodness and warmth pervade her restaurant creation. Dark and homey, it consists of two small rooms with beige walls, dark green ceiling and trim, and close-together, white-clothed tables topped with glass. In summer, there's a new canopied, screened patio for outdoor dining. Chef Peter Hansen prepares an interesting menu. Main courses ($11.95 to $18.95) vary from roasted chicken over penne with rosemary four-cheese sauce and seafood cacciatore on fresh tomato-basil linguini to fennel-encrusted salmon with two-pepper coulis, grilled T-bone steak florentine, rolled veal stuffed with spinach and pinenuts, and grilled lamb chops with roasted garlic. The mixed grill of lamb chop, pork tenderloin, Tuscan sausage and breast of chicken comes with grilled polenta and four sauces.

Among starters ($4.95 to $8.95) are sautéed calamari over capellini and spinach, grilled portobello mushrooms on spinach and balsamic sauce, and bruschetta with topping of the day. For dessert, try the amaretto bread pudding, chocolate-chestnut-truffle torte or tirami su. A short Italian and California wine list is priced from $15 to $45.

Lunch daily, 11:30 to 3:30, May-September, weekends rest of year; dinner nightly, 5 to 10, closed Monday and Tuesday in winter.

The Bay Voyage, 150 Conanicut Ave., Jamestown. (401) 423-2100.

The best Sunday brunch in Rhode Island -- as voted four years running by readers of Rhode Island Monthly -- is one claim to fame of this beauty of a restaurant, ensconced in a renovated century-old hotel with a commanding view of Newport across Jamestown harbor. Another is the consistently good food and service, offered by a staff with unusual staying power for a resort area. The formal dining room is elegant with aqua velvet chairs and floral china on white linens. The Bay Room with its original stained-glass windows and water view is most in demand, but the porch with black wrought-iron furniture is the place to be on a nice summer day.

Chef Roger Brown oversees a short but ambitious continental menu. Among main courses ($16 to $23) are grilled swordfish with citrus-wine butter, seafood

Expansive living room is furnished with comfort in mind at Elm Tree Cottage.

provençal over fresh lemon-basil pasta, lobster thermidor, chicken pimonte on a bed of steamed spinach, veal marsala, filet mignon béarnaise and rack of lamb provençal. Appetizers are predictable: shrimp cocktail, clams casino, oysters florentine and escargot bourguignonne, for example. Save room for dessert, perhaps amaretto/ice-cream pie, strawberry mousse or key lime pie.

The Sunday buffet brunch is $15.95 for quite a spread of treats from carved beef or ham to omelets cooked to order.

Dinner, Monday-Saturday 6 to 10; Sunday brunch, 10:30 to 2. Also closed Monday and Tuesday in off-season.

Lodging

Rooms in Newport are a glut on the market or scarce to come by, depending on the day and season. A deluxe room that goes for $225 a night on a summer weekend may be available for $100 or so on a winter weekday. The biggest "inns" tend to be time-sharing condos on the water; a couple of innkeepers own several inns. Breakfasts are usually continental and, in general, the owners are seldom to be seen. We focus here on some of the exceptions.

Elm Tree Cottage, 336 Gibbs Ave., Newport 02840. (401) 849-1610 or (800) 882-3356.

Here is one beautiful "cottage," situated in a quiet neighborhood a block from the sea. Large and comfortable rooms appointed in elegant country style and artist-innkeepers with outgoing personalities help make the place special. Priscilla and Tom Malone and their three young daughters acquired the mansion, built in 1882 and later owned by Mrs. Crawford Hill, the Pennsylvania Railroad heiress and member of Newport's 400. "Our entire house fit into this living room," Priscilla said, recalling their move from Long Island and how they furnished the huge home "from auctions and estate sales."

Furnish it they did, quite grandly yet unpretentiously. There's an 87-foot sweep from dining room to parlor, which ends at expansive windows overlooking Easton's Pond and First Beach. Chintz sofas and a grand piano welcome guests to a living room that could be pictured in a design magazine. To the side are a morning garden room great for lounging and a bar room furnished in wicker. Here the Malones put out munchies for guests to BYOB and sit at the great old bar with 1921 silver dollars embedded in its top and pictures of the former owner's Pekinese dogs reverse-painted on the mirror behind.

At three tables in the fireplaced dining room, the Malones serve extravagant breakfasts by candlelight: perhaps apple crêpes, heart-shaped waffles, Portuguese sweet bread french toast or apple crêpes in the shape of calla lilies. "No bacon and eggs here," says Priscilla. "I try to treat guests the way I want to be pampered when I'm away from home." Our autumn breakfast started with juice and homemade oatmeal (the dish arrived on a saucer delightfully decorated with five varieties of dried leaves) and culminated in delicious pumpkin waffles. The day's calligraphed menu went home as a souvenir.

On the second floor are four large bedrooms and a master suite; all with private baths and four with fireplaces. The suite, all 23 by 37 feet of it, is pretty in salmon and seafoam green. It has a Louis XV kingsize bed with a crown canopy, two sitting areas (one in front of the fireplace) and a huge bath with a dressing table and Austrian crystal legs on the washstand. Country French and English linens and antiques dress this and the other four rooms, which pale only modestly in comparison. The newest room is the main-floor corner library-bedroom, lovely in wine and teal colors and outfitted in an equestrian theme with a TV. After more than a year of renovations and flat-out work in getting the place furnished, Priscilla has fulfilled her desire to "fluff up the rooms" with such touches as dried flowers, mounds of pillows, racks with old hats and individual stained-glass pieces reflecting the couple's artistry. At our latest visit, her eye for fluff produced a goat cart in the foyer, brought in for fall to showcase the harvest.

Priscilla's background in fine arts and woodworking and Tom's in interior design have stood them in good stead for the inn's refurbishing as well as for their thriving stained-glass business.

Doubles, $165 to $300; two-night minimum on weekends. No smoking.

The Francis Malbone House, 392 Thames St., Newport 02840. (401) 846-0392.

The former St. Claire's nursing home, converted into an imposing residence by a physician, was acquired in 1990 by five partners who turned it into one of Newport's more inviting inns. Exquisitely decorated, it has eight rooms and a suite with private baths, six with fireplaces. For space and privacy go for the sunken downstairs suite (formerly the physician's office) with its private entry, a queensize four-poster bed facing the TV, a sitting area with a sofabed and two chairs, and a two-part bathroom with shower and dressing room-vanity.

Upstairs off a center hall on two floors are eight corner rooms, all with private baths, but only two with tubs. The front rooms are bigger and claim harbor views. Each is nicely furnished with antique queensize beds covered by monogrammed duvet covers in white. Baskets of Gilchrist & Soames toiletries are in each bathroom. Guests enjoy a couple of lovely, high-ceilinged front parlors, a library with TV and a handsome dining room that served as the kitchen when the house was built in 1760 for a shipping merchant. Innkeeper Will Dewey likes to show the hidden servants' stairway leading to the attic beside the tiled fireplace and the old bread oven in the hearth.

Will, a culinary graduate of Johnson & Wales University in Providence, serves a full breakfast at a long, linen-covered table in the dining room. The fare includes

Courtyard at Francis Malbone House.　　**Breakfast table at Cliffside Inn.**

fruits, breads, perhaps raspberry croissants or cinnamon-raisin strudels, and a main course ranging from eggs benedict to belgian waffles. Out back is a flagstone courtyard with a fountain and, a real plus for downtown Newport, a large shady lawn with colorful gardens.

Doubles, $140 to $175; suite, $225. No smoking.

Cliffside Inn, 2 Seaview Ave., Newport 02840. (401) 847-1811 or (800) 845-1811.

Big bucks and great taste have been rendered unto this Victorian charmer. Always one of our favorite B&Bs, it has been upgraded and made more comfortable by new owner Winthrop Baker. The summer villa, a short block from the ocean, was built in 1880 by a governor of Maryland. It later was owned by Newport artist Beatrice Turner, a fact that prompted its new owner to gather many of her paintings from hither and yon and mount a fascinating retrospective exhibit that commanded wide attention for the inn in 1993. The Cliffside now contains twelve bedrooms and suites, the four largest of which Win Baker considers the most upscale in Newport with their jacuzzi baths and sitting areas with TVs.

No room in the house has escaped his touch, be it the Governor's Suite with its working fireplace visible from both the bedroom and the jacuzzi or the newly enlarged Veranda Room, a great summer space with a bay window off the front porch. The inn's many floor-to-ceiling and bay windows bathe the rooms with light, blending rich Victoriana with an airy Laura Ashley freshness.

Guests gather in the large fireplaced parlor, cheerfully redecorated in shades of orange-coral and moss green with stunning faille draperies. Classical music or opera plays in the background as afternoon refreshments are served here or on the front veranda. Hot apple cider, lemonade or iced tea, depending on the season, are accompanied by such treats as shrimp in puff pastry, duck-liver pâté and brie with crackers.

A full breakfast is offered by resident innkeeper Stephan Nicolas, a Johnson & Wales hospitality graduate and son of a French chef and cookbook author. The meal starts with a help-yourself buffet of fresh fruit, juice, yogurt, granola and muffins. Then comes a hot dish like waffles, walnut pancakes, leek and bacon quiche, french toast or eggs benedict.

Doubles, $135 to $185; suites, $225 to $325.

The Inn at Old Beach, 19 Old Beach Road, Newport 02840. (401) 849-3479.

Look beyond the ornate Victorian facade, colorful in grayish beige, yellow and green, and you might see an old anchor embedded in the third-story turret of the home built as the Anchorage in 1879. It's one of the surprises that abound in this stellar B&B run very personally by Luke and Cyndi Murray.

They offer seven guest rooms with private baths. Cyndi says she likes "a lot of different styles." They are reflected in the English country decor in the rooms, named after flowers or plants and full of whimsical touches. In the Rose Room, a pencil-post canopy bed angles from the corner beneath a bamboo-beamed ceiling. Done up in black and pink, it has a fireplace and a handpainted dresser with hand-carved rose drawer pulls. Handpainted Victorian cottage furniture, a faux bookcase along one wall and an antique woodburning fireplace grace the Ivy Room. Check out the bishop-sleeve draperies with valances in the first-floor Wisteria Room, and the wicker loveseat and chair in the Forget-Me-Not Room. The newest rooms are two with separate entrances in a rear carriage house, part of which the Murrays converted into quarters for themselves and their infant son. These have TVs and a more contemporary air; the Sunflower, lovely in pale yellow and burgundy, contains a wicker queensize sleigh bed, a wicker loveseat and two chairs, and a sunflower motif, from the lamps on the nightstands to a hand-painted shelf. Cyndi decorates for the season, but the front hall's original stained-glass window representing the four seasons shines at all times.

Guests gather in a small front parlor or a new and larger Victorian living room where two plush chairs and a couch face a glass cocktail table resting on four bunnies. Here are a pretty tiled fireplace, a rabbit fashioned from moss and a copper bar in the corner. Outside are a back porch and a brick patio overlooking a pleasant back yard with a gazebo and a fish pond. The Murrays serve continental breakfast at four tables in the dining room or on the porch. It usually involves juice, fruit and pastries like muffins, croissants and coffee cake. The Murrays also have put together a categorized collection of restaurant menus, drawing on Luke's experience as a restaurant consultant and beverage manager for the Black Pearl.

Doubles, $130 to $140.

Rhode Island House, 77 Rhode Island Ave., Newport 02840. (401) 848-7787.

Cooking instructor Michael Dupré makes this elegant new B&B special for those with an interest in matters culinary. Trained at La Varenne in Paris, the former private chef for the Auchincloss family offers culinary weekends in winter and serves breakfasts to remember in a dining room with Chinese Chippendale chairs at tables for four. The meal starts with a buffet on the sideboard. Bowls of fresh fruit, homemade granola, scones, muffins, grapefruit custard, rice pudding and johnnycakes are mere preliminaries to the main event, perhaps a soufflé or egg-white omelet, macadamia french toast or fruit crêpes. These treats originate in a great professional kitchen, where Michael caters and gives cooking lessons, including wintertime classes in which everyone participates and then sits down to eat. "I used to peek in the windows and say 'I want that kitchen,'" Michael said as he told how he acquired the property in 1993. The kitchen came with an 1882 Victorian estate that a previous owner had turned into a low-profile B&B.

As most of the restoration work had been done. Michael, an avid collector, and partner John Rich had only to furnish the house. This they have done with taste and flair, in both common rooms and bedrooms. The great hall/foyer is remarkable for yellow faux-marble walls. Off one side is an airy sun room. In front is a cozy library. On the other side is an inviting living room with a remarkable set of elaborate arched windows.

Upstairs are five guest rooms with private baths and queensize beds, each with its own distinction. The bath in the small Mary Kay Room, for instance, occupies a sun porch and retains the original pink and gray fixtures. The antique headboard on the bed matches the chest of drawers in the creamy white and floral green front Garden Room. The Auchincloss Room is "dainty, lovely and nice -- just like her," says Michael of Mrs. Auchincloss, who was his favorite grande dame. It has a fireplace and a full bath with an enormous jacuzzi, as does the rear Hunter Room, masculine in hunter green and complete with a private balcony overlooking the back yard. All the rooms have large windows and are bright and airy, which is unusual for Victorian houses of the period.

Doubles, $110 to $185. No smoking.

The Victorian Ladies, 63 Memorial Blvd., Newport 02840. (401) 849-9960.

Helene and Donald O'Neill took fourteen months to gut and renovate these two Victorian beauties, one behind the other, before opening their nine-room B&B, all with private baths and TV. The front building contains a small parlor with a crystal chandelier and crystal sconces on the mantel and an adjacent dining room where an enormous 1740 hutch-sideboard of English pine displays plates and country knickknacks. Here Helene serves a full breakfast buffet. The fare includes fruits, juices, sweet breads, croissants and an egg dish, perhaps a soufflé or a particular guest favorite, sausage ring stuffed with eggs.

Helene had never decorated before, but she has done a super job on her rooms, with a prevailing pink and blue color scheme and striking window treatments. One of the nicest is the room she calls the honeymoon suite in the main house, which has a queensize bed and sitting area. With puffy curtains, dhurrie rugs in pastel colors or wall-to-wall rose carpeting, vials of dried flowers on the doors, potpourri, down comforters, eyelet ruffles, and thick pink and blue towels, it is all fresh, pretty and feminine. Her favorite room, upstairs in the rear Carriage House, has pink walls, lace curtains and an antique white gown and straw hat hanging from hooks on the wall. Although the theme is Victorian, the look is light and uncluttered.

The newest rooms are two deluxe suites upstairs in the rear caretaker's cottage just behind the Carriage House. Both contain lavender carpeting with which Helene paired a pale yellow color scheme in one suite and red and dark green in the other. Both have telephones as well as the televisions common to all rooms.

Don, a contractor, built the gazebo and the courtyard, and his green thumb shows in a profusion of flowers.

Doubles, $135 to $175.

Culpeper House, 30 Second St., Newport 02840. (401) 846-4011.

Winter dinners prepared by New England chefs are among the attractions at this house built in 1771 in the historic Point section of Newport. Restoration developer Ann Wylie oversaw its refurbishment for her brother-in-law, who bought it as an investment. Now Ann, a former publicist for a San Francisco hotel, is running the B&B as a retirement project.

She loves to show off the myriad historic details of her home, which is a curious blend of old and new, furnished as it is with her California possessions. Up a very steep staircase are two guest rooms, comfortable with feather beds, down comforters and modern bathrooms.

A lot of living and camaraderie go on in the small downstairs living room and the larger library/dining room. The latter is Ann's pride and joy with its shelves of good books (particularly strong on mysteries, Newport history and cooking) and a basket of tiny flags representing the countries from which her worldly guests have come. Here is where she serves French wine and cheese in the afternoon and a three-course breakfast in the morning. The fare might be orange juice and a fresh fruit platter with yogurt, homemade blueberry cake or muffins with English jams and marmalades, and french toast with grand marnier and rum, Spanish shirred eggs or hot porridge. "I've only begun to cook in this house," says Ann, who was looking quickly to expand her repertoire.

The visiting chefs she had lined up for her first season of weekend dinners in 1994 were excited about using the working fireplace in her kitchen. Each was planning his own menu, to be served with wine to eight people for $50 each.

Doubles, $100 to $115.

Gourmet Treats

With everything from delis to food boutiques, the Newport area is a paradise for the palate of the wandering gourmet. Among the possibilities:

Newport Mansions. On most visitors' must-see lists, several hold special culinary appeal. The dining rooms are on display, and at the Marble House is a gold ballroom in which the owner once gave a ten-course dinner for 100 dogs in full party dress. At the fabulous Breakers, you get to see a number of kitchens and butler's pantries, an area larger than most houses. The dining room at Kingscote, an oft-overlooked Greek Revival cottage, is one of the nicest rooms in all the mansions — decorated with Tiffany glass tiles and stained-glass panels of dahlias.

The Market on the Boulevard, 43 Memorial Blvd., is a large, very upscale grocery store with a market cafe and espresso bar, a bakery, deli and "gourmet to go." And what wonderful things do go — in our case, a dish of oriental beef with a vegetable medley for supper at home plus a ginger-pear tart and lemon-raspberry roulade for dessert. There are wonderful breads, choice meats, exotic produce, fresh pastas — you name it, Newport's beautiful (and ordinary) people come here to buy it. From salads to pastries to sandwiches (the last delightfully named for behind-the-scenes workers at the mansions), all the makings for a gourmet picnic, lunch or dinner are here.

Anthony's Seafood, Waite's Wharf, is a good fish market with a few deli items and specialty foods. Everything from codfish to oysters is available. It supplies the seafood for the 200-seat **Shore Dinner Hall** next door, a vast enclosed lobster pound with garage-size doors opening onto the harbor and colorful banners hanging from the ceiling. This is the kind of casual family waterfront place long needed in Newport. It offers a one-pound lobster for $8.95, as well as chowder ($2.25), fish and chips ($5.50), steamers, and hot dogs or fried chicken for the kids. A full lobster boil, including lobster, steamers, mussels, corn, potatoes, sausage and chowder, is $19.95. Sit at picnic tables and have yourself a feast without breaking the bank. Wine and beer are served. Open daily, April-October.

For casual dining, **Cappuccino's** at 92 William St. is a nice little breakfast and

Dining room at Kingscote is one of most appealing in Newport mansions.

lunch cafe in the uptown Bellevue Avenue area. The salads are great, the chicken-onion-bacon quiche was hearty and we drooled over the white-chocolate and strawberry bars. **Ocean Breeze Cafe** at 580 Thames St. stocks gourmet coffees and teas, baked goods and an array of sandwiches and salads. The **Wharf Deli** on Bowen's Wharf also has good sandwiches and a raw bar. Nearby, the aromas drifting through the door may draw you into the **Cookie Jar** for chocolate-chip, gingersnap or oatmeal-raisin cookies.

Fragrant dried flowers hang from the ceiling and jars of loose teas, herbs and teapots line the shelves at **Tea & Herb Essence,** 476 Thames St. Proprietor Laureen Grenus offers everything from passion fruit to hibiscus heaven teas to herbal remedies and health-care products, handmade soaps, gifts and more. Some of the herbs and flowers come from her gardens out front.

A most colorful kitchen shop is **Runcible Spoon** (the title taken from "The Owl and the Pussycat") at 180 Bellevue Ave. Amid the garlic salsa and the lobster platters, we were taken with a line of Portuguese pottery with tiny vegetables like radishes and scallions depicted thereon.

Take a side trip down Route 77 along the East Bay to the quaint hamlet of Tiverton Four Corners. Here is **Provender,** a specialty-foods store and upscale sandwich shop, where you can obtain lunch to eat in or take out. Farther along are **Walker's Farm Stand,** where the folks from suave Little Compton shop for produce and preserves, and **Olga's Cup & Saucer,** a small place next door, where you can stop for coffee, biscotti or pizzas. Nearby at 162 West Main Road in Little Compton is **Sakonnet Vineyards,** the largest and oldest continuously producing winery in New England. Its annual production of 30,000 cases includes some of the East's better wines, among them an estate chardonnay and a pinot noir, both retailing for $12.50. You can sample some of their offerings in a large tasting room with oriental rugs on the floors. The winery schedules occasional special events, including a Sakonnet Chefs series. It offers three guest rooms with private baths ($65 to $80) in **The Roost,** a B&B at the entrance to the vineyard grounds.

Cape Cod

New Capers on the Old Cape

The time was not all that long ago when dining on Cape Cod meant, for many, the three C's: Chillingsworth, the Christopher Ryder House and clam shacks.

When you thought of places to stay, you hoped to luck into a friend's summer house or you rented a cottage, preferably somewhere near the water. The few inns tended to be large and posh and were far outnumbered by all those funny-looking motels with glassed-in swimming pools near Hyannis.

Well, Chillingsworth is still there, better than ever. The Christopher Ryder House has been converted into condominiums, and the clam shacks are overshadowed by a burst of serious restaurants.

There are more summer houses, cottages, posh inns and funny-looking motels than ever, of course. But there's also a new breed of country inns — not full-service like their predecessors, but more than bed-and-breakfast houses.

In spring, the season starts gearing up, yet crowds and prices are less than during July and August. Then comes the summer crush, and the high season ends abruptly after Labor Day.

Knowledgeable visitors have long preferred the Cape in the off-season. They avoid the tourist trappings of Hyannis and Provincetown, whose restaurants this chapter purposely omits. For this is a time and a place for escape, for relative solitude, for respite in a sandy, seaside setting unsurpassed in New England.

Note: Although the Cape's season is lengthening every year and more places remain open year-round, the owners' plans may change. Restaurant hours vary widely. Reservations are required in advance for peak periods. Minimum stays for lodging are not unusual. Such caveats are overcome by planning, flexibility and/or luck.

People who haven't been to the Cape lately — or who haven't ventured far from the beach if they have — might be surprised by the "new" Cape that has emerged and co-exists with the old.

Dining

The Best of the Best

Chillingsworth, Route 6A, Brewster. (508) 896-3640.

The revitalized dowager of Cape Cod restaurants is now the site of what some reviewers call the best serious resort-area dining in New England. For two years in a row it outranked all 500 Boston restaurants in the Zagat survey. In 1993, it won a Distinguished Restaurants of North America award, along with the Chanticleer on Nantucket and three Boston restaurants, and was featured on the Great Chefs of the East television series.

For most, it is a special destination place — so special, in fact, that we stopped by to reserve a table six weeks in advance for a mid-October Saturday. As it turned out, we didn't get the specific time nor the table we had picked out, but that was our only complaint from a thoroughly memorable dinner that lasted past midnight.

The restored 1689 house is named for Chillingsworth Foster, son of its builder. Its quaint, unassuming, Cape Cod exterior gives little clue to the treasures inside — room after room full of priceless furnishings, antiques and museum pieces.

Chef Robert Rabin outside Chillingsworth.

The large Terrace Room in which we ended up dining is not, to our mind, as intimate or as special as one of the smaller rooms like the Empire, where we had booked, or the table for four in an alcove off the living room, which one innkeeper of our acquaintance calls the most exquisite in the world.

A hurricane oil lamp, Limoges china and a vase of flowers graced our heavily linened table. A harpist was playing in the background as the waiter asked if we had questions about the menu, which is typewritten daily. The meal consists of seven courses at a fixed price of $40 to $51.50, depending upon choice of entrée.

We chose a French vouvray ($23.50) to accompany our appetizers, grilled duck and pepper quesadilla with coriander and tomatillo salsa and a feuilleté of oysters with spinach and lemon-butter sauce with roe. A dozen appetizers were offered, from a jumbo ravioli of foie gras, chanterelles and veal to smoked sirloin carpaccio with truffle oil, truffle cheese, grated summer truffle and grilled bread.

The cream of mussel soup that followed was superb, as was the consommé of mushrooms. A second helping of the night's squash bread — after all, we weren't seated until 9:30 — was followed by a salad of four baby leaf lettuces, arugula, radicchio and sorrel, enriched with a crouton of warm chèvre and dressed with a zesty vinaigrette. A grapefruit sorbet with a sprig of mint, served in a crystal sherry glass, cleared the palate.

All that preceded was literally prelude to the main event — stunning entrées, lavishly and beautifully presented. The breast of duck was garnished with citrus rind and fanned out in slices around the plate, interspersed with kiwi and papaya slices. A side plate contained julienned carrots and a spinach soufflé with nutmeg and wild rice. Our other entrée was an equally imaginative treatment of lamb with veal kidneys, grilled with herbs from Chillingsworth's garden. With these we had a 1982 Rodney Strong cabernet ($27), the least expensive California vintage on a choice wine list priced well into the hundreds.

Others among the night's nine or ten entrées might be lacquered tunafish with julienned jícama, sea beans, fried kale and caramelized scallop sauce; sweetbreads and foie gras with asparagus and sweetbread and veal raviolis, and loin of veal with saffron risotto, garlic custard, asparagus and mushroom-veal sauce.

Desserts are anything but an anti-climax. One of us chose a raspberry tulipe, an intriguing presentation atop a speckled-striped pattern of napoleon. The other enjoyed a grand-marnier custard on a bed of strawberries. Before these came the "amusements" — a plate of gingerbread men, rolled cookies around citrus and macaroons. The finale was a serving of fantastic chocolate truffles, which were intense to the ultimate.

Chef-owner Robert (Nitzi) Rabin made the rounds of diners as they lingered over coffee. He and wife Pat, whose youthful appearances belie their fortyish years, work fourteen-hour days overseeing the expanding operation they purchased in 1975 following the death of the previous owner. Both worked summers at Chillingsworth, he advancing from busboy to captain to manager and managing to pick up an MBA at the Tuck School at Dartmouth. The Rabins travel every spring to France or California to continue to enhance their highly creative American version of new French cuisine. They ran the Cafe at the Queen Anne Inn in Chatham for a couple of summers, and in 1992 opened **Chills East Vail Bistro,** which Pat calls "a robust upscale bistro" at the East Vail Racquet Club in Colorado, where they spend the winter.

At Chillingsworth, they added a contemporary bistro and greenhouse lounge area with skylights, walls of glass and plants. Lunch and dinner are available here beside a garden terrace. The lunch menu embraces some of the dinner items as well as other creative fare at more affordable prices (appetizers, $5.75 to $6.75; entrées, $8 to $11.50). A broader bistro menu at night offers exotic appetizers in the $6 to $8.50 range and main courses from $9.50 for grilled poussin with field salad and warm mushroom vinaigrette to $19.50 for grilled veal chop with garlic mashed potatoes and red-onion marmalade. This is the place for those who find that the main Chillingsworth dining room serves too much food, or who don't like the precise seatings at awkward hours.

Beyond the lounge, the **Le Bistro** gift shop offers many Chillingsworth specialties for sale. Nitzi calls it "a nice catering business without the delivery problems." The shop was crowded on a summer Sunday with tourists seeking to get a taste of Chillingsworth without paying full price. Frankly, we'd go all-out and splurge — the experience is worth the tab.

Upstairs, the Rabins offer three elegant guest rooms and suites for overnight stays. Rates are $95 to $135, B&B.

Lunch, Wednesday-Sunday 11:30 to 2; dinner seatings, Tuesday-Sunday 6 to 6:30 and 9 to 9:30, fewer days off-season. Closed after Thanksgiving to Memorial Day.

The Regatta, Scranton Avenue, Falmouth. (508) 548-5400.

One of the Cape's best waterfront locations, a jaunty pink and white decor, inventive food and a smashing wine list — it's little wonder that Upper Cape folks rate this long-established restaurant right up there with Chillingsworth and keep it consistently crowded and lively. And to offer New England specialties in an historic setting, owners Wendy and Brantz Bryan took on a year-round venture in 1987, the Regatta at Cotuit (see below), which some now consider the best restaurant on Cape Cod.

The original Regatta takes its name, no doubt, from its location in a gray-

Window table for two at The Regatta at Falmouth.

shingled building with black and white awnings and a profusion of pink geraniums and purple impatiens beside Falmouth's inner harbor. The structure was totally rebuilt in 1992 after suffering severe damage during Hurricane Bob. Most of the 100 seats in the main dining room take advantage of the view.

Pink cloths, dusky rose napkins fanned in the water glasses, pink bows on the pillars and pink banquettes around the perimeter set the color scheme. Chairs and plates are white. Waitresses are outfitted in pink and waiters in black vests and bow ties. As the hurricane lamps are lit before dusk, the setting is colorful, to say the least.

Wendy Bryan is in charge of the wine list, which has many available by the glass since no hard liquor is served. The unusual selection, mainly French with a nod to California, is priced from $15 to $250.

Appetizers ($6.50 to $9.50) are oriented toward seafood: grilled shrimp and sea scallops with caramelized lemon, native corn and oyster fritters with tomato beurre blanc, and sautéed Jonah crab cakes with California greens. We gobbled up a rich chilled lobster and sole terrine, served with a saffron sauce garnished with truffles, and loved the grilled Cotuit bay oysters with black American caviar.

A complimentary sorbet follows the appetizer course. Our dinner could have ended happily there, but the entrées were equal to the task. The seafood fettuccine contained more shrimp, scallops, lobster and artichoke hearts than it did spinach pasta, and the seared Norwegian salmon came with oysters and a leek and chardonnay sauce. Vegetables, served on clear glass side plates, were two kinds of squash, piquant red cabbage and new potatoes.

Other entrées range from $18 for oven-roasted monkfish with raspberry and sage sauce to $25 for boneless loin of lamb en chemise with cabernet sauce. On our latest visit we sampled a palette of two fish, each with its own sauce (yellowfin tuna with pinot-noir sauce and roasted shallots, and swordfish with caramelized-lemon and white-butter sauce), and the grilled breast of pheasant.

Desserts ($4.50 to $6) are inventive as well: among them, raspberry-chocolate torte with crème anglaise, fallen chocolate soufflé cake with kahlua crème anglaise, and a selection of homemade ice creams and sorbets. Best bet is a tasting trilogy of three favored desserts ($8.50). Ours brought a chocolate truffle cake, almond torte with framboise sauce and hand-dipped chocolate strawberries. With dessert comes coffee in delicate cups.

The nautical flags fluttering outside in the breeze are a wonderful sight, matched by the wildly colored trousers of Brantz Bryan, who explains that he wears them "to make people laugh and feel at ease." He and Wendy were the first restaurateurs on our travels to anticipate the economic slowdown, holding the line on prices and even reducing them at the low end following the 1987 stock-market crash. Since rebuilding following the hurricane, they have added lunch service in summer, with an appealing menu priced from $5.95 to $12.95. Perhaps such flexibility is why the Bryans have been so successful at the Regatta for more than 25 years.

Lunch daily, 11:45 to 2:30; dinner nightly, 5:30 to 10. Open mid-May to mid-September.

The Red Pheasant Inn, 905 Main St. (Route 6A), Dennis. (508) 385-2133.

The exterior is strictly old New England — a rambling, red 200-year-old saltbox house and barn. Inside is a reception area-living room (used for wine tastings), a couple of dining rooms and an enclosed porch, a mix of bentwood chairs and white linens, barnwood and walls with painted flowers, hanging plants and flickering oil lamps. It's a very comfortable place with tables well spaced, background music at the right level and the service deft and unobtrusive.

The food is on the cutting edge, with inspired touches of regional New England cuisine. The creative hand in the kitchen belongs to chef Bill Atwood Jr., 42-year-old son of the founder, who left the stove to manage the front of the house with Bill's wife Denise. The Atwoods have been involved in the Red Pheasant since 1977.

Bill, elected to the Master Chefs of America, says his efforts have evolved over the years into a Cape Cod cuisine with "a truly local flavor." He smokes his own bluefish and cod cakes, mixes local cod and calamari in new presentations, makes smoked-venison sausage and stuffs quails with duck sausage.

For starters ($4.50 to $8.75), we were impressed with a caesar salad as good as we can make at home and the fried goat-cheese raviolis, an incredibly smooth-tasting presentation on a lovely tomato coulis, with asparagus spears and frizzles of leek radiating out. Other choices included carpaccio of venison, wild-mushroom strudel, smoked salt cod and bluefish cakes, and rillettes of salmon with its roe on field greens.

Among main courses ($13 to $22) were pan-roasted swordfish provençal, grilled yellowfin tuna with baby field greens and grilled vegetables, sautéed sole meunière, paupiettes of veal stuffed with crab meat and served with eggplant timbale, and native bouillabaisse in a tomato-saffron broth, served in custom-designed bowls from the nearby Scargo Pottery. Our choices could not have been better: roast boneless Long Island duckling served with a rhubarb, dried cherry and caramelized-ginger sauce and grilled pavé of beef with fried oysters, wrapped in leeks with bordelaise sauce. Side plates carried different assortments of grilled and roasted vegetables, including sliced potatoes, zucchini, yellow squash and green tomatoes, as well as some barely cooked green beans. Our only complaint was with an over-battered, tough asparagus spring roll that came with the duck.

Gallery dining room at Abbicci features hand-drawn maps of Italy on walls.

We were too full to sample the desserts, which for a warm summer night seemed rather heavy. Typical choices are flourless chocolate cake with raspberry coulis and crème anglaise, linzer torte, fresh fruit tart and a terrine of two chocolates with chocolate genoise and chocolate-butter cream with white-chocolate mousse.

The long, distinguished wine list, priced starting in the high teens, has been cited by Wine Spectator.

Dinner nightly from 5.

Abbicci, 43 Main St. (Route 6A), Yarmouth Port. (508) 362-3501.

Veteran Cape restaurateurs Marietta and Robert Hickey took over the beloved Cranberry Moose in 1989, returning to his hometown where he got his culinary start at its predecessor, the old Cranberry Goose, and where she had founded La Cipollina down the street. But, they said, the Moose never really prospered in its New American realm. Marietta longed to restore Italian fare but did not want to compete with La Cipollina. The opportunity arose in 1992 when La Cipollina was sold to become a Japanese restaurant. The Cranberry Moose closed for redecoration and a reconfiguration of the kitchen to handle more business. The restaurant reopened with a new name, a new look and a new menu. And a new lease on life.

"Business is up big-time," says Marietta, "even though the average check has dropped." No longer merely a special-occasion place, Abbicci offers a variety of dining options. Locals crowd into the 75 seats in four dining areas for earlybird specials that are the best value on the Cape, in the view of one innkeeper. Consistency has been a problem, although when Abbicci is at its best, it's one of the very best.

Robert Hickey and four assistants in the kitchen execute an ambitious menu created by Marietta, who oversees the front of the house. The two dozen entrées are priced from $12.95 for calves liver veneziana to $23.95 for grilled veal chop with mushrooms and madeira demi-glace or roast rack of lamb with a garlic, marjoram and pistachio crust. Other options include grilled tuna with a roasted-pepper and orange salsa, oven-roasted salmon with a mustard and herb cream sauce, veal saltimbocca, roast duck with a honey-apricot sauce and steak florentine. Fresh asparagus, haricots verts or sautéed seasonal greens come with.

The antipasti and pastas ($11.95 to $21.95) are first-rate here. Desserts are to die for, especially the apricot dacquoise, the chocolate pâté served on raspberry puree and the tirami su. Finish with the seductive Abbicci cappuccino, a heavily liqueured concoction that may finish you off. The extensive wine list is heavily Italian, well chosen in a broad price range.

We returned lately for a lunch that got off to a shaky start with too-loud jazz playing in the background and niggardly glasses of white wine for $4. Things got better with crumbly, piping-hot rolls and our main choices: a kicky steak sandwich with sautéed onions and peppers, served open-faced on sourdough bread with red potatoes ($7.75), and an assertive linguini and shellfish ($8.50), with all kinds of vegetables from squash and peppers to tomatoes and asparagus. Warm raisin gingerbread with lemon mousse and applejack brandy sauce was a memorable dessert.

The decor is spare, with splashes of yellow and blue amid the prevailing white walls, white tablecloths and an array of cactus plants. The subdued maps of Italy on the walls were hand-drawn by Marietta's son, a San Francisco architect who handled Abbicci's redesign.

Lunch daily, 11:30 to 2:30; dinner nightly, 5 to 9 or 10; Sunday buffet brunch, 11:30 to 2:30.

Cielo, East Main Street, Wellfleet. (508) 349-2108.

The word means "heaven" and that's what you'll find inside this small house that's an intriguing combination of café and art gallery, which, despite a succession of chefs, manages to endure and is thought to be better than ever. The latest is Mitch Rosenbaum, former chef at Good Housekeeping Institute's executive dining room. His partner and pastry chef, Laxmi Venkateshwaran, a native of India, trained at the New York Restaurant School. "The two of us do everything," says Mitch. "She waits on tables and does the desserts and I cook."

And cook he does — one prix-fixe ($32 to $39), four-course meal that changes nightly and, for the first time, gives two options for main courses. Dinner at our latest visit started with sesame beef and oyster roulade, followed by a salad of poached salmon on greens. Entrée choices were poppyseed turban of sole and shrimp, and osso buco braised with porcini mushrooms, merlot and pancetta. Dessert was a mocha-hazelnut napoleon. The next night's fare sounded equally tempting: sea scallop and artichoke bisque with chives, a watercress, arugula and tomato salad, tandoori swordfish steak or roast loin of lamb en croûte with portobello mushrooms, and fresh plum tart.

Patrons dine on an enclosed rear porch, overlooking the picturesque Wellfleet marshes. Two sittings are the norm, 6 and 8 o'clock the times for sixteen lucky people who generally arrive early to browse and look at the artworks, photos on the walls and pottery in the front gallery.

The Scandinavian-look decor, with floral tablecloths over burgundy, octagonal white plates, a small carafe containing carnations and masses of flowers around, is worthy of the food. Eating here is like being at a dinner party in a private home.

If you can't make the party at dinner time, settle for Sunday brunch. Or try one

Dining areas at Aesop's Tables.   **Arty backdrop for dining at Cielo.**

of Laxmi's changing $20 Indian buffets, served Tuesdays in summer and Wednesdays in the off-season.

Dinner by reservation, nightly at 6 and 8 in summer, Wednesday-Sunday in off-season. Closed December-March. BYOB.

Aesop's Tables, Main Street, Wellfleet. (508) 349-6450.

New American cuisine is featured in this highly rated seasonal restaurant in a large white house built about 1805 in the heart of Wellfleet. A warren of small dining rooms and an appealing porch display some of the charming collages of artist Kim Kettler, co-owner with her husband Brian Dunne. Upstairs is a tavern outfitted with plush Victorian chairs and sofas. For a summer treat, you can dine at outdoor tables on the front lawn.

Market availability determines the numerous specials that supplement the menu. Arty touches occasionally prevail, as in Monet's garden salad ($6.25) of exotic greens, sundried tomatoes and montrachet, and the poulet d'art ($15.75), chicken breast stuffed with kalamata olives and garlic. Aesop's local oysters, chilled or hot, are always fine appetizers; they may come in a sauce of soy and balsamic vinegar, topped with all colors and kinds of peppers including jalapeño. Other good choices ($6.25 to $7.75) are grilled grape leaves filled with feta and buffalo mozzarella with crostini, a tri-color terrine layered with grilled vegetables, goat cheese and pesto, and littlenecks steamed in black-bean/chile-pepper sauce.

Among main courses ($14.75 to $22.75) are roasted duck marinated in spiced wine, veal roulade stuffed with prosciutto, goat cheese and spinach, and pan-roasted lamb chops accompanied by grilled rosemary polenta and broiled figs. A friend tried the scallops with roe intact, a chiffonade of basil, roasted garlic and shallots and saffron spaëtzle and pronounced the dish a huge success. Vegetables and greens come from the owners' farm in Truro.

The pastry chef bakes outstanding breads, including sourdough baguettes and cranberry scones. She outdoes herself on desserts, among them a delicate cheesecake topped with raspberry-blueberry sauce, sweet citrus shortbread tart, cranberry-pecan tart with vanilla ice cream, and death by chocolate. Frozen mixed drinks and international coffees are featured, and the wine list is pleasantly priced.

Appetizers and light fare make up the **Tavern on the Terrace** menu, available upstairs in the tavern or on the terrace. Aesop's strata, a baked egg custard with fresh fruit or vegetables, and huevos rancheros are popular items at the buffet brunch ($13.95).

Dinner, nightly from 6; Sunday brunch, 10 to 2. Closed November-April.

Christian's, 443 Main St., Chatham. (508) 945-3362.

With an abiding interest in cooking and a degree from the Culinary Institute of America, all Christian Schultz needed was a restaurant. His father Walter provided it, purchasing the old Chatham Arms. Christian's mother did the decorating, his younger brother became the mâitre-d and his eventual bride became the office manager. The family project has since grown from something of a summer lark into an expanding, nearly year-round venture with the popular Upstairs at Christian's, a classic English bar, and an outdoor deck for drinks and light eating.

The main floor has two dining rooms, one of them an enclosed porch. Oriental rugs dot the floors and a mix of woven white, pink and blue cloths cover the tables. Classical music plays in the background.

A complimentary liver pâté served with crisp and buttery homemade melba toast comes with drinks. Appetizers ($7 to $8) range from chèvre wrapped in phyllo with sundried tomatoes and kalamata olives to escargots with penne noodles and feta cheese. We enjoyed crab beurrecks, wrapped in phyllo dough and presented on top of a lemon-butter sauce with red and green pepper strips, and a special called "cockles and such," in this case four Monterey oysters in a choron sauce. Crusty French bread preceded a salad of leaf lettuce and tomatoes, served with a zesty herb and cheese dressing.

Entrées, which change every few weeks, go from $19 for calves liver topped with a parma ham and red-onion marmalade to $26 for rack of lamb with a minted pesto-cream sauce. Christian might top his grilled swordfish with an anchovy, tuna and garlic sauce (the menu advises that you also can order the same swordfish "served plain"), and his seafood sauté combines lobster, shrimp and scallops flamed in tequila. We found superb both the fresh halibut, topped with asparagus and hollandaise, and the medallions of veal sautéed with shrimp, garlic, lemon and white wine. With these came side plates of green and yellow squash, carrots and rice, the vegetables living up to advance billing as some of the more interesting and nicely presented in the area.

A grand-marnier torte topped with a chocolate shell filled with grand marnier made a special dessert. Raspberry linzer torte, rum-caramel custard and a trio of mousses are others. An extensive wine list, half American and half European, is priced from $15 to $90.

After dinner, cordials and special coffees are an attraction at **Upstairs at Christian's** amid African mahogany paneling, shelves full of books, a handsome homemade curved oak bar, and a distinctive mix of eaves and niches with leather sofas and love seats. When we stopped in, a banjo player, "proud to be a preppy from North Chatham," sang rousing ditties while one of Walter Schultz's collection of old movies was shown in "The Critic's Corner."

Lately, an upstairs menu offers quite a variety of appetizers, pastas, fish and

Dining porch at Christian's in Chatham.

meat dishes in a wide range of prices from $4 to $12.50. The atmosphere is like dining in a library, and the food creative and affordable, although we must say our latest lunch on the canopied upstairs deck was on the pedestrian side.

Lunch in summer, 11:30 to 3; dinner nightly, 5 to 10. Downstairs closed Columbus Day to May. Upstairs open year-round.

The Regatta of Cotuit, 4631 Falmouth Road (Route 28), Cotuit. (508) 428-5715.

The Crocker House, a short-lived restaurant in a handsome 1790 Federal-style house on Route 28, was acquired in 1987 by Wendy and Brantz Bryan of the Regatta in Falmouth. "You couldn't have two more extremes," admitted Wendy. While the Falmouth restaurant features seafood and is summery, New Yorkish and on the waterfront, the Cotuit venture serves regional dishes and Americana on a year-round basis. It also has a full bar and a broad new tavern menu.

Seven dining rooms, one with only two tables, are beautifully appointed in shades of pink and green, with authentic print wallpapers, needlepoint rugs and furnishings of the period. Tables are set with pink and white Limoges china, crystal glassware and fine silver.

Chef Martin Murphy, formerly of High Brewster, has helped the Regatta earn a reputation for fine dining every bit as stellar as that of Chillingsworth, which is more widely known.

Entrées are priced from $17 for breast of chicken roulade to $25 for sautéed medallions of venison with lingonberry and port sauce. Among the possibilities are pan-seared sea scallops with scallion and herb sauce in puff pastry, Thai-style lobster and shrimp with ginger and Asian greens, sweetbreads and foie gras with sautéed apples and leeks, and filet mignon with a roasted-shallot glace. Specials could range from soft-shell crabs to seared buffalo tenderloin.

Among starters ($6 to $10.50) are wild-mushroom strudel with a sauce of five mushrooms, chilled oysters with a roasted-shallot crème fraîche, grilled quail with a wild-mushroom salad, seared beef carpaccio and tartare, and sautéed foie gras with warm greens, raspberries and figs. Desserts are similar to those of the Regatta at Falmouth, including house-made ice creams and sorbets and a trilogy of three favorites ($8.50). The chocolate seduction on a lovely patterned raspberry sauce and the crème brûlée garnished with red and gold raspberries and blackberries are among the best we've tasted.

The food here is of such a caliber and the choices so tempting that many opt for the five-course tasting menu for two or more. It's well worth the $48 tab.

At the other extreme -- and equally well received -- is the Regatta's new tavern menu, perfect for grazing. It modifies some of the regular appetizers and entrées and adds salads and sandwiches. The result is a selection of goodies, from crispy vegetable raviolis with spicy Vietnamese sauce to an open-face sandwich of Maine crab meat with smoked cheddar on focaccia, at prices from $4.50 to $14.50. Most are under $10.

The wine list, which emphasizes good reds, is priced from $18 to $78.

Dinner nightly from 5:30.

Other Dining Choices

Inaho Japanese Restaurant, 157 Route 6A, Yarmouth Port. (508) 362-5522.

The little white house that long harbored La Cipollina restaurant became the home in 1992 of a Japanese restaurant that relocated from Hyannis. Ugi Wantanabe, who had worked as a sushi chef in New York and Newport, and his Portuguese-American wife Alda live upstairs, in the European fashion, and travel every other day to Boston for fresh fish and provisions.

A long sushi bar where singles can be comfortable faces one wall of the rear dining room; three Japanese-looking booths flank the other. The far end is all windows gazing onto a courtyard garden, where spotlights focus on a few Japanese plantings (the Japanese garden in front seemed to be thriving better at our visit). There are two front dining rooms as well. The bare wood tables topped only with chopsticks and napkins hint that here you'll find the real thing.

An order of gyoza dumplings staved off hunger as we nursed a bottle of Chalk Hill sauvignon blanc from a small but well chosen wine list. One of us sampled the nine-piece sushi plate for $15; the sushi was fresh and delicious. The other was pleased with the bento box ($15.75) yielding salad, a skewer of chicken teriyaki, tempura and a California roll. Sashimi, teriyaki, tempura and katsu items completed the menu, priced from $11.50 to $18.75. Also available are shabu shabu and sushi special dinners, $39 for two. Desserts included a frozen chocolate cake as thick as fudge, served with vanilla ice cream, and a poached pear on ice cream with ginger sauce. But we could not be dissuaded from our favorite ginger ice cream, rendered here to perfection.

Dinner nightly from 5.

The Brewster Fish House Restaurant, 2208 Route 6A, Brewster. (508) 896-7867.

David and Vernon Smith took over what had been a retail fish market in 1984 and converted it into one of the Cape's best seafood restaurants. It's so low-key that, despite countless trips through the area, we were unaware of its existence until a knowing innkeeper tipped us off. Good thing, for we found a stylish little cafe where the young brothers, both self-taught chefs, man the kitchen and produce a simple yet satisfying array of the freshest fish available.

Small and personal, this is a pure place -- nothing like the take-a-number-and-

Wendy and Brantz Bryan outside Regatta of Cotuit.

hope-for-the-best of the ubiquitous fried-fish ilk. There's no meat on the menu, although one of the three nightly specials involves a beef, lamb or poultry dish. Otherwise it's all seafood, from $9.75 for fish and chips to $18 for steamed lobster with a shellfish garnish. In between are treats like grilled Atlantic salmon with spinach and pancetta, grilled swordfish with citrus-lobster butter, broiled halibut with a plum-tomato and herb sauce, baked pollock under a horseradish crust with a grilled corn and red-onion salad, and sautéed cornmeal flounder with soprasseta. The mixed grill combines swordfish, shrimp, scallops and andouille sausage with a soy, sesame and molasses dipping sauce. Specials at our visit were poached salmon with raspberry sauce and poached leeks, and grilled tuna over bok choy with sesame-soy sauce. Three pastas can be ordered as appetizers or main courses.

All the appetizers except one -- fried artichokes with a garlic and ginger ketchup -- involve seafood. Dill-and-brandy-cured salmon, crab cake with a mixed fruit and bell-pepper marmalade and fried calamari with a tomato and red-pepper aioli are favorites. Or you can start with chowder, lobster bisque or billi-bi.

The day's three desserts could be crème brûlée, flourless chocolate torte with raspberry sauce and lemon-lime or roasted-hazelnut cheesecakes. The wine list is as well chosen as the rest of the menu, and many are available by the glass.

Dining is at bare green tables set with linen napkins, candles and fresh flowers. Classical music or soft jazz plays in the background.

Lunch daily, 11:30 to 3; dinner, 5 to 9:30 or 10; closed Monday in off-season. Open April-November.

Flying Fish Cafe, Briar Lane, Wellfleet. (508) 349-3100.

Stop here for breakfast, lunch or dinner and find creative cooking at affordable prices. Co-owners Lisa Brown and Patricia Foley say they "cater to vegetarians and more experimental eaters." Everything is made on the premises, and baked goods are available in the adjacent bakery.

For breakfast, try the sunrise special (two eggs, toast and homefries, $1.99) or the Flying Fish omelet with cream cheese, bacon and guacamole ($5.50). Chef Lisa is partial to the "green eggs and ham" dish and the scrambled tofu with veggies. Lunch runs from a BLT ($3.75) and a "boring" burger (lettuce, tomato and no cheese) to Jamaican jerked chicken and salad plates of chicken, tuna or smoked turkey ($6.75).

The Flying Fish is at its best at night, when candlelight and linens take over. The short menu ($12.50 to $18.50) might list Thai scallops sautéed with lemon grass, jalapeños and tomatoes, caramelized in a sauce that's "a lot like our chef (slightly spicy, slightly sweet)," seafood penne, Mediterranean chicken, lobster romantique with leeks and tomatoes in a ginger-cinnamon beurre blanc over black-pepper fettuccine, and filet mignon with a two-mustard, green-peppercorn sauce. Start with "mussels from heaven" splashed with pernod or the Californian, montrachet baked in radicchio leaves with tomato-shallot sauce. Finish with blueberry-lime pie, mile-high chocolate cake or a fruit cobbler fresh from the bakery.

Breakfast, 7 to noon; lunch, noon to 3; dinner, 6 to 9:30 or 10. Closed Monday for dinner. Open mid-April to mid-October.

Nauset Beach Club, 221 Main St., East Orleans. (508) 255-8547.

When Doug and Beth Campbell left their Michigan restaurant to retire to the Cape in 1986, they bought the old Wry and Ginger restaurant for their son. He eventually left, and Jack and Annamaria Salemi joined them from Michigan. All four are hands-on restaurateurs, Jack being the chef and responsible for down-to-earth, affordable Italian bistro fare that packs in the crowds.

Success spawned a batch of renovations, and now the summery little house on the way to Nauset Beach has a new entry and service bar, a wood-fired oven and two dining rooms seating 55. Walls are terra cotta, tablecloths are green and pails of fat crayons are on each table for doodling on the white butcher paper.

The oversize menu with big type for easy reading is short and to the point. There are five pastas ($11.50) and a risotto of the day. For a casual treat, how about the Nauset Beach club sandwich ($16.50) — lobster meat, pancetta and arugula served atop country bread with a sundried tomato dressing? The dozen entrées ($13.50 to $18) include zuppa di pesce, lobster or scampi over linguini, scallops with wild mushrooms and cheese tortellini, chicken pancetta atop angel-hair pasta, osso buco and veal saltimbocca. Start with an arugula and gorgonzola salad, spiedini or focaccia, clam cakes served with caponata or a lobster-potato tart with warm citrus vinaigrette.

The restaurant is known for its desserts, which include dark coffee ice cream with homemade caramel sauce, cranberry cobble with ginger ice cream and torta cioccolato, flourless chocolate cake served with chocolate gelato and chocolate sauce. The perfectly serviceable roster of wines printed on the menu is supplemented by a wide-ranging cellar list priced from $15 to $96. The restaurant stages wine-tasting dinners in the off-season.

Dinner nightly, 5:30 to 9 or 9:30. Closed Sunday and Monday, November-April, Sunday in May.

The Arbor, Route 28 at Route 6A, Orleans. (508) 255-4847.

Our kind of food — meaning assertive and out of the ordinary — is served in this old sea captain's house with an attached barn. The several dining rooms (one on a porch with slanting floor, one in a paneled room with a fireplace, one in a quiet back room with four tables for two) are unusual, to say the least. Decor is sort of early-to-late flea market; the owners scour flea markets, especially Brimfield, and have they got a collection! From old toys to 1,000 early cans, the stuff covers every possible surface. Even the tablecloths are flowered cotton like those our grandmothers used to have in the kitchen — each is different and has to be ironed on a mangle. It's funky but charming, and the food is highly rated.

With the extensive menu came a tray decorated with grapes and bearing three small glasses of the wines of the night, so you could taste before you chose — a nice idea that, we regretted to hear, has been discontinued. We ordered a glass of the chardonnay ($3) and liked it enough that we ordered a bottle. The wine cellar is extensive with a special list of rare bottles priced in the hundreds of dollars. A complimentary tray of pickled peppers and crudités with a dip as well as large buttermilk biscuits sustained us until we could dig into the appetizer, a hot seafood platter ($9.95 for two). Two each of clams casino, oysters rockefeller, crab-stuffed mushrooms and stuffed mussels were delicious. A good caesar salad and a house salad of romaine with crushed pineapple and shredded carrots with a honey-fennel dressing preceded the entrées.

The choice embraces a staggering 41 items, from five pastas and five veal dishes to five cajun-style offerings and three of "the Arbor's best" — two preparations of lobster and one of pasta, each bearing a name (including lobster Kendall for the late co-owner Kendall Bowers). The prices are $12.95 to $18.95, and you wonder how they can do it so cheaply, as well as how they can succeed so handsomely with so extensive a repertoire.

One of us had bouillabaisse, which came in a huge crock — it was crammed with so much seafood she could eat only about a quarter of it, and was given a doggy bag (make that a plastic Stop & Shop container) to take home. The other had oysters and scallops Stephen in a cream sauce on pasta and loved it. A shared dessert of a meringue shell filled with coffee ice cream and praline sauce was heavenly. The bill, including wine and tip, came to about $70.

Don't be deceived by the exterior of the Arbor and its grotto-like **Binnacle Tavern,** all covered with buoys. Inside is some mighty interesting food.

Dinner nightly, 5 to 10, weekends only in off-season. Closed January to Valentine's Day.

The Impudent Oyster, 115 Chatham Bars Ave., Chatham. (508) 945-3545.

With a name like the Impudent Oyster, how could this small restaurant down a side street in Chatham miss? An avid local following jams together at small, glass-covered tables under a skylit cathedral ceiling, beneath plants in straw baskets balancing overhead on the beams.

The changing international menu, based on local seafoods, blends regional, French, Mexican, Chinese, Indian and Italian cuisines, among others.

We couldn't resist starting with the drunken mussels, shelled and served in an intense marinade of tamari, fresh ginger, Szechuan peppercorns and sake. We were disappointed to find it had been removed from recent menus in favor of Portuguese mussels, steamed with chorizo sausage in a spicy tomato sauce. The Mexican chicken, chile and lime soup, spicy and full of interesting flavors, was one of the best we've tasted. Other unusual starters ($5.95 to $7.95) include curried mussel stew, oysters sardinia, grilled shrimp tapachula with cilantro and a southwestern barbecue sauce, swordfish and avocado seviche, and Caribbean plantains served with a fresh mango and papaya salsa.

Entrées run from $14 to $23 (for a house specialty, bouillabaisse). Szechuan scrod, yellowfin tuna in soy sauce and cumin, crab-stuffed sole with asparagus and brie, and salmon pesaro with tomato and cheese tortellini are some of owner Peter Barnard's changing offerings. Local seafood is obviously featured, but there are chicken and steak dishes, a pasta with grilled duck, and a wonderful-sounding mesclun salad garnished with grilled shrimp, tuna and chicken. At one visit we liked the feta and fennel scrod, a Greek dish touched with ouzo, and the swordfish broiled with orange and pepper butter. A plate of several ice creams made with fresh fruits was a cooling dessert.

Creativity extends to the wine list, which, like the food, is reasonably priced (many in the low to mid teens, with a few up to $50), and to the lunch menu with a changing array of salads, sandwiches and entrées. This is the kind of food of which we never tire, although we might prefer to have it in a more tranquil and less crowded setting.

Lunch daily, 11:30 to 3; dinner, 5:30 to 10.

Campari's, 352 Main St., Chatham. (508) 945-9123.

Talented chef Bob Chiappetta cooks in an open kitchen in this pleasant Italian bistro in the Dolphin inn and motel. By day it's the Bittersweet Cafe, serving breakfast. At night it turns cozy and intimate as diners partake at tables covered with red-checked cloths and candles in chianti bottles amid hanging plants, two working fireplaces and a couple of prominently displayed aquariums. Italian opera music plays in the background. Cocktails are served in summer at **Alfresco's,** an appealing screened porch in front.

The kitchen, open to the dining room and imparting tantalizing odors throughout, resembles the household kitchen it once was. It provides inspiration and recreates childhood memories for Bob, who recalls watching with interest the preparation of family meals in various regions of Italy. His short menu reflects such ethnic specialties ($17 to $25) as broiled swordfish siciliana served with capellini, chicken tuscano, veal orvieto and scampi luciano, the last a mix of tiger prawns and lobster meat served with wine-simmered mussels on a bed of capellini. The five changing entrées come with soup and salad. Crab cakes parmigiana and raviolis are possible starters. Bob's wife Lisa bakes the desserts, perhaps a honey-nut pie. She also oversees the short Italian wine list.

As if they weren't busy enough with breakfast and dinner, the couple also have opened **Carmine's,** a new cappuccino and pizza place with Italian pastries, desserts and gelatos in the Galleria at 595 Main St., Chatham.

Breakfast daily, 8 to 1; dinner nightly except Monday, 6 to 9; off-season, Wednesday-Saturday 6 to 9.

Vining's Bistro, 595 Main St., Chatham. (508) 945-5033.

We've had lobster in countless forms, but never before wrapped in a flour tortilla with spinach and jalapeño jack cheese and here called a warm lobster taco. With homemade two-tomato salsa sparked with cilantro, it made a delightful lunch (and also is a favorite appetizer for dinner). The warm roasted-scallop salad with grilled eggplant and yogurt dressing, served on wilted bok choy, was also a lunchtime winner.

Steve Vining, who was formerly at La Grand Rue in Harwichport, runs what has been rated the best wood-grill bistro on the Cape. It's upstairs in the Galleria, with rattan chairs at dark wood tables, beamed cathedral ceilings and tall windows onto Main Street. Other windows look into an atrium art gallery in front,

Dining room is quirky at The Arbor. **Front dining room at Bramble Inn.**

and through a doorway into a new bar area with tables. That's for overflow, we guess, since there already was a prominent bar that always seems to be occupied in the main dining room.

Many dishes are prepared on the open grill, using woods like hickory, cherry and apple. Appetizers, also available in entrée portions, include aforementioned warm lobster taco, curried shrimp cakes and "pasta from hell" with smoked chicken, hot sausage and banana-guava ketchup. The seafood pasta ($14.50) stir-fried with sesame, tamari and ginger sounds great. Main courses run from $12.50 for spit-roasted chicken with garlic mashed potatoes to $16.50 for grilled Atlantic salmon with roasted-tomato hollandaise or jade sauce. Favorites are Caribbean barbecued shrimp with coconut, mango and pineapple salsa and Thai fire pot with chicken, sausage and seafood in a hot and sour broth of lemon grass. Or sup on Thai beef salad, grilled chicken and spinach salad or Siamese vegetable sauté. Dessert could be maple-pecan bread pudding or chocolate-pudding cake.

The beer and wine list are as creative as the rest of the menu, ranging widely in scope and price.

Lunch, Wednesday-Sunday 11:30 to 2:30; dinner nightly, 5:30 to 10. Closed January-March.

Bed and Board

The Bramble Inn & Restaurant, Route 6A, Box 807, Brewster 01631. (508) 896-7644.

White linens, stunning floral china in the Victoria pattern from Czechoslovakia, candles in hurricane lamps and assorted flowers in vases grace the five small dining rooms seating a total of 60 at this inn renowned for its restaurant. Ruth and Cliff Manchester, who got their start at his parents' nearby Old Manse Inn, have continued the tradition launched by former owners Karen Etsell and Elaine Brennan, who wrote the book on "How to Open a Country Inn" and soon afterward sold to pursue their artistic and antiquing interests.

Ruth Manchester is an inventive cook, whose four-course, prix-fixe dinners ($36 to $45, depending on choice of entrée) draw a devoted following and rave press reviews. Her soups are triumphs: perhaps chilled cherry with port and crème fraîche, four-onion soup with brie croutons or a lettuce and scallion bisque. Other starters might be Vermont goat-cheese tapenade with french bread, a trio of smoked-mozzarella raviolis with basil-pesto cream, grilled duck sausage with raisin-sage brioche and homemade chutney and -- a unique dish -- New England seafood chili: cod, clams and tuna in a spicy tomato sauce with black beans, jack cheese and sour cream.

The nine main-course choices could include grilled shrimp with cilantro-chipotle butter, Thai lard-na seafood stew, pan-roasted veal with shiitake mushrooms, medallions of venison with mashed sweet potatoes and a warm red cabbage salad, and New York sirloin on a country-bread crouton with ham, mushrooms and béarnaise sauce. The assorted-seafood curry combines cod, scallops, shrimp and lobster in a light curry sauce with banana, coconut, almonds and chutney.

Among desserts are white-chocolate coeur à la crème (a recipe requested by Bon Appétit magazine), chocolate-chambord truffle tart, lemon-soufflé tart and fresh fruit tarts. The small, paneled Hunt Room houses a service bar. The limited but serviceable wine list offers good values.

Upstairs in the main 1861 house are three guest rooms with sloping floors, furnished in a comfortable country style. Five more rooms are in the 1849 House, a Greek Revival structure two doors away. The Manchesters lately added five more rooms in the 1793 Pepper House. All have private baths and air-conditioning. Guests enjoy a full breakfast on the cheery dining porch of the main inn.

In 1993, Sue Johnson, who had worked with her mother for two years in the kitchen at the Bramble Inn, returned to the family's early beginnings when she reopened the restaurant at the Old Manse Inn. She was serving à la carte meals there with a Mediterranean flair.

Dinner nightly by reservation, 6 to 9, Thursday-Saturday in spring and fall. Closed January to mid-April. Doubles, $85 to $125.

High Brewster, 964 Satucket Road, Brewster 01631. (508) 896-3636.

Only a discreet sign in front of the large brown Colonial house on a hill with beautifully landscaped grounds gives a clue that this is more than someone's private home. And for 25 years, it was indeed the home of William Arbuckle and Walter Hyde, two gentlemen in the old-fashioned sense of the word, who — with little fanfare, no advertising and much acclaim from those in the know — welcomed guests to their home for dinner four nights a week.

After the death of his partner, Walter ran the restaurant for a couple of seasons until he sold it in 1987 to pursue his painting and decorating interests. It was purchased by two local couples, who upgraded the guest rooms, installed a professional kitchen and extended the meal hours. The dining experience in the 1738 house overlooking Lower Mill Pond remains the essence of Cape Cod, much as it was when we first dined here, although not so personal.

Chef Elizabeth White's fare is contemporary American and quite complex, as in a summer appetizer of cherrywood-smoked pork tenderloin on green apple chutney and Boston brown bread, served with a coarse-grain fig mustard. The four-course dinner is priced from $33 to $39, depending on choice of entrée. At our summer visit, you could start with grilled shrimp on black-bean cakes with sonoma cornmeal muffins, warm goat-cheese salad or potato gnocchis on a bed

Outdoor terrace at High Brewster looks toward Lower Mill Pond.

of wilted spinach tossed with basil pesto and shredded mozzarella, among others. Following a salad of local greens with organic edible flowers and chèvre, the seven main-course choices included grilled swordfish on spicy peanut sauce with tri-color tagliatelle, sautéed halibut with strawberry-mint beurre blanc and New England succotash, breast of Long Island duck with nectarine chutney, grilled veal chop with rosemary-chèvre polenta and grilled tenderloin with boursin cheese and baked potato pancakes. New York cheesecake, Nantucket oatmeal-spice cake, peach-melba mousse and crème caramel are among the desserts.

Traditionally, High Brewster lacked a liquor license but allowed patrons to bring their own. Now it serves beer and wine, inside in the cozy lounge or outside in summer on a small terrace overlooking the scenic pond.

New in 1993 were three-course dinners with an appealing array of options for $19.50 on Wednesdays and Thursdays in the off-season.

The 18th-century Cape Cod house, its age wearing well, contains three cozy, low-ceilinged dining rooms seating a total of 60. Tables are of deeply polished dark wood, and those in the keeping room are set with crisp white linens and Blue Willow tableware. Dark beams, wide paneling and barn boards are displayed to advantage by candlelight and track lights, as are the oil paintings and antiques all around.

Upstairs are four refurbished guest rooms with sloping ceilings and a lived-in, historic feel. Two have private baths and two smaller rooms share. Outside are an efficiency cottage for two as well as two houses sleeping up to four, rented by the night or week. Breakfast of the guest's choice is included with the rooms.

Dinner nightly, 6 to 9, Memorial Day to Columbus Day; Wednesday-Sunday in off-season. Doubles, $80 to $100; cottage and houses, $135 to $160.

Wequassett Inn, Pleasant Bay, Chatham 02633. (508) 432-5400 or (800) 225-7125.

Cape Cod has perhaps no more majestic water view amid more elegant surroundings than from the restored, 18th-century "square top" sea captain's mansion that houses this venerable inn's dining room. Light lunches and cocktails are served on a colorful, canopied outdoor terrace amid pink geraniums framing a view of Pleasant Bay.

Floor-to-ceiling windows on three sides is all the decor necessary in the expansive main dining room that looks quite summery with beige chairs, linens from France and oil lamps. A tiered deck off the lounge, planned for 1994, would be a treat for lunch overlooking the water.

Fresh seafood and continental cuisine are the themes of chef Frank McMullen, a Culinary Institute of America graduate who came here from Pier 66 in Fort Lauderdale. Our dinner began with a special terrine, one part scallop and the other part salmon, garnished with grapefruit and a tangy sauce, and escargots with pinenuts in puff pastry.

Among entrées ($18.50 to $22.75, except $34 for lobster wellington), we liked the grilled double lamb chops with orange and rosemary demi-glace and the twin beef tenderloins with smoked-cheddar sauce, both accessorized with crisp snow peas, carrots, cauliflower and roast potatoes. Other options were four enticing pastas, grilled scallops with pesto beurre blanc and Italian salsa, blackened mixed-seafood grill with mango-cilantro sour cream, Norwegian salmon baked on a cedar plank, and veal chop with morel sauce.

Desserts included cranberry mousse in an almond tuile with a red and white sauce underneath looking as lacy as a doily, and a frozen chambord mousse in a parfait glass. With all the candles lit and reflecting in the windows, it was a romantic atmosphere in which to linger over cappuccino and cordials.

We only had to amble off to our room, one of several in duplex cottages right by the bay, with a deck almost over the water. The 104 handsomely furnished rooms with all the amenities are in eighteen Cape-style cottages, motel buildings and condo-type facilities. They range from water-view suites to tennis villas with cathedral ceilings and private balconies overlooking the woods and courts.

Lunch daily, 11:30 to 2; dinner, 6 to 10. Doubles, $150 to $290, suites $350 to $470, EP. Open May-October.

The Bradford Inn and Motel, 26 Cross St., Chatham 02633. (508) 945-1030 or (800) 562-4667.

An exceptionally attractive motel-inn, this growing establishment with its cheery exterior of yellow awnings and fine gardens is well situated in a residential section just off Chatham's Main Street.

Always upgrading, innkeepers William and Audrey Gray added four deluxe rooms with fireplaces, canopy beds and TVs hidden in armoires in the Jonathan Gray House, which they built to look old and named Jonathan, Bill Gray explained, "because the name sounds old." They also added the Lion's Den, a lounge for reading and games, and opened a two-bedroom cottage as the Captain's Hideaway. Their latest gem is the adjacent **Mulberry Inn,** a deluxe B&B with two guest rooms, a suite and fireplaced parlor (doubles, $159 to $180).

Five large rooms are in the Bradford House in front, which we found cozy with a fireplace on a fall evening, while four are in the Carriage House near the pool. Eleven more are in the L-shaped motel building in back. All are individually decorated and have private baths, television, phones and air-conditioning.

A complimentary breakfast is served in the 1860 Captain Elijah Smith House, which serves as the Grays' home and office. Breakfast, also available to the public, includes choice of eggs (from omelets to eggs benedict), french toast and wonderful pancakes like apricot or apple with cinnamon sugar and sour cream. Belgian waffles with bananas and pecans in brandy and brown sugar, made from scratch, are a highlight of the Sunday brunch. Guests linger over coffee on the garden patio beside the small pool, savoring the extravagant roses and watching the birds feed.

With the opening of **Champlain's,** the Grays added two more dining areas to

Wedgewood Inn at Yarmouth Port.

the original poolside breakfast room. The full-service restaurant is homespun with Hitchcock chairs, white woven mats over mulberry cloths, captain's chairs, a fireplace and a big fish tank that "everyone likes to watch," says Audrey. The Grays' son, Robert, is chef for the dining venture named for explorer Samuel de Champlain, who sailed into Chatham's Stage Harbor in 1606.

His extensive dinner menu is priced from $14.50 for fire-roasted breast of chicken to $23.95 for seafood diablo, the chef's specialty served over linguini. Poached salmon, lobster crumb pie, curried chicken, veal with crab meat and chargrilled breast of duck are other possibilities. All meals include breads, salad, sorbet, starch and vegetables. Dessert could be a meringue glacé or a tart apple-cranberry pie with french vanilla ice cream.

Breakfast, 8 to 11; dinner nightly, 5:30 to 9:30, fewer nights in off-season. Doubles, $120 to $189.

Lodging

Among the many places to stay on the Cape, here are some of special appeal for vacationing gourmets.

Wedgewood Inn, 83 Main St. (Route 6A), Yarmouth Port 02675. (508) 362-5157.

Built in 1812, this distinguished white house with black shutters was restored from top to bottom in 1983. The result was one of the first in the new breed of Cape Cod B&Bs offering superior lodging.

All six air-conditioned guest rooms are spacious with private baths and sitting areas. A third-floor room affords a view of Cape Cod Bay. The two main-floor rooms have screened porches and one has a separate sitting room. Four rooms hold working fireplaces and pencil-post beds. All are comfortably and artfully furnished with quilts, upholstered wing chairs, oriental rugs on wide-board floors and spiffy period wallpapers, mostly in shades of Wedgwood blue, pink and white. A charming rear room with a double and single bed is done in Laura Ashley style. Fresh flowers and fruit are in each room, and a tea tray with munchies is offered about 4 p.m.

The cream-colored dining room is particularly attractive, with windsor chairs at tables for two set with china patterned with swallows (from the Country Diary of an Edwardian Lady) and sunlight streaming through a plant-filled bow window.

Four kinds of pastries, cold cereals, fresh fruit and yogurt are set out on the sideboard for breakfast. Guests have a choice of scrambled eggs, french toast or belgian waffles. Innkeepers Gerrie and Milton Graham (she a former teacher and he a retired FBI agent who played pro football with the Ottawa Rough Riders and the old Boston Patriots) have added Williamsburg gardens and a walk leading to a new entry and common room with oriental rugs, a small TV and a Colonial air. Lately, they built a gazebo in the perennial gardens, and were planning to add three large fireplaced rooms, each with jacuzzi and balcony or patio, in a rear barn.

Doubles, $105 to $150.

Cobb's Cove, Powder Hill Road, Barnstable Village 02630. (508) 362-9356.

Down a country lane off Route 6A, this house was built to look old in 1974 by engineer Henry Chester, whose wife Evelyn is innkeeper.

You can tell they have a sense of humor when you see the Scargo Pottery bird feeder in the back garden. It's a replica of St. Basil's in the Kremlin and the birds (including "Cardinal Richelieu") really flock to it.

In the dining room-library is a piano surrounded by a fascinating collection of books of all kinds, many of the coffee-table variety. Behind it is the Keeping Room with its Count Rumford fireplace, unusually shallow and designed to send out much heat, and beyond that is the sunny terrace where guests keep an eye on the many feathered visitors.

Six unusually large guest rooms are on two floors. The honeymoon suites on the third floor afford spectacular views of Barnstable Harbor and Cape Cod Bay, each with two chairs in front of a huge window from which to enjoy it. Windows dip to the floors in all the rooms. Most walls are of barnsiding for a pleasantly rustic look, the floors are tiled and the closets huge. King or queensize beds, loveseats or wing chairs, antiques, pottery, vases of pampas grass, baskets of pine cones, terrycloth robes, magazines and bowls of nuts make each room special. Bathrooms are modern and sometimes divided; each tub has a whirlpool, and Pears soap and bath oil are provided.

Guests are served wine in the afternoon and a full breakfast, sometimes peach crêpes with mint, fish cakes with scrambled eggs or french toast made with raisin-nut bread.

Outspoken Henry, in his other guise as Henri-Jean, serves dinners by request to groups of six to eight or more. The gala five-course meal with wine ($50 a head) could include Portuguese soup, asparagus vinaigrette, a whole bass garnished with herbs from the garden, salad and a fruit tart or crème caramel with espresso or sambuca-laced coffee.

"We try to get a full table," says Evelyn. "The fun is having our guests sitting down together." Knowing the Chesters, it would be a lively dinner party indeed.

Doubles, $149 to $189.

Ashley Manor, 3660 Olde Kings Highway (Route 6A), Box 856, Barnstable 02630. (508) 362-8044.

One of the more gracious houses on the north shore was turned into a serene and elegant B&B by Fay and Don Bain, dropouts from the New York corporate scene. Ashley Manor was built around a Balm of Gilead tree, tall enough to serve as a landmark for navigators entering Barnstable harbor. Unfortunately, it fell in a storm, but six-feet-high boxwood and a privet hedge set off the house beautifully and enhance a sense of privacy.

In summer, breakfast is served on a delightful brick terrace in back of the house, with a fountain garden, a tennis court and spacious lawns beyond. In other

seasons, guests breakfast by the fire on Chippendale chairs in the dining room, the original 1699 part of the house, with candles lit in elaborate crystal candelabra. Don is the chef ("I'm the sous chef," says Fay, who does the pancakes and muffins). It's a fairly elaborate affair — "almost like an early brunch," says Don -- accompanied by the house coffee with "our own spices." We enjoyed watching the birds flit in and out of a remarkable Scargo cathedral birdhouse as we feasted on fresh orange juice, a stuffed baked apple, the best raspberry muffins we've ever tasted (the Bains even packed a couple to go), Don's delicious and not too sweet homemade granola

Breakfast table at Ashley Manor.

and, the crowning glory, stuffed crêpes with farmer's cheese, strawberry sauce and sour cream. Other main courses include omelets that Fay says are the world's best (light, soft and fluffy, with changing fillings), quiche or a french-toast sandwich with cream cheese, nuts and currants.

Both a keeping room and a well-furnished living room with a grand piano and three navy blue sofas contain fireplaces; the massive one in the living room has a beehive oven. Decanters of wine, sherry and port are set out for guests. Five bedrooms are in the main house; a cottage out back comes with a small kitchenette. The spacious master bedroom in which we stayed on the main floor has a floor that is painted, stained and turpentined, giving it an elegant sheen; the same treatment is in the living room as well. By the fireplace in the master bedroom is a secret stairway leading to the second floor.

Upstairs are four bedrooms with private baths, three with working fireplaces and one with an outdoor balcony. All are welcoming, but we especially like the one with a kingsize canopy bed, a beautiful breakfront, two pumpkin-colored velvet wing chairs beside the fireplace, and deep blue wallpaper and bedspread. Interestingly furnished in antiques, all rooms have flowers, magazines, bedside candies, coffee and tea service, and wine glasses tied with white ribbons. Some rooms sport colorful Nantucket spackled floors.

The personable innkeepers serve fruit and nuts in the afternoon, and sometimes mingle with guests over wine and cheese.

Doubles, $115 to $175.

Beechwood, 2839 Main St., Barnstable 02630. (508) 362-6618.

A magnificent weeping beech and a huge copper beech are on the grounds of this Queen Anne charmer, taken over by Anne and Bob Livermore from Connecticut. Breakfast is served in the pretty wood-paneled dining room, with draped lace curtains, white eyelet cloths over blue linens and a pressed-tin ceiling.

Fresh juice, poached pears, cranapple muffins, raspberry-cheese coffee cake, ham and cheese strata, apple-filled pancakes, waffles and the like make for a hearty repast, changing every day.

All six distinctive guest rooms have private baths and are furnished with interesting antiques, fresh flowers, Crabtree & Evelyn toiletries and refrigerators. In the Rose Room, the queen canopy bed is draped with lace and is high enough that you need a booster stool to climb into it. Add a red sofa, a huge bathroom and a fireplace, and you have a perfect room for honeymooners. The Marble Room, light and airy, harbors an old brass bed and marble fireplace. Handpainted cottage furniture adorns the Cottage Room, where you can see the weeping beech and Cape Cod Bay through a lavender and gold glass window. More colored-glass windows are in the Eastlake Room with its carved Eastlake-style furniture and tortoise-shell dresser set. The wood-paneled Garret on the third floor yields a grand view of the bay, and its bed is dressed with paisley linens and comforter. The newest Lilac Room has a kingsize bed draped in chintz and a bathroom with a clawfoot tub and a separate shower room.

Afternoon tea is served by the hearth in the parlor or on the wraparound veranda, where a hammock and rockers await and wind chimes sing in the breeze. Guests may play croquet on the lawn.

Doubles, $105 to $140.

The Brewster Farmhouse Inn, 716 Main St. (Route 6A), Brewster 01631. (508) 896-3910 or (800) 892-3910.

In an area where antiquity is cherished, it's refreshing to come across a country-modern B&B with a more contemporary feeling. Robert Messina and Joseph Zelich, who owned a large motel with restaurant in North Eastham, took over an abandoned house that we first encountered as Pineapple Place, a B&B. Behind its prim and proper 1850 exterior is a smashingly remodeled and decorated California-type interior with a central cathedral ceiling. The airy main room has a dining area with a table for eight, where gourmet breakfasts are served, and a gathering room with comfortable sofas and chairs facing a fireplace. Oriental rugs accent the Mexican tile floors. Through sliding glass doors onto an enormous deck (where breakfast is taken in warm weather), one can see the large pool and hot tub. At the side are prolific flower and vegetable gardens.

Sophistication extends to the inn's creative brochure, which contains watercolors faithful to the facilities and colors of each room. The five guest air-conditioned rooms (three with private bath and two that share and can be rented individually or as a suite) are nothing short of gorgeous. One, up its own staircase, is a real hideaway with a hand-carved, queensize acorn bed and the two arm chairs that are the norm in all rooms. We fell for the main-floor garden room with a canopied, kingsize rice-carved bed, a comforter matching the valances and curtains, and its own private deck near the pool. Amenities include terrycloth robes, hair dryers, toiletries, sherry and Godiva chocolates at nightly turndown. TVs are available in each room.

Joe's breakfasts are a treat. At our visit, fresh melons and plums and a variety of breads and croissants preceded the main course, individual quiches with ham, jalapeños, pesto and grilled tomato, accompanied by sautéed zucchini and tomatoes from the garden. Portuguese sweet-bread french toast was on the docket for the next morning. Bob bakes most of the pastries for afternoon tea, perhaps pear tarts one day and a cheesecake the next.

Doubles, $125 to $140; suite, $160. Smoking restricted.

The Captain Freeman Inn, 15 Breakwater Road, Brewster 01631. (508) 896-7481 or (800) 843-4664.

The innkeeper teaches cooking classes and serves Saturday-night dinners at this twelve-room inn in an 1860s sea captain's home, grandly reborn in 1992 into a place of great comfort and warmth. Carol Covitz, formerly in computer marketing in New York, teamed up with Tom Edmondson from Texas to reopen the inn following a total renovation. Trained by her grandmother, a professional chef, she conducts cooking schools on winter weekends. Her 1994 series featured the cuisines of Tuscany, the Mediterranean region and the Orient.

Guests share the bounty of her expertise at breakfast, the menu for which is placed in the rooms each day. At our visit it started with a variety of fresh juices, ginger-poached pears and exquisite little blueberry muffins served with crumbly strawberry and orange/grand-marnier butters. Homemade oatmeal and cranberry granola accompanied. The main event this day was a prosciutto and cheddar quiche; other days could see eggs Brewster with a cranberry compote, prosciutto and tabasco-hollandaise sauce; cinnamon french toast with homemade blueberry-rum syrup, or homemade granola pancakes with dried cranberries and currants. Tom furnishes the herbs, wild berries and fruits from his gardens and trees on the two-acre property.

Saturday BYOB dinners in winter for house guests cost $24 for four courses. A typical menu involves corn and sweet-potato chowder, orange and walnut salad, cornish hen glazed with cranberries and cognac over grilled polenta, and a choice of cranberry/chocolate-chip torte or homemade ginger ice cream.

Guest rooms come in three configurations. The Orleans, with shiny, patterned inlaid parquet floors and a high, hand-carved ceiling medallion from Italy, is typical of the six mid-range rooms with private baths. It has a lace-canopy queensize bed, a reading area with a loveseat and a wing chair, a small TV and five tiny straw hats on the wall of a bathroom outfitted with Whitemor & Keach toiletries. Most deluxe are three air-conditioned suites at the rear, each with its own whirlpool spa on an enclosed balcony, a fireplace with sitting area, reading lamps with three-way bulbs, cable TV/VCR, telephone, mini-refrigerator, queen-size canopy bed and full bath. Carol, who did the decorating, is partial to floral patterns, roman shades on the windows, lace swag curtains and straw hats. Three more rooms on the third floor share a hall bath and are available only May-October.

The common areas are comfortable as well, from the Victorian parlor to the fireplaced dining room to the wraparound veranda outfitted in wicker and wrought iron. Guests enjoy a swimming pool, woodland trails and a Victorian specimen garden along a hillside in back. Afternoon refreshments might be iced tea or hot mulled cider with almond biscotti and a basket of fruit.

Doubles, $75 to $115; suites, $185. No smoking.

The Nauset House Inn, Beach Road, Box 774, East Orleans 02643. (508) 255-2195.

Here's an inn with exceptional personality and character, reflecting the tastes and energies of its owners, Diane and Al Johnson, lately joined by their daughter and son-in-law, Cindy and John Vessella.

Well-known for her stained-glass objects, artistic Diane has refurbished the inn with many of her works. She and Cindy stenciled most of the sweet bedrooms where quilts, crewel work and afghans abound. Named for native wildflowers, eight of the fourteen rooms in the main inn and a couple of cottages have private

Conservatory sitting area at Nauset House Inn.

bathrooms with showers. Diane painted a trompe-l'oeil cabinet on the wall of the Sea Oats Room to make it appear bigger. The biggest, the Beach Plum, has a kingsize bed and sofa with a crazy quilt on the wall.

Breakfast ($4.50 extra per person, $2.50 for continental) is served in the beamed, brick-floored dining room with its huge open hearth, looking for all the world like a British pub. Guests have so enjoyed Diane's unusual dishes (hardy sausage pie, potato casserole, strawberry frosty) that she has published the recipes in a small cookbook. We can attest to her veggie frittatas and raspberry pancakes.

The dining room separates the plush and comfortable living room, where guests congregate around the fire and play board games, from the fabulous Victorian glass conservatory, filled with wicker furniture and plants centered by a weeping cherry tree. The rhododendron and clematis were in bloom at one visit; at another, grapes from the vines garnished the breakfast plates.

Every afternoon around 5:30, Diane sets out hors d'oeuvre like guacamole, an olive-nut spread, or a cream-cheese and chutney spread with crackers for a BYOB happy hour. Guests write spirited reviews in a guest book called "Where Did You Eat and How Did You Like It?"

The inn is so comfy and the grounds so pretty that you might not want to leave, but Nauset Beach is nearby. Don't miss the shop out back where Diane sells her stained glass, painted furniture, picture frames, little boxes and other handicrafts.

Doubles, $55 to $95. Closed November-March.

The Captain's House Inn of Chatham, 371 Old Harbor Road, Chatham 02633. (508) 945-0127.

"We liked Chatham and particularly this inn," says Jan McMaster, new innkeeper with her husband David, a former California computer company CEO. They took over a going concern from David and Cathy Eakin, the founding innkeepers who transformed the 1839 house built by Captain Harding. The Eakins had freshened up the place with white eyelet-edged curtains, paint and polish, refinished all the wide-board pine floors and opened in 1983 to a full house. Repeat guests as well as the McMasters were wowed by the improvements and expansion that turned this into one of the few AAA four-diamond country inns in New England.

Set on two acres of green lawns and shrubbery in a residential section, the Captain's House is dignified and quiet. All sixteen guest rooms have private baths, French toiletries, pretty sheets, thick towels and comfortable chairs for reading. Many have canopy beds, and a few have fireplaces. Five ultra-deluxe rooms, a couple with beamed and peaked ceilings, have been fashioned from a rear carriage house. Another coveted room is in the 1930 Captain's Cottage, where the sumptuous suite looks like an English library with dark wood paneling, a working fireplace, plush sofa, wing chair, canopied four-poster and oriental rug.

Jan McMaster, faithful to her British background, serves a true English tea in the afternoons. She also has enlarged the breakfast offerings to include things like quiche, frittata and hot apple crunch along with the usual breads and fresh fruits. The McMasters added classical music, planned to enlarge the sunny dining porch, where linens and flowers adorn individual tables, and were setting out to make the gardens a focal point of the inn. "And that lawn was made for croquet," says Dave, who already added complimentary bicycles for guests to use. The McMasters are continuing the Eakins' tradition of staffing their inn with English students from the University of Bournemouth, which happens to be Jan's hometown. They also will continue to own their Fleur de Lys Inn and pub at Dorchester-on-Thames near Oxford.

Doubles, $125 to $195. Closed January to mid-February.

The Inn at Fernbrook, 481 Main St., Centerville 02632. (508) 775-4334.

Grounds landscaped by Fredrick Law Olmsted, a mansion where Cardinal Spellman entertained the cream of the crop, and breakfasts to savor — that's The Inn at Fernbrook, converted to an inn in 1987 by Brian Gallo and Sal DiFlorio. Add the fact that Sal is a professional massage therapist and has his practice at the inn and, well, you can expect a relaxing time.

Breakfast is "the best part," says Brian, who serves fruit courses of gingered rhubarb with egg cream, orange sections with sambuca or baked apples with rum. Maybe he'll bring out dutch babies with marmalade and powdered sugar, eggs benedict with homefries, brandied french toast, oatmeal pancakes or eggs goldenrod, which is creamed eggs with chipped beef. Irish sodabread or raisin-buttermilk scones might accompany, and the coffee is hazelnut.

Situated on gorgeous grounds (enjoy the heart-shaped Sweetheart Rose Garden and the little fish pond filled with Japanese koi), the Queen Anne Victorian offers five rooms and suites and a cathedral-ceilinged garden cottage. The Spellman Suite was a chapel when the Cardinal used the mansion, willed to the Diocese of New York by the previous owner, Dr. Herbert Kalmus, inventor of technicolor. It has a fireplace in the corner, a pyramid ceiling, stained-glass windows and a canopy bed. It's on the ground floor, with its own entrance. The Kalmus Suite is on two levels and is done in shades of blue, and the homey Marston Room affords a good view of the rose garden. On the third floor is the large Olmsted Suite, with two bedrooms, a living room with fireplace, walls of bookcases and a rooftop deck overlooking the duck ponds. Cream sherry awaits in each room.

Check out the collection of French porcelain bottles depicting soldiers of Napoleon in the Victorian parlor with its fine antiques, polished wood floors and oriental carpets. Then take your afternoon tea or lemonade to a wicker rocker on the side porch. Pretend you're Gloria Swanson (who was entertained here along with many other early Hollywood luminaries) and living the high life. For a while, it's possible.

Doubles, $115 to $135; Olmsted Suite, $185.

The Simmons Homestead Inn, 288 Scudder Ave., Hyannis Port 02647. (508) 778-4999 or (800) 637-1649.

"I can't abide empty spaces," says Bill Putman, who has filled every available space, and then some, at this winner of a B&B. Built by a sea captain, the restored country estate was acquired in 1988 by Bill, then recently widowed, and turned into a B&B of great personality.

Part of the personality comes from Bill, an outgoing, marketing type who proudly displays his varied collections throughout the house. But most comes from the inn and its furnishings. Start with the 32-foot-long living room, comfortable as can be and now a jungle of hanging plants as "the only empty spaces left are on the ceiling." The room is notable for all the brass birds on the mantel and inanimate wildlife everywhere, a remarkable tapestry of animals done by his first wife, and large parrots from Pavo Real. Parrots are a theme repeated in many rooms. For instance, they are on the chandeliers in the 20-by-40-foot dining room, which has a fantastic collection of mugs depicting different fruits to coordinate with the fruit du jour china. Here guests gather at two tables for a full breakfast with perhaps cheese omelets or blueberry pancakes. Bill does the cooking — "I learned quickly," says he, although he did defer once to a guest, Dinah Shore. He serves complimentary wine in the early evening on the breezy porches in summer and in front of the roaring fireplace in winter.

It is the ten guest rooms with private baths that are most unusual. Room 3, the elephant room, has a working fireplace and a queensize four-poster with a fishnet canopy. Its theme is elephants, and they are everywhere — inside the shutters, on the windows, on the mantel. Room 6 is the rabbit room, with a kingsize bed and bunnies all around. Room 7, Bill's concession to country decor, has a cherry four-poster bed and a country goose theme. It also serves as a transition to Room 8, which is simply wild: beneath the cathedral ceiling is a loft that's a jungle of plants and animals, including a purple rhinoceros. Animals are appliquéed all over the walls, the queensize bed is purple and the floor is painted green, but somehow it all works. Traditionalists might prefer the new rooms in the old servants' quarters. Room 10, the largest and brightest, has its own little patio bedecked with spirea. It's outfitted in white wicker with a kingsize bed and blue summery prints.

Bill, a former race-car driver, displays the hoods of his race car and Paul Newman's on the upstairs landing and racing photos in a long upstairs hallway. There's also a bulletin board with letters from guests, and a map with pins showing where guests have come from. Not to mention several plants adorned with tiny white lights. "I wanted to create a place where you feel at home," Bill says. Although it's not like any home we know, we'd be quite at home as guests.

Doubles, $85 to $130.

Mostly Hall, 27 Main St., Falmouth 02540. (508) 548-3786 or (800) 682-0565.

This 1849 house with the wraparound veranda looks as if it came right out of New Orleans. As a matter of fact, it was built by a sea captain as a wedding present for his bride from New Orleans, and is named for its extra-large hall. Innkeepers Caroline and Jim Lloyd say it got its name from a young child who entered the home and blurted, "why, Mama, it's mostly hall!"

Side porch overlooks Olmsted-designed grounds at Inn at Fernbrook.

Off that hall with a thirteen-foot-high ceiling are a guest room and a long living room with striped velvet sofas, oriental rugs and Victorian furnishings. The six refurbished corner guest rooms have private baths, queensize canopy four-posters and two comfortable chairs for reading.

An enclosed widow's walk with peach-colored walls, two comfortable arm chairs and a TV/VCR is a great retreat, from which you can see the gazebo out back.

Lemonade or tea are served in the living room or on the veranda, as is a full breakfast in the morning. Caroline might whip up cheese blintzes, muffins with warm blueberry sauce, eggs-benedict soufflé or stuffed french toast. She says she goes two weeks before repeating a recipe -- twenty of which are included in her cookbook, "Mostly Hall Breakfast at 9," now in its second printing after selling 1,000 copies. She also packs breakfasts to go for guests daytripping to Martha's Vineyard or Nantucket.

Doubles, $105. Closed January to mid-February. No smoking.

The Inn at West Falmouth, Box 1111, West Falmouth 02574. (508) 540-7696.

The outside is a typical large, shingled turn-of-the-century summer mansion nestled in cedar trees high up on Telegraph Hill off Blacksmith Shop Road, bordered with lush impatiens and yielding a distant view of Buzzards Bay. The inside is a stunner, one of the more smashingly decorated and luxurious inns we have encountered.

Opened in 1986 by Lewis Milarado of Middletown, Conn., this inn, which he likens to a small European hotel, is favored by corporate and wedding groups. It has a lot going for it — nine fabulous bedrooms, some with fireplaces and balconies, a clay tennis court, a small heated swimming pool enclosed by a wooden deck with smart lounging chairs, another large deck for gazing at the bay, a conservatory, a screened porch furnished in wicker, a wonderful living room filled with the latest books and sofas and nooks for reading, and a breakfast room with murals of parrots and a faux-marble floor. Add the incredible arrangements of flowers everywhere (from Lewis's extensive gardens in season; from Boston where he goes weekly in winter to bring them all back) and guest passes to one of the area's nicest beaches, and you have a nearly perfect place in which to get away from it all.

Walk up the grand staircase to the guest rooms on the second and third floors, past landings with topiary trees and plump pillows on the window seats. The spacious bedrooms are done in French, English and Oriental antiques, and each offers a jacuzzi tub in the bathroom. Comfortable sitting areas have good reading lamps. Some beds are draped with a colorful rainbow fabric, some have embroidered covers and about six eyelet-edged pillows, the floors are covered with gorgeous area rugs — it's all too sophisticated for words. On the fourth floor is a lookout with window seats and a telescope.

Lewis, who took the house apart and put it back together again during its restoration, serves a continental breakfast of juices, fresh fruit, croissants and muffins at tables for two set with white linens and Villeroy & Boch china in the attractive breakfast room. His decorating trademark is shells, which are everywhere you look. He serves dinner upon request to parties of four or more, $45 per person from appetizer to dessert. The menu is negotiable, he says. "I'll cook anything but Middle Eastern." He also specializes in small business meetings, which accounts for the inn's low profile.

The Inn at West Falmouth does not even have a sign to direct you to it (get directions from the innkeeper, who likes to keep things quiet and peaceful for his guests). It's perfect for a getaway in every sense of the word.

Doubles, $150 to $185; two-night minimum on weekends.

Gourmet Treats

The Cape is full of kitchen and specialty-food shops, along with every other type of shop imaginable. Among our favorites:

The Green Briar Jam Kitchen, 6 Discovery Road, East Sandwich. The first stop on the Cape might be this charmingly low-key place, where four paid cooks and many volunteers employ turn-of-the-century methods, to produce jams, continuing a tradition begun in 1903. You get to see the old wood stove that founder Ida Putnam started with, as well as probably the oldest solar-cooking operation in the country — the hot-house windows in which ingenious racks slide in and out to make the prized sun-cooked strawberries with vodka, as well as blueberries with kirsch. Of course, you get to watch — and smell — some of the 20,000 bottles of jams, chutneys and relishes as they are lovingly prepared for sale in the gift shop. You also see Thornton Burgess's framed, handwritten description of the Jam Kitchen in 1939: "It is a wonderful thing to sweeten the world which is in a jam and needs preserving." Adjacent to the kitchen is the **Green Briar Nature Center,** including the Old Briar Patch conservation area, home of Peter Rabbit and his animal friends. Kitchen open Monday-Saturday 10 to 4, Sunday 1 to 4; winter hours vary. Shop open Monday-Friday 9 to 4, year-round.

The **Lemon Tree Village** complex on Route 6A in Brewster is worth a visit. The **Lemon Tree Pottery** is full of interesting pottery and other crafts. The **Cook Shop** is a kaleidoscope of kitchen things, table linens, baskets and glassware.

Pranzo, with tables inside and out, is a great place for an interesting lunch. We enjoyed a grilled eggplant and mozzarella sandwich ($4.50) and a salad sampler (any three for $4.95) that yielded smoked turkey, curried rice with chicken, and Chinese noodles and vegetables. A raspberry square made for a tasty dessert.

The open-air showroom of **Scargo Stoneware Pottery** is quite a sight off Dr. Lord's Road South in Dennis. Harry Holl and his family have been producing the stunning stoneware for decorative and kitchen purposes since 1952. Harry, whose majestic bird feeders grace the back yards of some of our favorite B&Bs in the area, has been turning his hand to painting lately, while his four daughters and a son-in-law continue at the potter's kiln.

More gorgeous pottery, wine goblets of blown glass, jewelry, lamps, environment boxes and other works, all by American craftsmen, are offered at the **Artful Hand Gallery** at Main Street Square, Orleans. We gladly could have bought practically everything in the store.

If you like smoked fish or cheese, stop at the expanded **Sveden's Seafood** on Route 6A, Wellfleet (at the traffic light), where Ron and Nancy Sveden do the smoking. Their smoked-bluefish pâté makes a great nibble at cocktail time. They offer deli sandwiches as well as the usual range of fish and shellfish, plus marinated or stuffed mussels, lobster dip, chowder and lobster bisque base, seafood salad, Norwegian whole-grain bread, and homemade chocolate-chip/peanut-butter cookies. Nancy has at the ready a sheet of her recipes for cooking seafood.

In Wellfleet, **Hatch's Fish Market** has fresh herbs, homemade pesto, baby vegetables, fruit popsicles and smoked mussel pâté as well as every kind of fish imaginable, including a tray of sushi for $8.

The Chocolate Sparrow in North Eastham is where dietitian Marjorie Sparrow produces her luscious chocolates, penny candies, saltwater taffy and more. Now she has opened The Chocolate Sparrow Espresso, the quintessential coffee and candy shop along Route 6A at Lowell Square, Orleans. We stopped at the coffee bar here for fat-free cranberry muffins and a latte and watched touring families devouring the candies and terrific ice-cream concoctions, among them a raspberry-sorbet lime rickey and a frozen espresso shake.

Fancy's Farm Stand, 199 Main St., East Orleans, and Route 28, West Chatham, are the Cape's ultimate produce stands, purveying potpourris and wreaths (we coveted a huge one with all kinds of geese for $100), fancy cheeses and local jellies, baked goods and soups. You can make up a meal to go with, perhaps, kale and corn chowder, the offerings from an extensive salad bar, and a pastry or piece of pie.

Chatham Cookware, 524 Main St., Chatham, offers all kinds of kitchen items and colorful pottery as well as fine foods to eat in or to go. Proprietor Vera Lynne Champlin no longer gives cooking demonstrations in her open kitchen based on the one at La Varenne, but she and her staff certainly put out some delectable terrines, soups, salads, quiches and desserts. There are a few tables in a little pink room at the rear and on a side courtyard.

Art and Meredith Fancy's new **Cornfield Market** complex at 1297 Main St. in West Chatham is a gourmet haven for gourmets. **The Pampered Palate** is an excellent deli and gourmet foods shop. Owner Virginia Sharpe, who honed her cooking knowledge in Paris, offers all sorts of nifty foods to go, from pumpkin-pecan muffins to cranberry-glazed stuffed game hens. Fireworks coleslaw and fiesta corn are among the salads; cheese tortellini with sundried-tomato pesto is one of the pastas. Pick up a Queen Anne sandwich (avocado, smoked turkey and fresh tomato salsa on a whole-wheat baguette, $4.95) and a slice of orange yogurt cake for a super picnic. Supplement this fare with impeccable produce from the large **Fancy's** farm market, the all-natural baked goods and sweets at **Cookies and Creams** or the extensive selection at **Chatham Fish and Lobster** next door and you have the makings for a great party.

Located upstairs at the Cornfield, **Chatham Winery** offers tastings of its interesting fruit wines, such as cranberry mead, red currant and belle of Georgia peach, an award-winning dessert wine. At our latest visit, Glenn and Susan Smith-Elion were singing the praises of their Midnight Blues, a $9 blend of red grapes and blueberries, which had just won a silver medal in an international wine competition in Toronto. Their 30 wines are priced from $7 to $10. The Chatham blush comes in a bottle shaped like a lobster.

Stop in Hyannis at **Virgie's Deli/Barnstable Grocery** in the Village Market Place at North and Steven streets. It's a wonderful gourmet grocery, displaying lots of good salads and sandwiches, ham and swiss croissants, dozens of cheeses and even devonshire cream from England. There are a couple of tables for partaking. We love the smells here, from jars of herbs and coffee beans for grinding to bins of candies and nuts.

La Petite France at 207 North St. in Hyannis lives up to its name. The aromas of fresh breads nearly overpower, as Lucien DeGioanni turns his little bakery and cafe into a haven for francophiles. The blackboard lists the day's soups, salads and sandwiches. We lunched splendidly on a sandwich of tuna salad with poppyseeds and a cup of chowder and half a chicken-salad sandwich with walnuts and raisins, each $3.75 and served with good little side salads. Ebullient Lucien proudly displays a thank-you letter from the pastry chef at the White House to "one of the best French bakers and baker oven engineers." He'd been called in just before the Clinton inauguration to set up a bakery oven, a skill he had plied for a manufacturer when he came to this country a decade ago. He makes up for his out-of-the-way location in One Financial Place by purveying top quality and a French joie de vivre that's contagious.

Do you think, as we do, that Cape Cod potato chips are absolutely the best? Then stop in Hyannis at their place of origin, **The Cape Cod Potato Chip Co.,** Breed's Hill Road, in an industrial park area off Route 132. There's an informative, self-guided tour of the plant, which evolved from Steve and Lynn Bernard's storefront kitchen that started in 1980 producing 200 bags of Cape Cod Potato Chips a day. Still hand-cooking their chips in kettles one batch at a time, they produce 80,000 bags a day and go through 48 million pounds of potatoes a year. This is big business, and we were surprised by the number of people touring on a summer day. You can pick up samples as well as buy more in the gift shop at tour's end.

Our favorite shop for browsing at the Cape is **Tree's Place,** Route 6A at 28, Orleans. An art gallery, a tilery (the largest selection of designer tiles in the country, they say) and a gift shop occupy several rooms filled with such diverse items as Russian lacquer boxes, jewelry, Swiss musical paper weights, Hadley stoneware, Salt Marsh Pottery, carved birds — even tartan ties. We love the biscuit baskets of glazed stoneware made by Eucalyptus Pottery in California. You can choose any of the tiles to be framed for use as a trivet. One of us could spend hours mooching around here, but the other always says that it's time to be moving on.

Table at Straight Wharf Restaurant overlooks Nantucket harbor.

Nantucket

The Ultimate Indulgence for Gourmets

For an off-shore island with a year-round population of 6,000 (augmented by up to 40,000 high-livers and free-spenders in the summer), Nantucket has an uncommon concentration of uncommonly good restaurants.

Ever since French chef Jean-Charles Berruet took over the rose-covered Chanticleer Inn in the hamlet of Siasconset in 1969, knowledgeable diners have been flocking to Nantucket in droves. Other restaurateurs and culinary businesses have followed.

"I don't know of another resort area that can beat Nantucket for good restaurants per square mile," says Neal Grennan, chef-owner of Le Languedoc.

Given its small size and island remoteness, "it's amazing," adds Chick Walsh, owner-manager of the highly acclaimed 21 Federal, who started as mâitre-d' at the old Opera House restaurant in 1970 when it was the only game in town. "When I first arrived here, we couldn't have had a restaurant like this. We used to have difficulty flying in Haagen-Dazs ice cream. Now, fancy food products are at our doorstep, and we make ice cream ourselves. Twenty-five years ago, the local population wouldn't have supported this restaurant, and now they do. The whole food awareness has changed."

Indeed it has. The island now has a dozen superior restaurants, another dozen good ones, and countless more of the pedestrian variety.

At one of our visits, two cookbooks by Nantucket chefs had just been published and another was in the works. And the 21 Federal restaurant had opened a "branch" in Washington, D.C., leaving its culinary mark on the mainland.

What other seaside resort dines so fashionably late? Many restaurants don't open for dinner until 6:30 or 7 — the 4:30 early-bird specials of Cape Cod don't play here. Dining is an event and a pricey one, given local chefs' preoccupation with fresh and exotic ingredients, their island location and a captive, affluent audience.

We have friends who vacation at Nantucket for a month every summer, eating out almost every night, and relishing every minute of the ultimate gustatory experience. Book a room, reserve the ferry or an airplane seat, bring your wallet and indulge in the gourmet splendors of Nantucket yourself.

Dining

The Best of the Best

The Chanticleer Inn, 40 New St., Siasconset. (508) 257-6231.

Lunch in the rose garden is a local tradition, as is an after-dinner drink in the old Chantey Bar, lately rechristened the **Grill Room.** But the four-course dinners and the extraordinary wine cellar are what draw the knowing from hither and yon to the world-class restaurant generated by Jean-Charles Berruet since he took over in 1969.

Prix-fixe dinners are $60 "and worth every penny," all kinds of fans had told us. The setting, the service and the food could not be more perfect, which is exactly the way Jean-Charles wants it.

You are greeted at the door and directed to your table: in the sought-after, formal main-floor dining room with a fireplace at the end and a greenhouse on one side (rather brightly illuminated, we thought — the better to see and be seen, perhaps?), or in the convivial, informal grill (a bit too bistro-ish, we felt, considering the tab), or in the upstairs dining room to which we were assigned, serene in peach and white and dim enough to be just right.

The complex, complicated French menu and the endless wine list are so staggering that both first-timers and knowing regulars put themselves in the hands of a solicitous, knowledgeable staff to help with their selections. Easier to decipher are the grill menu (available only in the grill on a first-come basis, and the room fills up early with regular patrons) and the three-course light-cuisine menu, a small selection of three courses for $50.

We, like most, chose to go the prix-fixe route. A tiny cheese gougère was served with drinks, "compliments of the chef." For starters, one of us had Nantucket oysters served in a warm mussel broth topped with American sturgeon caviar (a small portion, but ever so delicious). The other had lobster and sole sausage poached with a puree of sweet red peppers (ever so presented, but super).

From a choice of twelve entrées (all of which we gladly could have sampled), we decided on the Nantucket-raised pheasant, stuffed with mushrooms, herbs and ricotta, and the roasted tenderloin of lamb served with a venison sauce. A triangle of potato pancake, spinach and ratatouille niçoise accompanied. The salad of greens with two kinds of cheeses that followed was unwieldy to eat because the leaves were too large.

For dessert, the assortment of fresh sorbets was a pretty plate of small scoops interspersed with fresh fruit on a raspberry sauce. Creole-style lime meringue pie was an ethereal second choice. Over demitasses of decaf and espresso, we savored an experience that ranks with the ultimate in fine dining.

Not that it's for everyone. Without background music, the atmosphere is hushed until the room fills up. The tastes are complex and the portions small. The prices are steep (à la carte, appetizers, $19 to $35; entrées, $25 to $35; desserts, $15 to $20, and wines, $20 to $400). Riffling through the thousand selections on the

Chef Jean-Charles Berruet takes break outside Chanticleer Inn.

wine list — winner of Wine Spectator's Grand Award — is so mind-boggling that you're apt to ask the waiter to make the decision for you, and he'll likely choose on the high side.

And yet, young and old alike go back time after time, such is the spell of the Chanticleer and the output of the energetic owner and his kitchen staff of eleven. Jean-Charles proudly showed us his expansive facility, including a big walk-in cooler in back. "You can tell how good a kitchen is by the condition of its cooler," said he; his was organized and spotless.

If you can't get in for dinner (tables are booked far in advance), splurge for lunch in the garden, beneath trellised canopies of roses and surrounded by impeccably manicured hedges. Entrées are $15 to $20, and you might try lobster en croûte with arborio risotto, a mousse of eel and salmon rolled in a crêpe, or scrambled eggs put back in the shell and topped with sevruga caviar, garnished with a puree of potatoes with olive oil.

If you can't get there for a meal, pick up some of the delicacies at **Chanticleer to Go,** the in-town gourmet shop run by the chef's daughter, Nathalie. Or you might buy a copy of Jean-Charles's beautiful cookbook, *Here's to Nantucket: Recipes for the Good Life and Great Food.* This could be the slogan for all Nantucket. And Jean-Charles certainly knows the recipes.

Lunch, noon to 2 in summer; dinner, 6:30 to 9:30. Closed Wednesday. Open late May to mid-October. Reservations and jackets required.

21 Federal, 21 Federal St., Nantucket. (508) 228-2121.

If Chanticleer is the venerable old-timer, 21 Federal is the acclaimed newcomer. It did so well that only two years after opening in 1985 it added a second establishment in Washington, D.C. Executive chef Bob Kinkead was dispatched to the D.C. operation, called 21 Federal as well, which consistently won high ratings in the nation's capital until it closed in 1993 and reopened as Kinkead's in a new Foggy Bottom location.

Owner-manager Chick Walsh runs a tight ship back on the island. Known for its new American grill cuisine, 21 Federal presents a limited menu, but one that's compelling and not in the vanguard of Nantucket's high prices. There are six intimate dining rooms — some with their white-linened tables rather close together — on two floors of museum-quality, Federal period decor. In summer, lunch is served on a nifty outdoor courtyard ringed with impatiens, where tables are topped by herbs in clay pots and classical music wafts across the scene.

Our courtyard lunch arrived on in large wicker trays on white-linened tables. The pheasant and wild rice soup of the day ($5.50) was sublime, as was the linguini salad with shrimp and pinenuts ($10.50). The five-salad sampler ($9.50) was less interesting, the chicken with green salsa and oriental noodles outshining the ratatouille and the eggplant, which were a bit too much of the same thing. Calvados ice cream and an intense pineapple-mint sorbet served with wonderful small coconut or lemon squares topped off a flavorful meal.

Chef Michael Getter changes the short dinner menu daily. For openers ($9 to $14), you might start with lobster and corn bisque with brioche crostini, wild-mushroom risotto with roasted garlic, Texas prawns with lobster oil and coral, Hudson valley foie gras with champagne grapes or the signature parma ham with arugula, parmesan cheese and balsamic vinegar.

Entrées ($18 to $28) could be grilled swordfish with poblano pesto and grilled corn salsa, soft-shell crabs with Chinese black-bean sauce, spit-roasted chicken with fresh figs and mashed potatoes, and charred leg of lamb with rosemary polenta and eggplant tapenade. A cafe-bistro menu offers a handful of lighter selections at much lighter prices in the off-season. Dessert ($6) might be a Georgia peach cobbler with praline anglaise, apple tarte tatin with cider sabayon, chocolate oblivion torte or cinnamon crème caramel with plum sauce. The fare changes with the seasons, but always appeals and asserts.

Lunch daily, 11:30 to 2:30; dinner, 6 to 10. Open April-December.

The Second Story, 1 South Beach St., Nantucket. (508) 228-3471.

Still more assertive fare — a couple of local fans allow as how some think it's outrageous — is doled out by chef-proprietor David Toole in his second-floor walkup across from the harbor. The space, done up in Nantucket pink and green, is illuminated entirely by candles in enormous hurricane chimneys.

The setting could not be more romantic and the menu, which changes nightly, is the kind on which everything appeals, influenced by regional cuisines from around the world, including Thai, Vietnamese, French and Italian. Starters ($9 and $10) might be grilled shrimp and cucumber soup with coriander, salmon stir-fried with sorrel and mustard and served over fried wontons, warm lobster pâté with sautéed spinach and a goat-cheese bruschetta, grilled oysters with a zesty catalan salsa, and rice noodles tossed with duck, shrimp, spinach, mushrooms and peanuts in a curry-lime-basil vinaigrette.

Entrées ($17 to $24) include peppered tuna grilled with a horseradish and sundried-tomato vinaigrette, sautéed duckling with sweet and sour grapefruit-shallot sauce, grilled pork tenderloin with a pecan compote and cheddar mashed potatoes, and lobster and black-bean enchilada with a goat-cheese and cilantro sauce.

We can vouch for the hot country pâté (a huge slab of goose, duck, chicken and sausage), served piping hot and bathed in a creamy green-peppercorn sauce; the scallops au gratin with tomato, avocado, garlic and cream, and the Thai shrimp with black-bean and coriander sauce, so spicy that it left the mouth smoldering long into the night.

Setting is elegant in dining rooms at 21 Federal.

Our amaretto soufflé turned out neither hot nor cold, but more like a mousse with a hint of amaretto. Other tempting desserts ($7) were grand-marnier crème caramel, pumpkin-ginger spice cake with vanilla ice cream and spiced wine sauce, and an Asian napoleon (layers of fried wontons with a citrus pastry cream, fruit and a ginger-raspberry sauce).

Dinner nightly except Monday, seatings at 7 and 9:15; Sunday brunch and lunch seasonally. Open April-December. No smoking.

American Seasons, 80 Centre St., Nantucket. (508) 228-7111.

Upstaging many Nantucket restaurants lately has been this small newcomer, opened by brothers Stuart and Everett G. Reid III in 1988 and now run by Everett and his wife, Linda Bridges. It's off the beaten path, but a find for those who want distinguished, ever-changing regional cuisine at affordable prices.

A Culinary Institute of America graduate who had worked in Boston, New York at the Summer House in Siasconset. Everett does the cooking with the help of eleven assistants, while Linda oversees the front of the house and the fascinating all-American wine list, which has won Wine Spectator awards.

The couple recently redecorated their 50-seat dining room, adding high-backed banquettes as room dividers and polyurethaned tables whose tops are game boards. A local artist painted the table tops as well as a stunning wall mural that portrays what we thought to be the Napa valley but turned out to be a hillside in Oregon. A couple of dim wall sconces and candlelight provide illumination.

As our meal unfolded, we discovered why people had told us that the presentations were so striking and that every plate was different. It turned out it wasn't the plates (most are white) but the decorative garnishes on the rims that made them look different.

Interestingly, the menu is categorized by four regions -- Pacific Coast, Wild West, New England and Down South -- each with two or three appetizers and entrées. You're supposed to mix and match, pairing, say, a New Orleans oyster loaf with fried collard greens and bayou slaw ($7.50) with a New England sandwich of goat cheese, roast eggplant, tomatoes and watercress dressing ($8). One of us happily made a dinner of three first courses: a bowl of smooth, chilled tomato and leek soup with herb brioche croutons and goat cheese, with sprinkles of parsley on the accompanying plate. This was followed by lobster and black-bean hash with a poached egg and spicy ketchup, the plate decorated with stripes of red pepper puree interspersed with specks of green herbs. Then came an interesting salad of wild greens, smoked cheddar and crab meat, decorated with carrots, green onions, celery and more. The other diner had wild-mushroom and tomato pasta with garlic, olive oil and Pacific manila clams ($16). Two long strips of chives were crossed on top of the pasta, which entered the annals as one of the most powerful-tasting ever. A side dish of crisp carrots, zucchini, beets, summer squash, turnips and a section of corn on the cob accompanied.

We shared a dessert of raspberry-mango shortcake with raspberry coulis, presented artistically with fresh fruit on a square plate decorated with squiggles of chocolate and crème anglaise. Other choices included chocolate devil's food cake with hazelnut buttercream, chocolate banana tart with fresh strawberries, and cinnamon-pecan pie with vanilla-rum ice cream.

All but two entrées were priced in the teens, grilled Texas venison with a whiskey barbecue sauce ($22) and grilled veal chop with goat-cheese potato croquettes ($26) being the exceptions. Other possibilities included grilled West Coast tuna with pesto and black olives, Yankee pot roast with creamed horseradish and parsley potatoes, fried trout with a sauce of smoked tomatoes, shrimp and green onions, and grilled Maine salmon with a fennel and lobster sauce and black-olive risotto.

Dinner nightly, 6 to 10, April to January. Closed Wednesday in off-season.

Le Languedoc, 24 Broad St., Nantucket. (508) 228-2552.

After a brief stint with a hired chef, longtime chef-owner Neal Grennan is back in the kitchen, where he can keep better rein on what he admits are Nantucket's steep prices and where he produced one of our best meals in Nantucket a few years back.

An autumn dinner began with an appetizer of smoked Nantucket pheasant with cranberry relish, very good and very colorful with red cabbage and slices of apples and oranges on a bed of lettuce. For entrées ($19.75 to $28.50), one of us tried the noisettes of lamb with artichokes in a rosemary sauce and the other enjoyed sautéed sweetbreads and lobster in puff pastry. Nicely presented on piping-hot white oval plates, they were accompanied by snow peas, broccoli, pureed turnips, yellow peppers, sweet potatoes and peach slices. We ended with a dense chocolate-hazelnut torte spiked with grand marnier.

Recently, we liked the sound of cream of crab soup, a seafood phyllo bundle with lemon chèvre and smoked-corn confetti, and sautéed Catskill foie gras with orange marmalade and grilled potato bread, followed by fennel-crusted salmon with spaghetti squash and savoy salad, truffled loin of rabbit with sundried cherries and roast rack of lamb with a white-bean ragout.

The dessert list included banana-butterscotch meringue tart with caramel drizzle, vanilla crème brûlée and three-chocolate terrine with praline chantilly.

These treats are served in four small upstairs dining rooms amid peach walls and white trim, windows covered with peach draperies and valances, and changing art from a local gallery. Windsor chairs are at well-spaced tables topped by candles in hurricane lamps and vases, each containing a salmon-hued rose.

The downstairs has a small pub-like dining room with checkered cloths. Off

Local artist painted mural and table tops at American Seasons.

the side entrance is a canopied terrace for summer lunches. Everyone loves the cafe menu, from which you can dine very well for under $15.50; perhaps on a pork quesadilla with black beans or lobster-scallion hash on a bed of fresh corn.

Lunch, 11:30 to 2:30; dinner nightly, 6:30 to 10. Open mid-April through January.

The Boarding House, 12 Federal St., Nantucket. (508) 228-9622.

When it opened in 1973, the Boarding House was the summer's success story and provided our first great meal on Nantucket. It since has moved around the corner to considerably larger quarters, and several owners (and chefs) have come and gone. It's better than ever lately, having been taken over by Seth and Angela Raynor, he a former sous chef at 21 Federal and both having worked at the Chanticleer.

A beauty it is, its cathedral-ceilinged Victorian lounge with small faux-marble tables on a flagstone floor opening into a sunken dining room. The latter is striking as can be in rich cream and pink, with a curved banquette at the far end in front of a mural of Vernazzia, a culinary destination featured in Gourmet magazine the month after the mural went up. The Raynors own the originals but sell lithographs of the exclusive Nantucket series "Streets of Paris," which hangs on the walls. Villeroy & Boch china of the Florida pattern graces the nicely spaced tables, which allow for one of Nantucket's more pleasant dining situations.

Equal to the lovely setting is the cooking of Seth, who said he was "honored but amazed" to be chosen one of 30 chefs to appear on the Great Chefs of the East television series only nine months after opening his restaurant in 1992. We certainly liked our latest dinner here: mellow sautéed crab cakes with scallion crème fraîche and grilled quail with crisp fried onion rings and baby mixed greens, among starters from $6 to $9, and pan-roasted salmon with Thai curried cream and crispy rice noodles and a spicy Asian seafood stew with lobster, shrimp and scallops, among entrées from $19 to $26.50. Accompanying was a powerful

Caymus sauvignon blanc ($19) from a well-chosen wine selection with less than the normal Nantucket price markup. Coffee ice cream with chocolate sauce and a dense chocolate-kahlua terrine were worthy endings. Other starters included a tempura of haricots verts with parmesan dipping sauce, lacquered shrimp with Thai pesto noodles, and warm lobster and duck salad with goat cheese, pinenuts and truffle-oil vinaigrette. Signature main dishes are grilled lobster tails, grilled swordfish with lemon-basil aioli and olive-oil mashed potatoes, and grilled tenderloin with thyme jus and a wild-mushroom potato gratin.

The outdoor terrace is appealing for a bistro lunch and drinks. We've also found it a felicitous setting for an after-dinner liqueur while watching the late-night parade pass by.

Lunch daily in summer, noon to 2; dinner nightly, 6 to 10. Closed mid-October to mid-November. No smoking.

Straight Wharf Restaurant, Straight Wharf, Nantucket. (508) 228-4499.

Chef Marian Morash of television and cookbook fame put this summery restaurant on the culinary map. She left in 1987 to finish a seafood cookbook, but the menu style and the spiffy decor remained the same.

The interior is a pristine palette of shiny floors and soaring, shingled walls topped by billowing banners. The banners are the work of Elaine Gifford, owner with husband Jack, and the striking paintings are the work of an island artist.

We wish that the June night we dined had been warm enough to eat outside on the canopied, rib-lit deck beside the water, that the service had been more prompt, and that the acclaimed vegetables were more exciting than plainly cooked broccoli and carrots. But the complimentary bluefish pâté with drinks, the grilled salmon with tarragon-mustard sauce and the lobster crêpes were first-rate, the peach bavarian laden with raspberry sauce was outstanding and, a nice touch, the elaborately written bill came with two chocolate shells.

More recently, lobster and fish cakes with tomato-basil beurre blanc, Malpeque oysters with mignonette sauce and pan-fried shrimp wontons were among the starters ($7 to $10). Entrées ranged from $22.50 for pan-fried tuna with wasabi crème fraîche and pickled ginger to $28 for a two-pound steamed lobster. Besides other seafood choices, roast rack of lamb with roasted garlic and grilled tenderloin with pearl onions and saga blue sauce were offered. Chocolate soufflé cake with vanilla crème anglaise, fresh fruit tartlet and melon, kiwi and berries with blackberry cream and cookies are favored desserts ($6).

The bar menu, served from 7 to 10, is very popular (there's apt to be a long wait to get in, and the bar is noisy). It yields some of the same appetizers and desserts as the dining room plus five entrées "from the grill" at half the price, like broiled salmon with pesto pasta salad and goat cheese, grilled lemon shrimp and grilled leg of lamb with new potatoes, asparagus and roasted garlic.

The wine list is a pricey indulgence, mainly American but with the standard imports and even a sauvignon blanc from Israel.

Dinner nightly except Monday by reservation, seatings at 6:45 and 9:15. Open mid-June to mid-September. Bar open to mid-October; no reservations.

Company of the Cauldron, 7 India St., Nantucket. (508) 228-4016.

The former quarters of the Boarding House lately have been occupied by this intimate little restaurant, in which the night's prix-fixe menu is posted outside the door about 9 a.m. and patrons make reservations for the nightly seatings and take what's served, which is reputed to be excellent.

Archways and mural evoke Mediterranean feeling at Boarding House.

Behind a wrought-iron shelf divider laden with flowers at the entry are a number of small tables rather close together, colorful with a mix of pink and green floral mats and overcloths atop white linens or bare wood. Copper pots, cauldrons and ship's models hang from the stucco walls, and it's all very dark and romantic.

A typical dinner ($38) brings wild mushroom and brie soup with fresh thyme, Nantucket greens with red and yellow cherry tomatoes and shallot-dill vinaigrette, almond-hazelnut crusted salmon with lime beurre blanc, scallion rice and snow peas, and lemon bread pudding with blueberry sauce. Another could be lobster ravioli, green salad with chive croutons, grilled loin lamb chops with roasted garlic and fresh mint sauce, black-olive polenta and asparagus, and orange crème brûlée. The small but select wine list is rationally priced.

Dinner nightly; seatings at 7:30, or at 7 and 9:15 on busy nights. Open Memorial Day to Columbus Day.

The Club Car, 1 Main St., Nantucket. (508) 228-1101.

Creative chef Michael Shannon is a local institution at this sumptuous establishment entered through a red train car used as a lounge (open from noon and lately the scene of sandwich lunches — ham or turkey on Portuguese bread) and a lively piano bar. Beyond is an expansive dining room of white-over-red-linened tables topped by enormous wine globes, upholstered cane-back chairs, an array of large artworks and a colorful shelf of copper pans.

The menu, which changes often, has traditionally ranked as the town's priciest. Appetizers start at $8.50 for sautéed calves brains with tomato concasse and go to $22.50 for fresh New York State foie gras. Grilled quail with fried polenta, cold Nantucket lobster with asparagus flan and "squid in the style of Bangkok" are among the possibilities.

Entrée prices have been lowered since our previous visits. Lately they ranged from $17.50 for veal kidneys and mushrooms stir-fried with rice and spinach greens to $30 for grilled sirloin bordelaise with fried shallots. Other choices might be grilled swordfish with citrus vinaigrette and fried spaëtzle, shrimp scampi provençal and veal sweetbreads with belgian endive.

Finish with one of a dozen desserts, perhaps fresh berries with devonshire cream, crème brûlée or chocolate-mousse cake with creme anglaise.

Dinner nightly, 6 to 10. Open Memorial Day to mid-October.

The Beach Plum Cafe, 11 West Creek Road, Nantucket. (508) 228-8893.

Just what the doctor ordered for Nantucket's surfeit of pricey restaurants is this casual new cafe, where the food sparkles and the prices make you think the island does have a middle class, after all. Owned by Jack Gifford, it started as a bakery for his various Straight Wharf enterprises, but was put on the dinner map by CIA-trained chef Jean Dion, a Cape Codder who formerly was at Chillingsworth and the Boca Raton Hotel and Club.

That's quite a background for a chef at an unpretentious little cafe on a residential side street at the southern edge of town. The plain wood tables are nicely spaced and bear green tea towels as napkins and perhaps a vase of alstroemeria and a candle.

Service was as casual as the decor, but we were rewarded with what Jean called his "upscale food at low-end cost." Exceptional were two appetizers, the ravioli of the evening ($6.50) with feta cheese, sweet peppers and a fabulous sauce of chutney and tomato beurre blanc, and sautéed veal sweetbreads ($7.75) with leeks, mushrooms and cognac in puff pastry. Among entrées ($12.95 to $14.95), we liked the mildly spicy peppered flank steak and the pan-seared loin of lamb with roasted shallot and rosemary sauce. Both came with the Beach Plum's trademark potatoes, sliced and baked in olive oil in a convection oven, plus snow peas and fresh-off-the-cob island corn. Very crusty, hot bread with a crock of butter preceded. A bottle of the house red (one of our favorites, Heitz Cellar's Ryan's Red for $14) accompanied.

Although this is a bakery and the desserts are said to be stellar, most offerings were gone that night and we weren't tempted by anything as mundane as blueberry pie. But even without dessert, lighting a bit too bright and recorded music too loud for middle-aged ears, we'd gladly go back again and again.

Feather-light buckwheat pancakes with wild blueberries, walnut-apple french toast made from baguettes and Mexican omelets are featured at breakfast.

Breakfast, Monday-Friday 7 to 11, Saturday to 12:30; dinner nightly, 6 to 9; lunch in fall and winter; Sunday brunch. No reservations.

Cioppino's, 20 Broad St., Nantucket. (508) 228-4622.

This house in the heart of the town's restaurant district has been home to many an eatery. Its latest incarnation by Tracy and Susan Root (he the mâitre-d' at Chanticleer and she a bartender at the Summer House) raised the hopes of fans that it might endure.

Dining is in a couple of small rooms on the main floor, pretty in white, black and mauve. Upstairs are larger rooms, one with a skylit peaked ceiling and a stunning mural of what looks to be a Monet's Garden by a Nantucket artist. In season you can dine at umbrellaed tables on the rear patio.

At a September lunch, the special fried oysters with béarnaise sauce ($9) was a nouvelle presentation with rice, broccoli, strained zucchini and swirled yellow squash. Also excellent was the caribbean shrimp and avocado salad ($8.75). Good sourdough rolls came first; a mellow key lime pie was the finale. The folks at the next table were exclaiming over the soup and half a sandwich ($7.50 for conch chowder and roast beef with boursin) and the shrimp, tomato and mozzarella pizzetta ($10.50). On our way out, we paused to look at the wine labels inlaid in the bar, representing only a few of the owner's collection of 12,000 labels.

At dinner, a three-course prix-fixe menu ($34) changes every two weeks. We would gladly have sampled the seared raw tuna miso, the roast stuffed pheasant with mushroom and chestnut mousse and the chocolate-truffle terrine with mango coulis offered at our visit. There's also an à-la-carte menu, priced from $17 for oven-roasted chicken with lemon and fresh herbs to $25.50 for tournedos of beef with Maine lobster or roast rack of lamb with mint and rosemary sauce. Hazelnut-crusted fillet of salmon, braised rabbit and San Francisco cioppino also appealed. Start with sautéed scallops niçoise or a marinated conch salad. Finish with warm pecan pie with bourbon ice cream or the chocolate-kahlua fantasy cake.

Lunch daily, 11:30 to 2:30; dinner nightly from 5:30; Sunday brunch. Open May-October.

India House, 37 India St., Nantucket. (508) 228-9043.

The Sunday garden brunches are legendary, but this 1803 house with two small, candlelit dining rooms is praised for dinner fare as well.

You might start with lobster-artichoke crêpe, a trio of seafood cakes with three sauces or carpaccio of fish with a quail egg. Entrées are priced from $14 for wild Russian boar ribs with grilled-pineapple barbecue sauce to $23 for tournedos of beef singapore with ginger and sake. Planked swordfish with cashew-pecan glaze and lime beurre blanc and lamb with dijon and red rose mint sauce are house specialties. Dessert could be a sweet-potato/pecan pie, autumn harvest cake or fresh raspberry soufflé.

The Sunday brunch ($9.95) involves seven choices from eggs benedict to grilled tenderloin of pork with bourbon apples and herbed scrambled eggs.

The daily breakfasts here are not to be overlooked. The prix-fixe menu yields fresh orange juice, homemade fruit breads and muffins, beverage and a choice of eggs benedict, fruit pancakes, Mexican omelet or a fruit boboli breakfast pizza.

On warm nights when the old house can get steamy, many patrons prefer the outdoor garden cafe.

Breakfast, Monday-Saturday 8:30 to 10:30; dinner nightly, 6:30 to 9:30; Sunday brunch, 9 to 1.

American Bounty Restaurant, 60 Union St., Nantucket. (508) 228-3886.

CIA-trained chef Philip Aviles, who worked at the Waldorf and yacht clubs around New York City, took over the leased restaurant operation in the Tuckernut Inn and launched a short but exciting menu.

His initial 1993 offering featured such starters ($4 to $7) as smoked corn and mussel chowder, rock shrimp sandwiches in crisp potato crusts, grilled smoked quail with horseradish crème fraîche and grilled medallions of goat cheese and sundried tomatoes. Main courses ($15 to $20) included pan-seared salmon with horseradish crust, salmon roe and warm cucumber crème fraîche; grilled shrimp with crostini of red-pepper polenta and smoked roasted-tomato coulis, and roasted filet of veal with smoked quail and lobster sausages. Among desserts were tirami su, chocolate torte and a light chocolate mousse wrapped in a crêpe with butterscotch sauce. The wine list is as well-chosen as the rest of the fare.

The dining room, despite its name, looks like a country French bistro. It's unusually colorful with light pink tablecloths, striking prints on the walls and floral fabrics on the valances that match the backs of the chairs and of the unusual four-seat benches acquired from a salvage company.

Dinner, Tuesday-Sunday 5:30 to 9:30. Open April through Christmas Stroll.

The Woodbox, 29 Fair St., Nantucket. (508) 228-0587.

Nantucket's oldest inn (1709) provides atmospheric meals in three of the town's oldest dining rooms that bear the patina of age. Pine-paneled walls, low beamed ceilings and brass candlesticks are the norm; the rear room fashioned from the original kitchen adds an open hearth. White quilted mats, candles in hurricane lamps and a fresh rose grace every table. No wonder the Woodbox was voted "most romantic" for dining on the island.

Chef Joseph Keller offers a short but traditional menu. You might start with smoked lox with horseradish mustard sauce or a goat-cheese tart with kalamata olives and sundried tomatoes. For the main course ($17.50 to $24.50), how about scampi with sherry-mustard-tarragon sauce, grilled quail, veal chop, rack of lamb provençal or, the house specialty, beef wellington? Dessert could be crème brûlée, bananas foster or fruit crumb cake.

Dinner, Tuesday-Sunday, seatings at 6:45 and 9, Thursday-Saturday in off-season. Closed January to Memorial Day.

Other Dining Choices

Even the most confirmed Nantucket gourmet must tire of fancy, high-priced meals. Luckily, the island has other possibilities, among them:

Black-Eyed Susan's, 10 India St., Nantucket. No phone.

Some of the talk about dining in Nantucket in 1993 focused on Black Eyed Susan's, a small storefront run by partners Susan Handy and chef Jeff Worster, both with long backgrounds in local restaurants, the most recent being the Summer House. The space was formerly a breakfast bar, said Susan, and "all we had to do was clean it up." They still serve breakfast, probably a bit more fancy than before, with the likes of sourdough french toast with orange Jack Daniels butter and pecans ($4.50) and a spicy Thai curry scramble with broccoli and new potatoes. Most dishes come with a choice of hash browns or blackeyed peas, and you can add garlic, cilantro and/or salsa to your omelet for 50 cents each.

From his open kitchen behind the counter, Jeff, a chef-taught chef with experience in Los Angeles, where he got a lot of his creative ideas, offers such pasta dishes as wild-mushroom ravioli on carrot-ginger puree with organic greens and romano cheese ($14.95, or $9.95 for a half order). Moroccan lamb stew on minted couscous, poppyseed-seared salmon on parmesan mashed potatoes and oyster gumbo were a few of the intriguing dishes (all $13.95) on his fall dinner menu, and we liked the sound of lemon-parsnip soup with peppered grilled tomato. Lighter eaters could order a huge hearts of romaine salad with caesar dressing (a whole head of romaine, says Susan) for $7. There's one dessert a night, perhaps a cobbler or bread pudding.

For dinner, there's a social, European cafe atmosphere, and singles love to eat at the long bar. Summer diners face waits of more than an hour; says Susan; "you put your name in and then go off and have a cocktail somewhere." She added that the idea was to be here for the local population more than for the tourists, but the word has gotten out.

Breakfast daily, 6:30 to 1 or 2; dinner, 6 to 10. No smoking. No credit cards. BYOB. Closed six weeks in winter.

The Morning Glory Cafe, 14 Old South Wharf, Nantucket. (508) 228-2212.

The wharf patio is where everyone who is anyone seems to gather for breakfast to exchange gossip from the night before. They sit at tables that have blue and white cloths painted on them and wake up with good strong coffee and Morning

Glory muffins, made from carrots, raisins, nuts, apples and coconut — everything but the kitchen sink, says owner Liz Gracia. All kinds of fruit pancakes and fancy egg dishes also are popular.

Inside, Liz works in an open kitchen beside a small cafe with striking trompe-l'oeil paintings on the walls, done by an artist neighbor. Lunch brings tarragon-chicken and smoked turkey caesar salads, quiche, sandwiches and pizzas with unusual toppings like beef teriyaki and Chinese mushrooms, or clams and artichokes, from $6.95 to $9.95. Dinner entrées change weekly: half a dozen offerings from wonton lasagna to Szechuan tenderloin with fresh vegetables to pork tenderloin with an oriental plum sauce to spicy shrimp with a hot garlic and ginger sauce ($10.95 to $16.95). Cheesecakes, black-bottom pies and the Morning Glory pie of ricotta, chocolate chips, heavy cream, amaretto, almond flavoring and a graham-cracker crust are favored desserts.

Breakfast, 7 to 11:30; lunch, 12:15 to 3; dinner, 5:30 to 10. Open Memorial Day to mid-September. BYOB. No credit cards.

Sconset Cafe, Post Office Square, Siasconset. (508) 257-4008.

The founder of the Morning Glory Cafe, Pam McKinstry, moved on to the Sconset Cafe, where she packs in habitués at eight tables for three meals a day amid a casual green and white decor, track lighting and arty accents. We enjoyed a delicious lunch of chicken fajitas salad in a tortilla shell ($8.50) and boboli (a pizza-like creation with pesto and artichoke hearts, $7.25). Finishing touches were homemade rum-walnut ice cream with chocolate sauce and a slice of frozen key lime pie, both heavenly.

Dinners from $16 to $24 could be tuna au poivre, grilled salmon with a Mediterranean sauce, spicy seafood stew over shell pasta, confit of duck, veal portofino and loin of lamb provençal. Start with filetto carpaccio, crab cakes rémoulade, pot stickers or the cafe ravioli with artichokes and cheese. But save room for desserts like fresh peach pie, bête noir and bread pudding flavored with grand marnier. Many of the recipes are detailed in the cafe's three cookbooks.

Lunch daily, 11 to 3; dinner, 6 to 9:30. Closed late September to May. BYOB. No credit cards.

Still more changes of pace:

Espresso Cafe, 40 Main St., Nantucket. (508) 228-6930. The foods of the caterer, Fast Forward, have moved into town to this snazzy location with a mod interior in black and white and an appealing, two-level rear garden patio that's an oasis away from the hustle and bustle, with ivy twining all over the stucco walls. We know people who go here just for the desserts, perhaps, lemon-almond pound cake or one of the humungous cookies with cappuccino or espresso. Scones, bagels and Mexican eggs are among the breakfast items. At lunch, we were impressed by a garden burger with Mexican sage cheese and salsa ($6.95) and a grilled spinach and mozzarella sandwich with garlic and roasted red peppers ($5.25), both served with zesty cafe potatoes. Another time, a big chocolate-chip cookie and a mocha cappuccino ($2.40) made a nice mid-afternoon break. Light entrées supplement the lunch items in the evening. Open daily, 8 a.m. to 11 p.m.

Off Centre Cafe, 29 Centre St., Nantucket. (508) 228-8470. Another of Nantucket's ubiquitous cafes seemingly sprouting like daffodils, this small place offers creative breakfasts in the $5 to $7 range — perhaps nectarine pancakes, huevos rancheros with black beans, breakfast burritos or caramelized-banana popovers. The kitchen and the counter are bigger than the six-table cafe, which is augmented by a sidewalk cafe in the summer. It branches out with Mexican dinners, the standards plus a few fancier offerings from $8.95 to $15.95. In the off-season, soups, pizza, enchiladas and blue-plate specials are served at lunch. Breakfast daily, 7 to 11:30; dinner, Monday-Saturday from 6; Sunday brunch, 8 to 1. Breakfast and lunch in off-season..

Chin's, 126 Chin's Way, Nantucket. (508) 228-0200. Ensconced in a house across from the Finast market south of town is this pleasant restaurant owned by Chin Manasmontri, a Chinese native of Thailand, who has been cooking and catering on the island since 1972. This is the real thing for the island's only Chinese and Thai foods (entrées, $9.95 to $18, the latter for seafood steamed with wine sauce and ginger in a clay pot). They're served in a Chinese decor that's surprisingly glamorous, save for the glass tops over the linens and the coffee cups and upside-down water tumblers at each setting. Lunch and dinner daily.

Claudette's on the Porch, Post Office Square, Siasconset. (508) 257-6622. Casual fare is served up on the front deck by John Pearl. He learned to cook from his legendary mother, Claudette, who started in 1967 and built this thriving little establishment from scratch. Ice-cream-parlor chairs and little round tables are the setting for muffins, lemonade, iced tea, soups like homemade turkey, and sandwiches (meat loaf, veggie, ham and cheese, $5.25). A box lunch ($6) yields a sandwich, veggie sticks and a brownie or Claudette's famous lemon cake, the recipe for which was published in Gourmet magazine. Open daily 9 to 5, shorter hours in off-season. Open May to mid-October.

Something Natural, 50 Cliff Road, Nantucket. (508) 228-0504. Gourmet magazine requested the recipes for the carrot cake and the herb bread made at this rustic cottage at the edge of town. There are old school desks on the deck and a few picnic tables on the grounds for enjoying one of the fifteen sandwiches ($4.50 to $6.25 whole, $2.50 to $3.50 for a half), available on the wonderful whole-wheat berry, oatmeal, rye, pumpernickel, herb and Portuguese breads served at many a restaurant in town. You also can get salads, fresh lemonade and, for breakfast, muffins and raisin rolls. Open daily 8 to 6 in summer, shorter hours in off-season. Open May-October.

Bed and Board

The Wauwinet, Box 2580, Wauwinet Road, Nantucket 02554. (508) 228-0145 or (800) 426-8718.

Gloriously situated on a strip of land between Nantucket Bay and the Atlantic, the Wauwinet House had seen better days before it was acquired by Stephen and Jill Karp of Weston, Mass., island vacationers who restored the place to the tune of many millions of dollars for a grand reopening in 1988.

The original building in a rural section of parkland was gutted to make a dining room with french doors and windows taking advantage of the view, a common sitting room with a fireplace, and 24 air-conditioned rooms with private baths, antique pine armoires, and iron or wicker headboards. Five cottages containing eleven more rooms and suites were added across the road.

Our "superior" room — as opposed to deluxe or suite — was not large but was nicely located on a third-floor corner facing the harbor so that we were able to watch spectacular sunsets at night. Fresh and pretty, it had a queensize bed, wicker and upholstered armchairs, and a painted armoire topped with a wooden swan and two hat boxes (one of the inn's decorating signatures). The modern bathroom contained a multitude of thick white towels and a basket of Crabtree

Toppers is luxurious dining room at the Wauwinet.

& Evelyn amenities. During turndown service, the towels were replenished, mints placed by the bed and the radio turned on.

All the rooms we saw had different, striking stenciled borders (some turning up in the most ingenious places), interesting artworks and sculptures, ceiling fans, and such fillips as clouds painted on the ceiling. Remote-control TVs and VCRs are hidden in armoires and trunks.

Outside are chairs lined up strategically on the back lawn and a beachside grill where drinks and snacks are available. You can swim from a dock in the bay, or walk a couple of minutes from the hotel through the dunes to the most gorgeous, endless and unoccupied strand we've seen on the Atlantic coast. A 21-foot runabout will transport guests to town or to a remote beach for the day. You can play tennis or rent a sailboat.

A full breakfast is included in the room rate. Guests may order any item from a menu spanning a spectrum from strawberry and rhubarb pancakes to egg-white omelets with spa cheese and fresh vegetables.

General manager Russell Cleveland (earlier of Williamsburg Inn and Salishan Lodge renown) ensures that everything is first-rate as far as lodging goes. The restaurant and its Wine Spectator award-winning wine list are overseen by his wife Debbie, food and beverage manager.

Toppers, named for the owners' dog, is a refined summery setting for some of the island's best food. Two elegant, side-by-side rooms harbor masses of flowers and well-spaced tables with upholstered chairs in blue and white. The outdoor terrace overlooking lawn and bay is favored for lunch and drinks.

The dinner menu, printed daily, is priced from $24 for smoke-roasted cornish hen with sour cherries and cream to $32 for grilled arctic char with matchstick potatoes and fried capers.

Among appetizers, we savored the lobster and crab cakes with smoked corn and a super mustard sauce, grilled quail on a toasted brioche, and grilled shrimp with buffalo mozzarella and grilled pizza. Chilled oysters with pickled ginger mignonette and incendiary blackened swordfish with crayfish and grilled cornbread didn't come off quite as well. The caesar salad ($8.50) is so good that some order it with every meal.

Seafood dishes like grilled salmon with spicy black beans and striped bass with a hot vegetable relish confirmed that the chef likes to leave a fiery after-taste. Another night we enjoyed the grilled rack and leg of lamb with a tomato-eggplant timbale and peppered veal chop with cognac-mustard cream. Both were accompanied by baby vegetables (tiny pattypan squash and sliced carrots about as big as a fingernail) and a wedge of potatoes.

Desserts like pineapple-papaya sorbet, pecan-praline ice cream and crème brûlée are refreshing endings.

Wonderful salads -- among them, great northern bean with smoked salmon, shrimp mandarin, lamb tabbouleh and Thai grilled pork -- are featured on the lunch menu ($11.50 to $16). A special treat for visitors to town is a cruise to the Wauwinet for lunch. The launch departs from Straight Wharf daily at 10:30. The food and cruise price is $29.

Lunch daily, noon to 2; dinner nightly, 6 to 9:30, jackets required; Sunday brunch, 10:30 to 2:30. Doubles, $290 to $590, B&B; suites, $490 to $1,000. Three-night minimum, summer weekends. Open April through Christmas Stroll.

The Summer House, Ocean Avenue, Box 313, Siasconset 02564. (508) 257-9976.

A more romantic setting for dining could scarcely be imagined than the front veranda of this low-slung, Southern-style house or its summery interior dining room awash in white and green. It's a mix of white chairs (some with colorful upholstered seats) and painted floors, good 'Sconset oils and watercolors on the whitewashed walls, and fresh flowers and plants everywhere.

We chose one of the handful of tables on the veranda that yielded a view of the moon rising over the ocean we could hear lapping at the foot of the bluff across the road. The setting remained etched in our memory longer than our dinner, which was more ordinary than the tab would have suggested. Owner Peter Karlson insists the dining situation has improved since our stay.

You're paying for the setting as well as the food, of course: appetizers ($8 to $14) like marinated shrimp with caramelized vidalia onions, lamb and fennel sausage on riesling-braised cabbage, or sautéed foie gras on a white-grape and blood-orange vinaigrette; entrées ($22 to $31) like sautéed striped bass sauced with kalamata olives and roasted yellow tomatoes, seared tuna glazed with passion fruit and served with an orange-soy butter sauce, grilled black-angus sirloin roast with a five-peppercorn/cognac sauce and rack of lamb on a bed of fresh rosemary with black-currant/mint sauce.

A brandy tart with dollops of whipped cream, blueberries and slices of kiwi was a memorable choice from a dessert selection that included crème brûlée, key lime pie on a raspberry coulis, chocolate sin cake with crème anglaise, and pecan tart with bourbon ice cream and fresh berries. The extensive wine list is priced from $16 for Entre Deux Mers to $400 for a 1979 Pomerol Château Petrus.

Our meal was enlivened by the piano stylings of Sal Gioe, an island institution who was playing in the white rattan-filled lounge and whose 84-year-old fingers still fly across the keyboard of a new grand piano. We were content to toddle off to our room in one of eight Bermuda-like cottages strung in a horseshoe pattern around a garden between restaurant and sea.

Beneath a canopy of trees and ivy with bridal veil spilling over the roofs, the charming, rose-covered cottages have been redecorated with antiques, eyelet-

Summery dining room at Summer House in Siasconset.

embroidered pillows and lace-edged duvets on the beds, lace curtains, and painted floors and chests. Interesting roof lines, stained glass, leaded windows, and little nooks and crannies add to the charm. Modern amenities include telephones and renovated bathrooms, each with a marble jacuzzi.

Jimmy Cagney cherished the privacy of the cottage-suite named in his honor. Although each has its own or a shared small terrace, we felt on display reading on ours as arriving diners passed at cocktail hour. There are no real sitting areas, either public or private, inside the cottages or main building.

A continental breakfast buffet — fresh fruit, granola, bran cereal and muffins — is offered in the morning on the sun-drenched veranda, where you can savor the sun rising over the open expanse of azure-blue ocean. It's a magical setting, like none other we know of on the East Coast.

Lunch is available on a newly expanded and landscaped bluestone terrace beside the pool, sequestered halfway down the bluff in the dunes, a long stone's throw from the beach. Everything's pricey ($6 to $17), but there's a good selection and the eight-ounce burger ($8) is advertised as the best on the island. Look at it this way: lunch patrons get to use the pool (others are charged $15), and the view is free.

Lunch at poolside, daily noon to 4; dinner, 6 to 10. Doubles, $300 to $325; suites, $350 to $400. Open mid-May to mid-October.

Cliffside Beach Club, Jefferson Avenue, Box 449, Nantucket 02554. (508) 228-0618.

The Cliffside Beach Club, situated for 70 years on the marvelous open beach on the north shore, has been owned since 1954 by the Currie family, whose offspring now run a deluxe small inn-hotel and an oceanfront restaurant.

Club members coveted the same umbrella and assortment of chairs and used to wait years to reserve one of the more prestigious spots on the west beach, according to general manager Robert F. Currie. Now guests don't have to wait — they simply walk out of their rooms onto the beach. Some of the old bathhouses have been converted into fourteen contemporary bedrooms with cathedral ceilings and modern baths. All the beds, doors, tables, vanities and even the pegs for the beach towels were built by Nantucket craftsmen. Angled wainscoting serves as the headboards for the built-in queensize beds. Prints by local artists and oriental rugs on the dark green carpets set off the old wood walls. Wicker furniture, antique wooden toys and black leather couches are among the appointments.

Nine air-conditioned beachfront studio apartments, each with a private deck and the phones and TVs characteristic of all the rooms, were added in 1987. Two suites were added in 1990, and a new exercise room is said to be one of the busiest spots in town.

A continental breakfast is served in the club's spectacular high-ceilinged lobby that Monique Currie decorated in South of France style. It has quilts on the ceiling and is full of smart wicker furniture and potted flowers, so prolific and splashy that tending them has "become my full-time job," says Monique.

Lunch and dinner are available to guests and the public at **The Galley on Cliffside Beach,** situated between the club and the studio apartments, with an L-shaped, canopied deck facing the ocean. Here you sit on blue wicker chairs at tables with floral cloths, backing up to planters filled with petunias and geraniums with hanging pink paper globes overhead. It's enchanting by day or night.

We thoroughly enjoyed a couple of the best bloody marys ever (spicy and generous for $5) before a lunch of salade niçoise and chicken salad Hawaiian ($11 and $12). Service is by waiters who spend their winters working at a club in Palm Beach, which helps explain the level of professionalism here.

For dinner, French chef Daniel Fouquenot specializes in "cuisine of the sun" from the south of France. Start with crispy beer-batter calamari, home-cured gravlax prepared in the Icelandic style or fish soup with toasted baguette and rouille ($8 to $11). Continue with the spicy farandole of seafood rich with saffron, the roast duck with sundried cranberries or the rack of lamb dijonnaise ($19 to $30). Finish with homemade cognac ice cream, French blueberry-peach pie or chocolate-soufflé cake ($6.50).

Owner Jane Currie Silva's son David is the sous chef; the acclaimed grilled yellowfin tuna with scallion pancake, braised bok choy and honey-soy-ginger glaze is his recipe. Another son, Geoffrey, is the mâitre-d. Many of the Galley's paintings and the menu cover are by Belgian artist Lucien van Vyve, the first chef at the old Opera House here, whom Jane considers her mentor.

Lunch daily, noon to 2; dinner nightly, 6:30 to 10, mid-June to mid-September. Doubles, $230 to $355; suites, $400 to $585; lodging, late May to mid-October.

The White Elephant, Easton Street, Box 359, Nantucket 02554. (508) 228-2500 or (800) 475-2637.

This venerable complex beside the harbor has been upgraded with the refurbishing of the 26 posh rooms in the Breakers annex, a hotel concierge-style operation outfitted with canopied four-poster beds, plush sofas, modern baths and twin sinks. Continental breakfast is served in the lounge, and there are stocked minibars in the rooms.

Traditionalists may prefer the fifteen rose-covered cottages scattered about the nicely landscaped property, done up with wicker and some with bay-windowed living rooms overlooking the water. Twenty-two comfortable rooms, recently

Canopied outdoor deck offers seaside dining at The Galley on Cliffside Beach.

redecorated in colors of peach and green (even the armoires hiding the TVs are painted in these colors) and air-conditioned, are available in the main hotel.

Also redecorated is the **Regatta** dining room, elegant in hunter green and white, with tables on several levels for water views beyond the harborfront terrace. The room is serene with little amethyst oil lamps, Limoges service plates and striking porcelain flowers lying on each table. A guitarist plays during dinner.

A new chef was pleasing customers and the prices had been toned down at our latest visit. Dinner entrées ranged from $17.75 for spicy roasted pork loin with sweet onions and wilted greens to $26.50 for lobster and asparagus feuilleté with chive beurre blanc. Other choices might be blackened tuna with harissa butter and pineapple salsa, sautéed halibut with roasted tomato and fennel sauce, grilled duck with orange-cranberry sauce, loin of venison with roasted shallots and artichokes, and rack of lamb with white beans and rosemary, served with apple relish. Start with sautéed squid with grilled polenta, thyme-crusted quail with red-pepper coulis or tempura wild mushrooms with wasabi dipping oil ($6.75 to $11.75). A new bistro menu with some interesting choices is offered in the porch area at night. The pool has been relocated to open up the view of the harbor from the dining room. The expanded terrace in its place, with a setting like that of a yacht club, is one of the prettiest places in town for lunch, although we thought our Thai chicken and seafood salads rather paltry for the price ($9.50 and $10.50). The waiter gladly obliged when we asked for seconds on rolls.

Lunch. Monday-Saturday 11:30 to 2:30; dinner nightly, 6:30 to 9:30; Sunday brunch. Doubles, $245 to $305 in hotel, $235 to $435 in cottages, $335 to $435 in the Breakers. Open mid-June to mid-October.

Ships Inn, 13 Fair St., Nantucket 02554. (508) 228-0040.
Built in 1831 by whaling captain Obed Starbuck, this was nicely restored in 1991 by chef-owner Mark Gottwald and his actress-wife Ellie. It now claims some of Nantucket's most comfortable accommodations as well as a good restaurant.

The ten guest rooms with private baths, named after ships that Starbuck commanded, contain many of original furnishings. They have been refurbished with new wallpapers and tiled baths and come with interesting window treatments, Neutrogena toiletries and mini-refrigerators in cabinets beneath the TV sets. Most have reading chairs and half have desks. All but two tiny single rooms are more spacious than most Nantucket bedrooms.

Guests enjoy afternoon tea with coffee cake and cookies. Innkeeper Meghan Moore sets out a continental-plus breakfast of fruit, cereal, scones and muffins.

Dinners here have received considerable attention since the Gottwalds took over. Chef Mark, who trained at Le Cirque in New York and at Spago in Los Angeles, oversees the cooking duties with a sizable kitchen staff. Among entrées ($15.50 to $22), you might find crispy salmon sauté with cabernet sauce and grilled vegetables, Nantucket sole steamed with watercress puree and lobster oil, oven-roasted pork loin with creamed spinach and braised apples, grilled skirt steak with horseradish bordelaise, and loin of lamb with lentils and eggplant puree. Or consider a pasta, perhaps porcini-risotto with grilled chicken and roasted endive or lobster fettuccine with grilled plum tomatoes and roasted garlic sauce. Start with fried calamari with ponzu sauce or a sauté of wild mushrooms with creamy polenta. Finish with raspberry sorbet or chocolate-soufflé cake. A well-chosen but pricey wine list starts in the twenties.

The dining room is attractive with apricot walls over white wainscoting, exposed beams, a white fireplace in the center of the room, candles in the many-paned windows, and white-linened tables dressed with candles and fresh flowers. There also are tables for eating in the adjacent Dory Bar.

The Gottswalds, who tend to lead a bi-coastal life because of her acting career, winter with their young children in Vero Beach, Fla., where they opened Ellie's, a new American restaurant on the waterfront, in the winter of 1994. They and their staff go back and forth between Vero Beach and Nantucket.

Dinner, nightly except Tuesday, 5:30 to 9:15. Doubles, $125. Open Memorial Day to Columbus Day.

Lodging

Westmoor Inn, Cliff Road, Nantucket 02554. (508) 228-0877.

The location at the edge of town is one of the drawing cards at this substantial inn, with fourteen guest rooms on the second and third floors, all with private baths and some quite spacious by Nantucket standards. Other draws are the continental breakfasts in the cheery solarium dining room, the afternoon wine and hors d'oeuvre with the innkeeper in the elegant living room, the small library-TV room dressed in wicker, and the inviting rear patio and gardens.

Guest rooms and a suite vary in size (some are quite small), but all are lavishly furnished with a mix of modern and antique furnishings and have telephones. Most contain king or queen beds and one suite has a jacuzzi. We liked Room 206 with a kingsize bed and a fireplace. The bathroom in its neighbor is as big as the bedroom, but surprisingly, most have showers only rather than tubs (a pattern repeated at many local inns). Abundant toiletries are in each bathroom.

Innkeeper Nancy Holdgate feels quite at home since her husband grew up in the house (his parents established it as an inn in 1952). Although she doesn't stay on premises, she attends the nightly wine and cheese party, which runs from 6 to 7 and "becomes a real gathering," she says. Also special is the breakfast, beautifully served on tables with white cloths and decorative overlays in the skylit

Greenhouse breakfast room at Westmoor Inn.

solarium, where three walls of windows afford a panoramic view. It's apt to include fresh fruit, wild blueberries, cereals, yogurt and an elaborate spread of croissants, muffins, breads and scones, and two kinds of fruit muffin.

"This house is unique here because of its grand open public rooms and its grand scale," says Nancy.

Doubles, $115 to $235. Open late April through October.

Centerboard Guest House, 8 Chester St., Box 456, Nantucket 02554. (508) 228-9696.

A Victorian guest house of quiet country elegance is how its brochure describes it. That doesn't entirely do justice to this appealing B&B, which is a cut above the rest in town. Each of the seven air-conditioned guest rooms has private bath, color TV, phone and refrigerator, and is furnished with panache by owner Marcia Wasserman, a Long Island artist and interior designer.

We lucked into the main-floor suite, with a library-style living room in dark woods and hunter green, a bedroom with a queensize canopy feather bed, and a glamorous bathroom in deep green marble, with a jacuzzi in one section, a large marble-tiled shower in another, and the sink and toilet in still another. The suite had two TVs, plush masculine furnishings, and no fewer than six bouquets of fresh and dried flowers scattered here and there.

The upstairs rooms are romantic, if not quite so glamorous. All with queens or two double beds, they show decorative flair, with lacy pillows and the odd mural on the wall. Refrigerators with soft drinks, baskets of Gilbert & Soames toiletries, a bowl of toffee and a welcoming basket of apples and cheeses are in the rooms. A studio apartment in the basement has built-in double beds and a small kitchen.

Resident innkeeper Reggie Reid puts out a bountiful continental-breakfast buffet: bowls of fresh fruit salad, cereals, granola, cranberry and coconut muffins, and Portuguese bread for toasting. This can be taken in the dining room, on the front porch or at the window seat in the living room.

Doubles, $165; suites, $265.

Martin House Inn, 61 Centre St., Box 743, Nantucket 02554. (508) 228-0678.

Hard work and T.L.C. by new owners Ceci and Channing Moore have upgraded this 1803 mariner's home, a guest house since the 1920s and heretofore rather short of creature comforts. No more. The Moores, who lived previously in Hong Kong and Wilmington, Del., have taken to it with heart and soul.

Exceptionally pretty are the large open front foyer and the long front parlor and dining area, with sponged royal blue walls and lovely oriental rugs. The dining-room table is set for eight, although some prefer to eat on a tray at one of the wicker chairs on the side veranda. An expanded continental breakfast of two fresh fruits, two cereals, granola, Nantucket breads and homemade muffins is the fare.

The Moores offer thirteen guest rooms, nine with private baths and most with queensize beds. We saw a couple of spacious rooms with canopy beds, fireplaces, cherry dressers and either a loveseat or two plush club chairs. Four rooms on the third floor share baths. One room with two double beds could accommodate four people, and two single rooms are offered at $45 a night.

Doubles, $75 to $140.

Cobblestone Inn, 5 Ash St., Nantucket 02554. (508) 228-1987.

Wooden lighthouses line the stairs at this B&B, lovingly tended by Robin Hammer-Yankow, a Chamber of Commerce officer and civic booster, and her husband Keith, a local attorney. Their 1725 house beside a cobblestoned street offers five guest rooms, all with private baths and queen canopy beds and nicely furnished with period pieces. Painted Colonial windows and beams, oriental rugs and swag curtains that match the canopies are some of the decorative touches. History shows up in the wide-plank floors, narrow closets and tilted doorways.

Given its in-town location and the cobblestoned street, we were surprised to find our second-floor room so utterly quiet, that is until the church bells tolled at 7 a.m. We were ready to arise anyway to prepare for Robin's continental breakfast, served family style at a long table in the dining area behind the living room. Fresh fruit, orange juice, homemade granola, cereals and melt-in-the-mouth pumpkin and zucchini breads were the fare.

Guests spread out in a living room with TV, a sun porch with wicker furniture and quite a collection of Nantucket menus and brochures, and a brick patio overlooking the garden.

Doubles, $100 to $140. No credit cards. No smoking.

Cliff Lodge, 9 Cliff Road, Nantucket 02554. (508) 228-9480.

Eleven guest rooms, designed for comfort and decorated with flair, are offered at this 1771 sea captain's house in a residential neighborhood overlooking town and harbor. Rooms are notable for spatter-painted floors, Laura Ashley wallpapers, frilly bedding, fresh flowers and antiques. Many boast kingsize beds and fireplaces, and all have private baths, telephones and remote-control TVs neatly built into the walls or concealed in armoires.

Innkeeper Gerrie Miller serves a buffet breakfast in one of the sitting rooms, or guests can adjourn to the patio. Fresh fruit, cereal, granola and muffins are typical fare. She offers hot or iced tea and cocktail snacks in the afternoon.

Few inns have so many neat places to sit and relax, inside or out. There are five sitting rooms on three floors, a rooftop deck with a view of the harbor, reading porches and a brick patio beside a secluded garden.

Doubles, $100 to $150.

76 Main Street, 76 Main St., Nantucket 02554. (508) 228-2533.

Located in the heart of Nantucket's historic district, not far from the famed Three Bricks of residential Main Street, is this grandly restored 1883 sea captain's home, handsome in a new coat of white paint with gray shutters. It contains eleven guest rooms, each with queensize beds, upholstered chairs, antiques and private baths.

The showplace is a large, main-floor front corner room with a canopied four-poster and Victorian furnishings, renting for $135 a night. Off an impressive entry hall are a formal Victorian parlor and a kitchen with a dining area, where innkeeper Shirley Peters offers a continental breakfast of fresh fruits and granola, homemade blueberry coffee cake and a variety of muffins.

Out back, between the inn and a motel-style annex with six redecorated family units, is a flagstone patio — a welcome refuge amid flowers and shade trees for a summer afternoon.

Doubles, $115 to $135. No smoking.

Anchor Inn, 66 Centre St., Nantucket 02554. (508) 228-0072.

Charles and Ann Balas, who used to own the Nantucket Fine Chocolates store, are the hands-on innkeepers at this venerable B&B and feel their in-residence position sets the inn apart. Built by a whaling ship captain, this was the home in the 1950s of the Gilbreths of "Cheaper by the Dozen" fame, who wrote of their experience in the book *Innside Nantucket.*

Eleven guest rooms, named after whaling ships, have private baths, queen or twin beds, and period furnishings amid the original random-width floorboards and antique paneling. Charles's homemade muffins are served to the accompaniment of classical music in a side porch with cafe curtains. Chocolates are likely to be put out at night in the front parlor.

Doubles, $95 to $135. Open April-December.

Seven Sea Street, 7 Sea St., Nantucket 02554. (508) 228-3577.

Matthew Parker and his wife Mary oversee this post and beam guest house, which was opened in 1987 on the last vacant lot in town by the Parker family, who also run the Tuckernuck Inn and the Parker Guest House.

You enter into the dining room in which Matthew serves the blueberry and cranberry muffins he bakes for continental breakfast, as well as coffee cake and fresh fruit, nicely presented on Villeroy & Boch china.

The house has eight guest rooms with queensize fishnet canopy beds, TVs, phones and painted furniture that Matthew assembled himself. All have refrigerators and modern baths with a vanity outside. Guests may use a couple of small common rooms on the second floor, the widow's walk with a view of the harbor in the distance, an indoor hot tub and a pleasant garden patio. While Matthew tends to the innkeeping, his wife edits the slick Nantucket Journal magazine, of which he is co-publisher and business manager.

Doubles, $165. No smoking.

Gourmet Treats

Rarely have we seen a place so chock full of gourmet shops, specialty-food takeouts, caterers and other services pertaining to matters culinary.

At **Chanticleer to Go** at 15 South Beach St., Nathalie Berruet manages her family's gourmet takeout shop. Most of the food is different from that at the renowned Chanticleer ("we cater more to the tourists here," Nathalie explains). But the foods "reflect the Chanticleer flair," as in coq au vin, osso buco and beef bourguignonne, which are made at the inn in 'Sconset. She also sells some of the same wines and her pastry chef here sends some of his desserts to the restaurant. You'll find basic sandwiches in the $5 range, some not-so-basic salads, soups, wonderful appetizers, rotisserie chicken and duck, and pastries galore. Open Monday-Saturday 10 to 8, Sunday noon to 6. Closed November to April.

Many cheeses, gazpacho, Thai noodle and curried couscous salads, muffulettas, apple-peach muffins and sandwiches in the $5.75 range are available from **Provisions,** behind the bandstand on Straight Wharf. Also part of Elaine and Jack Gifford's food complex here are the **Straight Wharf Fish Store,** where lobster rolls were going for $9.50 and fish fillet sandwiches for $6.75 last we knew, and **Stars,** an ice cream and frozen yogurt shop with a porch where you can sit right by the water.

The **Bagel Basin** at 2 East Chestnut St. is the latest takeout endeavor of the folks at 21 Federal. The basic bagels go for 75 cents. The toppings, from pineapple/cream cheese to smoked mozzarella with pesto and sundried tomatoes, add a dollar or a few. There's a benedict bagel for breakfast, along with a variety of bagel sandwiches for lunch. Open daily, 6 a.m. to 6 p.m.

For our money, the best homemade ice creams and yogurts in town are served at **The Juice Bar,** a pastry and ice-cream shop at 12 Broad St. across from the Whaling Museum. We enjoyed an oversize cup of different fruit sorbets after one dessert-less dinner. Frozen yogurt with a choice of more than 25 toppings and island-baked pastries are available at **Yogurt Plus,** a sitdown place that formerly was a restaurant at 6 Oak St.

Satisfy your sweet tooth at **Sweet Inspirations** at 26 Centre St. You can indulge in handmade chocolates, pecan and caramel tuckernucks, award-winning cranberry-chocolate truffles, chocolate-almond buttercrunch, and an exclusive line of Nantucket fruit preserves and chutneys.

The **Complete Kitchen** at 25 Centre St. is run by Mary Murray, who used to own the wonderful Good Food Store in Darien, Conn. Here she offers Nantucket jams, jellies and ketchup made just for the store, caviars, crème fraîche and California tortas with fresh basil, garlic and pinenuts or smoked salmon, mustard and dill. All those items the beautiful people need for their cocktail parties are here, as are a good selection of cookbooks and cookware. Around the corner is the **Nantucket Gourmet,** with an abundance of teas, coffees, cookware, housewares and gourmet goodies, with a lot of high-tech kettles, toasters and such as well as a practical oyster opener for $13.95.

The **Lion's Paw** at the foot of Main Street carries wonderful handpainted pottery, including great fish plates. We think it's the nicest of several gift shops of interest to gourmets.

Only in Nantucket would you not be surprised to find **Cold Noses,** a small gourmet shop for cats and dogs near Straight Wharf. As well as gourmet natural dog cookies, you'll find "doggie duds," cat beds, pearls pour le pouch and perfect purrls for cats, and even cologne from Paris for Minnie or Bowser.

Although its wines don't seem to turn up in local restaurants, **Nantucket Vineyard** produces 3,500 cases a year. Dean and Melissa Long grow five varieties of vinifera grapes, but import most from Long Island and Washington. Prices at the winery at the side of their home at 3 Bartlett Farm Road go from $5 to $12 for a merlot. Tastings are offered Monday-Saturday 10 to 6, Sunday noon to 5.

Boston skyline as viewed from the Rotunda at Boston Harbor Hotel.

Boston and Cambridge
Baked Beans to New Cuisine

If Los Angeles is our last culinary frontier, as one food magazine has suggested, Boston is our first. This city situated not far from where the Pilgrims landed has had more than 350 years to refine and redefine itself, to become civilized in cuisine as well as in culture.

No American city has given its name to, nor been associated with, more indigenous foods. Boston baked beans, Boston scrod, Boston lettuce, Indian pudding, Boston brown bread and Parker House rolls got their start here. The nation's first French restaurant dates back to 1793 in Boston. The Parker House opened in 1854 as New England's first leading hotel and dining room. The famed Durgin-Park can safely proclaim it was "established before you were born." And Locke-Ober still serves lobster savannah in the same manner it did when one of us first had it there as a teenager more decades ago than we care to remember.

Boston's food scene has perhaps changed more in the last dozen years than in its first 350, however. Some of the staples remain, but the new regional cuisine is everywhere — reigning a tad preciously in some of the East's great restaurants (most of them creatures of the 1980s and '90s), simply evolving or being accommodated in more traditional places. Boston was among the first to take to bistro cooking, even before its restaurants started the trend toward downscaling as its economy softened in the 1990s. Local restaurateur Patrick Bowe made Newsweek magazine with his innovative "hard times" menu in 1991.

Boston remains at the heart of an emerging New England cuisine — overtly at high-profile places like Jasper's, where Jasper White is elevating basic New England cooking to new heights, and with less fanfare at countless other restaurants where chefs seek out the best regional ingredients and recipes.

A number of the city's chefs are on the cutting edge of cuisine, several having

407

been ranked by national magazines among the country's best. Lydia Shire, who led the revolution in Boston food circles while at the acclaimed Seasons, returned to Boston to open her own restaurant after a brief stint in southern California, where she could not find as good local provisioners. Some of the city's hotels are in the forefront of the city's growing culinary reputation.

Until lately, Bostonians with a sense of adventure satisfied their palates across the Charles River in Cambridge, where academia helped spur culinary experimentation. Now they enjoy it in the heart of Boston as well.

Dining

The Best of the Best

L'Espalier, 30 Gloucester St., Boston. (617) 262-3023.

The first — and, many think, still the best — of Boston's great restaurants, L'Espalier offers cuisine, setting and style for a special occasion. It makes such demands upon your palate that we could not imagine dining here every week, as some habitués are known to do. Not to mention the fact that the money we spent for a birthday dinner for two could have fed a couple of hundred souls at a soup kitchen we know of.

L'Espalier began in 1978 under the auspices of Tunisian-born French chef Moncef Meddeb, who sold it a decade later to his former sous chef, Frank McClelland. Frank and his wife Catherine, who live upstairs with their young children, devote fulltime-plus to the effort. "We're putting lots of energy into upgrading every aspect of the cuisine, service and decor so that we have something very special here," says Frank, whose youth and unassuming demeanor belie his stature as one of the top 25 chefs in the nation in Food & Wine magazine's estimation.

Despite tough times, they have taken the upscale market and made it virtually their own. L'Espalier is the only major Boston restaurant left that has a totally prix-fixe menu. It charges $56 for three courses or $72 for the dégustation menu, for which the chef chooses the courses, taking three appetizers, a main course and a selection of desserts from the regular menu. Since we wanted to taste as much as possible, we put ourselves in the chef's hands.

You might start with a cappuccino of chanterelles and white truffles, a vegetarian broth with a foamy topping of essence of mushrooms and truffles steamed in the manner of cappuccino, enhanced with Wellfleet oysters baked with cider and cracked white-pepper glaze. That could be followed by roasted New York foie gras with quince tatin and pomegranate savory sauce. Next, how about glazed Maine lobster in curry and carrot juice with lobster and avocado mousse and a watercress-tarragon sauce? A sorbet of blood orange and fruit coulis with star anise prepares the palate suavely for the main event, perhaps roast rack and loin of lamb in fava beans with artichoke and vidalia onion soufflé, grilled tomato, black pepper and fresh oregano, or roasted Atlantic salmon in corn-basil crust with overnight baked tomato salad. Then follows a selection of cheeses and desserts, perhaps coconut mille-feuille with passion-fruit mousse and mango, an apricot, honey and poppyseed torte with white-chocolate crème anglaise and raspberries, and a trio of intense rhubarb-ginger, pineapple and honeydew sorbets with berries and fruit coulis.

The menu descriptions belie the complexity of flavors and tastes. Frank cooks in an intellectual style, working daily in a test kitchen on taste and composition so that the diner senses the essence of the food. Perfection is his goal (he received

Frank and Catherine McClelland pause for dessert at L'Espalier.

the new Boston Globe food critic's only four-star review so far). He is also has a passion for vegetables. Indeed, his restaurant is the first mainstream establishment we've encountered that offers a dégustation vegetarian menu, $62 for four remarkable courses plus dessert.

No matter what you choose, whether the roast stuffed rabbit loin with kale and vegetables or the grilled rack of venison molé with morel risotto, asparagus spring roll and chervil puree, you can be assured of the ultimate in flavors.

The lamb, rabbit, produce -- most grown organically -- come from L'Espalier's own purveyors. Frank personally buys the selections for the thirteen-page wine list, especially strong on Bordeaux and wines from Alsace and Rhône, well aged in three cellars. Although he has eleven professional cooks in the kitchen, he works a station and personally oversees every dish that goes out. You also can be assured that he's on the scene — when he goes to France for his annual busman's holiday to study with three-star chefs, he closes the restaurant.

His renovated Victorian townhouse has a supremely elegant atmosphere in which to sample this changing blend of classic French and nouvelle cuisine. After buzzing a doorbell to gain entry, diners climb to the second floor, which has two high-ceilinged dining rooms in shades of taupe and cream, or to the third floor, where the dining-room walls are a warm lacquered and stenciled terra cotta and the kitchen is next door. There are marble fireplaces, carved moldings, beautiful flower arrangements in niches, pin spotlights on tables set with damask linens and fresh flowers, and comfortable and luxurious lacquered chairs with curved arms.

From the complimentary fennel and leek mousse wrapped with smoked salmon and topped with ossetra caviar that accompanies cocktails to the petit fours that gild the bill, diners here relish a rare culinary treat.

Dinner nightly except Sunday, 6 to 10:30. No smoking.

Jasper's, 240 Commercial St., Boston. (617) 523-1126.

Jasper White's temple of contemporary New England cookery has been a winner since it opened in 1983 to instant four-star reviews from both Boston newspapers and accolades from the national press. He started in Boston at the Copley Plaza after training at the Culinary Institute and on the West Coast, was the first chef at the Harvard Bookstore Cafe, and opened Seasons at the Bostonian Hotel with Lydia Shire before embarking on his own venture. His national reputation was cemented in 1989 when Harper & Row published his impressive cookbook, *Jasper White's Cooking from New England.*

The restaurant's decor is notable for the huge blown-glass sculptures perched on five shelves in a niche running the length of the main wall. They are the work of glass artist Dan Dailey. The sculptures provide splashy color to a dining area with light exposed-brick walls, red lacquered chairs with pretty patterned seats, and white-linened tables topped with floral china from Germany. Altogether there are three dining areas plus four booths recently added to the lounge.

In the gospel according to Jasper, basic New England cookery is enhanced by international flourishes, as in Portuguese pork with clams and garlic, Alentejo style; grilled lobster sausages with warm savoy cabbage-potato slaw, and sautéed moulard duck foie gras with beets and crackling.

Innovation begins with the fresh bread sticks, the flavor of which changes nightly (perhaps cheddar cheese, onion or spinach). There's a choice of about a dozen appetizers, from a silken, saffron-scented lobster bisque ($10) to salt cod cakes with hot greens and bacon. We liked the tortellini with rich rabbit sauce, filled with creamy ricotta and sharp romano cheeses and garnished with julienned rabbit, and a signature dish of grilled duck salad with papaya and cranberries.

Entrées are a changing panoply of creative regional cuisine, from $16 for a big bowl of fresh and smoked haddock chowder to $34 for pan-roasted lobster with chervil and chives. Rabbit pot pie, grilled rare tuna steak with pasta and beans, and a deluxe shellfish platter with lobster sausage, baked clams, fried Maine shrimp, tempura mussels and broiled scallops, are other favorites. One of us sampled breast of squab with poached oysters in zinfandel sauce, a unique presentation served with wild rice pilaf and an oh-so-precious side salad of arugula, mache and radicchio with a mild vinaigrette topped with two tiny squab legs. The other had grilled Rhode Island quail with bitter greens and sweet-potato fritters. Superlative shoestring potatoes, creamy garlic mashed potatoes, onion rings and even baked beans might accompany.

Desserts are more limited: a pear upside-down cake, chocolate pot au crème, hot pineapple tartlet with coconut ice cream, and rice pudding with tangerines. We settled for a selection of homemade ice creams and sorbets: kiwi, coconut and champagne, intense and refreshing. With the bill came an orange rind encrusted in bitter chocolate and a mini-pastry of dates and nuts.

Dinner at Jasper's is a treat, from enjoying unobtrusive, down-to-earth service amid sophisticated decor to relishing culinary adventure with every bite.

Dinner, Monday-Saturday 6 to 10 or 11.

Dining is elegantly casual at Hamersley's Bistro.

Hamersley's Bistro, 553 Tremont St., Boston. (617) 423-2700.

Anticipating the trend to downscaled food, this bistro was an instant hit when it opened in 1987 in the South End, so much so that it up and moved to much larger quarters in 1993. Now ensconced in what had been an empty studio in the Center for Performing Arts, it's a friendly, with-it, 120-seat place run very personally by two redheads, Gordon Hamersley, once apprentice to Wolfgang Puck at Ma Maison in Los Angeles and then executive sous chef to Lydia Shire at Seasons, and his English-born wife Fiona, former New England director of the American Institute of Wine and Food. He and his assistants wear red baseball caps in the open kitchen along the side of the long dining room (the ceiling at his former place was too low for a white toque, he explained). The bobbing baseball caps came to symbolize a refreshing lack of pretense.

In typical bistro style, large squares of white paper are clipped over the tablecloths, the silverware is rolled inside white napkins, bottles of S. Pellegrino water serve as centerpieces, track lights provide illumination and the noise level is high enough that you can't really overhear the couple at the next table. Fiona presides at the bar, which is now part of a cafe that offers the same menu but without the $16.50 food minimum of the dining room and without reservations.

"We serve high-quality food stripped down to the basics," Gordon says. "Rustic, peasant food" is what he calls it. We call it gutsy.

Our dinner began with a memorable grilled mushroom and garlic "sandwich" on country bread, not really a sandwich but two toasted bread slices flanking an abundance of mushrooms and watercress ($8.50), and a tasty but messy whole braised artichoke stuffed with olives and mint ($8). Cured foie gras with muscat-grape aspic, frisée salad with smoked bacon and poached egg, a soupe de poisson with aioli that a well-traveled friend called the best she'd ever had and a crisp potato galette with ossetra caviar and crème fraîche are other recommended starters ($7.50 to $16.50).

Among main courses ($17.50 to $24.75), we loved the duckling with turnips, endive and apple slices — an enormous portion, including an entire leg and crisp

slices of breast grilled and blackened at the edges like a good sirloin steak —
and a Moroccan lamb stew with couscous and harissa that everybody raves about.
The roast chicken with garlic, lemon and parsley is said to be a standout. Other
possibilities range from sautéed skate with beets and horseradish crumbs to osso
buco and polenta cooked in a clay pot and seared beef tenderloin with
fire-roasted onions and herb butter. A new section of the menu categorized as
"pasta, grains and vegetarian plates" includes rabbit and goat-cheese lasagna with
lentil sauce and oven-cooked couscous with quail, prunes and almonds,

Given the comfort level of most of the menu, we were surprised by the
unfamiliar and somewhat confusing wine list ($18 to $68). The Hamersleys seek
out the unique among European wines and there was scarcely a vintner we
recognized. Symbols distinguish the type of grape for the uninitiated.

Except for a warm fig tart with almonds and honey, most of the desserts seemed
mundane for $6 (things like souffléed lemon custard and Sophie's favorite
homemade cookies). But for the rest of the meal, we'd gladly go back — and
back again.

Dinner nightly, 6 to 10 or 10:30. No smoking.

Biba, 272 Boylston St., Boston. (617) 426-7878.

Lydia Shire is back where she belongs. Enticed away from Seasons at the
Bostonian Hotel in 1986 to launch the Four Seasons Hotel in Beverly Hills,
Boston's leading culinary light returned in 1989 to open a restaurant of her own.
And it's one like no other, which is not surprising to those who know Lydia.

The two-story emporium in the tony Heritage on the Garden shopping-
residential complex seats 50 in a main-floor bar serving tapas and such, and 150
in a wildly colorful dining room up a curving staircase. The bar features a Winston
Churchill-style smoking couch, a mural of chubby, well-fed people, a lineup of
photos taken by Lydia on her various travels, and framed shopping bags from
the late Biba, her favorite London store.

The Biba Food Hall upstairs is notable for a glassed-in wine cellar along the
curving staircase, an open space with a tandoori oven, pale yellow walls, ceilings
with patterns taken from Albanian carpets, warm woods and white-clothed tables
covered with butcher paper and placed rather close together. The tables bear a
salt dish, a diminutive pepper grinder and, strangely, two ash trays.

Lydia refutes those who classify her decor as Southwest; "if anything, it's
Mediterranean in feeling," she counters. Her menu defies classification as well.
Instead of appetizers and entrées it's categorized according to fish, Biba classics,
meat, offal, starch, legumina and sweets. Full of surprises, it's hard to follow (and
figure) but delightfully quirky, as in -- we quote -- mondongo...uncommon tripe
soup with plantain and avocado, monk wrapped in streaky bacon with pan-
roasted oysters and cider sauce, focaccia cooked to order in iron skillet with rind
of parma ham and fresh autumn figs, duck roasted in sal de mer with sauce of
crushed wine grapes and pan drippings, hanger steak with marrow toasts on
Russian black bread, mix of greens with fork-split aged cheddar, hot baked puffed
tart of swiss chard with roasted autumn beet roots and such, bollito mixto of
parsley and pignoli stuffed pigs feet, chuck, shank and tongue with salsa verde,
and unusual salad of chestnut whipped potato in crisp potato shell, dark garden
greens and grilled bacon...with or without. Without what, you might wonder. But
you get the idea.

At a springtime lunch, we devoured the yummy onion, tandoori and French
breads that preceded our entrées: chickpea and potato rolled in thin pasta with

Chef Lydia Shire at Biba.   **Chef Todd English at Olives**

Moroccan tenderloin of lamb ($14) and citrus salmon with crackling skin and parsley cakes ($16.50). Each was artfully presented on rectangular white plates and was an explosion of tastes. A $16 bottle of Hogue fumé blanc from the Yakima Valley accompanied from a fairly priced and unusual wine list. We finished a memorable meal with a terrific warm tarte tatin with cinnamon ice cream ($7) and a cassis and champagne sorbet with linzer cookies ($8).

Dinnertime brings the ultimate grazing menu, as Lydia breaks all the rules regarding appetizers, entrées and such. Under fish, you might order a fry of native smelts and Cape scallops ($13) or lobster with scotch whiskey and white-bean ravioli in leaves of green chard ($32). Ditto for meat: handcut tartare of beef on toasted soured potato bread served with Wellfleet oysters ($14.50) or roasted rack of venison with hot buttered crespelle of date, walnut and mustard fruits ($32). Legumina items vary from crisped artichoke flower with slivered truffled raw porcini to curried skewered onions charred in the tandoori oven.

While food reviewers swoon and restaurateurs of our acquaintance think this is the most exciting eating in New England, mere mortals are not universally charmed. Some think it's quite awful for a restaurant to present a menu with three items listed as "offal." Others complain of a high decibel level and slow service. But we found that the dining experience fully measured up to its high advance billing.

And success spawned another Shire venture: **Pignoli,** described as an upscale Italian restaurant with dining room, cafe, bakery and bar, scheduled to open around the corner on Park Plaza in the spring of 1994. Same restaurant designer, same Lydia theme, but the smaller menu was to change more often and feature pasta and seafood, in a slightly lower price range. Open daily for lunch and dinner, as well as takeout.

Lunch, Monday-Friday 11:30 to 2:30 (Saturday in bar only); dinner nightly, 5:30 to 10 or 11; Sunday brunch, 11:30 to 3.

Olives, 10 City Square, Charlestown. (617) 242-1999.

Celebrated chef Todd English builds three wood fires a day in the open kitchen of his newly relocated and expanded restaurant at the foot of America's oldest

413

main street, just across the Charles River from Boston. One fire is in the brick oven, a second is in the grill he designed himself and the third is for a rotisserie — all the better for his roasts and grills fired by such New England hardwoods as apple, oak and ash. And all the better for his stand-in-line clientele who appreciate robust cooking and spirited surroundings.

Olives moved two blocks down the street in 1992 to larger quarters, with double the number of seats (110) and probably quadruple the space. As Olives went more upscale in price and setting, the original Olives downscaled into Figs, a cafe/pizzeria. Todd and wife Olivia, both Culinary Institute of America graduates, opened in 1989 after he had put Michela's in Cambridge on the culinary map. Olives takes no reservations. Lines start forming at 4:30 and the place is filled many nights by 6.

Once inside the high-ceilinged space with walls of brick and tall windows on two sides, you'll find a mix of plush and rustic. Upholstered banquettes and booths are situated side-by-side with bentwood chairs at bare wood tables. Lights in the form of stars hang over the bar, which is separated from the dining room by a divider with arched windows. Most of the color comes from the crowd and the activity in the huge open kitchen at the rear.

Diners much on marinated olives and crusty focaccia as they watch Todd and crew whip up starters ($6.50 to $7.95) like roasted onion and smoked-bacon soup with four-cheese crostini, tuna carpaccio on crispy flatbread with mesclun greens, warm parmesan pudding with sweet-pea sauce and wood-grilled prosciutto salad with shallot vinaigrette, green beans and walnut sticks. Homemade pastas come in two sizes and in such unusual combinations as tortelli of butternut squash, sweet Maine crab angolotti and braised goose ravioli, the last with a sauce of seared foie gras and black-truffle essence.

The chef, known for the bold and robust flavors of Italy where he did most of his training, has mellowed a bit from the time when he said "I couldn't see myself doing all that nouvelle, prissy stuff. It just wasn't lusty and full-bodied enough."

Now many of his entrées ($15.50 to $19.75), still hearty and abundant in portions, have been prissied up. Wood-oven-roasted halibut is served on a warm asparagus salad with five-grain timbale and roasted littleneck vinaigrette. Char-grilled turkey chops studded with garlic and rosemary come atop fondutta risotto budino with stir-fry asparagus, haricots verts, favas and country-ham glaze. The spit-roasted ribeye of pork rests on a caraway-crusted mashed-potato tart with confit of leeks and cucumber salad. The night's specials ($19.50 to $25.95) are as precious and pricey as any in Boston: black pearl salmon and littleneck clams served on creamy polenta with braised salsify/white-truffle crème and haricots verts; pan-crisped Maine sea scallops with a chanterelle glaze over a potato and oxtail galette with a frisée and bacon vinaigrette.

Desserts here ($6) are a high point: perhaps pumpkin-brioche pudding with pumpkin anglaise and poached cranberries, tirami su crêpe soufflé with rum-raisin sauce and espresso glaze, or fried banana ravioli with banana flan gâteau.

Not content to rest on his many laurels (Food and Wine, Esquire and the James Beard Foundation have elevated him to the ranks of America's best chefs), Todd opened a third restaurant in 1993, Isola, in Edgartown on Martha's Vineyard. Another Figs was in the works for a Charles Street location in Boston.

This is not leisurely or intimate dining (the lights are bright and the music loud to discourage lingering). But there's no denying the food, which is the rage in Boston as well as the wave of the future.

Dinner, Tuesday-Saturday 5:30 to 10. Beer and wine only.

Anago Bistro, 798 Main St., Cambridge. (617) 876-8444.

First there was Panache, acclaimed local chef Bruce Frankel's early paean to nouvelle/regional cuisine. Then, after a laudable venture in haute New England cuisine at the ill-fated Colony in Boston, he downscaled a bit with 798 Main. The challenge seemingly gone, Bruce "retired" (way too early) in 1992, turning the place over to his chef of nine years, Bob Calderone. The space remains virtually the same, but the new spirit earned Anago a ranking as one of the nation's top new restaurants in 1993 by Bon Appétit magazine.

From a small kitchen Anago fulfills one of the area's more appealing menus — and certainly one of its more affordable. Consider some of the autumn entrées: wood-grilled lobster with fresh spaghetti, sweet corn, spinach and plum tomatoes; baked grey sole and garlic shrimp with black trumpet mushrooms, snap peas and potatoes; grilled duck breast with mashed celery root, savoy cabbage, roasted carrots and parsnips, and grilled venison steak with roasted beets, green beans and chanterelles. The price range is $14.50 to $21. Add a modest bottle of wine from a list that holds good values — many in the mid-teens — and two can dine at a superior restaurant for as little as $50 to $60.

Start, perhaps, with sweet-corn and smoked-salmon polenta, pan-roasted manila clams with broccoli rabe, or wood-grilled crostini with wild-mushroom ragout and sautéed greens ($7.25 to $10). Finish with caramel pot au crème with biscotti, tirami su with berry sauce or apple and pear crisp with homemade vanilla ice cream (all $5).

We'll never forget a cream of mushroom soup — the true essence of the fungus, topped with heavy cream and a dash of nutmeg in a beautiful pattern — and a thick poached salmon, barely cooked, garnished with wispy fennel leaves and served with a thin hollandaise sauce, rice cooked in red wine and glistening crescents of sautéed cucumber. Also soul-warming for lunch on a winter day was the homemade pasta with garlic confit, rich and flavorful but not overpoweringly garlicky. Topped by fresh basil leaves, it also was accompanied by crisp cucumber pieces. Wood-grilled pizza with roasted mushrooms, asparagus and goat cheese and grilled pork chop with warm apple and pear compote were other lunch offerings ($7.50 to $9.75) that day.

Named for the nickname of Bob's great aunt, this is a serene place with little interior trace of its heritage as an industrial building just off Central Square. Forty-two diners can be seated at tables covered with white butcher paper over white cloths. Pale yellow walls rise above sponged terra-cotta wainscoting. Seasonal arrangements are displayed to advantage in mirrored niches. Co-owner Susan Finegold oversees the dining room with warmth and attention to detail.

Lunch, Tuesday-Friday 11:30 to 2; dinner, Tuesday-Thursday 6 to 10, Friday and Saturday 5:30 to 10:30. No smoking.

The Blue Room, 1 Kendall Square, Cambridge. (617) 494-9034.

"This is our grown-up restaurant," advises chef-owner Chris Schlesinger. Known for fiery equatorial cuisine at his East Coast Grill and at Jack and Earl's Dixie Barbecue across town, he calls his new, larger venture "more international, more French and Mediterranean. Our world grill and bar."

Call it what you will, but call it fun. Chris and his chefs still cook everything over a live fire in a state-of-the-art open kitchen. He points to his "line fire" -- a twenty-foot-long bank of burning coals with an oak wood grill, wood-fired oven, a smoker on top, a vertical spit -- all visible from the facing food bar. This is where one best catches the spirit of the place. It's less noisy and more refined than the East Coast Grill, Chris hopes, and certainly less close and claustrophobic. But it's lively and mod, with 85 seats at bare tables set with silverware and chopsticks stuffed into canisters and not much else (the wine is poured in juice glasses). There's a tropical mural in the cocktail lounge at one end; otherwise the decor is mostly windows, brick walls and kitchen.

Dining is an adventure, starting with appetizers ($6.25 to $7.50) like tuna tartare with pickled ginger and soy spinach, an Arabic salad and dip plate, Asian noodle salad with smoked chicken and peanut vinaigrette, and catalonian shrimp with romesco and garlic. Or try the arugula salad with fried squid, the seared rare filet mignon salad or the "straight forward green" with maytag blue cheese.

Among main dishes ($13.50 to $19), the plato de sabores latinos best represents Schlesinger's testament to the grill: a panoply of smoked onion, tortillas, grilled pineapple, papaya, cornbread salad, black beans, pickled slaw, chipotle salsa and salsa verde accompanying chicken garlic sausage or chile-glazed pork tenderloin. Other possibilities are Indonesian-style grilled tuna steak, pecan-crusted red snapper with grilled banana and lime marmalade, spit-roasted tea-soaked chicken with scallion fried rice and sesame greens, and lamb two ways: spicy braised shank and grilled skewered leg with couscous, parsley salad and sweet and hot apricots. Thai red curry shrimp over a crispy noodle cake with glazed mango is one of the pasta/noodle dishes.

For dessert ($4.95), how about pumpkin flan with maple syrup, carrot cake with stewed cherries and cream-cheese topping or something called khulfee ice cream (pistachio, cardamom and honey) with pistachio biscotti and chocolate sauce?

Buttermilk pancakes with roasted bananas are the signature dish at the popular live jazz brunch on Sundays. Big Mike's Sunday supper yields an interesting, all-you-can-eat buffet for $19.75.

Dinner, Monday-Saturday 5:30 to 10 or 10:30; Sunday, brunch 11 to 2:30, dinner buffet, 4 to 9.

Michela's, 245 First St., Cambridge. (617) 494-5419.

Owner Michela Larson put this large northern Italian restaurant with a gourmet takeout shop in the former Carter Ink building on the culinary map when it opened in 1987. Things went downhill briefly after founding chef Todd English left to open Olives, but current chef Jody Adams, formerly sous chef at Hamersley's Bistro, is earning applause for her Mediterranean-style dishes with an emphasis on Tuscany and Umbria.

Although the sidewalk cafe with its umbrellaed tables beneath the lofty atrium appealed for takeout, we chose the elegant square cavern of a dining room, colorful with yellow walls, red pillars, black chairs, exposed beams on the ceiling and a mural of a 15th-century Siena scene at one end. Prim white tables are set with square water glasses and heavy silver.

A mozzarella salad with fresh tomatoes, basil, black olives and peppers ($6) and goat-cheese ravioli with spinach pasta in a sauce of wild mushrooms ($9.50) made a flavorful lunch. So did a pasta with a ragout of veal, grilled quail and artichokes served on a tomato coulis ($11.50), followed by a honeydew sorbet that was almost as creamy as ice cream.

The wine list, with an emphasis on Italians, has some distinguished Californias and, happily, a number of worthy offerings in the teens.

The flavors also sing at dinner time, as in such starters ($7 to $12) as roasted red pepper stuffed with rabbit stew on tuscan beans; duck and farro soup with

Amazing space along with powerful food is offered at Rocco's.

favas, swiss chard and pecorino cheese; a pizza with four cheeses, caramelized onions and truffle oil, and aquacotta, a porcini broth with polenta, taleggio cheese, poached egg and truffle oil. Entrées ($18 to $24) could be tuscan fish stew with saffron couscous gnocchi, seared salmon with braised cabbage and celery root, roast duck with balsamic vinegar and duck-liver crostini, and grilled sirloin steak with truffled mashed potatoes and mushroom relish.

Desserts range from chocolate-espresso torta with cappuccino ice cream to cranberry-hazelnut frangipane tart.

A different but wide-ranging menu (antipasti, pizzas and entrées, $8 to $12) is offered for lunch and dinner in the sidewalk cafe, where no reservations are taken. You also can get lunch from Michela's excellent takeout shop and specialty-foods store next door. There she sells pottery from Italy and coffee mugs from Bennington Potters, as well as assorted vinegars, preserves and such.

Dinner, Monday-Saturday 6 to 10 or 10:30. Cafe and takeout, 7 a.m. to 10 p.m.

Rocco's, 5 Charles St. South, Boston. (617) 723-6800.

"Amazing Grace" was playing on tape as we gazed up at the satyrs and nymphs on the ceiling mural, two stories high. Amazing space, we thought. Owner Patrick Bowe, former manager of Harvest in Cambridge (and lately its new owner), wanted a place that was "playful and colorful." And that it is, along with a bit of the bizarre. Huge windows are framed with incredible draperies, gigantic bronze chandeliers hang from the ceiling and avant-garde sculptures (from changing displays) decorate the bar and environs. The polished bare wood tables are ringed with comfortable bow-back chairs and topped with dishtowel-size napkins. Each table sports a decoration (perhaps a carousel horse, a marble urn, a cement pig or a pewter fish pitcher) that is for sale, the prices listed on the back of the menu.

The unconventional interior is a visual feast, and so is the menu. New chef Barbara Lynch (a Todd English protégé from Michela, Olives and Figs) has added artistic richness and flair to the international-turned-Italian menu. On a day that was raining cats and dogs, we took refuge for a heart-warming lunch of fettuccine tossed with mushrooms, scallions and pieces of game hen ($9.50), and a fabulous version of chili (pork, beef, chicken and black beans, very spicy and garnished with raw red onion, guacamole, and both blue corn and regular tortilla chips, $5.75). A "country" salad ($6.50) sported several kinds of exotic lettuces, barley, dates, goat cheese spread on croutons and a truffle vinaigrette. Comfort food can't get more comforting than the warm pumpkin Indian pudding, fragrant with spices, accompanied by hard sauce and bourbon-vanilla ice cream. Add a glass of the house Corvio wine, and we were ready to face the soaking streets again.

At dinner, mix and match starters ($7.50 to $8.50) like pan-seared fennel-risotto cake with shrimp and tomato salad, roasted clams with fried polenta, chicken-liver soufflé with caramelized onions, a crispy pizzetta and wild-mushroom raviolis with salsa verde and roasted potatoes. Main courses ($15 to $20) could be Genovese fish stew in saffron broth, grilled salmon with braised fennel, stuffed pork loin with warm fig chutney, veal saltimbocca, and grilled beef tenderloin with truffle mashed potatoes and roasted asparagus. To go with you'll find one of the top wine lists in the city, a quirky and expensive affair compiled by wine steward Cat Silirie (frequently honored as Boston's best). Its Italian listings were ranked by a national trade magazine as the finest in the country.

For dessert ($3 to $8), how about the killer chocolate trio, the homemade caramel gelato served on a florentine cookie plate or the cranberry-orange bread pudding with white-chocolate sauce? Finish with a cup of cappuccino, lean back and look at the incredible ceiling, and appreciate one of Boston's more original restaurants.

Lunch daily, 11:30 to 2:30; dinner nightly, 5:30 to 11:30.

Upstairs at the Pudding, 10 Holyoke St., Cambridge. (617) 864-1933.

The top floor of Harvard's famed Hasty Pudding Club building was converted in 1982 into a northern Italian restaurant of lasting renown, thanks to founders Mary-Catherine Deibel and Deborah Hughes, veterans of the old Peasant Stock restaurant in Somerville.

There's nothing peasanty, however, about dining in the Pudding's venerable refectory, its beamed cathedral ceiling hung with brass chandeliers and its soaring green walls decorated with posters from Pudding shows long gone. Widely spaced tables set with pink linens, gleaming crystal and silver create a clublike atmosphere in pink and green.

Chef Mark Newton changes his extensive menu nightly. The meal begins with a freebie, perhaps a plate of marinated kalamata olives and a marinated artichoke heart amidst a sunburst of roasted red peppers and anchovy filets. For first courses, try any of the tagliatelles (said to be as good as those in Bologna), especially the version with basil, plum tomatoes, St. André cheese, parmesan and toasted pine nuts). The grilled bruschetta with fennel relish and herbed goat cheese, and grilled duck breast served on watercress with sherried ginger dressing also are recommended.

Entrées run from $16 for linguini with littlenecks, spinach, pancetta and garlic crostini to $24 for sautéed beef tenderloin with pancetta and rosemary. Other wintertime choices included pan-seared Atlantic salmon with mustard-dill sauce, roasted pork loin with chèvre and port sauce, and osso buco braised with cider and tarragon. The plate overflows with interesting accompaniments, artfully arranged: maybe crispy potato cakes or garlic mashed potatoes, fresh young asparagus, baby carrots, a spoonful of yam puree, braised leeks, salsify, wild Italian mushrooms and red peppers.

Among desserts ($6 to $8) are charlotte au chocolate, chocolate-soufflé cake with an orange-coffee nape, vanilla pot de crème with honey-walnut biscotti, and profiteroles with mocha ice cream and bittersweet-chocolate sauce.

The Pudding also offers a tasting menu for $42, consisting of one choice from each category as well as salad.

A summertime asset is the new roof deck and herb garden, a serendipitous and romantic hideaway for al-fresco dining. The Pudding also has expanded its hours and added lunch and brunch service. The special "rapido lunch" -- soup and a sandwich "served within five minutes" -- puts $7 to good use.

Lunch, Monday-Friday noon to 3; dinner nightly, 6 to 10; Sunday brunch, noon to 2

Another Season, 97 Mt. Vernon St., Boston. (617) 367-0880.

The colorful French murals on the walls of this Beacon Hill townhouse make you think you're dining in a small and intimate art gallery. The meals combine the artistic and culinary talents of English-born chef-owner Odette D. Bery, for whom this is her third and best Boston restaurant effort.

Its name is appropriate, for since she opened the romantic refuge with three small dining rooms in 1977 she has devoted herself to changing seasons and tastes. She also is known for her occasional series of cooking demonstrations.

Her eclectic and changing regular menu offers appetizers for $7.50 to $8.50; perhaps peppered smoked mackerel with hot potato salad and arugula or spicy shrimp in orange marinade with avocado and mixed greens; $14 to $23 for entrées like crayfish jambalaya, grilled salmon with red-pepper pesto and saffron couscous, chicken breast stuffed with leeks, spinach and mozzarella, and tenderloin of beef with apricot-walnut whiskey sauce. It's a melding of continental, Mediterranean, Asian and regional American influences into a cuisine that is hers alone.

One terrific winter dinner began with shrimp aioli with a great garlicky sauce and a fantastic watercress mousse with prosciutto. Then came an excellent house salad topped with julienned celery root. Main courses were a fine beef tenderloin sautéed with red peppers and juniper berries, and chicken breast with a sauce of brie, chives and fresh thyme. We shared a super marjolaine for dessert after finishing a bottle of beaujolais from a primarily French wine list (with a few from California and Oregon) starting in the high teens.

The tables, most tiny and close together, are decked out in white napery and fresh flowers. The spotlights illuminating the murals make some tables rather bright. And you may have to wait in the tiny front ante-room with quarry tile floors and a few seats. Odette Bery's meals transcend such quibbles, however.

Lunch, Tuesday-Friday noon to 2; dinner, Monday-Saturday 6 to 10.

Cafe Budapest, 90 Exeter St., Boston. (617) 734-3388.

The late Edith Ban, a Hungarian who came to Boston after the 1956 uprising and who was the grande dame of Boston restauranteurs, had a reputation for imperiousness, one no doubt enhanced by her commanding presence always garbed completely in white. So we were stunned after staggering through a January blizzard for a 1 p.m. lunch reservation to learn that Mrs. Ban had decreed that the first patrons of the day were to be her guests, and that we were they.

Many are the times since that we and friends have dined in regal splendor in our favorite oak-paneled dining room, all red and white with old Hungarian flasks, walking sticks, wine jugs and decorative plates on the walls. The tradition has been maintained by Mrs. Ban's sister, Dr. Hedda Rev-Kury, who practices medicine by day and restauranteuring at night.

Our first memorable lunch began with a hearty peasant soup topped with fried noodles and exquisite chicken paprikas crêpes. It continued with gypsy baron rice pilaf and the authentic beef goulash that an Austrian friend who manages a fine hotel thinks is the greatest. The finale was a sensational Hungarian strudel, accompanied by fragrant Viennese coffee, made from beans ground fresh hourly and served in glass cups.

Meals here are fit for royalty, and the setting is so old-world romantic that you'd almost expect to see Zsa Zsa Gabor dallying with an admirer in one of the intimate alcoves off the lounge (actually, she has dined here, on chicken paprika, we're told). At night, when things get busy and up to 500 meals may be served, the Hungarian menu carries french accents. For appetizers, you can get the great chicken paprikas crêpe ($7), or you can try Hungarian goose liver with truffles ($12) or caviar à la russe ($12.50).

Most of the 26 entrées ($19.50 to $33) are Middle European, things like sweetbreads à la hongroise under glass, veal gulyas and wiener schnitzel vying for attention with broiled lemon sole and châteaubriand with mimosa salad. Each comes with different vegetables and salads. One night, three in our party declared spectacular the veal served with rice, string beans and carrots tied in a bundle, and a special salad of grapes and endive arranged like a star. Most of the unusual desserts like a champagne torte or crêpes with farm cheese and raisins are in the $5.50 range.

If you have any romance in your soul, you'll love Cafe Budapest — particularly the small pink dining room with pink chairs off the lounge, almost too pretty for words, and the Empire-style lounge where, ensconced in gilt and brocade chairs, you can have dessert crêpes flambéed tableside while a pianist and violinist entertain nearby.

Lunch, Monday-Saturday noon to 3; dinner, 5:30 to 10:30, Friday and Saturday to midnight, Sunday 1 to 10:30.

Other Dining Choices

East Coast Grill, 1271 Cambridge St., Cambridge. (617) 491-6568.

"Grills just want to have fun" is the motto on the menu and the T-shirts of the staff at this former Inman Square luncheonette that's hot, hot, hot. The hottest dish in New England is said to be an appetizer called sausage from hell ($5.25), served with banana-guava ketchup and West Indies bread salad and fired by the house-bottled Inner Beauty Real Hot Sauce — the label cautions: "This is not a toy. This is serious." So it is, so much so that the second time we bought a bottle we dropped down a degree to "mild." The mustard-colored liquid fire derives its wallop from scotch bonnet chiles, which make jalapeños taste like tofu in

In kitchen at Blue Room is Chris Schlesinger (left), who also owns East Coast Grill.

comparison. Those with less incendiary tastes can start with smoked pork tenderloin served with cucumber and radish salad or grilled chicken livers with a seared green salad.

Chef-owner Chris Schlesinger, grandson of the late Harvard historian Arthur Schlesinger, is co-author of *The Thrill of the Grill* and *Salsa, Sambals, Chutneys and Chow Chows* cookbooks. He bases his changing menu on equatorial cuisine — food from hot places. "The closer you get to the equator," says he, who has traveled there frequently, "the more spicy and intense the flavors are." He offers three kinds of barbecue: North Carolina shredded pork flavored with vinegar and hot peppers ($12.95); Memphis pork spare ribs, authentic and succulent, and Texas beef brisket with sweet barbecue sauce (both $14.25). The uninitiated can try a sampler of all three ($14.95). Other entrées ($13.50 to $18.95) include Chilean sea bass thrilled on the grill with pickled cucumber salad, spit-roasted jerk-rubbed pork loin with candied yams and peppered strip loin with wild-mushroom steak sauce and "damn good" fries. Cool off with a dessert like pumpkin bread pudding, guava caramel custard or apple-pear-cranberry cobbler. Most of the wines are priced in the teens, but there are far more boutique beers, the beverage of choice.

The place is a funky melange of geometric shapes in earthy colors on the walls, splashes of neon, a marble-topped bar with diner stools, small tables and a rear wall of stainless steel that reflects the flames from the open-pit barbecue. The galvanized hanging lights were fashioned by a local artist from ice-cube trays, forks, graters and other kitchen utensils.

Although it's not for the faint of heart (or palate), the 43 seats are packed nightly -- a staggering 225 dinners were served the Saturday night before we were there. If you can't get in, take out from **Jake and Earl's Dixie Barbecue,** which Chris and partner Cary Wheaton run next door. Open daily from 11:30 to 11, it's named for his pet Labrador and her father, and looks as if it would be quite at home in his native South.

Dinner nightly, 5 to 10 or 10:30.

Harvest, 44 Brattle St., Cambridge. (617) 492-1115.

The earliest (1975) and trendiest of the new Cambridge restaurant breed, Harvest has long been *the* place to see and be seen. Tucked behind a Crate & Barrel store, it is furnished in Marimekko, bentwood, stoneware, tiles, zippy prints and one entire wall of tiny colored lights — all very high-tech, as was typical of designer-owners Jane and Ben Thompson. The Thompsons sold the place in 1993 to Patrick Bowe, owner of Rocco's in Boston, who had managed Harvest for them for five years in the early 1980s. He brought in his executive chef, Chris Fallon, and started freshening up the '70s decor.

You can sit in the main dining room, a smaller room or the cafe-bar (and, seasonally, in an outdoor garden where the trees are strung with white lights). For an Easter Weekend lunch, we chose a pillowed banquette near the bar and enjoyed hearing classical guitar and excerpts from "The Messiah" on tape.

The menu, adorned with pictures of the season's harvest, changes monthly. The terrine was a great rough country pâté, and we thoroughly enjoyed a huge artichoke served with a mayonnaise and tomato sauce, ringed by crisp vegetables chilled in a vinaigrette, and an entrée of sautéed salmon sprigged with fresh dill and served with hot mashed avocado and crisp carrots. The combination was ahead of its time — that being 1979 and pre-nouvelle — but Harvest has always anticipated trends and has spawned some of Boston's top chefs.

The new menu is equally innovative, while reflecting more hearty fare at lower prices. Among starters ($5 to $9) are grilled shrimp served hot over chipotle polenta with charred bitter greens and sour cream, beet and butternut-squash ravioli with goat cheese in a roasted onion and thyme broth, and duck galantine stuffed with pork, liver and dried cranberries. Main courses ($14.50 to $27) included curried red snapper with couscous and a green curry-basil sauce, lobster and crabmeat manicotti, roasted pheasant with shallot and sage sauce, and rack of lamb with roasted garlic risotto. The mixed grill teams squab, quail and venison.

Desserts could be cranberry-walnut tart or rum-spiked tirami su. We remember a delightful chocolate-mint cheesecake from an earlier visit. Nine wines are available by the glass and there's an extensive cellar, as well as all the correct domestic and imported beers.

A wide-ranging menu featuring lower-priced fare is available nightly in the **Harvest Cafe.** You also can get a quick bite or food to go at **Harvest Express,** where we liked the looks of the creative calzones, torta rustica and vegetarian strudel.

Lunch, Monday-Saturday 11:30 to 2:30; dinner nightly, 6 to 10 or 11; Sunday brunch, 11 to 3. Express, Monday-Saturday 8:30 to 7.

Maison Robert, 45 School St., Boston. (617) 227-3370.

Formal and a tad forbidding, this has been a bastion of classic French cuisine since it opened in 1972 in one of Boston's first building restorations, the Old City Hall. Wrote architectural critic Ada Louise Huxtable at the time: "Those who said it couldn't be done are enjoying tournedos and a good little burgundy at Maison Robert." And many still are, such is the draw of chef-owner Lucien Robert from Normandy for a coterie of expense-account businessmen plus tourists off the Freedom Trail, attracted by the colorful umbrellas on an outdoor terrace.

The Empire-style Bonhomme Richard dining room with its lofty molded ceiling, three majestic crystal chandeliers and twenty-foot-high draperies is elegant and expensive. Ben's Cafe downstairs is less so.

The basics of the upstairs menu, printed in French with English translations, have not changed since one of us dined regally more than fifteen years ago as the guest of an entertaining businessman. But there are innovations: perhaps corn and parmesan soufflé with smoked tomato sauce, grilled veal chop with pear and ginger compote, and sweetbreads with a chestnut and truffle sauce. Prices of the twenty entrées range from $17 for roulade of chicken breast with spinach and pinenuts to $30 for rack of lamb provençal.

The ambitious menu details fourteen appetizers from $4.25 for soup du jour to $18 for pâté of foie gras, not counting the $45 tab for beluga caviar with blinis. Fifteen desserts range from $4.50 from fruit tart of the day to $9 for soufflé grand marnier. The handsome, sleek wine list delivers some of Boston's most reasonable prices at the low end, as well as old and rare vintages to $600.

Ben's Cafe, bright and cheery, is the domain of M. Robert's daughter Andrée, who's doing some highly rated cooking (and lately became executive chef for the entire restaurant). Her prix-fixe cafe menu changes monthly. With things like goose lasagna with pearl onions and mushrooms or sea bass poached with leeks and mushrooms, it's a tad more au courant than that upstairs. And the prices -- four courses with several choices each for $15 or $22 -- are a positive steal.

Lunch, Monday-Friday 11:30 to 2:30; dinner, Monday-Saturday 6 to 10 or 10:30.

Dali Restaurant and Tapas Bar, 415 Washington St., Somerville. (617) 661-3254.

"We are proud to be a real Spanish restaurant," says courtly owner Mario Leon Iriarte, born in Bilbao and raised in Argentina. He and partner Tamara Bourso opened in 1989 and do no advertising, yet word has gotten around, to the point where restaurateurs throughout the Boston area consider it one of the best.

The nondescript facade on a busy street at the Cambridge-Somerville line masks an interior of great appeal. People gather at the tapas bar with its copper plate tiles made in Seville and the crooked picture of Dali on the wall behind. Hanging over the bar is an incredible assortment of items: serrano hams, wine skins, slabs of salt cod, dried flowers, ropes of garlic, baskets of corks, strands of glass beads and copper pans.

Eleven cold and twenty-one hot tapas ($3.50 to $5.50) are on the regular menu, and every day a dozen or so more are on an "inspiraciones" list. Served in natural clay bowls, they vary from mesclun salad to scallops in saffron cream to wood-roasted peppers with shrimp to pork sausage with figs to garlic soup to white asparagus with shrimp dressing. To go with, there are more than 25 kinds of sherry and 60 wines, many under $15 and all Spanish.

That's not all — two dining rooms with tiled tables are beyond the tapas bar. The decor must be seen to be believed: curved rails here, Daumier reproductions of Don Quixote there, a wonderful mural of a bacchanal by Mark Steel, walls the color of "blood of the bulls," a plaster arch that makes one think of the Alhambra, a laundry line hung with unmentionables that Mario calls "lost and found" — it's wild and wonderful, and quite charming. "People come just to see the roses in the bathrooms," says Mario.

Most popular among entrées ($11 to $17) is pescado a la sal, Dali's signature dish: red snapper baked in a crust of salt that is broken when the dish comes to the table, leaving the fish, pure and simple, smelling of the ocean. Also popular is shrimp in a romesco sauce of Barcelona origin that includes pimento, almonds, spices, onions and garlic, and is like pink velvet, according to the owner. Rabbit is braised in juniper berries, cinnamon, serrano chiles, sherry vinegar and red wine, and could be accompanied by mashed-potato rosettes and red cabbage and apples. Of course, there's paella in two traditional versions, valencia and del oceano, plus a third with gingered lamb. Beef tenderloin with dried figs, apricots and prunes in a brandy cream sauce and rare angulas, sautéed baby eels from Spain and available in this country only at Dali, are new additions to the menu. End with flan, crêpes filled with fruit and topped with chocolate sauce and orange liqueur, or a dish of quince paste and manchego cheese.

Dinner, Monday-Saturday 5 to midnight.

Icarus, 3 Appleton St., Boston. (617) 426-1790.

A statue of the mythological Icarus, poised for flight, looms above tree branches lit with tiny white lights high on the rear wall. It oversees this chic restaurant that has done very nicely since it moved to expanded quarters here from nearby Tremont St. The sunken, split-level room full of rich dark wood is a mix of booths and round mission oak tables. The tables are left bare except for dusky pink napkins folded sideways between fluted silverware. Recessed aqua lighting outlines the perimeter of the ceiling.

It's an altogether pleasant backdrop for the fare of longtime chef Chris Douglass, whose low public profile masks his standing as one of the best in town. His menu is brief but the equal of any in the city: entrées ($17.50 to $23) like grilled salmon with sesame-ginger vinaigrette and crab pot stickers, lobster over squid-ink pappardelle with roasted red peppers and savoy cabbage, sautéed breast and roasted leg of duck with wild-rice pancakes, grilled veal chop with porcini sauce and white-bean puree, and juniper-crusted venison with cranberries and walnuts.

Appetizers ($8.50 to $9.75) are unusual: grilled turkey and fig sausage with mustard and lentils, hazelnut-toasted sweetbreads with watercress and orange salad, grilled shrimp with mango and jalapeño sorbet, and polenta with braised exotic mushrooms. Lighter eaters (and spenders) can go for the potato, leek and bacon soup with crème fraîche or the mesclun salad with an orange and sherry vinaigrette (each $4.50).

Save room for dessert, perhaps chocolate gâteau with crème chantilly, Asian pear crisp with anise streusel and ginger ice cream, pumpkin semifreddo with bourbon-maple anglaise and spiced walnuts, or white-chocolate soufflé with caramel sauce and cashew praline.

Many of the dinner starters turn up on the small menu ($7 to $9.50) for Sunday brunch, which is immensely popular with South End neighbors.

Dinner, Monday-Friday 5 to 10 or 11, Saturday 5:30 to 11; Sunday, brunch 11 to 3, dinner 5:30 to 10:30.

Azita Ristorante, 560 Tremont St., Boston. (617) 338-8070.

One of the newest restaurants in this South End block is run lovingly by Azita Bina and her brother Babak. Azita had been a founding partner of Ristorante Toscano, a Tuscan charmer on Beacon Hill. But this is very much her place — small (50 seats), pristine and personal.

The decor is sleek in white and black, with pink walls and a white pressed-tin ceiling. Pink and white linens dress the well-spaced tables, each set with heavy silver, white china and a vase with a single orchid. Changing artworks and recessed plants provide accents. A new rear solarium with curtained ceiling contains six tables overlooking a garden. Azita cooks in a narrow, semi-open kitchen behind a front display counter.

Start with her salty scacciata and Italian breads before digging into chicken over arugula, a delicious plateful for $7.75 at lunch. For a winter lunch, we also liked

Azita Ristorante is sleek in black and white.

the Tuscan pasta e fagioli soup ($4.50), followed by a plate of carpaccio ($5.25). Dessert was a superior tirami su.

At night, the antipasti ($5.75 to $8.25) include warm foie gras over puree of borlotti red beans and wild mushrooms over grilled polenta. The dozen pastas top off at $12 for linguini with lobster and tomatoes in a vodka cream sauce. Main courses ($14.95 to $19.95) could be brook trout in orange and vermouth sauce, grilled cornish hen with rosemary, roasted pork loin with blueberry sauce, roasted veal with gruyère and truffle sauce, and grilled venison steak and sausage with horseradish sauce. The Italian and California wines are affordably priced.

Lunch, Monday-Saturday 11:30 to 2:30; dinner, 5:30 to 10 or 11.

Jae's Cafe & Grill, 1281 Cambridge St., Cambridge. (617) 497-8380.

One look and we were smitten. How could you help but like a place where three long tropical fish tanks divide the bar from the dining room, the white brick walls are handpainted in multi-color abstracts by the owner and three chefs man the 40-item sushi bar? This is the new-in-1993 Jae's, a contemporary and expanded outpost of the original Jae's at 520 Columbus Ave. in Boston's South End. Here, Korean-born Jae Chung has added grills to his Korean-Japanese-Thai offerings.

Artistry in the kitchen seems to come naturally to Jae, who studied fine arts in college. It turns up in all kinds of decorative (and tasty) morsels, from Jae's tidbits (an appetizer sampler for $11.95) to his ginger custard, dark-chocolate mousse and lemon framboise for dessert. In between are all kinds of noodle, pad thai, vegetable, fried rice and curry dishes, pleasantly priced from $7.50 to $12.95. We wanted to lunch on one of the lunch box combos, but the menu had preceded their arrival, for some obscure reason. Upon the waitress's recommendation, we settled on the Party Boat 1, $30 for two, a feast of impeccably fresh sushi that arrived in a wooden boat and was almost more than two could finish. A glass of house wine accompanied from an exceptionally appealing -- and affordable -- American wine list priced mainly in the teens. We also would have liked to have tried the spicy squid Korean style, the basil Wellfleet clams with mixed vegetables or noodles, the grilled shrimp scampi, the tuna or salmon tartare, the dumplings with curry sauce -- in fact, almost everything on the menu. That, however, would take a number of return visits, something the locals are better able than we to do. They take seriously the restaurant's slogan: "Eat at Jae's...and live forever."

Lunch, Monday-Saturday 11:30 to 4; dinner nightly, 5 to 10:30; late-night sushi, 10:30 to 1; Sunday brunch, 10 to 3.

Emporio Armani Express, 214 Newbury St., Boston. (617) 437-0909.

What to make of this designer restaurant, an adjunct opening to and from the adjacent Armani designer store? It's as showy as its fans had proclaimed. It's as trendy as its press notices indicated. The Italian fare is wide-ranging, to mixed reviews. And there's something about it that makes the visitor feel he's intruding, as if he were trying to crash the private preserve of the "in" crowd.

Granted, it was 2:30 on a Friday afternoon and we'd already eaten. But journalistic research demanded a look. Two long and narrow floors: one a hip and crowded bar/cafe with tiled floor, whirring ceiling fans and many of the young, beautiful people -- perhaps (young) ladies who lunch? Upstairs, a dining room that is understated yet luxurious to the max: sponged beige walls with bleached pine wainscoting below, well-spaced tables bearing rich, cream-colored cloths and napkins folded in layers ever so correctly, a few mirrors and plants for decor, with windows onto Newbury Street. And everywhere waiters and busboys in striking brown, uh, whatchamacallits. Dress military outfits? We asked. "Uniforms," was the considered reply. No one knew them by any other name. They only knew they were Giorgio Armani originals.

The upscale Italian menu -- with English translations -- details all the usual suspects and then some. At lunch, pastas, risottos, pizzas, panini and salads are in the $6.25 to $12.95 range and entrées, $11.50 to $15.50. That's not likely to break the bank of any of the local trendoids. Dinner pastas and risottos at $9.95 to $16.95 won't either. But add one of the antipasti ($9.95 to $14.95), say carpaccio of tuna or prosciutto with grilled porcini mushrooms, a salad of baby lettuce with broiled dover sole ($10.50) or the shellfish soup ($11.50). Order an entrée ($18 to $29), perhaps grilled ahi tuna in a lemon vinaigrette or beef steak grilled and fanned, topped with arugula and drizzled with olive oil. Indulge with a bottle from the Italian-California wine list, nicely arranged by prices from $18 to $200. Finish with tirami su or crespellini, a crêpe wrapped with sweet mascarpone cheese and toasted pecans in strawberry sauce. Linger over cappuccino and a special grappa. Bet your brush with the rich and famous of Italy will set you back a few hundred thousand lire.

Open daily, 11:30 to 11, Friday and Saturday to midnight, Sunday to 10; Sunday brunch, 11:30 to 5.

Mirabelle, 85 Newbury St., Boston. (617) 859-4848.

Pair the chairman of the National Restaurant Association with a 23-year-old chef whose skills exceed his years. Add a "neighborhood restaurant" concept serving three meals a day on weekends. The result is this winner of a small, elegant yet comfortable restaurant that opened in 1993 in fancy digs on Newbury Street.

In his past catering days, proprietor Stephen Elmont served thousands of people, from Maria Shriver to Jacqueline Kennedy. Now he and chef Tom Tenuta, who quit the Johnson & Wales culinary program to become immersed in the food business, provide what they call adult comfort food that reflects customers' favorites. That translates to a wide range of contemporary and classic European cuisine with an emphasis on fresh seafood and vegetarian fare.

It also involves an emphasis on New England bounty. We were there for one of the New England food festivals that change weekly in winter. The meal began with butternut-squash soup and Maine crab cakes with cilantro mayonnaise. Roasted Vermont lamb persillade was accompanied by brussels sprouts with roasted chestnuts, candied baby carrots and garlicky mashed potatoes, followed by a salad of wild greens with Hubbardston goat cheese. The apple bread pudding topped with homemade vanilla ice cream and a sampler of five sorbets -- from Ethiopian coffee to concord grape -- finished a delicious feast.

The regular dinner menu ($14.50 to $23.95) ranges from the simple (coq au vin, baked lemon sole and calves liver) to the sublime (seared fillet of salmon with fennel and mustard beurre blanc, seared duck breast with cranberries and lemon verbena, and roasted veal chop stuffed with prosciutto, apples and sage).

Stop here for weekend breakfast, anything from lemon scones to brioche french toast, from Irish oatmeal to eggs benedict. Lunch is a mixed bag as well, from roasted duck salad to veal stew with herbed risotto.

Besides the food, some innovations are being pioneered here. If the wine prices ($12 to $33) look unusually reasonable for Boston, be advised that they are for half bottles and those are all that are served. The idea is to inspire wine exploration. The prices are supposedly less than half the cost of a full bottle.

Also be advised that a fifteen percent service charge is added to each check and is retained by the restaurant. The proprietor says he accumulates the charges to pay higher salaries to the entire staff.

Breakfast, Saturday 9 to 11 and Sunday 9 to 3; lunch, Monday-Saturday 11 to 4; dinner, Monday-Saturday from 6, Sunday from 5. No smoking.

Cornucopia on the Wharf, 100 Atlantic Ave., Boston. (617) 367-0300.

After a lengthy birthing period in all-but hidden quarters downtown on West Street, this little winner up and moved in 1993 to the waterfront. Chef Stuart Cameron retained his small and stylish contemporary American menu in the new 300-seat venue on two floors. The goal was to snare tourists and become Boston's leading seafood house with a water view. It survived the transition, despite initial skepticism from colleagues.

Tables are situated near windows around the perimeter of a dining room that surrounds an interior bar-lounge. Rich wood panels on the diagonal and edging the ceiling accent the yellow walls of windows looking onto harbor and skyline; here and there are other accents in a cornucopia of colors.

The menu changes seasonally. For a December lunch, we had a wonderful oyster and fennel soup and a fried squid salad with Asian black-bean dressing for starters, followed by a chicken breast grilled with Indian spices ($8), served with crisp carrots and vegetables and a cucumber salad, and egg fettuccine with a spicy tomato, herb and clam sauce ($7.50). Portions were small, but the waiter brought seconds (and thirds) of the good French bread. A $16 bottle of muscadet was fine. Desserts included a chestnut torte "fort" with gingersnap logs and pear coulis, milk-chocolate and pistachio tart with cinnamon-espresso anglaise, and a hot maple-buckwheat crêpe with poached quince and vanilla ice cream.

At dinner, entrées ($12.95 to $21) might be bouillabaisse, roasted monkfish wrapped in cob-smoked bacon, roasted salmon with horseradish crust and caramelized red-onion sauce, pepper-crusted tuna steak with poached pear and bitter greens, and roasted filet mignon topped with melted brie, wild mushrooms and sundried tomatoes. The menu suggests a wine with each appetizer and entrée, by the bottle or glass.

Lunch, Monday-Friday 11:30 to 2:30; dinner nightly, 5:30 to 10 or 10:30; Saturday and Sunday brunch..

Sonsie, 327 Newbury St., Boston. (617) 351-2500.

What's this? A "kitchen/bar/bakery" on Newbury Street? Opened by Boston's leading nightclub entrepreneur? Overseen by one of the city's top chefs? With healthful foods?

The name provides a clue -- a Celtic word for relaxed and comfortable. A front wall of french doors opens onto Newbury Street. An air-curtain allows patrons to sip cappuccino at little marble tables just inside as they "watch the world go by right out front, even in the dead of winter," in the words of young owner Patrick Lyons. Inside is a corner salon harboring a clutch of antique stuffed leather club chairs for lounging. A multi-colored curtain parts to yield a vista of bar and dining room beneath a high pressed-tin ceiling. The vision is one of terra-cotta colors, wainscoted walls, close-together tables, red swagged draperies and Moroccan hand-blown glass chandeliers.

This is like nothing Boston heretofore had seen. And upon opening in December 1993, it promised quickly to become a Boston scene. Chef Bill Poirier, whom we first met at Seasons at the Bostonian Hotel, directs a cast of dozens -- big enough to staff an entire hotel without the rooms, says Lyons, who obviously was putting his money where his mouth is. Poirier's wide-ranging international menu covers all the bases, from whole roast onion soup with gruyère and toasted bread crumbs and wild-mushroom tamales with chipotle-chile salsa through intriguing pastas, brick-oven pizzas and main dishes to decadent desserts. A notice on the menu says the dishes are designed to keep fat and cholesterol levels low; "we use little or no dairy products and lean meats whenever possible." The only beef word on the menu turns up in an appetizer of crisp beef dumplings with coriander and Chinese mustard. Pastas ($6.75 to $12) tend to be things like bucatini with Italian pickled peppers, cauliflower and roasted tomato or hand-cut black-pepper noodles with smoked duck and swiss chard. Main dishes ($12.50 to $17) include sake-steamed salmon fillet with cucumber nori rolls and toasted sesame, and grilled loin of cured pork with rosemary and fennel. In the contemporary Boston food idiom, the layered codfish cake comes with "melting onions and lobster jus;" the "big chowder plate" with sea bass, shrimp, oysters and vegetable crackers, and the "seven-hour lamb leg" is "braised in its own juices." The Vietnamese spring rolls with fresh mint are "available vegetarian." Featured is a vegetarian tasting menu, $22 for soup, two appetizers and the vegetable mixed grill.

Indulge in at least a semi-good-for-you dessert ($6), perhaps apple phyllo crunch with warm caramel sauce and whipped cream, warm dark-molasses pie with double vanilla ice cream, citrus-lemon cake with sundried cherries and lemon curd, or a five-flavor fruit sorbet with frosted mint leaves.

There's lot to look at: a cache of daily newspapers from across the world, a 1902 hand-carved oak mantel from a Commonwealth Avenue mansion behind the bar, a waterfall of colored water droplets on the way to the downstairs bakery, a ladies' room papered with racy tabloid covers and polyurethaned toilet seats embedded with coins or, ouch, barbed wire. "We wanted to inject a little theater," deadpans Patrick.

Breakfast, lunch and dinner daily, 7 a.m. to 1 a.m.

Ristorante Pomodoro, 319 Hanover St., Boston. (617) 367-4348.

Boston's famed North End has never really attracted true connoisseurs. Its staggering array of Italian eateries tends to seem all the same, with predictable and interchangeable menus of veal parm and red sauce redux. Some are large and gaudy, more are small and basic, and a handful are true. Lately, a few newcomers -- the kind of contemporary Italian places that abound elsewhere in Boston and around the country -- have infiltrated.

The hands-down best is Pomodoro, a lovable hole in the wall with 24 seats and, by comparison, a large and open kitchen. Here is where proprietress Siovhan Carew, an unlikely Irishwoman with her own ideas about Italian food after a stint as a waitress at the nearby Daily Catch, and chef Richard Hanson, whose mother was Italian by way of The Bronx, have pooled their talents since 1992. The printed dinner menu looks like many another hereabouts, although the results are quite a cut above. It is the specials, handwritten nightly, and particularly the game dishes that aspire to the heights. Start perhaps with a tossed salad of seared tuna carpaccio with chickpeas and onions or the house-smoked sea bass with a roasted red-pepper vinaigrette on a bed of organic mesclun greens. Continue with oven-roasted swordfish with a warm salad of eggplant and tomatoes, served with herbed risotto and asparagus, or a seared venison chop with a wine sauce of sundried tomatoes and pinenuts, served with garlic mashed potatoes, braised radicchio and sugar snap peas. The pasta special could be a ragout of beef, veal and pork cooked in red wine with fresh herbs and served over bow-tie pasta. The prices are $4.95 to $10.95 for appetizers and $9.95 to $15.95 for menu entrées, $17.95 to $19.50 for specials.

The wine list is mostly Italian and surprisingly extensive, with prices in the teens and twenties. As is the case with a number of its peers, Pomodoro offers no desserts or coffees, and we were advised the rest rooms are somewhere "across the street." After all, the food is foremost. With black close-together tables and rows of striking spoons and forks painted as sculptures on the walls, this is one convivial and appealing little place.

Open daily, 11 to 11.

Terramia, 98 Salem St., Boston. (617) 523-3112.

Another North End newcomer, this is even newer (1993) than Pomodoro, a bit larger and more refined, and with an entire menu that's every bit as cutting edge. Eating here is a serious affair, but is just as personal as Pomodoro, thanks to chef Mario Nocero from Salerno and hostess Carla Agrippino, friends and owners.

You're not likely to find spaghetti or chicken cacciatore here. Instead, savor such antipasti ($6.50 to $10) as veal carpaccio with tuna sauce, bresaola with parmigiano and pears, sea scallops filled with porcini mushrooms and potato gratin, or baby octopus, steamed in plum-tomato sauce. All of the pasta, riso and polenta dishes entice, particularly the skewer of rabbit and homemade sausage with wild mushrooms over fresh polenta.

Other main courses ($12 to $19.50) could be a standout salted cod with potatoes, onions and truffle oil; baked salmon with zucchini and leeks in fumet sauce; grilled shrimp and scallops in a pepper sauce with couscous; swordfish steamed with olives and rosemary in parchment paper, or grilled lamb with garlic and rosemary. The wine list is primarily Italian, priced in the teens and twenties.

Space constraints prevent Terramia from serving dessert and coffee, two commodities in abundance at specialty shops and espresso bars throughout the North End. The tables here, though close, seem not quite as tight as in other

North End spots. The space is colorful with a terra-cotta tile floor, beamed ceiling, white over green tablecloths and abstract paintings on the walls.

Dinner nightly, 5 to 10 or 11.

Hotel Dining

Aujourd'hui, Four Seasons Hotel, 200 Boylston St., Boston. (617) 338-4400.

A window table at Aujourd'hui is a prospect on the finer things in Boston life, among them a view of the swan boats plying the pond of the Public Garden and the cooking of world-class chefs. The latter seem to come and go, as is inherent in chain-hotel restaurants. The departure of Boston-born chef Mark Baker, whom Food & Wine magazine had portrayed as one of the young stars on the dining scene, caused short-lived concern, but new chef Jamie Mammano was equal to the challenge.

The second-floor restaurant's setting is serene: floral-fabric banquettes, rich oak paneling, Royal Doulton china atop white damask cloths and floor-length skirts, nicely spaced tables, and a solicitous staff in outfits that match the colors of the 110-seat room.

At lunch, we loved the subtle creamless tomato and fennel soup with toasted focaccia ($5.50) and smoked duck pieces encased in tiny herbed rice pancakes with a sesame-flavored dipping sauce ($7.75). Entrées were a tasty grilled pork tenderloin with plum-pepper marmalade and potato pancakes ($16.50) and a special of medallions of wild boar with pearl onions and madeira ($18), accompanied by tiny beans, baby carrots and small roasted potatoes. The fruit tart that we'd admired in the enticing pastry display near the entry was perfection, filled with oversize blackberries, blueberries and strawberries in a pastry cream with a shortbread-like crust. The sorbet lover among us freaked out on the day's trio — pear, mixed berry and mango.

The regular menu is supplemented by specials, including a number of marked selections containing reduced levels of calories, cholesterol, sodium and fat.

Dinner begins, compliments of the chef, with a freebie like salmon mousse with black-pepper vodka and crème fraîche. In the evening, first courses run from $10.50 for Mediterranean shellfish stew or tuna tartare with smoked onion and poblano-pepper relish to $13.50 for acorn squash and lobster risotto in its shell. We found both the Thai spring roll with duck confit and the pappardelle with braised rabbit, chanterelles and barolo wine extraordinary.

Our main dishes ($26 to $38) were a burst of flavors: a special of grilled lamb chops with crispy potato sticks and feta and dried tomato flan, and roast ribeye of veal with port wine, onions and sage. The mascarpone and espresso cheesecake, the warm mango tart and the grand-marnier nougat soufflé came highly recommended, but we settled on a trio of delicious frozen parfaits. A tray of candies accompanied the bill.

The wine list, one of Boston's best, includes a full page of wines by the glass and two pages of domestic chardonnays. We found a couple of good sauvignon blancs and a pinot noir in the mid-twenties.

The Four Seasons has Viennese dessert buffets (eighteen fabulous desserts, of which you may choose two for $7.75 or four for $14 — the idea is to share) on weekends from 9 to midnight in its airy **Bristol Lounge,** where afternoon tea is served by the fireplace daily from 3 to 4:30. An elegant Sunday brunch for $25 is considered one of the best in the city.

Lunch, Monday-Friday 11:30 to 2:30; dinner nightly, 6 to 10:30 or 11; Sunday brunch, 11:30 to 2:30.

Window tables at Aujourd'hui overlook Boston Public Garden.

Julien, Hotel Meridien, 250 Franklin St., Boston. (617) 451-1900.

The setting is historic: the former Members Court of the stately Federal Reserve Building built in 1922 and patterned after a Renaissance palace in Rome, across from the site of Boston's first French restaurant, opened in 1793 by French-émigré Jean-Baptiste Julien. But its spirit is highly contemporary, with French chef André Chouvin taking his cue from the Meridien's consulting chef, Marc Haeberlin, owner of a Michelin three-star restaurant in Alsace, who visits Boston several times a year.

Some of Boston's most distinguished food is served in this formal room with towering gilded ceiling, five crystal chandeliers and lattice work on the walls with lights behind. Mushroom velour banquettes or Queen Anne wing chairs flank tables set with unusually heavy silverware, monogrammed china, tiny shaded brass lamps and Peruvian lilies.

Ample drinks come with a complimentary hors d'oeuvre — a small vegetable quiche at our visit. If you're not up to an appetizer ($12 to $18 for the likes of terrine of venison with seasonal greens or lobster with artichokes, fresh tomatoes and basil), splurge on one of the masterful soups ($8 and $9), perhaps pea soup with essence of lobster or pheasant consommé with game-stuffed savoy cabbage.

Entrée prices have edged up a bit after dropping across the board in the early 1990s here, as they did at many of Boston's most expensive restaurants. For $21 to $32, you might find fillet of sturgeon with caviar sauce, a signature salmon soufflé, braised rabbit with truffles, young wild-boar chop served with a puree of celery root and chestnuts, and filet of lamb stuffed with spinach mousse. We'll never forget our lobster ravioli, the lobster reconstructed from its head and tail, the body made from ravioli filled with lobster mousse, the legs and feelers represented by green beans and asparagus or snow peas, and the whole topped with tomatoes and truffles — presentation personified.

High-ceilinged dining room at Julien.

Desserts from the menu and a pastry cart ($8.50 to $10) include brandied cherry soufflé with a sour cherry sauce, a gingerbread charlotte with a tulipe of dried fruits and a sauternes sabayon, or pear tartlet with vanilla-bourbon ice cream. We tried a delicious almond ice-cream cookie and two mille-feuilles, pastries layered with whipped cream and peaches in one case and strawberries and raspberries in the other. The bill is sweetened with a plate of homemade candies and cookies.

Although offering an impressive variety of French wines that won Wine Spectator's Best of Award of Excellence, the sommelier also recommends a number of Californias.

The formal atmosphere and service are lightened somewhat by piano music in the adjacent Julien bar, the bank's former counting room, where two original N.C. Wyeth murals embellish the walls.

Lunch, Monday-Friday noon to 2:30; dinner nightly, 6 to 10:30 or 11.

Seasons, Bostonian Hotel, North Street, Boston. (617) 523-4119.

This is the culinary heart of the Bostonian Hotel, its curved, windowed dining room on the fourth floor looking out over Quincy Market. Part of the ceiling is stainless steel and part glass, and an odd-shaped drapery affair moves back and forth electrically, depending on sunshine and temperatures.

Generally well-spaced tables seat 125 on several tiers to take full advantage of the view. Silver-rimmed service plates, heavy cutlery and a pristine freesia in a bud vase on each table add to the feeling of warm, contemporary elegance. Service is by an army of fresh-faced, tuxedoed waiters.

The food has been ranked among Boston's best since noted chef Jasper White helped open Seasons in the mid-1980s. Successors including Lydia Shire and Bill Poirier maintained the same kind of concept and a menu that changes with the seasons. New chef in 1993 was Peter McCarthy, who joined Seasons as a line cook after graduation from the Culinary Institute of America and worked his way through the ranks in six years. An advocate of cooking light, he uses almost no butter or cream. His menu format is unusual in that prices are listed as $28 for two courses, $35 for three and $39 for four. Further inquiry reveals that entrées cost $23 and other courses $7.

At our stay, an appetizer of smoked fish — red sturgeon with scallops and salmon in a horseradish-champagne vinaigrette, with a side presentation of cucumbers, watercress and capers — was superb, as was the smooth lobster and sweet-corn chowder. French, pumpernickel and whole-wheat rolls followed. Among main courses, we liked the signature roast duckling with ginger and scallions, surrounded by Chinese vegetables, and grilled red snapper with thin johnnycakes and mustard greens. A sensational array of sorbets — papaya, pear, apple and raspberry — was most refreshing. Cappuccino and decaf coffee were served in silver pots. The not unreasonable bill arrived with chocolate truffles and a macadamia-nut pastry on a doily.

The choice all-American wine list is enormous, with no fewer than 50 California cabernet sauvignons priced from $27 to $150. Some are available by the half bottle or the magnum.

Dinner nightly, 6 to 10 or 11.

Lodging

Boston Harbor Hotel, 70 Rowes Wharf, Boston 02110. (617) 439-7000 or (800) 752-7077.

A more sumptuous hotel could scarcely be imagined. The floors are marble, the sides of the elevators are brocade, and the walls of the public spaces are hung with fine art and antique nautical prints (a constant source of interest to passersby). Redwood furniture surrounds the 60-foot lap pool and a very large lounge at the rear of the main floor has huge sofas in plums, golds and teal blues for relaxing as you enjoy live piano music and absorb the view of boats and airplanes around the harbor.

Luxury and care extend to the 230 rooms and suites on Floors 8 through 16 (the lower floors are offices). Our oversize room had lovely reproduction antiques, a sofa and an upholstered chair with good reading lamps in a sitting area, a kingsize bed and an enormous bathroom full of amenities from fine soaps to terrycloth robes and a hair dryer. Breakfronts concealed the TV and a minibar, atop which were three kinds of glasses — highball, lowball and wine. Luggage racks, removable hangers, soundproof windows that open and enormous towels are other assets. Doorways are recessed well back from the corridor.

Drinks are served in a handsome bar on the main floor, and private parties and special events take place in the two-story Rotunda, a copper-domed observatory with views of harbor and city. Guests enjoy the health club and spa, which besides a lap pool has steam rooms and saunas, a hydrotherapy tub and an exercise room with the most up-to-date equipment available, including bicycles with TVs mounted on them.

The hotel's **Rowes Wharf Restaurant** is masculine and clubby with dark mahogany walls, recessed lighting in the ceiling, and a deep blue decor from chairs to vases to carpeting. Chef Daniel Bruce's dinner menu features seafood, from an appetizer of shrimp and crab ravioli over green and white asparagus ($13) to a fricassee of lobster and chorizo with sweet-corn pudding (at $29 the highest-priced main course). For a winter lunch, we began with Maryland crab cakes with a spicy rémoulade and kippered sable and caviar with johnnycakes and crème fraîche. Fine main dishes ($14.75 to $16.75) were poached coho salmon with fennel and lime and grilled shrimp and sea scallops with marjoram over olive pasta. A chocolate-chestnut dacquoise and a trilogy of strawberry, raspberry and blackberry sorbets were grand endings.

In 1994, the hotel was host to the fifth annual Boston Wine Festival, fifteen weeks of wine tastings, dinners, seminars and other events involving many of the world's leading winemakers.

Rowes Wharf is "elaborate, dramatic, even operatic," gushed the Boston Globe's architectural critic shortly after its 1987 opening. It is "an expression of the new wealth of Boston." Stay here, indulge, and you'll surely feel part of it.

Doubles, $225 to $375.

Four Seasons Hotel, 200 Boylston St., Boston 02116. (617) 338-4400.

From the hotel's eighth-floor health spa that has Caribbean-style patio furniture around a swimming pool and a jacuzzi, you can look out over the Boston Public Garden and, at night, the lights of Boston. "Very romantic while relaxing in the jacuzzi," said our informant.

It's also very serene and comfortable, this grand hotel with 288 guest rooms and suites reflecting the understated style of a traditional Beacon Hill guest bedroom. All rooms have Henredon cherry furniture, writing tables, TV in an armoire, a minibar, two telephones, hair dryers, windows that open, terrycloth robes and such, and the 64 Four Seasons mini-suites add alcove seating areas. Executive suites with a living room contain two TVs, although we never found ours hidden away in a cabinet and pulled the other out from the bedroom. That was the only glitch in an experience that lived up to its AAA five-diamond rating.

The luxurious health spa has treadmills with TVs and VCRs, and spin-dry machines for wet swimsuits. Public rooms are quietly decorated with antiques and fine art. A five-foot crystal chandelier lights the grand stairway to the second-floor Aujourd'hui restaurant.

Doubles, $260 to $365; suites, $390 to $430.

Ritz-Carlton Hotel, 15 Arlington St., Boston 02117. (617) 536-5700 or (800) 241-3333.

The Ritz is not just a hotel. It's an institution — *the* place where proper Bostonians put up visitors or go themselves for lunch in the cafe, tea in the lounge, or drinks and dinner in the Ritz Bar and the Dining Room. Even with all the new hotel competition in which the Ritz risked becoming passé, it remains Boston's bastion of Brahmin elegance.

The elevator operators wear white gloves — yes, there are still elevator operators, to say nothing of white gloves — as they take guests up to the 278 rooms, perhaps one of the 48 fireplaced suites billed for romance. Could romance be why the Ritz perpetuates its tradition of nightly dancing in the lounge and weekly Thursday tea dances in the French and Adam Room? And why the Ritz presents "a weekend of social savvy" for budding social climbers aged 8 to 12?

Yes, romance and the Ritz are legendary: Rodgers and Hammerstein wrote many of their musical favorites here, and in the 1930s and '40s, more romantic Broadway musicals were worked on at the Ritz than at any other location in the country.

So it comes as little surprise that the Boston Globe rated the Ritz tops for romance in head-to-head competition with the Four Seasons after the latter joined the Ritz in the five-diamond inner circle of hotels in 1989 (the Ritz has since lost a diamond). The Globe found the Four Seasons best for business and scored it ahead of the Ritz in every category except romance and, surprisingly, food.

The martinis in the Ritz Bar are legendary, as is English tea while a harpist plays in the Victorian parlor-salon (full tea, $16.50; light tea, $12.50).

French provincial furnishings, imported fabrics, distinctive artworks, windows that open onto a view of the Public Garden and all the amenities of a four-diamond hotel are here, even if some think they've seen better days.

Doubles, $260 to $380.

Atrium at Inn at Harvard imparts feeling of Italian courtyard.

Hotel Meridien, 250 Franklin St., Boston 02110. (617) 451-1900.

The 1922 Federal Reserve Bank building, a National Historic Landmark, was reincarnated 60 years later to the tune of $40 million into the elegant Meridien, run in European splendor by Air France.

Rather hard to find in the heart of the Financial District, it has 326 guest rooms on nine floors, with more than 150 variations from two-story loft suites to rooms on the three top floors with sloping windows and mansard roofs. Contemporary sofas, artworks (striking caricatures by local artist Ken Maryanski), live plants and minibars are in each room. Beds are made up in the French style (an extra sheet on top of the blanket), and maids provide turndown service at night with mints and a written weather forecast. A French news sheet is distributed to the rooms, and French cable television is available in the evening. The large bathrooms contain scales, baskets of assorted amenities and telephones. The third-floor health club has a glassed-in pool with skylights.

The Meridien, always known for its gastronomic flair, offers a chocolate lover's weekend package from September through May. It features the ultimate chocolate bar, an all-you-can-eat buffet of light and dark chocolate desserts, served Saturdays from 2 to 5 for $12.50 in the **Cafe Fleuri.** Maui cake (chocolate and coconut), chocolate torte with Bailey's Irish Cream and cinnamon, and a "vintner's cake" made with chocolate and cognac, each identified by a handwritten label, are among the creations. A nine-station Sunday brunch ($31.50), voted Boston's best, is served in the cafe's interior courtyard-atrium soaring six stories high.

Doubles, $205 to $255.

The Inn at Harvard, 1201 Massachusetts Ave., Cambridge 02138. (617) 491-2222 or (800) 222-8733.

Add innkeeping to Harvard University's script of accomplishments. The university has opened a fine hotel with the atmosphere of a private club, cloistered at

435

the edge of Harvard Square. Enter the arched, four-story palazzo that blends nicely with the buildings of Georgian red brick with white trim indigenous to the Harvard campus. Ahead lies a stunning four-story skylit atrium that imparts the feeling of an Italian courtyard. Rich cherrywood balconies and mullioned windows accent the sponged terra-cotta walls, hiding from public view the 113 guest rooms on all sides. Shelves of books and colorful murals line the main floor. Sofas, wingback and Queen Anne-style chairs are grouped for conversation in this soaring lobby to end all lobbies. And lo! Tables along one side are set with white linens and china for dinner. You're home -- away from home.

Architect Graham Gund, a Harvard alum, met the challenge of creating the warm atmosphere of an inn living room in what could be a stark hotel lobby. The atrium is a true gathering spot, both because it is so inviting and because seating is at a premium in some of the guest rooms, at least those we saw. The bedrooms, all pleasantly decorated in sand tones, come with queensize or two double beds, armoires holding TVs and modern bathrooms with pedestal sinks. Some offer outdoor balconies. There are amenities aplenty: terry robes, turndown service, chocolates on the pillows, Dickens & Hawthorne toiletries and complimentary newspapers. Each room contains an original print from the 17th or 18th century, on loan from Harvard's Fogg Art Museum, which also is responsible for the prints of Harvard personages and scenes lining corridors and public spaces.

Breakfast is offered in the lobby. Many guests opt for the European buffet ($10.95), an elaborate spread including cheeses, meats, granolas, fruits and pastries. A full menu is available as well. The library side of the lobby is the setting for candlelight dining at tables spaced among the books near an oversize baroque statue of Bacchus, which oversees all. Chef Susan Connors prepares a short menu for inn guests. The six entrées ($16 to $21) might include basil-smoked grilled salmon, a mixed grill of quail and sausage, and grilled beef tenderloin with a warm lobster-potato salad. Lighter fare also is available, and there's a concise but well-chosen wine list. Inn guests enjoy dining privileges at the Harvard Faculty Club next door.

Doubles, $129 to $219.

The Bostonian Hotel, at Faneuil Hall Marketplace, Boston 02109. (617) 523-3600 or (800) 343-0922.

Its location next to Quincy Market could lead you to think this is good for families, but the Bostonian is quiet, deluxe and, above all, grown-up. Although the 153 rooms on three floors are rather small, they are beautifully decorated and equipped, and the bathrooms with deep tiled tubs, French soaps and huge towels are a delight. In most rooms, french doors open onto tiny balconies with wrought-iron railings and planters filled with flowers. The television set is tucked discreetly into the armoire. There are two telephones (one in the bathroom), two AM/FM radios (one in the bathroom). You get the picture.

Since its 1982 opening, the Bostonian has been acclaimed for its European style, its small residential lobby with a corner fireplace around which are comfortable wing chairs, its spacious Atrium Lounge where you can sink into upholstered chairs and sofas to order a fine wine by the glass, espresso or a light lunch, and especially for Seasons, its renowned rooftop restaurant.

Eleven suites come with fireplaces and some have oval tubs and jacuzzis. The hotel is basically in two wings — one called the contemporary, especially attractive to business travelers, and one in the 19th-century Harkness wing.

Doubles, $235 to $290.

The Lenox Hotel, 710 Boylston St., Boston 02116. (617) 536-5300 or (800) 225-7676.

Built in 1900 as Boston's answer to the Waldorf-Astoria, this totally renovated, family-owned hotel is on the way up again after a period of being overshadowed by the large new chain hotels. It's personally run by the Saunders family, who also own the neighboring Copley Square Hotel and the huge Boston Park Plaza Hotel & Towers. This is billed as their intimate, boutique property, which is not as far-fetched as it sounds. We found it to have a nice, friendly feeling, and we especially liked its central location, right beside Lord & Taylor and just a short block from Newbury Street.

A just-completed, multi-million-dollar renovation shows off the 222 rooms on eleven floors to best advantage. High ceilings, glittering chandeliers, armoires or chests of drawers, walk-in closets (with a few removable hangars), windows that open (some in the bathrooms), useful amenities (mouthwash and hair dryers) and bedtime candies with nightly turndown service imbue the hotel with a charm that earned the hotel a surprising place in Norman Simpson's *Country Inns and Back Roads* guide.

The corner room in which we stayed was large and unusually quiet, and contained one of the hotel's 36 woodburning fireplaces. There was enough space for one of the plush loveseats we saw in smaller rooms, instead of the two stiff wooden-arm chairs with which ours was equipped. Most rooms are furnished in Drexel Colonial reproduction style; some are done in French provincial.

The 50-seat dining room called the **Upstairs Grill** is an unexpectedly charming hideaway. It's designed to resemble a 16th-century English pub with beamed ceiling, brick walls and shelves of fascinating artifacts, and it's altogether warm and welcoming, with little of the preciousness you may discern in other hotel dining rooms. Chef David Schmidt came on board from Cape Cod in 1994 with a new dinner menu featuring dishes grilled over specialty woods. Appetizers ($4.95 to $6.50) include smoked cheese en croûte baked over alderwood, served with a fruit coulis, and grilled swordfish cakes with green onion mayonnaise. You can even order a caesar salad with grilled swordfish on top. Seafood, meats and poultry grilled over hickory and maple woods come with choice of house sauces or compound butters; prices range from $8.50 for turkey loin steaks to $13.50 for yellowfin tuna steak. Even the accompanying vegetables are grilled.

Doubles, $155 to $215.

A Rural Retreat

Stonehedge Inn, 160 Pawtucket Blvd., Tyngsboro 01879. (508) 649-4400 or (800) 648-7070.

If you tire of the city or want to escape to a spa to work off the calories, consider this relatively undiscovered, elegant hideaway off the beaten path near Lowell, a 40-minute drive northwest of Boston. Here you'll find a refined restaurant and 30 luxurious, European-style suites in local developer Gilbert Campbell's $10 million hotel modeled after an English manor. The owner breeds horses in Florida, and inn guests may see horses grazing in the pastures on his 40-acre farm out back.

The public areas are sumptuous indeed, from a fireplaced rear library with carved windows onto the back forest, where tea is served in the afternoon for $9.95, to the most country-plush cocktail lounge (again with fireplace) in which it has been our pleasure to sip an after-dinner brandy. A health club with an

437

indoor-outdoor pool and spa (and eventually perhaps a spa package) was in the works for 1994.

The guest accommodations are extra-large and extra-quiet. Most have balconies onto the sylvan outdoors, a few harbor gas fireplaces and two at the end come with screened porches. Our Capri suite, surely one of the largest, contained a sofa facing two wicker chairs across a pair of antique cocktail tables -- perfect for a business meeting, we think, but rather uncomfortable for a couple trying to watch the evening news on the TV, which was hidden in the armoire at right angles to us but head-on to the bed. The bed was one of the most comfortable in which we've slept, an extra-wide and extra-long kingsize in the California style, made up in the French fashion and with two of the softest pillows ever. All but six suites have these beds (the others hold two doubles). Ours also came with a bathroom so huge that we almost felt lonesome, a mirrored jacuzzi tub and an uncommon number of amenities, from robes to bath scales. The walk-in closet contained removable hangers, an ironing board and a small iron. No one mistakenly leaves Stonehedge with the room key -- it's attached to an avocado-sized hunk of wood that bulges from the pocket.

Three meals a day are served in **Silks,** an expansive and most serene dining room with well-spaced booths and tables, striped arm chairs that are ever so comfortable and a conservatory on two sides yielding views onto the tranquil property. Named for the jackets and caps worn by jockeys, it carries out the owner's equestrian theme with a few pictures of horses and jockeys on the walls. A glass table in the center holds a spiral wreath dotted with berries and little birds at one visit, Christmas decorations at another. It's an auspicious setting for the lofty fare proffered by young executive chef James Overbaugh and an army of exuberant waiters. The prices are hardly rural ($7.95 to $9.95 for appetizers, $18.75 to $24.50 for entrées), but then neither is the cooking.

Our weeknight dinner got off to a good but slow start with a slice of seafood terrine with two excellent sauces, compliments of the chef. One thick slice of bread was doled out to each with two kinds of swirled butter, cinnamon and plain. Confusion resulted in a long wait before we got our wine, an $18 Australian shiraz from an outstanding but expensive 18,000-bottle wine cellar. Another long wait ensued before the arrival of our first courses, a superior roasted eggplant soup with parmesan cheese and basil cream and an interesting salad of goat cheese with boston lettuce and radicchio. Our main courses were two of the chef's favorites, a grilled veal chop with pears and pearl onions and roasted duckling with candied orange, dried cranberry and chestnut stuffing. Dollops of pureed beets and a very garlicky spaghetti squash with shiitake mushrooms accompanied. The duck also came with dressing and abundant wild rice; a potato-cheese cake supplemented the veal chop. These were such hefty platefuls we couldn't begin to finish, and had to groan when one of the waiters offered a roll after being stingy earlier with the bread. From a choice of such heavy desserts as pecan cheesecake, apple strudel and bûche de noël, we shared a plate of intense raspberry sorbet -- three large scoops on a dinner plate garnished with a sprig of mint. Six little pastries gilded the bill.

Upon returning to our room, the lights had been dimmed, music was playing on the radio, a little plate of cookies and fruit was at bedside and that capacious, comfy bed had been turned down. Our dreams were never sweeter.

Doubles, $139 to $169. Lunch, Monday-Saturday 11:30 to 3, dinner, Tuesday-Thursday 6 to 9, Friday and Saturday 5:30 to 10; Sunday, brunch 10 to 3, dinner, 5:30 to 8:30. Jackets required for dinner.

Horses graze in pasture behind rural Stonehedge Inn.

Gourmet Treats

Faneuil Hall Marketplace, the East's second busiest tourist destination after Disney World, is a festival arena for the gourmet, from the great **Crate & Barrel** store to the approximately twenty restaurants and thirty snackeries, salad bars and food stalls in Quincy Market. As you stroll through, pick up a wild berry bagel from **Finagle a Bagel,** a non-alcoholic banana daiquiri from the **Monkey Bar,** an empanada from **Latino's Taste,** or mussels with garlic butter from **Boston & Maine Fish Co.** There probably aren't any foods you can think of that you can't find here, and prices are gentle. Boston Cooks purveys a selection of cookbooks and cooking accessories. The restaurants, though frequented by tourists, are nothing to write home about, with the possible exceptions of historic **Durgin-Park** and the trendy Tex-Mex **Zuma.**

Under the market's north canopy is **Le Saucier,** where Lisa Lamme stocks, at latest count, more than 500 sauces from 27 countries. There are many items to taste; we tried a potent potion called "Hot as Hell! the hottest chile sauce on earth," and eyed a couple more called Dare Double Dare Sauce and Across the Border Got-Cha Jalapeño Sauce. The place also offers mustards, oils and vinegars, salsas, condiments, New England products and gift baskets.

One of the better places in the waterfront area to pick up lunch or a snack is **Rudi's** at 30 Rowes Wharf, near the Boston Harbor Hotel. Billed as a boulangerie, pâtisserie and croissanterie, Rebecca Thomas's upscale spot offers delectable salads and colorful pastries in a curved display case, along with gourmet foods and books. You can eat in at a few tables or take out to the waterfront.

Across town are the fashionable stores at **Copley Plaza,** Boston's answer to Chicago's Water Tower Place, and the grandly redone **Shops at Prudential Center.** Tony **Heritage on the Garden** includes a Waterford-Wedgwood shop.

As precious as the clothing is **Cafe Louis,** 234 Newbury St., at the rear of the first floor of the ultra-suave men's clothing store called Louis. It's in with the really-in shopping crowd. Pause here for a scone, bagel or organic granola ($4.50) with yogurt and fruit for late breakfast. Or lunch on a salad or sandwich, very exotic and very dear at $7.95 to $12.50.

The 100 block of increasingly fashionable Newbury Street holds special interest for food lovers. An artist from MacKenzie-Childs Ltd. in New York's Finger Lakes region was painting a table in the front window during a special exhibition when we visited **LaRuche** at 168 Newbury, notable for unique place settings and decorative accessories.

The Coffee Connection (165 Newbury St. and countless other locations around town) is the place to go for coffee beans, muffins, croissants and great dessert pastries. The espresso-cappuccino bar is considered one of the city's best. More espresso and coffee can be found next door at **Kaminsky's Finest of Fine Foods,** which translates mainly to sweets (wonderful biscuits and pastries) plus dried pastas. **Kitchen Arts** at 161 is full of neat gadgets, including a good little hand-held knife sharpener ($8.95) that went home in our shopping bag.

Literally a wall's worth of jars holds jelly beans, gum drops and other colorful candies at **Chocolate by Design,** 134 Newbury. But it is the chocolates made by Linda and Steve Weinstein in their Swampscott factory that most folks are after. We ogled a chocolate camera and a chocolate cellular phone before settling on a couple of dark-chocolate/macadamia truffles.

For soups and salads, you can't beat **Souper Salad,** which has ten locations in the Boston area including one with a sidewalk cafe at 119 Newbury. Locals consider it unusually good and we know why, after observing an impressive salad bar ($4.99, or $5.49 with soup -- about a dollar more evenings and on weekends). There's quite an array of quiches, club sandwiches, desserts, and beer and wine. Open daily, 10:30 to 8 or later.

"The menu is our best seller," advertises the **Harvard Book Store Cafe** at 190 Newbury St., one of the first of its genre. We've usually been so buried in books that we never noticed until lately the two back rooms devoted exclusively to dining, in addition to the tables we had seen amid the front bookshelves and outside on the sidewalk. Now overseen by Moncef Meddeb, former owner of L'Espalier, and Pierre Jospe, the menu is surprisingly varied, from falafel and hummus to salade niçoise, from a BLT with arugula on focaccia to a smoked-salmon club on whole wheat ($5.95 to $8.50). Dinner specials ($12 to $16) could be cod cakes with New England egg and caper sauce, roasted pork loin with walnuts and pesto, or veal tajine with artichokes, peas, lemon and mint. Open daily to 11 or midnight.

A "best office takeout" award helps account for the throngs at **Caffe Gianni,** 500 Boylston St. Besides the predictable espresso bar is a lineup of deli stations, from salads (the North African chicken looked great) to sandwiches ($4.25), an express salad and sandwich bar, and at one end a pizza station

Another of its ilk is **Caffe Marino,** a slick and big, cafeteria-style emporium serving espresso, deli items, pastas and pizzas at 30 Dunster St. in Cambridge, just off Mount Vernon Street in the new Shops by Harvard Yard. It's an offshoot of the northern Italian Ristorante Marino and Market at 2465 Massachusetts Ave., Cambridge.

Worth a trip across the Cambridge line to Somerville is **Panini,** a small bakery at 406 Washington St., where you can get a latte, a loaf of one of a dozen fabulous breads, a lemon scone, a ginger-cornmeal cookie, a piece of vegetarian pizza or focaccia ($2) topped with any number of things like herbs, olives, pesto, tomato or onion. There are a half-dozen tables for eating here.

440

Red brick buildings surround pond in picturesque Harrisville.

Monadnock Region

A Step Back in Time

The weathered sign under the flaming sugar maple is symbolic.

Appropriate and rustically low-key, it identifies the John Hancock Inn, New Hampshire's oldest. But the sign is almost superfluous, since the village of Hancock is so uncommercialized that the inn rivals the nearby white-spired Congregational Meeting House as the dominant feature and few could mistake its three-story, pillared Colonial/Greek Revival facade.

The only 20th-century establishment, if you can call it that, along Hancock's quarter-mile-long main street is the Hancock Store, a slightly updated version of the old general stores that still prevail in the Monadnock Region of southwestern New Hampshire. Otherwise, the village remains much as it was when John Hancock was its principal land owner and the inn opened in 1789.

"The Quiet Corner," they call the Monadnock area, of which Hancock is at the heart. Also "the Currier and Ives Section." Both with good reason.

Many of the trappings of contemporary civilization have passed this region by; so have many tourists. To find enough good places to eat, we had to stretch the Monadnock area's borders a bit (and, sadly, three of the area's better restaurants closed in 1993). During our explorations through the heart of the region, we noticed only two motels worthy of the name, nary a fast-food outlet, and only a single shopping center, that on the outskirts of Peterborough, the region's biggest town (population 5,000).

Instead there are picturebook villages with Colonial houses, churches and perhaps a general store, antiques shops but rarely a boutique or gift shop, the occasional inn or restaurant, countless streams, lakes and hills, and Mount Monadnock, the ubiquitous, 3,165-foot mountain that is supposedly the world's second most climbed. It seems fitting that the area's most popular tourist attraction is the Cathedral of the Pines, an outdoor shrine on a garden-bedecked knoll of

441

pines east of Rindge; the sounds of the carillon are soothing and the view of Grand Monadnock awesome. Even there, in the 1850s Cathedral House on the grounds, is one of the area's growing number of B&Bs.,

It's a real pleasure to encounter the old mill town of Harrisville, which is striking for its red brick structures, as opposed to the white frame buildings elsewhere in the region and perhaps epitomized in nearby Dublin, New England's highest village and home of Yankee magazine. In Harrisville, the brick buildings surrounding the duck pond lend an air of old England.

The Quiet Corner is ripe for such rural discoveries. You can find tranquil, postcard New England settings around almost every turn. And like the rest of Monadnock, many of the restaurants and inns are rustic and low-key, capitalizing on the fact they have changed little over the years. Nor have their prices.

They invite you to relive the old days.

Bed and Board

Chesterfield Inn, Route 9, West Chesterfield 03466. (603) 256-3211 or (800) 365-5515.

Young corporate dropouts Phil and Judy Heuber from Connecticut stayed in 80-odd country inns before deciding to purchase the two-year-old Chesterfield Inn in 1987, proclaiming the nine guest rooms here "the finest we've seen."

Stunning they are, thanks to architect Rodney Williams of Vermont's Inn at Saw Mill Farm, whose work here bears many Williams touches: cathedral ceilings and exposed beams and barn boards in most of the spacious guest rooms, each with a comfortable sitting area, three-way reading lamps, full baths (two with jacuzzis) beyond a separate dressing area, period antiques and quilts. All have kingsize or two double beds. There are fireplaces in four, and balconies in two, for contemplating the rural scene. The main entry lobby and sitting room has a twenty-foot-high ceiling, a brass chandelier and a beehive-style fireplace.

The Heubers have stocked mini-refrigerators in the rooms with a variety of beverages and have outfitted the bathrooms with Gilchrist & Soames toiletries. All rooms have televisions and telephones, all different and some cleverly tucked away in boxes. "These are really elegant and beautiful rooms," says Judy, "but we want them to be comfortable and livable."

The latter was a prime consideration when, in 1992, the Heubers added a new structure to the side with four spacious rooms in the same style. All come with corner fireplaces and private brick patios overlooking the gardens -- "great places to sit and watch the sunset," says Judy.

Borrowing another page from the Inn at Saw Mill Farm, the Heubers set out to create a serious restaurant as the inn's focal point. First they brightened up the sun porch dining room and added three more small dining rooms in the parlors of the original 1780s house as well as a fourth to the rear. Then, for 1994, they were expanding to the rear off the lobby, adding a living room, a commercial kitchen and a new dining room with windows on three sides and french doors onto a patio. Now 50 people can dine by candlelight at tables set with crisp white linens, Dudson floral china, big wine globes and crystal water glasses. No longer do house guests have to traipse through the kitchen to reach the dining room -- a situation that yielded culinary camaraderie with chef Carl Warner, who liked to explain the nightly specials and trade recipes. The chef now has a professional kitchen and the Heubers have transformed the old restaurant into new living quarters for their young family.

Innkeepers Phil and Judy Heuber outside Chesterfield Inn.

The short dinner menu changes every two months. A complimentary starter like smoked salmon pâté is on the table as guests are seated. Appetizers ($4 to $7) might be lobster and corn chowder, crab cakes with rémoulade sauce, Indonesian chicken satay and gorgonzola cappelletti with spinach, tomatoes and basil. Entrées ($17 to $21) could be scallops with spicy black-bean oyster sauce, shrimp with couscous, grilled pork chop with balsamic vinegar and sour cherry sauce, and venison loin with cranberry-port-wine chutney.

For dessert, try Carl's fresh berry trifle, flourless chocolate cake with custard sauce, pumpkin cheesecake or walnut pie. The wine list is a well-chosen mix of American and French, with some not often seen Californias among the selections starting in the teens.

Until the birth of their first child in 1990, Judy served and often cooked the hearty breakfast, taken in the cheery sun porch or outside on a terrace ("now that task falls to me," reports Phil). The main course might be french toast soaked in triple sec, blueberry pancakes, a fancy omelet or featherbed eggs (similar to a cheese and egg strata). Corn fritters, potato pancakes, hash browns, granola and homemade muffins might accompany.

Dinner, Tuesday-Saturday 6 to 9. No smoking. Doubles, $110 to $150; suites, $150 to $165.

The Ram in the Thicket, Maple Street, Milford 03055. (603) 654-6440.

It's hard to imagine a more unlikely spot than the old mill section of Wilton or a more unlikely innkeeper than the onetime minister of Abraham Lincoln's old church. The Ram in the Thicket, a Victorian mansion with nine guest rooms and a creative restaurant, is run by the Rev. Dr. Andrew Tempelman (whose Biblical background inspired the inn's name) and his wife Priscilla.

Upstairs are nine antiques-filled guest rooms, three with private baths and the rest sharing two. But it is for the food that the Ram in the Thicket rates plaudits.

Priscilla's taste determines both the decor in her elegant dining rooms and the fare that emanates from her kitchen. The intriguing menu — reasonably priced ($15 to $19) and including choice of soup or appetizer and salad — is a heady international mix that changes monthly and includes dishes with Greek, Mexican, Indonesian and Korean accents, among others. "We've done more than 300 different menus," Andrew noted at our latest visit.

Chicken liver pâté, a porridge of curried lentils, apples and cabbage baked with garlic and cranberries, spicy sausage braised in mustard-wine sauce, and pear piquant (poached in white wine, sugar and freshly cracked peppercorns, and exquisitely different, as the menu advised) were among the appetizers the autumn evening we were there. We tried stuffed grape leaves and a house special at the time called "shortasnails" — stuffed mushrooms created when the chef was short of snails. Three small mushrooms on a bed of lettuce were stuffed with snails in a garlicky concoction; both they and the stuffed grape leaves had unusual character.

The bread basket contained slices of poppyseed bread and squares with parmesan cheese and dill; the latter were so melt-in-your-mouth tender and so unusual that we asked for seconds. The choice of salads included one of greens and a mass of slivered carrots notable for a Korean sweet and sour dressing, and salad Tyrol, a surprising combination of garbanzo beans, sauerkraut and chopped vegetables in a marinade on a bed of lettuce. The Harvard and Yale salad mixed broccoli, cauliflower and beets with a fragrant sesame dressing.

Entrées entice as well. There's no such thing as typical here, but one night's menu mixed Moroccan shrimp with garlic-ginger sauce, roasted pork tenderloin in Japanese plum wine, chicken Adriatica, Polish hunter's stew, sautéed beef with a sour-cream sauce, Lucifer lamb (with a devilish marinade, baked with a parsley-crumb coat) and tenderloin of beef with a spicy garlic dipping sauce.

Priscilla says she always seeks out the new and rarely repeats an item, so no longer does she serve the spicy Indonesian beef satay or the Greek gypsy lamb (with vegetables and feta cheese baked in a huge parchment pocket) that we so enjoyed.

The wine list holds good values. Andrew offers Cribari for $2 a glass, as well as a bottle of Château Lafite for $98.

The desserts (all $3.50) might include dark-chocolate mousse covered with white-chocolate mousse and a whisper of frangelico, a blackberry and blueberry trifle saturated with peach schnapps, toffee-coffee pie and Dutch cheesecake laced with rum.

After paying one of our most reasonable dinner bills in months, we chatted at the bar with Andrew Tempelman, who related how he and his wife uprooted themselves and their three young sons from the Midwest in 1977 because they were "totally smitten with the romantic side of New England." The former minister of the church that President Lincoln had attended in Springfield, Ill., he also was on the staff of the large Fourth Presbyterian Church in Chicago before moving to Monadnock.

"This is a fun, relaxed place where every night's a dinner party," says Andrew. A more innovative dinner party for the price would be hard to come by.

Dinner, Wednesday-Sunday 5:30 to 8:30 or 9:30. Doubles, $60 to $75.

John Hancock Inn, Hancock 03449. (603) 525-3318 or (800) 525-1789.

New Hampshire's oldest operating inn doesn't look that old (1789) because of the later addition of a mansard roof. Its elegant, pillared facade enhances the main street of the picturesque hamlet of Hancock, which is well worth a stroll around. It also doesn't feel that old, thanks to the redecorating and upgrading done by new owners Linda and Joe Johnston, formerly of the New England Inn at Intervale, N.H. They have lavished much time and money in redoing the inn, from top to bottom, to create in Lynn's words, "a genuine inn experience for our guests."

Victorian mansion houses the Ram in the Thicket inn and restaurant in Wilton.

They started with the taproom, "because we strongly believe that an inn should be an inn -- with a common room." While older folks can imbibe, they (or their youngsters) can gather for checkers and other board games, or simply read in the corner. At our visit, remarkable Linda was painting a Rufus Porter-style mural around the walls of the tap room; it bore an uncanny resemblance to the artist's trademark murals that adorn the upstairs Rufus Porter bedroom and those at other hostelries in the area.

The Johnstons also were putting new emphasis on the inn's dining. They have gussied up all three dining areas, sponging the walls of the main room a Colonial red color, nicely trimmed in grayish-blue, which with a blazing hearth is a favorite in winter. In summer, we prefer the beamed dining room in the rear, the linoleum floor of old gone but the barnwood walls retained. Windows look onto the lawns as house guests enjoy a breakfast buffet of homemade granola, scones, juices, fruits and a cooked-to-order dish, perhaps banana-pecan pancakes with sausage or a sausage and egg casserole.

The dinner fare has been upgraded as well since we supped here a few years back. Instead of vegetable juice, cellophane-wrapped crackers with crocks of Wispride and tossed salads of iceberg lettuce, now you can order Maryland crab cakes with sesame butter, baked brie with fresh fruits and mushroom pâté with roasted-garlic toast points from a menu that changes with the seasons. The dozen or so entrées ($13.95 to $16.95) include salmon with lemon-dill sauce, stuffed rainbow trout, garlic shrimp served on a warm mushroom salad and garnished with red and yellow peppers, lamb shanks osso-buco style, roasted duck glazed with maple syrup, chargrilled delmonico steak or, the house specialty (brought here from the New England Inn), Shaker cranberry pot roast -- "which outsells anything else on the menu, two to one," says Linda.

Desserts are her preserve. At our visit, she had made deep-dish blueberry crisp, strawberry shortcake and pecan pie.

Most of the inn's ten guest rooms are done in handsome period furniture and one has walls covered with murals painted by Rufus Porter in the mid-19th century. The Johnstons have added telephones, air-conditioning, queensize or twin beds, bath toiletries and cassettes with tapes for music. The rooms look far more comfortable than when we stayed here a decade ago. We'll never forget being awakened on the hour all night by the Paul Revere bell in the nearby church steeple -- "gently lulling you to sleep," as the inn's fancy new brochure puts it.

Small sitting areas with books and magazines (one with a TV) are on the landings of the second and third floors for those who shun the action in the main-floor taproom. Within walking distance of the inn is Norway Pond, where we swam in refreshingly cool and clear water.

Dinner nightly, 6 to 9, Sunday 5 to 8. Doubles, $85 to $105. No smoking.

The Birchwood Inn, Route 45, Temple 03084. (603) 878-3285.

Judy and Bill Wolfe, originally from New Jersey, have been operating this red brick inn, built around 1800 and now listed on the National Register, since 1980. They have earned wide acclaim for their bargain-priced dinners, served to the public as well as inn guests.

The small dining room, its walls covered by Rufus Porter murals, is candlelit. The blackboard menu usually lists three entrées that could be seafood chautauqua (a medley of shrimp, scallops and lobster in herbed butter sauce over rice), roast duckling with grand-marnier sauce and tournedos of beef béarnaise. Meals start with relishes like cottage cheese with horseradish and curried kidney beans and a choice of two homemade breads from Judy's repertoire of 100. Then comes juice or soups, among them minestrone, French onion, black bean, she-crab and lobster bisque (offered only on Saturdays). Dessert could be an apple-raspberry cobbler, tortes, cheesecake, cream-cheese/pecan pie and ice cream with a homemade sauce, perhaps rum-maple.

The four-course meal costs $15.95 to $17.95, depending on choice of entrée. "We do everything ourselves — that's how we can keep these prices," Bill explained.

Upstairs are six small guest rooms with private baths. Each is charmingly decorated around family collection themes: a seashore room, music room, editorial office (with an ancient typewriter and wallpaper of front pages) and the like. A newer bedroom on the ground floor, where a large shop used to be, has TV, private bath and a brightly-colored quilt, with old produce signs on the walls. Room rates include a full country breakfast, which also draws the locals (as you might expect, considering prices in the $3 to $4 range).

A quaint piano with sheet music is ensconced in the country parlor, and in front is a small shop and game room.

Breakfast, Tuesday-Sunday, 7:30 to 9:30; dinner, Tuesday-Saturday 6 to 8:30. BYOB. Doubles, $60 to $70. No credit cards.

Maplehurst Inn, Main Street, Antrim 03440. (603) 588-8000.

An inn since 1794, the old Maplehurst Inn in the center of Antrim was grandly renovated and upgraded in 1987 to become the Antrim Inn. Financial difficulties did in one set of owners, and in 1993 local industrialist Stephen Crowell bought the inn and renamed it the Maplehurst. He made no changes to the good-looking public rooms and fourteen luxurious guest rooms with private baths, deciding instead to concentrate on reviving the full-service restaurant. A screened dining area on the front veranda, which proved to be a hit with summer visitors, was added.

The spacious, beamed main dining room is dressed in pink linens crossed by rose runners, with dark blue napkins in the stemware matching the candles in

John Hancock Inn is state's oldest.

the hurricane chimneys. Rose balloon curtains enhance the windows and well-worn oriental rugs cover the floors.

The dinner menu is American with a continental flair. Entrées ($11 to $15) include grilled garlic shrimp, poached Atlantic salmon, blackberry-peppercorn duckling, pan-seared filet mignon with wild mushrooms and roast rack of lamb. Among appetizers are New England crab cakes, salmon fritters with roasted pepper sauce, spicy seared shrimp with guava and pineapple sauce, and a smoked sampler of pork, duck, beef and chicken. Desserts include chocolate terrine with raspberry coulis, a chocolate and Bailey's mousse, and maple cake with ice cream. The wine list is serviceable and affordable.

Elsewhere in the inn, two parlors contain plush sofas and chairs and the front porch is full of upholstered wicker. Guest rooms on the second and third floors are named for ducks (Mallard, Greenwinged Teal, Black Scooter) and furnished accordingly, right down to the duck soaps in the bathrooms. The visitor is struck by the attractive colors, fresh flowers, carpeted floors, patterned sheets, thick towels, wing chairs beside three-way reading lights and antique beds. Each room has a telephone, television and air-conditioning.

Lunch, Monday-Saturday 11:30 to 2; dinner, 6 to 10; Sunday, brunch 11:30 to 2, dinner 5 to 8. Doubles, $55 to $75.

Colby Hill Inn, The Oaks, Box 778, Henniker 03242. (603) 428-3281 or (800) 531-0330.

Vastly upgraded lately in terms of food, hospitality and decor, this sixteen-room inn with a good dining room was a working farm until 1959 and the old barn is still attached to the inn. You go through it to get to the secluded swimming pool, with views of hills and meadows and a pond that is used for ice-skating.

Built about 1800, this is a cheery, cozy inn with two sitting rooms, one with a flickering fire and the other with games, television and rear windows looking onto gardens and a new gazebo. Business transplants from Maryland, Ellie and John Day and their daughter Laurel, took over the inn in 1990 and have infused it with enthusiasm and good taste. They redecorated six rooms in the rear carriage house and ten rooms in the main inn with antiques. All have private baths and telephones, and the two most prized in the main house have working fireplaces.

One with an ornate brass kingsize bed is especially appealing in blue and white Waverly fabrics.

Pots of coffee and tea and a cookie jar full of the best crunchy oatmeal-raisin cookies are at the ready for guests in the entry to the dining room. A full country breakfast is served in the morning. A couple of large, friendly dogs are very much in evidence in the common rooms.

The dining room has become increasingly known for good food under the aegis of CIA-trained chef Michael Mack, who has been with the Days since they took over. The dozen or so dinner entrées ($11.95 to $21.95) include a signature breast of chicken stuffed with lobster, leeks and boursin; poached salmon with mustard-cream sauce, scrod provençal, roast lamb with rosemary sauce and New Zealand loin of venison served with wild-mushroom sauce.

The starters are more limited but no less enticing, among them lobster bisque, seafood crêpe and wild mushrooms tossed with fresh cracked-pepper pasta. Ellie Day prepares the scrumptious desserts, always a cheesecake (pecan-pumpkin-praline at our autumn visit) and perhaps apple crumb pie, cream-puff swans with raspberry puree, blueberry-cream pie and a dense fudge cake with chocolate ganache and vanilla butter cream, swirled with chocolate sauce. The short but good wine list, priced in the teens and twenties, includes a chardonnay and cabernet from Henniker's New Hampshire Winery.

All this is served in a couple of serene dining rooms, one a wainscoted tavern room and the other a stenciled room with big windows onto the back gardens. Twining grapevines above the windows are strung with tiny white lights all year. Cream-colored linens, pink napkins, candles in hurricane lamps and oriental runners add to the country elegance.

Dinner, Wednesday-Saturday 5:30 to 8:30, Sunday, 4:30 to 7:30. Doubles, $85 to $140. No smoking.

The Inn at Crotched Mountain, Mountain Road off Route 47, Francestown 03043. (603) 588-6840.

This rambling red brick inn, with a renovated red and white barn attached, is at the 1,300-foot level with the former Crotched Mountain ski area almost at the front door, so the air is sparkling and the view, 40 miles across the Piscataquog Valley, is grand.

Owners Rose and John Perry are both schooled in the restaurant business and their dining room is highly regarded in the area. Lately they have curtailed its operations to weekends only, leaving house guests somewhat high and dry -- and hungry -- at other times, now that several nearby restaurants have closed.

The aromas emanating from the kitchen portend a culinary master at work. Chef Rose's nightly specials strike us as more interesting than the regular menu: things like lobster strudel, grilled tuna with cucumber dressing, babi ritja (an Indonesian dish with pork and ginger) and pot stickers supplementing the regular shrimp scampi, cranberry pot roast, chicken teriyaki, calves liver with onion and bacon, and filet mignon béarnaise. Entrée prices ($12.95 to $16.95) include cellophane-noodle or apple-curry soup, salad with one of the inn's homemade dressings, homemade breads and vegetables grown on the premises. A surcharge brings appetizers like herring in wine, shrimp cocktail or smoked mussels.

Guests eat in two dining rooms or at a couple of tables set up in the huge living room, which has a fireplace at either end and lovely oriental rugs. A display case shows off jars of the Perrys' homemade goodies, including jams, tarragon vinegar and celery seed dressing, which are for sale. The inn has eight other working

Twining grapevines are strung with tiny white lights in Colby Hill Inn dining room.

fireplaces, four of them in the guest rooms (of which there are thirteen, eight with private baths). Both a continental and full breakfast are included in the rates.

Two clay tennis courts and a large swimming pool taking full advantage of the view give guests a choice of activities. This is a place where you can really feel secluded and almost on top of the world.

Dinner, Friday-Saturday 6 to 8. Doubles, $100 to $120, MAP on weekends; $60 to $70, B&B on weekdays. Closed April and November. No credit cards.

Monadnock Inn, Main Street, Box B, Jaffrey Center 03454. (603) 532-7001.

This rambling inn erected in the 19th century in rural Jaffrey Center is known for its food. "My chefs have free rein in the kitchen," says innkeeper Sally Roberts, a former New Jersey school teacher.

The changing dinner menu includes such entrées ($14.75 to $19) as seafood sauté, poached or grilled salmon béarnaise, chicken mandalay, provimi veal cutlets sautéed with mushrooms and sweet vermouth, filet mignon with choice of toppings and rack of lamb with garlic aioli and mint jelly. Homemade breads, soup or salad, and a choice of starch come with. Among starters are baked brie, smoked salmon, duck sausage and escargots.

Flans, cream puffs, crème caramel, Viennese chocolate cake and a frozen meringue guava are special desserts. Gourmet magazine requested the recipes for the inn's stuffed loin of pork vouvray and chocolate mousse.

For Sunday brunch, we tried the eggs benedict ($5.75), which came not with Canadian bacon but thin slices of Smithfield ham, and an excellent hot salmon mousseline ($6.75), with a hollandaise sauce, homefries and crisp slices of yellow squash. A carafe of the house white from the limited wine list was quite adequate.

The pretty, country-style dining rooms have stenciled walls and wide-plank floors, tables with pink woven mats over white or blue cloths, fresh flowers and candles in hurricane lamps.

There are a cozy bar and a comfortable living room with a fireplace, always going in cool weather, and a piano but no television — Sally Roberts likes her guests to talk with each other.

The fourteen guest rooms (some singles) on the second and third floors are fairly basic and vary in size and decor; a few have been redone on the third floor. They come with one double or two twin beds. About half have private baths.

Lunch, Monday-Friday 11:30 to 2; dinner, Tuesday-Saturday 5:30 to 9; Sunday, brunch 10 to 1, dinner 5 to 8. Doubles, $55 to $65.

Fitzwilliam Inn, RR 1, Box 27, Fitzwilliam 03447. (603) 585-9000.

Dating to 1796, this obviously is an inn of the old school — and looks it, from its charming bar and dining room to the 28 upstairs guest rooms, fourteen with private baths. All kinds of stenciling, cows on the shower curtains and wreaths of dried flowers brighten what many would consider an old-fashioned, spartan feeling to the bedrooms. The larger rooms with two double beds are twice the size of the standards, which are just big enough to hold one double bed.

The main floor is a ramble of rooms, including a front library with an old English rebus over the fireplace. It's a seemingly nonsensical inscription that guests delight in trying to figure out (one of the inn's postcards gives the answer). Local crafts are sold in a gift shop. There's a fenced-in swimming pool in back.

Wagon-wheel chandeliers, hanging baskets, stenciling and a dark beamed ceiling mark the 65-seat dining area with its bare floors and wood tables. The dinner menu arrives on a paddle board listing fifteen entrées from $8.25 to $15.95 (add $3 for a complete dinner, including appetizer, dessert and beverage). The choice includes things like scrod, chicken marsala, lobster newburg and veal oscar. People return year after year for the black diamond steak marinated in soy and herbs and the roast duck stuffed with scalloped apples and served on a bed of brown sauce.

Innkeeper Barbara Wallace, an opera singer, makes the desserts. Among them are a mixed fruit cobbler with a nut topping, toasted coconut-almond cream pie and fudge cake with mocha icing.

Lunch, Monday-Saturday noon to 2; dinner, 6 to 9, Sunday noon to 8. Doubles, $40 to $55.

Dining

The Boilerhouse at Noone Falls, Route 202 South, Peterborough. (603) 924-9486.

A heron catching fish at the foot of Noone Falls just beyond our window table caused a good bit of diversion for people lunching here. "He comes every day," advised our waitress — which was just as well, for we needed a distraction to make up for a somewhat mediocre meal. Lunch, since discontinued, may have been an aberration, for owner Sandy King has plenty of backers for her claim that the Boiler House serves "the best food in southwest New Hampshire."

The setting and the scenery couldn't be nicer — an expansive, second-level dining room with white-linened tables and black lacquered chairs facing huge windows onto the waterfall.

Votive candles cast neat shadows at night, when diners feast on interesting food as well as the lovely setting. The menu appeals with entrées ($13.95 to $18.95) like fillet of Norwegian salmon sautéed with lemon ginger and an orange tamari sauce, served with asparagus and garlic-roasted potatoes; shrimp, scallops and

Window table at Boilerhouse at Noone Falls.

salmon with a puree of fresh tomatoes, served over roasted red-pepper fettuccine, and pork tenderloin rolled in mustard and herbs, served with orange and pommery mustard sauce. House specialties are medallions of New Zealand venison, served over wild mushrooms with wild rice; roast rack of lamb served with a potato, carrot and rosemary pancake, and grilled breast of duck with the chef's fruit sauce of the day.

New Orleans-style crab cakes, house-cured gravlax, grilled chicken and summer squash served with a chiffonade of spinach and a black-olive vinaigrette, and a gratinée of three-onion soup (vidalia, Spanish and Bermuda) are favorite starters. Save room for one of the desserts, which here are more interesting than most in the area. They include the chef's homemade ice creams (perhaps fresh peach with almonds or bittersweet-chocolate with kahlua), chocolate-truffle torte with raspberry cream sauce, frozen raspberry and honey-almond parfait, and white-chocolate pâté on blackberry sauce. We remember fondly the chef's special dessert of minted pineapple and grapes in peach schnapps from our otherwise forgotten lunch.

Honored by Wine Spectator, the wine list is far better than New Hampshire's average and priced accordingly. And, an endearing touch, the names of all the staff, from the chef to servers and bartenders, are listed on the front of the menu. Owner King includes herself under "kitchen staff."

Outside the entrance in the Boilerhouse arcade is her casual **Café at Noone Falls,** where at lunch time you can get soups, salads, sandwiches on freshly baked breads or croissants, and desserts to eat at little tables or to go.

Dinner, Tuesday-Saturday 5 to 8 or 9; Sunday brunch, noon to 2:30.

Latacarta, 6 School St., Peterborough. (603) 924-6878.
Inspired cookery and a decided New Age feel emanate from this restaurant, owned by Japanese master chef Hiroshi Hayashi, in the old Gem Theater. He moved to Peterborough from Newbury Street in Boston where, he says, "I never

had to serve meat, but I do here." Offering what he calls an "epicurean collage," he is a student of cosmic philosophy (explained on the back of the menu) and gives seminars in natural-foods cooking at his home.

Latacarta is a simple place, with bentwood chairs, mulberry walls on which are some sensational Japanese prints, track lighting, lace cafe curtains and many plants. A gorgeous kimono made by Hayashi's wife is spotlit in a niche.

A lunchtime taste of the two soups of the day, cream of butternut squash and a chunky fish chowder, made us wish we could stay for dinner. But we returned another time for a lunch of black-bean soup, the Latacarta tofu sandwich ($4.75) with a salad of lettuce, tomato and parsley-sesame dressing on the side, and the special of linguini with vegetables provençal ($6), served with a salad — all in more than generous portions. The delicious and piping-hot pear crunch with ice cream ($3.50) was enough for two to share.

Specials augment the regular evening fare ($10.95 to $16.95), but you'll always find vegetable or shrimp tempura, ginger chicken on whole-wheat pasta, pasta of the night, fresh fish like baked salmon with snow peas and mushrooms, and a colorful vegetarian dinner. The last, $12.95 at our visit, produced a zucchini boat filled with mushrooms, tomatoes, eggplant and cheddar cheese, vegetables in phyllo, green beans and roasted almonds with olive oil, plus soup and salad. Hummus served with pita bread is a popular appetizer, but we'd likely try the gyoza or the shrimp tempura with sweet-potato and carrot fritters. A large salad is topped with tofu, which the chef calls "sage's protein." Using little salt and sugar, he and his staff turn out desserts like mocha custard, apple pandowdy, banana supreme and cheesecake with fresh fruit sauce.

A typical dish at an elaborate Sunday brunch is linguini with smoked salmon, snow peas, broccoli, zucchini and mushrooms, with a fresh dill sauce.

A light menu is served most of the day in the adjacent bar/cafe. Nibble on enchiladas, a hummus and cheese platter or fish and chips while you listen to the New Age music or, on some nights, live music. The short wine list is more sophisticated than you might expect.

"There's a lot going on here," the hostess informed at our latest visit. Hayashi's building is now called the Tensing Art and Culture Center. The Tensing Gallery upstairs shows Japanese art, and the Peterborough Community Film Society presents classic movies Wednesday-Sunday night in the theater portion of the building behind the restaurant.

Lunch, Tuesday-Friday 11 to 5, Saturday noon to 5; dinner, 5 to 9 or 9:30; Sunday, brunch 11 to 5, dinner 5 to 7. Cafe open daily except Monday for cocktails and light meals, 11:30 to 9.

The Colonel Shepard House, 29 Mount Vernon St., Milford 03055. (603) 672-2527.

One of the more attractive new restaurants we've come across lately is housed in a substantial 1757 Colonial at the edge of downtown Milford. The food, according to all reports, measures up.

Brothers Charlie and Steve Burns opened the place in 1992 to quick acclaim, pouring a ton of money into its restoration and furnishing. Three serene dining rooms and an enclosed porch are lovely with white linens, fancy place settings, swagged draperies and almost more oriental rugs than the eye can behold, including one measuring fourteen by twenty-two feet that's restfully under foot on the enclosed porch. In the rear is a paneled and beamed tavern outfitted with sports pennants and mounted game heads.

The kitchen is under the able direction of chef Bob Bellisle, who formerly had the Peregrine House restaurant in Goffstown. The menu is fairly ambitious for the prices charged. For starters ($4 to $7), consider the caramelized five-onion soup finished with three cheeses, wild-mushroom sauté, smoked trout or escargots. Main courses ($14 to $18) include shrimp piccata over fettuccine, seafood thermidor, strawberry chicken, pork medallions with apple-brandy sauce, veal medallions with wild mushrooms, tournedos of beef au poivre and rack of lamb.

Dining room at Colonel Shepard House.

Dessert could be chocolate truffle, toasted almond torte and seasonal pies, all homemade by a local woman. The wine list, far better than the area's norm, is priced from $15 to $60.

Upstairs are three large guest rooms, one with private bath and two sharing. The original master bedroom has both a kingsize bed and a twin day bed and its own balcony over the porch. Another comes with a king bed, two club chairs and a wing chair. All contain the oriental rugs that seem to be the brothers' trademark. A continental breakfast is included in the rates.

Dinner, Tuesday-Sunday 5 to 9. Doubles, $65 to $75.

Del Rossi's Trattoria, Route 137 at Route 101, Dublin. (603) 563-7195.

The aroma of garlic wafts through this pretty Colonial house — the setting for some fine Italian fare, cooked up by chef David Del Rossi, co-owner with his wife Elaina. The two Jaffrey natives also run a music store, which is probably why they feature live music (mostly folk) on Friday and Saturday nights.

The main dining room, with its wide-plank floors and post and beam construction, is plain and comfortable with sturdy captain's chairs at the tables, some left bare and some with linens and burgundy napkins. There are a couple of smaller rooms plus a sun porch with a stained-glass window, where we enjoyed lunch.

For dinner, you might begin with polenta topped with a fresh tomato and basil (from the chef's garden) sauce and melted mozzarella, and go on to a pasta ($6.95 to $10.50) — all made in house — like spinach and cheese gnocchi or black-pepper raviolis stuffed with cheese and prosciutto.

Entrées ($10.95 to $14.95) include haddock Italian, scallops broiled in a wine sauce topped with bread crumbs and grated pecorino romano, pork scaloppine with onions, peppers and provolone, and chicken breast stuffed with ricotta, spinach and prosciutto. Loaves of homemade Italian bread, vegetable of the day and a side of pasta accompany. The wine list is most reasonable and beers are a bargain.

"Once you try my Sicilian cake, you want it again and again," says David. The homemade pound cake has ricotta cheese and chocolate filling between its layers and couldn't be more lush. Another favorite is Roman cheese pie, an old recipe featuring ricotta with a marsala wine crust on a bed of honey with grapes.

The menu for lunch, now served seasonally on a somewhat iffy basis, changes every day; there are always two salads, a frittata, a quiche, and a pasta. Our quiche of smoked oysters and cheese with a generous salad and a PLT version of a BLT (prosciutto, lettuce, and tomato on grilled garlic bread) were super.

Here is what we consider a "true" place, although one where music lately has been known to upstage the food.

Lunch occasionally, 11:30 to 2; dinner, Tuesday-Saturday 5 to 9, Sunday 4 to 8.

Twelve Pine, 1 Summer St., Peterborough. (603) 924-6140.

Although not a restaurant as such, this gourmet takeout spot is the new "in" place for food-lovers in town. Daniel Thibeault, who worked his way through art school in Boston in the employ of hotel restaurants, started a catering business at his home (from which is derived the name). Success prompted this downtown takeout, full of delightful aromas from exotic dishes.

You can pick up the makings for a picnic or get an entrée for dinner. The choices are legion. How about one of the soups (perhaps Russian peasant, gazpacho or tomato and cheddar), with a ham and potato tart or a crab meat quiche? Or one of about a dozen enticing salads? We made a picnic of three -- linguini with chicken and pesto, antipasto with shrimp and a red-cabbage slaw with capers and almonds -- and a couple of peanut-butter chocolate-chip cookies and trundled off to partake on the front steps of the nearby Unitarian Church as the world (or at least Peterborough's little share) went by. Moussaka, chicken rosemary, stuffed cornish game hens and baked salmon with rice are some of the heartier entrées ($4 to $6.25). Among delectable desserts are chocolate-raspberry cake and hazelnut torte.

Open Monday-Friday 11 to 6, Saturday 11 to 3.

The Folkway, 85 Grove St., Peterborough. (603) 924-7484.

Here's an interesting sprawl of dining rooms, a lounge, a garden patio and an upstairs music and crafts shop. Although not truly in the gourmet class, the food is interesting and the almost nightly entertainment by folk singers, both known and not so known, is popular. In fact, the Folkway had gained such stature that when its owner died in 1988 and it closed, a non-profit foundation was formed to reopen it in 1990.

The cuisine encompasses salads and light fare as well as such entrées ($8.95 to $15.95) as mushroom ravioli, tofu and noodles with fresh ginger and vegetables, grilled shrimp with pesto-cream sauce, roast loin of lamb with wild mushrooms and grilled sirloin au poivre.

You also can order light: stir-fries, grilled chicken salad, pastas or various items from a cafe menu in the $3.25 to $7.95 range.

Good desserts include strawberry-amaretto cake, chocolate-mousse pie, chocolate/peanut-butter pie and strawberry shortcake.

The main dining and entertainment room is fairly spartan but with a certain character, for want of a better word. There's courtyard dining in summer. In front is the **Queen of Hearts Café,** a funky place sporting all kinds of spool tables and serving an abbreviated menu.

Lunch, Tuesday-Saturday 11:30 to 2:30; dinner, Tuesday-Saturday 5:30 to 8:30 (shows at 8 or 8:30); cafe menu, 11:30 to 9; bar menu after 9; Sunday brunch, 11 to 2.

Café Pierrot, Pine Valley Mill, Wilton. (603) 654-9411.

Part of a food and entertainment center with several shops under the collective name Souhegan Market Place, the cafe has been nicely fashioned from part of an old mill. The high ceilings, white brick walls and exposed pipes lend a charming setting for candlelight dinners.

The wide-ranging menu is quite with-it and the specials enticing, such as shrimp with opal basil-pesto and squash blossoms over linguini or lasagna with roasted garlic and roasted peppers. Main courses ($7.95 to $13.50), many of them vegetarian, range from stir-fries and curries to chicken with whole-grain mustard, trout amandine and filet mignon. The tortellini with artichokes, olives and capers can be had as is or with shrimp or broccoli and pinenuts. There are lots of soups (perhaps oriental vegetable noodle or curried chicken and apple) appetizers, chilis and individual pizzas. Light fare includes "Punchinello's hat plate," two phyllo turnovers filled with spicy beef, creamy chicken, spinach and feta or the day's special -- garlic, onions and mushrooms, at our visit.

A large display case near the kitchen holds the day's salads and desserts. Among the latter we ogled the Italian chocolate-raspberry torte, the margarita-mousse pie, the mocha-fudge-truffle torte and the deep-dish lemon-cream pie. Live entertainment is presented following a buffet dinner on weekends in **The Stage at Café Pierrot,** a huge space fortunately well separated from the smaller cafe.

Open weekdays, 11 to 9, Thursday to 10, Friday and Saturday to 11; also, Saturday breakfast, 9 to 11; Sunday brunch 9 to 2:30, dinner 5 to 9.

Aesop's Tables, 12 Depot St., Peterborough. (603) 924-1612.

This is a coffee bar and tea room like no other. For one thing, it's in a corner of the Toad-Stool Bookstore, and is a comfy refuge of mismatched tables and chairs with a hand-me-down sofa along one side. For another, chef-owner Kin Schilling makes all her goodies at home and brings them here each day.

"The best cappuccino this side of the Continental Divide, surrounded by literary giants," is how she bills her cafe. Besides coffees, she offers teas, bagels, sandwiches and more from a short blackboard menu. She's known for her muffins, which might incorporate "blueberries I picked this morning in Hancock." You also can order frittata, tabbouleh, a tuna sandwich and a different soup daily, made from organic vegetables.

This has become a community gathering place. "You sit down and soon everybody starts talking to each other," says Kin.

Open weekdays, 8:30 to 5, Saturday 10 to 3.

Lodging

Amos A. Parker House, Route 119, Fitzwilliam 03447. (603) 585-6540.

A travel agent in Chicago, Freda Houpt had been nearly everywhere in the world except India and New England when she first visited her son in Boston. After that visit, she went home, sold her house the next day and wound up in Fitzwilliam, where she runs one of the region's most appealing B&Bs.

A Renaissance woman if ever there was one, energetic Freda does everything at the four-room B&B herself. She still finds time to develop and tend the incredible gardens in back, dabble in sculpture and host workshops on drying flowers. And, on a rare busman's holiday in 1993, she traveled around Russia staying at B&Bs.

Her 1780 house, backing up to fields and forests at the western edge of town, is a beauty. The main floor harbors a cozy "great room" (her words) with comfortable furniture, wood stove, barnwood walls, shelves of books and old crockery, and dried flowers hanging from the beams. There also are a charming fireplaced dining room painted a striking burnt orange, a kitchen in which guests tend to congregate, and a TV room with sliding doors to a rear deck overlooking the gardens and a pond "with 22 frogs and seven goldfish," Freda specifies.

The main floor also contains a suite with a private entrance. It has a large bedroom with queensize bed, a sitting area with a sofabed and a fireplace, a small kitchen and stenciling all around. Upstairs are two front guest rooms with fireplaces and private baths (one a two-room affair with a w.c. and sink in one and the smallest shower ever in the other). Two back rooms form a new suite with a full bath and a bidet, a sitting room and elaborate stenciling by master stencilist Jeannie Serpa, who lived for a time in Fitzwilliam. Oriental rugs warm the wide-plank floors and lace-edged pillows and comforters cover the beds. Fresh flowers, colorful towels and terrycloth robes in every room are among caring touches. As guests arrive, a silver tray on the dining room table awaits with hot or cold drinks, fruit, cheese, crackers and cookies.

Breakfast is quite a feast, starting with cold fruit under a glass dome garnished with flowers in the summer and hot fruit like apricot and blueberry compote in long-stemmed Waterford glasses in the fall. The main course might be a "pullapart," a huge puffy pancake done in an iron skillet and sprinkled with lemon and powdered sugar, spinach-soufflé crêpes with mushroom sauce, garnished with vegetables like snow peas or squash with walnuts and cranberries, or an apple-soufflé pancake with sour cream. Another favorite is a dish of rice and dried fruits topped with maple syrup, accompanied by a medley of breakfast meats. Freda loves to experiment, so who knows what yummy dishes you will find at the breakfast table.

Doubles, $65; suite, $80.

Hannah Davis House, 186 Depot Road (Route 119), Fitzwilliam 03447. (603) 585-3344.

This elegant, 1820 Federal house just up the street from the Amos Parker was restored into a B&B in 1990. Newcomers Kaye and Mike Terpstra hit it off immediately with their neighbor, and the Amos Parker and Hannah Davis have been helping each other ever since (their brochures even recommend each other). Kaye trades tomatoes for Freda Haupt's flowers and stores in her freezer the blueberries that Freda picks, which they then share.

The Terpstras did a remarkable job of restoration. They have an enormous, open country kitchen made cozy by prolific plants (including one hanging from a butcher scale). Guests breakfast here at a large table beside the fireplace.

Afternoon treats are served in a common room or on the rear deck overlooking colorful gardens and a bog created by a resident beaver. Another common room holds a piano and stereo system.

Upstairs are three guest rooms with private baths. All the beds are angled into the corners and the large bathrooms have clawfoot tubs and pedestal sinks. Kaye's collection of quilts, teddy bears and an old nightdress and cap decorate the rooms. A high chair in the hall contains all the necessities a guest might forget, including a hair dryer, a steam iron and a wine pull.

Two large and airy guest suites out over the garage and loft have private entrances. One has a deck, nice oak furniture, an angled bed, a sofa and another bed tucked into a corner. Mount Monadnock is on full view from the window of the bathroom, which, Kaye quips, has the best seat in the house. The lofty bedroom in the new Loft Suite opens onto a sitting room below with a queensize sofabed, walk-in closet and a bathroom with clawfoot tub and separate, glass-enclosed shower.

Benjamin Prescott Inn occupies Greek Revival house on a rural property.

The Terpstras serve afternoon refreshments, from popcorn to chocolate-chip cookies. Their hearty breakfast the day we visited included juice, homemade granola and apple sauce, cinnamon-raisin bread and banana bread with fresh ginger, pears poached in syrup and ginger, and french toast stuffed with ham and cheese topped with a dijon sauce. Nasturtiums and snow peas garnish the main courses, which could be scrambled eggs with green beans, ratatouille-stuffed crêpes or a sandwich of stuffed french toast with peaches and cream cheese. An occasional treat is stuffed french toast with seafood and cream cheese.

Doubles, $60 to $75; suites $90. No smoking.

The Benjamin Prescott Inn, Route 124 East, Jaffrey 03452. (603) 532-6637.

This handsome pale yellow 1820s Greek Revival house in a rural setting east of town was the first of Monadnock's upscale B&Bs. Since 1988 it's been run by Barry and Janice Miller, he with 26 years in the hotel business — half of them at Henry Ford's Dearborn Inn in Michigan.

The Snyders have added their own hallmarks and upgraded the ten guest rooms, all with private baths and ranging from standard size to a suite that can sleep eight. Rooms are stenciled and furnished with antiques, handsome quilts, items from the owners' seemingly myriad collections and interesting touches like handpainted antique irons used as door stops. The John Adams Attic Suite on the third floor is a delight with a living room-wet bar and a balcony overlooking the rural backyard, plus another room with a kingsize bed. Both rooms have unusual sleeping alcoves that Barry calls "closet beds" — a Scottish practice using the eaves to cram in extra sleeping space.

A full country breakfast is served at a large table in the dining room or at smaller tables in the common sitting room with a fireplace and color TV. Juices and three of Janice's fruit breads precede the main course, perhaps scotch eggs, eggs benedict or Prescott rarebit, or a bread dish like cinnamon-sourdough french toast shaped in a fan of maple leaves, multi-grain waffles with raspberry butter, or dutch apple pancakes made with granny smith apples. Check out Barry's collection of sands from across the world, stocked in test tubes and displayed on three shelves in the common room. And don't miss the inn's mailbox across the street, an intricate replica of the house itself.

Doubles, $60 to $75; suites, $80 and $130.

Apple Gate Bed & Breakfast, 199 Upland Farm Road (Route 123), Peterborough 03458. (603) 924-6543.

Tiny electric candles glow year-round in the windows of this handsome 1832 Colonial surrounded by prolific gardens, trees and apple orchards. The wraparound veranda with its dark green Adirondack chairs is a perfect spot for taking in the rural surroundings.

Apples are the theme inside, done in exquisite taste by Dianne and Ken Kegenhausen, formerly of Long Island, where she was a music teacher and he a police officer. Colorful stenciling leads guests up the front staircase to three of the four fresh-looking guest rooms, all with private baths. We like best the buttery yellow Cortland corner room with a queensize bed, hooked rugs on the wide pine floors and basket of Woods of Windsor amenities in the bath. The small McIntosh room with a clawfoot tub in the bath is barely big enough for a three-quarter bed.

Particularly attractive are the main-floor common rooms, including a fireplaced parlor opening into a library, where a stuffed bear is perched on the bench at the piano. A full breakfast is served by candlelight beside the fireplace in the beamed dining room, where the table is set for six or eight.

Doubles, $60 to $75.

The Greenfield Inn Bed & Breakfast, Route 31, Greenfield 03047. (603) 547-6327.

Here is a B&B with personality, that of gregarious Vic Mangini, innkeeper-promoter with his wife Barbara, and of their inn furnished with what she calls "Victorian whimsy." That translates to tiny dresses hanging in the front hall, miniature tea sets, cut-glass bowls and perfume bottles in the windows, teddy bears and dolls on the beds, decorated eggs hanging from the dining room chandelier and pink satin ribbons from lace curtains.

"Everything's for sale," says Vic as he shows off every nook and cranny of the rambling, 175-year-old farmhouse. "Except for the inn and Vic, and he might be!" He also probably should have excluded the antique bedspread hanging in the upstairs hall, so proud is he of its history. It was handmade by Bob Hope's mother-in-law, and was sent by the Hopes after one of their visits with their friends the Manginis in Greenfield.

The Hopes have stayed in the two front rooms, the king-bedded Delilah & Sampson and the queen-size Juliet & Romeo, both with private baths and television sets and dressed to the nines in lace, fringe and floral wallpapers. "My wife likes lace," Vic says in an understatement.

Orphan Annie's Room, nicely outfitted in wicker, has the only bathroom with a tub. A canopy of embroidered netting hangs from the ceiling in Casanova's Room, one of the four rooms sharing two baths. All told, there are nine guest rooms, five with private baths. One is a two-level apartment fashioned from an old hayloft, with a kitchen, two daybeds and a loft bedroom accommodating six.

Sherry, candy and apples are in all the rooms, reflecting the Manginis' extra efforts to provide a place for "a relaxing, romantic escape for working people."

The main floor has a chock-full living room with TV, VCR, organ, wood stove, magazines and candies but, oddly, only a couple of chairs upon which to sit. Off the dining room is a wicker room, where you can sit and enjoy tea if you wish. Also good for lounging are the original front wraparound veranda and a new rear deck off a glass-walled meeting room available for conferences and receptions. Antiques, jams, soaps, crystal — you name it — are on display and

Herbal luncheons are served at Pickity Place.

for sale in the breakfast room. Barbara prepares breakfast, served buffet style. It involves five kinds of homemade muffins, mini-bagels, cranberry-almond coffee cake, cereal, fresh fruit and an egg casserole.

Doubles, $49 to $69; suite, $79 to $99.

Gourmet Treats

Pickity Place, Nutting Hill Road, Mason. (603) 878-1151.

Usually it's "over the river and through the woods" to Grandmother's house, but in this case it's up, up, and up a mountain on some horrendous dirt roads and, if you didn't see the odd small sign tacked to a tree, you would swear you were on a wild goose chase.

It's worth the jolts, for eventually you come to a 1786 house and barn embracing a restaurant, herb shop, museum, garden shop, greenhouse and, in the Little Red Riding Hood Room (because Elizabeth O. Jones used the house to illustrate her version of the book), you guessed it, a big bad wolf in a nightcap, lying in grandmother's canopied bed.

The shop smells marvelous, with its wares of herbal teas, potpourris, pomanders, soaps, dried apple wreaths, and even a dill pillow (which apparently will help soothe a baby to sleep). We picked up a tea drinker's gift box ($12.95 — four teas, bamboo strainer, honey and honey dipper) for a tea-loving grandpa.

And, shades of our local, well-loved Caprilands in Coventry, Conn., Pickity Place offers herbal luncheons, five courses for about $15. You're encouraged to bring your own wine (not too much, or you'll never negotiate down the mountain). In a room where bunches of herbs hang on the walls and a huge swag of bay leaves is over the mantel, you will be served foods appropriate to the season (and often in honor of the ancient farming festivals of Europe). The October menu, for instance, might have creamy spinach dip, tomato-barley soup, eight-grain bread, herbed pasta salad, a choice of beef crêpes with horseradish sauce or vegetable stroganoff, spinach mornay and pumpkin squares.

Seatings at 11:30, 12:45 or 2, daily except major holidays year-round. Reservations required.

For a taste of rural New England, **Parker's Maple Barn,** Brookline Road,

Mason, is a favorite stop of many for breakfast — for pancakes, of course. Besides old-fashioned home cooking in a 19th-century barn, there's a country store with gifts and maple items produced on site. Open February-December, Monday-Friday 8 a.m. to 9 p.m., Saturday 7 to 9, Sunday 7 to 8.

Peterborough is the center of the area's cultural and shopping attractions. The **Sharon Arts Center** on Route 123 south of town has a super shop with items from the League of New Hampshire Craftsmen and exhibits in the Kilian Gallery. **The North Gallery at Tewksbury's,** Route 123, is a favorite shop of many, representing more than 500 American craftsmen and carrying everything from cards to toys to paintings to collectibles and a small section of specialty foods and jams, not to mention all the crafts, on three floors of a newly reconstructed, post and beam barn. Other good gift shops in and around Peterborough are the **Black Swan** and **At Wit's End.**

Harlow's Deli & Wide World Cheese Co. on School Street is a European-style cheese shop with an increasing emphasis on a deli serving bagels, sandwiches, homemade soups like Senegalese, chili, stroganoff and goulash. Caterer Harlow Richardson also offers a few gourmet items and fresh bread from a Portuguese bakery. The specialty is a Pita Burro (get it?), Mexican goodies in a toasted pocket with sour cream and salsa. Sit at one of the handful of tables and you'll think you're in the old world. Open Monday-Friday 7 to 4 (Wednesday to 2), Saturday 10 to 2.

Maggie's Farm Natural Foods at 14 Main St. is a large and good natural-foods store with healthful cookbooks, vinegars, sundried tomatoes, salsas and such, plus organic produce, wines and coffee. Next door is **Cook's Complements,** an exceptionally nice kitchen shop. Proprietor Janet Quinn stocks all the proper equipment from gadgets to coffee makers to pretty placemats.

Some of the salads at local restaurants bear the name Rosaly, as in "Rosaly's Garden" at Latacarta or simply "Rosaly Salad at Folkway." They contain fresh organic baby greens, tomatoes, cucumbers and whatever and come from the certified organic gardens of Rosaly S. Bass just southeast of Peterborough along Route 123. **Rosaly's Farm Stand,** the retail adjunct to the twenty-year-old Rosaly's Garden enterprise, is a fascinating stop for people interested in exotic produce and flowers. It also offers cookies, scones and the odd prepared foods and vinegars, among them hot pepper. We bought some Yukon gold potatoes, lavender peppers and pattypan squash and admired the pick-your-own flower and herb gardens, a well-marked showplace of prolific blooms and color. Open daily in season, 10 to 6.

The fledgling **New Hampshire Winery,** 38 Flanders Road, Henniker, bills itself as northern New England's only grape winery. Wines are made on site and tours are offered. Local connoisseurs say that the winery's cabernet is quite good, but that the chardonnay is inconsistent. Open daily 10 to noon and 1 to 6, Sunday noon to 5, July-December. Hours vary rest of year.

Summer Suite at Inn at Harbor Head yields view toward ocean from Cape Porpoise.

Southern Maine
Sophistication by the Sea

It wasn't so long ago that proper Bostonians thought fine dining ended at Portsmouth and the New Hampshire-Maine state line.

The Southern Maine coast was known for lobster shacks and seafood road-houses, and about the only restaurants of note were the Whistling Oyster in Ogunquit and the Roma Cafe in Portland.

How times have changed. The restoration of the historic Old Port Exchange area in Portland has spawned a proliferation of restaurants, both fine and casual, in Maine's largest city. And the sophistication of summer resort areas like Ogunquit and Kennebunkport has attracted new restaurants and inns.

Many of the better establishments simply did not exist fifteen years ago. A restaurant supplier said that in one boom year in the late 1980s, twelve major restaurants had popped up along the Maine coast since the previous summer. The boom continues, with more opening in the recessionary years of 1992 and 1993, when other locales barely held to the status quo.

Now a center of culinary interest — from intimate restaurants serving contemporary American cuisine to casual spots, gourmet shops, delis and inventive vegetarian eateries — Portland offers more quality and variety than most cities its size.

The other centers of culinary interest are in York-Ogunquit and Kennebunkport, two of the more luxurious summer colonies along the coast. Ogunquit's famed Whistling Oyster has closed, but worthy successors remain. And George Bush and his summer neighbors in Kennebunkport no longer have to go to Ogunquit for a fine meal — they have plenty of good restaurants of their own.

There's more sophisticated dining along the southern Maine coast than until lately it has been given credit for.

461

Dining

The Best of the Best

Arrows, Berwick Road, Ogunquit. (207) 646-7175.

Two young chefs who apprenticed with Jeremiah Tower at Stars in San Francisco came east in 1988 to take over this off-again, on-again restaurant with great potential. Clark Frasier and Mark Gaier quickly fulfilled that potential, presenting no doubt the most exciting — and probably the most expensive — food in Maine.

Certainly their setting is hard to beat: a 1765 Colonial farmhouse that imparts a vision of pastoral paradise just west of the Maine Turnpike. Through large leaded panes reminiscent of the mission style, patrons in the spacious rear dining room look out onto fabulous gardens. On the entry table, magnificent flowers and branches of berries rise to the ceiling from a bowl flanked by produce spilling out of baskets. The dark wood ceiling, wide-plank floors, handsome mismatched service plates, crisp white linens and fresh flowers are as pretty as a picture.

Surrounded by trees, fields and flowers (spotlit from above and below at night), diners feast on the view of jaunty blackeyed susans and a sea of zinnias as well as some of Maine's most sophisticated fare. Formally clad waiters in black and white take orders without making notes, quite a feat since the New American menu with Pacific Rim overtones changes nightly.

For starters ($6.95 to $8.95), how about lobster minestrone with roasted bell peppers, asparagus and pancetta or steamed Maine shrimp dumplings with rice wrappers, scallions, carrots, ginger and three sauces? We liked the tea-smoked quail with a garlic-ginger vinaigrette and red-chile mayonnaise (the description cannot do justice to its complexity) and one of the evening's three salads, a trio of Japanese delicacies: zucchini with soy, carrot with sweet peanut dressing and mushroom with green onion. Each was a visual as well as a gustatory work of art, as was each dish to come, although nit-pickers might complain of small portions and a tendency toward preciousness.

Among the six tantalizing entrée choices ($19.95 to $26.95), you might find deep-fried soft-shell crabs with garlic, ginger and Chinese black beans or paella with saffron risotto, littleneck clams, mussels, chorizo, shrimp and scallops. The roasted duck with molasses glaze, wild rice, snow peas and a macadamia-nut vinaigrette was a masterpiece. The only dish we weren't wild about was the grilled tenderloin of beef, which we thought had too intense a smoky taste. The accompaniment of fire-roasted red onion, grilled radicchio, green and yellow beans, tarragon mayonnaise and the best thread-thin crispy french fries ever more than compensated.

A dessert of pineapple, peach-plum and mango sorbets, each atop a meringue and each with its own distinctive sauce, was a triumph. But we'd return anytime for any of pastry chef Bernice Fehringer's masterpieces, say the trio of pears (pear mousse, sorbet and sautéed compote), the strudel of warm black mission figs with honey-vanilla ice cream or the fresh cherry egg roll with star-anise ice cream, each $7.50 but worth every pretty penny.

The wide-ranging, Wine Spectator award-winning wine list is affordably priced.

At meal's end, personable chef-owners Clark and Mark table-hop and chat about food with their clients. Clark, who studied cooking in China, hails from California. Mark trained with Madeleine Kamman and was executive chef at the late Whistling Oyster in Perkins Cove.

Mark Gaier and Clark Frasier with the day's bounty at Arrows.

On the walls of the bar are autographed menus from other great restaurants and chefs. The reviews that have come Arrows' way attest that this pair measures up to the best of them.

Dinner nightly, 6 to 10; fewer nights off-season. Open late April through Thanksgiving.

Cape Neddick Inn and Gallery, Route 1 at Route 1A, Cape Neddick. (207) 363-2899.

Combine an artistic setting and an innovative menu and you have one of the most appealing restaurants in southern Maine. That's just what Pamela Wallis and Glenn Gobeille did, recreating their original restaurant that burned to the ground in May 1985 and reopening by that Thanksgiving.

The dining room on two levels has windsor chairs at nicely spaced tables covered with beige cloths, a remarkable variety of old china for service plates, glass candlesticks, rose napkins and cobalt blue water glasses. Vases of flowers, potted palms, fancy screens, and paintings and sculptures illuminated by track lights make you feel as if you're dining in a gallery, which you are (the artworks are for sale). A more casual dining area in a smaller room with a bar is perfect for enjoying the new "light side" menu, but both menus are available in either room and are designed for devotees of mix and match.

The menus executed by longtime chef Burton Richardson change every six weeks. The nightly specials of fish, veal tenderloin, tournedos and pasta vary, the preparation not decided until that afternoon.

A complimentary plate of raw vegetables with dip accompanies drinks. Soups might be lamb broth with roasted vegetables or mushroom-barley with pinenuts. Appetizers ($5 to $8) at one visit included pâté of foie gras, grilled shrimp with jalapeño sauce, chilled smoked salmon with chèvre and an extraordinary macadamia-lobster tart served on mushroom duxelles. Then came house salads bathed in fresh basil-caesar or cucumber-dill dressings.

Entrées run from $15 for chicken breast marinated in spices and lime and served with vegetable dahl and yogurt to $23 for châteaubriand on herbed french toast with peppercorn-mustard sauce. We passed up one of the night's specials of swordfish grilled with ginger and gin for a fantastic fettuccine with lobster, shrimp, scallops, scallions, peas and artichokes and a Korean-style lamb kabob on rice with sesame sauce and a spicy vegetable relish. Served on large oval plates, these came with glazed parsnips, broccoli and yellow beans. Those with lighter appetites or pocketbooks could opt for such "light side" choices as beef tenderloin tips and shiitake mushrooms in phyllo turnovers with horseradish sour-cream sauce or raviolis stuffed with duck meat and sundried tomatoes -- a satisfying meal when preceded by an appetizer or salad.

"Don't forget Varel's desserts," the menu correctly advises. Sous chef Varel McGuire's creations include a dynamite peach pie, lemon tart with apricot glaze, kahlua cheesecake with hot fudge sauce, plum crumble with ginger-custard sauce, what Pamela touts as "a state-of-the-art dacquoise," chocolate-cognac ice cream and strawberry-wine sorbet. The wine list is appealing and fairly priced.

Dinner nightly in summer, 6 to 9 or 9:30, Wednesday-Sunday in winter; Sunday brunch, noon to 3, mid-October to May.

Cape Arundel Inn, Ocean Avenue, Kennebunkport 04046. (207) 967-2125.

A Portland caterer of our acquaintance thinks the Cape Arundel has the best breakfasts this side of home, and we think the setting couldn't be nicer. The simple dining room with lots of windows has nothing to detract from the view of the sparkling ocean outside, with a bird's-eye peek at George Bush's Walker Point compound. We're partial to the fried codfish cakes served with baked beans and broiled tomato ($6.25), a standard on the menu, and at our latest visit enjoyed an omelet generously strewn with wild mushrooms.

If breakfast here is a great way to start the day, dinner is the way to end. Try for a window table and watch wispy clouds turn to mauve and violet as the sun sets, followed perhaps by a full golden moon rising over the darkened ocean. Chef Ron Bogart is back in the kitchen and satisfying diners' palates after a brief hiatus during which we heard that the food had slipped.

An excellent warm pheasant salad on radicchio with Thai dressing ($7.95) and wild-mushroom crostini ($6.25) got our dinners off to a good start. The highlights were sweetbreads with a tart grapefruit sauce and rack of lamb with pear and mint chutney, accompanied by rice pilaf, crisp ratatouille, and julienned carrots and turnips. Other entrées ($15.95 to $23.50) include medallions of salmon with a sauce of ginger, scallions, tamari and cilantro; shrimp and scallops with pesto, tomatoes and fresh pasta; sautéed duck with jasmine-honey glaze and orange-cranberry compote, and roast veal chop with leek and pernod sauce.

Dining is innovative and setting is artistic at Cape Neddick Inn and Gallery.

Chocolate-almond torte, fruit shortcake and brandy pound cake are among the offerings on the changing dessert tray.

The inn also offers seven guest rooms with private baths and ocean view, as well as a wing with seven motel rooms with private balconies.

Breakfast daily, 8 to 10:30, Sunday to 11; dinner, Monday-Saturday 5:30 to 8:30 or 9. Doubles, $125 to $145. Open mid-May to Columbus Day.

Seascapes, On the Pier, Cape Porpoise, Kennebunkport. (207) 967-8500.

The smashing table settings at this elegant seaside restaurant won a national tabletop competition sponsored by Restaurant Hospitality magazine as "the prettiest tables in America." No wonder. The striking plates and candle holders are of handpainted Italian pottery in heavenly colors, the napkins are ringed with fishes, and the unusual wine glasses are fluted. Angela and Arthur LeBlanc, then owners of the Kennebunk Inn, found them on their travels and knew they were perfect for their new restaurant, with its sea of windows onto the waterscape. The colorful table -- pictured on the cover of our book, *The Restaurants of New England* -- is the match for the view of boats in quaint Cape Porpoise Harbor.

Chef Ray Wieczoreck has overseen the kitchen since 1990 and enjoys a reputation for fare that is consistent though a tad pricey. Excellent dark wheat rolls get dinner here off to a good start. For appetizers ($5.95 to $9.95), we've enjoyed a stellar seafood chowder, soup of the day (tomato and cheddar), curried belon oysters with cucumber sauce and zesty steamed mussels with spicy salsa and andouille sausage, and thought the Maine crab cakes with crispy outsides and a tomato-rosemary sauce even better than the Chesapeake Bay variety. A sorbet precedes the entrées ($17.95 to $21.95). At one dinner they were a classic Mediterranean bouillabaisse with rouille and a breast of chicken coated with pistachio nuts and stuffed with scallops; at another, a rich lobster tequila over linguini, a garlicky shrimp Christina with feta, cilantro and tomatoes, and grilled salmon with a sesame-soy-sherry marinade and a trio of julienned vegetables.

We're usually too full after the main courses to order dessert, but you might succumb to an ethereal strawberry torte, blueberry cheesecake, chocolate decadence or polenta pound cake with berry sauce. The select, primarily American wine list is reasonably priced.

Next door, the LeBlancs operate **The Lively Lobster,** a seafood shanty. In the walkout basement beneath Seascapes is the casual **Cape Porpoise Pub.**

Lunch daily, noon to 3, late June to late October; dinner nightly, 5:30 to 9 or 10, Wednesday-Sunday in May and June. Closed late October to April.

Cafe Always, 47 Middle St., Portland. (207) 774-9399.

This mod, new-wave-style cafe with white butcher paper over white tablecloths, napkins tied with black cords and halogen lights illuminating large floral designs on the walls has been packing in appreciative diners since it opened in 1985.

Little wonder. Chef Cheryl Lewis, who owns the 32-seat establishment with partner Norine Kotts, provided one of our more memorable meals in years.

The green salad tossed with sundried tomatoes, toasted pinenuts, sweet peppers and parmesan cheese ($4.75) was so good that the person who said she would share it didn't. Ditto for the grape leaves stuffed with goat cheese, lamb and walnuts ($6). Accompanied by warm French and rye breads, it turned out these were mere preliminaries to the main events ($14 to $20): roast pork tenderloin stuffed with sundried tomatoes and spinach in a red wine sauce, a masterpiece served with crisp snap peas and shredded carrots, and Thai chicken sautéed in red chile oil and served with a curried-coconut cream sauce, so spicy that the partaker (who really likes incendiary food) was sniffling and her eyes were tearing all through the meal.

The pièce de résistance was a trio of flavorful desserts: an incredibly intense grapefruit sorbet, a plum sorbet in which you could actually detect the plum, and peach ice cream, all garnished with a perfect raspberry and wafer-thin peach slices. Even the house Geyser Peak red wine at $13 a bottle was outstanding.

New in 1993 was a four-course, prix-fixe ($25) tasting menu that changes monthly. A Mediterranean meal was offered when we were there. It involved a selection of marinated olives, mussels simmered in Moroccan spices and served with bruschetta, swordfish stuffed with capers and parmesan cheese, and citrus sorbet with a fresh basil sauce.

Chef Lewis, who trained in Boston, changes her short menu daily. "No food rules" is her motto, and she likes to experiment with tastes and presentation. "When the plates are put in front of people, they're happy with the way it looks," she says. And the way it tastes — as long as they're into assertive food like grilled yellowfin tuna steak served with a fiery Japanese wasabi and pickled ginger sauce or a lobster and goat-cheese burrito with fresh mango salsa and a crunchy black-bean salad. An appetizer at one of our visits was called simply "three ways to eat eggplant" and cost $8.75 to find out. This is inspired cuisine, but not for the faint of palate.

Dinner nightly, 5 to 10.

Back Bay Grill, 65 Portland St., Portland. (207) 772-8833.

A new, 20-foot-long mural along one wall attests that this grill isn't in Back Bay Boston. Done by local artist Ed Manning Jr., it is a fanciful rendering of restaurant scenes and characters that are very much the Back Bay Grill. It's also so life-like that it makes the room seem bigger, according to owner Joel Freund, who commissioned it in 1993.

New wave look at Cafe Always.   **Prize-winning table setting at Seascapes.**

The mural is a focal point of this highly regarded establishment, which is quite urbane with high ceilings, track lighting, antique mirrors, modern upholstered chairs (obtained from an office furniture company) and mahogany tables. Roses and candles are atop the tables.

Chef Scott Anderson changes his handsomely printed menu monthly. Entrées ($15.95 to $20.95) might be bluefin tuna with sundried-tomato aioli and grilled radicchio, scallop and lobster cakes with organic spinach and rémoulade sauce, a skewer of grilled lamb with white-bean salsa and New York sirloin with gorgonzola butter and roasted pancetta. These could be accompanied by haricots verts, julienned carrots, corn with sugar-snap peas and grilled red potatoes.

Start perhaps with chilled cantaloupe soup in summer, black-bean and pancetta soup in winter. Marinated Mediterranean lamb salad, duck-filled corn crêpe with cumin and grilled-onion salsa, and pizza with spicy tasso, ricotta and caramelized onions might be other appetizers, in the $5.75 to $8.25 range. Desserts (around $5.50) include an acclaimed crème brûlée, raspberry gratin with mascarpone custard, chocolate profiterole with caramel and nougat ice cream, and apricot and bittersweet-chocolate sorbets.

The wine list, which changes every week or two, is quite extensive and fairly priced from $13.50 to $165. Many wines are available by the glass.

Dinner, Monday-Saturday 5:30 to 9:30 or 10.

Wharf Street Cafe, 38 Wharf St., Portland. (207) 773-6667.

Pair a former Minneapolis caterer with big ideas and a little lunch spot known for its sandwiches. The result is this newly relocated winner on the "in" street in the Old Port Exchange, where a single block harbors six restaurants (with more on the way) and live music and a strolling crowd make for festive weekend evenings.

Caterer Steve Massing teamed with Janet Berry, who had run the cafe as a sandwich shop. They moved to larger quarters across the street in 1994.

For dinner the cafe sheds its earthy image in favor of tablecloths, dimmed lamps and blues music on the stereo. A copy of Food Arts magazine is on each table. Steve changes his short dinner menu every few weeks. His contemporary

American fare bears California, Southwest and Pacific Rim influences. The "petite" course ($2.95 to $6.95) could be chilled cucumber gazpacho, spicy crab-meat tacos with lime and cilantro, shrimp and rice spring rolls with peanut sauce, and herb pizzette with goat cheese, roasted tomatoes and pinenuts.

The "grande" course ($10.95 to $16.95) numbers seven choices, with at the most one meat dish and usually a couple of vegetarian. Tempting at our visit were pistachio-crusted salmon with citron soy sauce and soba noodles, Atlantic swordfish with roasted tomato butter sauce, fresh asparagus and garlic potato turnovers, and lobster and brie raviolis with caramelized-onion sauce, roasted grapes, green beans and toasted almonds.

Desserts include homemade fruit pies, chocolate bread pudding with chianti-poached pears and crème caramel with fresh berries.

The relocated cafe continues to serve soups and sandwiches and added a couple of "hot items more in keeping with the dinner menu," Janet said. Although it holds only 48 diners, it spills onto the street in summer. At our visit, Steve was hoping to add a vegetarian-gourmet foods shop nearby.

Lunch, Monday-Friday 10:30 to 3; dinner, Tuesday-Sunday 5:30 to 9:30. BYOB.

Street and Co., 33 Wharf St., Portland. (207) 775-0887.

Pure, pure, pure is the feeling of the small "eating establishment" opened by Dana Street in 1989 in the Old Port Exchange. You enter past an open grill and kitchen and face a blackboard menu, both good indicators. Ahead is a small basement room with bare pegged floors and 40 seats, where strands of herbs and garlic hang on a brick wall. In 1994, Dana acquired the adjacent space formerly occupied by the Wharf Street Cafe, which moved across the street. That gave him twenty more seats as well as a wine bar that doubles as a waiting area. Outside are twenty more seats along Wharf Street for summer dining, and the tables might turn four times on a busy night.

The freshest of seafood and a purist philosophy draw a steady clientele. The night we visited, the blackboard listed lobster fra diavolo, $34.95 for two, and five fish dishes grilled or cajun -- tuna, swordfish, salmon, sole or scallops, each $14.95. Other choices were scallops with pernod and cream, sole française, mussels over linguini, and shrimp with tomatoes and capers, $12.95 to $15.95. Sometimes there's a pasta alfredo, the only non-seafood item. Meals come with French bread, tossed salad with a balsamic vinaigrette and fresh vegetables (asparagus, zucchini and red bell peppers at our visit) sautéed in butter and white wine.

Equally straightforward are such appetizers as mussels, steamers and crab sauté. Most of the wines are priced in the teens.

Dinner nightly, 5:30 to 10 or 11.

Cafe Brix, 545 Gorham Road, South Portland. (207) 773-2262.

The upscale Cornerbrook shopping strip across from the Maine Mall is an unlikely location for a stylish restaurant. But partners Charles Neureuther and CIA-grad Michael Reed had scored with the seasonal Diamond's Edge Restaurant on Great Diamond Island in Casco Bay in 1992 and decided to open on the mainland in 1993. They gutted and rebuilt a long fishhook-shaped storefront and emerged with a restaurant of uncommon style.

"People are overwhelmed by the change," Chuck said. Two local women did the faux finish on the rag-rolled yellow walls tinted with burgundy to pick up the color of the carpeting and match the faux-marble bar facing the entry. One entire wall is a mural. Hidden around the corner in back are tall windows onto the woods with a faux grapevine curled with sunflowers painted along the top. Sleek black upholstered chairs are at well-spaced tables dressed in pale yellow cloths over white. The yellow and burgundy flowers in the bud vases carry out the color scheme.

It's a luscious-looking backdrop for some acclaimed food prepared by wunderkind chef Diane Davis, age 26. Dinner might start with lobster risotto with romano, mushroom-filled raviolis with pistachios and sundried-tomato/pesto cream, and seafood stew with cream and saffron. Toasted pinenuts are tossed with mesclun greens in one of the salads. Main courses ($12.95 to $18.95) could be poached salmon with a chervil and dill wine sauce, grilled swordfish with coriander butter and braised shiitake mushrooms, veal sweetbreads with porcini mushrooms over puff pastry and grilled lamb chops with green-peppercorn sauce.

Among desserts are chocolate-toffee torte, brandied apple tart and frozen lemon mousse. The wine list is serious business here, as you might expect from a restaurant that takes its name from a wine term, the Brix scale.

Lunch, Monday-Friday 11:30 to 3; dinner, Monday-Saturday from 5.

Other Dining Choices

Hurricane, Oarweed Lane, Perkins Cove, Ogunquit. (207) 646-6348.

This trendy spot opened by the people who run the Horsefeathers restaurant chain (Portland and North Conway) was acquired in 1991 by Brooks and Luanne MacDonald, he the working chef who has elevated its already high reputation. "Our view will blow you away -- our menu will bring you back" is its slogan, a realistic claim based on our earlier meal there and the crowds waiting to be seated for lunch at 2 o'clock on a September weekday at our latest visit.

Every table has a view in two small summery rooms beside the ocean. Most desirable is the enclosed but breezy porch. The all-day menu is divided into soups, salads and small plates, with entrées added for dinner. You could make a good lunch or supper of lobster gazpacho ("so hot it's cool"), a five-onion soup with gorgonzola crust (which a friend found surprisingly flavorless), the house salad of field greens with roasted shallots and pistachios and grilled chicken satay, baked shrimp and crab with artichoke hearts and three cheeses, or a napoleon of smoked salmon with lemon-chive crème fraîche.

More substantial are the dinner dishes ($13.95 to $19.95), among them cuervo and lime-glazed swordfish with black-bean and white-corn salsa, lobster-stuffed pasta shells with gorgonzola cream, chargrilled veal chop with an armagnac demi-glace and rack of lamb with cabernet sauce. Hearth-baked sourdough bread, house salad, potato and vegetable come with.

Among desserts are tirami su, crème brûlée and mile-high cheesecake.

Lunch daily, 11:30 to 4; dinner, 5:30 to 10:30.

Frankie & Johnny's, 1594 Route 1 North, Cape Neddick. (207) 363-1909.

This new gourmet natural-foods restaurant isn't much to look at -- a manufactured home beside the highway, painted with colorful triangles and sporting a Haagen-Dazs sign in front. But stop, venture in and enjoy a healthful meal at unbelievably low prices, either inside in a whimsical dining room, outside at a couple of picnic tables or to go.

Personable Frank Rostad handles the front of the house while John Shaw, formerly with the late Laura Tanner House restaurant in Ogunquit, cooks in a state-of-the-art kitchen. Everything here is made from scratch and almost all of it on site, say these purists (it took them fourteen months to find an all-natural cone to serve with their Haagen-Dazs ice cream). They even squeeze juices at their juice bar.

John produces "gourmet food that's good for you." The soups could be vegetarian or vegan (dairy-free). Six salads ($3.75 to $5.75) range from tabbouleh and hummus to blackened chicken on assorted greens. Under spaëtzles ($7.75) you'll find chicken, shrimp, seafood diablo and vegetable harvest. Favorites among entrées ($6.25 to $8.75) are poached or blackened Atlantic salmon and blackened chicken served over sweet and sour cabbage with potatoes and feta cheese. This interesting pair are best known for their trademarked crustolis ($7.50), ten-inch-round French bread crusts made from unbleached flour and not unlike pizzas. For dinner, we ordered one with shrimp, pesto and goat cheese and another with capers, olives, red onions and feta cheese, split a house salad and had more than enough left over for lunch the next day. Dinner is by candlelight and the food is serious, but it's dispensed in a relaxed and playful environment. Decor in the pine-paneled room is nil except for a few abstract oils by Frank's sister at one end and a handful of rocks and perhaps a miniature dinosaur on each table. "It's hard to take yourself seriously with rocks and a little dinosaur in front of you," says Frank, whose aim is to help customers enjoy healthful food and have a good time. It's also hard to imagine that reservations are advised, but this place is very popular.

Open in summer, Monday-Saturday 11 to 9, Sunday 2 to 9; closed Tuesday and Wednesday in off-season and Dec. 21 through March. BYOB. No smoking.

Madd Apple Cafe, 23 Forest Ave., Portland. (207) 774-9698.

An American bistro with a Southern accent is offered by Martha and James Williamson in a pleasant space beside the Portland Performing Arts Center. The accent comes from Jim's background in the South; hence all the barbecue items from secret family recipes and the fresh catfish, crawfish, boudin blanc, cornbread and sweet-potato pie. They're served up in two small rooms containing half a dozen tables each, crisp white linens, mauve and white walls, and interesting art.

At dinner, you might start with escargots bourguignonne, mussels provençal, creole-style red-bean soup or Caribbean salad composed of corn, avocados, bananas, tomatoes, cucumbers, sprouts, scallions and greens, or perhaps a special of barbecued lamb ribs. Entrées run from $10.95 to $17.95. They might be shrimp cakes with rémoulade sauce and red beans, pan-fried rainbow trout creolaise, frog's legs meunière, marlin with citrus sauce, pork loin diablo, sautéed chicken livers and steak New Orleans, sautéed with mushrooms and scallions and served with a brandy-worcestershire sauce. Carolina chopped pork barbecue is usually available at lunch and barbecued Denver lamb ribs at dinner.

Bananas foster, key lime pie, profiteroles and espresso cheesecake are signature desserts.

In New Orleans style, background jazz is played on the sound system. Before turning to cooking, Jim, a jazz guitarist and composer, taught at Berklee School of Music in Boston.

Lunch, Tuesday-Friday 11:30 to 3; dinner, Tuesday-Saturday 5:30 to 9.

Katahdin, Spring and High Streets, Portland. (207) 774-1740.

A creative hand is at work in the kitchen as well as with the decor in this offbeat new restaurant. Chef-owners Gretchen Bates and Dan Peters named it for Maine's highest mountain to reflect Maine home cooking and, according to the bartender, "mountains of food" and "the summit of fine dining."

Decor is colorful at Katahdin.

They shop daily for fresh ingredients (we spotted their van at the downtown Portland Farmer's Market). These turn up in such specials as oyster stew with fresh peas, pan-seared bluefish with a mustard-thyme crust, grilled halibut with leeks and peas in a white-wine cream sauce and vegetarian lasagna with swiss chard, mushrooms, gouda and a sweet red-onion cream sauce. The regular menu ($9.95 to $13.95) also appeals, from grilled medallions of pork tenderloin wrapped in bacon and served with jalapeño butter to london broil marinated with ginger, scallions and garlic. There's always a blue-plate special ($9.95) served with a cup of soup and a salad -- smothered beef and onions at our visit. Appetizers and pastas tempt as well: perhaps lobster spring rolls, goat-cheese flan with greens and sliced tomatoes, pan-fried oysters with sour cream-mustard sauce or buckwheat pasta tossed with pepper-cured ham, crimini mushrooms, leeks and cream.

No one leaves hungry, for dinners are served with buttermilk biscuits, Aunt Nina's pickles, salad, starch and vegetable. But save room for dessert, perhaps mint-orange sherbet or blueberry-cinnamon frozen yogurt or the chocolate mountain -- a brownie shell filled with chocolate mousse, fudge sauce, whipped cream and nuts.

There's lots to look at in this dining area, where mismatched chairs and upholstered armchairs flank tables whose tops are painted with different fruit and vegetable designs. A large 1950s mural graces one wall, while others bear quilts and changing artworks. A selection of oldies but goodies, played on tape rather loudly, sets a vibrant backdrop.

Dinner, Monday-Saturday 5 to 10 or 11.

Alberta's Cafe, 21 Pleasant St., Portland. (207) 774-5408.

This funky cafe, named for the mother of one of the founders, was voted "most bohemian" by a local magazine. The description surprised co-founder Tom Russell, who hailed from Cambridge and since has departed for Soho Kitchen and Cafe, a *really* bohemian place he opened in Halifax.

His partners, Jim Ladue and Bob Corey, have upgraded the decor. Framed black and white photos are arranged artistically on the sponged cranberry walls, a divider is painted with intricate design to resemble marble, and windsor chairs face tables draped in beige and brown linens at night, But an aquarium atop the bar remains a centerpiece and coats are hung on funky racks in a place utterly without pretension.

The food is a mixed bag of inspiration and value. Among entrées priced from $15.95 to $18.95 are medallions of grilled swordfish layered with crab meat and asparagus, chunks of grilled salmon and snow peas with pasta and herb cream, grilled bluefin tuna with grilled vegetables marinated in sake and tamari, Asian noodles with shrimp and cashews, grilled strip sirloin with horseradish dressing, and mixed grill of pork loin, lamb kidney, rabbit and chicken.

A section of the menu is labeled starters or light meals ($3.95 to $6.95). Among choices are green-chile and tomatillo ragout with grilled sweet corn and seared rock shrimp, garnished with blue corn chips and sour cream, and grilled lamb kidneys on roasted garlic toast. A nice touch: an extra $5 turns a light meal into a full meal. Much of the dinner menu is available in smaller portions for lunch.

Desserts are refreshing, as they ought to be to cool down such assertive fare: ginger ice cream with chocolate sauce, mocha-pecan pie with ice cream and the house special, death by chocolate (served frozen).

Since a fire destroyed the owners' Good Egg Cafe on Congress Street, Alberta's has been serving breakfast. At our latest visit we devoured the smoked ham and cheddar omelet served on a homemade toasted English muffin ($2.95) and a fiery "eggs from hell" with roasted chile sauce, cheddar, salsa and sour cream, served on a crisp fried corn tortilla with delicious pinto beans on the side ($3.95).

Breakfast, Monday-Friday 6 to 11:30, weekends, 7 to 2; lunch, Monday-Friday 11:30 to 2:30; dinner nightly, 5 to 11.

Walter's Cafe, 15 Exchange St., Portland. (207) 871-9258.

Noisy and intimate, this "now" kind of place has been packed to the rafters since it opened by Walter Loeman and Mark Loring in 1990. It doesn't advertise and doesn't have to, its spirited food at pleasant prices producing lengthy lineups at peak periods.

We faced a twenty-minute wait for a weekday lunch in July, but were glad we waited. A BOLT ($5.75) -- bacon, lettuce, tomato and red onion sandwich with sweet cajun mayonnaise -- arrived in a pita, served with a pickle and gnarly fries. The "chilling pasta salad" ($6.75) yielded a zesty plateful tossed with chicken, avocado and red peppers.

From our table alongside a brick wall in the long and narrow high-ceilinged room we could see the cooks splashing liberal amounts of wines into the dishes they were preparing in the open kitchen. Green plants backlit on a shelf above the kitchen area provided accents amid the prevailing brick. Glass covered the black vinyl tablecloths.

Dinner entrées ($10.75 to $14.95) are categorized by "flippin' pans" and "thrill of the grill." Among the possibilities are "crazy chicken" with prosciutto, sweet peas, red wine and cream over angel-hair pasta, grilled chicken ya-ya with dried figs, brazil nuts and sweet peppers over egg noodles, shrimp and scallop florentine over linguini, grilled pork tenderloin with a spicy hazelnut glaze, and sirloin steak stuffed with sundried tomatoes, mushrooms and gorgonzola.

Irish cream cheesecake, orange mousse with wild blueberries and varied chocolate creations comprise the dessert list. Lots of nice wines are priced in the teens and twenties.

Lunch daily, 11 to 3; dinner, 5 to 10.

Pepperclub, 78 Middle St., Portland. (207) 772-0531.

"World cuisine" is the theme of this hip new organic-vegetarian-seafood establishment, part of the Middle Street "Restaurant Row." It's the creation of Jaap Helper, a Danish-born chef-artist who owned the late, great Vinyard restaurant nearby. He re-emerged here with his paintings and a partner, former

Soaring barn is home of White Barn Inn's acclaimed dining room.

art editor Eddie Fitzpatrick, to produce something of a showplace of culinary design. Fresh flowers on the table, a crazy paint job with many colors on the walls and a bar made of old Jamaican steel drums, painted and cut in half, create a vivid setting.

The food is colorful as well. The blackboard menu lists such starters as curried corn chowder, Caribbean shrimp cakes, vegetarian samosas with beet chutney, hummus salad, pizza rustica and Moroccan vegetable stew. Main dishes ($7.95 to $9.95) could be Maine shrimp with pasta and pesto, kashmiri chicken, North African stuffed peppers, chicken and leek pie, Tunisian couscous, mahi-mahi with ginger and cilantro, pinto-bean flautas with salsa fresca, English country pork pie and roasted red-pepper and spinach lasagna.

Among desserts are strawberry-raspberry pie and mocha-butternut crunch.

Dinner nightly, 5 to 9 or 10. No credit cards. No smoking.

Bed and Board

White Barn Inn, Beach Street, Box 560 C, Kennebunkport 04046. (207) 967-2321.

Long known for its restaurant, the White Barn has been vastly upgraded in terms of accommodations lately. Such has been the infusion of money and T.L.C. by the hands-on Australian owner, personable Laurie Bongiorno, and his wife Laurie Cameron, that the inn was quickly accepted into the prestigious Relais & Châteaux, the world-wide association chain of deluxe owner-operated hotels. In 1992, the restaurant became the first in northern New England to win five diamonds from the AAA. In 1993, it was the first to be accorded five stars for all three categories of food, service and atmosphere from the Maine Sunday Telegram.

The 24 rooms in the main inn and outbuildings vary considerably, as their range in prices indicates. The seven fireplaced suites in May's Annex, a refurbished carriage house, are the height of luxury. Each has a library-style sitting area, chintz-covered furniture, fireplace, dressing room, spacious bath with a marble jacuzzi, Queen Anne kingsize four-poster bed and a television set hidden in the armoire. We felt quite pampered in the Green Room here, thanks to a personal note of welcome from the innkeeper, fresh fruit, Poland Spring water, terry robes, Gilchrist & Soames toiletries and a couple of cookies when the bed was turned down. Four large renovated rooms in the Gatehouses also claim fireplaces and jacuzzis, as well as cathedral ceilings, queensize sleigh beds and sitting areas with wing chairs. The thirteen rooms upstairs in the inn, though nicely furnished and cheerfully decorated with whimsical hand-painted furniture, are not as spacious or sumptuous.

A lavish continental breakfast is served in the elegant Colonial dining room. Fresh orange juice and slices of cut-up fruits are brought to your table by a tuxedoed waiter. You help yourself to assorted cereals, yogurts and an array of muffins and pastries the likes of which we've seldom seen before -- including a sensational strawberry-bran muffin with a top the size of a grapefruit and a cool crème d'amandes with a sliced peach inside.

Dinners of considerable note are served in the adjacent three-story barn, where you can look out through plate-glass windows onto a deck, laden with impatiens and spotlit at night. Farm implements and artifacts hang from the rafters. Tables, spaced well apart, are set with silver and pewter, cut crystal and Villeroy & Boch china, white linens and oil lamps. The convivial gather at the gorgeous solid brass bar (even the small tables in the bar are brass-topped). The truly jovial gather around the baby grand piano after dinner and sing along with the pianist if so inclined.

New chef Gethin DuValle Thomas took over the kitchen in 1993 after three years at the acclaimed Adirondack in Washington, D.C. He has added stronger flavors and Southwest touches to fare that had been rather subtle, "awakening some tastebuds here," says Laurie. He testified that the food is better than ever, and we've been mighty impressed by many a dinner here in the past.

The menu, which changes weekly, offers nine soups, salads and appetizers in the $7.95 to $12.95 range and nine entrées from $19.75 to $31.95. Each is tantalizing, and you'll likely have as difficult a time choosing as we did. Crunchy French bread and a neat little bonus from the chef (in our case, a gingery lobster spring roll on a red-pepper puree) are a sign of things to come. You might start with a chowder of Maine corn with jalapeño, coriander and poached oysters or a lightly seared medallion of foie gras with a lingonberry/port-wine compote, baby lettuces and marinated asparagus tips. A choice of champagne sorbet (presented in a glass dish shaped like a daffodil) or a fine house salad on a chilled glass plate comes next. For main courses, how about seared striped bass with saffron potatoes, creamy savoy cabbage and a tomato-basil vinaigrette; grilled breast of duck with garlic whipped potatoes, sautéed spinach, sundried cherries and ginger sauce, or grilled veal rib chop with haricots verts, wax beans, oyster mushrooms, garlic-roasted parisienne potatoes and a port-wine sauce? This is food fit for royalty -- conceived, executed, served (and priced) accordingly.

The treats continue for dessert ($6.45 to $7.95), perhaps a chilled champagne timbale with peaches and raspberry coulis, a frozen white-chocolate and grand-marnier cake with a compote of Maine strawberries and rhubarb or a rich chocolate marquis tart with toasted hazelnuts and frangelico whipped cream. Such extravagances call for another -- perhaps a bottle of Château d'Yquem for $290, as listed with the dessert wines. The well-chosen wine list, priced from $20 to $300, is especially strong on American chardonnays and cabernets.

Dining here is theatrical and delivered with grace and ceremony. With candles flickering and classical music playing, the setting and service are equal to the food.

Dinner nightly, 5:30 or 6 to 9:30 or 10:30. Closed Monday and Tuesday in winter. Doubles, $110 to $150; Gatehouse rooms, $175; suites, $260.

Kennebunkport Inn, Dock Square, Kennebunkport 04046. (207) 967-2621 or (800) 967-2621.

This attractive inn with a convenient in-town location just off the main square has expanded in size to the point where it now has valet parking in summer, but its acclaimed restaurant keeps getting better. On busy nights it's so popular that tables are set up in the elegant new lounge for the overflow.

Against a backdrop of candlelight and classical music, dining is in two small, pretty rooms off either side of a wide entry hall. Fringed valances and lace curtains, Laura Ashley wallpaper and stenciling, hurricane lamps and well-spaced tables done up in white over beige create a light and festive feeling.

Innkeepers Martha and Rick Griffin, who travel to France for new ideas, have garnered quite a culinary reputation. Our dinner began with good crusty rolls and excellent mixed green salads, one just of greens with an almond and orange-honey dressing and the other with tomatoes, hard-boiled egg and a creamy dill dressing. They were enough that we skipped such appetizers as shrimp pâté with peanut sauce and gravlax served on cucumber rounds.

The grilled duck breast with a piquant raspberry sauce was artfully presented, and the mustard-ginger rack of lamb was extraordinary — five individual chops of about two bites each, very tender and rare, served with steamed herbed new red potatoes, and sautéed squash and tomatoes. Other possibilities priced from $16.95 to $24.95 include the inn's traditional bouillabaisse, charbroiled swordfish with Japanese ponzu sauce, grilled veal chop with shiitake mushrooms and grilled beef tenderloin with a port-wine and mustard sauce.

The dessert cart yielded a white-chocolate mousse with strawberries in kirsch, good but not very chocolatey, and an ethereal key lime pie, plus English trifle and strata pie. The house wine by the liter was good and the best value on a rather expensive wine list. A pub menu is available in the Victorian piano bar.

The inn has 34 rooms, all with private baths and TV. The nine newest, larger and more deluxe than the rest, have four-poster beds. A small octagonal swimming pool with a large wooden deck fits snugly between the graceful 19th-century mansion housing the main inn and a motel-style annex.

Breakfast specials include a basque pepper omelet and garlic popovers with scrambled eggs and chives.

Breakfast daily, 8 to 9:30, Sunday to 10:30; dinner nightly in summer, 6 to 9, closed Sunday night in off-season. Dining room closed November-April. Doubles, $79.50 to $165, EP.

The Inn by the Sea, Route 77, Cape Elizabeth 04107. (207) 799-3134 or (800) 888-4287.

Nearly $7 million went into Maine's newest luxury resort, which opened in

Every suite at Inn by the Sea has deck or balcony facing ocean..

1987 on the site of the former Crescent Beach Inn. And it looks it, from the marble-tiled lobby and the fourteen Audubon hand-colored engravings gracing the inn's walls to the luxury suites with two TVs (the one in the sitting room hidden in the armoire) and no fewer than three telephones. There's an ocean view from every patio and balcony.

Handsomely done in Maine shingle style, the angled complex consists of 25 one-bedroom suites in the main building and eighteen two-bedroom suites in four attached cottages. The loft suites on the second floor are most in demand, each with a kitchenette, a large living room opening onto a private balcony and a loft bedroom upstairs. We liked our garden suite facing the lawn and ocean on the first floor, its living room — with reproduction Chippendale furnishings and a blue chintz sofa — with sliding doors allowing us to walk right outside onto a patio. Its small bedroom with a four-poster bed was quite adequate, even though the windows opened onto the parking lot. We do think they could provide brighter lights for reading -- or do they expect everybody to retire to the unique rooftop library, where hors d'oeuvre and cocktails are available at night? The library comes with a TV, comfy rattan chairs and shelves full of books, including some good mysteries. The angled windows frame the ocean, and the outdoor deck with built-in benches has the best view of all.

You can swim in a pleasant pool, saunter down a boardwalk to a private entrance to the beach at Crescent Beach State Park, and play croquet on the regulation croquet lawn with an English gazebo at the end. The little tea garden with rose bushes and fish swimming in a fountain pool is a quiet retreat.

Breakfast and dinner are served in the Audubon Room, a harmonious space striking in white, with very comfortable chairs and a porch around two sides. Tables are topped with white linens, lovely English bone china and fresh flowers. The dinner fare has been elevated since we last dined here, the choices ranging from $15.95 for pan-seared brook trout with citrus beurre blanc to $21.95 for grilled veal chop with vegetable mirepoix and radicchio.

Breakfast is hotel style at hotel prices ($4.95 to $9.95, for eggs benedict, the house specialty; $12.95 with lobster). You can cook in your room, though few do, or go up the road as we did to the locally popular Spurwink Country Kitchen, where two of us enjoyed a more than ample breakfast for less than the price of a continental back at the inn, where they do things up big. Even the bill comes on an oversize computer printout.

Breakfast, 7 to 11; dinner, 5:30 to 9:30. Doubles, $160 to $220; cottage suites, $290 to $370.

Lodging

Wooden Goose Inn, Route 1, Cape Neddick 03902. (207) 363-5673.

Here is the stuff of which design-magazine editors' dreams are made. A parlor displays a magnificent collection of crystal candlesticks on a square glass table. Bedrooms sport fabric pillow shams matching the window treatments. One has a custom-designed corner headboard to make more room for a queensize bed, and a carpeted bathroom with a freestanding clawfoot tub and two rocking chairs. The gorgeous, glass-enclosed dining room overlooking an English garden contains wrought-iron tables set with white linen, Lenox china and Waterford crystal. Every room is decorated to the nth degree.

That this seven-bedroom B&B is such an extravagance of eclectic furnishings and decor should come as no surprise. Jerry Rippetoe was a decorator in New York and New Jersey before he and Anthony Sienicki acquired the ramshackle home in 1984. "It took ten painters seven days just to scrape the house," Jerry recalls. "It was horrendous." Nonetheless, they opened within two weeks with four guest rooms, and have been going strong ever since. Lately the pair bought 750 yards of fabric to redo three bedrooms and learned to use a sewing machine when they found it would cost $11,000 to have done what they wanted. Their do-it-yourself window treatments, billowing canopies and coordinated pillows -- most in their favorite colors of hunter greens and burgundies -- are incredible. Tony also builds the remarkable decorative birdhouses that are scattered about the house and are for sale.

Each air-conditioned room has a queensize bed, private bath and a sitting area. Suffice to say that the Wooden Goose offers the ultimate in good taste and comfort, even if we find some of the rooms a bit dark and closed-in for summer stays. The house has been turned cocoon-like to the inside since it's right up against Route 1. "We're trying to create a romantic mood," says Jerry. You can always enjoy the two parlors or the airy dining room. Or go out to the lush gardens (the nasturtiums at one visit were so profuse as to be unbelievable), in the midst of which is a trickling pool bordered by rocks, umbrella-covered tables with yellow chairs, and loungers scattered about.

"People always bring us geese as gifts," says Jerry. "We incorporate them into the inn" — and the results are ingenious.

Afternoon tea is taken in the Terrace Room or the gardens. Eleven varieties are offered, as are such changing treats as a chocolate ganache with macadamia crust and caramel sauce, a tart of granny smith apples and lemon, chocolate sheba with crème anglaise and other fancy desserts prepared by Tony.

Breakfasts are as luscious as they are varied. The day we visited, it started with fresh orange juice, date bread, cinnamon muffins and strawberries romanoff, culminating in eggs oscar accompanied by steamed broccoli and homefries. The next day, peach and cherry soup was the fruit course; the entrée, potato pancakes topped with poached eggs and hollandaise sauce, with sausage and sautéed peppers and onions. This is beginning to sound more like dinner, but recent favorites include lobster quiche, poached fillet of sole stuffed with Maine shrimp and topped with dill hollandaise, crab cakes with dijon mustard sauce, chicken breast with peaches and zucchini and sour-cream sauce, and baked swordfish with mustard topping, curried potatoes and vegetables. Their special roulade -- a soufflé with ham, mustard, shallots, and parmesan cheese -- is rolled, baked, topped with gruyère, then broiled and sliced. It looks like a jelly roll and "is heaven," says Jerry.

Doubles, $110. Closed in January and some weekdays in off-season.

Hartwell House, 116 Shore Road, Ogunquit 03907. (207) 646-7210 or (800) 235-8883.

The British flag flies alongside the American in front of this sophisticated B&B on the main road between the center of Ogunquit and Perkins Cove. Owners Jim and Tricia Hartwell have an English background, which explains their extensive use of English antiques in the thirteen guest rooms and three suites, all with modern baths, and the lush lawns and sculpted gardens out back, which provide the profusion of flowers inside.

The enclosed front porch is gorgeous with its arched windows, colorful French chintz on the loungers and wicker chairs, and an array of plants and flowers. Here is where guests gather for an afternoon pick-me-up of iced tea, poured from a glass pitcher topped with strawberries and orange slices on a silver tray. Everything except the wood floor in the stunning living room is white. The formal dining room has one long table, willowware china and a silver service on the sideboard. Hooked rugs dot the wide-board floors. Guests gather here or on the porch for a full breakfast of fresh fruit and a hot dish, perhaps stuffed crêpes, frittatas, baked chicken in puff pastry or belgian waffles. Managers Alec and Renée Adams also serve intimate, five-course dinners for eight on Saturday nights in the winter as part of a weekend package.

Some of the nine rooms in the main house have private balconies looking over the rear yard. Across the street in a new addition to the house where the managers reside are seven more luxurious rooms, including three suites. Trisha's favorite is the James Monroe Suite, a two-level affair all in white.

Doubles, $110 to $135; suites, $155 to $175. Closed two weeks in mid-January.

The Captain Lord Mansion, Pleasant Street, Box 800, Kennebunkport 04046. (207) 967-3141 or (800) 522-3141.

Rick Litchfield and his wife Bev Davis bought this inn, which they consider "probably the finest example of Federal architecture on the coast of Maine, if not the country," in 1978. It was then a home for elderly women; five stayed on for the next two years while the couple went to work and totally restored the place, putting in private baths for each of the sixteen bedrooms.

Two chocolates are placed every evening in the bedrooms, which are elegantly furnished in antiques, some with four-poster or canopied beds. Eleven have working fireplaces, and are so in demand in the autumn and winter that 30 cords of wood are consumed annually. The corner rooms in this square, cupola-topped yellow mansion are especially spacious and airy. All have period reproduction wallpaper and nice touches like sewing kits, Poland Spring water, and a tray with wine glasses and a corkscrew.

Guests gather beneath crystal chandeliers in the richly furnished parlor for herbal tea or Swedish glögg, or beside the fire in the Gathering Room.

Lately, the Captain Lord has opened two annexes with six ultra-deluxe rooms and suites. The first was the **Captain's Hideaway,** which contains two honeymoon quarters in a house that Rick calls "our gourmet B&B" and bills as even more romantic than the mansion. The second-floor suite is entered through an enormous bathroom complete with fireplace and a raised, two-person whirlpool tub; beyond is a room with a queensize canopy bed and another fireplace. Hideaway guests enjoy a gourmet breakfast, perhaps cheese strata or eggs benedict, by candlelight.

The newest addition, **Phoebe's Fantasy,** offers four guest rooms, all with king or queen beds and fireplaces. Guests here take breakfast at a seven-foot harvest table in a gathering room with chintz sofa, fireplace and television.

Breakfast for guests in the main inn is served family-style in the big, cheery kitchen. The fare includes soft-boiled eggs, apple-cinnamon pancakes, cheese strata or quiche as well as french vanilla yogurt, nutri-grain cereals and all kinds of muffins and breads.

Doubles, $125 to $199; suite, $249.

The Captain Jefferds Inn, Pearl Street, Box 691, Kennebunkport 04046. (207) 967-2311.

Breakfast is a big deal at this inn, run by two antiques dealers who bought the gracious sea captain's home in 1980 and moved in their collections.

Innkeeper Warren Fitzsimmons cooks breakfast in the small but efficient and spotless kitchen. Clad in a white jacket, partner Don Kelly serves it formally in the handsome dining room, which is rather incredible — we've never seen so many gorgeous antiques. Guests sign up for 8 or 9 o'clock seatings to enjoy specialties like frittata with mushrooms or zucchini, eggs benedict, quiche, french toast grand marnier or blueberry crêpes.

Warren, a decorator and antiquarian, has made the 1804 sea captain's mansion into a colorful and comfortable spot, one that once was pictured on the cover of House Beautiful magazine.

All twelve guest rooms have private tiled baths and canopy beds; four have fireplaces. All are luxurious, with chaise lounges, Laura Ashley linens, woolen blankets and four pillows on each bed. The partners' collection of antique white cotton spreads and quilts is so vast that they change them around periodically. Three large suites are available in an adjacent carriage house.

Afternoon tea with cookies and finger sandwiches is served in the cooler months in the living room with its amazing collection of majolica or in the cheery solarium, a great expanse of wicker furniture with decorated plates on the wall and everything positioned perfectly. A brick terrace and expansive lawn are fine for lounging in summer. The widow's walk provides a view of the river.

Doubles, $85 to $125; suites, $125 to $145; two-night minimum in summer. Closed November and January-March.

Old Fort Inn, Old Fort Avenue, Kennebunkport 04046. (207) 967-5353 or (800) 828-3678.

Away from the hubbub of town and out near the ocean in a secluded, landscaped setting with a large pool and tennis court, this is the kind of place that appeals to Californians, to say nothing of Connecticut friends who have returned year after year. David and Sheila Aldrich, transplanted Californians, have furnished fourteen large and luxurious guest rooms and two suites in a stone and brick carriage house with style and such nice touches as velvet wing chairs, stenciling on the walls and handmade wreaths over the beds. Each room has a phone, color TV and deluxe wet bar with microwave, since this is a place where people tend to stay for some time (there's a two-night minimum in summer). A plate of chocolate-chip cookies greets guests at check-in; chocolates are at bedside at night.

Besides the pool, the gathering spot of choice is the main lodge in a converted barn. At the entry is a reception area and Sheila's antiques shop. Beyond is a large rustic room with enormous beams, weathered pine walls and a massive brick fireplace — the perfect setting for some of her antiques.

It's also where the Aldriches set up their breakfast buffet: homemade muffins, fruit breads and croissants plus a selection of fresh fruits — bananas, apples, two kinds of melon, strawberries and pineapple when we were there. The homemade granola is consumed at a rate of twenty pounds a week. Pick up a wicker tray lined with calico, help yourself to the goodies and relax around the lodge or on the outdoor deck beside the pool.

Doubles, $120 to $230. Closed early December to early April.

The Inn at Harbor Head, 41 Pier Road, R.R.2, Box 1180, Kennebunkport 04046. (207) 967-5564.

Chocolate french toast for breakfast? Yes — it's from the repertoire of Joan Sutter who, with husband David, runs one of the more special B&Bs in Maine. Honeymooners are smitten with it, and it's easy to see why. The Sutters' picturesque shingled home is on a rocky knoll right above Cape Porpoise harbor, and it is lovely to swim from their float or to loll in a hammock or a comfy garden chair and watch the lobster boats go by. There are a pleasant living room and a large library, where two chairs face the window for a good look at the harbor.

Breakfasts are served at 9 at a long table in the dining room amidst gorgeous flower arrangements, soothing New Age music and lots of fine china, crystal and silver. The fruit course might be poached pears with grand-marnier custard sauce, broiled bananas or melon balls with a ginger, lime and honey sauce. With luck, you'll be there when Joan serves her homemade roast-beef hash with poached eggs and salsa, or creamed chicken and mushrooms on sourdough rounds. Puff pastry with eggs, feta cheese and spinach or dutch babies with fresh peaches and melba sauce are other goodies. And the chocolate french toast is topped with raspberries and served with crisp bacon. "I want everything to look pretty," says Joan, an artist who has also painted wonderful murals throughout the house. And pretty her dishes are, garnished with nasturtium blossoms and the like.

Five bedrooms have private baths and are decorated to the ultimate. The Greenery, where we stayed, has a little sitting area and a queensize bed covered in white with tons of lacy pillows. The barnwood walls are painted a deep green, and Joan's mural of fir trees by the shore highlights the side of the peaked ceiling. The luxurious bathroom has a step-up jacuzzi. The entrance to the Garden Room is paved with stones, which with exotic plants give it an oriental feeling. French doors open onto a private deck. The Summer Suite upstairs, with the best view of the harbor, is painted with clouds and comes with a kingsize bed and a huge bathroom with skylight, bidet and jacuzzi. The murals of Cape Porpoise in the fireplaced Harbor Suite are exquisite.

Bedrooms at Pomegranate Inn in Portland are a kaleidoscope of design.

Rooms are outfitted with thick towels, terrycloth robes, books and magazines, good reading lights, clock radios, a decanter of sherry and fresh flowers from Joan's new backyard cutting garden, The Sutters also put out wine and cheese and crackers in the afternoon. When you are out for dinner, they turn down your bed and leave chocolates on a silver tray. Some guests stay for two weeks, the Sutters say, and we can understand why.

Doubles, $125 to $160. Two-night minimum. No smoking.

Pomegranate Inn, 49 Neal St., Portland 04102. (207) 772-1006 or (800) 356-0408.

Isabel and Alan Smiles, a most urbane couple, picked Portland as the small city in which to launch a B&B when they decided to move from Connecticut. They "turned the conventional idea of a bed and breakfast on its side and created a funky, relaxed and stylish inner-city space," in the words of the Portland Press-Telegram. They also made heads turn in local art circles, not to mention those of their B&B colleagues.

Called the "queen of the B&Bs" by no less than the New York Times, the Pomegranate is an art lover's paradise — part museum, part gallery, part antiques collection and part inn. The last attribute gives the unlikely-looking, 1884 Italianate Victorian with Colonial Revival facade its new raison d'être. It's filled with antiques (Isabel was in the decorating and antiques business in Greenwich) and contemporary art collected by the couple. Naturally, says Alan in his British accent, "lots of the art museum people like to stay here."

The six bedrooms on the second and third floors, all with modern tiled baths, are a kaleidoscope of design. Each is unique, mixing antique rugs, colorful fabrics, antique and contemporary furnishings, charming eccentricities and prized artworks. Even the bed configuration is mixed: three rooms come with queensize beds and the others are kingsize, double or two twins. A large new room and a deluxe, two-room suite have been added in the renovated carriage house across the terrace from the main inn.

Walls in five of the guest rooms were handpainted by Portland artist Heidi Gerquest and are themselves works of art. Most striking is one on a chocolate-colored wall with a swirl design taken from a pattern on a Japanese kimono. Paisley, birds and flowers are painted in other rooms, and the hallways are sponged a golden color. Isabel's daughter, Amy Russack, painted faux finishes on moldings, fireplace mantels and columns.

Since none of the rooms backs up to each other, Alan notes, there is ample privacy and the setting in Portland's residential West End is quiet. Telephones plus televisions mounted on black pedestals appeal to the business traveler.

Breakfast is served between 8 and 9:30 at a long hand-painted Italianate table or at a couple of small tables for those who prefer solitude. Alan is the chef, turning out poached eggs with capers, a variety of quiches, broiled tomatoes on polenta or pancakes with sautéed pears.

Doubles, $95; suite, $145.

Gourmet Treats

Along with its restaurants, the restored Old Port Exchange area of Portland is the center of shops appealing to those interested in food. The owners of **The Whip and Spoon,** a fascinating shop for serious cooks at 161 Commercial St., say "if it's worth using in the kitchen, we have it." From fifteen-cent lobster picks to expensive food processors, you can find everything including magazines for cooks, a great collection of cookbooks and local products like herbs and spices from Ram Island Farm in Cape Elizabeth. All kinds of supplies are available for beer-makers, too. This store is one you could spend hours in, browsing and buying.

Maine Potters Market, 376 Fore St., stocks wondrous pottery from potters across the state in the old Mariner's Church. The ovenware is lead-free and safe to use in oven and dishwasher. More colorful pottery is available at Maxwell's Pottery Outlet across the street.

Smoked fish at rather hefty prices is offered at the new factory outlet of **Appledore Smoked Foods,** 260 Commercial St.

Modeled after a European coffee bar, the **Portland Coffee Roasting Co.** at 111 Commercial St. draws locals as well as tourists for a coffee fix or the "eggspresso breakfast" (scrambled eggs, bagel and small coffee, $3.25). Later in the day and evening, tall windows reveal the passing scene as you sip cappuccino or cafe au lait at modern little tables beneath a high pressed-tin ceiling. As we nursed a latte and caffe mocha outdoors on a ledge with a view of the waterfront and the sounds of the seagulls, we could picture ourselves back in Seattle, the latte capital of the world.

For a terrific hamburger, drop into **Ruby's Choice** at 116 Free St., which bills itself as having the "world's greatest hamburgers." In the cavernous room with its pressed-tin ceiling, there's a fixings bar to add on salsas, exotic mustards, hot peppers and the like, as well as a good salad bar. Seafood chowder, burritos, grilled chicken and fresh-cut french fries are other items on the limited menu. Wash down your meal with a Molson's ale or a glass of Chantovent wine.

Go into the **Port Bake House** at 265 Commercial St. to get one of the magnificent cheesecake brownies, a frangipane tart, a white-chocolate mousse cake or a honey macaroon. Breads like Irish oatmeal, peasant rye and nine-grain sesame are $1.15 to $2.45. The soups, salads and sandwiches -- from veggie hummus to turkey avocado, $2.95 to $4.25 -- here are scrumptious.

Della's Catessen at 9 Deering Ave. is a fun place where Della Parker, who was a sous chef at Cafe Always, sells homemade pastas and sauces, good salads, soups, dishes like Armenian lentil stew, and desserts like chocolate-espresso terrine. She makes her own pizzas and calzones, all vegetarian. Pâtés and other dishes from Cafe Always are available here, as are beers and wines, herbs, oils, vinegars and exotic jars of pickled fiddleheads, cajun ketchup and rhubarb chutney.

Christine's Dream, a tiny place serving breakfast and lunch at 41 Middle St., is the dream come true for Christine Burke. While her husband Christopher greets customers, she cooks up a storm in the kitchen. We relished the salsa eggs scramble ($3.65), laden with cheese and flanked with homefries, and the peach pancakes ($3.55) like mother used to make. Lunch time brings a short menu priced from $4.25 for chili with vegetables to $5.25 for a tabbouleh plate with pita bread and hummus or Chinese chicken salad with pasta. Eggs benedict is a bargain $4.25 at weekend brunch. The Burkes occasionally serve dinner of the customer's choice by reservation. Open Tuesday-Friday 7 to 2:30, Saturday and Sunday brunch, 9 to 2.

Maine Food Importers/Model Market, 111 Middle St., is called "the best damn grocery in the state of Maine" by Saul Goldberg, who might be prejudiced because he owns it. Food and wines from across the world (an extensive selection of Chinese seasonings, Amore pasta, beluga caviar and bins of Davis-Bynum cabernet) are on hand in this crowded store, which has been in business since 1928.

In Kennebunkport, Suzie Anderson, a former baker at the Port Bake House in Portland, now provides desserts for some of the best restaurants in southern Maine from her **Chase Hill Bakery** at the top of Chase Hill Road. All of her desserts looked luscious, but on the early September day we stopped by for lunch we were surprised there weren't any sandwiches. They also had no way to heat the food in the display case, so we had to settle for a cold slice of vegetable-broccoli-mushroom pizza, a cold quiche and chilled cream of cucumber soup.

Two Kennebunkport stores are of special interest to gourmets. Herbal teas, jams, jellies, sauces and more from her family's Callaway Gardens Country Store in Georgia are featured at Susan Elton Warren's **Sassafras Tea Company** on Ocean Avenue. Lou Lipkin sells her remarkable handpainted tiles that would dress up a designer kitchen, fine porcelain pottery, stoneware, mugs, berry pots and more at Goose Rocks Pottery, Wharf Lane.

Wonderful pastries accompany the cream tea ($6) and the Edwardian tea ($10.50) at the **Rose Arbor Tea Room,** Route 9 in Kennebunkport's Lower Village, a delightful place full of lacy Victorian decor. Owner Stacy Zauzmer also offers soups, salads and various platters (ploughman's or pâté and cheeses) for lunch, coffees and desserts at night, and treats like Scotch eggs, a smoked-salmon plate, and spinach and cheddar quiche at her weekend buffet breakfasts. Tea daily, noon to 6; dessert to 10, weekend breakfast, 8 to 11:30.

The way proprietor John Audley figures it, there are ten trillion possible combinations in his food at **Pizzoodles,** at the Shipyard in the Lower Village. Patrons choose the toppings for his brick-oven gourmet pizzas, perhaps caramelized onion, chèvre, sundried tomatoes, spam (yes, spam), wild mushrooms and more (he even offered a gator pizza over the 1993 Labor Day Weekend, a few months after opening). He makes his pastas the Italian way, offers a variety of sauces, pasta salads, panini (Italian sandwiches -- the toppings chosen from the pizza selections and spread on foccacia, $3.25), coffees, bagels and pastries. There are tables inside or out upon which to enjoy. Open daily, 7 a.m. to 9 or 10 p.m.

The high-end, dark beers are particularly good, we're told, at the new **Kennebunkport Brewing Co.** at the Shipyard, facing the river in the Lower Village. You can tour the main-floor brewery and sample the beers upstairs at its Federal Jack's Brew Pub, where lunch and dinner are available daily at sturdy wood communal tables in a big room beside the water.

If you love raspberries as much as we do, don't miss **Whistling Wings Farm** at 427 West St., Biddeford. Don and Julie Harper started with a card table and umbrella in their driveway; now people come from across the world, among them George and Barbara Bush, "our down-the-road neighbors." Julie gets up at 1 in the morning to do the day's baking, producing 30 to 40 dozen muffins, 50 to 100 turnovers, 30 to 40 loaves of bread and an equal number of pies. "Many days there's nothing left by 1:30," says Don, who oversees the growing retail and mail-order business. He says their toppings, syrups and raspberry vinegars are totally different from others on the market — the last is like raspberry with a touch of vinegar, not the other way around. "The secret is in the berries and our cooking methods." Get a turnover or a dish of homemade raspberry ice cream and take it to a picnic table beside a little pond, where ducks and geese make their presence known. Open daily, 7 to 6.

Lobster Spots

Two Lights Lobster Shack, Two Lights Road, Cape Elizabeth. (207) 799-1677. Near Two Lights State Park and almost in the shadow of the two lighthouses south of Portland, this is located on a bluff overlooking nothing but rocks and open ocean. You can eat inside, but we prefer sipping a drink outside at a picnic table (BYOB) as we await our order. This is a great place to bring youngsters because they can clamber around on the rocks while waiting for dinner and because the Lobster Shack offers hot dogs, hamburgers, fried chicken and clam cakes as well as boiled lobsters, chowder and steamers. A lobster dinner was $11.95 at our last visit. Open daily from 11 to 8, mid-May to mid-October, to 8:30 in July and August.

Nunan's Lobster Hut, Route 9, Cape Porpoise. (207) 967-4362. The decor is rustic, to put it mildly, and kind of schlocky with paraphernalia like you wouldn't believe (a friend who waitressed here 35 years ago has her picture on the wall, along with all the others through the years). But people from movie stars to common folk start lining up before Hoppy Nunan, daughter-in-law of the late founder, Captain Nunan, opens the doors at 5 o'clock. Lobsters trapped by her son Richard are cooked to order; some think they are the best in Maine. Steamed clams, lobster stew, salads and sensational homemade pies are among the offerings. Beer and wine are available. Open daily in season, 5 to 10.

The Lively Lobster, On the Pier, Cape Porpoise. If you like your lobster in an informal outdoor setting, head right to the pier at Cape Porpoise. This is the former site of Tilly's Shanty, taken over by Angela and Arthur LeBlanc of the adjacent Seascapes restaurant in 1991. Here they feature steamed lobsters, lobster rolls, fried seafood and what Arthur touts as the best onion rings "made from scratch." You place your order and sit at a battered picnic table inside or out beside the water. Or you take it next door into a new room below Seascapes called the Cape Porpoise Pub, where wine and beer are offered daily in summer from 2 to 8. Lively Lobster open daily in season, 7 a.m. to sunset.

Everyone likes to eat lobster beside the ocean at Two Lights, Cape Elizabeth.

Mid-Coast Maine

Where the Real Maine Starts

The sandy beaches of Southern Maine yield to Maine's more typical rocky coast north of Portland. There are those who say that this is where the real Maine starts.

The coastline becomes more jagged, its fingers protruding like tentacles toward the sea between inlets, rivers and bays. Poke down remote byways to Bailey Island, Popham Beach, Westport, Christmas Cove and Pemaquid Point. You'll find life more quiet here and the distances between points long and roundabout. One look at the map as you eye the shore across the inlet and you'll understand why the natives say "you can't get theah from heah" — except by boat.

Here also are two of Maine's leading tourist destinations — crowded Boothbay Harbor, a commercial fishing village surrounded by choice and remote shoreline beyond and on either side, and upscale Camden, where the mountains meet the sea and the windjammer fleet sets sail from the colorful harbor.

These two resort areas have long been favored by visitors, whose arrival has produced the inevitable influx of souvenir stands and golden arches nearby. But the mid-coast's increasing gentrification also has attracted new and better restaurants, inns and B&Bs.

Side by side with busy Boothbay and Camden are postcard fishing hamlets like Ocean Point and Port Clyde. The shipbuilding towns of Bath, Rockland and Belfast co-exist with salt-washed villages like Rockport and South Harpswell.

Before you head Down East, tarry along Maine's mid-coast.

Dining

The Best of the Best

Fiddlehead Farm, 15 Independence Drive at Route 1, Freeport. (207) 865-0466.

Chef-owners Chris and Laura Washburn honed their culinary backgrounds at restaurants across the country before returning to her native Maine to acquire this charmer in a rural homestead across from the huge L.L. Bean corporate headquarters on the eastern edge of town. Dining is at white-linened tables in small rooms with wide-board floors, ladderback chairs, balloon draperies and sprightly wallpapers. An arresting picture of a girl on the shore looking out to sea nearly covers one wall.

The garden-ringed outdoor deck, where tables are topped with Poland Spring umbrellas, was the setting for a fine lunch. Classical music played as we sampled a bowl of gazpacho with yogurt and a zesty spinach salad with feta cheese and dried cranberries ($4.95) plus a wonderful garden salad with grilled breast of turkey and crumbled bacon ($6.95). Soups here are interesting: besides a classic lobster bisque, there might be one of peanut butter, carrots and leeks, and another of zucchini and sausage, the latter so good that customers order it by the carton to take home.

The dinner menu is short and sweet. Entrées are priced from $16.95 for chargrilled pork tenderloin with leeks, capers and glace de viande to $21.95 for lobster strudel, grilled black-angus strip steak with green- and red-peppercorn sauce or roasted veal rib chop with garlic, shallots and tomato glace. A favorite is angel-hair pasta with lobster and scallops nestled amid roasted shallots, mushrooms and red peppers.

Among starters are Maine crab cakes with a light mustard-wine sauce and sundried-tomato/basil tortellini with prosciutto, mushrooms, asparagus, roasted peppers and parmesan cream. Desserts could be a rich flourless chocolate perfection cake with oatmeal crisp, blueberry-raspberry bread pudding with whipped cream, tirami su and a neapolitan cheesecake layered with blackberries and chocolate. A good wine list starts in the high teens.

Fiddlehead Farm's thriving Country Cafe is a good spot for breakfast or lunch in more basic surroundings.

Lunch, Monday-Friday 11 to 3; dinner nightly, 5 to 9. Cafe open daily from 6 or 7 a.m. to 8 p.m. No smoking.

The Osprey, Robinhood Marine Center, off Route 127, Robinhood. (207) 371-2530.

The water view here has been described as the best of any restaurant in Maine, and indeed the sight of Riggs Cove on two sides and the view of an osprey on a nest atop a green channel marker are idyllic on a summer's afternoon or evening. That the food is worthy of the setting is a bonus.

The Osprey's space — an inner dining room, a narrow side porch and an enclosed deck above a marine center — has been continually upgraded over its fifteen-year existence. Gone is the original linoleum and oilcloth decor. Now the tables are covered with white linens topped with white china and small carafes containing field flowers. Even the backs of the chairs are slipcovered in white. The overall air is of simple, yet sophisticated, summer charm.

Chef Michael Gagné, well known in the area for his catering and cooking classes, presides over an ambitious, contemporary menu that has gone beyond its original New American base to embrace oriental cuisines (some dishes are marked "very peppery" and "seriously spicy hot"). He makes his own breads, pastas, sausages and ice creams, and turns out more than 30 changing dinner entrées a night, as well as a delectable array of appetizers, salads and pastas.

Michael invites customers to "mix and match appetizers, pastas and salads to make up a meal that fits your appetite." The smoked coastal sampler served with a baguette and horseradish-mustard mousseline ($9) is sensational, as are the corn-fried oysters with fresh salsa and chipotle cream ($8). Among entrées ($18 to $21), we found the gutsy scallops niçoise in puff pastry with saffron rice and the grilled chicken with sundried tomatoes over fettuccine both so ample as to require doggy bags, since we wanted to save room for the trio of ice creams — ginger, raspberry swirl and childhood orange.

Porch dining at The Osprey.

Because of the water view, we find the Osprey more appealing at lunch than after dark. For a midday meal on the screened porch, the cold cucumber soup with dill was thick, garlicky and had a real bite, the perfect foil for a smoked-sausage sampler. The fettuccine with Maine clams and garlic was terrific. A basket of hot bagels and corn muffins laced with corn kernels came with. Grand-marnier cake with chocolate sauce and crème anglaise and the strawberry tart with crème pâtissière were sweet endings.

Quite a selection of wines is available by the glass, and the wine list has less than the usual markup. Somehow the Poland Spring mineral water, served throughout the meal as a regional touch, didn't make it in place of plain water. But that was about our only quibble involving an exciting restaurant that received a then-perfect four-star rating for food, service and atmosphere from the Maine Sunday Telegram.

Lunch daily in summer, 11:30 to 2:30, Friday and Saturday in off-season; dinner nightly, 5:30 to 9; Sunday brunch, 11:30 to 2:30. Closed Monday and Tuesday in off-season and November-March. No smoking.

Batchelder's Tavern, Route 126, Litchfield. (207) 268-4965.

Dutch-born businessman Dirk Keijer and his wife Clare, a former Philadelphia lawyer, purchased this 1808 Federal house and barn in 1992 as the site to fulfill a dream: to run a fine country French restaurant and a small B&B. They quickly succeeded in the former, earning the first five-star award for food given by the Maine Sunday Telegram within six months of opening. They were on their way to the latter in the winter of 1994, readying four guest rooms with private baths (and three with fireplaces) upstairs in the handsome main house, plus two fireplaced rooms with private bath downstairs. Guests enjoy a fireplaced common room and, in season, a heated swimming pool and hot tub.

The Keijers got the restaurant on line first, restoring the attached barn as well as the first floor of the house to seat 100 diners. Fine art hangs from the weathered pumpkin pine walls of the unadorned post and beam barn, which has been gentrified with white tablecloths, candles and fresh flowers. French doors yield views across the screened summer dining deck overlooking the illuminated gardens, grounds and pond.

It's an elegant setting for the food of native Maine chef Paul Siegler, a Culinary Institute of America grad. He takes his cues from the Keijers' love for fine food honed from their work and travels in Europe. "Classic French with a strong Mediterranean flair" is how Clare describes it. The menu is simple and understated, as in such starters ($4.95 to $6.95) as escargots bourguignonne, steamed mussels marinière with herbed shallot cream, Maine smoked salmon with capers and red onions, and sautéed Vermont chèvre garnished with thyme and spring greens dressed with dijon vinaigrette. The dozen main courses are priced from $14.95 for Boston scrod sautéed with pommery-mustard cream sauce to $24.95 for medallions of beef tenderloin with a sauce of morels, wild mushrooms and truffles. Swordfish provençal, poached salmon with ginger and green-peppercorn sauce, chicken chasseur, medallions of pork tenderloin with honey-apple curry sauce and rib veal chop milanese with penne pasta are other summer possibilities. Specials might be Clare's catalonian lobster with a fresh tomato-saffron sauce, Dirk's dover sole with lobster and tarragon cream sauce, and bouillabaisse served with rouille and aioli. Such autumn game treats as elk, buffalo, antelope and partridge are accompanied variously by brussels sprouts, Swedish lingonberries, chestnut puree, spaëtzle and root vegetables.

Homemade desserts include creamy cheesecake with raspberry coulis, Dutch chocolate-pistachio mousse cake, French crêpes with three-berry sauce and crème de cassis, double-chocolate torte with blackberry glaze and fresh black-berries, mocha-hazelnut torte and homemade sorbets.

The wine list is choice and affordably priced from the mid-teens to $60. A reserve list carries more pricey vintages.

Dinner, Tuesday-Saturday from 5; Sunday, brunch 11 to 2:30, dinner from 2:30. Doubles, $65 to $100.

Jessica's, 2 South Main St. (Route 73), Rockland. (207) 596-0770.

A loyal following from miles around is drawn to chef-owner Hans Bucher's European bistro in a pleasant Victorian home atop a hill south of town. The front veranda has a barber's chair and deck chairs scattered about for pre-dinner drinks, which are also available upstairs in a spiffy parlor. Three small rooms seat 40 diners at bare wood tables set with cloth mats, fresh flowers and small candles.

As Hans's menu has evolved, the early bundnerfleisch and raclettes from his Swiss background have evolved into more intricate treats like lobster ravioli, an appetizer served in a sauce of sherry, garlic, coriander and tarragon -- so good that one innkeeper of our acquaintance said she would gladly make it her dinner. Other worthy starters are tapenade, served with sliced goat cheese and crostini, and a cassoulet pâté made of lamb, duck and pork, served with a bean vinaigrette and roasted leeks. Or try the focaccia, Italian flatbread topped with plum tomatoes and basil or eggplant, goat cheese and black olives.

Among main courses ($10.50 to $15.50), we've heard nothing but raves for the lamb provençal and the tournedos, the latter served amid a cluster of artichokes, onions, mushrooms and potatoes in one presentation. Also memorable are paella, veal Zurich and paysanne pork stew, a robust potpourri of pork, bratwurst, bacon and vegetables served with garlicky mashed potatoes. One section of the menu details eight pasta and risotto items, from seafood basque ladled atop homemade pasta to a grilled duet of quail, served with fennel sausage and a light risotto.

Desserts are the province of Hans's wife, Sheila. She might offer a smooth crème brûlée, a rich chocolate-truffle cake topped with white-chocolate mousse, a walnut torte or grand-marnier parfait.

Dinner nightly except Tuesday, 5:30 to 9.

Cassoulet, 31 Elm St., Camden. (207) 236-6304.

Classic country cooking is featured at this small restaurant, which more than doubled in size when owners Sally and Bob Teague enclosed the garden in back.

Cassoulet's rear garden has been enclosed for summer dining.

Now a screened porch, it's summery as can be with pink deck chairs and dusky pink tablecloths, an abundance of hanging plants, fresh flowers all around and, adding to the romance, the starry night sky visible through openings in the roof. It's the dining location of choice in summer, far more airy than the intimate and colorful interior dining room with its moss green banquettes and chairs, cacti in the windows, flowers in little carafes and striking pictures of flowers on the walls.

When he's in the kitchen, chef Bob Teague features "classic country cooking" with an Italian accent, which has been highly rated. Caponata with crostini and polenta with grilled mushrooms are among appetizers in the $5 range. We started with mozzarella galettes with sundried-tomato pesto -- excellent, though we would have liked a bit more pesto -- and a tossed salad with blue cheese dressing.

Nightly specials supplement the short list of entrées ($12 to $18); perhaps baked halibut with pesto and tomatoes, and baked scallops en casserole with garlic, scallions, mushrooms and marsala. Cassoulet, made with lamb, pork and garlic sausage, heads the regular entrees, which might include broiled salmon en croûte, bouillabaisse in a rich saffron-seafood broth, seafood taverna (shrimp or scallops tossed with pasta, feta and parmesan cheese), filet mignon with sautéed mushrooms and black-peppercorn sauce, or lobster alfredo. The shrimp à la grecque, a house specialty, was good but could have used some rice or pasta to go with, while the pasta of the day -- fettuccine with scallops -- proved a triumph.

Sally's desserts are winners — perhaps a flourless chocolate-raspberry torte, strawberry shortcake with a citrus biscuit or divine decadence, a fudgy cake with brandy-soaked apricots. Frozen lemon mousse, intense and refreshing, was a perfect choice. Many of the well-chosen wines, priced from the mid-teens, are available by the glass.

Lately, reports are that both the kitchen and service have slipped. That garden-like porch helps compensate, however.

Dinner, Monday-Saturday 6 to 9:30.

Nickerson Tavern, Route 1, Searsport. (207) 548-2220.

In late 1993, new ownership took over this highly regarded restaurant located in a white Colonial captain's homestead dating from 1838. Jim Bouras, new general manager, retained the kitchen staff and pledged to keep the same decor and format that had been successful for founding chef-owner Tom Weiner.

Entrées on the changing menu, served with salad, run from $12.50 to $18.50 (for lobster sautéed with dill and cognac or chargrilled filet mignon seasoned with red, green and black peppercorns). The kitchen likes to combine meats and fruits in intriguing ways. The raspberry-hazelnut chicken (breast of chicken coated with crushed hazelnuts and sauced with raspberries and shallots) is a favorite of patrons, as are veal with cider and apples and roast duckling glazed with cointreau and fresh pears. Other choices include fillet of Atlantic salmon wrapped in rice paper and sautéed with a citrus-ginger vinaigrette, grilled pork tenderloin with pineapple chutney and cioppino, served with couscous.

A spicy Thai shrimp satay, crab cakes with roasted-pepper puree, and brie in puff pastry with apples and almonds are favorite appetizers. You may not need an appetizer, however, after you finish the complimentary crisp vegetables and crackers with a fresh herb dip.

The dessert cart is laden with such delectables as chocolate-mousse cake, strawberry-lemon bavarian and grand-marnier/chocolate mousse. Also available are homemade ice creams, among them ginger and coffee/heath-bar crunch, and sorbets. American wines predominate on the reasonably priced wine list.

Dinner nightly in summer, 5:30 to 9; Thursday-Sunday in winter. Closed Valentines Day through March. No smoking.

Other Dining Choices

Kristina's, 160 Centre St., Bath. (207) 442-8577.

When we first met Kristina's, it was a tiny bakery with a few tables and a display case where such things as sticky buns were displayed. You can still get sticky buns from the bakery at the entrance, but now there are two dining rooms (by far the nicest is the non-smoking), a front deck with a tree growing through it and, upstairs, **Harry's Bar,** an attractive room that is all blond wood and deck chairs, with windows looking out onto green trees. Jazz groups play here at night.

You can still take out many good things from the display cases (Mexican confetti salad, for example), but you can sit down for breakfast, lunch or dinner. For the first, have a Mexican omelet, strawberry waffles or a seafood quiche ($3.50 to $6.95). Soups, quiches, salads (smoked trout or crab meat in avocado), sandwiches and burgers make up the lunch menu.

At dinner start with one of the changing seafood bisques, steamed clams in Bass ale, cornmeal and basil crêpes with ratatouille and chèvre, or grilled lamb sausage in zinfandel sauce with pistachios. Entrées ($11.95 to $18.95) include sesame-crusted scallops, grilled salmon steak au poivre with lime vinaigrette, sautéed lobster and avocado over scallion fettuccine, Caribbean pepper pot (seafood in coconut milk and scotch-bonnet-pepper broth with sweet potatoes and coconut johnnycakes), grilled lamb chops with roasted-eggplant puree on minted tabbouleh and Jamaican mixed grill on coconut-basmati rice. You know you're in creative culinary hands when haddock Kristina teams that Maine staple with crab meat and serves it in a brandied mushroom sauce. Desserts from the bakery case are gorgeous.

For weekend brunch, try the Swiss panfkuchen (a pancake filled with berries), Kristina's french toast made with cinnamon swirl bread, huevos rancheros or four kinds of benedicts, including crab meat.

Breakfast daily, 8 to 11; lunch, 11:30 to 2:30; dinner, 5 to 9. Harry's Bar, with light menu, open weekdays to 10, weekends to midnight.

Le Garage, Water Street, Wiscasset. (207) 882-5409.

It has a French name, but American food. It's really an old automobile dealer's garage, but the yellow exterior and striped awnings are most inviting and the expansive interior illuminated entirely by candlelight is positively magical. Best of all, perhaps, is the view from the airy, wraparound porch of the Sheepscot River and the huge deteriorating hulks of two schooners, a scene cherished by photographers and anyone else who eats at Le Garage.

The menu is enormous and rarely changes from year to year, except for the prices — and those not by much. "I'm not trying to be gourmet," says owner Cheryl Lee Rust, who presides at the front desk of her establishment now well into its second decade. "I like people to relax and enjoy themselves."

More than two dozen entrées are listed on the dinner menu, priced from $10.25 for ratatouille or creamed finnan haddie to $17.95 for sautéed lobster or sirloin steak with lobster newburg. Dinner starts with hot biscuits and a house salad, so you might not need any of the two dozen appetizers ranging from hummus with raw vegetables and crackers to lobster stew and oysters on the half shell. Our garlic lamb kabobs were perfect, and we remember fondly from years ago a ham, chicken, artichoke heart and cheese casserole that's only lately been superseded on the menu by chicken pie. Seafood and steaks come in many variations, most simply but well prepared. The poached haddock with newburg sauce and the crab meat casserole with spinach, mushrooms and cheese sauce are excellent.

The choice on the wine list is extensive,. with very little markup in price. Desserts include Indian pudding, crêpes, cheesecake and the like. Service is by a young staff outfitted in denim shirts with big paisley bow ties.

Downstairs is Le Bar, an expansive place with a simpler decor, serving quite an array of appetizers, salads, sandwiches, crêpes and light suppers for $6.95.

Lunch daily, 11:30 to 3; dinner, 5 to 10. Closed Monday in winter.

Ristorante Black Orchid, 5 By-Way, Boothbay Harbor. (207) 633-6650.

Rather New Yorkish in a seaside kind of way is this intimate Italian trattoria run by chef-owner Steven DiCicco, a Culinary Institute of America grad. The unpretentious interior is done up in black and white, with pink stenciling on the walls, beams strewn with odd-looking grapevines and baskets of hanging fuschias. The upstairs cafe and raw bar overlook the downtown harbor scene.

The highly rated food includes fourteen pasta dishes with salad, from $9.95 for fettuccine alfredo to $21.95 for seafood over linguini. Shrimp and scallops sauté, pork tenderloin with raisins and pinenuts, petite filets diavolo and seven veal dishes head the entrées ($12.50 to $23.95).

Desserts include amaretto bread pudding and chocolate-chambord torte.

Dinner nightly except Tuesday, 5:30 to 10; raw bar from 5. Open mid-May to mid-October.

Harbor View Tavern, 1 Water St., Thomaston. (207) 354-8173.

Want good food with a water view? Try this hard-to-find, funky eatery with a darkened dining room/tavern that's too atmospheric for words and, beyond, an enclosed porch overlooking the water. It's a favorite with locals, and probably only locals could find it down an unmarked roadway near the town landing.

Would-be diners line up outside at peak periods. Inside the entry, an upside-down perambulator is on the ceiling. Beyond, every conceivable inch of wall space is covered with old license plates, photos, books, signs, masks and such. But there's much up-to-date in this old boat-building facility, from the day's sports page from USA Today posted in the men's room to the garnishes and artful presentations of the lunches we were served. The chicken and basil pasta salad ($7.95) was garnished with sliced strawberries, oranges and watermelon; ditto for crab cristo ($6.95) that came with french fries and coleslaw. Two candies arrived with the bill.

Votive candles in little pewter dishes flicker at dinnertime when there is a varied menu of appetizers, light fare and entrées ($12.95 and $13.95) like stuffed haddock, scallops au gratin, chicken imperial and sirloin steak St. Jacques, smothered with scallops and mushroom-cream sauce. We're told the place is famous for its brownie à la mode, grapenut parfait, "strawberry fields forever" cake and apple crisp.

Lunch daily, 11:30 to 4; dinner, 5 to 10. Shorter hours in winter.

Cafe Miranda, 15 Oak St., Rockland. (207) 594-2034.

The beige and green colors of the exterior of the cute little house are repeated inside this surprisingly trendy little cafe at the edge of downtown Rockland. Opened in 1993 by chef Kerry Altiero and his wife, Evelyn Donnelly, a craftswoman by day, the cafe quickly drew throngs from throughout the meat-and-haddock Rockland area for its laid-back atmosphere and the gutsy cooking emanating from the wood-fired brick oven in the open kitchen.

At our lunchtime visit, patrons were extolling the carrot-ginger soup served with herbed flatbread ($3.50) and the bruschetta with grilled chicken, artichoke spread and greens ($6.50). At night, the expanded menu denotes small plates, medium plates and big plates, ranging from appetizers for one to dinner for one or appetizers for two, at prices from $2.50 to $10. Kerry cooks almost everything in the brick oven, even the fish of the day, going through a cord of wood a month. His offerings range widely, from pasta with sundried tomato, ricotta and chèvre and hearts of artichoke to risotto crab cakes served on wilted greens with olivado sauce. Try the rich seafood stew, the herb-roasted chicken served with mushroom-spinach risotto, or the picadillo, a chili-stew of braised turkey in tomato with vegetables, green olives and black beans seasoned with cumin and garlic. Lest Cafe Miranda be categorized as strictly Italian, Kerry notes Thai and North African influences, as in a pork dish with gorgonzola, polenta and three chiles with avocado salsa or grilled salmon with mandarin oranges, cilantro and roasted peppers and served with couscous.

Evelyn's talents are evident in the desserts, perhaps zabaglione with fresh fruit, white-chocolate cheesecake or ice cream with homemade Italian cookies.

Cloth napkins and candles grace the blond wood tables at night. Single diners enjoy gathering at one of the three counters -- two smack in the middle of the room and one facing Kerry in the kitchen. There's a varied, reasonably priced beer and wine list.

Lunch, Tuesday-Saturday 11 to 2; dinner, Tuesday-Sunday 5:30 to 9:30. No smoking.

The Waterfront Restaurant, Harborside Square off Bay View Street, Camden. (207) 236-3747.

This restaurant is notable for its large outdoor deck shaded by a striking white canopy resembling a boat's sails, right beside the windjammers on picturesque Camden Harbor, and for its inexpensive, international menu. Local purists say the location surpasses the food, though we've been happily impressed each time we've eaten here.

Billowing canopy shades deck at Waterfront Restaurant in Camden.

At lunch, the most costly entrées are fried clams and crab cakes (both $10.95, including salad or gazpacho and french fries). Seven delectable salads in glass bowls are dressed with any of four outstanding dressings: sweet-and-sour bacon, lemon-parmesan, vinaigrette and blue cheese.

At night, when most of the luncheon salads are still available, the menu turns more eclectic. Among appetizers are calamari and shrimp, mussels marinière, baked brie and soups, perhaps chilled raspberry accented with grand marnier, plus a superlative smoked-seafood sampler that was our choice for sharing. Entrees ($12.95 to $16.95) we've enjoyed were Maine crab cakes with creamy mustard sauce, an assertive linguini with salmon and sundried tomatoes, shrimp with oriental black beans over angel-hair pasta and a special of swordfish grilled over applewood with rosemary, which was juicy and succulent. Jerked chicken and filet of beef with a sweet red-pepper salsa are the only meat offerings. Mint-chocolate-chip pie with hot fudge sauce and whipped cream proved to be the ultimate dessert at one visit; the next time we passed and walked up the street to Camden Cone for some raspberry frozen yogurt.

All sorts of shellfish, including a smoked-fish sampler, and light fare from hamburgers to lobster rolls are available at the oyster bar and outdoor grill.

The Waterside is understandably a most popular spot on a sunny summer day. Its owners have opened a similar place, The Cannery, downstate at Lower Falls Landing in Yarmouth.

Lunch daily, 11:30 to 2:30; dinner, 5 to 10.

Mama & Leenie's, 27 Elm St., Camden. (207) 236-6300.
A small cafe with a cheery atmosphere, this opens at 8 for breakfast (blintzes with fruit and sour cream are in the $4 to $5 range, as are waffles with fruit), and continues with lunch and light dinner.

Mama does such dishes as Mama's special peasant soup with beef, kielbasa and vegetables. Leenie, her daughter, bakes goodies like fresh raspberry or Maine blueberry pies with whipped cream and New England pumpkin-pecan pie. For lunch, try the pasta-primavera salad with Leenie's garlic, olive oil and raspberry vinegar dressing or the green garden salad "of whatever looked good at the market — you'll have to trust us."

Bring your own wine for dinner, when you might find Indonesian marinated chicken on a skewer or a bowl of chili with homemade bread. Leenie is a master baker, as evidenced by the apricot strudel with coconut and walnuts, the double-chocolate-fudge brownies with orange zest and the pineapple upside-down cake. The fresh berry pies with real whipped cream are masterpieces. Peanut-butter granola cookies or butter shortbreads are good with a cup of Green Mountain coffee, perhaps on the small patio with its yellow tables. Check out Leenie's artwork on the walls and the display of greeting cards she designed.

Open daily, 8 a.m. to 9:30 p.m., Sunday 8 to 4; fewer hours in off-season. BYOB. No smoking.

Chez Michel, Route 1, Lincolnville Beach. (207) 789-5600.

This country French restaurant was opened in 1990 by Michel and Joan Hetuin, he a former chef at the Helm restaurant in Rockport. It's a simple room crowded with formica tables and pink-painted wood chairs with green upholstered seats.

For lunch, we enjoyed an avocado-tomato-cheddar melt ($3.95) and a fried clam roll ($4.95), plus Joan's fantastic raspberry pie with a cream-cheese base and an extra-good crust ($2.50).

A subsequent dinner began with great french bread, two slabs of rabbit pâté resting with cornichons on oodles of lettuce, and house salads dressed with creamy Italian and pepper-parmesan. A special of salmon béarnaise arrived on a bed of spinach. The only disappointment was the bouillabaisse, more like a spicy cioppino with haddock substituting for most of the usual shellfish. Other dinner entrées ($9.95 to $13.95) include vegetarian couscous, scallops provençal, mussels marinière, chicken chasseur, beef bourguignonne, lamb kabob and steak au poivre. Desserts might be strawberry torte, caramel custard and chocolate mousse. The short, mainly French wine list is priced in the teens. Stick to the French offerings; our California chardonnay proved nearly undrinkable.

Open daily except Monday, 11:30 to 9.

Bed and Board

Harraseeket Inn, 162 Main St., Freeport 04032. (207) 865-9377 or (800) 342-6423.

In Freeport, where the demand for rooms can hardly keep up with the onslaught of shoppers, sisters Nancy Gray and Jody Dyer of Connecticut's Inn at Mystic got their foot in the door in 1984 with an elegant, five-room B&B. Five years and $6.5 million later, a handsome, three-story white building connecting a couple of smaller existing structures houses a fine 85-seat restaurant, an informal tavern and 54 posh guest rooms and six suites.

The original 1850 Greek Revival farmhouse is now overshadowed by the new building, where standard rooms have two double beds or one queensize with blue and white fabric half-canopies, a single wing chair, and baskets of Lord & Mayfair amenities on the pedestal sinks in the bathrooms. Our large third-floor room offered a kingsize bed with a partial-canopy headboard and botanical prints, a sofa and wing chair beneath a Palladian window, a fireplace, a wet bar and a small refrigerator, remote-control TV hidden in an armoire, and an enormous bath with a jacuzzi. Turndown service produced chocolates at night.

Buffet table is ready for lunch at Harraseeket Inn.

Fine artworks, fresh flowers and many of Nancy Gray's personal antiques are evident throughout. Afternoon tea with quite a spread of pastries and sandwiches is served in a large and sumptuous drawing room notable for mahogany paneling. Downstairs is the dark, attractive Broad Arrow Tavern, outfitted with old snowshoes, paddles, fly rods and a moosehead. "It's my life in review," says Nancy, recalling her upbringing in a Maine sporting camp. The extensive tavern menu features hot-rock cooking. Casual lunch and dinner are served here and outside in a garden courtyard beside a croquet lawn.

The stylish main-floor dining room, divided into three sections, is pretty as a picture. Substantial black windsor chairs and a few banquettes flank tables set formally with white linens, heavy silver, silver service plates and pink stemware.

This has been the setting for some of the most innovative, highly rated food in Maine since the arrival of executive chef Sam Hayward, who had made quite a name for himself at the late 22 Lincoln in nearby Brunswick. Sam wearied of having his own restaurant and leapt at the chance to star in the Harraseeket's state-of-the-art, two-story kitchen, which he calls "a tremendous piano to play on." Here he presents an ambitious menu that is as challenging (even difficult) to read as it is exciting in the execution. If it all seems overwhelming, what with caesar salad with a choice of seared breast of duckling or lobster and pesto, consider the evening's prix-fixe menus. Legacies of Sam's days at 22 Lincoln, they come in four or six courses ($21.95 and $39.95, and both well worth the tab). The six-course repast at our latest visit included chilled seared moulard foie gras with muscat vinaigrette, lightly curried carrot soup, Maine mesclun with herb vinaigrette, grilled Atlantic tuna with warm three-bean salad, three New England dessert cheeses with fresh berries and, finally, chocolate-mint decadence. Those with less demanding palates could settle for Scotian chowder (haddock with potatoes, leeks, sweet corn and cob-smoked bacon), roasted half chicken with pear wine and mascarpone, and strawberry shortcake. Most entrées are priced from $14.95 for seafood-stuffed tomatoes to $22.95 for roasted Maine lobster or $24.95 for venison with fresh eggplant pancakes and juniper. Châteaubriand, Maine lobster risotto, pappardelle and rack of lamb are prepared tableside.

Sam makes the refreshing sorbets, ice creams and ice milks in house and uses many local purveyors for organic produce, berries, seafood and game (he devotes an entire page in the menu to listing their names and products). A pioneer in hosting wine-tasting dinners in Maine since 1982, he has continued them at the Harraseeket. His wine lists have won Wine Spectator awards annually since 1983.

A full breakfast buffet, from fresh fruit and biscuits to scrambled eggs and french toast, is included in the rates. The buffet lunch at $10.95 is exceeded in beauty and bounty only by the Sunday brunch ($14.95, with music by a classical guitarist).

Lunch, daily 11:30 to 2:30; dinner, 5:30 to 9. No smoking in dining room. Doubles, $135 to $175; suites, $225.

Lawnmeer Inn and Restaurant, Route 27, Box 505, West Boothbay Harbor 04575. (207) 633-2544 or (800) 633-7645.

Virtually every table has a water view in the long pine-paneled dining room of this Southport Island restaurant with high-back chairs and linened tables. Redone in burgundy and white with green napkins that match the carpet, it's dramatic by day and dim and romantic by candlelight at night.

Chef Bill Edgerton supplements the regular menu with a page of daily specials — things like angel-hair pasta with roast duckling, olive oil and garlic, $4.95 as an appetizer, and a trio of fish (swordfish with pesto, tuna with soy and garlic, and sole with crabmeat and tomato, $16.95 as an entrée), both of which proved exceptional. When one of us chose the fish trio over the lobster Johnny Walker but wanted to sample the sauce, the chef obliged with a taste on the side.

We also can vouch for the shrimp in parchment with julienned vegetables, new potatoes and crisp yellow squash and zucchini, and the poached salmon with dill-hollandaise sauce, among entrées priced from $9.95 to $18.95.

Vermont maple crème brûlée, a flourless chocolate torte with raspberry puree, blueberry bread pudding with crème anglaise, grand-marnier mousse and key lime pie are among the delightful desserts.

Owners Lee and Jim Metzger renovated thirteen inn rooms and suites, all with private baths. Twenty more modern rooms are in two motel buildings on either side of the inn, and there's a charming cottage for two with a kingsize bed and a sun deck at the water's edge. Lee, who is constantly upgrading, has recovered the beds in the motel buildings in lovely fabrics. She did the stunning, free-flowing stenciling that graces many of the rooms and bathrooms as well as the diverse wreaths in each room. Breakfast is extra, but the roast-beef hash topped with two poached eggs and the tomato and herb omelet with whole-wheat toast are well worth the $4.95 tab.

Dinner nightly, 6 to 9; Sunday brunch, 8 to 11. Doubles, $65 to $100; cottage, $110. Open mid-May to mid-October.

The Newcastle Inn, River Road, Newcastle 04553. (207) 563-5685 or (800) 832-8669.

From welcoming macaroons upon arrival to a doggy bag of white-chocolate pound cake to take on your way, food is foremost at this charming country inn. In between, you're likely to eat as well -- and as much -- as you have in your life. To heck with the extra pounds, this is the place and the time for a gastronomic splurge.

Dining is a gastronomic splurge at The Newcastle Inn.

The food is orchestrated -- and executed -- to perfection by Chris Sprague, a former law-firm office manager, and her husband Ted, a onetime Cape Cod school teacher. Since taking over the aging Federal-style Colonial in 1988, they have upgraded its fifteen guest rooms, all with private baths and furnished with a mix of antiques and New England crafts. Canopy beds, hand stenciling, floral wallpapers and wreaths on the doors are some of their attributes. In 1993, when the Spragues moved their living quarters into a building next door, the main-floor space they vacated left a second guest living room with an outside deck beside a busy bird feeder and the Damariscotta River and, more important, a second dining room. Now the inn's six tables have become twelve and, unless the dining room is unusually busy, guests no longer have to double up at tables for four and eat with strangers.

At our stay, six tables in the original rear dining room were occupied by deuces, and even the strains of Vivaldi could not overcome the hushed atmosphere. The meal was paced, service perfect and the food quite remarkable. The five-course, prix-fixe meal ($35) is served at 7 following a 6 o'clock cocktail hour with complimentary hors d'oeuvre in the living rooms and an enclosed side porch.

The menu for the evening is handwritten on a card at each table. Although there is no choice, vegetarians can be accommodated, as can those who would rather have a steak, or those who can only be happy with a boiled lobster. Our meal started with skewers of five large shrimp laced with dill and garlic and a fantastic cold cream of Vidalia onion soup with crisp bits of bacon floating in it. Cream biscuits accompanied an exotic salad of many lettuces and a creamy dressing. By this time, we barely had room for the juicy rack of lamb with its elegant sauce incorporating shiitake mushrooms, tender as could be and teamed with barely cooked snow peas. A very large slice of satiny chocolate-hazelnut terrine was a super ending.

Her cooking finished, Chris changes out of her kitchen duds and visits with guests over coffee in the country-fresh, candlelit dining room. It has a quilt on one wall and Wolfard oil lamps. Each white-linened table is topped with a red rose and Villeroy & Boch Cortina china.

"It's like throwing a dinner party every night," said Chris. She does all the cooking herself, with serving and cleanup assistance from a couple of waitresses. The food is not the kind one would consider eating every day, as we discovered the next day at breakfast. "We prepare things you wouldn't get at home," explained Ted. That meant a choice of juices, fresh peaches with crème anglaise, homemade granola with more peaches, a mound of white-chocolate pound cake (that went into the doggie bag) and an ample hot blueberry pudding with country ham. The pudding was too much even for the big eater among us to finish.

Chris, who is of Greek descent, knows she serves too much food, "but I can't help myself. I love making all of it. I explain to people they need to eat slowly and they don't have to finish everything. That's the trouble with being Mediterranean. I keep hearing this voice that says, 'feed, feed, feed.'"

And feed she does, whether it be an oyster bisque followed by roasted salmon with black pepper and almonds on celery root-puree, or a chilled cantaloupe soup with champagne followed by tenderloin of pork sauced with port and dried cranberries and served with sautéed beet greens. Some of her recipes, as well as her philosophy, are contained in her new cookbook, *Chris Sprague's Newcastle Inn Cookbook*, published by Harvard Common Press. Energetic Chris, who refers to herself and Ted as workaholics, does not plan to expand her reach beyond her grasp, but rather to "refine what we do." Shortly upon opening, they banned smoking and the American Cancer Society designated theirs the first smoke-free business in Maine in 1988.

The Newcastle Inn is an unpretentious, relaxed kind of a place where guests like to read and contemplate the river from hammocks or Adirondack chairs on the lawn and watch the many birds in the feeder off the deck.

Dinner by reservation, Tuesday-Sunday at 7, weekends only in off-season. No smoking. Doubles, $150 to $190, MAP; $90 to $130, B&B.

The Belmont, 6 Belmont Ave., Camden 04843. (207) 236-8053 or (800) 238-8053.

An 1886 Victorian house on a residential side street, Camden's oldest inn has been charmingly restored into a small and intimate full-service village inn with six guest rooms and a dining room of distinction. The process was started in 1979 by David and Kerlin Grant, who put the inn, then called Aubergine, on the culinary map as a pioneer in nouvelle cuisine. Chef Gerry Clare and partner John Mancarella took over in 1988, upgrading the rooms and changing the cuisine from French to American.

The six upstairs guest rooms, all now with private baths, have been "dressed up a bit," in John's words. They're nicely decorated with a mix of traditional and new, floral wallpapers and a light, sunny quality in keeping with the yellow exterior. The two third-floor rooms we once occupied with our sons have been converted into one extra-large room. A suite has a separate sitting room. Fresh towels are supplied with turndown service at night.

Guests often sip drinks while sitting on the old-fashioned swing on the front porch. A comfortable parlor-type reception room leads into the main dining room, serene and lovely with well-spaced tables dressed in white linens, floral china and tall flowers sprouting from clear-glass vases. The adjacent sun porch that we like best has a handful of pristine white tables and chairs.

Fresh raspberries and blueberries are breakfast treat at the Belmont.

Chef Clare's menu changes every few days. Some of it is inspired, like an appetizer of grilled oysters in pancetta with two sauces (a triumph, as it should have been for $8.50) and a white gazpacho with delicious homemade croutons. Pad Thai noodles with shrimp, chicken and peanuts, a warm Thai duck salad, Maine crab cakes and a savory three-onion tart are other starters.

We enjoyed grilled chicken with polenta and a tri-pepper compote — accompanied by julienned carrots, creamed spinach and new potatoes — and a special of poached salmon with a citrus sauce, very good but a smallish portion. The eight or so entrées are priced from $13 to $21 for the likes of grilled swordfish steak with cilantro compound butter, tamarind barbecued pork loin with drunken beans and jícama-corn relish, and pan-seared filet mignon with duxelles of mushroom toast and zinfandel bordelaise.

The sour-cream/blueberry cheesecake was sensational; not as successful was the strawberries Luxembourg. Other desserts were a warm plum tart, chocolate dacquoise, kahlua-espresso ice cream and a trio of sorbets. The wine list is distinguished and priced accordingly, though there are plenty of good choices in the teens and twenties.

For continental breakfast, we loved the fresh raspberries and blueberries with cream, the wonderful hot croissants with berry preserves, and a pot of strong, fragrant coffee.

Dinner nightly except Monday, 6 to 9:30. Doubles, $95 to $125; suite $145. Open May-October.

Reunion Inn & Grill, 49 Mechanic St., Box 711, Camden 04843. (207) 236-1090.

Noted local chef David Grant reappeared on the Camden dining scene in 1993, six years after leaving Aubergine in hopes of starting a restaurant in Portland or Boston." I was walking around in Portland for two years with cash in my pocket and nobody would sell me a building," he relates. "Then I saw this building and bought it." The building is a renovated 1800s mill house along up-and-coming Mechanic Street. David and his wife Kerlin, a bank executive, designed the structure to their specifications.

The result is an L-shaped dining room with an historic feeling, a semi-open kitchen beyond the bar, an outdoor terrace for light dining beside the Megunticook River and three contemporary suites upstairs.

The food is paramount here, as you'd expect from the man who pioneered with nouvelle and regional cuisine back in the late 1970s at Aubergine. But David has changed with the times, aiming for "a casual, friendly place for people who want interesting food at reasonable prices." The short dinner menu changes nightly. You might start with cold butternut-squash soup with fresh chervil, corn and salmon cakes with honey and whole-grain mustard, or lamb sausage in pastry with fresh mint. For main courses ($11 to $16), how about grilled bluefin tuna with sundried tomatoes, salmon with Pemaquid oysters and basil, pork chops with orange and ginger, or a mixed grill of flank steak and calves liver with wild mushrooms? Dessert could be strawberry-rhubarb pie, chocolate cheesecake or cinnamon-poached pears with vanilla ice cream and chocolate sauce.

The post and beam dining room is a bit austere with black and white checked napkins on blond wood tables, bare windows and wide-board floors. Tables are close together and the place, though spacious, can get noisy. Light eaters can retire to a few tables on the deck beside the rushing river for drinks and a short menu of sandwiches and appetizers.

Upstairs are three suites, designed as "a home away in Camden for the independent traveler." Each has a full bath, sitting room, queensize bed, cable TV, air-conditioning and phones -- "all the kinds of things we never had at our other place," says David. Most of the furniture and the striking paintings originated in Maine, thanks to the couple's evolution into "severe regionalists," as he describes it. "We started with a very clear idea of what we wanted and went ahead and did it."

And the name? It came to him as he was driving along listening to a tape about Joshua Slocum encountering the Reunion Islands as he was sailing around the world. "My father had a boat called Reunion. I was coming back, joining some of my old staff. So it was the right name."

Dinner, Tuesday-Sunday 5:30 to 10. Doubles, $90 to $120. Open May through mid-February.

The Youngtown Inn, Route 52 and Youngtown Road, Lincolnville 04849. (207) 763-4290.

The restaurant here, which we enjoyed so much when it opened a decade ago, reopened in 1992 after being abandoned for five years. The dining rooms are exceptionally pretty, the setting is rural and the food is French-inspired, though somewhat inconsistent, according to local consensus. It's run by Manuel Mercier, a chef who trained in Cannes, and his wife Mary Ann, a former Wall Street bond trader whom he met on a cruise ship.

The two pristine dining rooms and a sun porch seat 60 at well-spaced tables covered with white linens, oil lamps and fresh flowers. Floral stenciling and oriental rugs add color.

The short menu lists ten entrées ($9.95 to $16.95), including salmon en papillote, seafood in puff pastry, beef bourguignonne en croûte, entrecôte madagascar and veal chop normande. The best value is the four-course prix-fixe menu ($25), which starts with crab cakes or lobster ravioli and a salad of mixed greens. The four entrée choices could be roast rabbit in a light mustard sauce or roast rack of lamb. Dessert brings a crème brûlée that one reviewer said was the best he ever tasted, chocolate-mousse cake or homemade sorbets on a meringue shell.

Four of the six upstairs guest rooms have private baths and three have balconies. Each is decorated simply but attractively. There's also a small second-floor common room opening onto a porch over the entry.

A full breakfast, from homemade croissants to omelets and waffles, is served to overnight guests.

Dinner, Tuesday-Sunday 5:30 to 9:30; Sunday brunch, 11:30 to 3. Doubles, $50 to $95.

Dining areas at Youngtown Inn.

Penobscot Meadows Inn, Route 1, Belfast 04915. (207) 338-5320.

Seven guest rooms with private baths, one of them a studio apartment under the kitchen, are offered by Dini and Bernie Chapnick in a turn-of-the-century inn they renovated in 1984. The rooms are notable for nice window treatments and handmade quilts. One with a king bed has a wood stove and a view of the bay. Guests enjoy a TV in the parlor and an expanded continental breakfast with fresh fruit, granola, hot cinnamon rolls and bagels with cream cheese.

It is primarily the dinners for which this inn is known, served in a cozy dining room with quilts on the walls, sprigged tablecloths over white and candles in hurricane chimneys. There are a few tables on the sun porch and many on an outside deck amidst umbrellas and flowers, affording a view of Penobscot Bay.

Chef Judy Peavey, a Johnson & Wales culinary graduate, makes her own ice creams, including a terrific ice-cream-roll cake with hot fudge. But first things first. Appetizers run from $4.50 for stuffed mushrooms to $9.50 for a smoked-seafood platter for two. You might start with crab crêpes with a sauce of green peppercorns and sweet red peppers, or triple satay of grilled chicken, shrimp and pork, served with a spicy peanut sauce.

For entrées ($12.95 to $19.95), how about pistachio-pesto shrimp over angel-hair pasta, herb-crusted lamb chops with apricot-apple sauce, raspberry chicken or Szechuan veal, stir-fried and wrapped in Chinese-style basil pancakes?

Then it's time for ice cream and espresso, or perhaps a four-liqueur coffee topped with whipped cream ($5).

Dinner nightly in summer, 5:30 to 9; closed Tuesday in winter. Doubles, $69 to $99.

Lodging

181 Main Street Bed & Breakfast, 181 Main St., Freeport 04032. (207) 865-1226.

The most engaging of all the B&Bs popping up around busy Freeport is this 1840 Greek Revival cape, opened in 1986 by Ed Hasset and David Cates. They offer seven upstairs guest rooms with private baths and queensize beds, nicely furnished but rather small, as rooms in some historic homes are apt to be. They compensate with extra common space -- twin front parlors, one like a library with TV and the other containing quite a collection of ceramic animals in a sideboard and a long coffee table made of glass atop an old ship's rope bed.

Two dining rooms dressed with calico tablecloths and Hitchcock chairs are the settings for breakfasts to remember. When we stopped in, the feast began with a choice of juices and zucchini muffins. A fruit platter bearing slices of three kinds of melon, kiwi, pineapple, strawberries and cherries followed the main dish, cheese strata with English muffins and bacon. The day before produced apple-walnut coffee cake and belgian waffles with baked apple and sausage.

Out back is a secluded swimming pool, surrounded by flowers.

Doubles, $95. No smoking.

Kenniston Hill Inn, Route 27, Box 125, Boothbay 04537. (207) 633-2159 or (800) 992-2915.

Two rope hammocks, small groupings of lawn chairs and rock gardens greet summer visitors to a 1786 shipbuilder's mansion. Inside are a common room with decoys over the open-hearth fireplace, a dining room and eight guest rooms, all with private baths.

New innkeepers Susan and David Straight took over when longtime owners Paul and Ellen Morissette consolidated their B&B operations at the new Five Gables Inn. The Straights kept most of the furnishings, added some things of their own and started offering dinners to guests and the public. The five-course meal (prix-fixe at $28) is available in the off-season in the fireplaced dining room. One night's dinner started with Maine mussels in a wine and cream sauce, country vegetable soup and a green salad dressed with a honey-dijon vinaigrette. The main event was scallops in puff pastry with maple-cream sauce, fresh asparagus and a puree of acorn and butternut squash. The dessert course yielded a mint-chocolate mousse with raspberry coulis.

Breakfast, served at a single seating at 9 in the dining room or living room, involves fresh fruits and breads and perhaps blintzes, zucchini-walnut pancakes, ham and swiss cheese in puff pastry, or peaches-and-cream french toast.

The guest rooms are full of interesting touches, one with a collection of dolls and another with a high pineapple bed that needs a step-stool on which to climb in. Four have working fireplaces and queen or king beds. Two more in a rear carriage house have private entrances. The front porch is full of rocking chairs and wrought-iron furniture.

Doubles, $65 to $95. No smoking.

Norumbega, 61 High St., Camden 04843. (207) 236-4646.

Ensconced in one of the finest "castles" along the Maine coast is this elegant B&B with great style and a combination lock on the front door to keep out curious passersby.

The cobblestone and slate-roofed mansion, built in 1886 for the inventor of the duplex system of telegraphy, was for a few years the summer home of journalist Hodding Carter. The hillside property was acquired in 1987 by Murray Keatinge, a Californian who summers in Camden.

Inside are endlessly fascinating public rooms (the woodwork alone is priceless), twelve large bedrooms and a penthouse suite, all with private baths, sitting areas and telephones and some with TVs. Named after castles, they were sumptuously

Breakfast is served in formal dining room at Norumbega.

decorated by Murray's late wife Elisabeth. The ones in back of the house have breathtaking views of Penobscot Bay. Most have fireplaces and canopy beds, all of them kingsize. The ultimate is the penthouse suite, a bit of a hike up a spiral staircase from the third floor. It has a kingsize bed, a regal bath with pillows around a circular ebony whirlpool tub big enough for two, a wet bar, a sitting room in pink and green, and a see-through, three-sided fireplace, plus a little porch with two deck chairs and a fabulous view of the ocean.

Guests have the run of the parlors and a library, an intimate retreat for two beside a fireplace on the landing of the ornate staircase, a second-floor reading room, and flower-laden rear porches and balconies on all three floors overlooking expansive lawns and the bay.

Soup, cookies, mineral water and soft drinks are offered in the afternoon, and wine and hors d'oeuvre in the early evening -- enough food that some guests have stayed here all evening without going out to dinner. But breakfast is the day's highlight. Served at a long table in the formal dining room or at a round glass table beside the telescope in the conservatory, it is a feast of juices and fruits, all kinds of breads and muffins, and, when we stayed, the best french toast ever, topped with a dollop of sherbet and sliced oranges. Eggs florentine or benedict, vegetable omelets, crêpes with an almond filling and peach topping, and ginger-apple pancakes are other favorites.

Amazingly, Norumbega is not a whit pretentious, thanks partly to Murray's ebullient personality. He commutes back and forth to California to run his businesses there, but spends most of the summer and fall here as a hands-on innkeeper. Although proud of "what we've accomplished in six years" (Glamour magazine called it one of America's top 25 inns), Murray says he believes in "keeping it informal. Guests appreciate the homey, country atmosphere." They often go into the kitchen and help the chef; in return, the refrigerator always contains bread pudding for guests to help themselves.

Doubles, $195 to $270; suites, $295 to $425..

Windward House, 6 High St., Camden 04843. (207) 236-9656.

Bountiful breakfasts and beautiful gardens await guests at this cool blue 1854 Greek Revival, a stylish B&B run by personable New Jersey transplants Jon and Mary Davis. "We spend at least half an hour telling our guests where to go and what to do," says Mary as she seats new arrivals in a nicely furnished parlor or a paneled library for orientation purposes before showing them to their rooms. Upstairs are five guest rooms, each with private bath, and a suite with queensize canopy four-poster and a sitting room. French doors open onto a private garden from the Wicker Room, decorated in pretty pastels. Another favorite is the Rose Room with a queen canopy bed and many antiques. Mints and Crabtree & Evelyn toiletries are in each room, and decanters of sherry and port are set out in the parlor. A couple of outdoor decks and a long back yard are pleasant places for summer visitors.

Mary, who was a caterer in New Jersey, serves a gourmet breakfast at 9 in the formal dining room where abundant plants, a gleaming silver service, lace curtains and a blue patterned rug catch the eye. Jon may beckon guests to the long table for "liver, lima beans and sprouts," but return guests -- of which the Windward has many -- know better. A typical eye-opener might be sliced melon and peaches, zucchini muffins, belgian waffles with blueberry-lemon nut sauce, sausage and applesauce-raisin nutbread. We were mighty impressed with a bowl of fresh fruit, the raspberry/cream-cheese coffee cake and peaches-and-cream french toast. Spanakopita, eggs olé with homemade salsa, blueberry crunch, ham and cheese soufflé, apple-puff pancakes and grand marnier-strawberry puffs are other favorites.

All the gorgeous flowers come from the Davises' extensive cutting gardens and a spectacular perennial garden that seems to have expanded at every visit.

Doubles, $85 to $130. No smoking.

A Little Dream, 66 High St., Camden 04843. (207) 236-8742.

Piles of thank-you notes on the table at the entry, books of love letters and poems, an abundance of lace and a welcoming lemonade, served in a tall glass on a plate with a sprig of mint, blueberries and strawberries, signify that this utterly charming place is special. It's a little dream for Joanne Fontana and her husband, Billy, a sculptor and handyman-remodeler. From the looks of all the dolls and teddybears, the Fontanas must have brought their entire inventory with them when they sold their toy stores in New York City and Boston. Joanne has decorated and accessorized their turreted Victorian house with great flair.

She pampers guests in a parlor furnished in wicker and chintz, an elaborate dining room beside a conservatory and a side porch. Three bedrooms in the house are decorated to the hilt with Victorian clothing, lace, ribbons and at least eight pillows on each bed. All have private baths, as do two more in a rear carriage house with wet bars and small refrigerators.

Breakfasts, served on lace-clothed tables topped with floral mats and heavy silver, are gala events here. Guests make their choices from a fancy menu placed in their rooms the night before The choice might involve lemon-ricotta soufflé pancakes with fresh raspberry sauce, banana-pecan waffles with maple country sausage, or three kinds of omelets: smoked salmon, apple-cheddar and ham-swiss. The coffee is breakfast blend or chocolate-raspberry or hazelnut; there's also a choice among four teas. Orange or cranberry juice, fresh fruit and muffin of the day come with.

Doubles, $95 to $139.

The Inn at Sunrise Point, Box 1344, Camden. (207) 236-7716 or (800) 237-8674.

This is the inn of inn reviewer Jerry Levitin's dreams. The California travel writer, who took over Norman Simpson's *Country Inns & Back Roads* guidebooks and ruffled the feathers of a few longtime innkeepers along the way, opened his own B&B in 1992 on four forested acres at the foot of a dirt road leading from Route 1 to Penobscot Bay in Lincolnville.

"I built what I'd like to stay at," says Jerry with characteristic candor. The result is mixed -- contemporary and Californian in style, but small and overpriced for some New England tastes. Jerry offers three rooms in the main house plus four cottages. The Winslow Homer Cottage that we occupied right beside the water featured a kingsize bed, a fireplace and an enormous bathroom with a jacuzzi for two and a separate shower. We were surprised there was no space to stash luggage other than in the bathroom, and the waterfront deck was so narrow as to be useless (the front porch of the main house compensated). Though small, the three upstairs rooms have fireplaces and music systems, queensize beds, swivel upholstered or wicker chairs in front of the window, built-in desks and armoires holding TVs and VCRs. Two new cottages added in 1993 possess queensize beds and the other inn amenities. All have been upgraded with paintings, deck chairs and accessories to "make the rooms more warm and homey," in the words of the resident innkeepers who take over when Jerry's traveling, which is much of the time.

The main floor offers a wonderful living/dining room that's mostly windows onto Penobscot Bay, a fireplaced, English hunting-style library and a small conservatory for tête-à-tête breakfasts. We feasted here on fruit, coffee-pecan bread, a terrific frittata with basil, bay shrimp and jack cheese, potatoes dusted with cayenne, crisp bacon and hazelnut coffee. Hors d'oeuvre are served in the afternoon.

Upon departure, we found a card under our windshield: "Our porter has cleaned your windscreen to allow you to get a clear picture of our Penobscot Bay."

Doubles, $150 to $200; cottages, $225 and $295. Open Memorial Day-October.

Gourmet Treats

In Freeport, home of outlets to serve almost every interest and then some, a large **Ben & Jerry's Ice Cream** stand is set up right beside L.L. Bean. All the flavors of one of Vermont's best-known exporters are available. A small cone at $2.25 and a large cone at $3.45 are not exactly outlet prices, however.

And you thought **L.L. Bean Co.** was just for great sportswear and equipment. This ever-changing and expanding emporium now has a gourmet food shop with Maine-made and New England mail-order products, including its own line of raspberry jams, bittersweet fudge sauce, maple syrup and the like. From saltwater taffy and dandelion greens to Bean's-blend coffee beans, this place has it — or will soon.

If you tire of the Freeport outlet scene, head for the little-known South Freeport Harbor wharf and the **Harraseeket Lunch & Lobster Co.** This is what coastal Maine is supposed to be like. There's a small dining room, but most people prefer to pick up their food at the lobster pound's outside service window and eat at picnic tables on the working dock. The owners are noted for their basket dinners, priced from $4.75 for clam cakes to $11.75 for seafood. Other favorites are a fishwich, clamburger royale and lobster roll ($8.95).

At the **Bohemian Coffee House** at 111 Maine St., Brunswick, site of the former Omelette Shop, you can pick up a bagel or sandwich to eat with your espresso, cappuccino, latte or café au lait. There's a BLT on a bagel or a veggie sandwich with artichokes, cheese, lemon and tomato. It being mid-morning, we settled for a double latte ($2.65) that was every bit as good as you can get in Seattle. Open weekdays 7 to 2 and 6 to midnight, Saturday 9 to midnight, Sunday 9 to 5.

English cheeses from a Covent Garden firm are one of the strengths of **Treats,** Main Street, Wiscasset. Owner Paul Mrozinski offered a taste of cashel blue and we had to buy some, it was so buttery and delicious. We also had to buy one of the "bodacious breads" that are made in Waldeboro, a crusty olive loaf (one of the others was rosemary and hazelnut). Salads, soups, entrées and the usual suspects are all sold here. Paul and his wife Sharon rent two B&B rooms with private baths in their home, the Marsden House, which is also an antiques shop, across the street. The $75 tab gets you a queensize bed, fireplace, private entrance and hearty breakfast.

Native produce, specialty foods, wine, candies, pâtés, smoked salmon and croissants abound at **Weatherbird,** a neat gourmet food store and gift shop in a sprawl of a building called Northey Square off Main Street in downtown Damariscotta. There are a few tables out front upon which to partake.

You'll find at least 42 flavors at **Round Top Ice Cream,** Business Route 1, Damariscotta. This is the original home of the ice cream favored by restaurants throughout the region, an unpretentious little spot on the farm where it began in 1924. The choices range from cappuccino to watermelon, ginger to raspberry. Cones come in three sizes, priced from 94 cents to $1.84. You also can get a banana split for $2.78 or $3.49.

"Color is our passion," say Chris and Richard Hilton of **Edgecomb Potters,** Route 27, Edgecomb. And colorful is their extraordinary glazed porcelain in various hues, shown inside and out at this must-stop place on the road into Boothbay Harbor. They have all kinds of pottery for kitchen and dining room, from garlic cellars and pâté dishes to snack trays and soup tureens, as well as decorative accessories.

The place for breakfast treats, salads, sandwiches and deli foods in Boothbay Harbor is **Cafe Elizabeth** at 15 McKown St. Elizabeth Digiulian offers a handful of tables inside and out. Unless you insist on lobster, we recommend picking up a picnic here and eating on the breezy front porch or finding a scenic spot, rather than tackling Boothbay Harbor restaurants filled with tour-bus patrons.

The **School House Farm** produce stand, a few miles west of Thomaston on Route 1, has baskets of fresh vegetables, local cheeses and eggs, jams and jellies, homemade breads, muffins and blueberry pies, as well as the lovely watercolors of flowers and local landscapes by owner Debbie Beckwith, whose gallery may be visited next door.

The Brown Bag at 606 Main St., Rockland, is everyone's favorite spot for breakfast, lunch, supper or a snack. The owners, four sisters, started with a deli in the middle and expanded into a restaurant on one side and a gourmet food shop on the other. The extensive menu lists healthful selections at prices from yesteryear. Stop here for an oversize blueberry muffin (85 cents), a lentilburger on a whole-wheat roll, a crab and cheddar melt or a slice of apple-raspberry pie ($1.95).

A striking plum-colored building with lavender trim houses **Miss Plum's Parlour** along Route 1 in Rockport. It's famous for its ice creams and yogurts, served at a takeout window and available in changing flavors from red raspberry chip to toffee bar crunch. Sundaes, frappes, root-beer floats, lime rickeys, banana splits and more may be taken to lavender-colored picnic tables at the side. Owners Elaine and Bill Pellechia have added a stylish little restaurant and a clever menu for inside dining. Come for a heart-healthy breakfast, a midday plum dog (frankfurter with chili, cheese, onion, salsa and sour cream, $3.50) or lobster roll ($8.95), or a crab-meat cobb salad, fried clams, or meatloaf and gravy for a light dinner anytime. Open daily 7 a.m. to 10 p.m. in summer and fall.

Rockport folks favor **The Market Basket** at the junction of Routes 1 and 90, a specialty-foods store where you'll find everything from zucchini-feta casserole and Texas salsa salad to Shaker cheddar soup and peach or strawberry pie

In Camden, **Harbor Provisions** at 64 Bay View St. is where sailors from the Camden Yacht Club next door pick up their provisions. You should, too, if you're looking for exotic cheeses, fresh salads, soups, smoked salmon and other makings for a fancy picnic. We admired roquefort chicken salad with red grapes and almonds and a broccoli salad with bacon and purple onions, as well as any number of sandwiches made to order.

Rooster Brother, a branch of the fabulous kitchen store and specialty-food shop of the same name in Ellsworth, is a draw at the Highland Hill Mall. Here you'll find wines, local food products and a selection of deli items for picnics or take-out.

Maine beers and ales are all the rage at **Sea Dog Brewing Co.,** which emerged no-expense-spared in 1993 in one of the former Knox Mill buildings at 43 Mechanic St. in Camden. Tours of the downstairs brewery are given daily at 11 and 4 and there's a brewtique for bar ware and apparel. Most visitors gravitate to the fancy tavern -- a mix of booths, beams, oriental runners and stone walls that's too atmospheric for words. The splashy waterfall outside the soaring windows adds to the effect. The brewery's Penobscot Maine lager, Windjammer Maine ale and Owl's Head light are featured, along with a variety of snacks and sandwiches ($4.50 to $8.95).

Two sisters run the **Camden Coffee Co.,** a versatile little cafe and bakery with an adjacent gallery at the Public Landing in Camden. You'll find a variety from gazpacho to blueberry-walnut scones, black-bean chili to lemon-raspberry cake, nicely priced and available to go or to eat at a few tables inside or out. Folks like to come here for dessert and cappuccino.

Black canvas deck chairs at two little marble tables on the front porch beckon visitors upstairs to the **Blue Angel Cafe** on the second floor of the Harbor Square Gallery, 58 Bay View St. Here you'll find more tables for two amidst some striking artworks, the better to enjoy morning espressos and lattes, innovative lunches (how about rainbow soup -- orange-carrot on one side, mint pea on the other?), afternoon tea or weekend dinners with beer and wine. The blackboard menu favors chicken, fish and vegetarian dishes, from the Blue Angel chef's salad with blue cheese and cashews sprinkled on top to an evening special of lobster with basil over shell pasta ($12.50).

For casual seafood, head for **Lobster Stu's** on the Camden wharf. The food is higher quality than at some of the better-known restaurants nearby, and you can enjoy it at picnic tables on the dock where windjammers come and go. Stu Brady's lobster rolls are a bargain $7.75 and his lobster dinners, $8.95 to $12.95.

Our favorite shop among many in Camden is **Heather Harland** at 37 Bay View St., a large establishment with unusual stock, especially kitchen items, tableware, linens and cookbooks. Our best placemats that look like tapestry were purchased here.

Down East Maine
Lobster, Plus

We know, we know.

You're going to Maine on vacation and you can't wait to clamp your teeth around a shiny red lobster. In fact, you can hardly think of anything else. Oh, maybe some fried clams or a bucket of steamers, but lobster is what you're really after.

So you'll stand in line to get into some dive for the $8.95 lobster special. You'll suck out the feelers and wrestle with the claws of your one-and-one-quarter-pound (if you're lucky) crustacean. You'll end up with about three ounces of lobster meat, debris all over your clothes and hands that reek for two days.

And you'll probably gush, "That was the *best* lobster I've ever had!"

Well, friends, we're here to tell you that there is life after lobster in Maine. A lot of fine, creative cooking is going on in the Pine Tree State, and in the last decade a number of excellent restaurants have emerged Down East along the coast, many of them with young and innovative chefs.

Also new are a number of suave inns and bed-and-breakfast places, which are giving visitors an alternative to the traditional cabins, campgrounds and motels that abound along the coast of Maine.

In this final chapter, we meander our way along the coast, peninsulas and islands, hitting the high spots from East Penobscot Bay and Deer Isle — which is the epitome of Down East Maine — to Acadia National Park, where tea on the lawn is still a tradition at the Jordan Pond House.

Dining

The Best of the Best

Firepond, Main Street, Blue Hill. (207) 374-9970.

Of all the restaurants we know, Firepond lingers in the memory as one of the most romantic — that is, when you can snag a table on the screened porch, which wraps around the bar-waiting area and a convivial inside dining room.

And, good news, Firepond is back, bigger and better than ever -- after a year-long shutdown in 1993. New chef-owner Craig Rodenhiser, who had been assistant chef at Firepond in 1991 and 1992, was overseeing a major renovation and expansion of the restaurant in the former mill complex at the start of 1994. He opened two new dining rooms on the main floor, one of them in a former gourmet shop, where shelves full of antique books line the walls and oriental carpets dot the original wood floors. French doors look onto a new outdoor dining terrace facing Main Street. Craig installed an additional small bar on the main floor and a new interior stairway to connect the two levels. He also renovated the kitchen to handle the extra seats and the debut of lunch service, plus mid-morning pastries and espresso. "We're shooting for the same high-quality food and casually elegant atmosphere as before," he promised.

Even with all the changes, we're still partial to that great porch beside the stream, until 1993 a fixture for dinner every summer as far back as we can recall. The setting is enchanting, with water rippling down the stream into the tidal pool below and spotlights highlighting the shining rocks.

Drinks here are always generous, and we enjoyed ours with a selection of pâtés

Porch at Firepond provides enchanting dinner setting beside creek.

($8.50) that included pork, chicken livers and vegetables, garnished by cornichons — plenty for two, along with crusty French bread. Other of Craig's starters include baked brie en croûte with raspberries and almonds, raviolis stuffed with smoked salmon and gruyère cheese, escargots in puff pastry, caesar salad prepared tableside and soup du jour, perhaps gazpacho or brandy-mushroom.

Among main courses ($12.95 to $19.95) you'll likely find things like scallops with leeks, medallions of veal with sundried tomatoes, grilled pork loin with chutney, roast Long Island duckling with raspberry-chambord sauce and a signature New Zealand rack of lamb, marinated in burgundy wine. At recent visits we've enjoyed a fabulous fettuccine with crab meat and pinenuts, a zesty chicken with walnuts in plum sauce and ginger, and the halibut espagnole, topped with mussels and a saffron beurre blanc.

Desserts could be a terrific chocolate-truffle dacquoise, lemon-raspberry cheesecake, raspberry decadence, crème caramel and Bailey's chocolate mousse. We've found the ginger ice cream to be a refreshing finish after the hearty main dishes, and the Jamaican coffee with Irish whiskey and tia maria a fitting end to a meal of intense flavors in a magical setting.

Lunch daily in season, 11 to 2:30; dinner nightly, 5 to 9:30, fewer nights after Columbus Day. Closed January to early May.

Jonathan's, Main Street, Blue Hill. (207) 374-5226.

Innovative cuisine, an award-winning wine list and now a cookbook. These are the claims to fame of Jonathan Chase, owner of this informal restaurant now in its second decade. The cookbook, *Saltwater Seasonings,* written in collaboration with his sister, Sarah Leah Chase, the Nantucket caterer and cookbook author, was much in evidence in kitchen stores across Maine after receiving accolades from Down East magazine as "quite possibly Maine's best regional cookbook in fifty years."

The book incorporates some of the menus that have made Jonathan's a culinary star. Take, for example, some of his dishes from the summer of 1993: an appetizer of Baja fish taco with fresh tomato salsa and minted yogurt and an entrée of lobster "fried over cold" with buttermilk biscuits.

For starters, we're partial to his crostini with roasted elephant garlic and chèvre, served with ripe tomatoes, and a remarkable smoked-mussel salad with goat cheese and pinenuts. Also good are the soups, a choice of cold minted pea or hot cauliflower and blue cheese at one visit. Among entrées ($13.95 to $17.95), Arizona skirt steak came with a dynamite salsa of tomatoes, chile peppers, garlic and tequila, while the rabbit braised with smoked bacon, sundried tomatoes, rosemary and garlic was served with carrots and red-skinned potatoes. Grilled swordfish with spicy mango-papaya relish, peppercorn duck with apricot-ginger glaze, grilled medallions of venison with sweet onions and potato pancakes, and braised lamb shank with beer and bourbon barbecue sauce are other possibilities.

Cantaloupe sorbet with macaroons and frangelico cheesecake are among the sweet endings. Winner of the Wine Spectator Award of Excellence, the wine list is exceptional and pleasantly priced — when did you last enjoy a Firestone merlot for $15.50?

Dining is in the restaurant's original front section, done up in nautical blue with captain's chairs, skylights and alcove windows filled with plants, or in an expansive rear addition. Its bow windows and pitched ceilings provide an airy contrast to the front's dark and intimate quarters.

Dinner nightly, 5 to 9. Closed Monday in winter.

George's, 7 Stevens Lane, Bar Harbor. (207) 288-4505.

This hard-to-find restaurant in a little Southern-style house behind the First National Bank offers what we — and almost everyone else, it seems — have long considered the best and most creative food on Mount Desert Island. Run by retired local high-school history teacher George Demas, it's a summery place with a Greek orientation, lately gone glamorous. George is still in the kitchen, never taking a night off, we're told.

White organdy curtains flutter in the breeze in several small dining rooms, Greek or classical guitar music plays on tape, and everything is served on clear glass plates atop pink-linened tables. A pianist entertains after 9 in the surprisingly New Yorkish piano room, and patrons can dine on a new outdoor terrace.

The bone-dry Hymettus white wine goes perfectly with George's traditional dishes like lobster strudel, mustard shrimp or paella. Other entrées ($16.95 to $29 for a grilled 22-ounce porterhouse steak) include seared lamb, duck breast with honey-rum mango sauce, veal medallions sautéed with blue cheese and garlic, and a variety of game dishes.

At one visit, hot crusty French bread and the best little Greek salads ever preceded the entrées: distinctive smoked scallops on fettuccine and a special of shrimp on a fresh tomato sauce with feta cheese, rice pilaf and New Zealand spinach with orange juice and orange zest.

The appetizers are assertive (perhaps kasseri cheese broiled with garlic, baked phyllo shells with lamb and tzatziki, seared tuna loin with pickled ginger and wasabi, and smoked-salmon pizzetta. Desserts are usually first-rate, from Mississippi mud cake with raspberry puree and lemon curd almond tuile to macadamia and chocolate ice-cream profiteroles and a phyllo "party cracker" with mascarpone and tropical fruits and, one night, an irresistible fresh blueberry and peach meringue.

New in 1993 was a prix-fixe dinner for $27.50. You could fashion your own dinner with an appetizer, main course and dessert, choosing from all but a few of the priciest items on the menu.

Dinner nightly, 5:30 to 11. Open mid-June through October.

The Porcupine Grill, 123 Cottage St., Bar Harbor. (207) 288-3884.

Owner Terry Marinke and her husband had a local antiques business, which provided the furnishings and impetus for this trendy grill. It takes its name from the nearby Porcupine Islands and since opening in 1989, has given George's competition for top honors in town.

"Everything is real," says Terry, showing the assorted antique oak drop-leaf tables and Chippendale chairs, the rugs on the honey-colored wood floors, the Villeroy & Boch china, and different fresh flowers scattered about the dining areas on two floors. Also, "everything's homemade with Maine ingredients where possible."

Antique bulls-eye glass dividers and period sconces help create a cafe atmosphere in the main-floor bar area, where many like to sip champagne cocktails pairing French sparkling and Maine raspberry wines or Porcupine punch (rum and fruit juices) before snacking on New England cheddar and black-bean fritters with creamy garlic and herb dipping sauce, salmon cakes with minted cucumber vinaigrette and pickled ginger, or a terrine of shiitake mushrooms, crab meat and cheese with a roasted tomato and sherry sauce, the mushrooms grown by Terry's husband.

We prefer the quieter upstairs, where on a busy night we lucked into a private dining room for two. Our appetizers, smoked salmon and johnnycakes with caviar and sour cream and a signature caesar salad topped with fried shrimp ($7.95), lived up to advance billing. Among entrées ($15 to $19.95), we were smitten with the grilled chicken with ginger-peach chutney and the sautéed shrimp and peas in a light garlic-cream sauce over fresh egg noodles. Other possibilities might be a lightly smoked roasted duck breast served over a warm wild-rice and walnut salad, skillet-roasted pork chop with cornbread stuffing and grilled porterhouse steak with smoked shiitake mushrooms.

A $15 McDowell fumé blanc accompanied our meal, chosen from a well-selected, expensive wine list augmented by "celebration wines." Desserts included a wonderful peach ice cream with ginger shortbread, white-chocolate cheesecake with blueberry sauce and coconut-strawberry shortcake.

Dinner nightly from 6; winter, Friday-Sunday from 6.

The Fin Back, 78 West St., Bar Harbor. (207) 288-4193.

Pink and green neon squiggles across the ceiling create a beachy effect at this small, with-it restaurant across from the harbor. Pink napkins stand tall in the wine glasses and white cloth mats accent tables with green marbelized tops.

Chef-owner Terry Preble bills his as Bar Harbor's first "full scenic restaurant with a smoke-free environment." It's a healthful, appealing setting for some inspired cuisine. You might start with wild-mushroom ravioli, homemade salmon sausage with a light orange-cream sauce, crab meat quesadilla or the Fin Back pizelle, two flour tortillas brushed with pesto, reggiano cheese and sundried tomatoes. Main courses ($14.95 to $18.95) come with salad, "just the right rice or potato," vegetable and French bread. How about charbroiled scallops with roasted pecans and tomatillo sauce, grilled chicken with red-chile/almond sauce and cubanella bread pudding, grilled lamb tenderloin with Thai curry and Maine blueberry chutney, or pork medallions with apricot-cranberry sauce? Pastas, served with salad and French bread, include seafood pernod and Maine lobster in a coral sauce.

Desserts ($4.75) could be a strawberry and cheese strudel, roasted nut tart with caramel sauce, peanut-butter/chocolate-mousse pound cake and kiwi sorbet.

Dinner nightly from 5:30. Open late May to late October. No smoking.

The Burning Tree, Route 3, Otter Creek. (207) 288-9331.

Among top choices on everybody's list of culinary havens is this simple restaurant in a rural setting south of Bar Harbor. There are tables on the long front porch, one section of which is a waiting area. Beyond are two small dining rooms, cheerfully outfitted in pinks and blues, their linened tables topped with tall, blue-edged water glasses. Local art and colorful paintings adorn the walls.

Such is the summer-cottage setting for what young chef-owners Allison Martin and Elmer Beal Jr. call "gourmet seafood" with a vegetarian sideline. The only meat dishes are two or three versions of chicken: grilled with Mexican molé sauce, Indian, and sautéed with basil and balsamic cream. But it's seafood that most customers are after -- basic like baked cod with black-bean sauce and lofty as in grilled swordfish with watercress-lime sauce. Prices are down to earth: $4 to $5 for most appetizers, $10.50 to $16 for entrées.

Our party was impressed with such starters as mussels with mustard sauce, grilled scallops and an excellent vegetarian sushi. The cioppino for $13 came so highly rated that two of us ordered it. The others chose grilled monkfish with a spicy tomato-lemon coulis and the cajun crab and lobster au gratin. The garden out back provides vegetables and herbs, and the owners use organically grown produce whenever possible. Entrées come with fresh vegetables (carrots and snow peas, at our visit) and a choice of garlicked potatoes or three-grain rice salad in a lemon vinaigrette.

Desserts are to groan over: perhaps nectarine mousse cake, Ukranian pop-pyseed cake, chocolate-orange cheesecake or fresh strawberry pie. A good little wine list, chosen with as much care as the menu, is priced mostly in the teens.

Dinner nightly, 5 to 10. Open June to mid-October.

Redfield's, Main Street, Northeast Harbor. (207) 276-5283.

The hottest dining ticket on the other side of Mount Desert Island was opened in 1992 by Scott and Maureen Redfield. Their trendy commissary and restaurant, located next to his father's Redfield Artisans showroom and beneath their Village View Inn B&B, would be quite at home on Nantucket, although the prices and lack of pretensions are refreshingly Down East.

Decor in two small dining rooms is simple yet sophisticated. Tiny lamps hanging from long cords over most tables illuminate some large, summery, impression-ist-style paintings and make the rooms rather too bright for our tastes. But they do highlight the food, which is worth the spotlight here. We staved off hunger with Maureen's fabulous French bread, exquisite house salads and a shared appetizer of venison carpaccio as we nursed the house La Veille Ferme wine. Lemon sorbet in a lotus dish prepared the palate for the main dishes: sliced breast of duck with fresh chutney and marinated loin of lamb with goat cheese and black olives, both superb. Strawberry sorbet and a chocolate-almond mint tart ended a memorable meal.

Scott, who used to cook at Cranberry Lodge of Asticou, changes his menus frequently. Grilled tuna niçoise salad, sole with lobster and crab meat provençal,

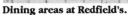
Dining areas at Redfield's.   Jean-Paul Lecomte outside his bistro.

salmon fillet with chardonnay-dill sauce, and filet of beef with smoked oysters and brie were on the docket for $13.95 to $17.50 at our latest visit. Starters included smoked-salmon phyllo florets, crab cakes with sherried cajun mayonnaise and spinach pesto puffs with smoked chile-pepper sauce.

The short lunch menu is equally appealing, and deli items from the commissary are perfect for picnics of distinction.

Open Tuesday-Sunday from 8:30 a.m.; dinner, 6:30 to 8:30.

Other Dining Choices

Jean-Paul's Bistro, Main Street, Blue Hill. (207) 374-5852.

Gaelic charm has come to Blue Hill with the opening of this delightful bistro by Jean-Paul Lecomte, taking full advantage of its view onto Blue Hill Bay. In his classic white Maine home with green shutters, the former waiter at some prestigious New York City restaurants, including the 21 Club, opened for lunch and tea in the summer of 1993 and had the locals buzzing. Jean-Paul takes care of the front of the house and several relatives, like his mother, father, brother and sister-in-law, help out.

You can come in at 11 a.m. for a cup of cappuccino and a chocolate croissant. For lunch, the simple menu might yield a salade niçoise, croque monsieur, chicken salad vinaigrette, bouillabaisse soup, or a roast-beef sandwich with melted brie. Dessert might be puff pastry with local strawberries. Prices are in the $3.95 to $5.95 range. From 3 to 5, drop in for a snack at one of the custom-made square wooden tables on the terrace, topped with a canvas umbrella, surrounded by beautiful flowers. Enjoy, as you really can't from any other establishment in town, the pristine view.

Inside, the dining room has cathedral ceilings, local art, white tablecloths, and blue and white spattered Bennington pottery for a simple and fresh yet sophisticated look. And it has big windows for enjoying the view. Wines and beers are available (the house wine is Boucheron for $10 a liter).

Jean-Paul was considering opening for prix-fixe dinners in 1994.

Coffee, lunch and tea, 11 to 5. Closed in winter.

513

Carrying Place Restaurant, 130 Cottage St., Bar Harbor. (207) 288-8905.

When Mardie Junkins was at the New York Restaurant School, the Maine restaurant scene was the subject for her thesis. "Now I'm living and working it," she said of the small restaurant she began in 1987 in a tan clapboard house in Ellsworth and moved in 1992 to Bar Harbor's restaurant row along Cottage Street. "We miss Ellsworth," Mardie said, "but we did more business here in January than we did there in August."

The relocated restaurant maintains the innovative regional menus and the simple, stylish decor. Dining is by candlelight at tables with windsor chairs amid bare floors, lace curtains and pear-colored walls with strawberry borders in various rooms of an 1882 house, plus a front porch and a "secret garden" at the side where umbrellaed tables provide shade for lunchtime service.

The dinner menu is categorized into salads, pastas, seafood, sautés and grills ($10.95 to $18.95). You might go all out on bouillabaisse, seafood crêpes, grilled pork with peanut sauce, sweetbreads, veal marsala or beef wellington. Or you could settle for a dinner salad of lobster-caesar or grilled tuna niçoise or a pasta dish like basil-pesto chicken with linguini, seafood primavera or shrimp carbonara. Desserts include tirami su, key lime pie and cream puffs with hot fudge, butterscotch or blackberry sauce. The short wine list is surprisingly far-reaching and pleasantly priced in the teens.

Upstairs at The Carrying Place are three large and cheery guest rooms with sitting areas, wicker furniture, armoires and old quilts on the Shaker beds. The B&B rates ($95) include breakfast, perhaps crêpes with raspberry sauce, homemade granola or popovers.

Dinner nightly from 5 in summer, Thursday-Monday from 6 rest of year.

Jordan Pond House, Park Loop Road, Acadia National Park. (207) 276-3316.

In striking contrast to the famed old Jordan Pond House with its birch-bark dining rooms, which burned to the ground in 1979, the replacement is strikingly modern, with high ceilings and huge windows. The incomparable setting remains the same, however, with green lawns sloping down to Jordan Pond and the Bubbles mountains in the background.

Lunch and dinner are served daily in season, but you'd be amazed at all the people who arrive for afternoon tea on the lawn (two popovers with butter and strawberry preserves and tea, $5), a Bar Harbor tradition.

The dinner menu is fairly standard, with lots of lobster dishes, steak, chicken and fish of the day, priced from $12.50 to $18. A relish tray, popovers and vegetables are accompaniments. If you're hungry, start with a smoked-seafood sampler ($6.50). Flickering candles, fresh flowers and the sunset over pond and mountains create an unforgettable setting.

For lunch, we like to sit outside on the "porch," which is more like a covered terrace. The last time we enjoyed a fine seafood pasta and a curried chicken salad, garnished with red grapes and orange slices, and shared a popover — good but a bit steep at $2, given that it was hollow. There's a full bar, and the large gift shop (one of several Acadia Shops on the island) is fun to browse in.

Lunch, 11:30 to 2:30; tea on the lawn, 2:30 to 5:30; dinner, 5:30 to 9. Open mid-June to mid-October.

The Bistro at Seal Harbor, Route 3, Seal Harbor. (207) 276-3299.

They have only eight tables and a kitchen not much bigger than that in a studio apartment, and they grow their own herbs in wine casks on the back porch. Such

Tea on the lawn is a Bar Harbor tradition, as viewed from Jordan Pond House.

is the homespun endeavor of Donna Fulton and Terri Clements, who teamed up in 1993 to open a bistro in the heart of old-money Seal Harbor. Formerly at the Fin Back in Bar Harbor, they offer a short and somewhat pricey (for the area) menu in a charming setting.

The storefront room is pristine with tables topped with white napkins, votive candles, fresh flowers and white china. Behind is a small service bar and aforementioned kitchen, snug with ten-burner stove. Donna handles the cooking chores, preparing half a dozen main courses ($16 to $21) like grilled salmon with pasta in garlic-basil cream, roasted swordfish with white beans and preserved lemon, bouillabaisse, and sautéed pork tenderloin with mangos and shallots. The Bistro salad comes with feta, apples and spiced pecans. Other appetizers range from polenta with marinara, gorgonzola and basil to smoked salmon with ginger-scallion pancake. Soup might be lobster with jalapeño peppers and corn. Desserts involve crème brûlée, seasonal tarts and pies, plus intense ice creams (coffee-almond-praline or ginger) and orange-buttermilk sorbet served with biscotti. A well chosen, all-domestic wine list is priced mostly in the twenties.

This is obviously a pure place, where the owners make everything from scratch. They even pick their own berries for the blueberry pie and grate their own vanilla beans for the extract . A local blacksmith crafted the striking wine-glass rack that hangs over the copper bar. Donna and Terri made the interesting table pottery during their winter off-season in Arizona.

Dinner, Tuesday-Sunday from 6. Open Memorial Day to October. No smoking.

Bed and Board

Castine Inn, Main Street, Box 41, Castine 04421. (207) 326-4365.

A pleasant front porch with polka-dot covered seats and a profusion of flowers welcomes guests to the Castine Inn, built in 1898 and operated continuously since. The welcome continues inside and out.

Owners Mark and Margaret Hodesh have redone the front parlor and spiffed up fourteen guest rooms, now all with private baths, opening hotel-style off a long wide corridor on the second floor. They also opened six more on the third floor. A fairly new addition is the sunny side deck with a view of Mark's elaborate gardens, which compete for attention with Margaret's striking murals of Castine in the dining room. The most recent change at this ever-upgrading inn is a new outdoor entry to the cozy, convivial pub.

Margaret's murals grace the walls, pillars and even a new service area in the pleasant dining room, the setting for creative cuisine. Although Mark is in the kitchen, he defers to chef Richard Langsner, "who has taken us to new heights. I'm a cook; he's a chef." Their offerings are as varied as crab cakes with mustard sauce ($4.50 as an appetizer, $14 as an entrée), billi-bi, roasted eggplant and garlic soup, lentil salad with goat cheese, roast pork loin with black beans and barbecue sauce, chicken and leek pot pie, roast duck with peach chutney and broiled Atlantic salmon with lemon and egg sauce. The price of the entrée ($12 to $18) includes biscuits, potato or rice and vegetable. One night we were there, broiled Stonington scallops with tomato-basil butter were on the menu, the scallops having been caught that day by a Stonington fisherman whose wife was a waitress at the inn.

Desserts include frozen lemon soufflé, chocolate bread pudding, apple crisp with cinnamon ice cream and fresh fruit cobblers and crisps. The appealing wine list starts in the low teens.

Dinner may be taken on the side deck. Later in the evening, desserts and nightcaps are served in the living room or on the front porch. Mark specially opened the dark and cozy pub, tucked away in a corner, to serve us an after-dinner brandy at one visit. This is an inn that's nothing if not accommodating.

Complimentary breakfast includes a choice of corned-beef hash every day, pancakes, sausages and fresh muffins.

Dinner nightly except Tuesday, 5:30 to 8:30. No smoking in dining room. Doubles, $75 to $110. Two-night minimum in summer. Open May to late October.

Pentagoet Inn, Main Street, Box 4, Castine 04421. (207) 326-8616 or (800) 845-1701.

All is serene and sophisticated in the public rooms, the highly regarded dining room and the guest rooms at this century-old inn run since 1985 by Lindsey and Virginia Miller from Arkansas.

He a physician and she a nurse, they refurbished in smashing seafoam shades the main-floor parlors, one a well-outfitted library and the other with a nifty window seat looking toward the harbor. The pristine dining room has an addition looking out over terraced gardens, and there's a sparkling new kitchen. The main inn holds eleven guest rooms, all with private baths and antique furnishings. We thought the bathroom off our kingsize turret room — with color-coordinated wallpapers, curtains and patterned rug and a basket of towels in shades of pink — a work of art. Perhaps the nicest rooms are the five behind the inn in the 200-year-old house called 10 Perkins Street.

Two-night minimum stays, MAP meal requirements, and a 6 p.m. cocktail hour with the innkeepers are intended, Virginia says, "to make this a highly desirable experience for our house guests," although some might find it a bit confining. Virginia did the decorating in the dining room, where the rose-colored walls are a backdrop for bare wood floors and well-spaced tables draped in white linens. Each place setting contains two wine glasses and a crystal water glass. To the rear, a newer dining area has six tables beside a small deck with gardens beyond.

Murals grace dining room at Castine Inn. **Turreted facade of Pentagoet Inn.**

Dinners are prix-fixe ($30 for the public) and start with a cocktail hour (cash bar) with the innkeepers in the library. Our dinner began with cold smoked quail with cranberry compote, followed by a superior barley and mushroom soup. Tournedos of beef, sautéed shrimp and pesto, and sautéed lobster with sherry were winning entrées. A salad of fresh mixed greens with raspberry vinaigrette followed the main course. Strawberry pie with whipped cream and chocolate/sour-cream cake with fudge frosting were dessert choices. The wine list is well-chosen and rather pricey.

Lobster is always one of the three entrée choices, as in lemon-garlic lobster or lobster pie. Others could be grilled Blue Hill Bay scallops in a marinade of scotch, ginger and soy; bourbon-orange-molasses-glazed pork chops, or brandy-buttered game hen with Southern pecan cornbread stuffing. Classical music is played through a compact disc system and occasionally there is live violin background music or chamber music during the reception, as the Pentagoet focuses on musical special events.

The good life continues with breakfast. The menu might include cantaloupe, homemade granola, sourdough blueberry pancakes or farmer's omelet and Canadian bacon. The toast, made from homemade whole-wheat bread, is delectable.

Dinner by reservation, nightly at 7. Doubles, $154 to $174, MAP. Open May-October. No smoking.

Pilgrim's Inn, Deer Isle 04627. (207) 348-6615.

An aura of history and an aroma of fine food emanate from this impressive, dark red 1793 house run with great taste and flair by Jean and Dud Hendrick. With a harbor in front and a mill pond in back, inviting common rooms and thirteen guest rooms (plus a small, deluxe seaside cottage down the street), it's a quiet place that beckons guests to stay for extended periods.

Jean and her chef, Terry Foster, are inventive in the kitchen, using local ingredients and grilling on an enormous barbecue on a new rear deck. Following cocktails at 6 in the downstairs common room or outside on the deck (where guests nibble on abundant hors d'oeuvre like bluefish pâté and mingle with Jean and Dud, who fixes great drinks), a single-entrée, prix-fixe dinner ($27.50 for the public) is served at 7 o'clock. You move into a charming dining room, a former goat barn with farm utensils and quilts on the walls, hand-hewn beams, mismatched chairs, tables with fresh flowers and ten outside doors that open to let in the breeze. Depending on the night, you might be served rainbow trout stuffed with lobster and crab, smoked boneless leg of lamb or mixed grill of duck confit, scallops and free-range chicken, often accompanied by a dynamite risotto and delectable vegetables.

Never will we forget a Sunday dinner of salad with goat cheese, homemade peasant bread, a heavenly paella topped with nasturtiums (such a pretty dish that it should have been photographed for Gourmet magazine) and a sensational raspberry-chocolate pie on a shortbread crust. Terry varies his menu annually and according to whim, but whatever is served, you can expect it to be a treat.

Homemade granola, scones, fresh melon and omelets are typical breakfast fare.

The handsome guest rooms, eight with private baths, are decorated in sprightly Laura Ashley style. Most in demand are the larger rooms at the back. Oriental rugs and quilts lend color to the prevailing simplicity. The main-floor library has an exceptional collection of books; another parlor is a showroom for local artists. The Hendricks have added appropriate art to every guest room. It's typical of the T.L.C. that they lavish on the inn as well as their guests. And they have fun, too -- their float as animals in an ark, honoring the inn's bicentennial, won first prize in Deer Isle's Fourth of July parade in 1993.

Dinner by reservation, nightly at 7. Doubles, $136 to $160, MAP; cottage, $180. Open mid-May to mid-October. No smoking. No credit cards.

Blue Hill Inn, Union Street, Box 403, Blue Hill 04614. (207) 374-2844.

This small village inn with eleven overnight rooms and a dining room of distinction marked its 150th anniversary in 1990. Never has it had such appeal since affable owners Mary and Don Hartley took over innkeeping duties and upgraded the kitchen.

The energetic Hartleys have enhanced the guest rooms, all with private baths and three with fireplaces, some with sitting areas converted from small bedrooms. Our rear bedroom -- occupied the previous night by Peter of Peter, Paul and Mary fame following their concert at the Blue Hill Fair Grounds -- was comfortable with a kingsize bed, two blue velvet wing chairs, colorful bed linens, plump towels and windows on three sides to circulate cool air, which was welcome after a heat wave. The others we saw also are nicely furnished with 19th-century antiques and traditional pieces reflecting what Mary calls "a homey Down East style." Homemade chocolates come with nightly turndown service.

It is dining for which the inn lately is best known. The Hartleys serve hors d'oeuvre (perhaps smoked mackerel or local goat cheese) with cocktails at 6 in the large parlor or outside on the side lawn. A leisurely, multi-course dinner ($35 for the public) begins at 7. Dining is by candlelight at white-linened tables in an enclosed sun-porch-style room where classical music plays in the background.

Chef André Strong, an American whose mother came from France, changes the hand-written menu nightly. Braised shiitake mushrooms with saffron risotto was the appetizer at our latest dinner, which was artistically presented and exceptionally tasty throughout. A blueberry-campari ice cleansed the palate for the main course, a choice of ethereal paupiettes of trout with salmon mousseline and mint

Pilgrim's Inn is in 1793 house.   Table at Asticou Inn has water view.

or tender noisettes of lamb with cob-smoked bacon, garlic and chèvre. A salad of local greens preceded the dessert, a remarkable frozen nougat with spiced orange rum -- so good that we requested the recipe and quickly realized we could never accomplish the feat at home.

Breakfast here is no slouch, either. Ours started with the usual juices, a plate of cut-up fresh fruit and a wedge of apple-custard pie that one of us thought was dessert. The main course involved a choice of eggs scrambled with garden chives in puff pastry, an omelet with chèvre or brie and Canadian bacon, waffles with strawberry topping or blueberry pancakes. Excellent french-roast coffee accompanied this repast fit for royalty.

The inn has excelled at themed wine dinners in the off-season, attracting an equal number of locals and out-of-town returnees. The Hartleys also offer seasonal concert weekends, schooner day trips and overnights on Penobscot Bay, and a women's relaxation getaway with massage. They were spearheading a townwide food and wine festival for October 1994.

Besides the main living room in blue and white with a fireplace, guests enjoy a sunny library-game room with comfortable chairs for lounging. Outside is a lovely perennial garden with lawn furniture, a gazebo and, at our visit, a profusion of huge yellow lilies.

Dinner nightly at 7, June-November; weekends and holidays in off-season; closed in winter. Doubles, $140 to $160, MAP.

Le Domaine, Route 1, Box 496, Hancock 04640. (207) 422-3395 or (800) 544-8498.

Here is a perfect getaway for gourmets: a country auberge with a handful of elegant upstairs guest rooms, some with private decks overlooking the rear gardens, and a main-floor restaurant and lounge purveying classic French cuisine and fine wines.

The red frame building semi-hidden behind huge evergreens seems as if it was lifted from provincial France and plunked down in rural Hancock, which is even down east from down east Bar Harbor. Inside is an extraordinarily appealing place in which to stay and dine.

Founded in 1945 by a Frenchwoman, Marianne Purslow-Dumas, Le Domaine is run now with equal competence by her daughter, Nicole Purslow, a graduate of the Cordon Bleu School and an advocate of country-French haute cuisine.

Beyond a delightful wicker sitting area where French magazines are piled upon tables is the long and narrow, L-shaped dining room, dominated at the far end by a huge stone fireplace framed by copper cooking utensils. Walls (red above, green below and separated by dark wood beams) are decorated with maps of France and pictures of folks in provincial costumes. A porch room in back, its tables covered with gaily colored cloths from Provence, takes full advantage of the sylvan view.

The menu changes frequently and features local produce from nearby gardens and herbs that grow by the kitchen door. Six or seven entrées in the $17.75 to $23 range are offered each night. They could include veal with wild mushrooms, steak au poivre, and poussin roasted with madeira and cream. We'd return any time for the sensational sweetbreads with lemon and capers, the grilled salmon with fennel, lamb chops dusted with rosemary, and a house specialty, rabbit with prunes marinated in brandy. Zucchini, snap peas and gnocchi might accompany.

The French bread is toasted in chunks and the rolls are marvelous. For starters ($5.50 to $7.50) on various occasions, we've tried malpeque oysters with a shallot-sherry vinegar dipping sauce, coquilles St. Jacques in a heavenly wine sauce, smoked trout and a salad of impeccable greens, including baby spinach, tossed with goat cheese and walnuts.

The cheesecake on raspberry sauce is ethereal, as is the frozen coffee mousse. Another visit produced a raspberry tart and frozen raspberry mousse with a meringue, plus perfect french-roast coffee. The wine list (mostly French, of course) is expensive, but some bargains are to be found.

Relaxing after dinner in the wicker sitting room with snifters of heady eau de vie, we almost didn't care about the cost ($7 each). We toddled upstairs to our overnight home in the king-bedded Tarragon Room, one of seven attractive, country-fresh guest rooms named after herbs.

All with private baths, they're exceptionally outfitted in chintz. The amenities you'd expect are here, including antiques, clock radios, books, French magazines, reading lamps on each side of the bed, French soaps and bath oils (and a night light in the shape of a shell), plus complimentary Perrier water. Behind a studied simplicity are incredibly sophisticated touches. On our rear deck, for instance, a spotlight shone on a tree growing through it and a piece of driftwood was placed perfectly on the stairs.

The next morning, we admired a circular garden surrounded by large rocks in back, looking casual but probably taking hours to plot. Through a forest of pine trees on 85 acres had been cleared a number of trails, one involving a long walk to a pond, with blueberries for sustenance along the way.

A breakfast tray was delivered to our deck, bearing bowls of peaches and raspberries, granola, crème fraîche, hot milk in a jug, homemade blueberry preserves, three of the flakiest croissants ever and a pot of fragrant coffee, all on floral china with linen napkins. Enchantment!

Dinner nightly, 6 to 9 (closed to public on Sunday). Doubles, $190, MAP. Open May-October.

Asticou Inn, Route 3, Northeast Harbor 04662. (207) 276-3344.

A bastion of elegance since 1883, this historic inn is grandly situated on a hillside at the head of Northeast Harbor. From the spacious dining room, you get a glorious view of the harbor goings-on from on high.

Wicker sitting area and curved bar lead into dining room at Le Domaine.

The $39.50 buffet every Thursday night draws people from all over Mount Desert Island. Thursday happens to be maid's night off hereabouts, so summer residents join inn guests for the extravagant spread followed by live music and an evening of socializing.

The pillared dining room is restful with handpainted murals of trees and flowers on the deep yellow walls, small oriental rugs, lovely floral china and tiny plants in clay pots. Jackets and ties are required at night.

Chef Lou Kiefer's dinner fare changes nightly and earns considerable acclaim. A typical menu might start with lobster crêpe, smoked-seafood antipasto with goat cheese and baked boursin with crab meat. Main courses ($18.50 to $23) could be lobster au poivre, grilled salmon fillet, broiled lamb chops with rosemary demi-glace and roasted beef tenderloin with cabernet sauce. Dessert possibilities are raspberry meringue glacé, chocolate-truffle torte and fresh fruit with cheeses.

We lunched on the outdoor terrace high above the sparkling harbor, choosing the buffet over the grilled sandwiches (both $12). The buffet included a choice of chicken-vegetable soup or a most refreshing chilled lime-yogurt soup, cold meats and many salads, beverage and choice of five or six desserts. The Sunday brunch ($14.50) is a panoply of treats, from eggs benedict and crêpes cooked to order to poached salmon, pastas and desserts.

Upstairs via a carpeted staircase or an ancient elevator are 50 simple guest rooms of varying configurations. Seventeen more rooms are available in guest houses and the striking, circular Topsider cottages (each with deck, full-length windows, attractive parlors and kitchenettes). One of the guest houses, **Cranberry Lodge,** operates as a B&B and a weekend dinner spot in the off-season. Lou Kiefer prepares three-course meals to be served on the heated, country-style porch or in front of a big fireplace in the dining room. Lit mostly by candles, it's rustic but elegant, with oriental rugs, fresh flowers and a total of 32 seats that are snapped up by locals in the winter. His short menu ($13.95 to $15.25) might yield seafood in pastry with fresh dill and lime sauce, breast of duck with mixed berry compote, and tenderloin of beef with béarnaise sauce.

Asticou's lavishly landscaped grounds offer a swimming pool and tennis. Guests return year after year, and the atmosphere seems somewhat that of a private club, although general manager Daniel Kimball has been making a determined effort to broaden the inn's appeal..

Doubles, $210 to $260, MAP; two-night minimum mid-June to mid-September. Off-season, $50 to $110, B&B. Open April-December. Lunch daily, 12:30 to 2; dinner, 7 to 9.

Bar Harbor Inn, Newport Drive, Bar Harbor 04609. (207) 288-3351 or (800) 248-3351.

Née the Bar Harbor Hotel and then the Bar Harbor Motor Inn, the name was changed again in 1986 to reflect the restoration of the original inn building, which now resembles its predecessor on the site, the private Oasis Club's Reading Room.

Owner David Witham made sure the expanded inn capitalized on both its history and its watery location, away from the hubbub on seven landscaped areas with the sea on two sides. Part of the older motel section was moved uphill to make way for a deluxe oceanfront lodge in 1988. Fifteen motel units remain, but the grandest accommodations are those in the lodge, where 64 spacious rooms on two floors have private balconies with a stunning view of rocks, water and islands. White lounge furniture outside, deep green draperies that match the dust ruffles on the beds, moiré wallpaper, rose carpeting, good art and big bathrooms with pink fixtures and fluffy towels characterize these rooms.

To our minds, they surpass even the 54 refurbished rooms in the main inn, furnished in Colonial elegance but with such accommodations to the times as cable TV, clock radios and phones.

Lunch and drinks are offered at the colorful **Terrace Grille** beside the pier.

The Reading Room, the inn's redecorated circular dining room, is lovelier than ever, all in deep cranberry colors enhanced by pots of chrysanthemums and the finest ocean panorama around. Dinner prices run from $14.95 for grilled chicken or broiled haddock to $19.95 for filet mignon or rack of lamb. Start with wild mushrooms, apples, and yellow peppers in cream sauce. Finish with strawberry-amaretto torte.

Lunch daily, 11:30 to 2:30; dinner, 5:30 to 9:30. Restaurant open April to Thanksgiving. Doubles, $139 to $225. Lodge open year-round.

Lodging

John Peters Inn, Peters Point, Box 916, Blue Hill 04614. (207) 374-2116.

Surrounded on two sides by water and 25 acres, this B&B is in an 1810 white-pillared and red-brick house that looks rather like a Southern plantation. Although close to Blue Hill, it's off by itself on its own idyllic hilltop peninsula. It also offers some of the nicest guest rooms and some of the most gourmet breakfasts around.

Energetic Barbara and Rick Seeger acquired the house in 1986, rebuilt the kitchen, added a dining porch, moved all the guest rooms upstairs and have a real winner of a place. To the original eight rooms they added six more in a rear carriage house in 1990. With fourteen rooms, the Seegers were eyeing the rear barn at our latest visit — possibly as the site for an antiques co-op. "No more rooms," says Barbara.

All rooms have private baths, most have king or queensize beds, half have fireplaces and some of those in the carriage house come with private decks. They are handsomely furnished, even the newer ones in back. There, you could have a room with queensize brass bed and a loveseat looking onto a private deck, or a larger room that's almost a studio apartment with queen bed, fireplace, kitchen with a dishwasher and dining table, and private deck.

We enjoyed our stay in the main house in the Blue Hill Room, which has a kingsize bed, working fireplace, lovely carpets, a wet bar and refrigerator, and a large rooftop deck looking up at Blue Hill. The deck is so pleasant that many guests bring dinner in and eat right there; "almost everyone who stays in this room eats a lobster dinner here at least once," says Barbara.

Caring touches include fresh fruit and flowers in the rooms, a small swimming pool, and a canoe and a couple of sailboats. Musicians from the nearby Kneisel Hall School of Music like to gather around the grand piano in the living room.

The Seegers and their staff put out a remarkable spread for breakfast, served on the enclosed side porch amid delicate blue and white floral china, heavy silver, etched water glasses and classical music. Our latest repast started with fresh orange juice, local blueberries and cream, and grilled blueberry and corn muffins. Then came a choice of nine entrées, from eggs any style to blueberry waffles, cheese eggs and a crabmeat/monterey-jack omelet. One of us liked the poached eggs with slender asparagus on whole-wheat toast, garnished with crisp bacon and edible flowers. The other ordered the lobster and artichoke omelet with hollandaise sauce. Garnished with lobster claws, it was so colorful that it cried out for a photo. It also was so good that he ordered it two mornings in a row. The waitress acknowledged that her father supplies the lobster and her mother the crab meat. Now that's down-home, with class.

Doubles, $85 to $135.

The Inn at Canoe Point, Route 3, Box 216, Hulls Cove 04644. (207) 288-9511.

Here is one of Mount Desert Island's few small inns right on the ocean, and it is a stunner of a place. Don Johnson, who started with a couple of B&Bs in Southwest Harbor, took over a private home in 1986 and turned it into a spiffy B&B with the best location imaginable and a wonderful deck that takes full advantage.

The stucco house with Tudor trim is set well back and below Route 3 in an acre and a half of woods flanking Frenchman Bay. The six guest rooms with private baths enjoy water views. We're partial to the front Master Suite with fireplace and deck and the side Garden Room, lately expanded with three walls of glass and its own door onto the garden and sea. The third-floor Garret Suite has wicker chairs, a neat captain's chest and a kingsize bed from which you can look out at an endless expanse of water. All are discreetly decorated in exquisite taste and muted colors so as not to detract from the view.

Guests enjoy a pleasant living room, which has an elegant grouping of seats around the fireplace and a notable crystal decanter collection, and the waterfront Ocean Room with a huge sectional, fireplace and stereo. The latter room is where breakfast is served at tables for four topped with candlesticks -- when the weather isn't suitable for eating on the spacious deck at water's edge.

Waterside deck at inn at Canoe Point has sweeping view of Frenchman Bay.

Breakfast might be spinach and cheddar quiche, eggs strata, cranberry-walnut pancakes, blueberry french toast or scrambled eggs, plus a fresh fruit salad. Decanters of port or sherry are in all the guest rooms, and Don serves iced tea on warm afternoons on the spacious deck.

Don recently sold his two inns in town, the Maples and Ridgeway, to concentrate on the Inn at Canoe Point. His dedication is paying off. At our early-July visit in 1993, he was fully booked for the entire summer and was taking reservations from disappointed turnaways for 1994.

Doubles, $105 to $195. No credit cards. No smoking.

Breakwater 1904, 45 Hancock St., Bar Harbor 04609. (207) 288-2313 or (800) 238-6309.

Fresh flowers abound and taped classical music fills the air as you enter one of Bar Harbor's more majestic seaside mansions, a 1904 English Tudor rescued from dereliction in 1992 by Bonnie and Tom Sawyer of Bangor. The public spaces of this showplace, built by John Kane, the great-grandson of John Jacob Astor, are impressive. A fire was blazing in the central fireplace of the "great living hall" on the cool summer day we visited. A large portrait of the new owners gazes down on two plush sofas in front, a 1918 Steinway grand piano beyond and guests as they descend the six-foot-wide cherry staircase past six chairs on the minstrel's landing, where musicians once entertained the Kanes. A side parlor, done up in burgundies and greens, harbors a multi-cushioned window seat from which to view Bald Porcupine Island through one of the mansion's countless leaded-glass windows. A custom-made billiards table is the focal point of the library. An oval oak table, especially made for the dining room, seats twenty at tapestry-covered chairs. Guests may use the butler's pantry, a space bigger than most kitchens. They also enjoy a huge piazza with granite walls and herringbone-brick floors, awash with chintz and wicker and overlooking the end of the town's Shore Path above Frenchman Bay.

Most of the six guest rooms, all with fireplaces and private baths, are in keeping with the scale, except for the small Abigail's Chamber, the former maid's room in the third-floor front corner, with a bathroom big enough for a shower only. Touches of whimsy like a rocking horse and teddybear in a crib mark the third-floor Nursery, side-by-side with the Nanny's Room. Ambassador Jay's Room holds a leather sofa, chair and deck. There are a clawfoot tub and a pull-chain toilet in the bath of the prized Mrs. Kane's Room; its more than 600 square feet of space features two settees, a tapestry spread on the tester bed matching the tapestry on an overstuffed sofa and chair, and a cheery decor in pinks and creams. Mr. Kane's Room, masculine in burgundy and blue, has a stuffed sofa and polo mallets on the wall. Mrs. Alsop's Room on the oceanfront is rich in rose and blue. It contains a kingsize mansion bed and two cushioned benches beside the fireplace. The decor was overseen by Bonnie Sawyer, who furnished it as a showcase for Drexel-Heritage furniture and County Inns magazine.

Warmth is provided by resident innkeepers Margot and Russell Snyder. They offer a full cold buffet of assorted juices, beverages, fresh fruit, two baked goods, homemade granola, cereals and yogurt. A hot entrée follows, perhaps eggs oscar or benedict, omelets, quiches or several variations of french toast. They also serve afternoon refreshments and host an evening social hour with wine and cheese or hors d'oeuvre on the veranda.

Doubles, $175 to $295. Closed January to mid-April. No smoking.

The Tides, 119 West St., Bar Harbor 04609. (207) 288-4968.

Listed on the National Register, this classic 1887 Greek Revival mansion faces Frenchman Bay head-on. A sensational wraparound veranda is full of upholstered wicker furniture that's all-matching to the max. Complete with its own fireplace, the veranda encloses a dining room with what must be a twenty-foot-long banquette along the window, plus a formal living room and entry foyer.

Guests have use of an upstairs living room with a huge sofa in front of a fireplace. Our room, the master bedroom, was the epitome of good taste, from the wing chairs, the queensize four-poster bed and coordinated Laura Ashley prints to the large dressing room with makeup table, the arrangement of daisies and mums, and the attention to every detail. There was even a small porch off the bathroom where we could sit and enjoy the salt air. And in the bathroom were Caswell-Massey toiletries and thick towels of deep burgundy. A welcoming sparkling cider came in a silver ice bucket with two crystal champagne glasses. The two other bedrooms are not as large but are equally well-equipped and outfitted in varied Laura Ashley prints.

Breakfast in the dining room is a feast — one day, bananas rolled in honey with toasted almonds and blueberry-stuffed french toast; the next day, strawberries zabaglione and sausage soufflé. Afternoon tea brings cookies or brownies, served on the veranda in summer or in front of the living-room fireplace in cool weather. New innkeepers Kim and John Bennett were leasing the place from its Bangor owners, Tom and Bonnie Sawyer, so had more of a stake in its operation than had their predecessors. The one-and-a-half-acre property, with lovely rolling green lawns and old lilac trees and Japanese maples, has 156 feet of bay frontage. You couldn't ask for a nicer place to unwind.

Doubles, $165 to $195. No smoking.

Ullikana Bed & Breakfast, 16 The Field, Bar Harbor 04609. (207) 288-9552.

Hospitable owner-innkeepers, creative breakfasts, a quiet in-town location near the water and a guest book full of grateful raves recommend this summery but substantial Victorian inn, tucked away in the trees between the Bar Harbor Inn and "the field," a meadow of wildflowers. Transplanted New Yorkers Roy Kasindorf and his Quebec City-born wife, Hélène Harton, bought the place in 1991 from a woman who had turned it into a B&B at the age of 86. They retained many of the furnishings, adding some of their own as well as artworks from artist-friends in New York.

Ten bedrooms with private baths have lots of chintz, wicker and antiques; some come with balconies, fireplaces or both. One dubbed Audrey's Room (for Roy's daughter) on the third floor contains two antique beds joined together as a kingsize and a clawfoot tub with its original fixtures, from which the bather can look out the low window onto Frenchman Bay.

The main floor harbors a wicker-furnished parlor with lots to look at, from collections (including two intricate puppets beside the fireplace) to reading materials, a dining room with shelves full of colorful Italian breakfast china and a kitchen from which Hélène produces the dishes that make breakfasts here such an event. They're served in summer outside on a terrace with glimpses of the water. Roy is the waiter and raconteur, doling out a fresh fruit dish, homemade granola muffins and a main course like waffles with fresh strawberries and whipped cream, an Italian omelet with homemade tomato sauce and mozzarella cheese, crêpes with frozen yogurt or a rum-cream sauce and, his favorite, puff pancakes with blueberries, raspberries and powdered sugar. Even the fruit dish is apt to be innovative; consider Hélène's grilled fruit brochettes bearing peaches, strawberries and kiwi marinated in honey, lemon and nutmeg and served with a ricotta-cheese sauce.

The couple have become avid Acadia promoters -- "we believe in this park and think it's paradise, " says Roy. Their enthusiasm rubs off on their pampered guests. And the meaning of the name of their own piece of paradise, christened in 1885, remains a mystery.

Doubles, $105 to $145. No smoking. Closed in winter.

Gourmet Pleasures

Potteries and crafts places abound in the vicinity of Blue Hill and Deer Isle. Foremost is **Rowantrees Pottery,** 9 Union St., Blue Hill, where Sheila Varnum and her associates continue the tradition launched in 1934 by Adelaide Pearson through her friend, Mahatma Gandhi. Named for the mountain ash tree above the green gate in front of the rambling house and barn, Rowantrees is especially known for its jam jar with a flat white lid covered with blueberries, as well as for unique glazes. **Rackliffe Pottery** on Route 172 also makes all kinds of handsome and useful kitchenware.

Local farmers, food producers and artisans gather at the **Blue Hill Farmer's Market** at the Blue Hill Fairgrounds Saturdays in July and August from 9 to 11:30 to sell everything from fresh produce and goat cheese to handmade gifts and patterned sweaters. It's a fun event for local color and foods.

The **Blue Hill Tea & Tobacco Shop,** in an aromatic modern shed attached to a home on Main Street, carries an abundance of teas, coffees and fine wines as well as rare tobaccos. Partners David Witter and William Petry also have related gift selections and do an extensive mail-order business.

Nervous Nellie's Jams and Jellies, Sunshine Road, Deer Isle, 348-6182, makes the products you see all over Maine the old-fashioned way. Founded by Peter Beerits, the business puts up 30,000 jars each year in the little house with a big kitchen. So many people were stopping in that Peter decided to serve refreshments as well. His **Mountainville Cafe** offers morning coffee and afternoon tea with homemade breads and pastries. Included is a frozen drink called a Batido ($2.50), a refreshing but caloric mix of cream cheese, freezer jam and crushed

Fine kitchenware is on display in Rowantrees Pottery showroom.

ice cubes. Besides all the wonderful jams (we especially like the wild Maine blueberry-ginger conserve and the hot tomato jelly), Peter's quirky sculptures outside make this kitchen and cafe worth a visit. We were intrigued by a sculpture of a lobsterman with huge red wooden claws for arms. Jelly kitchen is open most weekdays; cafe is open Monday-Saturday, noon to 4.

Fresh breads made from natural ingredients, soups and sandwiches, prepared foods, smoked fish, cheeses and wines comprise some of "the best foods of Maine," as billed by **Penobscot Bay Provisions,** a fine gourmet store on West Main Street in the culinary backwater of Stonington.

Rooster Brother, 18 West Main St., Ellsworth, is a store for cooks, serious and otherwise. Occupying a large Victorian building, it has a specialty food and wine shop downstairs and a wide variety of cookbooks and kitchen equipment upstairs. More than 60 cheeses are available. Lately, owners Pamela and George Elias have been concentrating on coffee roasting and an expanding bakery, where the store produces its own French bread. We came away with four types of dried chile peppers we had never before seen in the Northeast as well as a cookbook called *Hotter Than Hell.*

In Northeast Harbor, **Provisions** market offers good wines, gorgeous fruits and vegetables, meats, cheeses, herbs and even garlic cashews, as well as an excellent deli and bakery.

Café au lait and latte on Mount Desert? There is now, thanks to **Jumpin' Java,** an espresso bar that opened in 1993 in downtown Southwest Harbor and added the **Bouncin' Buns Bakery** with a move to larger quarters in 1994. Tom and Donna Wogan, ex-Californians who live on Swan's Island, offer espresso for $1.50 and latte for $2.25, among a host of coffees, beverages and baked goods at their year-round store where there are a few tables upon which to partake.

Coffees, wines, cheeses and a large selection of gourmet and natural foods are available at the **Alternative Market,** 99 Main St., Bar Harbor. It also has a mail-order desk for Maine-made products. *The* grocery store in Bar Harbor is the **J.H. Butterfield Co.,** a fixture since 1887 at 152 Main St. Definitely catering to the upper crust, it has a fine supply of gourmet foods, chocolates, picnic items and luscious fruits, and there are good sandwiches to go for picnics. Never have we seen so many varieties of Walker shortbreads and biscuits. There's also an extensive selection of beers and wines, including those from the nearby Bartlett Winery.

A winery in far Down East Maine? Yes, the **Bartlett Maine Estate Winery** in Gouldsboro, east of Hancock, is in the forefront in producing premium fruit wines. Finding conditions unsuitable for grapes, winemakers Robert and Kathe Bartlett substituted local apples, pears, raspberries and blueberries, and pioneered in making fine wines that have won best-of-show awards in the East (including, in 1989, the most medals of any winery in the New England Wine Competition and a total of 53 medals in nine years). They employ grape wine techniques in the production of 16,000 gallons annually, and the wines are aged in French oak.

MAINE ESTATE WINERY

The Bartletts consider their apple and pear Coastal White perfect for a picnic along the shore, and we're partial to the nouveau blueberry, fit for the finest of gourmet dinners. Prices range from $6.95 to $12.95 for blueberry French oak reserve.

Winery tours, Tuesday-Saturday 10 to 5, Sunday noon to 5, June to mid-October.

Dry English-style hard cider slowly ferments in oak barrels in the 19th-century cellar of the **Sow's Ear Winery,** which opened in 1990 along Route 176 in South Brooksville. Winemaker Tom Hoey, who sells his cider throughout the state, introduced two new wines in 1993, a dry rhubarb and chokecherry, a smooth and elegant fruit wine. You can sample the wines in a teeny tasting room enhanced by his wife's weavings and purchase a bottle for $7 to $10. Open Tuesday-Saturday noon to 6.

Lobster Pounds

Okay, okay, we can hear some of you thinking.

"Rabbits with prunes, for heaven's sake," you're sneering. "Billi-bi, what kind of garbage is that? Snap peas, schnap peas. We want *lobster.*"

We confess. Once each Maine trip we want lobster, too. But not a one-pound weakling. What we do is go to a lobster pound, order steamers and maybe onion rings and a couple of two-pound lobsters. We sit at picnic tables beside the water and watch the boats, and we pig out, just like everyone else.

In this area, our favorites:

Oak Point Lobster Pound, Route 230, Trenton. (203) 667-8548. This is where, some say, you get the best lobster in Maine, served with one of the best views in Maine: Mount Desert Island across the bay, with Cadillac Mountain and the Western Mountains showing to best advantage. The lobsters are boiled outside, but you eat inside in a rustic room rather brightly lit for our tastes. The lobster roll has all the meat from a whole lobster for $10.95; lobster stew is $14.50 and a whole shore dinner is $18.95. The stews and chowders are renowned here, as are the blueberry pie and chocolate-mousse pie. Although it's a simple place, the menu is fairly extensive and chef-owner Brian Langley teaches cooking in Ellsworth, so he knows what he's doing. And when did you ever see strawberry-amaretto torte on the menu at a lobster pound? There's a full liquor license. Dinner nightly from 5, mid-June to mid-October.

The **Tidal Falls Lobster Pound**, Hancock, is idyllic for its outdoor setting beside the reversing falls. Picnic tables shaded by birch trees are spaced well apart along the grassy waterfront, the better to view the cormorants on a nearby rock; a lined plastic bucket at the end of each table keeps this special place pristine. There's an enclosed pavilion for those who prefer. You order à la carte, anything from coleslaw (50 cents) to lobster ($7 a pound). We savored a midday repast of mussels with garlic butter ($3.95), a good, big crab roll ($6.95) and an even bigger lobster roll ($8.25). They don't pick the lobster meat out of the shell until you order and then they stuff oodles into the roll and put chips and a pickle on the side. Finish with a Harbor Bar or Dove Bar. BYOB and enjoy. Open daily in season, 11 to 8.

From the jaunty upstairs deck at **Thurston's Lobster Pound** on Steamboat Wharf in Bernard, you can look below and see where the lobstermen keep their traps. This is a real working lobster wharf. And if you couldn't tell from all the pickup trucks parked along the road, one taste of the lobster will convince you. You can get a lobster roll for $6.50 or a lobster dinner for $6.25 to $6.75 a pound, plus $3 for the extras. Steamers, mussels, chili, hamburgers and more are available at this true place opened in 1993 by Michael Radcliffe, great-grandson of the founder, and his wife Libby. A local couple, whose license plate said "Pies," was delivering the apple and rhubarb pies for the day when we stopped by. Pick out one of the twelve square tables for four on the covered deck and dig in. Open daily in season, 11 to 8.

Another good place for lobster, plus other goodies, is **Head of the Harbor,** Route 102, Southwest Harbor. You place your order at the outdoor steamer and grill and a waitress will deliver to the citronella-lit picnic tables on the expansive deck looking down toward Somes Sound or a screened porch adjacent. At our latest visit, we enjoyed a sunset dinner of stuffed shrimp with potato salad and sautéed scallops with french fries and three-bean salad (each $10.95), accompanied by a Napa Ridge chardonnay for $10.95 and followed by fresh raspberry pie. The lobster here is $7.95 a pound; add $2 for a complete dinner. Open daily in season, noon to 10.

Fisherman's Landing on the pier at 35 West St. in Bar Harbor is a lobster pound we've been going to since the '70s. From inside a cramped shack come succulent lobsters; you dine at picnic tables on the wharf, inside an enclosed pavilion or on an upstairs deck, sip wine or beer obtained from the adjacent bar, and watch all the harbor activities. For visitors, it's the essence of Down East Maine, all wrapped up in one convenient package. The lobster here is $6.25 to $7.50 a pound. The french fries are especially good, and hamburgers and other items are available. Open daily in summer, 6 to 9.

Index

Also by Wood Pond Press

The Restaurants of New England. This new book by Nancy and Richard Woodworth is the most comprehensive guide ever to restaurants throughout New England. The authors detail menu offerings, atmosphere, hours and prices for more than 1,000 restaurants in the same informative style that makes their other books so credible. Ratings designate several hundred for exceptional food, atmosphere, and/or value. Published in 1990; fully revised and updated in second edition in 1994. 490 pages of up-to-date information. $14.95.

Waterside Escapes: Great Getaways by Lake, River and Sea. The latest book by Betsy Wittemann and Nancy Woodworth relates the best lodging, dining, attractions and activities in 36 great waterside vacation spots in the Northeast, from the Chesapeake Bay to Cape Breton Island, from the Thousand Islands to Martha's Vineyard. Everything you need to know for a day trip, a weekend, or a week near the water is told the way you want to know it. Published in 1987; fully revised in 1996. 474 pages to discover and enjoy. $15.95.

Inn Spots & Special Places in New England. Much more than an inn guide, this book by Nancy and Richard Woodworth tells you where to go, stay, eat, and enjoy in the region's choicest areas. Focusing on 32 special places, it details the best inns, restaurants, sights to see, and things to do. Published in 1986. Fully updated in 1995. 488 pages of timely ideas. $16.95.

Inn Spots & Special Places/New York and Mid-Atlantic. The second volume in the series, the newest book by Nancy and Richard Woodworth guides you to the best places to eat and stay in 32 of the Mid-Atlantic's choicest areas, from New York to Virginia. Published in 1992. Fully updated in 1995. 504 pages of great ideas. $16.95.

Weekending in New England. The best-selling travel guide by Betsy Wittemann and Nancy Webster details everything you need to know about 24 of New England's most interesting vacation spots: more than 1,000 things to do, sights to see and places to stay, eat and shop year-round. First published in 1980; fully updated and expanded in 1993. 394 pages of facts and fun. $12.95.

The Originals in Their Fields

These books may be ordered from bookstores or direct from the publisher, pre-paid, plus $1.75 handling for each book. Connecticut residents add sales tax.

Wood Pond Press
365 Ridgewood Road
West Hartford, Conn. 06107
Tel: (860) 521-0389
Fax: (860) 313-0185
E-Mail: woodpond@pop.ntplx.net
Web Site: http://www.ntplx.net/~woodpond/